PRINCIPLES OF
macroeconomics

SECOND CANADIAN EDITION

KARL E. CASE
WELLESLEY COLLEGE

RAY C. FAIR
YALE UNIVERSITY

J. FRANK STRAIN
MOUNT ALLISON UNIVERSITY

MICHAEL R. VEALL
MCMASTER UNIVERSITY

Prentice
Hall

Toronto

Canadian Cataloguing in Publication Data

Main entry under title:

Principles of macroeconomics

2nd Canadian ed.
Includes index.
ISBN 0-13-025491-6

1. Macroeconomics.   I. Case, Karl E.   II. Title: Macroeconomics.

HB172.5.P74   2001   339   C00-933097-6

ISBN 0-13-025491-6

Vice President, Editorial Director: Michael Young
Executive Acquisitions Editor: Dave Ward
Director of Marketing: Michael Campbell
Developmental Editor: Maurice Esses
Production Editor: Jennifer Therriault
Copy Editor: Rodney Rawlings
Production Coordinator: Janette Lush
Page Layout: Wordstyle Productions
Photo Research: Linda Tanaka
Art Director: Mary Opper
Interior Design: Anthony Leung
Cover Design: Jennifer Federico
Cover Image: Romilly Lockyer/Imagebank

1 2 3 4 5   05 04 03 02 01

Printed and bound in USA

Statistics Canada information is used with the permission of the Minister of Industry, as Minister responsible for Statistics Canada. Information on the availability of the wide range of data from Statistics Canada can be obtained from Statistic Canada's Regional Offices, its World Wide Web site at http://www.statcan.ca, and its toll-free access number 1-800-263-1136.

Prentice
Hall

Brief Table of Contents

CONTENTS v

GLOBAL COVERAGE xii

PREFACE xv

ABOUT THE AUTHORS xxi

INTRODUCTION

PART One: Introduction to Economics 1

1. The Scope and Method of Economics 1
2. The Economic Problem: Scarcity and Choice 26
3. The Structure of the Canadian Economy: The Private, Public, and International Sectors 48
4. Demand, Supply, and Market Equilibrium 64
5. The Price System and Supply and Demand 97

MACROECONOMICS

Part Two: Concepts and Problems in Macroeconomics 113

6. Introduction to Macroeconomics 113
7. Measuring National Output, National Income, and the Price Level 132
8. Macroeconomic Problems: Unemployment and Inflation 153

Part Three: Macroeconomic Principles and Policy 174

9. Aggregate Expenditure and Equilibrium Output 174
10. The Government and Fiscal Policy 199
11. The Money Supply and the Bank of Canada 227
12. Money Demand, Interest Rates, Exchange Rates, and Monetary Policy 247

Part Four: Macroeconomic Analysis and Issues 273

13. Money, the Interest Rate, and Output: Analysis and Policy 273
14. Aggregate Demand, Aggregate Supply, and Inflation 289
15. The Labour Market, Unemployment, and Inflation 313
16. The Debt and Stabilization Policy 332
17. Household and Firm Behaviour in the Macroeconomy 346

Part Five: Macroeconomic Policy: A Closer Look 365

18. Issues in Macroeconomic Policy: Monetarism, New Classical Theory, and Supply-Side Economics 365
19. Economic Growth and Productivity 381

INTERNATIONAL ECONOMICS

Part Six: The Global Economy 401

20. International Trade, Comparative Advantage, and Protectionism 401
21. Open-Economy Macroeconomics: The Balance of Payments and Exchange Rates 425
22. Economic Growth in Developing Countries 451

CONCISE DICTIONARY OF ECONOMIC TERMINOLOGY 477

SOLUTIONS TO EVEN-NUMBERED PROBLEMS 483

INDEX 495

PHOTO CREDITS 505

Contents

GLOBAL COVERAGE xii

PREFACE xv

ABOUT THE AUTHORS xxi

INTRODUCTION

Part One: Introduction to Economics 1

1 The Scope and Method of Economics 1

Why Study Economics? 2
To Learn a Way of Thinking 2
To Understand Society 4
To Understand Global Affairs 5
To Be an Informed Voter 6

The Scope of Economics 7
Microeconomics and Macroeconomics 7
The Diversity of Fields in Economics 8

The Method of Economics 8

APPLICATION: THE FIELDS OF ECONOMICS 10

Theories and Models 11
Economic Policy 15

An Invitation 16

SUMMARY 17
REVIEW TERMS AND CONCEPTS 17
PROBLEM SET 18

APPENDIX 1A: How to Read and Understand Graphs 19

2 The Economic Problem: Scarcity and Choice 26

Scarcity, Choice, and Opportunity Cost 27
The Three Basic Questions 27
The Production Possibility Frontier 32
The Economic Problem 37

Economic Systems 38
Command Economies 38
Pure Market Economies: Laissez Faire 38
Mixed Systems, Markets, and Governments 40

GLOBAL PERSPECTIVE: EASTERN EUROPE AND RUSSIA: A MIXED PROGRESS REPORT 42

Looking Ahead 43

SUMMARY 44
REVIEW TERMS AND CONCEPTS 44
PROBLEM SET 45

3 The Structure of the Canadian Economy: The Private, Public, and International Sectors 48

The Private Sector in Canada 49
Canadian Households 49
The Private Sector Firm 51
The Legal Organization of Firms 52
A Profile of Canadian Private Sector Firms 53
Structural Changes in the Canadian Economy 54

The Public Sector: Taxes and Government Spending in Canada 56
The Size of the Public Sector 56
Government Structure and Expenditures 58
Sources of Government Revenue 59

The International Sector: Imports and Exports in Canada 61

From Institutions to Theory 62

SUMMARY 62
REVIEW TERMS AND CONCEPTS 63
PROBLEM SET 63

4 Demand, Supply, and Market Equilibrium 64

Firms and Households: The Basic Decision-Making Units 65

Input Markets and Output Markets: The Circular Flow 66

Demand in Product/Output Markets 67
Price and Quantity Demanded: The Law of Demand 69
Other Determinants of Household Demand 71
Shift of Demand Versus Movement Along a Demand Curve 73
From Household Demand to Market Demand 75

Supply in Product/Output Markets 75
Price and Quantity Supplied: The Law of Supply 78
Other Determinants of Firm Supply 78
Shift of Supply Versus Movement Along a Supply Curve 80
From Individual Firm Supply to Market Supply 80

Market Equilibrium 81
Excess Demand 81
Excess Supply 84
Changes in Equilibrium 85

Demand and Supply in Product Markets: A Review 87

Looking Ahead: Markets and the Allocation of Resources 88

APPLICATION: SUPPLY AND DEMAND IN THE NEWS 90

SUMMARY 91
REVIEW TERMS AND CONCEPTS 92
PROBLEM SET 93

APPENDIX 4A: The Simple Mathematics of Demand and Supply 93

5 The Price System and Supply and Demand 97

The Price System: Rationing and Allocating Resources 97
Price Rationing 97
Constraints on the Market and Alternative Rationing Mechanisms 100

GLOBAL PERSPECTIVE: THE MARKET COMES TO CHINA 102

The Canadian Farm Crisis: The Case of Prairie Wheat Producers 102
Prices and the Allocation of Resources 105

Supply and Demand Analysis: The Price of Gasoline 105

Looking Ahead 108

SUMMARY 108
REVIEW TERMS AND CONCEPTS 109
PROBLEM SET 109

CANADIAN CASE STUDY ONE: Gasoline Taxes and Gasoline Prices 110

WEB REFERENCES FOR PART ONE 112

MACROECONOMICS

Part Two: Concepts and Problems in Macroeconomics 113

6 Introduction to Macroeconomics 113

The Roots of Macroeconomics 114
The Great Depression 114
Recent Macroeconomic History 115

Macroeconomic Concerns 115

APPLICATION: THE GREAT DEPRESSION AND JOHN MAYNARD KEYNES 116
Inflation 116
Aggregate Output, the Business Cycle, and Output Growth 117
Unemployment 118

Government in the Macroeconomy 119

The Components of the Macroeconomy 120
The Circular Flow Diagram 120
The Three Market Arenas 121

An Introduction to Aggregate Demand and Aggregate Supply 123

The Canadian Economy: Trends and Cycles 124
The Canadian Economy Since 1970 126

SUMMARY 130
REVIEW TERMS AND CONCEPTS 130
PROBLEM SET 131

7 Measuring National Output, National Income, and the Price Level 132

Gross Domestic Product 132
"Final Goods and Services" 133
"Produced Within a Given Period of Time" 133
"By Factors of Production Located Within a Coutnry" 134

Calculating GDP 135
The Expenditure Approach 135

GLOBAL PERSPECTIVE: FOREIGN INVESTMENT IN CANADA AND CANADIAN INVESTMENT ABROAD 138

The Income Approach 139

From GDP to Personal Income 141

Nominal Versus Real GDP 142
Calculating Real GDP 143

Measuring the Price Level 144
The GDP Deflator 144
The Consumer Price Index 145

Limitations of the GDP Concept 147
GDP and Social Welfare 147
The Underground Economy 147
Per Capita GDP/GNP 148

Looking Ahead 149

SUMMARY 150
REVIEW TERMS AND CONCEPTS 151
PROBLEM SET 151

8 Macroeconomic Problems: Unemployment and Inflation 153

Recessions, Depressions, and Unemployment 154
Defining and Measuring Unemployment 154
Components of the Unemployment Rate 156
The Costs of Unemployment 158
Other Consequences of Recessions 162

Inflation 162
Defining Inflation 163
Price Indexes 163

APPLICATION: THE CPI WEIGHTS 164

The Costs of Inflation 166
Inflation: Public Enemy Number One? 167

Global Unemployment Rates and Inflation 167

Looking Ahead 168

SUMMARY 169
REVIEW TERMS AND CONCEPTS 169
PROBLEM SET 170

CANADIAN CASE STUDY TWO: Indexes of Economic Well-Being 171

WEB REFERENCES FOR PART TWO 173

Part Three: Macroeconomic Principles and Policy 174

9 Aggregate Expenditure and Equilibrium Output 174

Aggregate Output and Aggregate Income (Y) 175
Income, Consumption, and Saving (Y, C, and S) 176
Explaining Spending Behaviour 177
Planned Investment (I) 180
Planned Aggregate Expenditure (AE) 183

Equilibrium Aggregate Output (Income) 183
The Saving/Investment Approach to Equilibrium 185
Adjustment to Equilibrium 187
The Multiplier 188

Looking Ahead: The Government and International Sectors 193

APPLICATION: THE MULTIPLIER IN PRACTICE 194

SUMMARY 195
REVIEW TERMS AND CONCEPTS 196
PROBLEM SET 196

APPENDIX 9A: Deriving the Multiplier Algebraically 197

10 The Government and Fiscal Policy 199

Government in the Economy 200
Government Purchases (G), Net Taxes (T), and Disposable Income (Y_d) 201
Finding Equilibrium Output 203

Fiscal Policy at Work: The Multiplier Effects 204
The Government Spending Multiplier 204
The Tax Multiplier 207
The Balanced-Budget Multiplier 209

More on the International Sector 210

The Federal Budget 212
An Overview of the Budget 213
The Federal Budget Balance and the Federal Debt 213

APPLICATION: TAXATION IN CANADA 214

The Economy's Influence on the Budget Balance 215

APPLICATION: PROVINCIAL GOVERNMENTS AND FISCAL POLICY 216

Debt and Budget Balances in the Rest of the World 218

The Money Market and Monetary Policy: A Preview 218

SUMMARY 219
REVIEW TERMS AND CONCEPTS 220
PROBLEM SET 220

APPENDIX 10A: Deriving the Fiscal Policy Multipliers Algebraically (With Neither Taxes Nor Imports Depending on Income) 221

APPENDIX 10B: The Case in Which Tax Revenues (But Not Imports) Depend on Income 223

APPENDIX 10C: The Case in Which Imports (But Not Tax Revenues) Depend on Income 225

11 The Money Supply and the Bank of Canada 227

An Overview of Money 227
What Is Money? 228
Commodity and Fiat Monies 229
Measuring the Supply of Money in Canada 230

APPLICATION: DEBASEMENT, CLIPPED COINS, AND COUNTERFEITING 231

The Canadian Financial System 232

GLOBAL PERSPECTIVE: A CASHLESS SOCIETY 233

How Banks Create Money 234
A Historical Perspective: Goldsmiths 234
The Modern Banking System 235

The Bank of Canada 239
The Bank of Canada's Balance Sheet 240

How the Bank of Canada Controls the Money Supply 241
Open Market Operations 241
Transfers of Government Deposits 242
The Bank Rate 242
The Supply Curve For Money 243

Looking Ahead 243

SUMMARY 244
REVIEW TERMS AND CONCEPTS 244
PROBLEM SET 245

APPENDIX 11A: Deriving the Money Multiplier Algebraically 246

12 Money Demand, Interest Rates, Exchange Rates, and Monetary Policy 247

The Demand for Money 248
The Speculation Motive 248
The Transaction Motive 249
Transactions Volume, Output, and the Price Level 250
The Determinants of Money Demand (Review) 252

APPLICATION: BONDS AND MONEY MARKETS 252

The Equilibrium Interest Rate 254
Supply and Demand in the Money Market 255
Shifts in the Money Demand Curve 255
The Bank of Canada: Changing the Money Supply to Affect the Interest Rate 256
Fixed Exchange Rates 256
Flexible Exchange Rates 258

Looking Ahead: Bank of Canada Behaviour and Monetary Policy 261

GLOBAL PERSPECTIVE: MONETARY UNION 262

APPLICATION: THE MONETARY CONDITIONS INDEX 263

SUMMARY 263
REVIEW TERMS AND CONCEPTS 265
PROBLEM SET 265

APPENDIX 12A: The Various Interest Rates in the Canadian Economy 266

CANADIAN CASE STUDY THREE: The Asian Economic Crisis 270

WEB REFERENCES FOR PART THREE 272

Part Four: Macroeconomic Analysis and Issues 273

13 Money, the Interest Rate, and Output: Analysis and Policy 273

The Links Between the Goods Market and the Money Market 274
The Interest Rate and the Goods Market 274
Money Demand, Aggregate Output (Income), and the Money Market 277

Combining the Goods Market and the Money Market 278
Expansionary Policy Effects 279

APPLICATION: HOW INTEREST RATES AFFECT INVESTMENT: THE CASE OF NEW HOUSING 282

Contractionary Policy Effects 282
The Macroeconomic Policy Mix 283
The Macroeconomic Policy Mix in Canada in the New Century 284

More on the Determinants of Planned Investment 284

Looking Ahead: The Price Level 286

SUMMARY 286
REVIEW TERMS AND CONCEPTS 287
PROBLEM SET 287

14 Aggregate Demand, Aggregate Supply, and Inflation 289

The Aggregate Demand Curve 289
Deriving the Aggregate Demand Curve 290
The Aggregate Demand Curve: A Warning 291
Other Reasons for a Downward-Sloping Aggregate Demand Curve 292
Aggregate Expenditure and Aggregate Demand 293
Shifts of the Aggregate Demand Curve 294

The Aggregate Supply Curve 295
The Aggregate Supply Curve: A Warning 295
Aggregate Supply in the Short Run 296
Shifts of the Short-Run Aggregate Supply Curve 297

The Equilibrium Price Level 299

The Long-Run Aggregate Supply Curve 300

AD, AS, **and Monetary and Fiscal Policy 303**

ISSUES AND CONTROVERSIES: THE GREAT CANADIAN SLUMP 304

Long-Run Aggregate Supply and Policy Effects 305

Causes of Inflation 307
Demand-Pull Inflation 307

Cost-Push, or Supply-Side, Inflation 307
Expectations and Inflation 308
Money and Inflation 309
*Sustained Inflation as a Purely Monetary
Phenomenon 309*

Looking Ahead 309

SUMMARY 310
REVIEW TERMS AND CONCEPTS 311
PROBLEM SET 311

15 **The Labour Market, Unemployment, and
Inflation 313**

The Classical View of the Labour Market 314
The Classical Labour Market and the AS Curve 315
*Reconciling the Unemployment Rate to the Classical
View 316*

Explaining the Existence of Unemployment 317
Sticky Wages 317
Efficiency Wage Theory 318
Minimum Wage Laws 319
An Open Question 319

**The Short-Run Relationship Between the Unemployment
Rate and Inflation 319**

*ISSUES AND CONTROVERSIES: DOES THE MINIMUM
WAGE ELIMINATE JOBS? 320*

The Phillips Curve: A Historical Perspective 322
AS/AD Analysis and the Phillips Curve 323
Expectations and the Phillips Curve 326
*Is There a Short-Run Tradeoff between Inflation and
Unemployment? 326*
*The Long-Run AS Curve, Potential GDP, and the
Natural Rate of Unemployment 326*

*GLOBAL PERSPECTIVE: WHY IS UNEMPLOYMENT SO
MUCH HIGHER IN CANADA THAN IN THE UNITED
STATES? 328*

Looking Ahead 329

SUMMARY 330
REVIEW TERMS AND CONCEPTS 330
PROBLEM SET 331

16 **The Debt and Stabilization Policy 332**

The Federal Debt 332
The Burden of the Debt 333

Debt Management and Macropolicy 335
Economic Stability and Deficit Reduction 336

The Bank's Response to the State of the Economy 337

**Lags in the Economy's Response to Monetary and Fiscal
Policy 339**
Recognition Lags 341
Implementation Lags 341
Response Lags 341

SUMMARY 343
REVIEW TERMS AND CONCEPTS 344
PROBLEM SET 344

17 **Household and Firm Behaviour in the
Macroeconomy 346**

**Households: Consumption and Labour Supply
Decisions 346**
*The Keynesian Theory of Consumption:
A Review 347*
The Life-Cycle Theory of Consumption 347
The Labour Supply Decision 349
*Government Effects on Consumption and Labour
Supply: Taxes and Transfers 350*
Interest Rate Effects on Consumption 352

APPLICATION: READING THE STOCK PAGE 352

A Summary of Household Behaviour 353

Firms: Investment and Employment Decisions 353
Expectations and Animal Spirits 354
Excess Labour and Excess Capital Effects 355
Inventory Investment 357

*APPLICATION: SLOWDOWNS AND SKILLED
WORKERS 358*

A Summary of Firm Behaviour 359

SUMMARY 359
REVIEW TERMS AND CONCEPTS 360
PROBLEM SET 361

WEB REFERENCES FOR PART FOUR 362

**CANADIAN CASE STUDY FOUR: Recovery in Europe and
Deflation in Japan 363**

Part Five: Macroeconomic Policy: A Closer
Look 365

18 **Issues in Macroeconomic Policy: Monetarism, New
Classical Theory, and Supply-Side Economics 365**

Keynesian Economics 365

Monetarism 366
The Velocity of Money 366
The Quantity Theory of Money 367
Inflation as a Purely Monetary Phenomenon 369
The Keynesian/Monetarist Debate 369

New Classical Macroeconomics 370
The Development of New Classical Macroeconomics 370
Rational Expectations 371

APPLICATION: EXPECTATIONS AND FINANCIAL MARKETS 372

The Lucas Supply Function 373
Evaluating Rational-Expectations Theory 374
Real Business Cycle Theory 374

Supply-Side Economics 375
Evaluating Supply-Side Economics 376

Testing Alternative Macroeconomic Models 377

SUMMARY 378
REVIEW TERMS AND CONCEPTS 379
PROBLEM SET 379

19 Economic Growth and Productivity 381

The Growth Process: From Agriculture to Industry 381

The Sources of Economic Growth 383
An Increase in Labour Supply 383
Increases in Physical Capital 385
Increases in Human Capital 386
Increases in Productivity 386

Growth and Productivity in the Canadian Economy 388
Growth in Canada Since Confederation 388
The Productivity "Problem" 389

Economic Growth and Public Policy 390

ISSUES AND CONTROVERSIES: CAN WE REALLY MEASURE PRODUCTIVITY CHANGES? 392

Growth Policy: A Long-Run Proposition 393

The Pros and Cons of Growth 393
The Pro-Growth Argument 393
The Anti-Growth Argument 394
Summary: No "Right Answer" 396

SUMMARY 396
REVIEW TERMS AND CONCEPTS 397
PROBLEM SET 397

WEB REFERENCES FOR PART FIVE 398

CANADIAN CASE STUDY FIVE: Demography and Economic Growth 399

INTERNATIONAL ECONOMICS

Part Six: The Global Economy 401

20 International Trade, Comparative Advantage, and Protectionism 401

The International Economy: Trade Surpluses and Deficits 402

The Economic Basis for Trade: Comparative Advantage 403
Absolute Advantage Versus Comparative Advantage 403
Terms of Trade 408
Exchange Rates 408

The Sources of Comparative Advantage 412
The Heckscher-Ohlin Theorem 412
Other Explanations for Observed Trade Flows 412

Trade Barriers: Tariffs, Export Subsidies, and Quotas 413

Free Trade or Protection? 415
The Case for Free Trade 415

GLOBAL PERSPECTIVE: FREE TRADE IN CANADA 416

The Case for Protection 418

GLOBAL PERSPECTIVE: TRADE AND BORDERS 420

An Economic Consensus 421

SUMMARY 422
REVIEW TERMS AND CONCEPTS 423
PROBLEM SET 423

21 Open-Economy Macroeconomics: The Balance of Payments and Exchange Rates 425

The Balance of Payments 427
The Current Account 428
The Capital Account 429
The Global Balance of Payments 430

Equilibrium Output (Income) in an Open Economy 431
The International Sector and Planned Aggregate Expenditure 431
The Determinants of Exports and Imports 433

The Open Economy with Flexible Exchange Rates 434
The Market for Foreign Exchange 435
Factors That Affect Exchange Rates 438

GLOBAL PERSPECTIVE: MCPARITY? 440

Monetary and Fiscal Policy in the Open Economy 442

An Interdependent World Economy 446

SUMMARY *447*
REVIEW TERMS AND CONCEPTS *448*
PROBLEM SET *448*

22 Economic Growth in Developing Countries 451

Life in the Developing Countries: Population and Poverty 452

Economic Development: Sources and Strategies 454
The Sources of Economic Development 455
Strategies for Economic Development 457
Growth Versus Development: The Policy Cycle 460

Issues in Economic Development 460
Population Growth 460

GLOBAL PERSPECTIVE: CANADIAN FOREIGN AID *463*

Food Shortages: Acts of Nature or Human Mistakes? 464
Agricultural Output and Pricing Policies 464
Third World Debt 465

SUMMARY *467*
REVIEW TERMS AND CONCEPTS *468*
PROBLEM SET *468*

APPENDIX 22A: Marxian Economics 469

CANADIAN CASE STUDY SIX: International Trade Negotiations 473

CONCISE DICTIONARY OF ECONOMIC TERMINOLOGY 477

SOLUTIONS TO EVEN-NUMBERED PROBLEMS 483

INDEX 495

PHOTO CREDITS 505

Global Coverage

Because the study of economics crosses national boundaries, this book includes international examples in almost every chapter. The following list is a summary of global examples and discussions in the text.

CHAPTER	TOPIC
1	Understanding global affairs as a reason to study economics, 5
2	Introduction to comparative advantage, 29
	Alternative economic systems and economies in transition, 38
	Eastern Europe and Russia, a progress report, 42
3	The international sector: imports and exports in Canada, 61
4	Supply of and demand for Brazilian coffee, 85
	The basic forces of supply and demand throughout the world, 87
5	Market reforms in China, 102
	United States and European government policy and grain markets, 102
	Supply, demand, and the price of gasoline, 105
	OPEC, taxes, and the price of gasoline, 106
6	Hyperinflation in Bolivia, 116
	Open-economy circular flow models, 120
7	GDP and GNP in Lesotho and Japan, 134
	Foreign investment in Canada and Canadian investment abroad, 138
	Underground economy in Italy and Switzerland, 148
	International comparisons of per capita GDP and their shortcomings, 148
8	Global inflation and unemployment figures, 167
10	Introduction of the international sector in the planned aggregate expenditure model, 210
	Discussion on the open-economy multiplier, 211
	Debts and budget balances around the world (G-7 countries), 218
11	Commodity monies in the South Pacific and Africa, 229
	Debasement of currency in Bulgaria, 230
	Counterfeiting in England; development of paper money in Sweden, 231
	Barter in Russian in the 1990s, 233
12	Fixed and flexible exchange rates, 256, 258
	Links between Canadian and U.S. macroeconomies, 256
	Monetary union, 262
Case Study 3	The Asian economic crisis, 270
13	The trade balance and "crowding out," 279
	Effects of U.S. monetary policy on Canadian macroeconomic policy mix, 284

14	Role of oil prices in shifting the aggregate supply curve (OPEC oil shock), 298
	Role of immigration in shifting the aggregate supply curve, 298
	Deflation in Japan, 303
15	The wage tradeoff in less developed countries, 315
	Role of oil prices in an unstable Phillips curve (OPEC oil shock), 325
	Unemployment rates in Canada and the United States, 328
16	Canadian effects of U.S. monetary policy, 335
	U.S. deficit control legislation, 336
	Temporary U.S. income tax changes, 351
17	Labour costs in the Philippines, 354
Case Study 4	Recovery in Europe and deflation in Japan, 363
18	Expectations and financial markets, 372
19	World annual growth rates of productivity, 387
	Global problems associated with economic growth, 389
	Productivity gap between Canada and other countries, 390
20	Complete chapter on international trade, trade surpluses and deficits, comparative advantage, exchange rates, trade barriers and the World Trade Organization, economic integration (Canada–U.S. Free Trade Agreement, NAFTA, the European Union, APEC, and the Free Trade area of the Americas), and free trade vs. protection debate, 401–424
21	Complete chapter on the balance of payments (current and capital accounts), the gold standard, the Bretton Woods system, more on open-economy multiplier, determinants of imports and exports, trade feedback effects, foreign exchange markets, more on fixed vs. floating exchange rates, and the J curve, 425–450
22	Complete chapter on economic development; includes discussions of life in the developing countries, strategies for economic development, foreign aid to developing countries, the World Bank and IMF, debt crises, and Marxian economics in theory and worldwide practice, 451–472
Case Study 6	International trade negotiations, 473

Preface

Much has changed in the economies of both Canada and the world since the first edition of this book in 1998. The Canadian economy has continued to improve, although it still has not attained the lower unemployment rate of the United States. Public policy discussion has now entirely shifted from cutting government deficits to what to do with the surplus. The value of the Canadian dollar against the U.S. dollar is low by historical standards, while both exports and imports are at record highs. Outside Canada a strong U.S. economy contrasts with a deep recession in Japan, while the Asian crisis continues to have repercussions in Thailand, Indonesia, and Korea, even as growth is being restored in those countries after the crisis of the late 1990s.

This book provides an introduction to the principles of macroeconomics in the context of what is happening in Canada and the world. We have made every effort to maintain a balanced perspective. We feel this is especially important so that students can understand the arguments for as well as against activist aggregate demand policy. An introductory section (Chapters 1–5) provides the basics of microeconomics for students who have not yet covered that material, and part of the closing section (viz., Chapter 20) discusses the real theory of international trade. However, this volume focuses on macroeconomics and on the debate of whether the government can and should have some role in reducing unemployment and recession, stabilizing the economy more generally, and promoting long-term economic growth. Focal points include the economics of Keynes and the aggregate supply/aggregate demand model, but we also emphasize labour markets and unemployment, financial markets, and government debt. We devote more and earlier attention to the exchange rate than most first-year texts do, and throughout this volume we include a significant amount of international content. (See the complete listing of Global Coverage following the Table of Contents.)

While our priority is conveying the essential principles of macroeconomics, we believe that students should learn about institutions and events in the actual economy both in Canada and the rest of the world. Hence, not only do we frequently discuss policy and examples in the main body of the text, but we also provide:

- Application Boxes on topics ranging from an analysis of the Bank of Canada's goal of low inflation (p. 263) to an explanation of how to read the stock market page in newspapers (p. 352)
- Issues and Controversies Boxes on topics ranging from the effects of the minimum wage on the number of

available jobs (p. 320) to the effects of free trade on the Canadian economy (p. 416)
- Global Perspective Boxes on topics ranging from the European Monetary Union (p. 262) to the unemployment gap between Canada and the U.S. (p. 328)
- An analytical Case Study at the end of each Part— each accompanied by an annotated, highly selective list of Internet sites relating to the Case and to the other material in that Part
- Graphs and tables describing recent and long-term economic development in Canada as a whole, as well as individual Canadian provinces and other countries

The body of each chapter is composed as a single column and we have resisted cramming in extra graphs or using garish colour that may wear on the reader and distract from a focus on the essential principles. Students sometimes have difficulty with learning "too many" types of graphs. We think that graphical analysis should help consolidate knowledge, and so the analytics for all macroeconomics chapters concentrates on just three graphs: the supply and demand graph (sometimes for money markets or labour markets), the Keynes cross, and the aggregate supply/aggregate demand diagram.

Some instructors will want more detail on some topics than our chapters provide, and hence we provide a number of appendices, which in all cases can be skipped without loss of continuity. We also provide flexibility, as described in the following section, so that while a common choice of core-principle material might include 7 or 8 chapters, most of the issues chapters will be accessible if only 4 core chapters are covered, provided the students are familiar with supply and demand.

New to This Edition of Macroeconomics

We have made a number of changes to the second Canadian edition to improve it as a learning tool. We have reduced the amount of text to be covered by removing two infrequently used chapters and by significantly tightening the other chapters. The result is that the book is considerably shorter even though the following new learning features have been added:

- a list of learning objectives at the beginning of each chapter to complement the list of topics and subtopics.
- new Fast Facts boxes in the margins to reinforce text points with particularly vivid examples.
- two new optional appendices with algebraic derivations.

- more quantitative practice problems at the end of most chapters to give instructors more flexibility in choosing the mathematical level of the course.
- a new section of web references at the end of each Part.

None of the existing learning features has been removed. Margin definitions highlight important terms, which are also collected in the Concise Dictionary of Economic Terminology at the end of this book. For review purposes, each chapter ends with a list of terms, a list of equations and a point-form summary. There is also a dictionary of economic terms and answers to even-numbered review problems (with answers to odd-numbered problems in the Instructor's Resource Manual). We have replaced all the Canadian Case studies with new ones, each with more analytical guidance so the student can apply what has been learned. Each case study is designed so that it can be used with a new CBC video segment if desired.

The overall structure of the book is very similar so that instructors who have used the book before should have no trouble adjusting. Changes in content include:

- a sharper focus to the introductory chapters with more emphasis on the application of the production possibility frontier in Chapter 2 and a more concise overview of the Canadian economy, with an added consideration of income by occupation and income distribution, in Chapter 3.
- optional algebraic appendices for supply and demand in Chapter 4 and an extended supply and demand example (linked to that Part's case study) on the price of gasoline.
- expanded optional algebraic appendices on the fiscal multipliers in Chapters 9 and 10 and on the deposit and money multipliers in Chapter 11.
- a simple, updated discussion of Canadian monetary policy instruments (especially the Bank Rate) and an incorporation of the definitions of the most recent standard monetary aggregates.
- new or revised discussion of macroeconomic policy issues such as deflation (Chapter 14 and Case Study 3), the role of the Bank of Canada in the economic slowdown of the 1990s (Chapter 14), the proposal to "dollarize" the Canadian economy (Chapter 12), the effect of monetary policy on long-term versus short-term interest rates (Appendix to Chapter 12), and the natural rate of unemployment in Canada and the United States (Chapter 15).
- revisions in Chapter 10 and Chapter 16 to reflect recent government surpluses (as opposed to deficits), but here we also retain a focus on government debt.
- the deletion of the first edition's Chapter 18 (Further Topics in Macroeconomic Analysis), with its key terms and concepts now introduced in Chapter 17.
- an expanded discussion of growth including endogenous growth and productivity and the implications for public policy (new Chapter 19).
- the deletion of the appendix on World Monetary Systems and the incorporation of its main points in the text of Chapter 21.
- the deletion of the first edition's Chapter 24 (Economies in Transition and Alternative Economic Systems), with the section on Marxian terminology now condensed as an appendix to the new Chapter 22.

The Plan of *Principles of Macroeconomics,* Second Canadian Edition

ORGANIZATION

Many introductory economics programs are structured so that one term is microeconomics and another term is macroeconomics. If the macroeconomics term comes first, then normally it will also include an overall introduction to economics corresponding to at least some of our Chapters 1 through 5, material that also begins *Principles of Microeconomics.* Chapters 2, 4, and an abbreviated Chapter 5 (for the *Macroeconomics* volume) provide what most instructors will require before the study of macroeconomics can start: material on scarcity, opportunity cost, markets, and supply and demand. Chapter 1 is an overall "introduction to economics" chapter (and includes an appendix on understanding graphs), while Chapter 3 is a brief description of the private, public, and international sectors.

Turning to macroeconomics proper, most instructors will want to convey some understanding of the basic Keynesian model of the economy and the basic theory of fiscal and monetary policy. These theories are presented in Chapters 9 to 12, "the essential core." Unlike most other Canadian introductory textbooks, this book introduces the role of the exchange rate explicitly when interest rates are discussed in Chapter 12. This recognizes that in a small, open economy such as Canada's, the effects of monetary policy through the exchange rate are probably at least as important as the effects through interest rates. But allowing for the obvious openness of the Canadian economy and financial markets at this stage does not make the traditional analysis of monetary policy more complex. For example, we simply point out that an expansionary monetary policy may tend to increase aggregate demand *both* by reducing interest rates *and* by depreciating the exchange rate. Then the analysis proceeds in a very similar fashion to closed economy analysis. There is also some coverage of the important institutional aspects involved, including the government budget balance and debt and the role of the Bank of Canada. Therefore, upon completion of these four chapters, the student should have a basic understanding of the types of macroeconomic policy and be prepared for an informed discussion of their use.

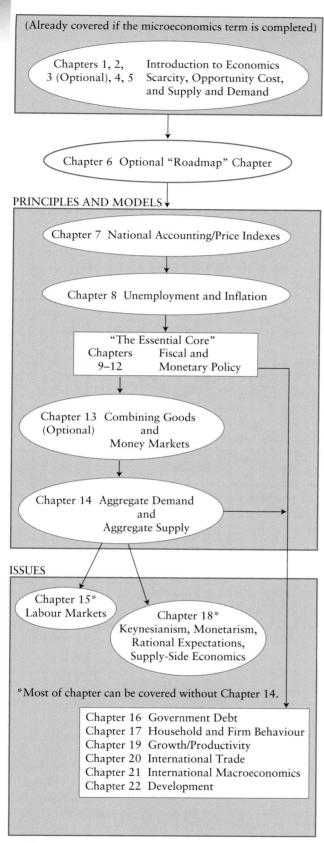

(Already covered if the microeconomics term is completed)

Chapters 1, 2, 3 (Optional), 4, 5 — Introduction to Economics Scarcity, Opportunity Cost, and Supply and Demand

Chapter 6 Optional "Roadmap" Chapter

PRINCIPLES AND MODELS

Chapter 7 National Accounting/Price Indexes

Chapter 8 Unemployment and Inflation

"The Essential Core" Chapters 9–12 — Fiscal and Monetary Policy

Chapter 13 Combining Goods (Optional) and Money Markets

Chapter 14 Aggregate Demand and Aggregate Supply

ISSUES

Chapter 15* Labour Markets

Chapter 18* Keynesianism, Monetarism, Rational Expectations, Supply-Side Economics

*Most of chapter can be covered without Chapter 14.

Chapter 16 Government Debt
Chapter 17 Household and Firm Behaviour
Chapter 19 Growth/Productivity
Chapter 20 International Trade
Chapter 21 International Macroeconomics
Chapter 22 Development

COURSE DESIGNS

We also recognize that every instructor will want to leave his or her own stamp on this course. Moreover, time is

Some Sample Courses

Primary Focus	Chapters
Macro stabilization policy with *AS/AD* model	Chapters 6 (optional), 7–12, 13 (optional), 18, plus selected issues chapters (15, 16, 19, and 21 are the most macro-oriented)
Macro stabilization policy without *AS/AD* model	Chapters 6 (optional and omit *AS/AD* part), 7–12, 13 (optional), 16, plus selected issues chapters, where the first part of Chapters 15 and 18 may be covered, as well as 17, 19, and 21, which are also macro-oriented
Long-run structural macroeconomic policy	Chapters 6 (optional and omit *AS/AD* part), 7–12, 13 (optional), the first part of Chapter 15, Chapters 16, 19, and selected issues chapters possibly including the first part of 18, as well as 20 and 22, which are less-macro-oriented chapters

tight in a course like this and few instructors will try to cover all chapters in this text. Therefore, we have structured the text to give instructors maximum flexibility in designing their own course. The chart here outlines a number of possible course designs.

It is possible to begin a course with Chapter 9 and make brief in-lecture references to measures such as GDP, the unemployment rate, and the CPI (defined along with many other terms in the Concise Dictionary of Economic Terminology). However, many instructors will wish to have a prior discussion of measurement (national accounting and price indexes in Chapter 7) and/or macroeconomic problems (unemployment and inflation, including labour market measurement and a brief stand-alone discussion of the CPI in Chapter 8). Similarly, some instructors will wish to cover basic aggregate demand/aggregate supply (*AS/AD*) model so that the course contains some explicit modelling of the price level as well as of output determination. This discussion is contained in Chapter 14. Hence, on the chart, Chapters 9–12 are described with Chapters 7, 8, and 14 as providing the "core principles and models" of the book.

What about Chapters 6 and 13? Chapter 6 is a "roadmap" chapter for macroeconomics. It may be used in whole or in part by instructors, particularly by those who intend to work through to the *AS/AD* model and who wish to outline the path to be followed. Chapter 13 is a description of the interaction of the money and goods markets, including the determination of interest rates, investment, and a discussion of "crowding out," in both a closed and an open economy. Chapter 13 concentrates on interest rate effects and can be omitted without disrupting the overall flow of the book.

The remaining macroeconomics chapters are "issues" chapters and extend the material in the core chapters. As indicated in the chart, almost all of these chapters require only Chapters 9–12 as background. Of the two chapters that use the *AS/AD* analysis of Chapter 14, in each case, the first part of the chapter can be covered without the *AS/AD* model. Chapter 15 begins with a discussion of labour market theories of unemployment and then uses the *AS/AD* model to introduce the Phillips curve. Chapter 18 starts with a discussion of Keynesianism versus monetarism and then employs the *AS/AD* model as part of the discussion of the rational expectations and supply-side (or real business cycle) approach.

Chapters 16 (government budget balance and debt), Chapter 17 (a more detailed analysis of consumption and investment behaviour), and Chapter 19 (growth) can all be covered with just the background of Chapters 9–12. These additional chapters provide a fuller discussion of topics sketched in the earlier chapters.

The last three chapters in the book are issues chapters on the global economy. Chapter 21 is on international macroeconomics. While this is an important area, it is not as vital to cover this material as it may be with other introductory texts, since the basic role of the exchange rate has been incorporated much earlier. Chapters 20 and 22 are common with the *Principles of Microeconomics* volume and cover the topics of "real" international trade and economic development.

How much of this material can be covered in a one-term course? Again, this is the instructor's choice and depends on the desired depth of coverage. The table above provides some suggestions for possible courses. We considered three broad types of emphasis: (a) macro stabilization policy with *AS/AD* analysis, (b) macro stabilization policy without *AS/AD* analysis, and (c) long-run structural macroeconomic policy. The last option is designed for instructors who feel more comfortable with an overall microeconomic emphasis within economics, but who nonetheless want to give students the basic tools to understand the Keynesian perspective and macroeconomic policy debates. For option (c), we assume that these instructors will want to omit *AS/AD* analysis.

In each case, if the macroeconomics term is the student's first exposure to economics, the course will probably begin with Chapters 1, 2, 3 (optional), 4, and the abbreviated Chapter 5, and fewer issues chapters will be chosen. Also, if instructors are including the "real" theory of international trade in the course, they may decide to include it in either term.

The Plan of *Principles of Microeconomics,* Second Canadian Edition

For professors who are teaching microeconomics, a new version of *Principles of Microeconomics* is also available.

The organization of the microeconomic material reflects our belief that the best way to understand how market economies operate—and the best way to understand basic economic theory—is to work through the perfectly competitive model first, including discussions of output *and* input markets and the connections between them, before turning to noncompetitive market structures. When students understand how a simple competitive system works, they can start thinking about how the pieces of the economy "fit together." We think this is a better approach to teaching economics than some of the more traditional approaches, which encourage students to think of economics as a series of disconnected alternative market models.

Doing competition first also allows students to see the power of the market system. It is impossible to discuss the things that markets do or do not do well until students have seen how a simple system determines the allocation of resources. This is our purpose in Chapters 6–11. Chapter 12 remains a pivotal chapter that links the world of perfect competition with the imperfect world of noncompetitive markets, externalities, imperfect information, and poverty, all of which we discuss in Chapters 13–17. In Chapters 18–20 students use everything they've learned in Chapters 6–17 to take a closer look at some of the fields of applied microeconomics (the economics of taxation, labour economics, and the economics of health care and immigration). Finally, in Chapters 21–22, we examine some topics in international economics. Although we've chosen to place these chapters at the end of the book, instructors can integrate them into their course at any time they feel is appropriate.

The Teaching Package

Each component of the teaching and learning package has been carefully crafted to ensure that the course is a rewarding experience for both instructors and students.

INSTRUCTOR'S RESOURCE MANUAL FOR MACROECONOMICS

An innovative instructor's resource manual is available for this text. The Instructor's Resource Manual (IRM) is the key integrative supplement in the teaching and learning package and has been designed with the *teaching* of economics in mind. Each chapter in the IRM corresponds to a chapter in the text. The manual includes chapter outlines with key terminology; teaching notes and lecture suggestions that provide ideas for applying theory, reinforcing key concepts, overcoming student misconceptions, initiating classroom discussion, and integrating outside readings and global examples into the lecture; additional problems with solutions; solutions to all odd-numbered problems in the text; and answers for all the analytical thinking questions that accompany the book's Case Studies.

The IRM also includes a section called "Extended Applications for Teaching Economics." This is a collection of instructors' favourite ideas, exercises, activities, experiments, and games that help economics come alive.

Test Item File 1 for Macroeconomics

The Case/Fair/Strain/Veall Test Item File is a comprehensive test bank. For each chapter, it provides approximately 100 multiple-choice questions, 10 true-false questions and 10 short-answer essay questions. The questions are classified into three levels of difficulty—easy, moderate, and difficult—and are page-referenced to the text. Problem sets (a series of questions based on a graph or scenario) can contain all three levels. Also included are challenging questions that require students to undertake several steps of reasoning, or to work backwards from effect to cause. The Test Item File is available in printed and electronic (word processing) formats.

Pearson Education Test Manager

The Test Item File is designed for use with the Pearson Test Manager, a computerized package that allows users to custom design, save, and generate classroom tests and to create gradebooks. The test program (which runs on Windows-based computers) permits instructors to edit and add or delete questions from the Test Item File, to edit existing graphics and create new graphics, and to export files to various programs, including Microsoft Word and Excel, and WordPerfect. Graphics capability ensures that all graphs included in the Test Item File can be printed next to the appropriate questions.

Test Item File 2 for Macroeconomics: Real-World Problem Sets

This ancillary provides approximately 50 questions for each chapter. Created to provide the instructor with an additional testing resource, the Real-World Problem Sets can be used as quiz/testing tools or as homework problems.

Each problem set is based on current events and/or newspaper or magazine clippings. Students are asked to analyze a scenario or minicase, draw or interpret graphs, and answer questions. Solutions are provided for each problem.

Transparency Masters for Macroeconomics and Microeconomics

Transparency Masters of all the figures and tables in both volumes of the text are available for classroom use.

PowerPoint Transparencies for Macroeconomics and Microeconomics

Also available is a series of PowerPoint presentations that summarize concepts and theories, emphasize

problem solving, provide visual support for lectures, and show the relevance of economics. The PowerPoint disk also includes additional sets of time-series data (not included in the textbook), drawn from a variety of sources. Lecture notes include a snapshot of each PowerPoint slide, provide lecture suggestions and discussion questions, and help instructors correlate the slides with the text and their classroom presentations.

CBC/Pearson Education Video Library for *Principles of Macroeconomics* and *Principles of Microeconomics*

CBC and Pearson Education have combined their experience in academic publishing and global reporting to create a special video ancillary to the text. The library consists of 9 video segments from the CBC programs *The National Magazine, News in Review,* and *Venture.* Each of the segments has been chosen to supplement a Case Study in the text.

On-Line Learning Solutions

Pearson Education Canada supports instructors interested in using on-line course management systems. We provide text-related content in WebCT, Blackboard, and our own private label version of Blackboard called CourseCompass. To find out more about creating an on-line course using Pearson content in one of these platforms, contact your local Pearson Education Canada representative.

The Learning Package

Study Guide for Macroeconomics

A comprehensive Study Guide has been prepared to reinforce the textbook and provide students with additional applications and exercises. Each chapter in the Guide corresponds to a chapter in the textbook and contains the following features:

- *Point-by-Point Objectives:* A list of learning goals for the chapter, along with a brief summary of the material, helpful study hints, tips, practice questions with solutions, and page references to the text

- *Practice Tests:* A series of multiple-choice, short-answer, discussion, and application questions designed to test students' grasp of the material and help them prepare for exams

- *Solutions:* Complete solutions—not just answers—to all questions in the Study Guide, complete with page references to the text

In addition, the Study Guide contains a Graphing Tutorial (for text Appendix 1A) that guides students through graphing techniques. "Graphing Pointer" sections in selected chapters feature additional tips and insights for students as they learn the graphical material in that chapter.

ECONOMICS CENTRAL

www.pearsoned.ca/economics — This site for introductory students and professors contains a wealth of on-line resources to help you study or teach economics. You will find the following features at this site:

- an instructor newsletter;
- actual exams from previous years for students to use as practice tests;
- on-line lessons for topics students often find challenging;
- links to breaking economic news around the world;
- an on-line tutor accessible through e-mail;
- tutorials on math and graphing;
- and lots more!

In addition, from this site you can go to our companion web site created specifically for *Principles of Macroeconomics*. Just follow the links! The companion web site contains self-test questions and special exercises for students, and a Syllabus Builder for instructors, all of which are tied directly to the second Canadian edition of Principles of Macroeconomics.

ACKNOWLEDGMENTS

We are grateful to the many people who offered support, helpful suggestions, references, data, and recommendations for the Second Canadian edition. The contributions of Deb Fretz of McMaster University were absolutely essential and we are deeply indebted to her. Brendon Cameron and Rosanna di Matteo provided valuable and timely assistance in our research. We also thank Joseph Attah-Mensah and Kevin Clinton (Bank of Canada); Paul Boothe (University of Alberta); Lois McNabb (Ministry of Forests, British Columbia); Tim Sargent (Department of Finance, Canada); Wulong Gu (Industry Canada); Livio di Matteo and Mike Shannon (both of Lakehead University); John Burbidge, Don Dawson, Martin Dooley, Andy Muller, Bill Scarth, and Byron Spencer (all of McMaster University); Chris Dimatteo and John Trim (ScotiaMcLeod); Michel Pascal and Karen Wilson (both of Statistics Canada); Dwayne Benjamin and Peter Dungan (both of University of Toronto); Arthur Sweetman (Queen's University); and Tom Crossley (York University).

We would also particularly like to thank the following instructors who provided formal reviews on all or part of the manuscript:

Mak Arvin (Trent University)
Bagala Biswal (Memorial University of Newfoundland)
Michael Bradfield (Dalhousie University)
Saud Choudhry (Trent University)
Patrick Coe (University of Calgary)
Don Dawson (McMaster University)
Torben Drewes (Trent University)
Hugh Grant (University of Winnipeg)
Susan Kamp (University of Alberta)
Brian Krauth (Simon Fraser University)
Dan Otchere (Concordia University)
Jim Sentance (University of PEI)
Larry Smith (University of Waterloo)
Christopher Worswick (Carleton University)

At Pearson Education Canada, we are grateful to Dave Ward, Acquisitions Editor; Maurice Esses, Developmental Editor; Jennifer Therriault, Production Editor; and Rodney Rawlings, Copy Editor, for their help in developing and producing this book.

We welcome comments about the Second Canadian edition. Please write to us care of Acquisitions Editor, Economics, Pearson Education Canada, Higher Education Division, 26 Prince Andrew Place, Don Mills, Ontario M3C 2T8.

Frank Strain
Michael Veall

About the Authors

Karl E. Case is the Marion Butler McLean Professor in the History of Ideas and Professor of Economics at Wellesley College. He also lectures on Econo-mics and Tax Policy in the International Tax Program at Harvard Law School and is a Visiting Scholar at the Federal Reserve Bank of Boston. He received his B.A. from Miami University in 1968, spent three years in the army, and received his M.A. and Ph.D. from Harvard University. In 1980 and 1981 he was a Liberal Arts Fellow in Law and Economics at Harvard Law School.

Professor Case's research has been in the areas of public finance, taxation, and housing. He is the author or coauthor of four other books, including *Economics and Tax Policy* and *Property Taxation: The Need for Reform,* as well as numerous articles in professional journals.

For the past 20 years, he has taught at Wellesley, where he was Department Chair from 1982 to 1985. Before coming to Wellesley, he spent two years as Head Tutor (director of undergraduate studies) at Harvard, where he won the Allyn Young Teaching Prize. He has been a member of the AEA's Committee on Economic Education and was Associate Editor of the *Journal of Economic Education,* responsible for the section on innovations in teaching. He teaches at least one section of the principles course every year.

Ray C. Fair is Professor of Economics at Yale University. He is a member of the Cowles Foundation at Yale and a Fellow of the Econometric Society. He received a B.A. in economics from Fresno State College in 1964 and a Ph.D. in economics from M.I.T. in 1968. He taught at Princeton University from 1968 to 1974 and has been at Yale since 1974.

Professor Fair's research has primarily been in the areas of macroeconomics and econometrics, with particular emphasis on macroeconometric model building. His publications include *Specification, Estimation, and Analysis of Macroeconometric Models* (Harvard Press, 1984) and *Testing Macroeconometric Models* (Harvard Press, 1994).

Professor Fair has taught introductory and intermediate economics at Yale. He has also taught graduate courses in macroeconomic theory and macroeconometrics.

About the Authors

J. Frank Strain is Professor and Head of the Department of Economics at Mount Allison University in Sackville, New Brunswick, where he has taught since 1985. He received a B.A. from the University of Prince Edward Island, an M.A. from the University of New Brunswick, and a Ph.D. from the University of Manitoba.

Dr. Strain's research has been in the areas of regional economics, public finance, labour economics, and Canadian economic history. He is the author or coauthor of 20 articles in professional journals and edited volumes. As well, he is the author of one book—*Integration, Federalism, and Cohesion in the European Community*—and coeditor of another—*The Canadian Welfare State: Past, Present, and Future*.

Dr. Strain teaches a wide variety of undergraduate courses at Mount Allison. In 1997, he was awarded the Paul Pare Medal for Excellence in recognition of his contributions to teaching and research.

Michael R. Veall is Professor of Economics at McMaster University. He received a B.A. from McMaster in 1976, an M.A. from the University of Western Ontario in 1977, and a Ph.D. from M.I.T. in 1981. Aside from teaching at McMaster, Professor Veall has taught at The University of Western Ontario, Queen's University, the Australian National University, and the University of Mannheim in Germany. He has also been a von Humboldt fellow both at Mannheim and at the University of Munich, and has held honourary visiting positions at the University of York in England and at the University of Western Australia.

Professor Veall's research has been primarily in the area of applied econometrics. He is the author of a number of articles in professional journals including the *Canadian Journal of Economics, Canadian Public Policy, Econometrica,* the *International Economic Review*, the *Journal of Public Economics*, and the *Review of Economics and Statistics*. He has been a consultant to a number of public-sector organizations including Ontario Hydro and the federal Department of Finance.

His proudest professional accomplishment is helping more than 2500 students survive and, he hopes, enjoy courses in introductory economics. He also teaches graduate econometrics at McMaster, and has taught graduate courses in public economics and international macroeconomics.

The Scope and Method of Economics

Learning Objectives

1 Summarize the importance of studying economic issues and describe how an economic way of thinking enables us to understand society and international affairs and thus become more informed voters.

2 Distinguish between the two main branches of economics.

3 Identify the roles played by theories, models, and empirical evidence in economics.

4 Describe the roles played by *positive* judgments and *normative* judgments in economic policy analysis.

5 *Appendix 1A*: Read and interpret graphs and linear equations.

Why Study Economics?
To Learn a Way of Thinking
To Understand Society
To Understand Global Affairs
To Be an Informed Voter

The Scope of Economics
Microeconomics and Macroeconomics
The Diversity of Fields in Economics

The Method of Economics
Theories and Models
Economic Policy

An Invitation

Appendix 1A: **How to Read and Understand Graphs**

The study of economics should begin with a sense of wonder. Pause for a moment and consider a typical day in your life. For breakfast you might have bread made in a local bakery with flour produced in Manitoba from wheat grown in Saskatchewan and bacon from pigs raised in Quebec packaged in plastic made in Ontario. You spill coffee from Colombia on your shirt made in Malaysia from textiles shipped from the Philippines.

After class you drive with a friend in a Japanese car on a highway system that took 20 years and billions of dollars' worth of resources to build. You stop for gasoline refined in New Brunswick from Venezuelan crude oil brought to Canada on a supertanker that took three years to build at a shipyard in Nova Scotia.

At night you call your brother in Mexico City. The call travels over fibre-optic cable to a powerful antenna that sends it to a transponder on one of over 1000 communications satellites orbiting the earth.

You use or consume tens of thousands of things, both tangible and intangible, every day: buildings, the music of a rock band. Thousands of decisions went into their completion. Somehow they got to you.

Fifteen million people in Canada—almost half the total population—work at hundreds of thousands of different kinds of jobs producing over a trillion dollars' worth of goods and services every year. Some cannot find work; some choose not to work. Some are rich; others are poor.

Every year Canadians import billions of dollars' worth of tropical fruit, electronic equipment, Hollywood movies, and other goods and services produced in other countries. High-rise office buildings go up in central cities. Condominiums and homes are built in the suburbs.

economics *The study of how individuals and societies choose to use the scarce resources that nature and previous generations have provided.*

Some countries are wealthy. Others are impoverished. Some are growing. Some are stagnating. Some businesses are doing well. Others are going bankrupt.

At any moment every society faces constraints imposed by nature and by previous generations. Some societies are handsomely endowed by nature with fertile land, water, sunshine, and natural resources. Others have deserts and few mineral resources. Some societies receive much from previous generations—art, music, technical knowledge, beautiful buildings, and productive factories. Others are left with overgrazed, eroded land, cities levelled by war, or polluted natural environments. All societies face limits.

Economics is the study of how individuals and societies choose to use the scarce resources that nature and previous generations have provided. The key word in this definition is *choose*. Economics is a behavioural science. In large measure it is the study of how people make choices. The choices that people make, when added up, translate into societal choices.

The purpose of this chapter and the next is to elaborate on this definition and to introduce the subject matter of economics. What is produced? How is it produced? Who gets it? Why? Is the result good or bad? Can it be improved?

Why Study Economics?

There are four main reasons to study economics: to learn a way of thinking, to understand society, to understand global affairs, and to be an informed voter.

To Learn a Way of Thinking

Probably the most important reason for studying economics is to learn a particular way of thinking. A good way to introduce economics is to review three of its most fundamental concepts: opportunity cost; marginalism; and information, incentives, and market coordination. If your study of economics is successful, you will find yourself using these concepts every day in making decisions.

■ **Opportunity Cost** What happens in an economy is the outcome of thousands of individual decisions. Households must decide how to divide up their incomes over all the goods and services available in the marketplace. Individuals must decide whether to work, whether to go to school, and how much to save. Businesses must decide what to produce, how much to produce, how much to charge, and where to locate. It is not surprising that economic analysis focuses on the process of decision-making.

All decisions involve tradeoffs. There are advantages and disadvantages, costs and benefits, associated with every action and every choice. A key concept that recurs again and again in analyzing the decision-making process is the notion of opportunity cost. The full "cost" of making a specific choice is what we give up by not making the alternative choice. That which we forgo, or give up, when we make a choice or a decision is called the **opportunity cost** of that decision.

opportunity cost *That which we forgo, or give up, when we make a choice or a decision.*

The concept applies to individuals, businesses, and entire societies. The opportunity cost of going to a movie is the value of the other things you could have done with the same money and time. If you decide to take time off in lieu of working, the opportunity cost of your leisure is the pay that you would have earned had you worked. Part of the cost of a university education is the income you could earn by working full-time instead of going to school. If a firm purchases a new piece of equipment for $3000, it does so because it expects that equipment to generate more profit. There is an opportunity cost, however, since that $3000 could have been deposited in an interest-earning account. To a society, the opportunity cost of using resources for medical care is the value of the other goods that could be produced with the same resources.

The reason that opportunity costs arise is that resources are scarce. *Scarce* simply means *limited*. Consider one of our most important resources—time. There are only 24 hours in a day, and we must live our lives under this constraint. A farmer in rural Brazil must decide whether it is better to stay on the land and continue to farm or to go to the city and look for a job. A hockey player at the University of Toronto must decide whether she will play on the varsity team or spend more time improving her academic work.

■ **Marginalism and Sunk Costs**   A second key concept used in analyzing choices is the notion of *marginalism*. In weighing the costs and benefits of a decision, it is important to weigh only the costs and benefits that are contingent upon the decision. Suppose, for example, that you lived in St. John's and that you were weighing the costs and benefits of visiting your mother in Vancouver. If business required that you travel to Winnipeg, the cost of visiting Mom would be only the additional, or *marginal*, time and money cost of getting to Vancouver from Winnipeg.

Consider the cost of producing this book. Assume that 10 000 copies are produced. The total cost of producing the copies includes the cost of the authors' time in writing the book, the cost of editing, the cost of making the plates for printing, and the cost of the paper and ink. If the total cost were $600 000, then the average cost of one copy would be $60, which is simply $600 000 divided by 10 000.

Although average cost is an important concept, a book publisher must know more than simply the average cost of a book. For example, suppose a second printing is being debated. That is, should another 10 000 copies be produced? In deciding whether to proceed, the costs of writing, editing, making plates, and so forth are irrelevant. Why? Because they have already been incurred—they are *sunk costs*. **Sunk costs** are costs that cannot be avoided, regardless of what is done in the future, because they have already been incurred. All that matters are the costs associated with the additional, or marginal, books to be printed. Technically, *marginal cost* is the cost of producing one more unit of output.

There are numerous examples in which the concept of marginal cost is useful. For an airplane that is about to take off with empty seats, the marginal cost of an extra passenger is essentially zero; the total cost of the trip is essentially unchanged by the addition of an extra passenger. Thus, setting aside a few seats to be sold at big discounts can be profitable even if the fare for those seats is far below the average cost per seat of making the trip. As long as the airline succeeds in filling seats that would otherwise have been empty, doing so is profitable—marginal revenue is greater than marginal cost.

■ **Information, Incentives, and Market Coordination**   Suppose you have been hired to direct traffic at a highway toll plaza with four toll booths. How would you carry out your task? If your goal is to minimize the time drivers spend in a line-up, you will direct cars to the shortest line, and thus keep all the lines at approximately the same length. But is a traffic director really needed to ensure this result? Drivers will want to spend as little time as possible in a lineup, and so they have an *incentive* to choose the toll booth with the shortest line. As they approach the booths, the drivers will observe the length of the line at each booth and use this *information* to choose which line to enter. If one line is much shorter than the others, cars will quickly move into it until all the lines are equalized. Thus the "visible hand" of the traffic director is not really needed to *coordinate* the choices of the individual drivers to ensure that their time spent in line is minimized.

In *The Wealth of Nations*, one of the most important economics books ever published, Adam Smith, an eighteenth-century Scottish philosopher, argued that prices, wages, and profits in a market economy often provide the incentives and information needed to ensure the type of coordination observed at the toll booths. For example, if people suddenly want more live musical entertainment and less DJ dance music, an economic planner could act as a traffic director and order people to offer more live music and less DJ dance music. But a planner is not necessary. The change in people's tastes creates profit opportunities. Lineups at live music venues will allow these venues to charge higher prices and earn higher profits while clubs supplying DJ dance music will face empty rooms and losses. In a process similar to what takes place at the toll booths—as the drivers move to the shortest line, eventually the length of wait at each line is the same—these profit opportunities will eventually be eliminated as venues try to increase profit by providing live music and avoid losses by supplying less DJ dance music.

sunk costs *Costs that cannot be avoided, regardless of what is done in the future, because they have already been incurred.*

A more dramatic real-life example is illustrated by the response to the OPEC (the Organization of Petroleum Exporting Countries) oil price hikes of 1973. In that year OPEC decided to reduce the supply of oil on world markets. The changes in prices and the new profit opportunities opened up by this decision provided the information and incentives required for Canadians to adjust to this important development. They responded to rising energy prices by increasing exploration for domestic oil and gas, searching for alternative energy sources, increasing purchases of home insulation, and using smaller and more fuel-efficient automobiles. The remarkable capacity of prices, wages, and profits in market economies to provide the information and incentives required to coordinate the decisions of individual decision-makers is one of the most important insights explored in this introductory course in economics.

However, market solutions are not always desirable because individual pursuit of private goals is not always consistent with the public good. Many social and environmental problems (for example, poverty, too little protection for fragile ecosystems and endangered species, etc.) and many of the activities of governments in Canada are tied closely to problems with market institutions. As your knowledge of economics grows you will find yourself thinking critically about market institutions and identifying how they sometimes work well and how they sometimes falter.

> The study of economics teaches us a way of thinking and helps us make decisions.

TO UNDERSTAND SOCIETY

Another reason for studying economics is to understand society better. You cannot hope to understand how a society functions without a basic knowledge of its economy, and you cannot understand a society's economy without knowing its economic history. Clearly, past and present economic decisions have an enormous influence on the character of life in a society. The current state of the physical environment, the level of material well-being, and the nature and number of jobs are all products of the economic system.

To get a sense of the ways in which economic decisions have shaped our environment, imagine that you are looking out of a window on the top floor of a high-rise office building in any large city. The workday is about to begin. All around you are other tall glass and steel buildings full of workers. In the distance you see the smoke of factories. Looking down, you see thousands of commuters pouring off trains and buses, and cars backed up on highway exit ramps. You see trucks carrying goods from one place to another. You also see the face of urban poverty: just beyond the highway is a large low-rent housing development and, beyond that, a group of old factories, many boarded up and deteriorating.

What you see before you is the product of millions of economic decisions made over hundreds of years. People at some point decided to spend time and money building those buildings and factories. Somebody cleared the land, laid the tracks, built the roads, and produced the cars and buses.

Industrial Revolution *The period in England during the late eighteenth and early nineteenth centuries in which new manufacturing technologies and improved transportation gave rise to the modern factory system and a massive movement of the population from the countryside to the cities.*

Not only have economic decisions shaped the physical environment, they have determined the character of society as well. At no time has the impact of economic change on the character of a society been more evident than in England during the late eighteenth and early nineteenth centuries, a period that we now call the **Industrial Revolution.** Increases in the productivity of agriculture, new manufacturing technologies, and the development of more efficient forms of transportation led to a massive movement of the British population from the countryside to the city. At the beginning of the eighteenth century, approximately two out of three people in Great Britain were engaged in agriculture. By 1812, only one in three remained in agriculture, and by 1900 the figure was fewer than one in ten. People jammed into overcrowded cities and worked long hours in factories. The world had changed completely in two centuries—a period that, in the run of history, was nothing more than the blink of an eye.

It is not surprising that the discipline of economics began to take shape during this period. Social critics and philosophers looked around them and knew that their philosophies must expand to accommodate the changes. Adam Smith's *The Wealth of Nations* appeared in 1776. It was followed by the writings of David Ricardo, Karl Marx, Thomas Malthus, and others. Each tried to make sense out of what was happening. Who was building the factories? Why? What determined the level of wages paid to workers or the price of food? What would happen in the future, and what should happen? The people who asked these questions were the first economists.

Similar changes continue to affect the character of life today. Digital technology is transforming everyday life with new products appearing almost every day. E-commerce is changing the way we buy and sell goods and services. Information is more accessible than ever before. For some, these changes are resulting in unemployment and lower incomes. For others, the changes have meant new opportunities and higher incomes. How does one make sense of this? Why are new technologies and new products being developed? Why does unemployment arise? What forces determine incomes? Why do some enjoy high incomes while others are poor?

> The study of economics is an essential part of the study of society.

TO UNDERSTAND GLOBAL AFFAIRS

A third reason for studying economics is to understand global affairs. Famine and poverty in Africa and Southeast Asia, political change in Eastern Europe, and war and genocide are some of the most important issues of our time. Like all global issues they have economic aspects and are impossible to understand without an understanding of economics.

Global affairs are becoming increasingly important. New telecommunications technologies, large movements of peoples, stronger economic linkages, and changes in the geographical pattern of production are contributing to a process popularly referred to as *globalization*. Not only are global affairs interesting in their own right, but international developments have larger consequences for Canadians than ever before.

All countries are part of the world economy, and an understanding of international relations must begin with a basic knowledge of the economic links between countries. For centuries, countries have attempted to protect their industries and workers from foreign competition by restricting imports. In recent years these restrictions have been reduced. Just after World War II many countries signed the General Agreement on Tariffs and Trade (GATT), which committed them to lowering trade barriers. The process continues today, and not always smoothly, under the World Trade Organization (WTO), which replaced GATT in 1995. Trade issues can arouse great passions, as was demonstrated during the WTO negotiations in Seattle in 1999.

Discussions of economic issues can result in passionate responses from participants. A move toward an open system of international trade at the WTO has provoked well-organized protests from citizens concerned that freer trade will damage the environment and result in more suffering in developing countries.

International economic linkages are increasingly important for the major industrial countries of Europe and North America. For example, in the early 1960s about 83% of goods and services produced in Canada were used in this country and the remaining 17% were sold abroad. By 2000, Canadians were selling 43% of their production abroad. Moreover, natural resource exports declined in relative importance as trade increased and exports of services and manufactured products became more important.

The search for profit-making opportunities has also become increasingly global. Canadians are investing heavily in other countries and citizens of other countries are investing more in Canada. Events that create a new climate for international investment, such as the end of the apartheid laws that legally separated the races in South Africa have an impact in Canada and abroad.

In some instances, the impact of developments abroad can be particularly large. The Iraqi invasion of Kuwait in 1990 and the resulting Persian Gulf War in 1991 sent world oil markets on a wild ride, and in part led to a *recession* (a period of decreased production and increasing unemployment). Today, the attempt by countries of Eastern Europe to create capitalist institutions that took centuries to build in the West is creating political uncertainty and increasing concern about nuclear accidents or terrorism.

Another critical global economic issue is the widening gap between rich and poor nations. Although some countries have been able to reduce the gap—notably Korea, Malaysia, and the so-called Asian Tigers—many have not. In 2000, world population was over 6 billion. Of that number, 4.5 billion lived in less developed countries and 1.5 billion lived in more developed countries. The 75% of the world's population that lives in the less developed countries receives less than 20% of the world's income. In dozens of countries, per capita income is only a few hundred dollars a year.

> An understanding of economics is essential to an understanding of global affairs.

TO BE AN INFORMED VOTER

For the past 25 years or so, the Canadian economy has been on a roller coaster. In 1973–74, the Organization of Petroleum Exporting Countries (OPEC) succeeded in raising the world price of oil by 400%. By 1974, prices in Canada were rising across the board at double-digit rates. Inflation again reached double-digit rates in 1980, at which time the economy plunged into a recession. By December 1982, 12.8% of the workforce was unemployed. Then, in the mid-1980s, the economy recovered and the unemployment rate fell to 7.5% by 1989.

In 1990, the Canadian economy went into another recession. Unemployment again rose rapidly reaching a peak in 1992 at a rate of 11.3%. A slow recovery followed and the economy began to create more jobs. By the turn of the century, unemployment had fallen to 6.8%, but this rate still looked high compared to that enjoyed in the United States, where only 4% of the workforce faced unemployment.

The performance of the Canadian economy was a major issue in every election in this period. Consequently, Canadian political parties had to address economic issues and each offered an economic strategy that it promised to pursue if elected.

Canadian parties continue to make economics a major platform plank. The economic strategies offered are remarkably diverse. The Ontario and Alberta Progressive Conservatives and the Canadian Alliance parties have proposed policies based on the belief that economic performance will improve dramatically if the role of government in society is reduced and the private sector given a bigger role. The New Democratic Party, on the other hand, suggests that increased reliance on the private sector will result in an unjust society and an economy that performs poorly; they propose a continuing role for government. The Liberals and the national Progressive Conservatives tend to fall somewhere in the middle.

Canadians always face a choice between competing strategies. Those without knowledge of economics have to base their choice on extraneous factors such as party loyalty, attitudes toward the previous prime minister, candidates' television appearances, and the rhetorical skill of the party leaders. Only those with some knowledge of economics possess the skills needed to assess critically the complex political platforms offered.

> When we participate in the political process, we are voting on issues that require a basic understanding of economics.

The Scope of Economics

Most students taking economics for the first time are surprised by the breadth of what they study. Some think that economics will teach them about the stock market or what to do with their money. Others think that economics deals exclusively with problems like inflation and unemployment. In fact, it deals with all these subjects, but they are pieces of a much larger puzzle.

Economics has deep roots in, and close ties to, social philosophy. An issue of great importance to philosophers, for example, is distributional justice. Why are some people rich and others poor, and whatever the answer, is this fair? A number of nineteenth-century social philosophers wrestled with these questions, and out of their musings economics as a separate discipline was born.

The easiest way to get a feel for the breadth and depth of what you will be studying is to briefly explore the way economics is organized. First of all, there are two major divisions of economics: microeconomics and macroeconomics.

MICROECONOMICS AND MACROECONOMICS

Microeconomics deals with the functioning of individual industries and the behaviour of individual economic decision-making units—business firms and households—and the effects of government economic policy on these units. Microeconomics explores the decisions that individual businesses and consumers make. Firms' choices about what to produce and how much to charge, households' choices about what and how much to buy, and government economic policies help explain why the economy produces the things it does.

> **microeconomics** *The branch of economics that examines the functioning of individual industries and the behaviour of individual decision-making units—business firms and households—and the effects of government economic policy on these units.*

Another big question that microeconomics addresses is who gets the things that are produced. Wealthy households get more output than poor households, and the forces that determine this distribution of output are microeconomics. Why does poverty exist? Who is poor? Why do some jobs pay more than others?

Think again about all the things you consume in a day, and then think back to that view out over a big city. Somebody decided to build those factories. Somebody decided to construct the roads, build the housing, and produce the cars. Why? What is going on in all those buildings? It is easy to see that understanding individual micro decisions is very important to any understanding of society.

Macroeconomics looks at the economy as a whole. Instead of trying to understand what determines the output of a single firm or industry or the consumption patterns of a single household or group of households, macroeconomics examines the factors that determine the country's output or domestic product. Microeconomics is concerned with *household* income; macroeconomics deals with *national* income.

> **macroeconomics** *The branch of economics that examines the economic behaviour of aggregates—income, employment, output, and so on—on a national scale and the effects of government economic policy on these aggregates.*

While microeconomics focuses on individual product prices and relative prices, macroeconomics looks at the overall price level and how quickly (or slowly) it is rising (or falling). Microeconomics questions how many people will be hired (or fired) this year in a particular industry or in a certain geographical area, and the factors that determine how much labour a firm or industry will hire. Macroeconomics deals with aggregate employment and unemployment: how many jobs exist in the economy as a whole, and how many people who are willing to work are not able to find work.

Like microeconomics, macroeconomics examines the impact of government economic policy; but it focuses on aggregates, examining how different government policies affect national income and output, total employment and unemployment, and the price level and inflation.

> Microeconomics looks at the individual unit—the household, the firm, the industry. It sees and examines the "trees." Macroeconomics looks at the whole, the aggregate. It sees and analyzes the "forest."

Table 1.1 summarizes these divisions and some of the subjects with which they are concerned.

Table 1.1 — **Examples of Microeconomic and Macroeconomic Concerns**

DIVISION OF ECONOMICS	PRODUCTION	PRICES	INCOME	EMPLOYMENT
Microeconomics	*Production/Output in Individual Industries and Businesses*	*Price of Individual Goods and Services*	*Distribution of Income and Wealth*	*Employment by Individual Businesses and Industry*
	How much steel How much office space How many cars	Price of medical care Price of gasoline Food prices Apartment rents	Wages in the auto industry Minimum wage Executive salaries Poverty	Jobs in the steel industry Number of employees in a firm Number of accountants
Macroeconomics	*National Production/Output*	*Aggregate Price Level*	*National Income*	*Employment and Unemployment in the Economy*
	Total industrial output Gross domestic product Growth of output	Consumer prices Producer prices Rate of inflation	Total wages and salaries Total corporate profits	Total number of jobs Unemployment rate

THE DIVERSITY OF FIELDS IN ECONOMICS

Individual economists focus their research and study in many diverse areas. Many of these specialized fields are reflected in the advanced courses offered at most colleges and universities. Some are concerned with economic history or the history of economic thought. Others focus on international economics or growth in less developed countries. Still others study the economics of cities (urban economics) or the relationship between economics and law. (See the Application box titled "The Fields of Economics" for more details.)

Economists also differ in the emphasis they place on theory. Some economists specialize in developing new theories, while others spend their time testing the theories of others. Some economists hope to expand the frontiers of knowledge, while others are more interested in applying what is already known to the formulation of public policies.

As you begin your study of economics, look through your school's course catalogue and talk to the faculty about their interests. You will discover that economics encompasses a broad range of inquiry and is linked to many other disciplines.

The Method of Economics

positive economics *An approach to economics that seeks to understand behaviour and the operation of systems without making judgments. It describes what exists and how it works.*

normative economics *An approach to economics that analyzes outcomes of economic behaviour, evaluates them as good or bad, and may prescribe courses of action.*

Economics asks and attempts to answer two kinds of questions, positive and normative. **Positive economics** attempts to understand behaviour and the operation of economic systems *without making judgments* about whether the outcomes are good or bad. It strives to describe what exists and how it works. What determines the wage rate for unskilled workers? What would happen if we abolished the corporate income tax? Who would benefit? Who would lose? The answers to such questions are the subject of positive economics.

In contrast, **normative economics** looks at the outcomes of economic behaviour and asks if they are good or bad and whether they can be made better. Normative economics involves judgments and prescriptions for courses of action. Should the government be involved in regulating the price of gasoline? Should the income tax be changed to reduce or increase the burden on upper-income families? Should Ontario Hydro be broken up into a set of smaller companies? Should we protect Canadian agriculture from foreign competition?

Of course most normative questions involve positive questions. To know whether the government *should* take a particular action, we must know first if it *can* and second what the consequences are likely to be. (For example, if Ontario Hydro is broken up, will there be more competition and lower prices?)

Some claim that positive, value-free economic analysis is impossible. They argue that analysts come to problems with biases that cannot help but influence their work. Furthermore, even in choosing what questions to ask or what problems to analyze, economists are influenced by political, ideological, and moral views.

While this argument has some merit, it is nevertheless important to distinguish between analyses that attempt to be positive and those that are intentionally and explicitly normative. Economists who ask explicitly normative questions should be forced to specify their grounds for judging one outcome superior to another. What does it mean to be better? The criteria for such evaluations must be clearly spelled out and thoroughly understood for conclusions to have meaning.

Positive economics is often divided into descriptive economics and economic theory. **Descriptive economics** is simply the compilation of data that describe phenomena and facts. Examples of such data appear in the *Canada Yearbook,* a large volume of data published by Statistics Canada every year that describes many features of the Canadian economy.

Where do all these data come from? Statistics Canada produces an enormous amount of raw data every year, as does the Bank of Canada and a number of federal government departments. The computer and the Internet now provide an invaluable means to access much of this economic information. However, keep in mind that information you might obtain from the Net is not always reliable or worthwhile. Nonetheless, there are some very good Web sites. Table 1.2 lists some sites that are worth exploring. Other Internet resources are listed at the end of each Part in this book.

Economic theory attempts to generalize about data and interprets them. An **economic theory** is a statement or set of related statements about cause and effect, action and reaction. One of the first theories you will encounter in this text is the *law of demand,* which was most clearly stated by Alfred Marshall in 1890: when

FAST FACTS

Statistics Canada estimated the median income of Canadian individuals in 1998 to be $20 100. The *median* is a measure designed to focus on a representative Canadian individual. Half of all Canadians earn more than $20 100; half earn less.

Source: *Statistics Canada, The Daily,* August 10, 2000.

descriptive economics *The compilation of data that describe phenomena and facts.*

economic theory *A statement or set of related statements about cause and effect, action and reaction.*

Table 1.2	Computers: Accessing Economic Information Through the Internet
Statistics Canada	www.statcan.ca/ This site provides access to statistical information on Canada including major monthly and quarterly economic indicators. You will also find here a detailed description of the Canadian Socio-economic Information System (CANSIM), the most important and comprehensive source of Canadian economic data. You should be able to get access to CANSIM through your school library.
Finance Canada	www.fin.gc.ca/ This site provides information on federal tax and expenditure policies as well as some links to the Internet sites of Canadian financial institutions and provincial governments.
Bank of Canada	www.bankofcanada.ca This site includes information on Canadian monetary policy, a variety of financial statistics, and a description of debt management policy.
Industry Canada	www.ic.gc.ca This site has the latest information on what Industry Canada is doing to position Canada as a frontrunner in the global, knowledge-based economy. There are also success stories about innovative Canadian companies and fact sheets that provide concise descriptions of many of Industry Canada's programs. The ministry's Strategis site provides business and consumer information.
Resources for Economists on the Internet	www.rfe.org This document—by Bill Goffe, Department of Economics, SUNY Oswego—is a comprehensive and regularly updated guide to information on the Internet, of interest to people working in economics.
Canadian Economics Association	www.economics.ca This site has links to most economics departments at Canadian universities and a variety of other useful sites.

A good way to convey the diversity of economics is to describe some of its major fields of study and the issues that economists address.

■ **INDUSTRIAL ORGANIZATION** looks carefully at the structure and performance of industries and firms within an economy. How do businesses compete? Who gains and who loses?

■ **URBAN AND REGIONAL ECONOMICS** studies the spatial arrangement of economic activity. Why do we have cities? Why are manufacturing firms locating farther and farther from the centre of urban areas?

■ **ECONOMETRICS** applies statistical techniques and data to economic problems in an effort to test hypotheses and theories. Most schools require economics degree students to take at least one course in statistics or econometrics.

■ **COMPARATIVE ECONOMIC SYSTEMS** examines the ways alternative economic systems function. What are the advantages and disadvantages of different systems? What is the best way to convert the planned economies of the former Soviet Union to market systems?

■ **ECONOMIC DEVELOPMENT** focuses on the problems of poor countries. What can be done to promote development in these nations? Important concerns of development economists include population growth and control, provision for basic needs, and strategies for international trade.

■ **LABOUR ECONOMICS** deals with the factors that determine wage rates, employment, and unemployment. How do people decide whether to work, how much to work, and at what kind of job? How have the roles of unions and management changed in recent years?

■ **FINANCE** examines the ways in which households and firms actually pay for, or finance their purchases. It involves the study of capital markets (including the stock and bond markets), futures and options, capital budgeting, and asset valuation.

■ **INTERNATIONAL ECONOMICS** studies trade flows among countries and international financial institutions. What are the advantages and disadvantages for a country that allows its citizens to buy and sell freely in world markets? Why is the Canadian dollar strong or weak?

■ **PUBLIC ECONOMICS** examines the role of government in the economy. What are the economic functions of government, and what should they be? How should the government finance the services that it provides? What kinds of government programs should confront the problems of poverty, unemployment, and pollution?

■ **ECONOMIC HISTORY** traces the development of the modern economy. What economic and political events and scientific advances caused the Industrial Revolution that began in eighteenth-century Great Britain? What explains the tremendous growth and progress of post–World War II Japan? What caused the Great Depression of the 1930s?

Several of the fields of economics are concerned with poverty in developing countries.

■ **LAW AND ECONOMICS** analyzes the economic function of legal rules and institutions. How does the law change the behaviour of individuals and businesses? Do different liability rules make accidents and injuries more or less likely? What are the economic costs of crime?

■ **THE HISTORY OF ECONOMIC THOUGHT,** which is grounded in philosophy, studies the development of economic ideas and theories over time, from Adam Smith in the eighteenth century to the works of economists such as Thomas Malthus, Karl Marx, and John Maynard Keynes. Because economic theory is constantly developing and changing, studying the history of ideas helps give meaning to modern theory and puts it in perspective.

inductive reasoning *The process of observing regular patterns from raw data and drawing generalizations from them.*

the price of a product rises, people tend to buy less of it; when the price of a product falls, they tend to buy more.

The process of observing regular patterns from raw data and drawing generalizations from them is called **inductive reasoning.** In all sciences, theories begin with inductive reasoning and observed regularities. For example, Aristotle believed that the speed at which objects fall toward the earth depends on their weight. But in a series of experiments carried out between 1589 and 1591, Galileo was able to show that bodies of very different weights seemed to fall at approximately the same speed when dropped from the Leaning Tower of Pisa. Over a century later, Galileo's data led Sir Isaac Newton to formulate the theory of gravity, which eventually became the basis of Albert Einstein's work.

Social scientists, including economists, study human behaviour. They develop and test theories of how human beings, institutions, and societies behave. The behaviour of human beings is by its nature not as regular or predictable as the behaviour of electrons, molecules, or planets, but there are patterns, regularities, and tendencies.

Theories do not always arise out of formal numerical data. All of us have been collecting observations of people's behaviour and their responses to economic stimuli for most of our lives. We may have observed our parents' reaction to a sudden increase—or decrease—in income or to the loss of a job or the acquisition of a new one. We all have seen people standing in line waiting for a bargain. And, of course, our own actions and reactions are another important source of data.

THEORIES AND MODELS

In many disciplines, including physics, chemistry, meteorology, political science, and economics, theorists build formal models of behaviour. A **model** is a formal statement of a theory. It is usually a mathematical statement of a presumed relationship between two or more variables.

A **variable** is a measure that can change from time to time or from observation to observation. Income is a variable—it has different values for different people, and different values for the same person at different times. The rental price of a movie on a videocassette is a variable; it has different values at different stores and at different times. There are countless other examples.

Because all models simplify reality by stripping part of it away, they are abstractions. Critics of economics often point to abstraction as a weakness. Most economists, however, see abstraction as a real strength.

The easiest way to see how abstraction can be helpful is to think of a map. A map is a representation of reality that is simplified and abstract. A city or province appears on a piece of paper as a series of lines and colours. The amount of reality that the mapmaker can strip away before the map loses something essential depends on what the map is going to be used for. If you want to drive from Fredericton to Sudbury, you need to know only the major highways and roads. You lose absolutely nothing and gain clarity by cutting out the local streets and roads. If, on the other hand, you need to get around in Montreal, you may need to see every street and alley.

Most maps are two-dimensional representations of a three-dimensional world; they show where roads and highways go but do not show hills and valleys along the way. Trail maps for hikers, however, have "contour lines" that represent changes in elevation. When you are in a car, changes in elevation matter very little; they would make a map needlessly complex and much more difficult to read. But if you are on foot carrying a 30-kilogram pack, a knowledge of elevation is crucial.

Like maps, economic models are abstractions that strip away detail to expose only those aspects of behaviour that are important to the question being asked. The principle that irrelevant detail should be cut away is called the principle of **Ockham's Razor** after the fourteenth-century philosopher William of Ockham.

But be careful. Although abstraction is a powerful tool for exposing and analyzing specific aspects of behaviour, it is possible to oversimplify. Economic models often strip away a good deal of social and political reality to get at underlying concepts. When an economic theory is used to help formulate actual government or institutional policy, political and social reality must often be reintroduced if the policy is to have a chance of working.

The key here is that the appropriate amount of simplification and abstraction depends upon the use to which the model will be put. To return to the map example: you may not want to walk around Halifax with a map made for drivers—the hill rising from the waterfront is steep!

model *A formal statement of a theory. Usually a mathematical statement of a presumed relationship between two or more variables.*

variable *A measure that can change from time to time or from observation to observation.*

Maps are useful abstract representations of reality.

Ockham's Razor *The principle that irrelevant detail should be cut away.*

All Else Equal: *ceteris paribus* It is almost always true that whatever you want to explain with a model depends on more than one factor. Suppose, for example, that you want to explain the total number of kilometres driven by automobile owners in Canada. The number of kilometres driven will change from year to year or month to month; it is a variable. The issue, if we want to understand and explain changes that occur, is what factors cause those changes.

Obviously, many things might have an impact on total kilometres driven. First, more or fewer people may be driving. This, in turn, can be affected by changes in the driving age, by population growth, or by changes in the law. Other factors might include the price of gasoline, the household's income, the number and age of children in the household, the distance from home to work, the location of shopping facilities, and the availability and quality of public transport. When any of these variables change, the members of the household may drive more or less. If changes in any of these variables affect large numbers of households across the country, the total number of kilometres driven will change.

Very often we need to isolate or separate out these effects. For example, suppose that we want to know the impact on driving of a higher tax on gasoline. This change would raise the price of gasoline at the pump, but would not (at least in the short run) affect income, workplace location, number of children, and so forth.

To isolate the impact of one single factor, we use the device of ***ceteris paribus,*** or "other things being equal". We ask: what is the impact of a change in gasoline price on driving behaviour, *ceteris paribus,* or assuming that nothing else changes? If gasoline prices rise by 10%, how much less driving will there be, assuming no simultaneous change in anything else—that is, assuming that income, number of children, population, laws, and so on all remain constant?

> Using the device of *ceteris paribus* is one part of the process of abstraction. In formulating economic theory, the concept helps us simplify reality in order to focus on the relationships that we are interested in.

Expressing Models in Words, Graphs, and Equations Economics is the most quantitative of social sciences, and as a consequence it makes extensive use of mathematics. The mathematics used in this course will not be very sophisticated; only basic high school math will be needed.

Mathematics is used in economics because the subject matter is fundamentally quantitative. Consider the following statements: "Lower airline prices cause people to fly more frequently." "Higher interest rates slow the rate of home sales." "When firms produce more output, employment increases." "Higher gasoline prices cause people to drive less and to buy more fuel-efficient cars." "When the Canadian dollar falls in value against the value of foreign currencies, firms that export products produced in Canada find their sales increasing." In each case the statement expresses a relationship between two variables that can be assigned numerical values. The ticket price is a number, and so is the number of trips. The amount of output is a number, and so is the level of employment, etc. Moreover, the statements not only involve variables that can be captured by numbers but also specify a relationship between the variables that involves a stimulus and a response or cause and effect.

Quantitative relationships can be expressed in a variety of ways. Sometimes words are sufficient to express the essence of a theory. However, it is often necessary to be more specific about the nature of a relationship or about the magnitude of a response. Consequently, if you flip through the pages of this or any other economics text, you will see countless tables and graphs and the occasional mathematical equation. The tables, graphs, and equations are important ways of specifically presenting relationships between quantitative variables.

In much of the text we rely on tables and graphs, and make only limited use of mathematical equations. This is because students often find the visual presentation of relationships using tables and graphs easier to comprehend than an equation. Moreover, they often find tables and graphs less intimidating. A review of basic graphing techniques is presented in the Appendix to this chapter.

ceteris paribus Literally, "other things being equal." Used to analyze the relationship between two variables while the values of other variables are held unchanged.

Because relationships can also be captured using mathematical equations, formal mathematics is extensively used by economists. Students comfortable with such mathematics may gain insights by translating tables and graphs into equations. For example, suppose households in some fictional economy spend or consume 90% of their income and save 10% of their income. We could then write:

$$C = 0.90Y \text{ and } S = 0.1Y$$

where C is consumption spending, Y is income, and S is savings. If we know the level of income, the equation can be used to tell us the levels of consumption and savings. For example, if we know income (Y) is $1 trillion, the equations can be used to determine that consumption equals $900 billion and savings equals $100 billion. As well, the equation tells us that every $1 increase in income results in a $0.90 increase in consumption and a $0.10 increase in savings. Writing algebraic expressions like these can help us understand the nature of the underlying process of decision-making. Understanding this process is what economics is all about.

To keep the level of mathematics used simple, all equations used in this text will be *linear*. Linear equations have the general form:

$$y = a + bx$$

where a is the value of y when $x = 0$ (the y-intercept when the relationship is graphed) and b is the change in the value of y when x changes by one unit (b is the slope when the relationship is graphed).

■ **Cautions and Pitfalls**   In formulating theories and models, it is especially important to avoid two pitfalls: the *post hoc* fallacy and the *fallacy of composition*.

Post Hoc *Fallacy*   Theories often make statements or sets of statements, about cause and effect. It can be quite tempting to look at two events that happen in sequence and assume that the first caused the second to happen. Clearly, this is not always the case. This common error is called the **post hoc, ergo propter hoc** (or "after this, therefore because of this") fallacy.

There are thousands of examples. The Toronto Maple Leafs have won seven games in a row. Last night, you went to the game and they lost. You must have "jinxed" them. They lost *because* you went to the game.

Stock market analysts indulge in what is perhaps the most striking example of the *post hoc* fallacy in action. Every day the stock market goes up or down, and every day some analyst on some national news program singles out one or two of the day's events as the cause of some change in the market: "Today the TSE Index rose five points on heavy trading; analysts say that the increase was due to Finance Minister Paul Martin's latest budget." But did the Martin budget really cause the increase in the TSE Index? If the stock market had fallen, presumably some reason would have been found to "explain" that as well (perhaps the reason would also have been Paul Martin's budget). Overall, it is difficult to link many daily changes in the stock market to specific news events.

Very closely related to the *post hoc* fallacy is the often erroneous link between correlation and causation. Two variables are said to be *correlated* if one variable changes when the other variable changes. But correlation does not imply causation. Cities that have high crime rates also have lots of automobiles, so there is a very high degree of correlation between number of cars and crime rates. Can we argue, then, that cars *cause* crime? No. The reason for the correlation here may have nothing to do with cause and effect. Big cities have lots of people, lots of people have lots of cars, and therefore big cities have lots of cars. Big cities also have high crime rates for many reasons—crowding, poverty, anonymity, unequal distribution of wealth, and the ready availability of drugs, to mention only a few. But the presence of cars is not one of them.

Fallacy of Composition   To conclude that what is true for a part is necessarily true for the whole is to fall into the **fallacy of composition.** Often what holds for an individual does not hold for a group or for society as a whole. Suppose that a large group of cattle ranchers graze their cattle on the same range. To an individual

post hoc, ergo propter hoc *Literally, "after this (in time), therefore because of this." A common error made in thinking about causation: if event A happens before event B happens, it is not necessarily true that A caused B.*

fallacy of composition *The belief that what is true for a part is necessarily true for the whole.*

rancher, more cattle and more grazing mean a higher income. But because its capacity is limited, the land can support only so many cattle. If every cattle rancher increased the number of cattle sent out to graze, the land would become overgrazed and barren, and everyone's income would fall.

> Theories that seem to work well when applied to individuals or households often break down when they are applied to the whole.

■ **Testing Theories and Models: Empirical Economics** In science, a theory is rejected when it fails to explain what is observed or when another theory better explains what is observed. Prior to the sixteenth century almost everyone believed that the earth was the centre of the universe and that the sun and stars rotated around it. The astronomer Ptolemy (A.D. 127–151) built a model that explained and predicted the movements of the heavenly bodies in a geocentric (earth-centred) universe. Early in the sixteenth century, however, the Polish astronomer Nicholas Copernicus found himself dissatisfied with the Ptolemaic model and proposed an alternative theory or model, placing the sun at the centre of the known universe and relegating the earth to the status of one planet among many. The battle between the competing models was waged, at least in part, with data based on observations—actual measurements of the movements of the planets. The new model ultimately predicted much better than the old, and in time it came to be accepted.

In the seventeenth century, building on the works of Copernicus and others, Sir Isaac Newton constructed yet another body of theory that seemed to predict planetary motion with still more accuracy. Newtonian physics became the accepted body of theory, relied on for almost 300 years. Then Albert Einstein did his work. The theory of relativity replaced Newtonian physics because it predicted even better. Relativity was able to explain some things that earlier theories could not.

Economic theories are also confronted with new and often conflicting data from time to time. The collection and use of data to test economic theories is called **empirical economics.**

empirical economics *The collection and use of data to test economic theories.*

Numerous large data sets are available to facilitate economic research. For example, economists studying the labour market can now test behavioural theories against the actual working experiences of thousands of randomly selected people. Macroeconomists continuously monitoring and studying the behaviour of the national economy pass thousands of items of data, collected by both government agencies and private companies, back and forth on disks and over telephone lines. Housing market analysts analyze data tapes containing observations recorded in connection with millions of home sales.

All scientific research needs to isolate and measure the responsiveness of one variable to a change in another variable *ceteris paribus*. Physical scientists, such as physicists and chemists, can often impose the condition of *ceteris paribus* by conducting controlled experiments. They can, for example, measure the effect of one chemical on another while literally holding all else constant in an environment that they control completely. Social scientists, who study people, rarely have this luxury.

While controlled experiments are difficult in economics and other social sciences, they are not impossible. For example, some economists examine certain types of behaviour, such as risk-taking and willingness to cooperate in controlled experiments involving individuals using techniques similar to those used in psychology laboratories. Other economists have been able to examine human behaviour in large-scale social experiments such as the Mincome experiment in Manitoba, where a number of citizens participated in an experiment designed to determine how a policy that guarantees a minimum income affects the amount of work people perform. However, social experiments are expensive and most questions in economics are not easily answered in a psychology lab. As a consequence, economists typically use another technique in their research: they try to observe the behaviour of groups of similar people under different circumstances. For example, if one province increases gasoline taxes and another does not, it may be that a subsequent difference in the growth rate of gasoline consumption can be attributed to the difference in taxes. But one must be very careful using this technique since other changes (for example, a change in relative incomes in the two provinces) can contribute to the different consumption behaviours. Statistical models and the computer are frequently used to try to hold other things equal in empirical economic research.

ECONOMIC POLICY

Economic theory helps us understand how the world works, but the formulation of *economic policy* requires a second step. We must have objectives. What do we want to change? Why? What is good and what is bad about the way the system is operating? Can we make it better?

Such questions force us to be specific about the grounds for judging one outcome superior to another. What does it mean to be better? Five criteria are frequently applied in making these judgments:

Criteria for Judging Economic Outcomes:	1. Efficiency
	2. Equity
	3. Growth
	4. Full employment
	5. Price stability

■ **Efficiency**   In physics "efficiency" refers to the ratio of useful energy delivered by a system to the energy supplied to it. An efficient automobile engine, for example, is one that uses up a small amount of fuel per kilometre for a given level of power.

In economics, **efficiency** means *allocative efficiency*. An efficient economy is one that produces what people want and does so at the least possible cost. If the system allocates resources to the production of things that nobody wants, it is inefficient. If all members of a particular society were vegetarian and somehow half of all that society's resources were used to produce meat, the result would be inefficient. It is inefficient when steel beams lie in the rain and rust because somebody fouled up a shipping schedule. If a firm could produce its product using 25% less labour and energy without sacrificing quality, it too is inefficient.

The clearest example of an efficient change is a voluntary exchange. If you and a friend each want something that the other has and you agree to exchange, you are both better off, and no one loses. When a company reorganizes its production or adopts a new technology that enables it to produce more of its product with fewer resources, without sacrificing quality, it has made an efficient change. At least potentially, the resources saved could be used to produce more of something.

Inefficiencies can arise in numerous ways. Sometimes they are caused by government regulations or tax laws that distort otherwise sound economic decisions. Suppose that land in Prince Edward Island is best suited for potato production and that land in Manitoba is best suited for wheat production. Clearly, a law that requires Manitoba to produce only potatoes and Prince Edward Island to produce only wheat would be inefficient. If firms that cause environmental damage are in no way held accountable for their actions, the incentive to minimize those damages is lost, and the result is inefficient.

Since most changes that can be made in an economy will leave some people better off and others worse off, we must have a way of comparing the gains and losses that may result from any given change. Most often we simply compare their sizes in dollar terms. A change is efficient if the value of the resulting gains exceeds the value of the resulting losses. In this case the winners can potentially compensate the losers and still be better off.

■ **Equity**   While efficiency has a fairly precise definition that can be applied with some degree of rigour, **equity** (fairness) lies in the eye of the beholder. Few people agree on what is fair and what is unfair. To many, fairness implies a more equal distribution of income and wealth. Fairness may imply alleviating poverty, but the extent to which poverty should be reduced is the subject of enormous disagreement. For thousands of years philosophers have wrestled with the principles of justice

efficiency *In economics, it means allocative efficiency. An efficient economy is one that produces what people want and does so at the least possible cost.*

equity *Fairness.*

that should guide social decisions. They will probably wrestle with such questions for thousands of years to come.

Despite the impossibility of defining equity or fairness universally, public policy makers judge the fairness of economic outcomes all the time. Rent control laws were passed because some legislators thought that landlords treated low-income tenants unfairly. Certainly most social welfare programs are created in the name of equity.

■ Growth As the result of technological change, the building of machinery, and the acquisition of knowledge, societies learn to produce new things and to produce old things better. In the early days of the Canadian economy, it took nearly half the population to produce the required food supply. Today less than 5% of the country's population is engaged in agriculture.

When we devise new and better ways of producing the things we use now and develop new products and services, the total amount of production in the economy increases. **Economic growth** is an increase in the total output of an economy. If output grows faster than the population, output per capita rises and standards of living increase. Presumably, when an economy grows there is more of what people want. Rural and agrarian societies become modern industrial societies as a result of economic growth and rising per capita output.

Some policies discourage economic growth and others encourage it. Tax laws, for example, can be designed to encourage the development and application of new production techniques. Research and development in some societies are subsidized by the government. Building roads, highways, bridges, and transport systems in developing countries may speed up the process of economic growth. If businesses and wealthy people invest their wealth outside their country rather than in its own industries, growth in their home country may be slowed.

■ Full Employment and Price Stability An economy may at times be unstable, either because it fails to assure resources are fully employed or because it experiences rising prices (inflation). During the 1960s, the Canadian economy grew steadily with low rates of unemployment and inflation. Consumer prices never rose more than 4.5% in a single year, and after 1961 the unemployment rate was less than 6% of the labour force. The 1970s and 1980s were much less stable. Canada experienced two periods of rapid inflation (over 10%) and a period of severe unemployment from 1982 through 1985. The beginning of the 1990s was another period of instability, with a recession occurring in 1990–1991. But by the year 2000 the Canadian economy was on a path of steady growth with unemployment falling and prices relatively stable. Many hope price stability and full employment will be features of the new century.

The causes of lapses from **full employment** and **price stability** and the ways in which governments have attempted to keep inflation and unemployment low are the subject matter of macroeconomics.

An Invitation

This chapter is meant to prepare you for what is to come. The first part of the chapter invited you into an exciting discipline that deals with important issues and questions. You cannot begin to understand how a society functions without knowing something about its economic history and its economic system.

The second part of the chapter introduced the method of reasoning that economics requires and some of the tools that economics uses. We believe that learning to think in this very powerful way will help you better understand the world.

As you proceed, it is important that you keep track of what you've learned in earlier chapters. This book has a plan; it proceeds step by step, each section building on the last.

economic growth *An increase in the total output of an economy.*

price stability *A condition in which there is little inflation in prices.*

full employment *A condition in which all resources available for use are being used.*

Summary

1. *Economics* is the study of how individuals and societies choose to use the scarce resources that nature and previous generations have provided.

Why Study Economics?

2. There are many reasons to study economics, including (a) to learn a way of thinking, (b) to understand society, (c) to understand global affairs, and (d) to be an informed voter.

3. That which we forgo when we make a choice or a decision is the *opportunity cost* of that decision.

The Scope of Economics

4. *Microeconomics* deals with the functioning of individual markets and industries and the behaviour of individual decision-making units: firms and households.

5. *Macroeconomics* looks at the economy as a whole. It deals with the economic behaviour of aggregates—national output, national income, the overall price level, and the general rate of inflation.

6. Economics is a broad and diverse discipline with many special fields of inquiry, which include economic history, international economics, and urban economics.

The Method of Economics

7. Economics asks and attempts to answer two kinds of questions: positive and normative. *Positive economics* attempts to understand behaviour and the operation of economies without making judgments about whether the outcomes are good or bad.

Normative economics looks at the results or outcomes of economic behaviour and asks if they are good or bad and whether they can be improved.

8. Positive economics is often divided into two parts. *Descriptive economics* involves the compilation of data that accurately describe economic facts and events. *Economic theory* attempts to generalize and explain what is observed. It involves statements of cause and effect—of action and reaction.

9. An economic *model* is a formal statement of an economic theory. Models simplify and abstract from reality.

10. It is often useful to isolate the effects of one variable or another while holding "all else constant." This is the device of *ceteris paribus*.

11. Models and theories can be expressed in many ways. The most common ways are in words, graphs, and equations.

12. Just because one event happens before another, the second event does not necessarily happen as a result of the first event. To assume that "after" implies "because" is to commit the fallacy of *post hoc, ergo propter hoc*. The belief that what is true for a part is necessarily true for the whole is the *fallacy of composition*.

13. *Empirical economics* involves the collection and use of data to test economic theories. In principle, the best model is the one that yields the most accurate predictions.

14. To make policy, one must be careful to specify criteria for making judgments. Five specific criteria are used most often in economics: *efficiency, equity, growth, full employment,* and *price stability*.

Review Terms and Concepts

ceteris paribus 12

descriptive economics 9

economic growth 16

economic theory 9

economics 2

efficiency 15

empirical economics 14

equity 15

fallacy of composition 13

full employment 16

inductive reasoning 10

Industrial Revolution 4

macroeconomics 7

microeconomics 7

model 11

normative economics 8

Ockham's Razor 11

opportunity cost 2

positive economics 8

post hoc, ergo propter hoc 13

price stability 16

sunk costs 3

variable 11

1. One of the scarce resources that constrains our behaviour is time. Each of us has only 24 hours in a day. How do you go about allocating your time in a given day among competing alternatives? How do you go about weighing the alternatives? Once you choose a most important use of time, why do you not spend all your time on it? Use the notion of opportunity cost in your answer.

2. Which of the following statements might be made by someone studying positive economics? Briefly explain your answer.
   a. The North American Free Trade Agreement (NAFTA) is likely to lead to increased exports of Canadian-made automobiles to Mexico.
   b. NAFTA is likely to make the people of Canada better off.
   c. The 1995 federal budget reduced unemployment insurance payments. This legislation is likely to increase employment.
   d. The unemployment caused by deficit reduction is unfair.
   e. The introduction of a toll system to pay for the TransCanada Highway in Nova Scotia is unfair because it will impose larger burdens on lower-income households.
   f. Increasing the toll on the bridges in Halifax by $1 is likely to reduce congestion in the city.

3. Selwyn signed up with an Internet provider for a fixed fee of $19.95 per month. For this fee he gets unlimited access to the World Wide Web. During the average month in 2000 he is logged onto the Web for 17 hours. What is the average cost of an hour of Web time to Selwyn? What is the marginal cost of an additional hour?

4. Suppose that all of the 10 000 voting-age citizens of Lumpland are required to register to vote every year. Suppose also that the citizens of Lumpland are fully employed and that they each value their time at $10 per hour. In addition, assume that nonvoting high-school students in Lumpland are willing to work for $5 per hour. The government has two choices: (1) it can hire 200 students to work at registration locations for five hours per day for 10 days or (2) it can hire 400 students for five hours per day for 10 days. If the government hires 200 students, each of the 10 000 citizens will have to wait in line for an hour to register. If the government hires 400 students, there will be no waiting time.

Assume that the cost of paying the students is obtained by taxing each citizen equally. The current government is very conservative and has decided to hold taxes down by hiring only 200 students. Do you agree with this decision? Why or why not? Is it efficient? Is it fair?

5. Suppose that a city is considering building a bridge across a river. The bridge will be paid for out of tax dollars, and the city gets its revenues from a sales tax imposed on things sold in the city. The bridge would provide more direct access for commuters and shoppers and would alleviate the huge traffic jam that occurs every morning at the bridge down the river in another city.
   a. Who would gain if the bridge were built? Could those gains be measured? How?
   b. Who would be hurt? Could those costs be measured? How?
   c. How would you determine if it were efficient to build the bridge?

6. Define equity. How would you decide if building the bridge described in question 5 were fair/equitable?

7. Describe one of the major economic issues facing the government of your city or your province. (*Hint:* You might look at a local newspaper. Most issues that make it into the paper will have an impact on people's lives.) Who will be affected by the resolution of this issue? What alternative actions have been proposed? Who will be the winners? The losers?

8. For each of the following situations, identify the full cost (opportunity costs) involved:
   a. A worker earning an hourly wage of $8.50 decides to cut back to half time in order to attend classes at York University.
   b. Samarah decides to drive to Kingston from Toronto to visit her son, who attends Queen's University.
   c. Tom decides to go to a wild fraternity party and stays out all night before his physics exam.
   d. Tova spends $200 on a new dress.
   e. The Confab Company spends $1 million to build a new branch plant that will probably be in operation for at least ten years.
   f. Alex's father owns a small grocery store in town. Alex works 40 hours a week in the store but receives no compensation.

9. A question facing many Canadian provinces is whether to allow casino gambling. Provinces with casino gambling have seen a substantial increase in

tax revenue flowing to provincial governments from this source. Since spending on gambling may divert expenditures from other areas the gain in revenue from gambling will be partially offset by a loss of tax revenues in other areas. Any net revenue can be used to finance schools, repair roads, maintain social programs, or reduce taxes.

a. Recall that efficiency means producing what people want at least cost. Can you make an efficiency argument in favour of allowing casinos to operate?

b. What non-monetary costs might be associated with gambling? Would these costs have an impact on the efficiency argument you made in part **a**?

c. Using the concept of equity argue for and against the legalization of casino gambling.

Appendix 1A	**How to Read and Understand Graphs**

Tables and graphs are extensively used in this text. They are used for a number of reasons. First, they illustrate important economic relationships. Second, they make difficult problems easier to understand and analyze. Finally, patterns and regularities that may not be discernible in simple lists of numbers can often be seen when those numbers are laid out in a table or on a graph.

A **graph** is a two-dimensional representation of a set of numbers, or data. There are many ways that numbers can be illustrated by a graph.

Time Series Graphs

It is often useful to see how a single measure or variable changes over time. One way to present this information is to plot the values of the variable on a graph, with each value corresponding to a different time period. A graph of this kind is called a **time series graph.** On a time series graph, time is measured along the horizontal scale and the variable being graphed is measured along the vertical scale. Figures 1A.1 and 1A.2 are time series graphs that present the total income in the Canadian economy for each year between 1975 and 1999.* These graphs are based on the data found in Table 1A.1. By displaying these data graphically, we can see clearly that (1) total personal disposable income has been increasing steadily since 1975, and (2) during certain periods, disposable income was increasing at a faster rate than during other periods.

Graphs must be read very carefully. For example, look at Figure 1A.2, which plots the same data as are plotted in Figure 1A.1. The only difference between the two graphs is that the scales used on the horizontal axes are different. (The distance separating each year in Figure 1A.1 is twice as large as the distance separating each year in Figure 1A.2.) As a consequence, it looks like income is growing more rapidly in Figure 1A.2 than in Figure 1A.1. This is not true, of course; the same data are plotted in the two graphs.

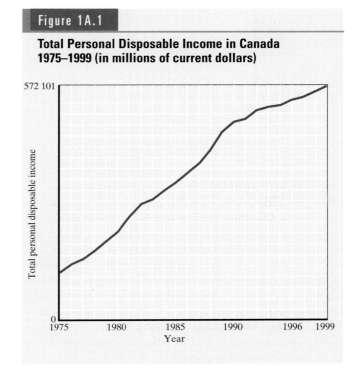

Figure 1A.1

Total Personal Disposable Income in Canada 1975–1999 (in millions of current dollars)

Source: Statistics Canada, *National Income and Expenditure Accounts,* Cat. no. 13-001.

When constructing or reading graphs, it is important to be aware of ways data can be distorted or misrepresented by the choice of units of measurement or scale.

The measure of income presented in Table 1A.1 and in Figures 1A.1 and 1A.2 is disposable income in millions of dollars. It is an approximation of the total personal income received by all households in Canada added together minus the taxes that they pay.

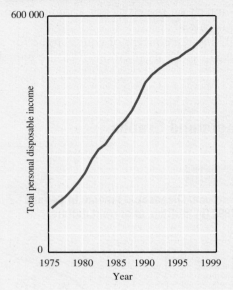

Total Personal Disposable Income in Canada, 1975–1999 (in millions of current dollars)

Source: Statistics Canada, *National Income and Expenditure Accounts,* Cat. no. 13-001.

Graphing Two Variables on a Cartesian Coordinate System

More important than simple graphs of one variable are graphs that contain information on two variables at the same time. The most common method of graphing two variables is the **Cartesian coordinate system.** This system is constructed by simply drawing two perpendicular lines: a horizontal line, or **X axis**, and a vertical line, or **Y axis**. The axes contain measurement scales that intersect at 0 (zero). This point is called the **origin.** On the vertical scale, positive numbers lie above the horizontal axis (that is, above the origin) and negative numbers lie below it. On the horizontal scale, positive numbers lie to the right of the vertical axis (to the right of the origin) and negative numbers lie to the left of it. The point at which the graph intersects the *Y* axis is called the **Y-intercept.**

When two variables are plotted on a single graph, each point represents a *pair* of numbers. The first number is measured on the *X* axis and the second number is measured on the *Y* axis. For example, the following points (*X, Y*) are plotted on the set of axes drawn in Figure 1A.3: (4, 2), (2, –1), (–3, 4), (–3, –2). Most, but not all, of the graphs in this book are plots of two variables where both values are positive numbers (such as [4, 2] in Figure 1A.3). On these graphs, only the upper right-hand quadrant of the coordinate system (i.e., the quadrant in which all *X* and *Y* values are positive) will be drawn.

Table 1A.1	Total Personal Disposable Income in Canada, 1975–1999 (in millions of dollars)

Year	Total Personal Disposable Income
1975	113 321
1976	128 239
1977	141 374
1978	159 466
1979	179 852
1980	203 653
1981	237 682
1982	262 861
1983	276 013
1984	300 346
1985	321 337
1986	338 093
1987	361 435
1988	394 235
1989	432 135
1990	451 976
1991	465 943
1992	478 158
1993	488 462
1994	495 246
1995	508 247
1996	513 300
1997	534 728
1998	552 778
1999	572 101

Source: Statistics Canada, *National Income and Expenditure Accounts,* Cat. no. 13-001.

Plotting Income and Consumption Data for Households

Table 1A.2 presents some data that were collected by Statistics Canada. In a survey of over 10 000 households, each household was asked to keep careful track of all its expenditures. The table shows average income and average spending for those households that were surveyed, ranked by income. For example the average income for the top fifth (20%) of the households was $96 647, and their average spending was $54 882.

Figure 1A.4 presents the numbers from Table 1A.2 graphically using the Cartesian coordinate system. Along the horizontal scale, the *X* axis, we measure average income. Along the vertical scale, the *Y* axis, we measure average consumption spending. Each of the five pairs of numbers from the table is represented by a point on the graph. Since all numbers are positive numbers, we need to show only the upper right quadrant of the coordinate system.

To help you read this graph, we have drawn a dashed line connecting all the points where consumption and income would be equal. This 45° line does not represent any data. Rather, it represents the line along which all variables on the *X* axis correspond exactly to the variables on the *Y* axis (e.g., [1, 1], [2, 2], [3.7, 3.7], etc.). The heavy coloured line traces out the data; the dashed line is only to help you read the graph.

A Cartesian Coordinate System

A Cartesian coordinate system is constructed by drawing two perpendicular lines: a vertical axis (the Y axis) and a horizontal axis (the X axis). Each axis is a measuring scale.

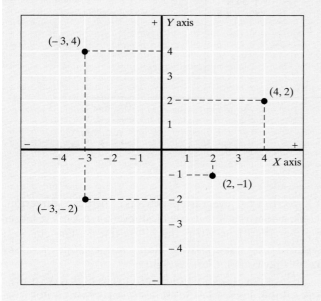

Household Consumption and Income

A graph is a simple two-dimensional geometric representation of data. This graph displays the data from Table 1A.2. Along the horizontal scale (X axis), we measure household income. Along the vertical scale (Y axis), we measure household consumption. *Note:* At point A, consumption equals $14 442 and income equals $12 104; at point B, consumption equals $23 178 and income equals $25 131.

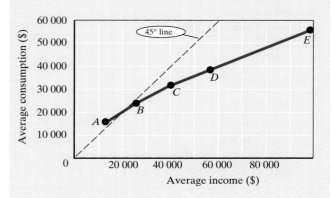

Source: Statistics Canada, *National Income and Expenditure Accounts*, Cat. no. 13-001.

There are several things to look for when reading a graph. The first thing you should notice is whether the line slopes upward or downward as you move from left to right. The coloured line in Figure 1A.4 slopes upward, indicating that there seems to be a **positive relationship** between income and spending: the higher a household's income, the more a household tends to consume. If we had graphed the percentage of each

group receiving welfare payments along the Y axis, the line would presumably slope downward, indicating that welfare payments are lower at higher income levels. The income level/welfare payment relationship is thus a **negative** one.

Slope

The **slope** of a line or curve is a measure that indicates whether the relationship between the variables is positive or negative and how much of a response there is in Y (the variable on the vertical axis) when X (the variable on the horizontal axis) changes. The slope of a line between two points is the change in the quantity being measured on the Y axis divided by the change in the quantity being measured on the X axis. We will normally use Δ (the Greek letter delta) to refer to a change in a variable. In Figure 1A.5, the slope of the line between points A and B is ΔY divided by ΔX. Sometimes it's easy to remember slope as "the rise over the run," indicating the vertical change over the horizontal change.

To be precise, ΔX between two points on a graph is simply X_2 minus X_1, where X_2 is the X value for the second point and X_1 is the X value for the first point. Similarly, ΔY is defined as Y_2 minus Y_1, where Y_2 is the Y value for the second point and Y_1 is the Y value for the first point. Slope is equal to

$$\frac{\Delta Y}{\Delta X} = \frac{Y_2 - Y_1}{X_2 - X_1}$$

Table 1A.2	Consumption Expenditures and Income, 1992*	
	Average Income	**Average Consumption Expenditures**
Bottom fifth	$12 104	$14 442
2nd fifth	25 131	23 178
3rd fifth	39 111	30 790
4th fifth	55 859	38 789
Top fifth	96 647	54 882

*Income and consumption data are for households. A *household* is a person or group of persons occupying a dwelling unit. A *dwelling* is defined as any structurally separate set of living premises with a private entrance from outside the building or from a common hallway or stairway inside.

Source: Statistics Canada, *Family Expenditures in Canada*, Cat. no. 62-555.

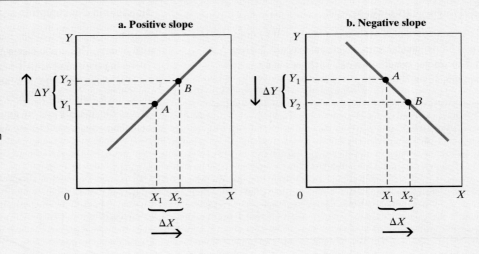

A Curve with a Positive Slope (a) and a Curve with a Negative Slope (b)

A positive slope indicates that increases in *X* are associated with increases in *Y* and that decreases in *X* are associated with decreases in *Y*. A negative slope indicates the opposite—when *X* increases, *Y* decreases and when *X* decreases, *Y* increases.

As we move from *A* to *B* in Figure 1A.5a, both *X* and *Y* increase; the slope is thus a positive number. On the other hand, as we move from *A* to *B* in Figure 1A.5b, *X* increases [$(X_2 - X_1)$ is a positive number], but *Y* decreases [$(Y_2 - Y_1)$ is a negative number]. The slope in Figure 1A.5b is thus a negative number, since a negative number divided by a positive number gives a negative quotient.

To calculate the numerical value of the slope between points *A* and *B* in Figure 1A.4, we need to calculate ΔY and ΔX. Since consumption is measured on the *Y* axis, ΔY is 8736 [$(Y_2 - Y_1) = (23\ 178 - 14\ 442)$]. Since income is measured along the *X* axis, ΔX is 13 027 [$(X_2 - X_1) = (25\ 131 - 12\ 104)$]. The slope between *A* and *B* is $\Delta Y/\Delta X = 8736/13\ 027 = +0.6706$.

Another interesting thing to note about the data graphed in Figure 1A.4 is that all the points lie roughly along a straight line. (If you look very closely, however, you can see that the slope declines as one moves from left to right; the line becomes slightly less steep.) A straight line has a constant slope. That is, if you pick any two points along it and calculate the slope, you will always get the same number. A horizontal line has a zero slope (ΔY is zero); a vertical line has an "infinite" slope, since ΔY is too big to be measured.

Unlike the slope of a straight line, the slope of a *curve* is continually changing. Consider, for example, the curves in Figure 1A.6. Figure 1A.6a shows a curve with a positive slope that decreases as you move from left to right. The easiest way to think about the concept of increasing or decreasing slope is to imagine what it is like walking up a hill from left to right. If the hill is steep (as it is in the first part of Figure 1A.6a), you are moving a lot in the *Y* direction for each step you take in the *X* direction. If the hill is less steep (as it is further along in Figure 1A.6a), you are moving less in the

Y direction for every step you take in the *X* direction. Thus, when the hill is steep, slope ($\Delta Y/\Delta X$) is a larger number than it is when the hill is flatter. The curve in Figure 1A.6b has a positive slope, but its slope *increases* as you move from left to right.

The same analogy holds for curves that have a negative slope. Figure 1A.6c shows a curve with a negative slope that increases (in absolute value)* as you move from left to right. This time think about skiing down a hill. At first, the descent in Figure 1A.6c is gradual (low slope), but as you proceed down the hill (to the right), you descend more quickly (high slope). Figure 1A.6d shows a curve with a negative slope that *decreases* in absolute value as you move from left to right.

In Figure 1A.6e, the slope goes from positive to negative as *X* increases. In 1A.6f, the slope goes from negative to positive. At point *A* in both, the slope is zero. (Remember, slope is defined as $\Delta Y/\Delta X$. At point *A*, *Y* is not changing [$\Delta Y = 0$]. Therefore slope at point *A* is zero.)

Some Precautions

When you read a graph, it is important to think carefully about what the points in the space defined by the axes represent. Table 1A.3 and Figure 1A.7 present a graph of consumption and income that is very different from the one in Table 1A.2 and Figure 1A.4. First, each point in Figure 1A.7 represents a different year; in Figure 1A.4, each point represented a different group of households at the *same* point in time (1992). Second, the points in Figure 1A.7 represent *aggregate* consumption and income for the whole nation measured in *billions* of dollars; in Figure 1A.4, the points represented average *household* income and consumption measured in dollars.

---

*The absolute value *of a number is its value disregarding its sign, that is, disregarding whether it is positive or negative: −7 is bigger in absolute value than −4; −9 is bigger in absolute value than +8.*

Changing Slopes Along Curves

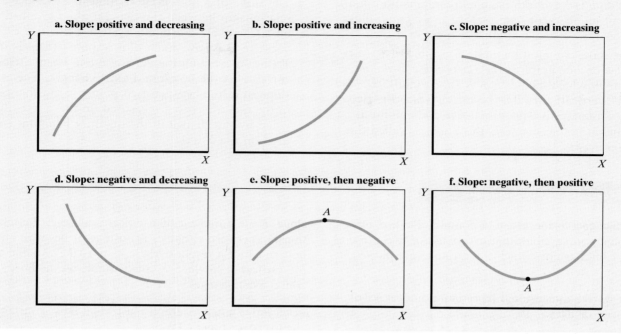

a. Slope: positive and decreasing b. Slope: positive and increasing c. Slope: negative and increasing

d. Slope: negative and decreasing e. Slope: positive, then negative f. Slope: negative, then positive

It is interesting to compare these two graphs. All points on the aggregate consumption curve in Figure 1A.7 lie below the 45-degree line, which means that aggregate consumption is always less than aggregate income. On the other hand, the graph of average household income and consumption in Figure 1A.4 crosses the 45-degree line, implying that for some households consumption is larger than income.

Table 1A.3	Aggregate Income and Consumption in Canada, 1965–1999 (in billions of dollars)	
	Aggregate National Income	*Aggregate Consumption*
1965	57.5	34.7
1970	89.1	51.9
1975	171.5	97.6
1980	309.8	172.4
1985	478.0	274.5
1990	669.5	399.3
1995	776.3	466.0
1999	957.9	558.6

Source: Statistics Canada, *Canadian Economic Observer, Historical Statistical Supplement, 1994–95*, Cat. no. 11-210, Table 1.

National Income and Consumption

It is important to think carefully about what is represented by points in the space defined by the axes of a graph. In this graph, we have income graphed with consumption, as was the case in Figure 1A.4, but here each observation point is national income and aggregate consumption in different years, measured in billions of dollars.

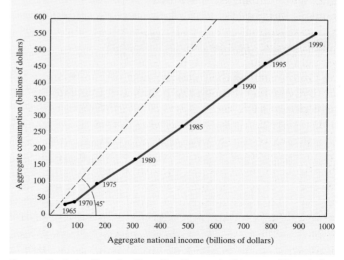

Source: Statistics Canada, *Canadian Economic Observer, Historical Statistical Supplement, 1994–95*, Cat. no. 11-210, Table 1.

Summary

1. A *graph* is a two-dimensional representation of a set of numbers, or data. A *time series graph* illustrates how a single variable changes over time.

2. The most common method of graphing two variables on one graph is the *Cartesian coordinate system,* which includes an X (horizontal) *axis* and a Y (vertical) *axis.* The points at which the two axes intersect is called the *origin.* The point at which a graph intersects the Y axis is called the *Y-intercept.*

3. The *slope* of a line or curve indicates whether the relationship between the two variables graphed on a Cartesian coordinate system is positive or negative and how much of a response there is in Y (the variable on the vertical axis) when X (the variable on the horizontal axis) changes. The slope of a line between two points is the change in the quantity being measured on the Y axis divided by the change in the quantity being measured on the X axis.

Review Terms and Concepts

Cartesian coordinate system A common method of graphing two variables that makes use of two perpendicular lines against which the variables are plotted. 20

graph A two-dimensional representation of a set of numbers, or data. 19

negative relationship A relationship between two variables, X and Y, in which a decrease in X is associated with an increase in Y, and an increase in X is associated with a decrease in Y. 21

origin On a Cartesian coordinate system, the point at which the horizontal and vertical axes intersect. 20

positive relationship A relationship between two variables, X and Y, in which a decrease in X is associated with a decrease in Y, and an increase in X is associated with an increase in Y. 21

slope A measurement that indicates whether the relationship between variables is positive or negative and how much of a response there is in Y (the variable on the vertical axis) when X (the variable on the horizontal axis) changes. 21

times series graph A graph illustrating how a variable changes over time. 19

X axis On a Cartesian coordinate system, the horizontal line against which a variable is plotted. 20

Y axis On a Cartesian coordinate system, the vertical line against which a variable is plotted. 20

Y-intercept The point at which a graph intersects the Y axis. 20

Problem Set

1. Graph each of the following sets of numbers. Draw a line through the points and calculate the slope of each line.

1		2		3		4		5		6	
X	Y	X	Y	X	Y	X	Y	X	Y	X	Y
1	5	1	25	0	0	0	40	0	0	0.1	100
2	10	2	20	10	10	10	30	10	10	0.2	75
3	15	3	15	20	20	20	20	20	20	0.3	50
4	20	4	10	30	30	30	10	30	10	0.4	25
5	25	5	5	40	40	40	0	40	0	0.5	0

2. For each of the following equations graph the line and calculate its slope.
   a. $P = 10 - 2q_D$ (Put q_D on the X axis)
   b. $P = 100 - 4q_D$ (Put q_D on the X axis)
   c. $P = 50 + 6q_S$ (Put q_S on the X axis)
   d. $I = 10\ 000 - 500r$ (Put I on the X axis)

3. For each of the graphs in Figure 1 on page 25, say whether the curve has a positive or negative slope. Give an intuitive explanation for the slope of each curve.

Figure 1

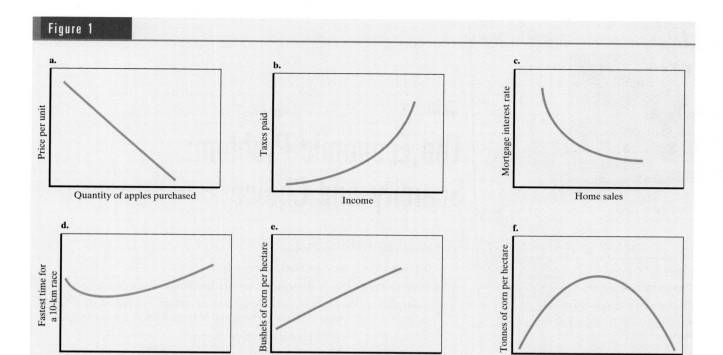

a. Price per unit / Quantity of apples purchased
b. Taxes paid / Income
c. Mortgage interest rate / Home sales
d. Fastest time for a 10-km race / Age
e. Bushels of corn per hectare / Days of sunshine
f. Tonnes of corn per hectare / Tonnes of fertilizer per hectare

2

The Economic Problem: Scarcity and Choice

Scarcity, Choice, and Opportunity Cost

The Three Basic Questions

The Production Possibility Frontier

The Economic Problem

Economic Systems

Command Economies

Pure Market Economies: Laissez Faire

Mixed Systems, Markets, and Governments

Looking Ahead

production *The process by which resources are transformed into useful forms.*

resources or **inputs** *Anything provided by nature or previous generations that can be used directly or indirectly to satisfy human wants.*

capital *Things that have already been produced that are in turn used to produce other goods and services.*

Learning Objectives

1 Define the three basic economic questions.

2 State the significance of scarcity, choice, and opportunity cost.

3 Distinguish between absolute and comparative advantage and explain why comparative advantage is critical in the theory of specialization and exchange.

4 Define and use the production possibilities frontier.

5 Identify the two main types of economic systems and describe the strengths and weaknesses of each.

Chapter 1 began with a broad definition of economics. As you saw there, every society has some system or mechanism that transforms what nature and previous generations provide into useful form. Economics is the study of that process and its outcomes. Economists attempt to answer the questions: What gets produced? How is it produced? Who gets it? Why? Is it good or bad? Can it be improved?

This chapter explores these questions further. In a sense, this entire chapter *is* the definition of economics. It lays out the central problems addressed by the discipline and provides the framework that will guide you through the rest of the book.

Human wants are unlimited, but resources are not. Limited, or scarce, resources force individuals and societies to choose. The central function of any economy, no matter how simple or how complex, is to transform resources into useful form in accordance with those choices. The process by which this transformation takes place is called **production.**

The term **resources** is very broad. Some resources are the product of nature: land, wildlife, minerals, timber, energy, even the rain and the wind. At any given time, the resources, or **inputs**, available to a society also include those things that have been produced by previous generations, such as buildings and equipment. Things that are produced and then used to produce other valuable goods or services later on are called *capital resources*, or simply **capital.** Buildings, machinery, equipment, tables, roads, bridges, desks, and so forth are part of the country's capital stock. *Human resources*—labour, skills, and knowledge—are also an important part of a country's resources.

Producers are those who take resources and transform them into usable products, or **outputs.** Private manufacturing firms purchase resources and produce products for the market. Governments do so as well. National defence, the justice system, police and fire protection, and sewer services—all are examples of outputs produced by the government, which is sometimes called the public sector.

Individual households often produce products for themselves. A household that owns its own home is in essence using land and a structure (capital) to produce "housing services" that it consumes itself. A symphony orchestra is no less a producer than General Motors. An orchestra takes capital resources—a building, musical instruments, lighting fixtures, musical scores, and so on—and combines them with land and highly skilled labour to produce performances.

producers *Those people or groups of people, whether private or public, who transform resources into usable products.*

outputs *Usable products.*

Scarcity, Choice, and Opportunity Cost

THE THREE BASIC QUESTIONS
All societies must answer **three basic questions:**

1. What will be produced?
2. How will it be produced?
3. Who will get what is produced?

three basic questions *The questions that all societies must answer: (1) What will be produced? (2) How will it be produced? (3) Who will get what is produced?*

Stated a slightly different way, every society must determine the allocation of scarce resources among producers, the mix of output, and the distribution of that output (Figure 2.1). There are a variety of ways society can answer these questions. As a consequence, it is necessary for Canadians to choose between possible institutional arrangements or economic systems. An important aspect of this choice is the extent to which answers to these questions are left up to individual producers and households and the extent to which government should be involved. The different types of economic systems are discussed in the second half of this chapter.

■ **Scarcity and Choice in a One-Person Economy** The simplest economy is one in which a single person lives alone on an island where no one has ever been before. Consider Ivan, the survivor of a plane crash, who finds himself cast ashore in such a place. Here, individual and society are one; there is no distinction between social and private. *Nonetheless, nearly all of the basic decisions that characterize complex economies must be made.* That is, although Ivan himself will get whatever he produces, he still must decide how to allocate the resources of the island, what to produce, and how and when to produce it.

First, Ivan must decide what he wants to produce. Notice that the word needs does not appear here. Needs are absolute requirements, but beyond just enough water, basic nutrition, and shelter to survive, they are very difficult to define. What is an "absolute necessity" for one person may not be for another. In any case, Ivan must put his wants in some order of priority and make some choices.

Next he must look at the possibilities. What can he do to satisfy his wants, given the limits of the island? In every society, no matter how simple or complex, people are constrained in what they can do. In this society of one, Ivan is constrained by time, his physical condition, knowledge, skills, and the resources and climate of the island.

Given that resources are limited, or scarce, Ivan must decide how to use them best to satisfy his hierarchy of wants. Food would probably come close to the top of his list. Should he spend his time simply gathering fruits and berries? Should he hunt for game? Should he clear a field and plant seeds? Clearly, the answers to these questions depend on the character of the island, its climate, its flora and fauna (are there any fruits and berries?), the extent of his skills and knowledge (does he know anything about farming?), and his preferences (he may be a vegetarian).

■ **Opportunity Cost** The concepts of *constrained choice* and *scarcity* are central to the discipline of economics. They can be applied when discussing the behaviour of

FIGURE 2.1

The Three Basic Questions

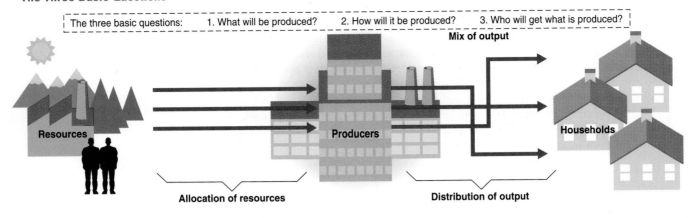

| The three basic questions: | 1. What will be produced? | 2. How will it be produced? | 3. Who will get what is produced? |

Resources

Producers

Mix of output

Households

Allocation of resources

Distribution of output

individuals like Ivan and when analyzing the behaviour of large groups of people in complex societies.

Given the scarcity of time and resources, Ivan has less time to gather fruits and berries if he chooses to hunt—he trades more meat for less fruit. There is a trade-off between food and shelter, too. If Ivan likes to be comfortable, he may work on building a nice place to live, but that may require giving up the food he might have produced. As we noted in Chapter 1, that which we forgo when we make a choice is the **opportunity cost** of that choice.

opportunity cost *That which we forgo, or give up, when we make a choice or a decision.*

Ivan may occasionally decide to rest, lie on the beach and enjoy the sun. In one sense, that benefit is free—he doesn't have to pay for the privilege. In reality, however, it does have a cost, an opportunity cost. Lying in the sun means using time that otherwise could have been spent doing something else. The true cost of that leisure is the value to Ivan of the other things he could have produced, but did not, during the time he spent on the beach.

In the 1960s, the United States decided to put a human being on the moon. This required devoting enormous resources to the space program, resources that could have been used to produce other things. The opportunity cost of placing a man on the moon was the total value of all the other things that those resources could have produced. Among other possibilities, taxes might have been lower. That would have meant more income for the population to spend on goods and services. Those same resources could also have been used for medical research, to improve education, repair roads and bridges, aid the poor, or support the arts.

In making everyday decisions it is often helpful to think about opportunity costs. Should I go to a residence party or not? First, it costs $4 to get in. When I pay out money for anything, I give up the other things that I could have bought with that money. Second, it costs two or three hours. Clearly, time is a valuable commodity for a student. I have exams next week and I need to study. I could go to a movie instead of the party. I could go to another party. I could sleep. Just as Ivan must weigh the value of sunning on the beach against more food or better housing, so I must weigh the value of the fun I may have at the residence party against everything else I might otherwise do with the time and money.

■ **Scarcity and Choice in an Economy of Two or More** Now suppose that another survivor of the crash, Colleen, appears on the island. Now that Ivan is not alone things are more complex, and some new decisions must be made. Ivan's and Colleen's preferences about what things to produce are likely to be different. They will probably not have the same knowledge or skills. Perhaps Colleen is very good at tracking animals, while Ivan has a knack for building things. How should they split the work that needs to be done? Once things are produced, they must decide how to divide them. How should their products be distributed?

The mechanism for answering these fundamental questions is clear when Ivan is alone on the island. The "central plan" is his; he simply decides what he wants and what to do about it. The minute someone else appears, however, a number of decision-making arrangements immediately become possible. One or the other may take charge, in which case that person will decide for both of them. The two may agree to cooperate, with each having an equal say, and come up with a joint plan. Or they may agree to split the planning, as well as the production duties. Finally, they may go off to live alone at opposite ends of the island. Even if they live apart, however, they may take advantage of each other's presence by specializing and trading.

> Modern industrial societies must answer exactly the same questions that Colleen and Ivan must answer, but the mechanics of larger economies are naturally more complex. Instead of two people living together, Canada has over 30 million. Still, decisions must be made about what to produce, how to produce it, and who gets it.

■ **Specialization, Exchange, and Comparative Advantage** The idea that members of society benefit by specializing in what they do best has a long history and is one of the most important and powerful ideas in all of economics. David Ricardo, a major nineteenth-century British economist, formalized the point precisely. According to Ricardo's **theory of comparative advantage**, specialization and free trade will benefit all trading parties, even when some are "absolutely" more efficient producers than others. Ricardo's basic point applies just as much to Colleen and Ivan as it does to different countries.

theory of comparative advantage *Ricardo's theory that specialization and free trade will benefit all trading parties, even those that may be absolutely more efficient producers.*

To keep things simple, suppose that Colleen and Ivan have only two tasks to accomplish each week: gathering food to eat and cutting logs to be used in constructing a house. If Colleen could cut more logs than Ivan in one day, and Ivan could gather more nuts and berries than Colleen could, specialization would clearly lead to more total production. Both Ivan and Colleen would benefit if Colleen only cuts logs and Ivan only gathers nuts and berries. But suppose that Ivan is slow and somewhat clumsy in his nut-gathering and that Colleen is better at both cutting logs *and* gathering food. Ricardo's point is that it still pays for them to specialize and exchange.

Suppose that Colleen can cut ten logs per day and that Ivan can cut only five. Also suppose that Colleen can gather 10 baskets of food per day and that Ivan can gather only eight (see table embedded in Figure 2.2). Assume also that Ivan and Colleen value baskets of food and logs equally. How then can the two gain from specialization and exchange? Think of opportunity costs. When Colleen gives up a day of food production to work on the house, she cuts ten logs and sacrifices 10 baskets of food. The opportunity cost of ten logs is thus 10 baskets of food if Colleen switches from food to logs. But because Ivan can cut only five logs in a day, he has to work for two days to cut 10 logs. In two days, Ivan could have produced 16 baskets of food (2 days × 8 baskets per day). The opportunity cost of ten logs is thus 16 baskets of food if Ivan switches from food to logs.

As Figure 2.2 makes clear, even though Colleen is *absolutely* more efficient at food production than Ivan, she should specialize in logs and let Ivan specialize in food. This way, the maximum number of logs and baskets of food are produced. A person or a country is said to have a comparative advantage in producing a good or service if it is *relatively* more efficient than a trading partner at doing so. Colleen is relatively more efficient at log production because the opportunity cost of switching from food to logs is lower for her than it is for Ivan.

Looking at the same problem from the standpoint of food production leads to exactly the same conclusion. If Colleen were to switch from cutting logs to gathering food, she would sacrifice ten logs to produce only 10 baskets of food. But if Ivan were to switch from cutting logs to gathering food, he would sacrifice 10 logs to produce a full 16 baskets! Even though Colleen has an absolute advantage in both cutting logs and producing food, Ivan has a comparative advantage producing food because for the same sacrifice of logs, Ivan produces much more food.

FIGURE 2.2

Comparative Advantage and
Opportunity Costs

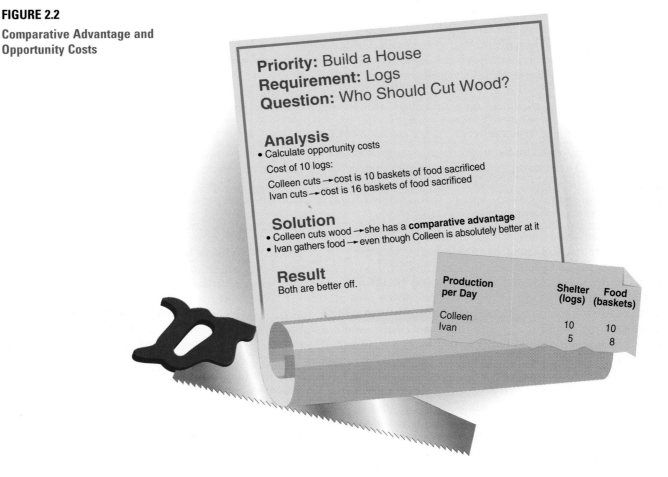

Priority: Build a House
Requirement: Logs
Question: Who Should Cut Wood?

Analysis
- Calculate opportunity costs

Cost of 10 logs:

Colleen cuts → cost is 10 baskets of food sacrificed
Ivan cuts → cost is 16 baskets of food sacrificed

Solution
- Colleen cuts wood → she has a **comparative advantage**
- Ivan gathers food → even though Colleen is absolutely better at it

Result
Both are better off.

Production per Day	Shelter (logs)	Food (baskets)
Colleen	10	10
Ivan	5	8

The theory of comparative advantage shows that trade and specialization work to raise productivity. But specialization may also lead to the development of skills that enhance productivity even further. By specializing in log cutting, Colleen will get even stronger shoulders. By spending more time at gathering food, Ivan will refine his food-finding skills. The same applies to countries that engage in international trade. A country that specializes in producing textiles will refine its skills in textile-making, while a country that specializes in growing corn will increase its corn-growing skills.

The degree of specialization in modern industrial societies is breathtaking. Consider the range of products and services available or under development today. As knowledge expands, specialization becomes a necessity. This is true not only for scientists and doctors but also in every career from tree surgeon to divorce lawyer. Understanding specialization and trade will help you to explain much of what goes on in today's global economy.

■ **Weighing Present and Expected Future Costs and Benefits** Very often we find ourselves weighing benefits available today against benefits available tomorrow. Here too the notion of opportunity cost is helpful.

While alone on the island, Ivan had to choose between cultivating a field and just gathering wild nuts and berries. Gathering nuts and berries provides food now; gathering seeds and clearing a field for planting will yield food tomorrow, if all goes well. Using today's time to farm may well be worth the effort if doing so will yield more food than Ivan would otherwise have in the future. By planting, Ivan is trading present value for future values. Working to gather seeds and clear a field has an opportunity cost—the present leisure he might consume and the value of the berries he might gather if he did not work the field.

The simplest example of trading present for future benefits is the act of saving. When I put income aside today for use in the future, I give up some things that I could have had today in exchange for something tomorrow. The saver must weigh the value of what that income can buy today against what it might be expected to buy later. Since nothing is certain, some judgment about future events and expected values must be made. What are interest rates likely to be? What will my income be in ten years? How long am I likely to live?

We trade off present and future benefits in small ways all the time. If you decide to study rather than go to the residence party, you are trading present fun for the expected future benefits of higher grades. If you decide to go outside on a very cold day and run eight kilometres, you are trading discomfort in the present for being in better shape later on.

■ **Capital Goods and Consumer Goods**   A society trades present for expected future benefits when it devotes a portion of its resources to research and development or to investment in capital. As we said earlier in this chapter, *capital* in its broadest definition is anything that is produced that will be used to produce other valuable goods or services over time.

Building capital means trading present benefits for future ones. Ivan and Colleen might trade gathering berries or lying in the sun for cutting logs to build a nicer house in the future. In a modern society, resources used to produce capital goods could have been used to produce **consumer goods**—that is, goods for present consumption. Heavy industrial machinery does not directly satisfy the wants of anyone, but producing it requires resources that could instead have gone into producing things that do satisfy wants directly—food, clothing, toys, or golf clubs.

consumer goods *Goods produced for present consumption.*

Capital is everywhere. A road is capital. Once built, we can drive on it or transport goods and services over it for many years to come. The benefits of producing it will be realized over many years. A house is also capital. When it is built, the builder presumes that it will provide shelter and valuable services for a long time. Before a new manufacturing firm can start up, it must put some capital in place. The buildings, equipment, and inventories that it owns are its capital. As it contributes to the production process, this capital yields valuable services through time.

In Chapter 1 we talked about the enormous amount of capital—buildings, roads, factories, housing, cars, trucks, telephone lines, and so forth—that you might see from a window high in an office tower. Much of it was put in place by previous generations, yet it continues to provide valuable services today; it is part of this generation's endowment of resources. In order to build every building, every road, every factory, every house, every car or truck, society must forgo using resources to produce consumer goods today. To get an education, you pay tuition and put off joining the workforce for a while.

Capital need not be tangible. When you spend time and resources developing skills or getting an education, you are investing in human capital—your own human capital—that will continue to exist and yield benefits to you for years to come. A computer program produced by a software company may come on a tangible disk that costs $0.75 to make, but its true intangible value comes from the ideas embodied in the program itself, which will drive computers to do valuable tasks over time. It too is capital.

The process of using resources to produce new capital is called **investment**. (In everyday language, the term *investment* is often used to refer to the act of buying a share of stock or a bond, as in "I invested in some Treasury bills." In economics, however, investment always refers to the creation of capital: the purchase or putting in place of buildings, equipment, roads, houses, and the like.) A wise investment in capital is one that yields future benefits that are more valuable than the present cost. When you spend money for a house, for example, presumably you value its future benefits. That is, you expect to gain more from living in it than you would from the things you could buy today with the same money.

investment *The process of using resources to produce new capital.*

Capital is able to generate future benefits in excess of cost by increasing the productivity of labour. A person who has to dig a hole can dig a bigger hole with a shovel than without a shovel. A computer can do in several seconds what it took hundreds of bookkeepers hours to do 15 years ago. This increased productivity makes it less costly to produce products.

> Because resources are scarce, the opportunity cost of every investment in capital is forgone present consumption.

THE PRODUCTION POSSIBILITY FRONTIER

A device called the **production possibility frontier (ppf)** is often used by economists to illustrate the principles of constrained choice and scarcity. The ppf is a simple graph that shows the maximum amounts of goods and services that can be produced given a society's scarce resources. Figure 2.3 shows a ppf for a hypothetical economy.

In the hypothetical economy described in Figure 2.3 only two goods—tomatoes and beef—can be produced. On the Y axis we measure the quantity of tomatoes produced, and on the X axis the quantity of beef. All points below and to the left of the curve (the coloured area) represent combinations of tomatoes and beef that can be produced in this economy given resources available and existing technology. Points above and to the right of the curve, such as point G, represent combinations that cannot be reached. If an economy were to end up at point A on the graph, it would be producing no beef at all; all resources would be used to produce tomatoes. If the economy were to end up at point F, it would be devoting all of its resources to the production of beef and none to the production of tomatoes.

Points that are actually on the production possibility frontier (such as A through F, which are graphed from the data in Table 2.1) can be thought of as points of both full employment and production efficiency. (Recall, from Chapter 1, that production efficiency involves producing a given mix of output at least cost.) Resources are not going unused, and no more of either product can be produced from existing resources. Points that lie within the coloured area but are not on the frontier represent either unemployment of resources or production inefficiency. An economy producing at point H can produce more beef and more tomatoes, for example, by moving to point E. This is possible only if resources were initially not fully employed or if resources were not being used efficiently.

■ **Unemployment** During the Great Depression of the 1930s, the Canadian economy experienced prolonged unemployment. Hundreds of thousands of workers who were willing to work found themselves without jobs. In 1933, nearly 20% of the civilian labour force was unemployed. Unemployment remained high until World War II, when increased defence spending created new jobs. In the mid-1970s and early 1980s, and through much of the 1990s, the economy experienced high levels of unemployment. In 1976, the annual unemployment rate reached a postwar high of 7.2%. By 1983 the rate had climbed to 11.9%, with 1.5 million people looking for work. In 1992, 1.6 million were unemployed.

In addition to the hardship that falls on the unemployed themselves, unemployment of labour means unemployment of capital. During the downturn of 1982, manufacturing plants in Canada were running at less than 73% of their total capacity. That meant that a considerable fraction of the country's industrial capital was sitting idle and, in effect, being wasted. Clearly, when there is unemployment we are not producing all that we can.

Periods of unemployment correspond to points inside the production possibility frontier, points like H in Figure 2.3. Moving onto the frontier from a point like H means moving up and to the right, achieving full employment of resources and increasing production of both capital goods and consumer goods.

■ **Production Inefficiency** Production inefficiency is another reason why an economy can fall short of the production possibility frontier. Suppose, for example, that the management of private sector firms fail to organize their firms' activities to produce at least cost. The economy will not produce all it potentially could have, and better management would result in more being produced. Production inefficiency is illustrated by the economy ending up at a point such as H in Figure 2.3—inside the production possibility frontier. Better management can increase the production of both beef and tomatoes, moving the economy to a point such as E.

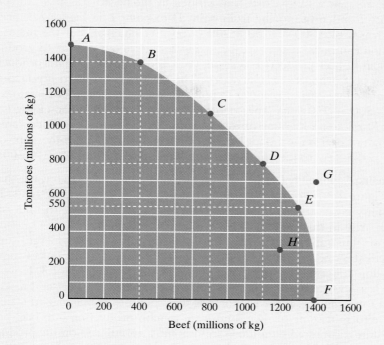

FIGURE 2.3

Production Possibility Frontier

The production possibility frontier illustrates a number of economic concepts. One of the most important is opportunity cost: producing more tomatoes means that less beef can be produced. Moving from *E* to *D*, production of tomatoes increases by 250 million kilograms. To produce these tomatoes, resources must be transferred from the production of beef. Moving from *E* to *D*, beef production declines by 200 million kilograms.

As another example, suppose that the land and climate in Prince Edward Island are best suited to tomato production, and that the land and climate in Alberta are best suited to beef production. (That is, Prince Edward Island has an absolute and comparative advantage in tomato production and Alberta has an absolute and comparative advantage in beef production.) If Parliament passes a law forcing farmers on Prince Edward Island to devote 50% of their land to beef production and forcing ranchers in Alberta to use 50% of their land to grow tomatoes, neither beef nor tomato production will be up to potential. Specialization based on comparative advantage is also necessary for productive efficiency and a position on the ppf.

■ **The Slope of the ppf and Opportunity Cost** Points that lie on the production possibility frontier represent points of full resource employment and production efficiency. But society can only choose one point on the curve. Because society's choices are constrained by available resources and existing technology, when those resources are fully and efficiently employed it can produce more beef only by reducing production of tomatoes. The opportunity cost of the additional tomatoes is the forgone production of beef.

Table 2.1	Production Possibility Schedule for Tomato and Beef Production	
Point on ppf	**Total Tomato Production (millions of kilograms)**	**Total Beef Production (millions of kilograms)**
A	1500	0
B	1400	400
C	1100	800
D	800	1100
E	550	1300
F	0	1400

The fact that scarcity exists is illustrated by the negative slope of the production possibility frontier. In moving from point D to point E in Figure 2.3, beef production increases by 1300 − 1100 = 200 (a positive change). But the increase in beef production can only be achieved by taking resources out of tomato production and using them in beef production instead. As a consequence, tomato production must fall when beef production is increased. The decrease in tomato production is illustrated in the move from point D to point E when production of tomatoes decreases by 550 − 800 = −250 units. The opportunity cost of the 200 million kilograms of beef is the 250 million kilograms of tomatoes not produced, or the opportunity cost of 1 kilogram of beef is the 1.25 kilogram of tomatoes lost. Notice the slope of the production possibility frontier, measured as the rise/run is equal to −250/200 = −1.25.

■ **Increasing Opportunity Costs** The data in Table 2.1 and the concave shape of the ppf in Figure 2.3 reflect an assumption of increasing opportunity costs. Increasing opportunity costs arise in many contexts and it is important to understand how they can arise in this example.

As an illustration of how increasing opportunity costs emerge, suppose our hypothetical economy is initially producing 1100 million kilograms of tomatoes and 800 million kilograms of beef, point C in Table 2.1 and Figure 2.3. Now imagine a change in tastes that results in increase in the demand for beef and a reduction in demand for tomatoes. If the economy is to respond to the change in tastes, farmers will have to shift some of their land from tomato production into beef production. Such a shift is captured by a move from point C to point D on the production possibility frontier (where 800 million kilograms of tomatoes are produced and 1100 million kilograms of beef). As this happens it becomes more and more difficult to produce additional beef. The best land for beef production was presumably already in beef production and the best land for tomato production already in tomatoes. As we try to produce more beef, the land used is less and less suited to that product. And as we take more and more land out of tomato production, we will be taking increasingly better tomato-producing land. All of this is to say that the opportunity cost of more beef, measured in terms of tomatoes, increases.

Try calculating the opportunity cost of additional beef production as we move along the ppf. The move from point C to point D involved acquiring 300 million kilograms of beef at a cost of 300 million kilograms of tomatoes; that is, each extra kilogram of beef was gained at an opportunity cost of a kilogram of tomatoes. But expanding beef production still more—shown by moving from point D to point E—results in a higher opportunity cost. We get an additional 200 million kilograms of beef (1300 − 1100) by sacrificing 250 million kilograms of tomatoes (800 − 550), so the opportunity cost of each additional kilogram of beef is 1.25 kilograms of tomatoes. Expanding beef production, moving from point E to point F on the ppf, further results in another increase in opportunity cost: an additional 100 million kilograms of beef is produced but at a cost of 550 kilograms of tomatoes, so each kilogram of beef gained involved an opportunity cost of 5.5 kilograms of tomatoes.

The shape of the production possibility frontier and the increasing opportunity cost results because resources are not equally productive in all activities. In our example differences in the productivity of land were critical. But land is not the only source of increasing opportunity costs. Workers are a resource, and they differ in ability and aptitude. Increasing opportunity costs can be expected in many resource allocation decisions.

■ **Economic Efficiency Versus Productive Efficiency** In Chapter 1 we defined an efficient economy to be one that produces what people want at least cost. Production inefficiency is just one reason an economy can operate inefficiently. An economy can also be inefficient if it produces a combination of goods and services that does not match the wants of its people — that is, by producing a the wrong point on the ppf.

For example, suppose a society produces at point F of the ppf in Figure 2.3. Because it is on the ppf, the economy is producing at least cost (there is no way to produce more with available resources and technology) and is achieving production efficiency. But if everyone in the society is vegetarian, producing all that beef and no tomatoes does not result in an efficiently operating economy. Indeed, the result is a total waste of resources (assuming that the society cannot trade beef for tomatoes produced by another society). Efficiency requires producing things people want at least cost.

It is important to remember that the ppf represents choices available within the constraints imposed by the current state of technology. In the long run, technology may improve, enabling the society to produce more. When that happens we have economic growth.

■ **Economic Growth Economic growth** is characterized by an increase in the total output of an economy. It occurs when a society acquires new resources or when society learns to produce more with existing resources. "New resources" may mean a larger labour force or an increased capital stock. The production and use of new machinery and equipment (capital) increases the productivity of workers. Improved productivity also comes from technological change and *innovation*—the discovery and application of new, efficient techniques of production.

There have been dramatic increases in the productivity of Canadian agriculture over the past 40 years due to the introduction of more efficient farming techniques, more and better capital (tractors, combines, and other equipment), and advances in scientific knowledge (new product varieties, new fertilizers, etc.). Figure 2.4 illustrates economic growth in our hypothetical tomato-and-beef-producing economy. Economic growth is captured by outward shifts in the ppf.

■ **Using the ppf to Think Like an Economist** The example used to introduce the production possibility frontier was based on an extremely simple hypothetical economy. It was not intended to be realistic; its purpose was to introduce the production possibility frontier. Our simple and concrete example highlighted the importance of scarcity, constrained choice, and opportunity cost when thinking about economic issues.

The ppf can be used as a starting point in the analysis of any economic issue. To illustrate the use of the ppf, we will discuss three applications in public policy analysis. Try to come up with your own and work through them carefully.[1]

1. Consider health care, one of the most important political issues in Canada today. A ppf for Canada with health care on one axis and other goods on the other axis is produced in Figure 2.5a. An economic analysis of this issue would begin by asking: Are we *inside* the ppf or are we operating *on* it? If we are inside, due to unemployment of resources or production inefficiencies, it is possible to have more health care without giving up other goods. If we are on the ppf, we can only have more health care if we shift resources out of the production of other goods and services and into health care (a movement from point A to point B)—in other words, there is an opportunity cost, and an economic analysis of health care would identify this cost (less expenditure on education, poverty reduction, environmental protection, computer games, etc.). Every society must choose the mix of health care and other goods and services and take opportunity costs into account when doing so. On the ppf "there is no free lunch"; if we want something we must be prepared to give something else up.

2. Let us look again at the choice between producing consumer and capital goods examined earlier in this chapter. A ppf highlighting this economic problem is shown in Figure 2.5b. If we are currently inside the ppf (at point C, for example) due to production inefficiencies or unemployment, it is possible to acquire additional capital goods without giving up consumer goods. But once we are on the ppf, we can acquire additional capital goods only if we take resources out the production of consumer goods and the expression "short-term pain for long-term gain" acquires significance.

economic growth *An increase in the total output of an economy. It occurs when a society acquires new resources or when it learns to produce more using existing resources.*

---

[1]*You will encounter the concept of a "frontier" a number of times as you work through this text. For example, we can easily define a* consumption possibility frontier *for a household that shows conbinations of two goods that the household can potentially consume given prices and income. The consumption possibility frontier—which is a straight line—is better known as the* consumers' budget constraint.

FIGURE 2.4

Economic Growth Shifts ppf Up to the Right

The production possibility frontier will shift outward if the available resources (more labour, land, capital, etc.) increase or if new knowledge that increases productivity is applied. The shifts in the ppf need not be parallel. In this example productivity increases were more dramatic in tomato production than in beef production.

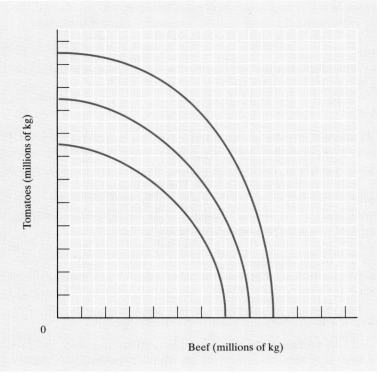

Tomatoes (millions of kg)

0

Beef (millions of kg)

3. Consider the critically important policy issue of environmental quality. As an example, a ppf highlighting environmental protection is shown in Figure 2.5c. If we are on the ppf (at a point such as *D*) additional environmental quality involves an opportunity cost (less production of other goods and services). Society must then decide if it wants to pay the cost.

Economists are often criticized by environmentalists for pointing out that there are costs that must be incurred. But it is not economists who decide how much environmental protection is produced. It is ultimately the people in the society who must choose. Indeed, large numbers of economists would, as individual citizens, favour a mix that involved more environmental protection and less other goods (automobile use, luxury goods, etc.).

Economists are also frequently criticized by environmentalists for being pro-growth. Economic growth, it is argued, generates environmental damage, and it is therefore inherently bad. The ppf in Figure 2.5c can be used to show that things are not so simple. Growth would be captured by an outward shift in the ppf. The economic growth might well involve additional production of goods that cause environmental damage but it could also allow society to produce more environmental protection. The net outcome would not necessarily be bad for the environment. As an extreme example, imagine that growth occurs due to a technological change affecting other goods but not environmental protection activities. This will generate the new ppf in Figure 2.5c. Even though the technological change had no impact on the productivity of environmental protection, it opened up possibilities for greater environmental protection. Indeed, the economic growth would allow additional protection to be had without giving up any other goods. This is clearly captured on the graph, since obviously economic growth allows the society to move from point *D* to reach a point such *E*. Of course, society might choose to produce at point *F*, where there is less environmental protection, or at point *G*, where there is substantially more. In a nutshell, the environmental issue is not growth per se but the mix of activities and outcomes it generates.

The production possibility frontier is one of the most important tools used by economists; every society has to continually deal with scarcity and opportunity costs. But there are different ways of organizing a society to deal with these issues. These will be introduced in the section of the chapter titled "Economic Systems."

a. Health care

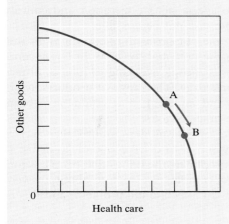

Other goods

Health care

b. Capital goods

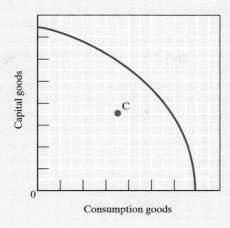

Capital goods

Consumption goods

c. Environmental protection

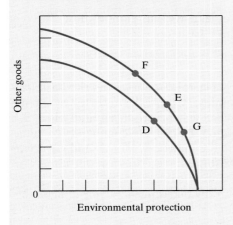

Other goods

Environmental protection

FIGURE 2.5

The ppf and Thinking About Policy

The production possibility frontier can be used to analyze any economic issue, since it emphasizes that some options are possible and others are not. Moreover, it highlights the tradeoffs (opportunity costs) that must be made.

Although it exists only as an abstraction, the production possibility frontier illustrates a number of very important concepts that we shall use throughout the rest of this book: scarcity, unemployment, inefficiency, opportunity cost, the law of increasing opportunity cost, and economic growth.

THE ECONOMIC PROBLEM

Recall that the three basic questions facing all economic systems are: (1) What will be produced? (2) How will it be produced? and (3) Who will get it?

When Ivan was alone on the island, the mechanism for answering these questions was simple. He thought about his own wants and preferences, looked at the constraints and limits imposed by the resources of the island and his own skills and time and made his decisions. As he set about his work, he allocated available resources quite simply, more or less by dividing up his available time. Distribution of the output was irrelevant. Because Ivan was the society, he got it all.

Introducing even one more person into the economy—in this case, Colleen—changed all that. With Colleen on the island, resource allocation involves deciding not only how each person spends time but also who does what. Labour must be allocated to the various tasks. And now there are two sets of wants and preferences. And even after two people decide what to produce, they have to decide how to divide it. If Ivan and Colleen go off on their own and form two completely separate, self-sufficient economies, there will be lost potential. Clearly, two people can do many more things together than one person can do alone. They may use their comparative advantages in different skills to specialize. Cooperation and coordination may give rise to gains that would otherwise not be possible.

When a society consists of millions of people, the problem of coordination and cooperation becomes enormous, but so does the potential for gain. In large, complex economies, specialization can go wild with people working in jobs as different in their detail as a painting is from a blank page. The range of products available in a modern industrial society is beyond anything that could have been imagined a hundred years ago, and so is the range of jobs.

The amount of coordination and cooperation in a modern industrial society is almost impossible to imagine. Yet something seems to drive economic systems, if sometimes clumsily and inefficiently, toward producing the things that people want. Given scarce resources, how exactly, do large, complex societies go about answering the three basic economic questions? This is the **economic problem**, and this is what this text is about.

Economic Systems

Now that you understand the economic problem, we can explore how different economic systems go about answering the three basic questions.

COMMAND ECONOMIES

In some modern societies government plays a big role in answering the basic economic questions. In pure **command economies**, a central authority or agency generally draws up a plan that establishes what will be produced and when, sets production goals, and makes rules for distribution. Planners in command economies use complex computer programs to determine the materials, labour, and energy inputs required to produce a variety of output targets. The final output targets are then set with an eye toward the same constraint that the single manager of a one-person economy faces—limited resources. Centrally determined income policies then establish how much compensation workers and managers receive for their labours.

Even in pure planned economies, people do exercise some choice. Commodities are sold at prices set by the government, and to the extent that they are able to pay those prices people are free to buy what is available. Sometimes more is demanded than is produced; sometimes goods are left on the shelves. These signals are used in the next plan to adjust output targets.

It is an understatement to say that the planned economies have not fared well over the last decade. In fact, the planned economies of Eastern Europe and the former Soviet Union—including the Russian Republic—have completely collapsed. (Another former command economy, that of Poland, has done better. For more details, see the Global Perspective box "Eastern Europe and Russia: A Mixed Progress Report.") China remains committed to many of the principles of a planned economy, but reforms have moved it sharply away from pure central planning.

PURE MARKET ECONOMIES: LAISSEZ FAIRE

At the opposite end of the spectrum from the command economy is the **laissez-faire economy.** The term *laissez faire,* which, translated literally from French, means "allow to do," implies a complete lack of government involvement in the economy. In this type of economy, individual households and firms pursue their own self-interest without any central direction or regulation; the sum total of millions of individual decisions ultimately determines all basic economic outcomes. The central institution through which a laissez-faire system answers the basic questions is the **market**, a term that is used in economics to signify an institution through which buyers and sellers interact and engage in exchange.

The interactions between buyers and sellers in any market range from simple to complex. Early explorers of Canada who wished to exchange with Aboriginals

economic problem *Given scarce resources how, exactly, do large, complex societies go about answering the three basic economic questions?*

command economy *An economy in which a central authority or agency draws up a plan that establishes what will be produced and when, sets production goals, and makes rules for distribution.*

laissez-faire economy *Literally from the French: "allow to do." An economy in which individual households and firms pursue their own self-interests without any central direction or regulation.*

market *The institution through which buyers and sellers interact and engage in exchange.*

One of the routes to economic growth is investment in capital. Despite low per capita income, Hanoi (Vietnam) is ordering cellular phones by the thousands, as well as more than 300 000 fibre-optic phone lines per year.

did so simply by bringing their goods to a central place and trading them. Today, a jewellery maker in Quebec may sell gold necklaces to a buyer through the Internet, which shows the product as an image on a computer screen—customers send in orders by e-mail and pay with a credit card. Ultimately, funds are transferred through a complicated chain of financial transactions. The result is that a buyer in Vancouver buys a necklace from an unseen jewellery producer in Quebec.

> Some markets are simple and others are complex, but they all involve buyers and sellers engaging in exchange. The behaviour of buyers and sellers in a laissez-faire economy determines what gets produced, how it is produced, and who gets it.

The following chapters explore market systems in great depth. A quick preview is worthwhile here, however.

■ **Consumer Choice**   In an unregulated market economy, consumers must make choices under conditions of scarcity; that is, given the income of consumers is never unlimited, they must choose to purchase some goods and services and not others. Since goods and services are produced only if producers can make a profit, consumers have a significant impact on producers. Clearly, you can't make a profit unless someone wants the product you are selling.

Some economists and political philosophers argue that consumers ultimately dictate what will be produced in an unregulated market economy by choosing what to purchase. This position—often called **consumer sovereignty**—suggests that producers are passive agents who simply respond to what consumers want. Not surprisingly, there are others who point out that firms spend billions of dollars every year on advertising in an attempt to manage consumer preferences. (Do you think firms are passive, or do they exert significant control over spending decisions?) Regardless of one's position on consumer sovereignty, it must be acknowledged that the purchasing decisions of consumers (consumer choice) play an important role in determining what is produced in an unregulated market economy.

consumer sovereignty *The idea that consumers ultimately dictate what will be produced (or not produced) by choosing what to purchase (and what not to purchase).*

■ **Individual Production Decisions**   Under a market system, individual producers must also figure out how to organize and coordinate the actual production of their products or services. The owner of a small shoe repair shop must buy the equipment and tools that she needs, hang signs, and set prices by herself. In a big corporation, so many people are involved in planning the production process that in many ways corporate planning resembles the planning in a command economy. Whether the firms are large or small, however, production decisions in a market economy are made by separate private organizations acting in what they perceive to be their own interests.

Individuals seeking profits also start new businesses. Since new businesses require capital investment before they can begin operation, starting a new business involves risk. Every day new businesses are born and others fail. A well-run business that produces a product for which demand exists will succeed; a poorly run business or one that produces a product for which little demand exists is likely to fail.

Proponents of market systems argue that private sector activity results in efficient production and the best response to diverse and changing consumer preferences. If a producer produces inefficiently, they argue, competitors will come along, fight for the business and will eventually take it away. Thus in a competitive market economy, competition forces producers to use efficient techniques of production. It is competition, then, that ultimately dictates how outputs are produced.

■ **Distribution of Output**   In a market system, the distribution of output—who gets what—is also determined in a decentralized way. The amount that any one household gets depends on its income and wealth. *Income* is the amount that a household earns each year. It comes in a number of forms: wages, salaries, interest, and the like. *Wealth* is the amount that households have accumulated out of past income through savings or inheritance.

A floating market in South East Asia.

Proponents of a pure market system argue that income is largely determined by individual choice. People choose to work for the wages available in the market only if these wages (and the things the wage will buy) are sufficient to compensate for what they give up by working. People will choose to acquire education or training only if it yields income sufficient to compensate for costs incurred. Moreover, they will choose the "right" type of education or training, since income will not be increased if the skill acquired is a skill no one wants.

Not all income comes from working. Individuals may also earn income by owning all or part of a business for which they do not work. Proponents of a pure market system argue that those who buy capital goods and services, or who lend part of their wealth, earn a return because they are putting their wealth at risk. Returns may come directly, as profit, or indirectly as interest or dividends on stock. We discuss these options in more detail in Chapter 3. In a market economy, people make independent decisions about what to with their wealth.

> In a pure market system, the basic economic questions are answered without the help of a central government plan or directives—the system is left to operate on its own with no outside interference. Individuals pursuing their own self-interest will go into business and produce the products and services that people want; others will decide whether to acquire skills or not, whether to work and whether to buy, sell, invest, or save the income that they earn.

price *The amount that a product sells for per unit. It reflects what society is willing to pay.*

■ **Price Theory**   The basic coordinating mechanism in a market system is price. A **price** is the amount that a product sells for per unit, and it reflects what society is willing to pay. Prices of inputs—labour, land, capital—determine how much it costs to produce a product. Prices of various kinds of labour, or *wage rates*, determine the rewards for working in different jobs and professions. Many of the independent decisions made in a market economy involve the weighing of prices and costs, so it is not surprising that much of economic theory focuses on the factors that influence and determine prices. This is why microeconomic theory is often simply called *price theory*.

MIXED SYSTEMS, MARKETS, AND GOVERNMENTS

The differences between command economies and laissez-faire economies in their pure forms are enormous. But in fact these pure forms do not exist in the world;

all real systems are in some sense "mixed." That is, individual enterprise exists and independent choice is exercised even in economies in which the government plays the major role.

Conversely, no market economies exist without government involvement and government regulation. Canada certainly has features of a market economy, but government also plays a critical role. The government directly produces many goods and services, employs workers, and raises revenue through taxation. The government also redistributes income by means of taxation and social welfare expenditures, and it regulates many economic activities.

One of the major themes in this book, and indeed in economics, is the tension between the advantages of unregulated markets and the need for government involvement in the economy. Advocates of markets argue that markets work best when left to themselves. They produce only what people want; without buyers, sellers go out of business. Competition forces firms to adopt efficient production techniques. Wage differentials lead people to acquire needed skills. Competition also leads to innovation in both production techniques and products. The result is quality and variety. But market systems have problems too.

> Even staunch defenders of the market system recognize that this system is not perfect. First, it does not always produce what people want at lowest cost—there are inefficiencies. Second, rewards (income) may be unevenly distributed, and some groups may be left out. Third, periods of unemployment and inflation recur with some regularity.

Many people point to these problems as reasons for government involvement. Indeed, for some problems government involvement may be the only solution. But government decisions are made by people who presumably, like the rest of us, act in their own self-interest. While governments may indeed be called upon to improve the functioning of the economy, there is no guarantee that they will do so. Just as markets may fail to produce an allocation of resources that is perfectly efficient and fair, governments may fail to improve matters.

■ **Inefficiencies** Markets may not produce all the goods that people want and are willing to pay for. There are some goods and services whose benefits are social, or collective, such as national defence, open park areas, a justice system, and police protection. These are called **public** or **social goods.** The fact that the benefits of such goods are collective presents the private market with a problem. Once a public good is produced, everyone gets to enjoy its benefits, whether they have paid for it or not. If police protection lowers a city's crime rate, all citizens of that city are safer.

public, or social goods *Goods and services whose benefits are social or collective.*

How, then, can a private business firm make a profit "selling" such a service to individual consumers? In most cases, it cannot. A private firm selling an automobile won't give it to you unless you pay for it. A producer of a public good doesn't have that option. Thus, if there is a public good that citizens decide they want, they must collectively arrange for its production. Traditionally, societies have funded public goods through governments, which are granted taxing authority.

Government intervention may also be necessary because private decision-makers in search of profits can make bad decisions from society's point of view. The market system provides an incentive to produce a product if, and only if, people are willing to pay more for it than the cost of the resources needed to produce it. This works to society's advantage as long as the resource costs reflect the *full* cost to society of producing the product. For example, if the environment is damaged during the production process and producers do not factor in these costs, profit-producing activities may not balance out to society's advantage. Governments involve themselves in markets to make sure that decision-makers consider all the benefits and costs of their decisions.

Markets work best when they are competitive. Competition forces producers to choose the most efficient methods of production. Inefficient producers are driven out of business by the forces of competition. Competition also leads to in-

Eastern Europe and Russia: A Mixed Progress Report

During the late 1980s, the communist command economies of Eastern Europe entered a period of dramatic reform. The process began in November 1989 when the Berlin Wall, which had separated communist East Berlin from capitalist West Berlin for nearly 30 years, was torn down. Then in 1991, the Soviet Union disintegrated, ending 75 years of communism and nearly half a century of Cold War with the West.

Many hoped that replacing a predominately command economic system with a predominately market economic system would result in a dramatic improvement in standards of living. A decade has passed and the transition to a set of independent economies oriented to the market is nearly complete. But the road to prosperity has been uneven and quite rocky. Some countries, including Poland, Hungary, and the Czech Republic, have done quite well. Poland, which was the first of the group to begin recording positive growth (in 1992), was growing at an annual rate of over 7% per year by the late 1990s. However, other countries, such as Albania, Bulgaria, and Romania, were still waiting for the first signs of growth:

People who visit planned economies frequently comment on the lack of variety in consumer goods. This problem has substantially decreased in Poland, which began its transition to a free market economy in the early 1990s.

The 1996 data show the division clearly. Foreign investment and rising buying power have transformed the larger cities of Hungary, the Czech Republic, and Poland into places with many of the accoutrements of the West: fast food restaurants, self-serve gas stations, Benetton stores, and apartment complexes outfitted with satellite dishes.

The average monthly wage in Poland is now well over $300, and people have access to adequate and cheap medical care. ...in chaotic Bulgaria ... many hospitals lack even such basics as X-ray film.

The biggest country making the transition from central planning to the market is, of course, Russia. The transition has not proceeded smoothly:

The officially recorded economy contracted for 8 years in a row, leaving it at the end of 1996 at about half the size it was in 1989—a steeper fall than in the U.S. or Canada during the Great Depression. Meanwhile prices, unemployment and the tally of unpaid wages has been rising.

Russia is now a market economy, whatever its imperfections. Moreover, much of the pain necessary to achieve such an economy may at last be over. In particular, inflation has dropped from 2505% in 1992 to an annual rate of 15% in April 1997.

Even more notable is the transfer of private property— the biggest in history. In just three years after 1991, 120 000 enterprises changed from state to private ownership.

What all this adds up to is that 22% of all Russians, or 32 million people, are living below the poverty line (defined as a minimum subsistence level of 394 000 rubles—$70 a month.) Among other things, as communists like to point out, this means falling meat and milk consumption: the average salary only buys about two-thirds as much meat as in Soviet days, and only about one-third as much milk.

Sources: Jane Perlez, "New Bricks Same Old Walls for Europe's Poor Nations," *New York Times,* January 24, 1997; "A Survey of Russia," *The Economist,* July 12, 1997.

novation and new products. However, powerful firms in a market system can gain control of their markets and block competition. A firm that gains control of a market may stifle innovation, charge higher prices than necessary, and cause a general misallocation of resources.

■ **Redistribution of Income**   Governments may also get involved in a market system because the final distribution of income (and thus of output) is considered inequitable. Market systems are based on the principle of individual self-interest and enterprise. Our rewards are supposed to be commensurate with how well we compete. But some people are not well equipped to compete—some are physically unable to work; some are mentally unable to hold a job. Moreover, not all have an equal opportunity to succeed; if you are born poor you will lack the financial capacity to invest in skills. Critics of pure market systems argue luck is more important than choice and that bad luck results in millions unable to get along economically.

Every government redistributes income to a certain extent. In Canada, social assistance, employment insurance, and a host of other programs have been designed to assist people who are poor or are temporarily without work.

Income redistribution is a subject of endless debate. Some claim that taxes on the rich and programs for the poor destroy the incentives that the market provides for hard work, enterprise, and risk-taking. Others argue that because many of the poor, particularly children, are in the position they are in through no fault of their own, cuts in income redistribution programs are cruel and unfair.

■ **Stabilization**   Macroeconomics explores the causes and consequences of unemployment and price inflation. In market economies, the level of unemployment is not planned, and prices are set freely by the forces of supply and demand. But governments may, through taxing and spending policies and by regulating the banking system, exert a stabilizing influence over prices and over the general level of output and employment. Like income redistribution, the desirability and the character of government involvement in the macroeconomy are hotly debated.

Looking Ahead

This chapter has described the economic problem in broad terms. We have outlined the questions that all economic systems must answer. We also discussed very broadly the two kinds of economic systems and some of the advantages and disadvantages of each. In the next chapter we turn from the general to the specific. There we discuss in some detail the institutions of Canadian capitalism: how the private sector is organized, what the government actually does, and how the international sector operates. Chapters 4 and 5 then begin the task of analyzing the way market systems work.

Summary

1. Every society has some system or mechanism for transforming what nature and previous generations have provided into useful form. Economics is the study of that process and its outcomes.

2. *Producers* are those who take resources and transform them into usable products or *outputs*. Private firms, households, and governments all produce something.

Scarcity, Choice, and Opportunity Cost

3. All societies must answer *three basic questions*: What will be produced? How will it be produced? Who will get what is produced? These three questions make up the *economic problem*.

4. One person alone on an island must make the same basic decisions that complex societies make. When society consists of more than one person, questions of distribution, cooperation, and specialization arise.

5. Because resources are scarce relative to human wants in all societies, using resources to produce one good or service implies *not* using them to produce something else. This concept of *opportunity cost* is central to an understanding of economics.

6. Using resources to produce *capital* that will in turn produce benefits in the future implies *not* using those resources to produce consumer goods in the present.

7. Even if one individual or country is absolutely more efficient at producing goods than another, all parties will gain if they specialize in producing goods in which they have a *comparative advantage*.

8. A *production possibility frontier* (ppf) is a graph that shows all the combinations of goods and services that can be produced if all of society's resources are used efficiently. The production possibility frontier illustrates a number of important economic concepts: scarcity, unemployment, inefficiency, increasing opportunity cost, and economic growth.

9. *Economic growth* occurs when society produces more, either by acquiring more resources or by learning to produce more with existing resources. Improved productivity may come from additional capital, or from the discovery and application of new, more efficient techniques of production.

Economic Systems

10. In some modern societies, government plays a big role in answering the three basic questions. In pure *command economies*, a central authority generally draws up a plan that determines what will be produced, how it will be produced, and who will get it.

11. A *laissez-faire economy* is one in which individuals independently pursuing their own self-interest, without any central direction or regulation, ultimately determine all basic economic outcomes.

12. A *market* is an institution through which buyers and sellers interact and engage in exchange. Some markets involve simple face-to-face exchange; others involve a complex series of transactions, often over great distance or electronically.

13. There are no purely planned economies and no pure laissez-faire economies; all economies are mixed. Individual enterprise, independent choice, and relatively free markets exist in centrally planned economies, and there is significant government involvement in market economies such as that of Canada.

14. One of the great debates in economics revolves around the tension between the advantages of unregulated markets and the need for government involvement in the economy. Markets produce what people want, and competition forces firms to adopt efficient production techniques. The need for government intervention arises because markets are characterized by inefficiencies and an unequal distribution of income, and they experience regular periods of inflation and unemployment.

Review Terms and Concepts

capital 26

command economy 38

consumer goods 31

consumer sovereignty 39

economic growth 35

economic problem 38

investment 31

laissez-faire economy 38

market 38

opportunity cost 28

outputs 27

price 40

producers 27

production 26

production possibility frontier (ppf) 32

public or social goods 41

resources or inputs 26

theory of comparative advantage 29

three basic questions 27

1. Kristen and Anna live in the Cavendish area of Prince Edward Island. They own a small business in which they make wristbands and potholders and sell them to people on the beach. Kristen can make 15 wristbands per hour, but only three potholders. Anna is a bit slower and can make only 12 wristbands or two potholders in an hour.

| | OUTPUT PER HOUR | |
	KRISTEN	ANNA
Wristbands	15	12
Potholders	3	2

   a. For Kristen, what is the opportunity cost of a potholder? For Anna? Who has a comparative advantage in the production of potholders? Explain.

   b. Who has a comparative advantage in the production of wristbands? Explain.

   c. Assume that Kristen works 20 hours per week in the business. If Kristen were in business on her own, graph the possible combinations of potholders and wristbands that she could produce in a week. Do the same for Anna.

   d. If Kristen devoted half of her time (10 out of 20 hours) to wristbands and half of her time to potholders, how many of each would she produce in a week? If Anna did the same thing, how many of each would she produce? How many wristbands and potholders would be produced in total?

   e. Suppose that Anna spent all 20 hours of her time on wristbands and Kristen spent 17 hours on potholders and three hours on wristbands. How many of each would be produced?

   f. Suppose that Kristen and Anna can sell all their wristbands for $1 each and all their potholders for $5.50 each. If each of them worked 20 hours per week, how should they split their time between wristbands and potholders? What is their maximum joint revenue?

2. Define *capital*. What distinguishes land from capital? Is a tree capital?

3. "Studying economics instead of going to town and partying is like building a boat instead of lying on the beach." Explain this statement carefully using the concepts of capital and opportunity cost.

4. Suppose that a simple society has an economy with only one resource, labour. Labour can be used to produce only two commodities—X, a necessity good (food), and Y, a luxury good (music and merriment). Suppose that the labour force consists of 100 workers. One labourer can produce either five units of necessity per month (by hunting and gathering) or ten units of luxury per month (by writing songs, playing the guitar, dancing, and so on).

   a. On a graph, draw the economy's production possibility frontier. Where does the ppf intersect the Y axis? Where does it intersect the X axis? What meaning do those points have?

   b. Suppose the economy ended up producing at a point *inside* the ppf. Give at least two reasons why this could occur. What could be done to move the economy to a point *on* the ppf?

   c. Suppose you succeeded in lifting your economy to a point on its ppf. What point would you choose? How might your small society decide the point at which it wanted to be?

   d. Once you have chosen a point on the ppf, you still need to decide how your society's product will be divided up. If you were a dictator, how would you decide? What would happen if you left product distribution to the market?

5. One of the justifications for government involvement in a market economy is that the market system is unlikely to produce "public goods" in sufficient quantity.

   a. Define a *public good*.

   b. A public good is not necessarily associated with government or the public sector. Explain why an economist would call a beautiful sunset a public good. Identify two other public goods not associated with the public sector.

   c. Why does the private market have a difficult time allocating resources to the production of public goods?

   d. Give five examples of goods provided by federal, provincial, or municipal governments that may yield public benefits.

   e. Assume that the production of public good X requires a certain amount of land, labour, and capital that the government will have to procure. How would you measure the full costs of this good's provision? (*Hint:* recall opportunity costs.)

   f. If you were a benevolent dictator, how would you go about determining if the production of a particular public good were worth it? How would you measure its benefits?

6. What progress has been made in recent years in Eastern Europe? Which countries are growing? Which are in decline? What factors seem to have contributed to the differences in success across countries?

7. Briefly describe the tradeoffs involved in each of the following decisions. Specifically, list some of the opportunity costs associated with the decision, paying particular attention to the tradeoffs between present and future consumption.

    a. After a stressful year in high school, Sherice decides to take the summer off rather than work before going to university.

    b. Frank is overweight and decides to work out every day and to go on a diet.

    c. Mei is very diligent about taking her car for routine checkups, even though it takes two hours of her time and costs $100 four times a year.

    d. Jim is in a big hurry. He runs a red light on the way to work.

*8. Match each diagram in Figure 1 with its description. Assume that the economy is producing or attempting to produce at point *A*, and most members of society like meat and not fish. Some descriptions apply to more than one diagram, and some diagrams have more than one description.

    a. Inefficient production of meat and fish

    b. Productive efficiency

    c. An inefficient mix of output

    d. Technological advances in the production of meat and fish

    e. The law of increasing opportunity costs

    f. An impossible combination of meat and fish

---

*Throughout the book, an asterisk designates a more challenging problem.

Figure 1

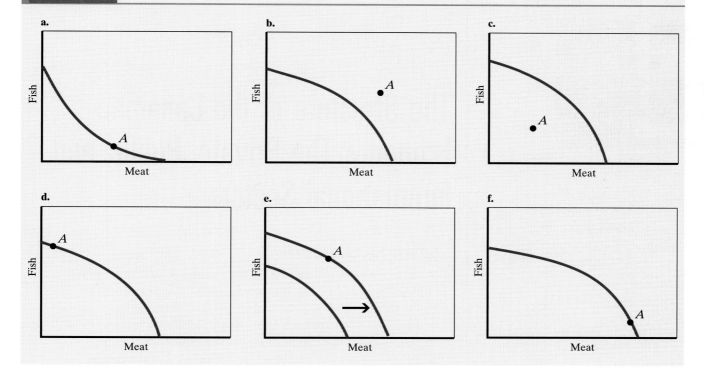

9. A nation with fixed quantities of resources is able to produce any of the following combinations of bread and ovens.

LOAVES OF BREAD (MILLIONS)	OVENS (THOUSANDS)
75	0
60	12
45	22
30	30
15	36
0	40

These figures assume that a certain number of previously produced ovens are available in the current period for breaking bread.

a. Using data in the table, graph the production possibility frontier (with ovens on the vertical axis).

b. Does the principle of increasing opportunity cost hold in the nation? Explain briefly. (*Hint:* What happens to the opportunity cost of bread — measured in numbers of ovens — as bread production increases?)

c. If this country chooses to produce both ovens and bread, what will happen to the production possibility frontier over time? Why?

d. A politician running for national office wants to reallocate resources to produce the maximum possible quantity of bread, with no production of ovens. His slogan is "You can't eat ovens!" If this politician is successful, explain what will happen to the production possibility frontier over time. Why?

e. Now suppose that a new technology is discovered that allows twice as many loaves of bread to be baked in each existing oven. Illustrate (on your original graph) the effect of this new technology on the production possibility curve.

f. Suppose that before the new technology is introduced, the nation produces 22 ovens. After the technology is introduced, the nation produces 30 ovens. What is the effect of the new technology on the production of bread? (Give the numbers of loaves before and after the change.)

3

The Structure of the Canadian Economy: The Private, Public, and International Sectors

The Private Sector

Canadian Households

The Private Sector Firm

The Legal Organization of Firms

A Profile of Canadian Private Sector Firms

Structural Changes in the Canadian Economy

The Public Sector: Taxes and Government Spending in Canada

The Size of the Public Sector

Government Structure and Expenditure

Sources of Government Revenue

The International Sector: Imports and Exports in Canada

From Institutions to Theory

Learning Objectives

1 Distinguish between the private and public sectors of the Canadian economy.
2 Describe the diversity of consumption and production activities engaged in by Canadian households.
3 Describe the three main legal forms taken by Canadian business firms.
4 State the main characteristics of the Canadian public sector.
5 Outline the sources of government revenue and the main areas of government expenditure.
6 State the significance of imports and exports in the Canadian economy.

The previous chapter described the *economic problem*. All societies are endowed by nature and by previous generations with scarce resources. A process called "production" combines and transforms these resources into goods and services that are demanded by the members of society.

At the end of Chapter 2, we briefly described the economic systems that exist in the world today. This chapter describes some basic characteristics of the Canadian economy, paying particular attention to the unique mix of private and public sector activities that have evolved in this country.

Microeconomics and macroeconomics are fundamentally concerned with people. As a consequence, we must begin our overview of the Canadian economy with a look at the individuals and households who make up Canadian society. It is the Canadian people who make economic decisions. They consume goods and services, they own and manage firms, they work, they volunteer, they save, they pay taxes, and they vote.

Because most production decisions in Canada are made by organizations characterized by independent ownership and control, we next turn our attention to private sector firms. **Private sector** firms come into existence when a person or a group of persons decides to produce a good or service to meet a perceived demand. These private sector firms may exist to make a profit or they may be nonprofit organizations. Chrysler Canada, the Catholic Church, fishers in Newfoundland, the corner drug store, and the babysitter down the street can all be considered private sector firms. In

private sector *Includes all independently owned profit-making firms, nonprofit organizations, and households; all the decision-making units in the economy that are not part of the government.*

essence, a private sector firm is any nongovernmental organization (or individual) that makes production decisions.

We then provide a brief overview of the Canadian public sector. The **public sector** is the government and its agencies at all levels—federal, provincial, and local. Government employees—tax assessors, public school teachers, post office workers, colonels in the army, supreme court justices, and the Prime Minister—work in the public sector. Just as the Ford Motor Company uses land, labour, and capital to produce automobiles, the public sector uses land, labour, and capital to produce goods and services such as police and fire protection, education, and national defence. The public sector in Canada also produces some things that are simultaneously produced by the private sector. Canada Post provides overnight express-mail service that competes directly with similar services provided by private firms such as FedEx and UPS.

Finally, we provide a brief introduction to the **international sector** and discuss the importance of imports and exports to the Canadian economy. From any one country's perspective, the international sector consists of the economies of the rest of the world. The Canadian economy has always been heavily influenced by events abroad. Economic changes in China and Eastern Europe, the election of a new president in the United States, the end of a recession in Japan, and other global events all have important implications for the functioning of the Canadian economy. In a very real sense there is only one economy: the world economy.

Recall the distinction drawn in Chapter 1 between descriptive economics and economic theory, and then notice what this chapter is not. We do not analyze behaviour in this chapter. Here we describe institutions only as they exist. We also try very hard to avoid any normative distinctions. We do not talk about proper or improper roles of government in the economy, for example, or the things that governments might do to make the economy more efficient or fair.

In Chapter 4, we begin to analyze behaviour. Before we begin the analysis in Chapter 4, however, it is important to have some sense of the institutional landscape. One purpose of studying economics is to understand the world and what people actually do. This chapter provides some important facts that describe the realities of the Canadian economy.

> **public sector** *Includes all agencies at all levels of government—federal, provincial, and local.*

> **international sector** *From any one country's perspective, the economies of the rest of the world.*

The Private Sector in Canada

CANADIAN HOUSEHOLDS

All 30 million Canadians belong to the most basic economic unit: the household. The typical Canadian household engages in a wide variety of economic activities. It purchases goods and services. It sells its time and ability to work for others who organize production and offer wages or a salary in exchange. It does its own work without pay. It may borrow or make loans. It may even own (or be part owner of) a private sector firm.

One of the most striking features of Canadian households is the remarkable diversity in their activities both as consumers and as producers. As consumers, Canadian households arrange their purchases of goods and services produced by private sector firms to generate the type of consumption they consider best suited to their needs and desires. Of course, the purchases any household can make are limited by income (and its ability to borrow). Thus the diversity in consumption patterns is a result of both differences in tastes and differences in income.

Diversity is still more dramatic when we look at the productive activities of Canadian households. Canada, like all modern economies, has a fine division of labour. There are almost as many specialized jobs as there are workers. Moreover, these jobs involve the use of not only an individual's unique physical and intellectual powers but also specialized tools.

Table 3.1 indicates the types of work Canadians are involved in. In 1996, the latest year for which good data were available, there were almost 15 million workers in Canada. Of these about 60 000 specialized in family medicine (physicians),

Table 3.1 — Occupations of Canadians, 1996

Management Occupations	**1 289 125**
Senior managers	145 180
Business, Finance, and Administrative Occupations	**2 718 250**
Accountants and auditors	119 265
Financial analysts, dealers, and traders	39 800
Secretaries	402 695
Clerical occupations	1 583 250
Natural and Applied Sciences and Related Occupations	**712 495**
Engineers	146 950
Architects	9 400
Health Occupations	**719 450**
Physicians	59 340
Pharmacists	20 625
Nurses	246 800
Occupations in Social Science, Education, Government Service, and Religion	**975 385**
Lawyers	58 820
Teachers	399 130
Occupations in Art, Culture, Recreation, and Sport	**86 315**
Musicians	29 265
Actors	6 815
Athletes	2 145
Sales and Service Occupations	**3 724 430**
Retail salespersons, sales clerks	554 370
Cashiers	274 390
Police officers	56 060
Trades, Transport, Equipment Operators, and and Related Occupations	**2 018 355**
Carpenters	114 325
Plumbers	27 955
Electricians	46 485
Occupations Unique to Primary Industry	**680 685**
Farmers	229 590
Underground miners/oil and gas drillers	20 900
Fishermen/fisherwomen	31 045
Logging and forestry workers	34 375
Occupations Unique to Processing, Manufacturing, and Utilities	**1 093 045**
Total	**14 017 535**

Source: Statistics Canada, Cat. no. 93F0027XDB96007. This table contains a small sample of the 1996 Census information on occupations. For more details on the occupations of Canadians see *www.statcan.ca/english/census96/mar17/occupa/table1/t1p00t.htm.*

60 000 worked as lawyers, 35 000 drove taxis, approximately 400 000 were secretaries, over 1.5 million were clerical workers, 550 000 were retail sales people, and about 275 000 were cashiers.

Not only is there remarkable diversity in the types of work people do but also there is remarkable diversity in wages and salaries earned. Table 3.2 presents information on average salaries for a selected set of occupations. In some occupations (judges, physicians, dentists) average incomes exceed $100 000 per year, while in others (cashiers, service station attendants, food and beverage servers) the typical person earns less than $20 000. Average income in all occupations in Canada is just over $26 000 and 58.1% of Canadians make less than $25 000.

A few Canadians have jobs with amazingly high wages and salaries. As illustrated in Table 3.3, Frank Stronach, Chairman of Magna International, received more than $34 000 000 in 1999. The income data in Table 3.3 do not really tell us who the richest Canadians are or what they earn. Income data are only available for senior managers in publicly traded corporations; no one knows the incomes of senior administrative workers in family firms. More importantly, the data

Table 3.2 — Incomes of Various Occupations in Canada, 1999

OCCUPATION	AVERAGE INCOME
Family physician	$107 620
Lawyer	$ 81 617
Investment dealer/trader	$ 75 911
Police officer	$ 63 518
Senior government manager	$ 63 195
Economist	$ 58 678
Mechanical engineer	$ 54 081
Auditor/accountant	$ 52 614
Chemist	$ 49 015
Head nurse	$ 46 196
Social worker	$ 38 960
Sheet metal worker	$ 37 159
Foundry worker	$ 37 072
Plumber	$ 34 872
Motor vehicle mechanic	$ 31 733
General office clerk	$ 27 842
Sales clerk	$ 25 624
Bank teller	$ 24 804
Taxi driver	$ 19 664
Cashier	$ 17 553
Bartender	$ 16 740
Food and beverage server	$ 14 891

Source: "The Rich List," *National Post*, April 22, 2000. *www.nationalpost.com/content/features/richlist/richlistmain.html*

in the table are for wages and salaries only; they do not include income paid in the form of stock options.

Wages and salaries are not the only source of income for Canadian households. For some Canadians, government programs such as Employment Insurance and social assistance are important sources of income. For others, ownership of private sector firms and/or financial assets (stocks, bonds, etc.) provides income in the form of profits, interest, and capital gains. Government programs tend to be an important source of income for low-income Canadians while profits and interest are most important for high-income Canadians.

Explaining the remarkable diversity in household consumption and production activities and developing an appreciation of the ways they are coordinated to produce coherent social outcomes are two of the most important reasons for studying economics. Another is that it will also contribute to your understanding of how prices of all kinds are determined including those for different kinds of labour and skills.

THE PRIVATE SECTOR FIRM

The private sector firm is a social institution that organizes production, hires workers, and provides profit income to its owners. As a consequence, private sector firms are critically important in the Canadian economy.

How is business organized in Canada? At this stage we will focus on two aspects of business organization: the types of firms that can be organized under

Table 3.3 — Some High-Income Canadians, 1999

TOTAL PAY	COMPANY	TITLE	PAY
Frank Stronach	Magna International	Chairman	$34 274 284
J. R. Shaw	Shaw Communication, Inc.	Exec. Chair and CEO	$26 604 918
Gerald Schwartz	Onyx	Chair, President and CEO	$11 068 805
Don Wright	Toronto Dominion Bank	Vice-Chairman	$ 7 323 160
J. S. Hunkin	CIBC	Chairman and CEO	$ 6 094 937
Peter C. Godsoe	Bank of Nova Scotia	Chairman and CEO	$ 5 617 613

Source: "The Rich List," *National Post*, April 22, 2000. *www.nationalpost.com/content/features/richlist/richlistmain.html*

Canadian law and the size of Canadian private sector firms. These aspects are important because an individual firm's behaviour will depend on its own legal structure, size, and relationship to other firms in its industry.

THE LEGAL ORGANIZATION OF FIRMS

Most private sector activity takes place within business firms that exist to make a profit. Some other private sector organizations that exist for reasons other than profit—clubs, cooperatives, and nonprofit organizations, for example—do produce goods or services. Because these organizations represent a small fraction of private sector activity, however, we focus here on profit-making firms.

> A business set up to make profits may be organized in one of three basic legal forms: (1) a proprietorship, (2) a partnership, or (3) a corporation. A single business may pass through more than one of these forms of organization during its development.

proprietorship *A form of business organization in which a person simply sets up to provide goods or services at a profit. In a proprietorship, the proprietor (or owner) is the firm. The assets and liabilities of the firm are the owner's assets and liabilities.*

■ **The Proprietorship** The least complex and most common form a business can take is the simple **proprietorship**. There is no legal process involved in starting a proprietorship. You simply start operating. You must, however, keep records of revenues and costs and pay personal income taxes on your profit.

A professor who does consulting on the side, for example, receives fees and has costs (computer expenses, research materials, and so forth). This consulting business is a proprietorship, even though the proprietor is the only employee and the business is very limited. A large restaurant that employs hundreds of people may also be a proprietorship if it is owned by a single person. Many doctors and lawyers in private practice report their incomes and expenses as proprietors.

In a proprietorship, one person owns the firm. In a sense, that person *is* the firm. If the firm owes money, the proprietor owes the money; if the firm earns a profit, the proprietor earns a profit. There is no limit to the proprietor's responsibility; if the business gets into financial trouble, the proprietor alone is liable. That is, if a business does poorly or ends up in debt, those debts are the proprietor's personal responsibility. There is no wall of protection between a proprietor and her business as is the case between corporations and their owners.

partnership *A form of business organization in which there is more than one proprietor. The owners are responsible jointly and separately for the firm's obligations.*

■ **The Partnership** A **partnership** is a proprietorship with more than one proprietor. When two or more people agree to share the responsibility for a business, they form a partnership. While no formal legal process is required to start this kind of business, most partnerships are based on agreements signed by all the partners, that detail who pays what part of the costs and how profits shall be divided. Because profits from partnerships are taxable, accurate records of receipts and expenditures must be kept and each party's profits must be reported to Revenue Canada.

In a partnership, as in a proprietorship, there is no limit to the liability of the owners (that is, the partners) for the firm's debts. But with a partnership it can be worse because each partner is both jointly and separately liable for all the debts of the partnership. If you own one-third of a partnership that goes out of business with a debt of $300 000, you owe your creditors $100 000 and so does each of your partners. But if your partners skip town, you owe the entire $300 000.

corporation *A form of business organization resting on a legal charter that establishes the corporation as an entity separate from its owners. Owners hold shares and are liable for the firm's debts only up to the limit of their investment, or share, in the firm.*

shares of stock *A certificate of partial ownership of a corporation that entitles the holder to a portion of the corporation's profits.*

■ **The Corporation** A **corporation** is a formally established legal entity that exists separately from those who establish it and those who own it. To establish a corporation, a corporate charter must be obtained. This is quite easily accomplished. A lawyer simply fills out the appropriate paperwork and files it with the right government office, along with certain fees. When a corporation is formed, **shares of stock** (certificates of partial ownership) are issued and either sold or assigned. A corporation is owned by its shareholders, who are in a sense partners in the firm's success or failure. Each share of stock entitles the holder to a portion of the corporation's profits. Shareholders differ from simple partners, however, in two important ways. First, the liability of shareholders is limited to the amount they paid for the stock. If the company goes out of business or bankrupt, the shareholders may lose what they have invested but no more than that. They are *not* liable for the debts of the corporation beyond the amount they invested. Second, the federal government levies special taxes on corporations. The federal government does not levy special taxes on proprietors and partners.

The federal corporate income tax is a tax on the **net income**, or profits, of corporations. The tax is approximately 28% of net income with a special rate of 12% available to small corporations. Each province also levies a corporate tax. Net income after taxes can be distributed to shareholders of the corporation as **dividends**—that is, the share of profits they receive from the corporation. Because dividends are also subject to taxation the Canadian tax system includes an adjustment to reduce the degree of "double taxation" that owners of corporations face.

The special privilege granted to corporations limiting their liability is often called a *franchise*. Some view the corporate tax as a payment to the government in exchange for this grant of limited liability status.

Corporate net income is usually divided into three parts. Some of it is paid to the federal and provincial governments in the form of taxes. Some of it is paid out to shareholders as dividends (sometimes called *distributed profits*). And some of it usually stays within the corporation to be used for the purchase of capital assets. This part of corporate profits is called **retained earnings**, or *undistributed profits*.

In 1999, corporations in Canada earned total profits at an annual rate of $101.4 billion. Out of this, $37.0 billion in taxes was paid, leaving $64.4 billion in after-tax profits. Of this amount, $33.2 billion was paid out to shareholders and the rest, $31.2 billion, was retained. In percentage terms, taxes accounted for 36.5%, while shareholders directly received 32.7% of total profits (Table 3.4).

The internal organization of a firm, whether it is a proprietorship, a partnership, or a corporation affects its behaviour and behaviour of potential investors. For example, because they are protected by a corporation's limited liability status, potential investors may be more likely to back high-risk but potentially high-payoff corporate ventures.

A PROFILE OF CANADIAN PRIVATE SECTOR FIRMS

The number of private sector firms in Canada is large; most of these are small in size. It is estimated that 78% of Canadian firms have fewer than five employees.[1] However, large firms account for most economic activity. For example, in 1987, there were over half a million incorporated firms operating in nonfinancial industries in Canada. The largest 1000 of these accounted for over half of the $1 trillion of revenue generated.[2] In the manufacturing sector, the largest 25% of establishments accounted for 92.4% of real gross output; the smallest 25% accounted for less than one-half of one percent of real gross output.[3]

Every year the *Financial Post* publishes a list of the 500 largest industrial corporations in Canada. The top ten—ranked by total revenue—are listed in Table 3.5.

net income *The profits of a firm.*

dividends *The portion of a corporation's profits that the firm pays out each period to shareholders. Also called* distributed profits.

retained earnings *The profits that a corporation keeps, usually for the purchase of capital assets. Also called* undistributed profits.

General Motors Canada is Canada's largest corporation.

Table 3.4	The Distribution of Corporate Profits, 1999		
		Billions of Dollars	Percent of Before-Tax Profit
Profits before tax		101.4	100.0
Minus profits tax		−37.0	−36.5
Profits after tax		64.4	63.5
Minus dividends paid		−33.2	−32.7
Undistributed profits		31.2	30.8

Source: Statistics Canada, *National Income and Expenditure Accounts, Annual Estimates*, Cat. no. 13-001-XBP.

[1] *Catherine Swift, President, Canadian Federation of Independent Business, quoted in Rod McQueen, "Small Business Sentinel," Financial Post, March 4, 2000, p. E8.*

[2] *Statistics Canada, "Corporations," Corporations and Labour Returns Act, Part 1, Cat. no. 61-210.*

[3] *Statistics Canada, Manufacturing Industries in Canada: National and Provincial Areas, Cat. no. 31-203-XPB.*

Table 3.5	Ten Largest Corporations in Canada by Revenue, 1999

RANK	COMPANY	REVENUE ($ MILLIONS)
1	General Motors Canada	33 765
2	BCE Inc.	27 454
3	Ford Motor Company of Canada	26 489
4	Nortel	26 073
5	Chrysler Canada	20 712
6	Trans-Canada Pipelines	17 228
7	Power Corp.	15 055
8	George Weston	14 726
9	Seagrams	13 431
10	Alcan Aluminum	11 554

Source: "The Financial Post 500," Financial Post, *National Post*, June 3, 1999, p. 99.

General Motors Canada tops the list with over $33 billion in revenue. BCE, the major player in the telecommunications industry in Canada, ranks second. In total, the top ten corporations account for over $206 billion in revenues.

Firm size raises many political and economic issues. Do large firms exert too much political influence? Do they have the power to set whatever prices they want? Do they face management challenges small firms can avoid? What forces caused the peculiar mix of large and small firms observed in Canada to evolve? Size is a particularly important concern at the industry level.

industry *All the firms that produce a similar product. The boundaries of a "product" can be drawn very widely ("agricultural products"), less widely ("dairy products"), or very narrowly ("cheese"). The term* industry *can be used interchangeably with the term* market.

The term **industry** is used loosely to refer to groups of firms that produce similar products. Industries can be defined broadly or narrowly, depending on the issue being discussed. For example, a company that produces and packages cheese is part of the cheese industry, the dairy products industry, the food products industry, and the manufacturing industry.

Whether we define industries broadly or narrowly, how firms within any industry behave is likely affected by how that industry is organized. For example, a firm with little or no competition is likely to behave differently from a firm facing stiff competition from many rivals. The term **market organization** is commonly used to describe how an industry is structured. A number of features of an industry are examined when determining its market organization, including the number of firms in the industry and their relative size, whether the products are virtually the same or differentiated, whether the firms can control prices or wages, whether competing firms can freely enter and leave the industry, and so forth. The relationship between market organization and behaviour is explored in detail in the microeconomics text.

market organization *The way an industry is structured. Structure is defined by how many firms there are in an industry, whether products are differentiated or are virtually the same, whether or not firms in the industry can control prices or wages, and whether or not competing firms can enter and leave the industry freely.*

STRUCTURAL CHANGES IN THE CANADIAN ECONOMY

Table 3.6 gives a breakdown of national income by major industry. The data point to a number of major changes in the structure of the economy over the past 125 years. First, the primary sector (agriculture, logging, fishing, trapping, and mining) has declined steadily in relative importance over the period. For much of the nineteenth century the Canadian economy was based on the production of primary products for export. Fur, fish, timber, and wheat were especially important. Production of these products—called *staples* by one of Canada's most famous economists, Harold A. Innis—directly involved large numbers of Canadians. It also indirectly involved many others, including those who produced inputs required in staple production, those who transported these goods to market, those who processed the staples into finished products, and those who provided goods and services to those in the staple trades. The importance of staple products in early Canadian economic history led many to consider Canada a staple-producing country and Canadians as "hewers of wood and drawers of water."

But in the twentieth century the relative importance of the primary sector declined and that of the manufacturing and service sectors grew. By 1956 only 13.1%

Table 3.6

Percentage Share of National Income by Major Sector, 1870, 1926, 1956, 1976, 1999

	1870	1926	1956	1976	1999
Primary Sector	46.2	23.4	13.1	8.5	6.1
Agriculture, logging, fishing, and trapping	45.3	20.2	8.8	4.3	2.5
Mining, quarrying, oil wells	0.9	3.2	4.3	4.2	3.6
Secondary Sector	22.6	38.7	47.3	39.2	35.4
Manufacturing	NA	21.7	28.5	20.9	18.2
Construction	NA	4.1	6.5	7.3	5.6
Transportation and communications	NA	12.9*	9.9	8.1	8.2
Electric power, water, and other utilities	NA	NA	2.4	2.9	3.4
Service Sector	31.2	37.9	39.7	52.3	58.5
Wholesale and retail trade	NA	11.6	12.5	11.9	12.3
Finance, insurance, and real estate	NA	10.0	10.1	12.0	16.2
Community, business, and personal services	NA	12.9	10.9	20.5	24.0
Public administration	NA	3.4	6.2	7.9	6.0

NA=not available
*Transportation and communications are combined with electric power, water, and other utilities.

Sources: M. C. Urquhart and K.A.H. Buckley, *Historical Statistics of Canada*, 1st ed. (Toronto: Macmillan, 1965); M.C. Urquhart and K.A.H. Buckley, *Historical Statistics of Canada*, 2nd ed. (Ottawa: Statistics Canada, 1983); and Statistics Canada, *National Income and Expenditure Accounts*, Cat. no. 31-201.

(i.e., 8.8% and 4.3%) of Canadian income was directly generated in the primary sector while 28.5% of Canada's national income originated in the manufacturing sector. Some of this manufacturing activity was still tied to the processing of natural resources but an increasing share resulted from the production of sophisticated consumer and producer goods (equipment and machinery).

Although many Canadians still believe that natural resource products are the linchpin of the Canadian economy, the data on structure indicate otherwise. In an attempt to illustrate the dramatic changes in the Canadian economy, economists like to ask people to name the most important Canadian export. Do you know what it is? People are generally amazed to discover that Canada's most important export is automobiles and automobile parts and they are still more amazed to learn that in 1999 the value of automotive exports was greater than the sum of exports of all agricultural products, all fish products, oil and natural gas, hydroelectricity, and lumber and other sawmill products. Today we are far from the staple-producing economy of the early nineteenth century.

Although Canada has a large and dynamic manufacturing sector, even this sector is in relative decline. In 1999 the relative share of the manufacturing sector had declined to 18.2% of total output. In contrast, the service sector has continued to grow in relative importance over the past 30 years. Indeed, service sector growth is one of the most striking features of recent Canadian economic history.

The growth of the service sector has sparked concern that "good" jobs are being lost and replaced by "bad" ones. Manufacturing has traditionally been thought of as a high-wage sector while the service sector is considered a low-wage sector. However, like the belief that Canadians are "hewers of wood and drawers of water," this view needs to be reconsidered. Doctors, lawyers, teachers, computer technicians and software designers, bankers, stockbrokers, budding rock musicians, and hamburger flippers at the local fast-food joint are all service providers. Thus, some service providers earn high incomes, some earn low incomes. Simple generalizations about the nature of service jobs can be misleading.

While some people are deeply concerned about the structural changes occurring in the Canadian economy, others see them as a natural consequence of continued economic growth and progress. For example, the decline in the relative importance of agriculture occurred as farmers learned more and more productive farming methods. As the need for farm labour declined so too did food prices. With lower food prices, people could spend their money on other things—manufactured goods and services. Because agriculture needed fewer workers, labour was available for employment in the new expanding sectors. Thus as the Canadian economy grew and developed, some sectors, such as agriculture, shrank in relative importance and others, such as manufacturing and services, grew in relative importance.

Modern economies are in a continuous state of change. Resources are always moving. Literally thousands of new firms are started every year and old, tired firms—not to mention young and inefficient ones—go out of business every day. Some firms grow rapidly in size, while others shrink. The purpose of this book is to help you understand this process. Why are new firms formed? Why do others go out of business? Why are some sectors expanding while others are contracting?

The Public Sector: Taxes and Government Spending in Canada

Thus far we have talked only about private firms. But this is only part of the story. The Canadian economy is best characterized as a mixed economy, because there is a large public sector that plays a major role in determining the allocation of resources, the mix of output, and the distribution of rewards. To understand the workings of the Canadian economy, it is necessary to understand the role of government.

The public sector in Canada operates on many levels—there is a national government in Ottawa, there are ten provincial and three territorial governments, there are thousands of municipal governments (cities, towns, and villages), and there are thousands more local school and hospital boards. Each of these public sector levels contributes in its own way to economic activity in this country. How big is the public sector? What do the different levels of government do? How do these governments finance their activities?

THE SIZE OF THE PUBLIC SECTOR

An economy's **gross domestic product**, or **GDP**, is the total value of all final goods and services produced in the economy in a given period of time, say a year. The concept of GDP is used extensively in macroeconomics. Here it is enough to say that GDP is used as a measure of a country's total annual "output." As you can see from Figure 3.1, public expenditure at all levels, as a percentage of GDP, increased from 21.3% in 1950 to 47.5% in 1990 and then declined to 42.2% in 1999. Thus, while the growth in the public sector between 1950 and 1990 was substantial, in recent years there has been a dramatic reversal. Between 1995 and 1999 the relative size of the public sector declined by 5.7 percentage points.

Government spending can be divided into three major categories: *purchases of goods and services*, *transfer payments* to households, and *interest payments* on the national debt. **Purchases of goods and services** make up that proportion of national output that government actually uses or "consumes" directly. They include new highways, the services of teachers and doctors, and all other goods and services purchased by the public sector. The wages and salaries of government employees are included in this category. **Transfer payments** are cash payments made directly to households—employment insurance benefits, social assistance, old age security, Canada and Quebec Pension Plan benefits, and the like. The government receives no current services in exchange for these payments. **Interest payments** on the public debt are also cash payments, but they are paid to those who own government bonds. Table 3.7 reveals how the government spending has changed in these three major categories since 1950.

Between 1970 and 1995 interest charges rose because of the large deficits. When governments spend more than they raise in revenue, they must borrow. They do so by issuing bonds, on which they must pay interest. Two major *recessions* (periods in which economic activity declines, tax revenues fall, and spending on social programs increases) and high interest rates played an important role in the rise in government debt in Canada and in the growth in interest charges. Control of debt became one of the major public sector issues.

gross domestic product (GDP)
The total value of all final goods and services produced by a national economy within a given time period.

government purchases of goods and services *A category of government spending that includes the portion of national output that the government uses, or "consumes," directly—ships for the navy, memo pads for the RCMP, salaries for government employees.*

government transfer payments *Cash payments made by the government directly to households for which no current services are received. They include old age security benefits, employment insurance, and the like.*

government interest payments *Cash payments made by the government to those who own government bonds.*

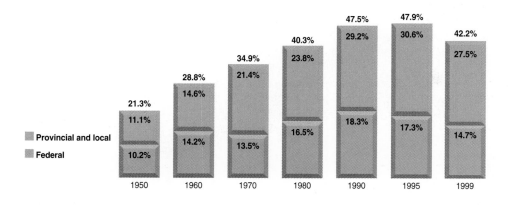

FIGURE 3.1

Total Government Expenditure as a Percentage of GDP, 1950–1999

Total government expenditures grew from 21.3% of GDP in 1950 to 47.9% in 1995. The sum of provincial and local government expenditure grew somewhat more rapidly than federal government expenditure.

Source: 1950–1980: David B. Perry, "Fiscal Figures: Changes in Government Spending Patterns," *Canadian Tax Journal* vol. 44, no. 2 (1996): 586, Table 6; 1990–2000: Authors' calculations based on Statistics Canada, *National Income and Expenditure Accounts*, Cat. no. 13-001.

The growth in debt in the late 1970s and early 1980s caused governments throughout Canada to adopt a fiscally conservative stance as they attempted to control spending while raising taxes. Unfortunately, high interest rates and high unemployment made debt control difficult. In 1995, Paul Martin, the Minister of Finance in the Liberal government, felt it necessary to take drastic action, and he introduced a budget that involved deep cuts in the civil service and transfer payments to individuals and the provinces. In the same year, the Progressive Conservative government of Mike Harris was elected in Ontario with a mandate not only to reduce debt but also to reduce the role of government in society. Governments everywhere followed the lead, and the public sector budgets began to move from a position of deficits to one of surpluses. In just four years, government expenditure as a percentage of GDP declined from 47.9% to 42.2%. For some, the shrinking public sector is cause for celebration; for others, it is a matter of deep concern.

Good statistics on the size of Canada's public sector are not easy to find, but Figure 3.2 presents some international comparisons based on taxes collected. Taxes support public sector activities and tax data are easy to find.

The data must be interpreted carefully. For example, Canadians and the citizens of many other countries pay for medical care and hospital insurance through taxes, whereas people in the United States do not. Ideally if data were available we would base comparisons on information both about taxes and about what people receive in return for their taxes.

The figures show total taxes collected by all levels of government as a percentage of gross domestic product (GDP). In 1980, tax collection in Canada amounted to 31.6% of GDP. This put Canada in tenth place among the 19 countries in the comparison. Between 1975 and 1991, taxes as a percentage of GDP increased in all 19 countries. In Canada, taxes rose from 31.6% to 36.1% of GDP.

Table 3.7	**The Size of the Canadian Public Sector, 1950–1999**						
	GOVERNMENT EXPENDITURES AS A PERCENTAGE OF GDP (EXCLUDING INTERGOVERNMENTAL TRANSFERS)						
	1950	*1960*	*1970*	*1980*	*1990*	*1995*	*1999*
Purchases of goods and services	9.0	12.2	17.1	17.7	25.3	24.1	21.9
Transfer payments to persons	5.3	7.8	7.8	9.0	10.8	12.3	11.1
Interest payments on debt	2.8	2.8	3.6	5.4	9.5	9.6	7.8
Other	4.2	6.0	6.4	7.6	1.9	1.4	1.4
Total	21.3	28.8	34.9	40.3	47.5	47.9	42.2

Source: 1950–1980: David B. Perry, "Fiscal Figures: Changes in Government Spending Patterns," *Canadian Tax Journal,* vol. 44, no. 2 (1996): Tables 5, 6, 9, and 10; 1990–2000: Authors' calculations based on Statistics Canada, *National Income and Expenditure Accounts*, Cat. no. 13-001.

FIGURE 3.2

Taxes as a Percentage of Gross Domestic Product, 1980 and 1994

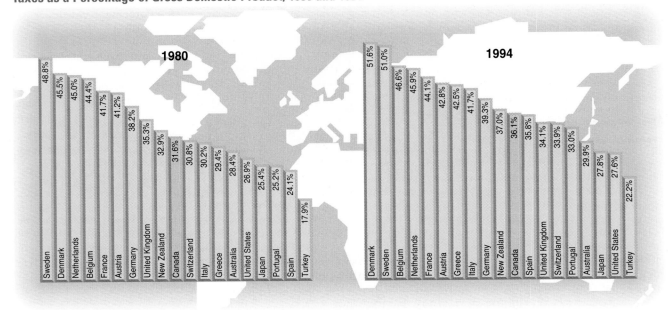

Source: Statistical Abstract of the United States, 1994, p. 867.

However, in the United States, the increase was virtually negligible—from 26.9% to 27.6%. (How would you account for the relatively small increase in the United States?)

GOVERNMENT STRUCTURE AND EXPENDITURE

When Canada was created in 1867 a critical document—the British North America (BNA) Act—divided public sector functions between the federal and provincial governments. A popular view of Canadian federalism suggests that most functions entrusted to the national government dealt with matters in which all Canadians had a common stake. Of these, national defence and an integrated Canadian economy were most important. The provinces, on the other hand, were given responsibility for local and cultural matters such as education, health, and social welfare, thereby limiting potential areas of conflict. Moreover, the provinces were given ultimate authority over municipal government, school boards, and hospital boards.

The BNA Act provided a constitutional framework for the development of the Canadian public sector. But it could not anticipate the many economic and social changes that were to occur after 1867. For example, while the Act assigned the largest revenue *sources* to the federal government, it left the provincial governments responsible for services for which it has since turned out they are ill-equipped to fund from their own resources — services that include the now critically important areas of health, education, and social welfare. In principle, the distribution of legislative powers in the BNA Act should have precluded the development of the welfare state, since provincial governments lacked the resources to support expansion of such a system and the national government lacked the authority to establish it in the first place. However, Canadian politicians proved remarkably innovative. The federal government was able to assume a key role in the welfare state, through constitutional amendment (e.g., a constitutional amendment gave the federal government the authority needed to implement a national unemployment insurance program), through fiscal transfers to provinces (in 1995, the federal government gave provincial and local governments over $30 billion to spend in areas in provincial jurisdiction), and through use of its so-called spending power (which allows the federal government to attach conditions—such as the conditions established in the Canada Health Act—to its transfers to the provinces). The result is an extremely complex system of government that involves conflict and cooperation, specialization and overlap, and, most importantly, continual change and adaptation.

Indeed, change is as important a characteristic of the public sector as it is of the private sector.

Table 3.8 divides total government expenditure as a percentage of GDP into two categories, "federal government" and "provincial/local/hospital" (PLH), to illustrate the relative importance of the two levels of government that enjoy constitutional status. The PLH sector is not subdivided here because the distribution of responsibilities among these three levels differs widely from province to province.

The table illustrates three important features of the structure of the Canadian public sector. First, the PLH sector is a much more important provider of goods and services than the federal government. This is not surprising given the provincial governments have primary responsibility for health, education, roads, and social services. Moreover, the activity of the PLH sector in this area has grown dramatically since 1950 in contrast to that of the federal government, whose goods and services expenditure accounts for a smaller proportion of GDP than it did in 1950. Second, the PLH sector has become increasingly active in directly transferring income. Finally, debt charges are most significant at the federal level.

SOURCES OF GOVERNMENT REVENUE

A breakdown of sources of government revenue in Canada in 1976/77 and 1995/96 is provided in Table 3.9. The biggest single source of revenue for governments in Canada in 1995/96 is the *personal income tax*, which accounted for 45.1% of federal government revenue and 20.4% of provincial government revenue. All personal income tax is collected by the federal government in all provinces except Quebec, which is responsible for its own provincial personal income tax collection. Personal income tax is withheld from most people's pay each week by their employers, who send it to Revenue Canada. Revenue Canada then distributes the provincial share to each of the provinces. Self-employed persons are responsible for sending Revenue Canada their own estimated taxes four times each year. Every year you add up our total income, subtract the items you are allowed to exclude or deduct, claim your tax credits, and figure out the tax you should have paid for the year. If you owe more than you paid, you must send the difference to Revenue Canada by April 30. If you paid more than you owe, you get a refund.

Corporations must pay special **corporate income taxes**. (Profits from other forms of business organizations—single proprietorships and partnerships—are taxed directly as ordinary personal income of the owners.) While personal income tax collections have been rising as a percentage of government revenue over the past 20 years, corporate income taxes have been falling in relative importance (see Table 3.9). The decline in the relative importance of the corporate tax has been a source of concern for many. However, it is important to distinguish between who

corporate income taxes *Taxes levied on the net incomes of corporations.*

Table 3.8	Activities of Different Levels of Government in Canada, 1950–1999						
	Government Expenditures as a Percentage of GDP						
	1950	1960	1970	1980	1990	1995	1999
Purchases of goods and services:							
Federal government	4.5	5.9	4.8	4.2	5.2	4.7	4.1
Provincial/local/hospital sector	4.5	6.3	12.2	13.5	21.1	19.9	17.8
Transfer payments to persons:							
Federal government	3.2	5.0	4.6	5.3	5.8	6.1	5.4
Provincial/local/hospital sector	2.1	2.8	3.2	3.7	4.0	6.2	6.4
Interest payments on debt:							
Federal government	2.2	1.9	2.1	3.2	6.2	5.4	4.5
Provincial/local/hospital sector	0.6	0.9	1.6	2.2	3.3	4.2	3.3
Other:							
Federal government	1.2	1.8	2.0	3.8	1.1	1.1	0.7
Provincial/local/hospital sector	3.0	4.2	4.4	4.4	0.8	0.3	0.1

Source: 1950–1980: David B. Perry, "Fiscal Figures: Changes in Government Spending Patterns," *Canadian Tax Journal*, vol. 44, no. 2 (1996): Table 10; 1990–2000: Authors' calculations based on Statistics Canada, *National Income and Expenditure Accounts*, Cat. no. 13-001.

Table 3.9	Sources of Public Sector Revenue, 1976/77 and 1995/96			
	Federal Revenues (% distribution)		Provincial/Local/Hospital Revenues (% distribution)	
	1976/77	1995/96	1976/77	1995/96
Personal income tax	42.0	45.1	16.0	20.4
Corporate income tax	15.0	9.8	5.0	3.3
General sales taxes	11.0	15.2	10.0	10.7
Excise taxes	6.0	5.4	5.0	4.6
Health and social insurance levies	7.0	13.4	5.0	5.2
Customs duties	6.0	2.2	0	0
Property taxes	0	0	14.0	17.0
Transfers from other levels of government	0	0	21.0	15.6
Other*	13.0	8.9	24.0	23.2

*Includes licences, sale of goods and services, natural resource revenues, return on investments.

Sources: Statistics Canada, *Public Sector Finance, 1995–96*, Cat. no. 68-212; Statistics Canada, *Public Finance Historical Data 1965/66–1991/92*, Cat. no. 68-512.

is legally responsible for writing a cheque to the government and who actually pays the tax by experiencing a loss in general well-being. This distinction, which in economics is known as the distinction between the *legal and economic incidence of a tax*, is critically important in debates about the corporate tax. Corporations are owned by individuals and it is individuals who ultimately must pay the tax. Moreover, a corporation may be able to pass on the tax by charging consumers higher prices or paying workers less than they would receive in the absence of the corporate tax. For example, if corporations can pass on the corporate tax to consumers or workers in low-income brackets then the relatively poor in our society may end up bearing a disproportionate share of the tax. We will return to the difference between legal and economic tax incidence in later chapters.

Sales taxes are another growing source of government revenue. The Goods and Services Tax (GST) and provincial sales taxes (currently in place in all provinces except Alberta) are known as general sales taxes since they are levied on a wide variety of goods and services. The federal government currently collects more than 15% of its total revenue from *general sales taxes*, and the PLH sector collects almost 11% of its revenue from this source. In addition, both levels of government collect revenue from taxes levied on the sales of specific products, such as cigarettes, alcoholic beverages, and gasoline. These taxes are known as **excise taxes**.

A fourth important source of government revenue is the **payroll taxes** used to finance social insurance programs such as employment insurance and the Canada and Quebec Pension Plans. Payroll taxes, which are based on wages and salaries paid, are paid by both employers and employees. They are presented as "health and social insurance levies" in Table 3.9. In 1995/96 about 13% of federal government revenue was collected through payroll taxes and about 5% of provincial revenue came from this source.

Some revenue sources are unique to a particular level of government. Only the federal government levies *customs duties* — taxes imposed on goods and services produced in other countries. Only provincial and local governments levy *property taxes* — determined as a percentage of the estimated or "assessed" value of commercial, industrial, and residential property. Property taxes are an important source of revenue for provincial and local governments. They accounted for 17% of PLH revenue in 1995/96.

The PLH sector also relies heavily on grants from higher levels of government. For example, the federal government estimates that it transfers over $30 billion to the provinces every year. In 1995/96 these transfers accounted for over 15% of PLH revenue. These government *transfer payments*—which include Equalization (a program designed to help the poorer provinces) and the Canada Health and Social Transfer (a grant intended to help provinces provide medicare, hospital insurance,

excise taxes *Taxes on specific commodities.*

payroll taxes *Taxes levied at a flat rate on wages and salaries. Proceeds support various government-administered social-benefit programs, including the social insurance system and the employment insurance system.*

postsecondary education, and provincial social assistance)—play a critical role in the Canadian federation.

Finally, governments collect revenue from a variety of other sources including profits from government enterprises such as lotteries, user fees imposed on users of public services, and royalties collected from firms selling natural resources owned by government.

Like all aspects of the Canadian economy, public sector revenue sources have changed dramatically over time. At Confederation, customs duties were the dominant revenue source. Today they are insignificant. The federal income tax was introduced in 1917 to generate a small amount of additional revenue to help pay for the costs incurred during World War I. Today it is the largest single source of revenue for the public sector.

The International Sector:
Imports and Exports in Canada

From almost the first moment Europeans arrived in Canada, Canadians have been engaged in trade with the rest of the world. We sell goods and services we produce to people residing in other countries, and they sell goods and services they produce to us. Indeed, international trade has been more important to Canada throughout its history than it has been to almost any other country in the world.

From 1750 to 1850 our economic history was dominated by England. We were part of the British Empire, and the Industrial Revolution in England generated a rapidly growing demand for natural resource products that could be produced in Canada. Meanwhile, the growing Canadian economy generated a demand for manufactured goods produced in England. Moreover, a significant proportion of the capital needed in the growing Canadian economy was financed by the English. Borrowing from the rest of the world has been an important aspect of the Canadian economy ever since.

Over time the patterns of trade changed, but the importance of trade to the Canadian economy did not. After 1850, the United States became increasingly important as a trading partner and as a source of foreign capital investment.

Because trade is so important to the Canadian economy, Canadians have always been sensitive to developments in the international economy. Three developments in recent years are particularly important in increasing the relative importance of trade. First, the rapid economic growth of Japan and other Southeast Asian states (such as Korea, Singapore, Taiwan, Hong Kong, China, and Malaysia) has increased the absolute importance of Pacific trade. Second, the emergence of regional trading blocs has influenced trade patterns. We are an integral partner in an emerging North American trading area currently involving the United States, Mexico, and Chile; many countries in Europe are members of the EU (European Union); and there is talk of the formation of a Pacific Rim trading area. The key feature of a trading bloc is that its participants are not subject to trading restrictions imposed on nonmembers. Finally, dramatic improvements in communications and other technologies have helped foster a general tendency known as *globalization*, meaning that goods, services, and capital are able to move across national boundaries much more easily than ever before.

Currently, Canadian exports equal about 43% of GDP, a very large share of total Canadian production. Imports are about 40% of GDP, a very large share of total expenditures of Canadian consumers, firms, and governments. The size and importance of the international sector of the Canadian economy is examined in more detail in Chapter 20.

Financial institutions play an important role in allocating savings in the private, public, and international sectors of the economy.

FAST FACTS

The following numbers are total exports as a percentage of total national output for selected countries in 1995:

Ireland	75%
Belgium	74%
United Arab Emirates	70%
Namibia	53%
Canada	**43%**
Thailand	42%
Korea	33%
Chile	29%
Germany	23%
India	12%
United States	11%
Japan	9%
Brazil	7%
Haiti	4%

From Institutions to Theory

This chapter has sketched the institutional structure of the Canadian economy. As we turn to economic theory, both positive and normative, you should reflect on the basic realities of economic life in Canada presented here. Why is the service sector expanding and the manufacturing sector contracting? Why is the public sector as large as it is? What economic functions does it perform? What determines the level of imports and exports? What effects do cheap foreign products have on the Canadian economy?

One of the most important questions in economics concerns the relative merits of public sector involvement in the economy. Should the government be involved in the economy, or should the market be left to its own devices? Before we can confront these and other important issues, we need to establish a theoretical framework. Our study of the economy and its operation begins in Chapter 4 with the behaviour of suppliers and demanders in private markets.

Summary

1. The *private sector* is made up of privately owned firms that exist to make a profit, nonprofit organizations, and individual households. The *public sector* is the government and its agencies at all levels—federal, provincial, and local. The international sector is the global economy. From any one country's perspective, the international sector consists of the economies of the rest of the world.

Canadian Households

2. Canadian households are engaged in a remarkably diverse set of consumption and production activities. There are thousands of occupations in Canada. Some are high-paying; others pay relatively poorly. The typical job in Canada pays about $26 000 per year. More than half of Canadians have jobs that pay less than this. However, some Canadians earn very, very high salaries. One Canadian earned $34 000 000 in 1999.

3. Some Canadian households also earn income because they own real assets (e.g., a business and its capital) or financial assets. Ownership of real and financial assets is not distributed evenly across Canadian households; ownership tends to be concentrated in the hands of the more affluent Canadians.

Private Sector Firms in Canada

4. Private sector firms are characterized by independent ownership and control. A proprietorship is a firm with a single owner. A partnership has two or more owners. Proprietorships and partnerships are fully liable for all the debts of the business. A corporation is a formally established legal entity that limits the liability of its owners. The owners are not responsible for the debts of the firm beyond what they invest.

5. Private sector firms can be large or small. Most firms in Canada are relatively small but some are very large.

The Public Sector: Taxes and Government Spending in Canada

6. The importance of the public sector in Canada has grown dramatically since World War II. Public expenditures at all levels increased from 21.3% of GDP in 1950 to 47.9% of GDP in 1995. Between 1995 and 1999 government expenditures at all levels fell.

7. The Canadian public sector is organized on a federal basis with many levels of government. The federal and provincial governments enjoy a special constitutional status. Provincial governments have ultimate responsibility for medical and hospital care, social welfare assistance, and education. The federal government has jurisdiction over national defence and an integrated economy. As well, the federal government is responsible for a number of income security programs such as Employment Insurance, Old Age Security, and the Canada Pension Plan.

8. Since 1950, expenditures on areas within provincial jurisdiction have grown faster than expenditures in areas falling within the jurisdiction of the federal government. Almost all the growth in federal government expenditure in this period can be attributed to increasing transfer payments (to persons and provincial governments) and to rising interest payments on the national debt.

9. The biggest single source of revenue for governments in Canada is the personal income tax. It accounts for over 45% of federal government revenue and over 20% of provincial government revenue. Sales taxes are now the second most important source of revenue for both levels of government.

The International Sector: Imports and Exports in Canada

10. Thousands of transactions between Canadians and virtually every other country in the world take place daily. Canada is and has always been a country that relies heavily on international trade. The United States is Canada's most important trading partner, and automobiles are Canada's most important export.

Review Terms and Concepts

corporate income
  taxes 59

corporation 52

dividends 53

excise taxes 60

government interest
  payments 56

government purchases of goods and
  services 56

government transfer
  payments 56

gross domestic product
  (GDP) 56

industry 54

international sector 49

market organization 54

net income 53

partnership 52

payroll taxes 60

private sector 48

proprietorship 52

public sector 49

retained earnings 53

shares of stock 52

Problem Set

1. Health care continues to be a major issue in 2000. Look up the latest figures on health care expenditures as a percentage of GDP. In your province what share of total government expenditure (federal, provincial, and local) is devoted to health care?

2. a. How many separate governments make decisions affecting your life?
  b. What are the five biggest functions of local government?
  c. What is the logic for assigning these functions to local government as opposed to provincial or federal government?

3. Do a short research project on one of the following large government services. What does the service accomplish or hope to accomplish? What is the basic logic for government involvement? How much was spent on the service in 2000 compared to 1995?
  a. Canada Council
  b. Canada Pension Plan
  c. Employment Insurance
  d. Parks Canada
  e. Canada Student Loan Program
  f. Trans-Canada Highway

4. NAFTA was much debated prior to coming into affect on January 1, 1994. What groups were opposed to it? Why? What are the basic arguments in favour of NAFTA?

5. Use the Internet to collect the most recent data on federal government expenditures and revenues and on international trade. Do the most recent data indicate major changes?

6. This chapter contains evidence on growth of both the public and the service sectors. How are these two developments related?

7. What are the differences between a proprietorship and a corporation? If you were going to start a small business, which form of organization would you choose? What are the advantages and disadvantages of the two forms of organization?

8. "Most firms are corporations, but they account for a relatively small portion of total output in Canada." Do you agree or disagree with this statement? Explain your answer.

9. In 1995 shareholders directly received only 26.1% of total corporate profits. What happened to the rest?

10. Several large corporations in Canada employ over 30 000 people. How do you think large corporations attempt to manage this number of people? Is there any similarity between the command economic systems discussed in Chapter 2 and the large corporation?

11. What do you think are the advantages and disadvantages of large firms? Of small firms?

12. How is it possible for government spending to increase as a percentage of GDP while taxes and government employment are both decreasing?

13. Why is the federal government spending less on interest payments now than it was five years ago? Explain.

Demand, Supply, and Market Equilibrium

Firms and Households: The Basic Decision-Making Units

Input Markets and Output Markets: The Circular Flow

Demand in Product/Output Markets

Price and Quantity Demanded: The Law of Demand

Other Determinants of Household Demand

Shift of Demand Versus Movement Along a Demand Curve

From Household Demand to Market Demand

Supply in Product/Output Markets

Price and Quantity Supplied: The Law of Supply

Other Determinants of Firm Supply

Shift of Supply Versus Movement Along a Supply Curve

From Individual Firm Supply to Market Supply

Market Equilibrium

Excess Demand

Excess Supply

Changes in Equilibrium

Demand and Supply in Product Markets: A Review

Looking Ahead: Markets and the Allocation of Resources

Appendix 4A

Learning Objectives

1 Describe the relationships between input and output markets in a simple market economy.

2 Explain the role of price and other factors in the basic theory of demand.

3 Distinguish between changes in quantity demanded (movements along the demand curve) and changes in demand (shifts in the demand curve).

4 Describe the relationship between individual and market demand.

5 Explain the role of price and other factors in the basic theory of supply.

6 Distinguish between changes in quantity supplied (movements along the supply curve) and changes in supply (shifts in the supply curve).

7 Describe the relationship between individual and market supply.

8 Describe the three market outcomes: excess demand, excess supply, and equilibrium.

9 Use the demand/supply market equilibrium model to analyze the impact of market changes on market prices, sales, and expenditures.

10 Appendix 4A: Use simple algebra to represent demand, supply, and market equilibrium.

Chapters 1 and 2 introduced the discipline, methodology, and subject matter of economics. Chapter 3 described the institutional landscape of the Canadian economy—its private, public, and international sectors. We now begin the task of analyzing how a market economy actually works. This chapter and the next present an overview of the way individual markets work. They introduce some of the concepts needed to understand both microeconomics and macroeconomics.

As we proceed to define terms and make assumptions, it is important to keep in mind what we are doing. In Chapter 1 we were very careful to explain what economic theory attempts to do. Theories are abstract representations of reality, like a map that represents a city. We believe that the models presented here will help you understand the workings of the economy just as a map helps you get where you want to go in a city. But just as a map presents one view of the world, so too does any given theory of the economy. Alternatives exist to the theory that we present. We believe, however, that the basic model presented here, while sometimes abstract, is useful in gaining an understanding of how the economy works.

In the simple island society discussed in Chapter 2, the economic problem was solved directly. Colleen and Ivan allocated their time and used the resources of the island to satisfy their wants. Ivan might be a farmer, Colleen a hunter and carpenter. He might be a civil engineer, she a doctor. Exchange occurred, but complex markets were not necessary.

In societies of many people, however, production must satisfy wide-ranging tastes and preferences. Producers therefore specialize. Farmers produce more food than they can eat in order to sell it to buy manufactured goods. Physicians are paid for specialized services, as are lawyers, construction workers, and editors. When there is specialization, there must be exchange, and exchange takes place in markets.

This chapter begins to explore the basic forces at work in market systems. The purpose of our discussion is to explain how the individual decisions of households and firms together, without any central planning or direction, answer the three basic questions: what will be produced, how it will be produced, and who will get what is produced. We begin with some definitions.

Firms and Households: The Basic Decision-Making Units

Throughout this book, we discuss and analyze the behaviour of two fundamental decision-making units: *firms*—the primary producing units in an economy—and *households*—the consuming units in an economy. Both are made up of people performing different functions and playing different roles. In essence, then, what we are developing is a theory of human behaviour.

A **firm** exists when a person or a group of people decides to produce a product or products by transforming inputs (i.e., resources in the broadest sense) into outputs (the products that are sold in the market). Some firms produce goods; others produce services. Some are large, some are small, and some are in between. But all firms exist to transform resources into things that people want. The Toronto Symphony Orchestra takes labour, land, a building, musically talented people, electricity, and other inputs and combines them to produce concerts. The production process can be extremely complicated. The first flutist in the orchestra, for example, uses training, talent, previous performance experience, a score, an instrument, the conductor's interpretation, and her own feelings about the music to produce just one contribution to an overall performance.

Most firms exist to make a profit for their owners, but some do not. Your university, for example, fits the description of a firm. It takes inputs in the form of labour, land, skills, books, and buildings and produces a service that we call education. Although it sells that service for a price, it does not exist to make a profit, but rather to provide education of the highest quality possible.

Still, most firms exist to make a profit. They engage in production because they can sell their product for more than it costs to produce it. The analysis of firm behaviour that follows rests on the assumption that firms make decisions in order to *maximize profits*.

An **entrepreneur** is one who organizes, manages, and assumes the risks of a firm. It is the entrepreneur who takes a new idea or a new product and turns it into a successful business. All firms have implicit in them some element of entrepreneurship. When a new firm is created—whether a proprietorship, a partnership, or a corporation—someone must organize the new firm, arrange financing, hire employees, and take risks. That person is an entrepreneur. Sometimes existing companies introduce new products, and sometimes new firms develop or improve on an old idea, but at the root of it all is entrepreneurship, which some see as the core of the free enterprise system.

At the root of the debate about the potential of free enterprise in formerly socialist Eastern Europe is the question of entrepreneurship. Does an entrepreneurial spirit exist in that part of the world? If not, can it be developed? Without it the free enterprise system breaks down.

The consuming units in an economy are **households**. A household may consist of any number of people: a single person living alone, a married couple with four children, or 15 unrelated people sharing a house. Household decisions are pre-

firm *An organization that transforms resources (inputs) into products (outputs). Firms are the primary producing units in a market economy.*

entrepreneur *A person who organizes, manages, and assumes the risks of a firm, taking a new idea or a new product and turning it into a successful business.*

households *The consuming units in an economy.*

The Toronto Symphony Orchestra is a firm. It combines inputs (land, labour, a concert hall, musically talented people, electricity, etc.) and uses them to produce outputs (musical performance).

sumably based on the individual tastes and preferences of the consuming unit. The household buys what it wants and can afford. In a large, heterogeneous, and open society such as Canada, wildly different tastes find expression in the marketplace. A six-block walk in any direction on any street in Montreal or a drive from Yonge and Bloor Streets north into rural Ontario should be enough to convince anyone that it is difficult to generalize about what people like and do not like.

Even though households have wide-ranging preferences, they also have some things in common. All—even the very rich—have ultimately limited incomes, and all must pay in some way for the things they consume. While households may have some control over their incomes—they can work more or less—they are also constrained by the availability of jobs, current wages, their own abilities, and their accumulated and inherited wealth (or lack thereof).

Input Markets and Output Markets: The Circular Flow

Households and firms interact in two basic kinds of markets: product or output markets and input or factor markets. Goods and services that are intended for use by households are exchanged in **product** or **output markets**. In output markets, competing firms supply and households demand.

To produce goods and services, firms must buy resources in **input** or **factor markets**. Firms buy inputs from households, which supply these inputs. When a firm decides how much to produce (supply) in output markets, it must simultaneously decide how much of each input it needs to produce the desired level of output. To produce automobiles, Chrysler Canada must use many inputs, including tires, steel, complicated machinery, and many different kinds of skilled labour.

Figure 4.1 shows the *circular flow* of economic activity through a simple market economy. Note that the flow reflects the direction in which goods and services flow through input and output markets. For example, goods and services flow from firms to households through output markets. Labour services flow from households to firms through input markets. Payment (most often in money form) for goods and services flows in the opposite direction. Payment for goods and services flows from households to firms, and payment for labour services flows from firms to households.

In input markets, households supply resources. Most households earn their incomes by working—they supply their labour in the **labour market** to firms that de-

product or **output markets** *The markets in which goods and services are exchanged.*

input or **factor markets** *The markets in which the resources used to produce products are exchanged.*

labour market *The input/factor market in which households supply work for wages to firms that demand labour.*

mand labour and pay workers for their time and skills. Households may also lend their accumulated or inherited savings to firms for interest or exchange those savings for claims to future profits, as when a household buys shares of stock in a corporation. In the **capital market**, households supply the funds that firms use to buy capital goods. In exchange, these households receive interest or claims to future profits. Households may also supply land or other real property in exchange for rent in the **land market**.

Inputs into the production process are also called **factors of production**. Land, labour, and capital are the three key factors of production. Throughout this text, we use the terms *input* and *factor of production* interchangeably. Thus, input markets and factor markets mean the same thing.

Early economics texts included entrepreneurship as a type of input, just like land, labour, and capital. Treating entrepreneurship as a separate factor of production has fallen out of favour, however, partially because it is unmeasurable. Most economists today implicitly assume that it is in plentiful supply. That is, if profit opportunities exist, it is likely that entrepreneurs will crop up to take advantage of them. This assumption has turned out to be a good predictor of actual economic behaviour and performance.

The supply of inputs and their prices ultimately determine households' income. The amount of income a household earns thus depends on the decisions it makes concerning what types of inputs it chooses to supply. Whether to stay in school, how much and what kind of training to get, whether to start a business, how many hours to work, whether to work at all, and how to invest savings are all household decisions that affect income.

As you can see, then:

> Input and output markets are connected through the behaviour of both firms and households. Firms determine the quantities and character of outputs produced and the types and quantities of inputs demanded. Households determine the types and quantities of products demanded and the quantities and types of inputs supplied.[1]

Demand in Product/Output Markets

In real life, households make many decisions at the same time. To see how the forces of demand and supply work, however, let us focus first on the amount of a single product that an individual household decides to consume within some given period of time, such as a month or a year.

> A household's decision about what quantity of a particular output, or product, to demand depends upon a number of factors:
>
> - The *price of the product* in question
> - The *income available* to the household
> - The household's *amount of accumulated wealth*
> - The *prices of other products* available to the household
> - The household's *tastes and preferences*
> - The household's *expectations* about future income, wealth, and prices

capital market *The input/factor market in which households supply their savings, for interest or for claims to future profits, to firms that demand funds in order to buy capital goods.*

land market *The input/factor market in which households supply land or other real property in exchange for rent.*

factors of production *The inputs into the production process. Land, labour, and capital are the three key factors of production.*

Colour Guide

Note that in Figure 4.1 households are depicted in *blue* and firms are depicted in *red*. From now on all diagrams relating to the behaviour of households will be in blue or shades of blue, and all diagrams relating to the behaviour of firms will be in red or shades of red.

---

[1]*Our description of markets begins with the behaviour of firms and households. Modern orthodox economic theory essentially combines two distinct but closely related theories of behaviour. The "theory of household behaviour," or "consumer behaviour," has its roots in the works of nineteenth-century utilitarians such as Jeremy Bentham, William Jevons, Carl Menger, Leon Walras, Vilfredo Pareto, and F. Y. Edgeworth. The "theory of the firm" developed out of the earlier classical political economy of Adam Smith, David Ricardo, and Thomas Malthus. In 1890 Alfred Marshall published the first of many editions of his* Principles of Economics. *That volume pulled together the main themes of both the classical economists and the utilitarians into what is now called "neoclassical economics." While there have been many changes over the years, the basic structure of the model that we build can be found in Marshall's work.*

FIGURE 4.1

The Circular Flow of
Economic Activity

Diagrams like this one show the
circular flow of economic activity,
hence the name *circular flow diagram.* Here, goods and services
flow clockwise: labour services
supplied by households flow to
firms, and goods and services
produced by firms flow to households. Money (not pictured here)
flows in the opposite (counter-
clockwise) direction: payment for
goods and services flows from
households to firms, and payment
for labour services flows from
firms to households.

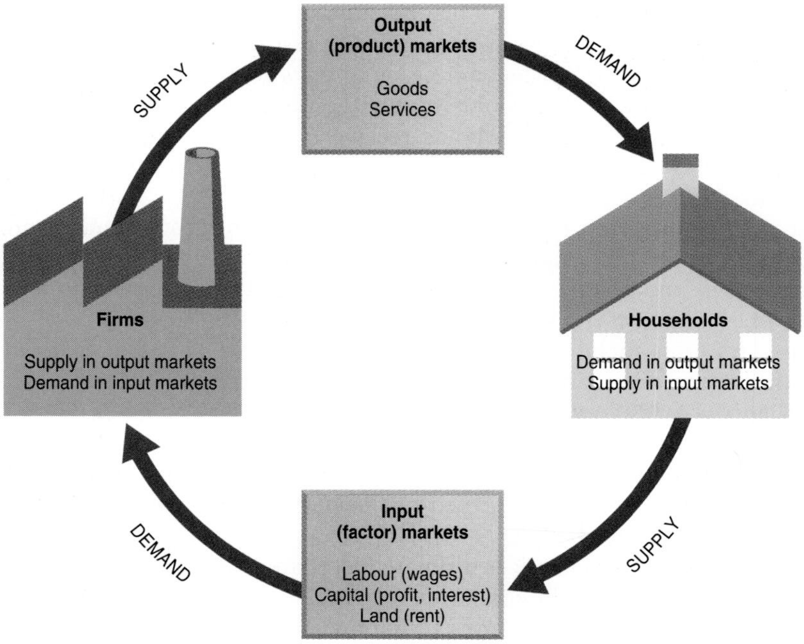

quantity demanded *The
amount (number of units) of a
product that a household would
buy in a given period if it could
buy all it wanted at the current
market price.*

Quantity demanded is the amount (number of units) of a product that a household would buy in a given period *if it could buy all it wanted at the current
market price.*

Of course, the amount of a product that households finally purchase depends
on the amount of product actually available in the market. But the quantity demanded at any moment may exceed or fall short of the quantity supplied. These
differences between the quantity demanded and the quantity supplied are very
important. The phrase *if it could buy all it wanted* is critical to the definition of
quantity demanded because it allows for the possibility that quantity supplied and
quantity demanded are unequal.

Our analysis of demand and supply is leading up to a theory of how market
prices are determined. Prices are determined by interaction between demanders and
suppliers. To understand this interaction, we first need to know how product prices
influence the behaviour of suppliers and demanders *separately.* We therefore begin
our discussion of output markets by focusing exclusively on this relationship.

■ **Changes in Quantity Demanded Versus Changes in Demand** The most important relationship in individual markets is that between market price and quantity demanded. For this reason, we need to begin our discussion by analyzing the likely
response of households to changes in price using the device of ceteris paribus, or
"all else equal." That is, we will attempt to derive a relationship between the quantity demanded of a good per time period and the price of that good, holding income, wealth, other prices, tastes, and expectations constant.

It is very important to distinguish between price changes, which affect the
quantity of a good demanded, and changes in other factors (such as income), which
change the entire relationship between price and quantity. For example, if a family
begins earning a higher income, it might buy more of a good at every possible price.
To be sure that we distinguish between changes in price and other changes that affect demand, we will throughout the rest of the text be very precise about terminology. Specifically:

Changes in the price of a product affect the *quantity* demanded per period.
Changes in any other factor, such as income or preferences, affect demand.
Thus we say that an increase in the price of Coca-Cola is likely to cause a decrease in the *quantity* of Coca-Cola demanded. Similarly, we say that an increase in income is likely to cause an increase in the demand for most goods.

PRICE AND QUANTITY DEMANDED: THE LAW OF DEMAND

A **demand schedule** shows the quantities of a product that a household would be willing to buy at different prices. Table 4.1 presents a hypothetical demand schedule for Anna, a student who went off to university to study economics while her boyfriend went to art school. If telephone calls were free (a price of zero), Anna would call her boyfriend every day, or 30 times a month. At a price of $0.50 per call, she makes 25 calls a month. When the price hits $3.50, she cuts back to seven calls a month. This same information presented graphically is called a **demand curve**. Anna's demand curve is presented in Figure 4.2.[2]

You will note in Figure 4.2 that *quantity* is measured along the horizontal axis, and *price* is measured along the vertical axis. This is the convention we follow throughout this book.

■ **Demand Curves Slope Downward**   The data in Table 4.1 show that at lower prices, Anna calls her boyfriend more frequently; at higher prices, she calls less frequently. There is thus a *negative, or inverse, relationship between quantity demanded and price*. When price rises, quantity demanded falls, and when price falls, quantity demanded rises. Thus demand curves slope downward. This negative relationship between price and quantity demanded is often referred to as the **law of demand**, a term first used by economist Alfred Marshall in his 1890 textbook *Principles of Economics*.

Some people are put off by the abstractness of demand curves. Of course, we don't actually draw our own demand curves for products. When we want to make a purchase, we usually face only a single price, and how much we would buy at other prices is irrelevant. But demand curves help analysts understand the kind of behaviour that households are *likely* to exhibit if they are actually faced with a higher or lower price. We know, for example, that if the price of a good rises enough, the quantity demanded must ultimately drop to zero. The demand curve is thus a tool that helps us explain economic behaviour and predict reactions to possible price changes.

Marshall's definition of a social "law" captures the idea:

> The term "law" means nothing more than a general proposition or statement of tendencies, more or less certain, more or less definite . . . a social law is a statement of social tendencies; that is, that a certain course of action may be expected from the members of a social group under certain conditions.[3]

It seems reasonable to expect that consumers will demand more of a product at a lower price and less of it at a higher price. Households must divide their incomes over a wide range of goods and services. If the price of a kilogram of beef rises while income and the prices of all other products remain the same, the household must sacrifice more of something else in order to buy each kilogram of beef. If I spend $9 for a kilogram of prime beef, I am sacrificing the other things that I might have bought with that $9. If the price of prime beef were to jump to $11 per kilogram, while chicken breasts remained at $5.99 (remember ceteris paribus—we are holding all else constant), I would have to give up more chicken and/or other items in order to buy that kilogram of beef. So I would probably eat more chicken and less beef. Anna calls her boyfriend three times when phone calls cost $7 each. A fourth call

demand schedule *A table showing how much of a given product a household would be willing to buy at different prices.*

demand curve *A graph illustrating how much of a given product a household would be buy*

Table 4.1

Anna's Demand Schedule for Telephone Calls

Price (per call)	Quantity Demanded (calls per month)
$ 0	30
0.50	25
3.50	7
7.00	3
10.00	1
15.00	0

law of demand *The negative relationship between price and quantity demanded. As price rises, quantity demanded decreases. As price falls, quantity demanded increases.*

---

[2]*Drawing a smooth curve, as we do in Figure 4.2, suggests that Anna can make a quarter of a phone call or half of a phone call. For example, according to the graph, at a price of $12 per call, Anna would make half a call and at $8 per call, about a call and a half. While fractional purchases are for goods that are divisible, such as phone calls—you might talk for one minute instead of two minutes— and products sold by weight, they are impossible for large purchases, such as automobiles. We use the term* lumpy *to describe goods that cannot be divided. You would not draw a smooth, downward sloping curve of a household's demand for automobiles, for example, because there might be only one (or at most two) points, and any points in between would be meaningless. Whenever we draw a smooth demand curve, we are assuming divisibility.*

[3]*Alfred Marshall,* Principles of Economics, *8th ed. (New York: Macmillan, 1948), p. 33. (The first edition was published in 1890.)*

FIGURE 4.2

Anna's Demand Curve

The relationship between price and quantity demanded presented graphically is called a *demand curve*. Demand curves have a negative slope, indicating that lower prices cause quantity demanded to increase. Note that Anna's demand curve is blue; demand in product markets is determined by household choice.

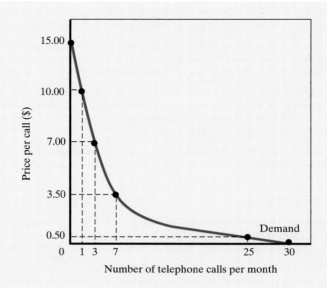

Number of telephone calls per month

would mean sacrificing $7 worth of other purchases. At a price of $3.50, however, the opportunity cost of each call is lower, and she calls more frequently.

Another explanation behind the fact that demand curves are very likely to slope downward rests on the notion of *utility*. Economists use utility as a measure of happiness or satisfaction. Presumably we consume goods and services because they give us utility. But as we consume more of a product within a given period of time, it is likely that each additional unit consumed will yield successively less satisfaction. The utility I gain from a second ice cream cone is likely to be less than the utility I gained from the first; the third is worth even less, and so forth. This law of diminishing marginal utility is an important concept in economics. If each successive unit of a good is worth less to me, I am not going to be willing to pay as much for it. It is thus reasonable to expect a downward slope in the demand curve for that good.

The idea of diminishing marginal utility also helps to explain Anna's behaviour. The demand curve is a way of representing what she is willing to pay per phone call. At a price of $7, she calls her boyfriend three times per month. A fourth call, however, is worth less than the third—that is, the fourth call is worth less than $7 to her, so she stops at three. If the price were only $3.50, however, she would keep right on calling. But even at $3.50, she would stop at seven calls per month. This behaviour reveals that the eighth call has less value to Anna than the seventh.

Thinking about the ways that people are affected by price changes also helps us see what is behind the law of demand. Consider this example: Craig lives and works in British Columbia. His elderly mother lives in Newfoundland. Last year, the airlines got into a price war, and the price of flying between Vancouver and St. John's dropped from $1500 to $750. How might Craig's behaviour change?

First, he is better off. Last year he flew home to Newfoundland three times at a total cost of $4500. This year he can fly to Newfoundland the same number of times, buy exactly the same combination of other goods and services that he bought last year, and have $2250 left over! Because he is better off—his income can buy more—he may fly home more frequently. Second, the opportunity cost of flying home has changed. Before the price war Craig had to sacrifice $1500 worth of other goods and services each time he flew to St. John's. After the price war he must sacrifice only $750 worth of other goods and services for each trip. The trade-off has changed. Both of these effects are likely to lead to a higher quantity demanded in response to the lower price.[4]

---

[4]*These separate effects are called the "income" and "substitution" effects of the price change. They will be formally defined and discussed in later chapters.*

In sum:

> It is reasonable to expect quantity demanded to fall when price rises, *ceteris paribus*, and to expect quantity demanded to rise when price falls, *ceteris paribus*. Demand curves have a negative slope.

■ **Other Properties of Demand Curves**   Two additional things are notable about Anna's demand curve. First, it intersects the *Y*, or price, axis. This means that there is a price above which no calls will be made. In this case, Anna simply stops calling when the price reaches $15 per call.

> As long as households have limited incomes and wealth, all demand curves will intersect the price axis. For any commodity, there is always a price above which a household will not, or cannot, pay. Even if the good or service is very important, all households are ultimately "constrained," or limited, by income and wealth.

Second, Anna's demand curve intersects the *X*, or quantity, axis. Even at a zero price, there is a limit to the number of phone calls Anna will make. If telephone calls were free, she would call 30 times a month, but not more.

> That demand curves intersect the quantity axis is a matter of common sense. Demands for most goods are limited, if only by time, even at a zero price.

OTHER DETERMINANTS OF HOUSEHOLD DEMAND

Of the many factors likely to influence a household's demand for a specific product, we have considered only the price of the product itself. Other determining factors include household income and wealth, the prices of other goods and services, tastes and preferences, and expectations.

■ **Income and Wealth**   Before we proceed, we need to define two terms that are often confused, *income* and *wealth*. A household's **income** is the sum of all the wages, salaries, profits, interest payments, rents, and other forms of earnings received by the household *in a given period of time*. Income is thus a *flow* measure: we must specify a time period for it—income *per month* or *per year*. You can spend or consume more or less than your income in any given period. If you consume less than the amount of your income, you save. To consume more than your income in a period, you must either borrow or draw on savings accumulated from previous periods.

Wealth is the total value of what a household owns less what it owes. Another word for wealth is **net worth**—the amount a household would have left if it sold off all its possessions and paid off all its debts. Wealth is a *stock* measure: it is measured at a given moment, or point, in time. If, in a given period, you spend less than your income, you save; the amount that you save is added to your wealth. Saving is the flow that affects the stock of wealth. When you spend more than your income, you *dissave*—you reduce your wealth.

Clearly, households with higher incomes and higher accumulated savings or inherited wealth can afford to buy more things. In general, then, we would expect higher demand at higher levels of income/wealth and lower demand at lower levels of income/wealth. Goods for which demand goes up when income is higher and for which demand goes down when income is lower are called **normal goods.** Movie tickets, restaurant meals, telephone calls, and shirts are all normal goods.

But generalization in economics can be hazardous. Sometimes demand for a good falls when household income rises. Consider, for example, the various qualities of meat available. When a household's income rises, it is likely to buy higher-quality meats—its demand for filet mignon is likely to rise—but its demand for lower-quality meats—chuck steak, for example—is likely to fall. Transportation is another example. At higher incomes, people can afford to fly. People who can af-

FAST FACTS

Statistics Canada estimates the total net worth of Canadians to be over $3 trillion or $100 000 per capita.

income *The sum of all a household's wages, salaries, profits, interest payments, rents, and other forms of earnings in a given period of time. It is a flow measure.*

wealth or **net worth** *The total value of what a household owns minus what it owes. It is a stock measure.*

normal goods *Goods for which demand goes up when income is higher and for which demand goes down when income is lower.*

ford to fly are less likely to take the bus long distances. Thus higher income may reduce the number of times someone takes a bus. Goods for which demand falls when income rises are called **inferior goods.**

■ **Prices of Other Goods and Services**   No consumer decides in isolation on the amount of any one commodity to buy. Rather, every decision is part of a larger set of decisions that are made simultaneously. Obviously, households must apportion their incomes over many different goods and services. As a result, the price of any one good can and does affect the demand for other goods.

This is most obviously the case when goods are substitutes for each other. To return to our lonesome first-year student: if the price of a telephone call rises to $10, Anna will call her boyfriend only once a month (see Table 4.1). But of course she can get in touch with him in other ways. Presumably she substitutes some other, less costly, form of communication, such as writing more letters or sending e-mail messages.

Consider another example. There is currently much discussion about the relative merits of cars produced in North America and cars produced in Japan. Recently, North American consumers have faced a sharp rise in the price of Japanese cars. As a result, we would expect to see consumers substitute North American–made cars for Japanese-made cars. The demand for North American cars should rise and the quantity of Japanese cars demanded should fall.

When an *increase* in the price of one good causes demand for another good to *increase* (a positive relationship), we say that the goods are **substitutes.** A *fall* in the price of a good causes a *decline* in demand for its substitutes. Substitutes are goods that can serve as replacements for one another.

To be substitutes, two products need not be identical. Identical products are called **perfect substitutes.** Japanese cars are not identical to Canadian cars. Nonetheless, all have four wheels, are capable of carrying people, and run on gasoline. Thus, significant changes in the price of one country's cars can be expected to influence demand for the other country's cars. Compact discs are substitutes for records and tapes, restaurant meals are substitutes for meals eaten at home, and flying from Toronto to Montreal is a substitute for taking the train.

Often, two products "go together"—that is, they complement each other. Our lonesome letter writer, for example, will find her demand for stamps and stationery rising as she writes more letters. Bacon and eggs are **complementary goods,** as are cars and gasoline, and cameras and film. During a price war between the airlines in the summer of 1994 when travel became less expensive, the demand for taxi service to and from airports and for luggage increased. When two goods are complements, a *decrease* in the price of one results in *increase* in demand for the other, and vice versa.

Because any one good may have many potential substitutes and complements at the same time, a single price change may affect a household's demands for many goods simultaneously; the demand for some of these products may rise while the demand for others may fall. For example, with the advent of the CD-ROM technology for personal computers, massive amounts of data could be stored digitally, and can be read by computers with a CD drive. When these drives first came on the market they were quite expensive, selling for several hundreds of dollars each. Now they are much less expensive, and most new computers have them built in. As a result, the demand for the CD-ROM discs (complementary goods) has soared. As more and more people adopt the technology and the price of CDs and CD hardware falls, fewer people are buying encyclopedias printed on paper (substitute goods), because many computer manufacturers now include a CD-ROM encyclopedia when you purchase one of their machines.

■ **Tastes and Preferences**   Income, wealth, and the prices of things available are the three factors that determine the combinations of things that a household is *able* to buy. You know that you cannot afford to rent an apartment at $1200 per month if your monthly income is only $400. But within these constraints, you are more or less free to choose what to buy. Your final choice depends on your individual tastes and preferences.

Changes in preferences can and do manifest themselves in market behaviour. As the medical consequences of smoking have become more and more clear, for example, more and more people have stopped smoking. As a result, the demand for cigarettes has dropped significantly. Fifteen years ago the major big-city marathons drew only a few hundred runners. Now tens of thousands enter and run. The demand for running shoes, running suits, stopwatches, and other running items has greatly increased.

Within the constraints of prices and incomes, it is preference that shapes the demand curve. But it is difficult to generalize about tastes and preferences. First of all, they are volatile. Five years ago, more people smoked cigarettes and fewer people had VCRs. Second, they are idiosyncratic. Some people like to talk on the telephone, while others prefer the written word; some people prefer dogs, while others are crazy about cats; some people like chicken wings, while others prefer legs. The diversity of individual demands is almost infinite.

■ **Expectations**   What you decide to buy today certainly depends on today's prices and your current income and wealth. But you also have expectations about what your position will be in the future. You may have expectations about future changes in prices, too, and these may affect your decisions today.

Examples of the ways expectations affect demand abound. When people buy a house or a car, they often must borrow part of the purchase price and pay it back over a number of years. In deciding what kind of house or car to buy, they presumably must think about their income today, as well as what their income is likely to be in the future.

As another example, consider a student in her final year of medical school living on a scholarship and summer earnings totalling $14 000. Compare her with another person earning $7 an hour at a full-time job, with no expectation of a significant change in income in the future. The two have virtually identical incomes. But even if they had the same tastes, the medical student is likely to demand different things, simply because she expects a major increase in income later on.

Increasingly, economic theory has come to recognize the importance of expectations. We will devote a good deal of time to discussing how expectations affect more than just demand. For the time being, however, it is important to understand that demand depends on more than just *current* incomes, prices, and tastes.

SHIFT OF DEMAND VERSUS MOVEMENT ALONG A DEMAND CURVE

Recall that a demand curve shows the relationship between quantity demanded and the price of a good. Such demand curves are derived while holding income, tastes, and other prices constant. If this condition of *ceteris paribus* were relaxed, we would have to derive an entirely new relationship between price and quantity.

Let us return once again to Anna (Table 4.1 and Figure 4.2). Suppose that when we derived the demand schedule in Table 4.1, Anna had a part-time job that paid $200 per month. Now suppose that her parents inherit some money and begin sending her an additional $200 per month. Assuming that she keeps her job, Anna's income is now $400 per month.[5]

With her higher income, Anna would probably call her boyfriend more frequently, regardless of the price of a call. Table 4.2 and Figure 4.3 present Anna's original-income schedule (D_1) and increased-income demand schedule (D_2). At $0.50 per call, the frequency of her calls (or the quantity she demands) increases from 25 to 33 calls per month; at $3.50 per call, frequency increases from seven to 18 calls per month; at $10 per call, frequency increases from one to seven calls per month. (Note in Figure 4.3 that even if calls are free, Anna's income matters;

---

[5]*The income from home may affect the amount of time Anna spends working. In the extreme, she may quit her job and her income will remain at $200. In essence, she would be spending the entire $200 on leisure. Here we assume that she keeps the job and that her income is higher. The point is that since labour-supply decisions affect income, they are closely tied to output-demand decisions. In a sense, the two decisions are made simultaneously.*

| Table 4.2 | Shift of Anna's Demand Schedule Due to Increase in Income | |

Price (per call)	SCHEDULE D_1 Quantity Demanded (calls per month at an income of $200 per month)	SCHEDULE D_2 Quantity Demanded (calls per month at an income of $400 per month)
$ 0	30	35
0.50	25	33
3.50	7	18
7.00	3	12
10.00	1	7
15.00	0	2
20.00	0	0

at zero price, her demand increases. With a higher income, she may visit her boyfriend more, for example, and more visits might mean more phone calls to organize and plan.)

The conditions that were in place at the time the original demand curve was derived have now changed. In other words, a factor that affects Anna's demand for telephone calls (in this case, her income) has changed, and there is now a new relationship between price and quantity demanded. Such a change is referred to as a **shift of the demand curve.**

It is very important to distinguish between a change in quantity demanded—that is, some movement *along* a demand curve—and a shift of demand. Demand schedules and demand curves show the relationship between the price of a good or service and the quantity demanded per period, *ceteris paribus*. If price changes, quantity demanded will change—this is a **movement along the demand curve.** When any of the other factors that influence demand change, however, a new relationship between price and quantity demanded is established—this is a *shift of the demand curve*. The result, then, is a *new* demand curve. Changes in income, preferences, or prices of other goods cause the demand curve to shift:

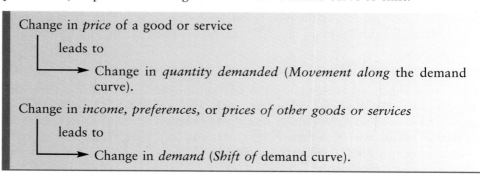

Change in *price* of a good or service

    leads to

        → Change in *quantity demanded* (*Movement along* the demand curve).

Change in *income, preferences,* or *prices of other goods or services*

    leads to

        → Change in *demand* (*Shift of* demand curve).

Figure 4.4 illustrates this point. In Figure 4.4a, an increase in household income causes demand for hamburger (an inferior good) to decline, or shift to the left from D_1 to D_2. (Because quantity is measured on the horizontal axis, a decrease means a move to the left.) Demand for steak (a normal good), on the other hand, increases, or shifts to the right, when income rises.

In Figure 4.4b, an increase in the price of hamburger from $4.49 to $6.50 a kilogram causes a household to buy less hamburger each month. In other words, the higher price causes the *quantity demanded* to decline from five kilograms to three kilograms per month. This change represents a movement *along* the demand curve for hamburger. In place of hamburger, the household buys more chicken. The household's demand for chicken (a substitute for hamburger) rises—the demand curve shifts to the right. At the same time, the demand for ketchup (a good that complements hamburger) declines—its demand curve shifts to the left.

shift of a demand curve *The change that takes place in a demand curve when a new relationship between quantity demanded of a good and the price of that good is brought about by a change in the original conditions.*

movement along a demand curve *What happens when a change in price causes quantity demanded to change.*

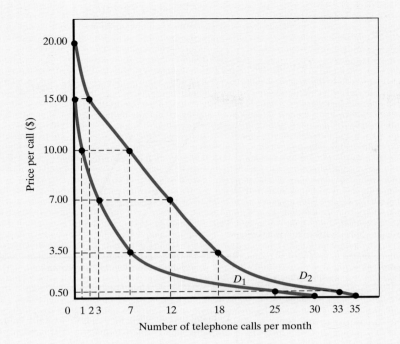

FIGURE 4.3

Shift of a Demand Curve Following a Rise in Income

When the price of a good changes, we move *along* the demand curve for that good. When any other factor that influences demand changes (income, tastes, etc.), the relationship between price and quantity is different; there is a *shift* of the demand curve, in this case from D_1 to D_2.

FROM HOUSEHOLD DEMAND TO MARKET DEMAND

Market demand is simply the sum of all the quantities of a good or service demanded per period by all the households buying in the market for that good or service. Figure 4.5 shows the derivation of a market demand curve from three individual demand curves. (Although this market demand curve is derived from the behaviour of only three people, most markets have thousands or even millions of demanders.) As the table in Figure 4.5 shows, when the price of a kilogram of coffee is $8.50, both A and C would purchase two kilograms per month, while B would buy none; at that price, presumably, B drinks tea. Market demand at $8.50 would thus be a total of two plus two, or four kilograms. At a price of $5.50 per kilogram, however, A would purchase three kilograms per month, B one kilogram, and C four kilograms. Thus, at $5.50 per kilogram, market demand would be three plus one plus four, or eight kilograms of coffee per month.

The total quantity demanded in the marketplace at a given price, then, is simply the sum of all the quantities demanded by all the individual households shopping in the market *at that price*. A market demand curve shows the total amount of a product that would be sold at each price if households could buy all they wanted at that price. As Figure 4.5 shows, the market demand curve is the sum of all the individual demand curves—that is, the sum of all the individual quantities demanded at each price. The market demand curve thus takes its shape and position from the shapes, positions, and number of individual demand curves. If more people decide to shop in a market, more demand curves must be added, and the market demand curve will shift to the right. Market demand curves may also shift as a result of preference changes, income changes, or changes in the number of demanders.

As a general rule throughout this book, capital letters refer to the entire market and lowercase letters refer to individual households or firms. Thus, in Figure 4.5, Q refers to total quantity demanded in the market, while q refers to the quantity demanded by individual households.

market demand *The sum of all the quantities of a good or service demanded per period by all the households buying in the market for that good or service.*

Supply in Product/Output Markets

In addition to dealing with households' demands for outputs, economic theory also deals with the behaviour of business firms, which supply in output markets and

FIGURE 4.4

Shifts Versus Movement Along a Demand Curve

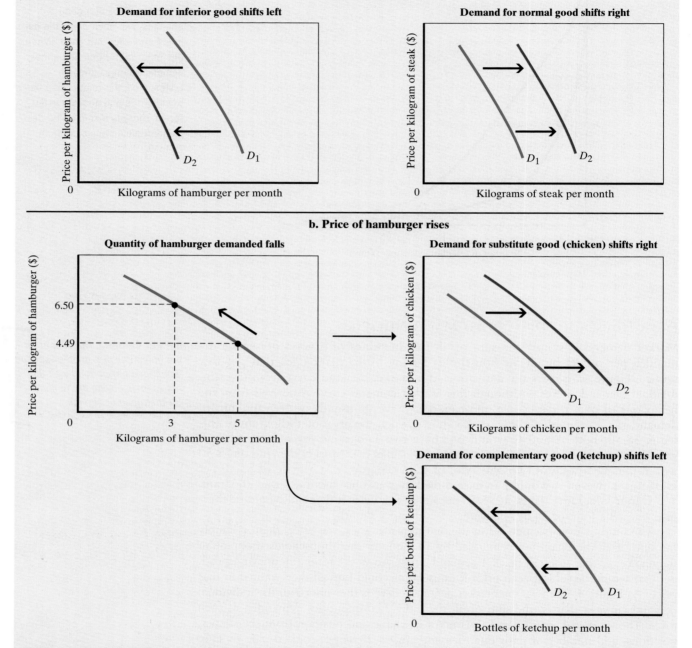

a. Income rises

Demand for inferior good shifts left

Price per kilogram of hamburger ($)

D_2 D_1

0 Kilograms of hamburger per month

Demand for normal good shifts right

Price per kilogram of steak ($)

D_1 D_2

0 Kilograms of steak per month

b. Price of hamburger rises

Quantity of hamburger demanded falls

Price per kilogram of hamburger ($)

6.50

4.49

0 3 5

Kilograms of hamburger per month

Demand for substitute good (chicken) shifts right

Price per kilogram of chicken ($)

D_2

D_1

0 Kilograms of chicken per month

Demand for complementary good (ketchup) shifts left

Price per bottle of ketchup ($)

D_2 D_1

0 Bottles of ketchup per month

a. When income increases, the demand for inferior goods *shifts to the left* and the demand for normal goods *shifts to the right.*
b. If the price of hamburger rises, the quantity of hamburger demanded declines—this is a movement along the demand curve. The same price would shift the demand for chicken (a substitute for hamburger) to the right and the demand for ketchup (a complement to hamburger) to the left.

FIGURE 4.5

Deriving Market Demand from Individual Household Demand Curves

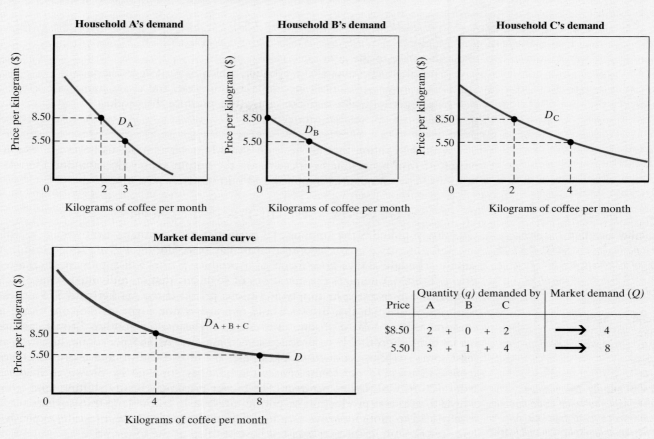

Price	Quantity (q) demanded by			Market demand (Q)
	A	B	C	
$8.50	2 +	0 +	2	→ 4
5.50	3 +	1 +	4	→ 8

Total demand in the marketplace is simply the sum of the demands of all the households shopping in a particular market. It is the sum of all the individual demand curves—that is, the sum of all the individual quantities demanded at each price.

demand in input markets (see again Figure 4.1). Firms engage in production, and we assume that they do so for profit. Successful firms make profits because they are able to sell their products for more than it costs to produce them.

Supply decisions can thus be expected to depend on profit potential. Because **profit** is the simple difference between revenues and costs, supply is likely to react to changes in revenues and changes in production costs. The amount of revenue that a firm earns depends on the price of its product in the market and on how much it sells. Costs of production depend on many factors, the most important of which are (1) the kinds of inputs needed to produce the product, (2) the amount of each input required, and (3) the prices of inputs.

The supply decision is just one of several decisions that firms make in order to maximize profit. There are usually a number of ways to produce any given product. A golf course can be built by hundreds of workers with shovels and grass seed or by a few workers with heavy earth-moving equipment and sod blankets. Hamburgers can be individually fried by a short-order cook or grilled by the hundreds on a mechanized moving grill. Firms must choose the production technique most appropriate to their products and projected levels of production. The best method of production is the one that minimizes cost, thus maximizing profit.

Which production technique is best, in turn, depends on the prices of inputs. Where labour is cheap and machinery is expensive and difficult to transport, firms are likely to choose production techniques that use a great deal of labour. Where machines are available and labour is scarce or expensive, they are likely to choose more capital-intensive methods. Obviously, the technique ultimately chosen deter-

profit *The difference between revenues and costs.*

mines input requirements. Thus, by choosing an output supply target and the most appropriate technology, firms determine which inputs to demand.

To summarize:

> Assuming that its objective is to maximize profits, a firm's decision about what quantity of output, or product, to supply depends on
> 1. The price of the good or service
> 2. The cost of producing the product, which in turn depends on
>   ■ The price of required inputs (labour, capital, and land), and
>   ■ The technologies that can be used to produce the product
> 3. The prices of related products

With the caution that no decision exists in a vacuum, let us begin our examination of firm behaviour by focusing on the output supply decision and the relationship between quantity supplied and output price, *ceteris paribus*.

PRICE AND QUANTITY SUPPLIED: THE LAW OF SUPPLY

Quantity supplied is the amount of a particular product that a firm would be willing and able to offer for sale at a particular price during a given time period. A **supply schedule** shows how much of a product a firm will supply at alternative prices. Table 4.3 itemizes the quantities of soybeans that an individual farmer such as Clarence Brown might supply at various prices. If the market paid $75 or less for a tonne of soybeans, Brown would not supply any soybeans. For one thing, it costs more than $75 to produce a tonne of soybeans; for another, Brown can use his land more profitably to produce something else. At $85 per tonne, however, at least some soybean production takes place on Brown's farm, and a price increase from $85 to $115 per tonne causes the quantity supplied by Brown to increase from 400 to 600 tonnes per year. The higher price may justify shifting land from wheat to soybean production or putting previously fallow land into soybeans. Or it may lead to more intensive farming of land already in soybeans, using expensive fertilizer or equipment that was not cost-justified at the lower price.

Generalizing from Farmer Brown's experience, we can reasonably expect an increase in market price to lead to an increase in quantity supplied. In other words, there is a positive relationship between the quantity of a good supplied and price. This statement sums up the **law of supply.**

The information in a supply schedule presented graphically is called a **supply curve.** Supply curves slope upward. The upward, or positive, slope of Brown's curve in Figure 4.6, for example, reflects this positive relationship between price and quantity supplied.

Note in Brown's supply schedule, however, that when price rises above $200 to $250, quantity supplied no longer increases. Often an individual firm's ability to respond to an increase in price is constrained by its existing scale of operations, or capacity, in the short run. For example, Brown's ability to produce more soybeans depends on the size of his farm, the fertility of his soil, and the types of equipment he has. The fact that output stays constant at 1200 tonnes per year suggests that he is running up against the limits imposed by the size of his farm and his existing technology.

In the longer run, however, Brown may acquire more land, or technology may change, allowing for more soybean production. The terms *short run* and *long run* have very precise meanings in economics; we will discuss them in detail later. Here it is important only to understand that time plays a critical role in supply decisions. When prices change, firms' immediate response may be different from what they are able to do after a month or a year. Short-run and long-run supply curves are often different.

OTHER DETERMINANTS OF FIRM SUPPLY

Of the factors listed above that are likely to affect the quantity of output supplied by a given firm, we have thus far discussed only the price of output. Other factors

---

quantity supplied *The amount of a particular product that a firm would be willing and able to offer for sale at a particular price during a given time period.*

supply schedule *A table showing how much of a product firms will supply at different prices.*

law of supply *The positive relationship between price and quantity of a good supplied. An increase in market price will lead to an increase in quantity supplied, and a decrease in market price will lead to a decrease in quantity supplied.*

supply curve *A graph illustrating how much of a product a firm will supply at different prices.*

Table 4.3

Clarence Brown's Supply Schedule for Soybeans

Price (per tonne)	Quantity Supplied (tonnes per year)
$ 75	0
85	400
115	600
150	800
200	1200
250	1200

that affect supply include the cost of producing the product and the prices of related products.

■ **The Cost of Production** Regardless of the price that a firm can command for its product, price must exceed the cost of producing the output for the firm to make a profit. Thus, the supply decision is likely to change in response to changes in the cost of production. Cost of production depends on a number of factors, including the available technologies and the price of the inputs (labour, land, capital, energy, and so forth) that the firm needs.

Technological change can have an enormous impact on the cost of production over time. Consider agriculture. The introduction of fertilizers, the development of complex farm machinery, and the use of bioengineering to increase the yield of individual crops all have powerfully affected the cost of producing agricultural commodities. Farm productivity in Canada has increased dramatically over the years. In 1925 wheat yields in Saskatchewan averaged 1265 kilograms per hectare, and in 1996 they averaged 2270 kilograms per hectare. Over the same period, barley yields in Alberta went from 1400 kilograms per hectare to 3340 kilograms per hectare.

When a technological advance lowers the cost of production, output is likely to increase. When yield per hectare increases, individual farmers can and do produce more. The output of the Ford Motor Company increased substantially after the introduction of assembly-line techniques. The production of electronic calculators, and later personal computers, boomed with the development of inexpensive techniques to produce microprocessors.

Cost of production is also affected directly by the price of the factors of production. When the price of oil rose so dramatically beginning in 1973, this affected the costs of production in many sectors of the economy. As a result, cab drivers faced higher gasoline prices, airlines faced higher fuel costs, and manufacturing firms faced higher heating bills. The result: cab drivers probably spent less time driving around looking for fares, airlines cut a few low-profit routes, and some manufacturing plants stopped running extra shifts. The moral of this story: increases in input prices raise costs of production and are likely to reduce supply.

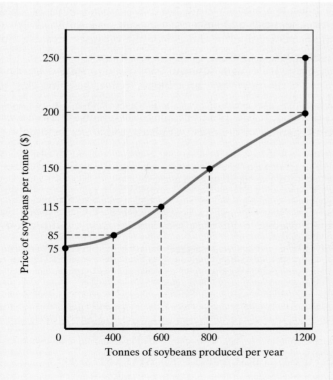

FIGURE 4.6

Clarence Brown's Individual Supply Curve

A producer will supply more when the price of output is higher. The slope of a supply curve is positive. Note that the supply curve is red. Supply is determined by choices made by firms.

■ **The Prices of Related Products**   Firms often react to changes in the prices of related products. For example, if land can be used for either corn or soybean production, an increase in soybean prices may cause individual farmers to shift land out of corn production and into soybeans. Thus, an increase in soybean prices actually affects the amount of corn supplied.

Similarly, if beef prices rise, producers may respond by raising more cattle. But leather comes from cowhide. Thus, an increase in beef prices may actually increase the supply of leather.

SHIFT OF SUPPLY VERSUS MOVEMENT ALONG A SUPPLY CURVE

A supply curve shows the relationship between the quantity of a good or service supplied by a firm and the price that good or service brings in the market. Higher prices are likely to lead to an increase in quantity supplied, *ceteris paribus*. Remember, the supply curve is derived holding everything constant except price. When the price of a product changes *ceteris paribus*, a change in the quantity supplied follows—that is, a *movement along* the supply curve takes place. But, as you have seen, supply decisions are also influenced by factors other than price. New relationships between price and quantity supplied come about when factors other than price change, and the result is a *shift* of the supply curve. When factors other than price cause supply curves to shift, we say that there has been a *change in supply.*

Recall that the cost of production depends upon the price of inputs and the technologies of production available. Now suppose that a major breakthrough in the production of soybeans has occurred; genetic engineering has produced a superstrain of disease- and pest-resistant seed. Such a technological change would enable individual farmers to supply more soybeans at *any* market price. Table 4.4 and Figure 4.7 describe this change. At $150 a tonne, farmers would have produced 800 tonnes from the old seed (schedule S_1 in Table 4.4); with the lower cost of production and higher yield resulting from the new seed, they produce 1100 tonnes (schedule S_2 in Table 4.4). At $85 per tonne, they would have produced 400 tonnes from the old seed; but with the lower costs and higher yields, output rises to 625 tonnes.

Increases in input prices may also cause supply curves to shift. What impact would an increase in the price of oil have on farmers? Since fertilizers are made in part from petrochemicals and since tractors run on gasoline, Farmer Brown would have faced higher costs than he did before the oil price increase. Such increases in production cost shift the supply curve to the left—that is, less is produced at any given market price. If Brown's soybean supply curve shifted far enough to the left, it would intersect the price axis at a higher point, meaning that it would take a higher market price to induce Brown to produce any soybeans at all.

As with demand, it is very important to distinguish between *movements along* supply curves (changes in quantity supplied) and *shifts in* supply curves (changes in supply):

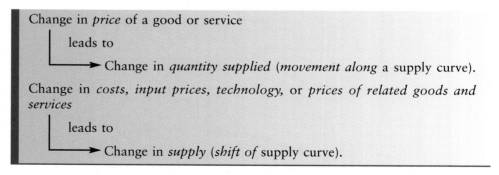

Change in *price* of a good or service

    leads to

        → Change in *quantity supplied* (*movement along* a supply curve).

Change in *costs, input prices, technology,* or *prices of related goods and services*

    leads to

        → Change in *supply* (*shift of* supply curve).

market supply *The sum of all that is supplied each period by all producers of a single product.*

FROM INDIVIDUAL FIRM SUPPLY TO MARKET SUPPLY

Market supply is determined in the same fashion as market demand. It is simply the sum of all that is supplied each period by all producers of a single product. Figure 4.8 derives a market supply curve from the supply curves of three individual firms. (In a market with more firms, total market supply would be the sum of the amounts produced by each of the firms in that market.) As the table in Figure 4.8 shows, at a price of $150 farm A supplies 3000 tonnes of soybeans, farm B supplies 1000 tonnes, and farm C supplies 2500 tonnes. At this price, the total amount supplied in the market is 3000 plus 1000 plus 2500, or 6500 tonnes. At a price of $85, however, the total amount supplied is only 2500 tonnes (1000 plus 500 plus 1000). The market supply curve is thus the simple addition of the individual supply curves of all the firms in a particular market—that is, the sum of all the individual quantities supplied at each price.

The position and shape of the market supply curve depends on the positions and shapes of the individual firms' supply curves from which it is derived. But it also depends on the number of firms that produce in that market. If firms that produce for a particular market are earning high profits, other firms may be tempted to go into that business. When the technology to produce computers for home use became available, literally hundreds of new firms got into the act. The popularity and profitability of the Internet has led to the formation of new service providers. When new firms enter an industry, the supply curve shifts to the right. When firms go out of business, or "exit" the market, the supply curve shifts to the left.

Market Equilibrium

So far we have identified a number of factors that influence the amount that households demand and firms supply in product (output) markets. The discussion has emphasized the role of market price as a determinant both of quantity demanded and quantity supplied. We are now ready to see how supply and demand in the market interact to determine the final market price.

We have been very careful in our discussions thus far to separate household decisions about how much to demand from firm decisions about how much to supply. The operation of the market, however, clearly depends on the interaction between suppliers and demanders. At any moment, one of three conditions prevails in every market: (1) the quantity demanded exceeds the quantity supplied at the current price, a situation called *excess demand*; (2) the quantity supplied exceeds the quantity demanded at the current price, a situation called *excess supply*; or (3) the quantity supplied equals the quantity demanded at the current price, a situation called **equilibrium.** At equilibrium, no tendency for price to change exists.

EXCESS DEMAND

Excess demand exists when quantity demanded is greater than quantity supplied at the current price. Figure 4.9, which plots both a supply curve and a demand curve on the same graph, illustrates such a situation. As you can see, market demand at $85 per tonne (5000 tonnes) exceeds the amount that farmers are currently supplying (2500 tonnes).

When excess demand occurs in an unregulated market, there is a tendency for price to rise as demanders compete against each other for the limited supply. The adjustment mechanisms may differ, but the outcome is always the same. For ex-

equilibrium *The condition that exists when quantity supplied and quantity demanded are equal. At equilibrium, there is no tendency for price to change.*

excess demand *The condition that exists when quantity demanded exceeds quantity supplied at the current price.*

Table 4.4	Shift of Supply Schedule for Soybeans Following Development of a New Disease-Resistant Seed Strain	
	SCHEDULE S_1	SCHEDULE S_2
Price (per tonne)	Quantity Supplied (tonnes per year using old seed)	Quantity Supplied (tonnes per year using new seed)
$ 75	0	150
85	400	625
115	600	900
150	800	1100
200	1200	1500
250	1200	1500

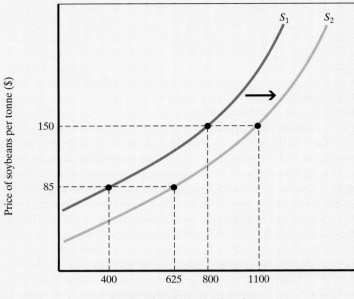

FIGURE 4.7

Shift of Supply Curve for Soybeans Following Development of a New Seed Strain

When the price of a product changes, we move *along* the supply curve for that product; the quantity supplied rises or falls. When any other factor affecting supply changes, the supply curve *shifts*.

ample, consider the mechanism of an auction. In an auction, items are sold directly to the highest bidder. When the auctioneer starts the bidding at a low price, many people bid for the item. At first there is excess demand: quantity demanded exceeds quantity supplied. As would-be buyers offer higher and higher prices, bidders drop out, until the one who offers the most ends up with the item being auctioned. Price rises until quantity demanded and quantity supplied are equal.

At a price of $85 (see Figure 4.9 again), farmers produce soybeans at a rate of 2500 tonnes per year, but at that price the demand is for 5000 tonnes. Most farm products are sold to local dealers who in turn sell large quantities in major market centres, where bidding would push prices up if quantity demanded exceeded quantity supplied. As price rises above $85, two things happen: (1) the quantity demanded falls as buyers drop out of the market and perhaps choose a substitute, and (2) the quantity supplied increases as farmers find themselves receiving a higher price for their product and shift additional acres into soybean production.[6]

This process continues until the excess demand is eliminated. In Figure 4.9, this occurs at $125, where quantity demanded has fallen from 5000 to 3500 tonnes per year and quantity supplied has increased from 2500 to 3500 tonnes per year. When quantity demanded and quantity supplied are equal and there is no further bidding, the process has achieved an equilibrium, a situation in which *there is no natural tendency for further adjustment*. Graphically, the point of equilibrium is the point at which the supply curve and the demand curve intersect.

The process through which excess demand leads to higher prices is different in different markets. Consider the market for houses in the hypothetical town of Boomville with a population of 25 000 people, most of whom live in single-family homes. Normally about 75 homes are sold in the Boomville market each year. But last year, a major business opened a plant in town, creating 1500 new jobs that

---

[6]*Once farmers have produced in any given season, they cannot change their minds and produce more, of course. When we derived Clarence Brown's supply schedule in Table 4.3, we imagined him reacting to prices that existed at the time he decided how much land to plant in soybeans. In Figure 4.9, the upward slope shows that higher prices justify shifting land from other crops. Final price may not be determined until final production figures are in. For our purposes here, however, we have ignored this timing problem. Perhaps the best way to think about it is that demand and supply are* flows, *or rates, of production—that is, we are talking about the number of tonnes produced* per production period. *Adjustments in the rate of production may take place over a number of production periods.*

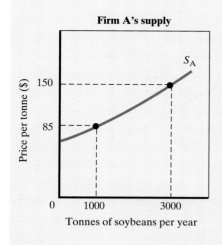

Firm A's supply

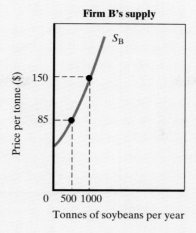

Firm B's supply

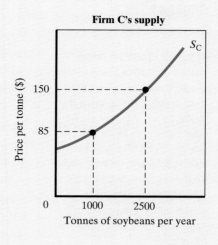

Firm C's supply

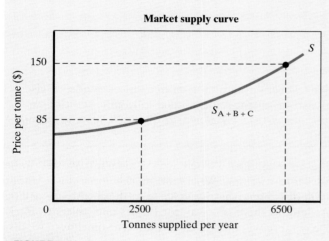

Market supply curve

Price	Quantity (q) supplied by			Market supply (Q)
	A	B	C	
$150	3000 +	1000 +	2500	⟶ 6500
$85	1000 +	500 +	1000	⟶ 2500

FIGURE 4.8

Deriving Market Supply from Individual Firm Supply Curves

Total supply in the marketplace is the sum of all the amounts supplied by all the firms selling in the market; it is the sum of all the individual quantities supplied at each price.

pay good wages. This attracted new residents to the area, and real estate agents now have more buyers than there are properties for sale. Quantity demanded now exceeds quantity supplied. In other words, there is excess demand.

Auctions are not unheard of in the housing market, but they are rare. This market usually works more subtly, but the outcome is the same. Properties are sold very quickly and housing prices begin to rise. Boomville sellers soon learn that there are more buyers than usual, and they begin to "hold out" for higher offers. As prices for houses in Boomville rise, quantity demanded eventually drops off and quantity supplied increases. Quantity supplied increases in at least two ways: (1) encouraged by the high prices, builders begin constructing new houses and (2) some people, attracted by the higher prices their homes will fetch, put their houses on the market. Discouraged by higher prices, however, some potential buyers (demanders) may begin to look for housing in neighbouring towns and settle on commuting. Eventually, equilibrium will be reestablished, with the quantity of houses demanded just equal to the quantity of houses supplied.

While the mechanics of price adjustment in the housing market differ from the mechanics of an auction, the outcome is exactly the same:

FIGURE 4.9

Excess Demand

At a price of $85 per tonne, quantity demanded exceeds quantity supplied. When *excess demand* arises, there is a tendency for price to rise. As price rises from $85 to $125, quantity demanded falls from 5000 to 3500 and quantity supplied rises from 2500 to 3500. When quantity demanded equals quantity supplied, excess demand is eliminated and the market is in equilibrium. Here, the equilibrium price is $125, and the equilibrium quantity is 3500 tonnes.

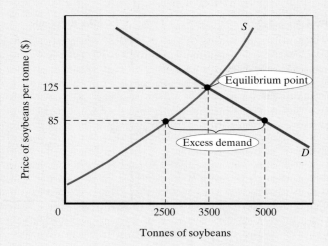

> When quantity demanded exceeds quantity supplied, price tends to rise. When the price in a market rises, quantity demanded falls and quantity supplied rises until an equilibrium is reached at which quantity demanded and quantity supplied are equal.

This process is called *price rationing*. When excess demand exists, some people will be satisfied and some will not. When the market operates without interference, price increases will distribute what is available to those who are willing and able to pay the most. As long as there is a way for buyers and sellers to interact, those who are willing to pay more will make that fact known somehow. (We discuss the nature of the price system as a rationing device in great detail in Chapter 5.)

Excess Supply

excess supply *The condition that exists when quantity supplied exceeds quantity demanded at the current price.*

Excess supply exists when the quantity supplied exceeds the quantity demanded at the current price. As with excess demand, the mechanics of price adjustment in the face of excess supply can differ from market to market. If automobile dealers find themselves with unsold cars in the fall when the new models are coming in, for example, you can expect to see price cuts. Sometimes dealers offer discounts to encourage buyers; sometimes buyers themselves simply offer less than the price initially asked. In any event, products do no one any good sitting in dealers' lots or on warehouse shelves. The auction metaphor introduced earlier can also be applied here. If the initial asking price is too high, no one bids, and the auctioneer tries a lower price. It's almost always true that certain items do not sell as well as anticipated during the Christmas holidays. After Christmas most stores have big sales during which they lower the prices of overstocked items. Quantities supplied exceeded quantities demanded at the current prices, so stores cut prices.

Across the province from Boomville is Bustville, where last year a drug manufacturer shut down its operations and 1500 people found themselves out of work. With no other prospects for work, many residents decided to pack up and move. They put their houses up for sale, but there were few buyers. The result was an excess supply of houses: the quantity of houses supplied exceeded the quantity demanded at the current prices.

As houses sit unsold on the market for months, sellers start to cut their asking prices. Potential buyers begin offering considerably less than sellers are asking. As prices fall, two things are likely to happen. First, the low housing prices may attract new buyers. People who might have bought in a neighbouring town see that there are housing bargains to be had in Bustville, and quantity demanded rises in response to price decline. Second, some of those who put their houses on the market may be discouraged by the lower prices and decide to stay in Bustville. Developers are certainly not likely to be building new housing in town. Lower prices thus lead to a decline in quantity supplied as potential sellers pull their houses from the market.

Figure 4.10 illustrates another excess supply situation. At a price of $150 per tonne, farmers are supplying soybeans at a rate of 4000 tonnes per year, but buyers demand only 2000. With 2000 (4000 minus 2000) tonnes of soybeans going unsold, the market price falls. As price falls from $150 to $125, quantity supplied decreases from 4000 tonnes per year to 3500. The lower price causes quantity demanded to rise from 2000 to 3500. At $125, quantity demanded and quantity supplied are equal. For the data shown here, then, $125 and 3500 tonnes are the equilibrium price and quantity.

Early in 1994, crude oil production worldwide exceeded the quantity demanded, and prices fell significantly as competing producer countries tried to maintain their share of world markets. Although the mechanism by which price is adjusted is different for automobiles, housing, soybeans, and crude oil, the outcome is the same:

> When quantity supplied exceeds quantity demanded at the current price, the price tends to fall. When price falls, quantity supplied is likely to decrease and quantity demanded is likely to increase until an equilibrium price is reached where quantity supplied and quantity demanded are equal.

CHANGES IN EQUILIBRIUM

When supply and demand curves shift, the equilibrium price and quantity change. The following example will help to illustrate this point.

South America is a major producer of coffee beans. A cold snap there can reduce the coffee harvest enough to affect the world price of coffee beans. In the summer of 1994, a major freeze hit Brazil and Colombia and drove up the price of coffee on world markets to a record $7.30 per kilogram.

Figure 4.11 illustrates how the freeze pushed up coffee prices. Initially, the market was in equilibrium at a price of $3.65. At that price, the quantity demanded was equal to quantity supplied (six billion kilograms). At a price of $3.65 and a quantity of six billion kilograms, the demand curve (labelled D) intersected the initial supply curve (labelled S_1). (Remember that equilibrium exists when quantity demanded equals quantity supplied—the point at which the supply and demand curves intersect.)

The freeze caused a decrease in the supply of coffee beans. That is, it caused the supply curve to shift to the left. In Figure 4.11, the new supply curve (the supply curve that shows the relationship between price and quantity supplied after the freeze) is labelled S_2.

At the initial equilibrium price, $3.65, there is now an excess demand for coffee. If the price were to remain at $3.65, quantity demanded would not change; it would remain at six billion kilograms. But at that price, quantity supplied would drop to three billion kilograms. At a price of $3.65, quantity demanded is greater than quantity supplied.

When excess demand exists in a market, price can be expected to rise, and rise it did. As the figure shows, price rose to a new equilibrium at $7.30. At $7.30, quantity demanded is again equal to quantity supplied, this time at 4.5 billion kilograms—the point at which the new supply curve (S_2) intersects the demand curve.

Notice that as the price of coffee rose from $3.65 to $7.30, two things happened. First, the quantity demanded declined (a movement along the demand curve) as people shifted to substitutes such as tea and hot cocoa. Second, the quantity supplied began to rise, but within the limits imposed by the damage from the

FAST FACTS

Prices can vary dramatically, as the average, minimum, and maximum prices of a barrel of crude oil for selected years reported below show.

Year	Avg. Price	Min. Price	Max. Price
1975	$ 7.67	$ 7.47	$ 7.93
1979	12.61	9.46	17.03
1981	31.80	28.25	34.70
1990	19.98	12.79	30.86
1999	15.53	8.58	22.55
2000	28.00	23.53	32.10

Source: *Louisiana State University, Centre for Energy Studies* (*maelstrom.enrg.lsu.edu*).

FIGURE 4.10

Excess Supply

At a price of $150, quantity supplied exceeds quantity demanded by 2000 tonnes. This excess supply will cause price to fall.

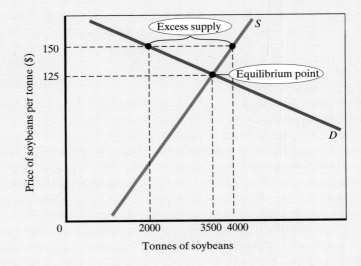

freeze. (It might also be that some countries or areas with high costs of production, previously unprofitable, came into production and shipped to the world market at the higher price.) That is, the quantity supplied increased in response to the higher price *along* the new supply curve, which lies to the left of the old supply curve. The final result was a higher price ($7.30), a smaller quantity finally exchanged in the market (4.5 billion kilograms), and coffee bought only by those willing to pay $7.30 per kilogram.

Figure 4.12 presents ten examples of shifts in either supply or demand and the resulting changes in equilibrium price and quantity. Examples of simultaneous changes in both supply and demand and their impact on equilibrium price and quantity are illustrated in Figure 4.13. Be sure to go through each graph carefully and ensure that you understand each.

FIGURE 4.11

The Coffee Market: A Shift of Supply and Subsequent Price Adjustment

Before the freeze, the coffee market was in equilibrium at a price of $3.65. At that price, quantity demanded equalled quantity supplied. The freeze shifted the supply curve to the left (from S_1 to S_2), increasing equilibrium price to $7.30.

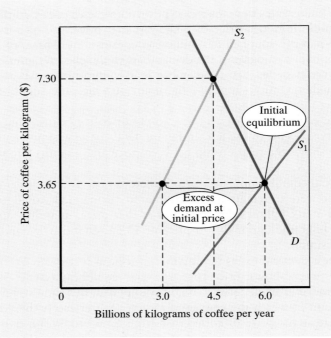

FIGURE 4.12

Examples of Supply and Demand Shifts for Product X

A. DEMAND SHIFTS

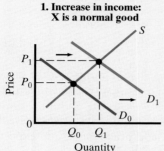

1. Increase in income:
X is a normal good

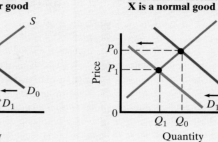

2. Increase in income:
X is an inferior good

3. Decrease in income:
X is a normal good

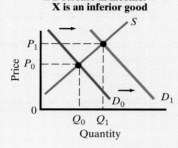

4. Decrease in income:
X is an inferior good

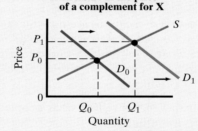

5. Increase in the price
of a substitute for X

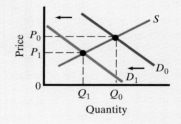

6. Increase in the price
of a complement for X

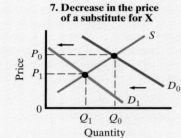

7. Decrease in the price
of a substitute for X

8. Decrease in the price
of a complement for X

B. SUPPLY SHIFTS

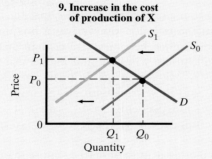

9. Increase in the cost
of production of X

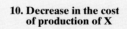

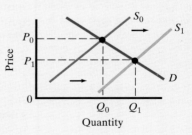

10. Decrease in the cost
of production of X

Demand and Supply in Product Markets: A Review

As you continue your study of economics, you will discover that it is a discipline full of controversy and debate. There is, however, little disagreement about the basic way that the forces of supply and demand operate in free markets. If you hear that a freeze in Florida has destroyed a good portion of the citrus crop, you can bet that the price of oranges will rise.[7] If a record wheat crop is expected, you can bet that wheat prices will fall. If fishers in British Columbia are not allowed to fish, you can bet that the price of fish will go up. (For additional examples of how the forces of supply and demand work, see the Application box titled "Supply and Demand in the News.")

Here are some important points to remember about the mechanics of supply and demand in product markets:

1. A demand curve shows how much of a product a household would buy if it could buy all it wanted at the given price. A supply curve shows how much of a product a firm would supply if it could sell all it wanted at the given price.
2. Quantity demanded and quantity supplied are always "per time period"— that is, per day, per month, or per year.
3. The demand for a good is determined by household income and wealth, the prices of other goods and services, tastes and preferences, and expectations.
4. The supply of a good is determined by costs of production and the prices of related products. Costs of production are determined by available technologies of production and input prices.
5. Be careful to distinguish between movements along supply and demand curves and shifts of these curves. When the price of a good changes, the quantity of that good demanded or supplied changes—that is, a movement occurs along the curve. When any other factor changes, the curves shift, or change position.
6. Market equilibrium exists only when quantity supplied equals quantity demanded at the current price.

Looking Ahead: Markets and the Allocation of Resources

You can already begin to see how markets answer the basic economic questions of what is produced, how it is produced, and who gets what is produced. A firm will produce what is profitable to produce. If it can sell a product at a price that is sufficient to leave a profit after production costs are paid, it will in all likelihood produce that product. Resources will flow in the direction of profit opportunities.

■ Demand curves reflect what people are willing and able to pay for products; they are influenced by incomes, wealth, preferences, the prices of other goods, and expectations. Because product prices are determined by the interaction of supply and demand, prices reflect what people are willing to pay. If people's preferences or incomes change, resources will be allocated differently. Consider, for example, an increase in demand—a shift in the market demand curve. Beginning at an equilibrium, households simply begin buying more. At the equilibrium price, quantity demanded becomes greater than quantity supplied. When there is excess demand, prices will rise, and higher prices mean higher profits for firms in the industry. Higher profits, in turn, provide existing firms with an incentive to expand and new firms with an incentive to enter the industry. Thus, the decisions of independent private firms responding to prices and profit opportunities determine *what* will be produced. No central direction is necessary.

Adam Smith saw this self-regulating feature of markets more than 200 years ago:

> Every individual . . . by pursuing his own interest . . . promotes that of society. He is led . . . by an invisible hand to promote an end which was no part of his intention.[8]

---

[7]*In economics you have to think twice, however, even about a "safe" bet. If you bet that the price of frozen orange juice will rise after a freeze, you will lose your money. It turns out that much of the crop that is damaged by a freeze can be used, but for only one thing—to make frozen orange juice. Thus, a freeze actually increases the supply of frozen juice on the market. Following the last two hard freezes in Florida, the price of oranges shot up, but the price of frozen orange juice fell sharply!*
[8]*Adam Smith*, The Wealth of Nations, *p. 456.*

FIGURE 4.13

Examples of Simultaneous Supply and Demand Shifts for Product X

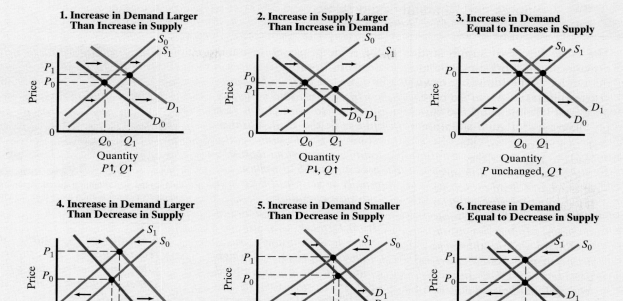

The term Smith coined, the *invisible hand*, has passed into common parlance and is still used by economists to refer to the self-regulation of markets.

■ Firms in business to make a profit have a good reason to choose the best available technology—lower costs mean higher profits. Thus, individual firms determine *how* to produce their products, again with no central direction.

■ So far we have barely touched on the question of distribution—*who* gets what is produced? But you can see part of the answer in the simple supply and demand diagrams. When a good is in short supply, price rises. As it does, those who are willing and able to continue buying do so; others stop buying.

The next chapter begins with a more detailed discussion of these topics. How, exactly, is the final allocation of resources (the mix of output and the distribution of output) determined in a market system?

The basic forces of supply and demand are at work throughout the world, as the following news articles illustrate. As an exercise, draw and label demand and supply diagrams for each situation.

1. An increase in demand leads to higher prices:

The home construction surge in much of Canada is hitting the wall as scarcity builds in one of the industry's most mundane products—gypsum wallboard. "Some shortages are occurring," Ken Meinert, president of CGC Inc., a leading Canadian supplier of wallboard, said Friday.

Production is being run at maximum capacity to meet the demand coming out of most parts of the country. But areas like Ontario, where the trade strikes stalled construction last year, are facing a tremendous pent-up demand".

...Prices have risen twice this year and are likely to increase twice more before December, builders say, raising the price to $11 a sheet from $9.

As you work through this example, note that the supply of gypsum wallboard in the short term is essentially fixed. Three reasons for this are noted in the article. First, producers are running "at maximum capacity." Second, "recent investments in the industry will not produce additional supply for at least another year." Third, "normally regional shortages of almost any product can be filled by shipping goods from another area. But the cost of transporting brittle, bulky, heavy, low-cost drywall makes this unattractive."

2. A decrease in demand leads to lower prices:

Potash Corp. of Saskatchewan Inc. said yesterday it plans to shut down five plants in the United States, some of them permanently, and eliminate more than 325 jobs to save $20 million annually in its phosphate and nitrogen operations.

...Lagging demand from farmers, who are suffering low commodity prices, higher gas prices, and tough competition, prompted Potash Corp.—one of the world's largest fertilizer makers—to adjust to weak prices and margins.

In this example, be careful to distinguish the changes in demand and supply from changes in the quantity demanded and the quantity supplied. Why, according to the article, is Potash Corp. reducing its production?

3. A small increase in demand and a large increase in supply results in lower prices:

Production is up, demand is weak and the world's largest exporter is about to sell its crop. So, watchers of the sugar market probably feel as if they are seeing reruns.

Just as it was last year, a record world sugar crop is expected; demand is barely growing; and Brazil, by far the largest exporter of sugar, is slated to sell the bulk of its harvest against the May and July contracts on New York's Coffee, Sugar, and Cocoa Exchange.

...Analysts warn of a tumble to 2.3 cents (a pound).

4. A combination of higher demand and lower supply results in higher prices:

Increased use of natural gas to replace coal in electricity generation increases demand for Alberta natural gas.

Natural gas is trading at record prices for future sales, and analysts say consumers could see an increase of as much as 40% over last year in some parts of the country.

...Much of the upward pressure on prices is coming from the U.S. market. As of the end of May, drilling activity in the United States was down 40% from last year. While drilling is beginning to improve, it is expected to take some time before production levels recover.

U.S. gas storage inventories have also fallen due to cool weather and increased demand, although revised weather forecasts yesterday sent natural gas futures lower.

More electricity generation is switching from coal to environmentally friendly natural gas, increasing demand.

Sources: [1]"Big Pent-Up Demand for Gypsum Wallboard," *National Post,* Financial Post, May 31, 1999, p. C2; [2]"Potash Corp. to Shut Five U.S. Plants, Cut 325 Jobs: Lagging Demand. Will Continue to Evaluate Conditions Before Final Decision," *National Post,* Financial Post, August 13, 1999, p. C4; [3]"Sugar Prices Sour on Record Crops—Barron's." *National Post,* Financial Post, March 6, 2000, p. C11; [4]Carol Howes, "Natural Gas Prices Expected to Rocket. Producers Refuse to Commit Supplies, Watching Prices," *National Post,* Financial Post, July 2, 1999, p. C4.

1. In societies with many people, production must satisfy wide-ranging tastes and preferences, and producers must therefore specialize.

Firms and Households: The Basic Decision-Making Units

2. A *firm* exists when a person or a group of people decides to produce a product or products by transforming resources, or *inputs*, into *outputs*—the products that are sold in the market. Firms are the primary producing units in a market economy. We assume firms make decisions to maximize profits.

3. *Households* are the primary consuming units in an economy. All households' incomes are subject to constraints.

Input Markets and Output Markets: The Circular Flow

4. Households and firms interact in two basic kinds of markets: *product or output markets* and *input or factor markets*. Goods and services intended for use by households are exchanged in output markets. In output markets, competing firms supply and competing households demand. In input markets, competing firms demand and competing households supply.

5. Ultimately, firms determine the quantities and character of outputs produced, the types and quantities of inputs demanded, and the technologies used in production. Households determine the types and quantities of products demanded and the types and quantities of inputs supplied.

Demand in Product/Output Markets

6. The quantity demanded of an individual product by an individual household depends on (1) income, (2) wealth, (3) the price of the product, (4) the prices of other products, (5) tastes and preferences, and (6) expectations about the future.

7. *Quantity demanded* is the amount of a product that an individual household would buy in a given period if it could buy all it wanted at the current price.

8. A *demand schedule* shows the quantities of a product that a household would buy at different prices. The same information presented graphically is called a *demand curve*.

9. The *law of demand* states that there is a negative relationship between price and quantity demanded. As price rises, quantity demanded decreases, and vice versa. Demand curves slope downward.

10. All demand curves eventually intersect the price axis because there is always a price above which a household cannot, or will not, pay. All demand curves also eventually intersect the quantity axis because demand for most goods is limited, if only by time, even at a zero price.

11. When an increase in income causes demand for a good to rise, that good is a *normal good*. When an increase in income causes demand for a good to fall, that good is an *inferior good*.

12. If a rise in the price of good X causes demand for good Y to increase, the goods are substitutes. If a rise in the price of X causes demand for Y to fall, the goods are complements.

13. *Market demand* is simply the sum of all the quantities of a good or service demanded per period by all the households buying in the market for that good or service. It is the sum of all the individual quantities demanded at each price.

Supply in Product/Output Markets

14. *Quantity supplied* by a firm depends on (1) the price of the good or service, (2) the cost of producing the product, which includes the prices of required inputs and the technologies that can be used to produce the product, and (3) the prices of related products.

15. *Market supply* is the sum of all that is supplied each period by all producers of a single product. It is the sum of all the individual quantities supplied at each price.

16. It is very important to distinguish between *movements* along demand and supply curves and *shifts* of demand and supply curves. The demand curve shows the relationship between price and quantity demanded. The *supply curve* shows the relationship between price and quantity supplied. A change in price is a movement along the curve. Changes in tastes, income, wealth, expectations, or prices of other goods and services cause demand curves to shift; changes in costs, input prices, technology, or prices of related goods and services cause supply curves to shift.

Market Equilibrium

17. When quantity demanded exceeds quantity supplied at the current price, *excess demand* exists and the price tends to rise. When prices in a market rise, quantity demanded falls and quantity supplied rises until an *equilibrium* is reached at which quantity supplied and quantity demanded are equal. At equilibrium, there is no further tendency for price to change.

18. When quantity supplied exceeds quantity demanded at the current price, *excess supply* exists and the price tends to fall. When price falls, quantity supplied decreases and quantity demanded increases until an equilibrium price is reached where quantity supplied and quantity demanded are equal.

Review Terms and Concepts

capital market 67

complements, complementary goods 72

demand curve 69

demand schedule 69

entrepreneur 65

equilibrium 81

excess demand 81

excess supply 84

factors of production 67

firm 65

households 65

income 71

inferior goods 72

input or factor markets 66

labour market 66

land market 67

law of demand 69

law of supply 78

market demand 75

market supply 80

movement along a demand curve 74

normal goods 71

perfect substitutes 72

product or output markets 66

profit 77

quantity demanded 68

quantity supplied 78

shift of a demand curve 74

substitutes 72

supply curve 78

supply schedule 78

wealth or net worth 71

Problem Set

1. Illustrate the following with supply and demand curves:
   a. Between 1998 and 2000 employment and income in Ontario rose, creating an increase in the demand for housing and raising home prices.
   b. In the mid-1990s, more and more people decided to lease their cars rather than buy them. When leases expire, people usually turn in their leased cars and lease new ones. During 1999, there was a big increase in used cars available for sale and the price of used cars dropped sharply.
   c. As more and more people bought home computers during the 1990s, the demand for access to the World Wide Web increased. At the same time a number of new Internet service providers entered the Internet access market, competing with more established service providers such as Sympatico and America Online Canada (**aol.ca**). Despite massive increases in demand, the price of access to the Web actually declined.
   d. Before economic reforms were implemented in the countries of Eastern Europe, regulation held the price of bread substancially below equilibrium. When reforms were implemented, prices were deregulated and they rose dramatically. As a result, the quantity of bread demanded fell and the quantity of bread supplied rose.
   e. Good weather on the Prairies in 1999 produced a very large wheat crop and pushed wheat prices down below $4.50 per bushel.

2. Housing prices in Toronto and Vancouver have been on a rollercoaster ride. Illustrate each of the following situations with supply and demand curves:
   a. In both cities an increase in income combined with expectations of a strong market shifted demand and caused prices to rise rapidly during the mid-to-late 1980s.
   b. By 1990, the construction industry boomed as more and more developers started new residential projects. But those new projects expanded the supply of housing just as demand was shifting as a result of falling incomes and expectations during the 1990–1991 recession.

3. There has been a great debate among housing policy analysts over the best way to increase the number of housing units available to low-income households. One strategy is to provide people with housing "vouchers," paid for by the government, that can be used to "rent" housing supplied by the private market. A second strategy is to have the government subsidize housing suppliers or simply to build public housing.

a. Illustrate both supply- and demand-side strategies using supply and demand curves. Which strategy will result in higher rents?

b. Critics of housing vouchers (the demand-side strategy) argue that because the supply of housing to low-income households is limited and will not respond at all to higher rents, demand vouchers will serve only to drive up rents and make landlords better off. Illustrate their point with supply and demand curves.

4. The following two sets of statements contain common errors. Identify and explain each.

a. Demand increases. This causes prices to rise. Higher prices cause demand to fall. Therefore prices fall back to their original levels.

b. The supply of meat in Russia increases. This causes meat prices to fall. Lower prices mean that Russian households spend more on meat.

5. In August of 1993, the Toronto Blue Jays were battling it out with the Boston Red Sox for first place in the American League East. On August 2, the Blue Jays played the Red Sox in Boston. All tickets to the Blue Jays game were sold out a month in advance, and many people who wanted to get tickets could not. The following week the Sox travelled to Ohio to play the Cleveland Indians (a team in last place). The Cleveland game broke records for low attendance. In fact, only 1600 went to that game in a stadium that seats 80 000! Fenway Park in Boston holds 36 000 people. Cleveland Stadium holds 80 000. Assume for sim-

plicity that tickets to all regular season games are priced at $20.

a. Draw supply and demand curves for tickets to each of the two games. You have enough information to identify a point on each demand and supply curve. Use the laws of demand to complete the demand curve and note that supply is fixed and does not change with price as you complete the supply curve.

b. Is there a pricing policy that would have filled the ballpark for the Cleveland game?

c. The price system was not allowed to work to ration the Blue Jays tickets. How do you know? How do you suppose the tickets were rationed?

6. Consider the effects of the following two programs that influence the cigarette market in Canada: (1) Health Canada administers an advertising program designed to discourage cigarette smoking, particularly by the young. (2) In Ontario, where most Canadian tobacco is grown, there is a marketing board system which effectively restricts the amount of land on which tobacco can be grown.

Show on a graph how the advertising program (if successful) and the marketing board restrictions are likely to affect the price and quantity of cigarettes consumed.

7. In 1999, a rare disease hits the Canadian cattle herd, causing a 20% decrease in Canadian beef production. As a result chicken prices rise. Illustrate this situation with supply and demand curves (draw diagrams for both markets).

Appendix 4A	The Simple Mathematics of Demand and Supply

The examination of an individual market using the concepts of demand and supply conducted in Chapter 4 was based on a series of graphs. It is also possible to conduct this analysis using some very simple mathematics. The demand and supply schedules and curves are just two ways of depicting what someone familiar with mathematics would call *demand and supply functions*.

In mathematics, a "function" is a certain type of relationship expressed by a special notation. For example, a mathematician might write $y = f(x)$ as a way of saying that the value taken by one variable, y, depends on the value taken by another variable, x. The notation $f(x)$ is read "a function of x." The f is not a number, but shorthand for the rule or formula used to go from the known x to the unknown y.

If the rule $f(x)$ is "$10 - 2x$," then $y = 10 - 2x$ and this explicitly specifies the relationship between x and

y: when $x = 0$, $y = 10$; when $x = 1$, $y = 8$, etc. The rule provides all the information needed to construct a schedule or a graph showing the relationship between x and y (construct the schedule and graph as an exercise). In this case, the function is *linear* and it generates a straight line when plotted on a graph.

Like mathematicians, economists also use functional notation as a convenient way of summarizing relationships. As we have seen, economists have a theory of demand which states that the amount of a product households want to buy is related to (or depends on) the price of the product, incomes, accumulated wealth, the prices of substitutes, the prices of complements, and expectations about future income, wealth, and prices. A demand function is simply the rule or formula that specifies the specific relationship between the amount households want to buy and the things that affect what they want to buy. For example, an economist might write

$$Q_x^D = f(P_x, Y, W, P_c, P_s, P_x^e, Y^e, W^e, P_c^e, P_s^e)$$

as a shorthand way of saying that the amount of a specific good (good x) the households want to buy (Q_x^D) depends on the price of that good (P_x), income (Y), wealth (W), the prices of complements (P_c), the prices of substitutes (P_s), and the expected future values of these variables ($P_x^e, Y^e, W_e, P_c^e, P_s^e$; where the e superscript is used to indicate that these are expected future values).

The demand function can also be made more explicit. A simple and convenient rule is to write the demand function as $Q_x^D = a - bP_x$. This is a linear function where households will purchase a units of good x when the price of good x is zero and where quantity demanded falls by b units with every unit change in price.

In this demand function, a and b are called *coefficients* or *parameters* while Q_x^D and P_x are variables. Once the values of a and b are explicitly assigned we can determine the amount of good x households will want to buy at each price. For example, if $a = 9000$ and $b = 500$, we can use the explicit demand function, $Q_x^D = 9000 - 500P_x$, to find that households will purchase 8000 units of good x when the price of x is 2; 4000 units when the price of x is 10; etc. Notice also that $b = -500$ tells us something about the behaviour of households: the households' will to reduce purchases by 500 units for every unit increase in the price of good x.

The simple and convenient demand function, $Q_x^D = a - bP_x$, can be thought of as a summary of the more general demand function $Q_x^D = f(P_x, Y, W, P_c, P_s, P_x^e, Y^e, W^e, P_c^e, P_s^e)$. The parameter, b, explicitly reveals how Q_x^D changes when P_x changes. But where are the other factors that economic theory suggests influence demand? In the simple demand function $Q_x^D = a - bP_x$, influence of these other factors is captured by the parameter a. The parameter a is sometimes called a *shift parameter*, since a change in $Y, W, P_c, P_s, P_x^e, Y^e, W^e, P_c^e, P_s^e$ will result in a change in the value taken by a. For example, if income (Y) increases and good x is a normal good, the value taken by a will increase. Similarly, if the price of a complement(P_c) rises a will take a lower value.

It is also possible to specify a supply function. The theory of supply presented in this chapter can be summarized by

$$Q_x^S = f(P_x, P_R, P_{inputs}, \text{technology})$$

where Q_x^S is the amount of good x firms are willing and able to supply, P_x is the price of good x, P_R is the price of related products, P_{inputs} is the price of inputs, and "technology" refers to the state of technical knowledge. One simple and convenient form the supply function might take is

$$Q_x^S = c + dP_x,$$

where the parameter d tells us how Q_x^S changes when price increases by one unit (the quantity supplied increases by d units for every unit increase in price) and c is the shift parameter (whose value depends on the price of related products, the prices of inputs and the state of technical knowledge, taxes, etc.).

Equilibrium in the market for good x exists when demand (Q_x^D) equals supply (Q_x^S). To find the equilibrium values of Q_x and P_x we follow the steps listed below.

- **Step 1.** Set ($Q_x^D = a - bP_x$) equal to supply ($Q_x^S = c + dP_x$). This yields the equation
$a - bP_x = c + dP_x$

- **Step 2.** Find the value of P_x when $a - bP_x = c + dP_x$. Subtracting c from both sides of the equation and adding bP_x to both sides of the equation will result in

$a - c = (b + d)P_x$

Now divide both sides of the equation by $(b + d)$ to yield the equilibrium value of P_x

$P_x = (a - c)/(b + d)$

- **Step 3.** Find the equilibrium value of Q_x. Substitute $P_x = (a - c)/(b + d)$ into Q_x^D or Q_x^S to find Q_x, the equilibrium value :
$$\begin{aligned} Q_x &= c + d\,[(a - c)/(b + d)] \\ &= (cb + cd + da - cd)/(b + d) \\ &= (cb + ad)/(b + d) \end{aligned}$$
$$\begin{aligned} Q_x &= a - b[(a - c)/(b + d)] \\ &= (ab + ad - ab + cb)/(b + d) \\ &= (cb + ad)/(b + d) \end{aligned}$$

If we fix the values of parameters, for example by setting $a = 9000$, $b = 500$, $c = -1000$, and $d = 300$, we can easily calculate the equilibrium price and equilibrium sales (and purchases): the equilibrium price is $12.50 and the equilibrium sales (and purchases) is 2750.

The linear demand and supply functions can be graphed quite easily. But we have to be careful to note that economists use the Y axis to measure price and the X axis to measure quantity (the amount demanded and supplied). Typically a person familiar with mathematics would measure the dependent variable (in this case the quantity demanded and the quantity supplied) on the Y axis and the independent variable (in this case price) on the X axis. But in the nineteenth century, Alfred Marshall in his *Principles of Economics* set a precedent for economists when he graphed demand and supply functions with price on the Y axis and quantity on the X axis. This peculiarity of economics must be remembered, since it involves inverting the axes and using inverse demand and supply functions.

Figure 4A.1 shows a plot of the demand and supply functions for the fixed parameters. The parameter

$a = 9000$ is the intercept of the demand curve on the X axis, the intercept for the Y axis is found by finding the price where Q^D_x is equal to zero, that is, $P_x = a/b = 9000/500 = 18$. In words: At a price of 18 or higher consumers will not buy any of good x. The slope of the demand curve is found by rearranging the demand function (subtract a from both sides of the original demand function and then divide both sides of the function by $-b$) to yield the inverse demand function: $P_x = a/b - 1/b \times Q^D_x = 18 - 0.002 \times Q^D_x$. The slope of the inverse demand function tells us that price must fall by 2/10 of a cent to induce consumers to buy an additional unit of good x and the distance from the X axis to the demand curve measures the maximum price consumers are willing to pay for the particular unit of the good measured on the X axis.

The supply function can be graphed by following the same steps used to graph the demand function.[1] We first find the Y axis intercept by finding the value of P_x where Q^s_x equals zero: $P_x = -c/d = 3.34$. In words, if the price is 3.34 (or less) the suppliers don't supply anything. We then find the inverse supply function by rearranging: $P_x = -c/d + 1/d \times Q^s_x = 3.34 + 0.00334 \times Q^s_x$. The slope of the inverse supply function[1] tells us that suppliers will increase supply by one unit for every 1/3 of a cent increase in the price.

The equilibrium calculated from the mathematical functions corresponds to the point at which the demand and supply curves intersect.

In the previous section of this chapter, a shift in either or both the supply and demand curves resulted in a change in the equilibrium price and equilibrium quantity. A shift in the supply or demand curves results from a change in the shift parameters (the intercepts a and c) of the linear demand and supply functions. Thus if we know that an increase in income will increase demand by 800, *ceteris paribus*, the increase in income will generate a new demand function and a new equilibrium price and quantity. Specifically, the new demand function will be $Q^D_x = 9800 - 500P_x$. At the original equilibrium price of $12.50, $Q^D_x = 9800 - 500(12.5) = 3550$ and $Q^s_x = -1000 + 300(12.5) = 2750$. Thus, there is an excess demand of 800 when $P_x = \$12.50$, so $12.50 cannot be the equilibrium price. The price that results in demand equal to supply is $13.50. At this new equilibrium price, the quantity bought and sold will be 3050. The price rise of $1 eliminated excess demand by inducing firms to increase quantity supplied by 300 and by inducing households to reduce quantity demanded by 500 units. The new equilibrium outcome is illustrated in Figure 4A.1.

Figure 4.A1

Graphing the Linear Model

The equilibrium found by solving the system of linear demand and supply equations corresponds to the equilibrium found by identifying the intersection of the demand and supply curves.

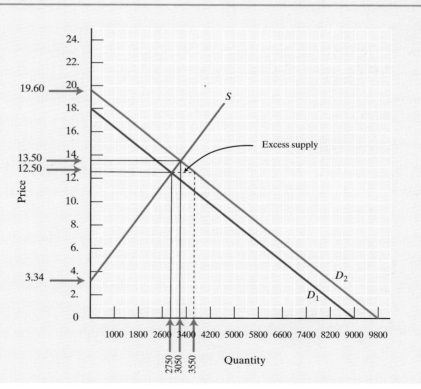

[1]*You will note that the X axis intercept is a negative number (–1000). Because this implies that the firms will want to supply – 1000 units of output when the price is zero, the mathematics seems to generate a result that defies common sense. This should encourage you to be very careful when using mathematics to describe economic behaviour: always be sure the implications of the mathematics make sense as a descriptor of behaviour. In this example, we just ignore the X axis intercept and assume that if the price is below 3.34 the suppliers do not supply anything.*

1. Suppose the demand and supply of eggs are described by the following equations:

$$Q_d = 100 - 20P$$
$$Q_s = 10 + 40P$$

where Q_d = millions of dozens of eggs people would like to buy; Q_s = millions of dozens of eggs farmers would like to sell; P = price per dozen eggs.

  a. Fill in the following table.

Price	Quantity Demanded	Quantity Supplied
$0.50	_____	_____
$1.00	_____	_____
$1.50	_____	_____
$2.00	_____	_____
$2.50	_____	_____

  b. Use the information in the table to find the equilibrium price and equilibrium quantity.

  c. Graph the demand and supply equations and identify the equilibrium price and quantity.

*2. Consider the market for pizza. Suppose that the market demand for pizza is given by the equation $Q_d = 300 - 20P$ and the market supply for pizza is given by the equation $Q_s = 20P - 100$, where Q_d = quantity demanded, Q_s = quantity supplied, P = price (per pizza).

  a. Graph the supply and demand schedules for pizza using $5 through $15 as the value of P.

  b. In equilibrium, how many pizzas would be sold and at what price?

  c. What would happen if suppliers set the price of pizza at $15? Explain the market adjustment process.

  d. Suppose that the price of hamburgers, a substitute for pizza, doubles. Assume that this leads to a doubling of the demand for pizza (i.e., at each price consumers demand twice as much pizza as before). Write the equation for the new market demand for pizza.

  e. Find the new equilibrium price and quantity of pizza.

———————

*Note: Problems marked with an asterisk are more challenging.

The Price System and Supply and Demand

Learning Objectives

1 Describe the role of price as a rationing device.
2 Describe the alternative rationing mechanisms.
3 Apply the demand and supply model in a variety of situations.
4 Explain the role of prices in the allocation of resources.

Every society has a system of institutions that determines what is produced, how it is produced, and who gets what is produced. Although in some societies these decisions are made centrally, through planning agencies or by government directive, in every society many decisions are made in a decentralized way, through the operation of markets.

Markets exist in all societies, and Chapter 4 provided a bare-bones description of how markets operate. In this chapter, we continue our examination of supply, demand, and the price system.

The Price System: Rationing and Allocating Resources
Price Rationing
Constraints on the Market and Alternative Rationing Mechanisms
The Canadian Farm Crisis: The Case of Prairie Wheat Producers
Prices and the Allocation of Resources

Supply and Demand Analysis: The Price of Gasoline

Looking Ahead

The Price System: Rationing and Allocating Resources

The market system, also called the *price system*, performs two important and closely related functions in a society with unregulated markets. First, it provides an automatic mechanism for distributing scarce goods and services. That is, it serves as a **price rationing** device for allocating goods and services to consumers when the quantity demanded exceeds the quantity supplied. Second, the price system ultimately determines both the allocation of resources among producers and the final mix of outputs.

price rationing *The process by which the market system allocates goods and services to consumers when quantity demanded exceeds quantity supplied.*

PRICE RATIONING

Consider first the simple process by which the price system eliminates excess demand. Figure 5.1 shows hypothetical supply and demand curves for lobsters caught off the coast of Atlantic Canada.

Lobsters are considered a delicacy. They are served in the finest restaurants, and people cook them at home on special occasions. As Figure 5.1 shows, the equilibrium price of live lobsters was $10 per kilogram in 2001. At this price, lobster boats brought in lobsters at a rate of 20 million kilograms per year—an amount that was just enough to satisfy demand.

Market equilibrium existed at $10 per kilogram, because at that price quantity demanded was equal to quantity supplied. (Remember that equilibrium occurs at the point where the supply and demand curves intersect. In Figure 5.1, this occurs at point C.)

Now suppose that in 2002 the waters off a section of the Atlantic coast become contaminated with a poisonous parasite. As a result, the Department of Fisheries and Oceans is forced to close 50 000 square kilometres of the most productive lobstering areas. Even though many of the lobster boats shift their trapping activities to other waters, there is a sharp reduction in the quantity of lobster supplied. The supply curve shifts to the left, from S_{2001} to S_{2002}. This shift in the supply curve creates a situation of excess demand at $10. At that price, the quantity demanded is 20 million kilograms and the quantity supplied is 10 million kilograms. Quantity demanded exceeds quantity supplied by 10 million kilograms (20 million minus 10 million).

The reduced supply causes the price of lobster to rise sharply. As the price rises, the available supply is "rationed." Who gets it? Those who are willing and able to pay the most.

You can see the market's price rationing function clearly in Figure 5.1. As the price rises from $10, the quantity demanded declines along the demand curve, moving from point C (20 million kilograms) toward point B (16 million kilograms). The higher prices mean that restaurants must charge much more for lobster rolls and stuffed lobsters. As a result, many people simply decide to stop buying lobster or order it less frequently when they dine out. Some restaurants drop it from the menu entirely, and some shoppers at the fish counter turn to lobster substitutes such as swordfish and salmon.

As the price rises, lobster trappers (suppliers) also change their behaviour. They stay out longer than they did when the price was $10 per kilogram. Quantity supplied increases from 10 million kilograms to 16 million kilograms. This increase in price brings about a movement along the 2002 supply curve from point A to point B.

Finally, a new equilibrium is established at a price of $13.75 per kilogram and a total output of 16 million kilograms. At the new equilibrium, total production is 16 million kilograms per year, and the market has determined who gets the lobsters. *The lower total supply is rationed to those who are willing and able to pay the higher price.*

FIGURE 5.1

The Market for Lobsters

Suppose that in 2002, 50 000 square kilometres of lobstering waters off the coast of Atlantic Canada are closed. The supply curve shifts to the left. Before the waters are closed, the lobster market is in equilibrium at the price of $10 and a quantity of 20 million kilograms. The decreased supply of lobster leads to higher prices, and a new equilibrium is reached at $13.75 and 16 million kilograms.

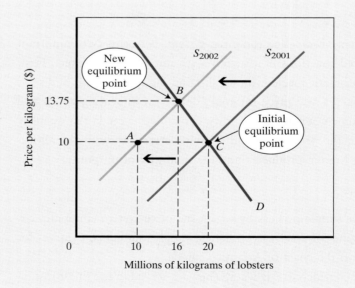

This idea of "willingness to pay" is central to the distribution of available supply, and willingness depends on both desire (preferences) and income/wealth. Willingness to pay does not necessarily mean that only the very rich will continue to buy lobsters when the price increases. Lower-income people may continue to buy some lobster, but they will have to be willing to sacrifice more of other goods in order to do so.

In sum:

> The adjustment of price is the rationing mechanism in free markets. Price rationing means that whenever there is a need to ration a good—that is, when excess demand exists—in a free market, the price of the good will rise until quantity supplied equals quantity demanded—that is, until the market clears.

There is some price that will clear any market you can think of. Consider the market for a famous painting such as Van Gogh's *Portrait of Dr. Gachet*. Figure 5.2 illustrates the operation of such a market. At a low price, there would be an enormous excess demand for such an important painting. The price would be bid up until there was only one remaining demander. The demander who gets the painting would be the one who is willing and able to pay the most. Presumably, that price would be very high. In fact, Van Gogh's *Portrait of Dr. Gachet* sold for a record US$82.5 million in 1990. If the product is in strictly scarce supply, as a single painting is, its price is said to be *demand-determined*; that is, its price is determined solely and exclusively by the amount that the highest bidder or bidders are willing to pay.

One might interpret the statement "There is some price that will clear any market" to mean "Everything has its price." But that is not exactly what it means. Suppose you own a small silver bracelet that has been in your family for many generations. It is quite possible that you wouldn't sell it for *any* amount of money. Does this mean that the market is not working, or that quantity supplied and quantity demanded are not equal? Not at all. It means simply that *you* are the highest bidder. By turning down all bids, you are setting your own price, revealing that the bracelet is worth more to you than to those who bid on it. To keep the bracelet, you must be willing to forgo what anybody offers for it.

When supply is fixed or something for sale is unique, its price is demand determined. Price is what the highest bidder is willing to pay. In 1990, the highest bidder was willing to pay $82.5 million for Van Gogh's portrait of Dr. Gachet.

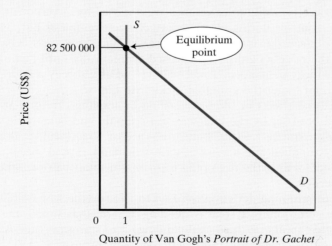

Quantity of Van Gogh's *Portrait of Dr. Gachet*

FIGURE 5.2

Market for a Rare Painting

There is some price that will clear any market, even if supply is strictly limited. In an auction for a unique painting, the price (bid) will rise to eliminate excess demand until there is only one bidder willing to purchase the single available painting.

On occasion, both governments and private firms decide to use some mechanism other than the market system to ration an item for which there is excess demand at the current price. (This was often the case in the former Soviet Union and other communist nations such as China. See the Global Perspective box titled "The Market Comes to China" for more details.) Policies designed to stop price rationing are commonly justified in a number of ways.

The rationale most often used is fairness. It is not "fair" to let landlords charge high rents, not "fair" for oil companies to run up the price of gasoline, not "fair" for insurance companies to charge enormous premiums, and so on. After all, the argument goes, we have no choice but to pay—housing and insurance are necessary, and one needs gasoline to get to work. While it is not precisely true that price rationing allocates goods and services solely on the basis of income and wealth, income and wealth do constrain our wants. Why should all the gasoline or all the tickets to the World Series go just to the rich? it is asked.

Various schemes to keep price from rising to equilibrium are based on several perceptions of injustice, among them (1) that price-gouging is bad, (2) that income is unfairly distributed, and (3) that some items are necessities, and everyone should be able to buy them at a "reasonable" price. Regardless of the rationale, the following examples will make two things clear:

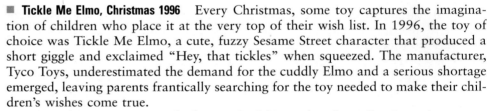

1. Attempts to bypass price rationing in the market and to use alternative rationing devices are much more difficult and costly than they would seem at first glance.

2. Very often, such attempts distribute costs and benefits among households in unintended ways.

■ **Tickle Me Elmo, Christmas 1996** Every Christmas, some toy captures the imagination of children who place it at the very top of their wish list. In 1996, the toy of choice was Tickle Me Elmo, a cute, fuzzy Sesame Street character that produced a short giggle and exclaimed "Hey, that tickles" when squeezed. The manufacturer, Tyco Toys, underestimated the demand for the cuddly Elmo and a serious shortage emerged, leaving parents frantically searching for the toy needed to make their children's wishes come true.

Tyco chose to maintain the list price of $35 rather than allowing prices to act as a rationing device. The list price became what economists call a **price ceiling**, or maximum price. Typically price ceilings are imposed by government. (Rent controls, and price controls during wartime, are classic examples.) But, as our toy illustration makes clear, this is not always the case. Had the market been allowed to operate freely, the price would have increased dramatically until quantity supplied was equal to quantity demanded. Those willing and able to pay a high price would have been the ones to get the available Tickle Me Elmos.

You can see the effects of the price ceiling by looking carefully at Figure 5.3. If the price had been set by the intersection of supply and demand it would have increased to approximately $100. But, at a price of $35, quantity demanded exceeded quantity supplied and a state of excess demand existed. Because Tyco and almost all retailers selling the toy opted to maintain the list price, other rationing devices were needed.

A number of rationing devices were used to allocate the scarce dolls. The most common nonprice rationing system is **queuing**, a term that simply means waiting in line. Desperate parents returned again and again to stores (a real cost to the parents) in search of the elusive toy. In Fredericton, New Brunswick, a Wal-Mart store advertised an Elmo special for one hour, beginning at 3 a.m. (yes, in the morning!). Three hundred shoppers showed up to compete for 48 Elmos. An unsuspecting employee suffered two cracked ribs and a concussion when the shoppers stampeded. Under this system Elmos went to those who were willing to get up at 3 a.m. and fight for the scarce product.

Meet Elmo

price ceiling *A maximum price that sellers may charge for a good, usually set by government.*

queuing *A nonprice rationing mechanism that uses waiting in line as a means of distributing goods and services.*

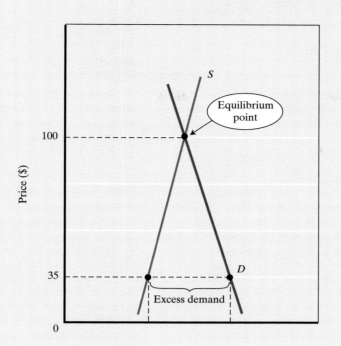

FIGURE 5.3

Excess Demand Created by a Price Ceiling of $35

If the price had been set by the interaction of supply and demand, the price of a Tickle Me Elmo doll would have been approximately $100. At $35, the quantity demanded exceeded the quantity supplied. Since the price system was not allowed to function, an alternative rationing system had to be found to distribute the available supply of the toy.

A second nonprice rationing device used was that of **favoured customers**. Some retailers simply reserved their limited stock of Elmos for friends, relatives, and favoured customers. Not surprisingly many customers tried to become "favoured" by offering side payments to store managers.

With so many people desperate for the Tickle Me Elmo toy, scalpers emerged. Some scalpers were able to find customers willing to pay over $500. In this case, resale was legal since the price ceiling was imposed by the producer and the retailers. However, if the ceiling had been imposed by government, resale at a higher price would have been illegal. But even when governments impose price ceilings and do their best to enforce them, new markets often emerge. These illegal or **black markets** generate prices determined by supply and demand.

While it is unlikely to be used for dolls, we should note a fourth nonprice rationing device: **ration coupons**. Ration coupons were employed in Canada in the 1940s when the government imposed wartime price ceilings on meat, sugar, gasoline, and many other items. The ration coupon entitled a family to a specific quantity of the product per month. The ration coupon was supposed to ensure that everyone received the same amount, regardless of income.

When ration coupons are used with no prohibition against trading them, however, the result is very similar to a system of price rationing. Those who are willing and able to pay the most simply buy up the coupons and use them to purchase gasoline, chocolate, fresh eggs, or anything else that is sold at a restricted price.[1] This means that the price of the restricted good will effectively rise to the market-clearing price. For instance, suppose that you decide not to sell your ration coupon. You are then forgoing what you would have received by selling the coupon. Thus the real price of the good you purchase will be higher (if only in opportunity cost) than the restricted price. Even when trade in coupons is declared illegal, it is virtually impossible to stop black markets from developing.

favoured customers *Those who receive special treatment from dealers during crises.*

black market *A market in which illegal trading takes place at market-determined prices.*

ration coupons *Tickets or coupons that entitle individual persons to purchase a certain amount of a given product per month.*

---

[1]*Of course, if you are assigned a number of coupons and sell them, you are better off than you would be with price rationing. Ration coupons thus serve as a way of redistributing income.*

Price rationing allocates goods and services to those who are willing and able to pay for them. One of the central premises of communism is that price rationing for basic necessities, such as food, is unfair; everyone should be able to afford such items as food and shelter. But regulating prices to "fair" levels below equilibrium means that quantity supplied will be less than quantity demanded.

In addition, preventing the price mechanism from operating requires that some other device other than price be used to ration available goods. Before the collapse of communism in the Soviet Union and Eastern Europe, people waited in long lines at state stores, which could not meet citizens' demands. The stores were not well stocked in part because farmers could get a much better price for their goods on the black market. The biggest problem with regulated prices, however, is that the incentive to produce is lost.

In 1997, China's paramount leader Deng Xiaoping died. More than any other leader in the communist world, Deng understood the importance of market prices as an incentive. In 1978, local officials associated with Deng began allowing rural peasants to grow grain on their own individual plots of land. The peasants could not own the land, and the government took a fixed amount of the grain they produced as a tax, but they were permitted to sell all surpluses in private markets at market prices. This policy had a dramatic effect on the level of output. As prices increased, so did the quantity supplied. Productivity soared, and Chinese agriculture began to grow dramatically.

Deng also knew that the industrial sector could not function without market prices playing a role. As of 1997, markets—not bureaucracies—determined the prices of nearly nine-tenths of all finished goods in China.

The mix of market and government institutions adopted in China proved to be beneficial. For 75% of Chinese, who make their living from the land, incomes have grown over 200 percent since 1978 to $1000 per year. Industrial incomes have risen even more. China's economy has grown at an average rate of over 9% since 1982. In 1997, it grew at an impressive annual rate of 10%.

Source: "Deng's China," *The Economist,* February 1997.

THE CANADIAN FARM CRISIS: THE CASE OF PRAIRIE WHEAT PRODUCERS

The Canadian Prairies are sometimes called the "breadbasket of the world," since a combination of climate and soil fertility allow Prairie farmers to produce high-quality wheat at a cost that is quite low relative to what farmers in the rest of the world can achieve. But despite the natural advantage, Prairie wheat producers are in the midst of a very difficult period. A survey of Prairie grain producers by the Canadian Wheat Board in 1999 revealed that 67% of farmers were losing money and that 47% felt they would be out of business if losses persisted for a couple of years. Unfortunately, current market prices are below the cost of production and this state of affairs seems unlikely to improve in the next few years.

A variety of factors lie behind the farm crisis in the Prairies, including a doubling of freight rates following the elimination of the Western Grain Transportation Act in 1995; higher costs for inputs such as fertilizer, chemicals, and machinery; and drought. But the most important factor is the low price of wheat on the world market: the inflation-adjusted price, about $56 per metric tonne, is approximately half that which existed in the mid-1970s.

Government policy in the United States and Europe is an extremely important factor in world grain markets. In 1999, the U.S. government spent about $33 billion on direct subsidies to farmers. In the same year, the European Union spent over $56 billion. (Canadian total farm income in 1999 was only $30 billion.) In relative terms, subsidies to farmers in the EU are equal to approximately 50% of gross farm receipts; in the U.S., subsidies account for over 35% of gross farm receipts; and in Canada, subsidies are less than 10% of gross farm receipts. Table 5.1 gives some indication of the relative levels of subsidization in wheat production.

The United States and Europe have a wide variety of agricultural subsidy programs. Traditionally, one of the most important policies used in the U.S. and Europe has been a *price floor*, which can be thought of as a minimum guaranteed

Table 5.1	Estimates of Subsidization in Wheat Production (US$/metric tonne)
European Union	$141
United States	61
Canada	8

Source: Greg Arason, "Grain Prices and Future Trends in the Agricultural Industry," a presentation to the Standing Committee on Agriculture and Agri-Food, p. 5.

price. Under a price floor program the government must buy wheat from the farmer at a preestablished price if the farmer offers the wheat for sale. Farmers will only offer the wheat to government if the market price is at or below the support price.

Figure 5.4a illustrates the theoretical impact of a price floor in a single isolated economy (imagine that this is Europe and that there are no exports from or imports to the European economy). Without government intervention the market will gravitate toward an equilibrium price at p_0 with sales (and purchases) of q_0 and total farm receipts equal to $p_0 \times q_0$. If the government introduces a price floor at p_s farmers will produce q_2 units of output and total farm receipts will be $p_s \times q_2$. Thus the first impact of the price support is higher farm incomes. Consumers buy q_1 units at a price of p_s: that is, they buy less at a higher price. The remaining $q_2 - q_1$ units are bought by the government and could be placed in storage, "dumped" on world markets, or given away. Taxpayers must foot the bill for this.

The theoretical model in Figure 5.4a suggests that Canadian wheat producers can suffer from low world prices if the excess supply of wheat arising because of the price support in Europe is sold on world markets. Figure 5.4b explicitly shows the impact of an increase in supply on world markets. The world wheat market is initially in equilibrium at a price of p_w^0 and sales of q_w^0. If the $q_2 - q_1$ units that went unsold in Figure 5.4a are dumped on world markets, the supply of wheat on world markets will increase by $q_2 - q_1$ units. This is illustrated in Figure 5.4b, where the world supply curve shifts out by the amount wheat dumped on the market. A new equilibrium emerges at a lower price of p_w^1. Although total sales are higher in the new equilibrium at q_w^1, the sales by suppliers who were participating in the market prior to the dumping actually fall to q_w^r. Thus suppliers who were participating in the world market prior to the dumping will experience lower prices and lower sales.

In Figure 5.4c an additional complication is introduced: it is assumed that, prior to the price floor being introduced, the consumers in the economy analyzed in Figure 5.4a (Europe, for example) can purchase the product on world markets at a price of p_w. From the demand curve it can seen that consumers purchase q_4' units of the good. But only part of this total is supplied by domestic producers; at a price p_w domestic producers are willing to supply at most q_0'. The $q_4' - q_0'$ units not supplied by domestic producers are purchased from foreign producers (imports). Total domestic farm receipts are $p_w \times q_0'$.

A policy that combines a price floor at p_s and restrictions on imports (no imports allowed) in this case not only results in higher prices for domestic farmers and consumers but also lowers exports for foreign producers. Notice that this policy eliminates the imports, $q_4' - q_0'$ units, and generates a surplus of $q_3' - q_2'$ which might be placed on world markets. The combined impact of restricting imports from foreign suppliers and dumping the surplus on world markets will depress world market prices by more than is illustrated in Figure 5.4b.

The theoretical analysis of price supports offers important insights into the crisis currently facing Prairie wheat producers. In the early 1960s the European Community introduced the Common Agricultural Policy to encourage European self-sufficiency in agriculture. A price floor was an important part of this policy. The policy was remarkably successful in achieving the goal of self-sufficiency: the EU went from being a net importer of agricultural products to being the world's largest exporter. But this came at a cost: Europeans faced high consumer prices and

FIGURE 5.4

Agricultural Policy and the Prairie Farm Crisis

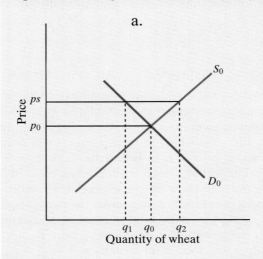

a.

A price support at price p_s will create a surplus of wheat of $q_2 - q_1$ and increase farm incomes from $p_0 \times q_0$ to $p_s \times q_2$.

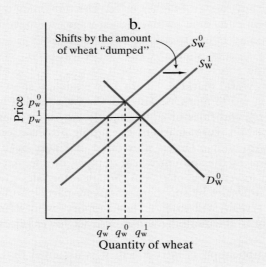

b.

Shifts by the amount of wheat "dumped"

If a surplus is dumped on world markets the world price will fall. The incomes of those participating in world markets before the dumping will fall from $p_w^0 \times q_w^0$ to $p_w^1 \times q_w^r$.

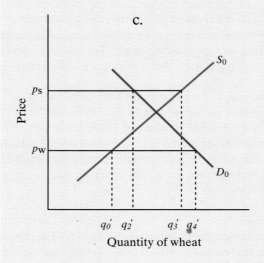

c.

A policy that combines restrictions on imports and a price support will result in a dramatic expansion of the agricultural sector in a country implementing these policies. In this example, output of wheat grows from q_0^1 to q_3^1.

high taxes to cover the cost of the price floor program, and Canadian farmers faced lower world prices.

In recent years the price support programs have come under attack during international trade negotiations, and the WTO now has rules that limit the use of price supports. Nonetheless, significant subsidies to wheat producers in Europe and the United States remain, and the effects of past price floor programs continue to have an effect on world wheat prices.[2]

In summary, the subsidization and price support programs of the U.S. and the EU have put their farmers at a considerable advantage relative to Canadian farmers. Consequently, many western Canadian farmers, despite being as efficient as their U.S. or EU counterparts, are facing bankruptcy.

PRICES AND THE ALLOCATION OF RESOURCES

Thinking of the market system as a mechanism for allocating scarce goods and services among competing demanders is very revealing. But the market determines much more than just the distribution of final outputs. It also determines what gets produced and how resources are allocated among competing uses.

Consider a change in consumer preferences that leads to an increase in demand for a specific good or service. During the 1970s, for example, people began going to restaurants much more frequently than before. Researchers think that this trend, which continues today, is partially the result of social changes (such as a dramatic rise in the number of two-earner families) and partially the result of rising incomes. The market responded to this change in demand by shifting resources, both capital and labour, into more and better restaurants.

With the increase in demand for restaurant meals, the price of eating out rose, and the restaurant business became more profitable. The higher profits attracted new businesses and provided old restaurants with an incentive to expand. As new capital, seeking profits, flowed into the restaurant business, so too did labour. New restaurants need chefs. Chefs need training, and the higher wages that came with increased demand provided an incentive for them to get it. In response to the increase in demand for training, new cooking schools opened up and existing schools began to offer courses in the culinary arts.

This story could run on and on, but the point is clear:

Price changes resulting from shifts of demand in output markets cause profits to rise or fall. Profits attract capital; losses lead to disinvestment. Higher wages attract labour and encourage workers to acquire skills. At the core of the system, supply, demand, and prices in input and output markets determine the allocation of resources and the ultimate combinations of things produced.

Supply and Demand Analysis:
The Price of Gasoline

In 1999, the price motorists in Canada faced at their local gas station rose dramatically. In January 1999 the typical retail price of regular gasoline in Canada stood at about $0.50 per litre. By June 2000 the average price had risen to over $0.75 per litre. Why did the price rise so dramatically? Canadians across the country were certainly asking this question at the time, and a popular theory was that Canadian gasoline companies were simply "ripping off" the consumers.

---

[2]*Under new WTO rules, agricultural support programs must be designed to minimize their impact on production decisions made by producers. A price support program results in an increase in production and is not neutral. The United States and Europe have responded by replacing price support programs with programs that base support on historical, not current, production levels. Under these policies, a farmer's production decision in the current year will not affect the subsidy; thus, the subsidy should not have an effect on current production decisions. However, past price support policies have determined the production levels used in these subsidy programs, so the impact of past price support policy persists despite the WTO rule changes.*

A "made-in-Canada" theory of the gasoline price increase does not, on closer examination, have much support. Canadian economists quickly discovered that motorists in every country in the world faced similar price increases. Thus, the forces contributing to the increase had to be global in scope.

Energy-and-oil-market analysts argue that the critical factor was a dramatic increase in the price of crude oil on world oil markets. On February 17, 1999 the price of crude oil was about US$11.53 per barrel, the lowest price in 70 years. By November the price had risen to over US$25 per barrel, and in early March 2000 the crude oil price passed the US$34 mark. Analysts also argue that the pattern of price changes reflects the operation of market forces: simple demand and supply.

As a concrete illustration of how formal demand supply analysis is used by economists, let us examine developments on world oil markets in 1999/2000. As a starting point take a snapshot of the state of the market on February 17. As illustrated in Figure 5.5a the market is in equilibrium with a spot price of US$11.53 per barrel with 76 million barrels purchased (and sold). The total revenue earned by oil producers (which equals the total expenditure of oil purchasers) is US$876.28 million per day. Notice that the total revenue (and total expenditure) can be captured by the area of the coloured rectangle, since the width of the rectangle is 76 million barrels and the length is US$11.53 (recall that the area of a rectangle is just the length times the width).

In the formal demand/supply model, prices rise if (1) there is a shift in the supply curve and/or (2) there is a shift in the demand curve. An economic analysis of developments on the crude oil market begins by identifying explanations for shifts in the demand and supply curves.

In March 1999 a meeting of OPEC in Vienna resulted in an agreement to lower crude oil production. OPEC supplies about one-third of all crude appearing on the market on any given day, and consequently it can have a significant impact on the market. Two large non-OPEC oil-producing countries, Norway and Mexico, also agreed to cut production. In combination, the OPEC/Norway/Mexico production cutback was expected to result in a decline in the supply of crude to world oil markets of about 4 million barrels per day.

The 4-million-barrel-a-day cut is illustrated as a shift in the supply curve of crude in Figure 5.5b where the original supply curve is labelled S_0 and the new supply curve S_1. Potential buyers were no longer able to buy all the crude they would like at the original market price of $11.53. The shortage of crude of 4 million barrels per day (labelled AB in Figure 5.5b) resulted in the price rising as buyers competed to get the reduced supply of oil available.

As prices rose, oil fields that had been unprofitable at a price of $11.53 began to become profitable. Consequently, oil-producing countries began supplying more oil to the world market. The impact of higher prices on the quantity of crude supplied is captured by a movement along the supply curve S_1 from B to C. Notice that the quantity of crude oil supplied is not very responsive to changes in price. The movement from B to C shows that an increase in price from $11.53 to $34 on the oil market only results in a 2-million-barrel-a-day increase in production.

Higher prices also have an effect on the quantity of crude oil demanded. This is captured by a movement along the demand curve, D_0, from A to C. Quantity demanded is not very responsive to price changes. The movement from A to C shows that the increase in price results in a reduction in quantity demand of about 2 million barrels a day.

The cut in production engineered by OPEC increased oil revenue dramatically. At the original price of $11.53, 76 million barrels were sold per day, yielding $876.28 million in revenue. At the new price of $34 and new sales level of 74 barrels per day, daily revenue is $2.516 billion.

The developments on the crude oil market obviously offered significant gains for oil-producing countries. However, the high oil prices are also a matter of concern for the oil producers. High prices encourage the development of alternative energy sources in the long term, they encourage conservation, and they might even push the world economy into a recession. None of these outcomes is in the long-term interest of oil producers.

FIGURE 5.5
World Oil Markets, 1999

a. Prices, sales, and revenues, February 17, 1999

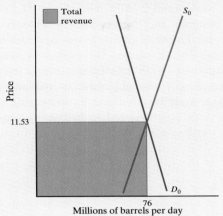

b. OPEC supply reduction: prices, sales, and revenues, November 1999

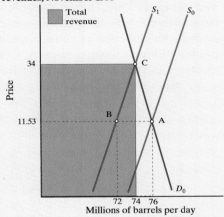

c. Combined OPEC supply increase and world demand increase, February 2000

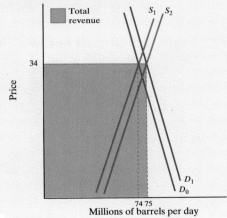

Concerns with high prices resulted in OPEC increasing production levels by over a million barrels per day in early 2000, but this only had a small impact on prices due to rapid growth in crude oil demand arising because economies throughout the world were growing. Figure 5.5c illustrates this case. A one-million-barrel-per-day increase in supply (a shift from S_1 to S_2) is matched by a one-million-barrel-per-day increase in demand (a shift from D_0 to D_1) due to strong economic performance in North America and the recovery of Asian economies from a period of very poor performance. The sales of crude rise by 1 million barrels per day but price is unchanged.

A detailed study of the 1999/2000 gasoline price increases by the Competition Bureau, an agency of the Government of Canada, is available online at **strategis.ic.ca /SSG/ct01699e.html**. The study concludes that "increasing retail gasoline prices in Canada after July 1999 can be attributed to increasing crude oil prices on world markets, which caused wholesale gasoline prices to rise throughout North America. Given the lack of evidence of anti-competitive behaviour, it is the conclusion of the Competition Bureau that the July 1999 price increases, while dramatic, were the result of normal market forces."

Looking Ahead

We have now discussed the nature of the market/price system and examined the basic forces of supply and demand. These basic concepts will serve as building blocks for what comes next. Whether you are studying microeconomics or macroeconomics, you will be studying the function of markets and the behaviour of market participants in more detail in the following chapters.

Since the concepts presented in the first five chapters are so important to your understanding of what is to come, this might be a good point at which to do a brief review of Part One.

Summary

The Price System: Rationing and Allocating Resources

1. In a market economy, the market system (or price system) serves two functions. It determines the allocation of resources among producers and the final mix of outputs. It also distributes goods and services on the basis of willingness and ability to pay. In this sense, it serves as a *price rationing* device.

2. Governments, as well as private firms, sometimes decide not to use the market system to ration an item for which there is an excess demand at current prices. Examples of nonprice rationing systems include *queuing*, *favoured customers*, and *ration coupons*. The most common rationale for policies or practices designed to avoid price rationing is "fairness."

3. Attempts to bypass the market and use alternative nonprice rationing devices are much more difficult and costly than it would seem at first glance. Schemes that open up opportunities for favoured customers, *black markets*, and side payments often end up less "fair" than the free market.

Supply and Demand Analysis: The Price of Gasoline

4. The basic logic of supply and demand is a powerful tool for analysis. For example, it can be used to help one understand why the price paid for gasoline by Canadian motorists rose dramatically in 1999.

Problem Set

1. Illustrate the following with supply and/or demand curves:
   a. A situation of excess labour supply (unemployment) caused by a minimum wage law.
   b. The effect of a sharp increase in heating oil prices on the demand for insulation material.

2. "Scalping, which is illegal in most provinces, may in fact serve a useful function." Do you agree or disagree? Explain.

3. Illustrate the following with supply and/or demand curves:
   a. The federal government "supports" the price of wheat by paying farmers not to plant wheat on some of their land.
   b. As the economy has begun to recover from recession, incomes are rising and expectations about the future are becoming more positive. As a result, home prices in many parts of the country are rising.
   c. The impact of an increase in the price of chicken on the price of hamburger.
   d. In a bill to be presented to the legislature, the MPPs of Ontario will be asked to vote on whether to abolish rent control. Under rent control, rents are held by law to levels below equilibrium. If rent control is discontinued, there will be an impact on housing demand and supply.
   e. Incomes rise, shifting the demand for gasoline. Crude oil prices rise, shifting the supply of gasoline. At the new equilibrium, the quantity of gasoline sold is less than it was before. (Crude oil is used to produce gasoline.)

4. "The price of blue jeans has risen substantially in recent years. Demand for blue jeans has also been rising. This is hard to explain, because the law of demand says that higher prices should lead to lower demand." Do you agree?

5. In an effort to "support" the price of some agricultural goods, Agriculture Canada has at times paid farmers a subsidy for the land they leave unplanted. The rationale is that the subsidy increases the "cost" of planting and that it will reduce supply and increase the price of competitively produced agricultural goods. Critics argue that because the subsidy is a payment to farmers, it will reduce costs and lead to lower prices. Which argument is correct? Explain.

Gasoline Taxes and Gasoline Prices

Between February 1999 and April 2000, gasoline prices in Canada rose by almost $0.25 per litre. As pointed out in Chapter 5, the price increase reflected the normal market forces of supply and demand with the market adjusting to a decision by the Organization of Petroleum Exporting Countries (OPEC) to cut supplies of crude oil. Not surprisingly, a lot of unhappy motorists blamed OPEC.

At meetings of the World Petroleum Congress, held in Calgary in April 2000, Rilwanu Lukman, the secretary-general of OPEC, fought back. He argued that Canadians should blame their government rather than oil producers for the record-high gasoline prices. "People should look at the taxation regime of their country and they will find that a lot of the money they are paying, they are paying to government."

Gasoline in Canada is heavily taxed. About 40% of the price of gasoline is accounted for by a combination of federal and provincial excise and general sales taxes. As a consequence, it should come as no great surprise to discover that many motorists and some politicians advocate reductions in gasoline taxes in periods when gasoline prices are high.

A proposal to lower taxes on gasoline appears, at first glance, to offer lower prices at the pump. After all, if taxes account for 40% of the price, eliminating taxes should reduce prices by 40%. Alas, this is not necessarily the outcome. Indeed, one possible scenario involves unchanged prices and consumption and a windfall gain for oil companies and OPEC.

FIGURE 1

Taxation and Gasoline Prices

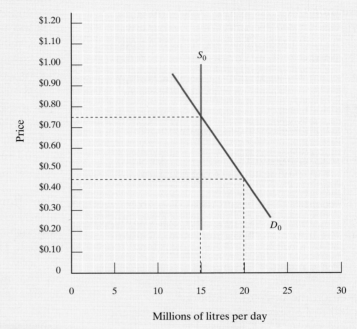

Millions of litres per day

FIGURE 2

Taxation and Gasoline Prices

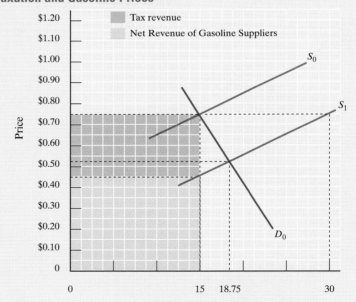

Millions of litres per day

The reason tax cuts may not have much impact on gasoline prices, especially in the short term, can be illustrated using a simple demand/supply model. Motorists demand gasoline. As price rises, they consume less; as price falls, they consume more. The demand for gasoline is captured by the demand curve D_0 in Figure 1. In the short term—and it is the short term that may be relevant when thinking about a policy of tax reduction to offset the rapid rise in gasoline prices—the supply of gasoline is essentially fixed, consisting of the inventories available to oil suppliers plus any en route. The short-term supply curve is then S_0 in the figure.

To analyze the impact of a tax cut, begin by identifying the pre–tax cut equilibrium. The pre–tax cut equilibrium in the model of the gasoline market is shown at a price of $0.75 per litre and total sales/consumption per day of 15 000 000 litres. Since approximately 40% of the price goes to taxes ($0.75 \times 0.4 = \$0.30$ per litre), gas stations earn about $0.45 per litre in net revenue.

The second step in the formal analysis of the tax cut involves asking: How can the tax cut be introduced in the model? One way of doing this is to assume that the price initially falls by the amount of the tax cut, that is, to $0.45 per litre. But this cannot be an equilibrium in the gasoline market. When the price falls, motorists demand more gasoline (a movement along the demand curve). In Figure 1 the demand rises from 15 000 000 litres per day to 20 000 000. But since supply cannot be increased in the short run, this causes a shortage of gasoline of 5 000 000 litres per day. The scarce gasoline must be rationed in some way, and in an unregulated market price is the rationing device. Thus price will rise. Indeed, price rises until demand again equals supply and the price where this happens is $0.75 per litre. All 15 000 000 litres available are sold and the net revenue of the gas stations has risen to $0.75 per litre. The gain to gas stations (and ultimately the oil producers) is exactly equal to the loss incurred in tax revenue.

Notice that gasoline consumers gain nothing from the tax cut in this example. In other words, gasoline taxes have no effect on the price

consumers pay. Price is determined by demand and supply, and in this example gasoline taxes have no effect on either demand or supply.

Our analysis of a gasoline tax cut illustrates the power of the simple economic analysis introduced in the first five chapters of the text. Apparently common-sense beliefs—such as the belief that gasoline tax cuts will instantly lower gasoline prices—do not always stand up to simple economic analysis. The elementary demand and supply model helps one think about issues in a systematic way and systematic thinking will almost always generate better conclusions.

Professional economists would not be completely satisfied with our analysis thus far, because it is based on the assumption that the supply is fixed in the short term. Over time, supply will increase, perhaps because a higher price diverts oil from the United States or because it leads to more production in Canada. Suppose supply does increase when prices rise (perhaps because some oil fields that were not profitable at a low price become profitable at a higher price). The upward-sloping supply curve (S_0) is added to the model in Figure 2. We begin our analysis of this case by again assuming that the gasoline market is in equilibrium at a price of $0.75 per litre with total sales of $15 000 000 litres. To identify the tax on the demand/supply diagram, note that we can draw a second supply curve parallel to the original supply curve but lower by the amount of the tax (which we assume to be $0.30 per litre). The lower supply curve, S_1, shows the amount suppliers are willing to supply at the net-of-tax price (i.e., at the price they actually receive as opposed to the price consumers pay). In equilibrium, the net revenue of the suppliers and the government tax collections are shown by the shaded rectangles in the diagram.

When the tax is eliminated, the supply curve S_1 becomes the industry supply curve. At a price of $0.75 per litre, suppliers are willing to supply 30 000 000 litres per day.

But if they do supply this amount there will be a surplus of gasoline of 15 000 000 litres. Since a surplus cannot persist we would expect the price to fall. The equilibrium price in this simple model occurs where the original demand curve (D_0) intersects the new supply curve (S_1)—at a price of $0.525 and sales of 18 750 000 litres per day.

A number of additional conclusions can be drawn from the simple model. Governments clearly lose $4.5 million in revenue per day as a result of the tax cut. Consumers buy an additional 3 750 000 litres at the new price of $0.525; thus consumers spend $1 406 250 less on gasoline as a result of the elimination of the tax on gasoline. Finally, the tax cut results in a gain of revenue of $3 093 700 for producers ($0.525 \times 18\,750\,000 - 0.45 \times 15\,000\,000 = \$3.09375$ million).

A sophisticated economic analysis of the tax cut would have to go much further than this. We would, for example, like to know how the government responds to the loss of revenue. Will it cut services or raise taxes in other areas to make up for the shortfall? How will consumers and producers use the leftover funds and extra revenue? The impact of the tax cut will not be restricted to the gasoline market, and one would like to know if the changes in other markets have implications (feedback effects) for the gasoline markets.

The simple model is powerful, but economic analysis typically requires one to do additional work when drawing conclusions.

Questions for Analytical Thinking

1. If, as the simple model suggests, a temporary tax cut is unlikely to eliminate price spikes that arise due to supply shortages, why would politicians advocate such tax cuts? (For one answer to this question see an op-ed article by American economist

Paul Krugman, "Gasoline Tax Follies," *New York Times*, March 15, 2000. This article can be accessed on the Web at **www.pkarchive.org/column/31500.html**.

2. In recent years, society has become increasingly interested in reducing fossil fuel consumption (since fossil fuel consumption results in serious environmental damage). Explain why environmentalists might favour tax increases (as opposed to cuts). Illustrate why a tax increase may not be very effective in the short term, when gasoline supplies are essentially fixed.

3. Write a brief essay explaining why the simple economic analysis of a tax cut and the conclusion that temporary tax cuts are unlikely to eliminate price spikes are more commonsensical than the popular belief that a tax cut will reduce prices by the amount of the tax cut.

Questions 4, 5, and 6 are for students who have taken microeconomics, and are familiar with the concept of elasticity. Elasticity is covered in Chapter 5 of the companion Microeconomics volume to this text.

4. Use the information provided in the case to estimate the elasticities of demand and supply.

5. When supply is not perfectly inelastic, a cut in the gasoline tax will increase consumption. Under what conditions is the tax likely to be an effective way of reducing gasoline consumption (to lessen environmental damage)? (*Hint*: Focus on the elasticity of demand for gasoline.)

6. The impact of a tax cut depends on assumptions about elasticity. Why will the decline in price be larger when demand is inelastic than when demand is elastic?

CBC Video: "The Price at the Pumps," *Marketplace*

Web References for Part One: Introduction to Economics

Economics involves the use of analytical tools (theory) to examine real-world economic phenomena. Statistical information is critically important. Statistics Canada's site (www.statcan.ca/), provides access to statistical information on Canada, including major monthly and quarterly indicators. Students using computers at most Canadian educational institutions can access the Canadian Socio-Economic Information System (CANSIM) using E-Stat (www.statcan.ca/english/ads/estat/index.htm). CANSIM is the most important and comprehensive source of Canadian enonomic data. The Organization for Economic Cooperation and Development (OECD) site (www.oecd.org/) contains useful international statistical information.

News organizations offer information and analysis of economic affairs that can be used to keep abreast of current events and controversies. Excellent sources are the Globe and Mail (www.globeandmail.ca/), the National Post (www.nationalpost.com/), and the CBC (cbc.ca/).

Students at Canadian educational institutions should also be able to access the CBCA (Canadian Business and Current Affairs) Periodical Index through their library's Web connection. The CBCA offers a searchable database of newspaper articles and wire stories. It is a valuable resource.

There are a large number of research institutes in Canada that offer more sophisticated analysis of economic issues than what is offered by news organizations. (It should be borne in mind that some of these institutes can receive funding from special-interest groups and their analysis can reflect a political agenda.) They include the C. D. Howe Institute (www.cdhowe.org/), the Fraser Institute (www.fraserinstitute.ca/), the Canadian Centre for Policy Alternatives (www.policyalternatives.ca/), and the Institute for Research on Public Policy (www.irpp.org/).

Many of the articles of Paul Krugman—an outstanding economist and prolific contributor to popular debate—are accessible to students just beginning to study economics. His writing can be found at the Official Paul Krugman Site (web.mit.edu/krugman/www/) and the Un-official Paul Krugman Site (pkarchive.org/).

Canadian economist Brian MacLean provides regular commentary on recent news articles that is useful, critical, and always entertaining. See Canada's Economy in the Newspapers (www.geocities.com/brian79/macecon.html) and MacLean's Economic Policy Page (www.geocities.com/brian79/).

For up-to-the-minute information and analysis of economic developments in the oil, gas, gasoline, and other energy markets: Crude Oil and Natural Gas Prices (oilprices.com/), Canadian Gasoline Prices (www.gaswatch.org/), and Natural Resources Canada (www.nrcan.gc.ca/es/).

For up-to-date information on and analysis of prices and Canadian agricultural policy, see the Canadian Wheat Board site (www.cwb.ca/) and the Agriculture Canada site (www.agr.ca/policy/epad/english/e-home.htm).

Introduction to Macroeconomics

Learning Objectives

1 Describe the development of Keynesian macroeconomic theory and policy within
the context of the Great Depression and more recent macroeconomic events.

2 Define *inflation*, *aggregate output*, and *unemployment rate*.

3 Define *fiscal policy*, *monetary policy*, and *growth (supply-side) policy*.

4 Describe circular flow.

5 Distinguish among the goods-and-services market, the labour market, and the
money market.

6 Use the aggregate demand and aggregate supply curves to describe movements
of aggregate output and the price level.

7 List three main determinants of long-run growth. Distinguish between long-run
growth and the business cycle.

We now begin our study of macroeconomics. We touched on the
differences between microeconomics and macroeconomics in
Chapter 1. **Microeconomics** is the branch of economics that examines the
functioning of individual industries and the behaviour of individual decision-
making units, typically business firms and households. With a few simple assumptions about how these units behave, we can derive useful conclusions
about how markets work, how resources are allocated, and so forth.

Macroeconomics, instead of focusing on the factors that influence the
production of particular products and the behaviour of individual industries, focuses on the determinants of total national output. Macroeconomics
studies not household income but *national* income, not individual prices
but the *overall* price level. It does not emphasize the demand for labour in
the steel industry but rather total employment in the economy.

Both microeconomics and macroeconomics are concerned with the decisions of households and firms. Microeconomics deals with individual decisions; macroeconomics deals with the sum of these individual decisions.

Aggregate is used in macroeconomics to refer to sums. When we speak
of **aggregate behaviour**, we mean the behaviour of all households and
firms taken together. We also speak of aggregate consumption and aggregate investment, which refer to total consumption and total investment in
the economy.

Microeconomists frequently use the working assumption that market
prices adjust to maintain equality between quantity supplied and quantity

---

**The Roots of
Macroeconomics**
The Great Depression
Recent Macroeconomic History

Macroeconomic Concerns
Inflation
Aggregate Output, the Business
Cycle, and Output Growth
Unemployment

**Government in the
Macroeconomy**

**The Components of the
Macroeconomy**
The Circular Flow Diagram
The Three Market Arenas

**An Introduction to Aggregate
Demand and Aggregate
Supply**

**The Canadian Economy:
Trends and Cycles**
The Canadian Economy Since
1970

microeconomics *The branch of
economics that deals with the
functioning of individual industries
and the behaviour of individual
decision-making units—business
firms and households.*

macroeconomics *The branch of
economics that focuses on the
determinants of such economic
aggregates as national income,
employment, the price level, interest rates, and exchange rates, and
on how government economic policy might be used to influence the
behaviour of these aggregates.*

Chapter 6
Introduction to Macroeconomics

aggregate behaviour *The behaviour of all households and firms taken together.*

sticky prices *Prices that do not always adjust rapidly to maintain equality between quantity supplied and quantity demanded.*

demanded. Macroeconomists, however, observe that many important prices in the economy often seem "sticky." **Sticky prices** are prices that do not always adjust rapidly to maintain equality between quantity supplied and quantity demanded. Most economists would assume that if the quantity of apples supplied exceeded the quantity of apples demanded, the price would fall and the market would clear, because the price of apples is not sticky. But the price of steel, with relatively few producers, appears to be sticky. Wages appear to be sticky too, perhaps because the "units" in the labour market are people rather than commodities. In any case, it appears as if wage rates do not always fall during periods of high unemployment, where the quantity of labour supplied appears to exceed the quantity of labour demanded.

Macroeconomics tackles the question of how government economic policy might be used to influence aggregate behaviour in ways that would affect such aggregates as unemployment and national income. This chapter will introduce the key macroeconomic concepts to be discussed in the remainder of the book.

The Roots of Macroeconomics

THE GREAT DEPRESSION

Great Depression *The period of severe economic contraction and high unemployment that began in 1929 and continued throughout the 1930s.*

Economic events of the 1930s, the decade of the **Great Depression**, spurred a great deal of thinking about macroeconomic issues. With the exception of the Maritimes, the late 1920s had been generally prosperous years for the Canadian economy and the nation's income was rising. Beginning in 1929, however, there was a downturn not only in the Canadian economy, but in the economies of many other countries of the world as well. A number of factors in 1929—the best-known of which were the stock market failures of late 1929—combined to turn a slowdown into the worst economic depression of modern times.

In 1933, the worst year of the Depression in Canada, unemployment stood at close to 20% of the labour force. From 1929 to 1933, production of new goods and services fell by almost 28%. One reason for this severe decline was Canada's close ties to the United States, generally agreed to be the only country in the world more severely affected than Canada. In the United States, the decline in production over the same period was nearly 50%.

■ **Classical Models**   Before the Great Depression, economists generally applied microeconomic models, sometimes referred to as "classical models," to economy-wide problems. (In fact, the word "macroeconomics" was not even invented until after World War II.) For example, classical supply and demand analysis assumed that an excess supply of labour would drive down wages to a new equilibrium level; as a result, unemployment would not persist.

But during the Great Depression unemployment levels remained very high for nearly ten years. In large measure, the failure of simple classical models[1] to explain the prolonged existence of high unemployment provided the impetus for the development of macroeconomics. Thus, it is not surprising that the application of what we now call macroeconomics was born in the 1930s.

■ **The Keynesian Revolution**   One of the most important works in the history of economics, *The General Theory of Employment, Interest and Money*, by John Maynard Keynes, was published in 1936. While other economists had explored similar ideas, it was the theoretical work of Keynes that had worldwide impact.

Much of macroeconomics has deep roots in Keynes's work. According to Keynes, it is not prices and wages that determine the level of employment, as classical models had suggested, but rather the level of aggregate demand for goods and services. Keynes also believed that governments could intervene in the economy and affect the level of output and employment. The government's role during periods when private demand is low, Keynes argued, is to stimulate aggregate

---

[1]*Classical models are also sometimes known as "market clearing" models because they emphasize that prices and wages adjust to ensure that markets always clear—that is, that the quantity supplied is equal to the quantity demanded.*

demand and, by so doing, to lift the economy out of recession. (See the Application box "The Great Depression and John Maynard Keynes.")

RECENT MACROECONOMIC HISTORY

During World War II, Keynes's views began to gain increasing influence over economists and government policy makers in Canada. Increased government spending during the war had a dramatic effect on reducing unemployment. Thus the belief arose that governments could intervene in their economies to attain specific employment and output goals.

In the next decades, the government used its power to tax and spend, as well as its ability to affect interest rates and control the money supply, for the explicit purpose of controlling the economy's ups and downs. The notion that the government could, and should, act to stabilize the macroeconomy was at the height of its popularity in the 1960s when unemployment was typically between 4% and 5%. The phrase **fine tuning** was coined to refer to governments' role in regulating inflation and unemployment. During this period, many economists believed that government could use the tools available to it to manipulate unemployment and inflation levels fairly precisely.

fine tuning *A phrase that refers to the government's role in regulating inflation and unemployment.*

■ **Disillusionment Since the 1970s** The 1970s witnessed the birth of a new phenomenon called **stagflation** (stagnation + inflation). Stagflation occurs when the overall price level rises rapidly (inflation) during periods of recession or high and persistent unemployment (stagnation). Until the 1970s, rapidly rising prices had been observed only in periods when the economy was prospering and unemployment was low (or at least declining). The problem of stagflation proved to be a vexing one, both for macroeconomic theorists and for policy makers concerned with the health of the economy. Policies designed to reduce inflation led to recessions in Canada in both 1980/82 and 1990/91, with especially the latter followed by a long period of slow economic growth with unemployment in excess of 9%. By 2000, inflation was low and unemployment had fallen to about 7%, but this was still well above the unemployment rates of the 1960s.

stagflation *Occurs when the overall price level rises rapidly (inflation) during periods of recession or high and persistent unemployment (stagnation).*

It was clear by the 1970s that the macroeconomy was considerably more difficult to control than textbook theory had led economists to believe. The events of the 1970s, the 1980s, and afterward have had an important influence on macroeconomic theory. Some of the faith in the simple Keynesian model and the "conventional wisdom" of the 1960s has been lost. Yet the central question remains: Even if fine tuning is not possible, can the government use its powers to influence economic activity (e.g., to reduce unemployment), and if so, how? This issue will be the main focus of our discussion of macroeconomics.

Macroeconomic Concerns

Three of the major concerns of macroeconomics are *inflation*, *output growth*, and *unemployment*. Government policy makers would like to have low inflation, and high output and employment. How effective the government can be in achieving these goals is a matter of considerable debate, but the goals themselves are clear.

One troublesome possibility should be kept in mind throughout our discussions:

> Almost all macroeconomic events are interrelated, and making progress on one front may make conditions worse on another front.

For example, some economists believe that the only way to cure inflation is to put the economy into a recession (thereby increasing unemployment and lowering output). Not all the good things we want may be compatible with each other, and thus macroeconomics is rife with tradeoffs.

The Great Depression and John Maynard Keynes

Much of the framework of modern macroeconomics comes from the works of John Maynard Keynes, whose *General Theory of Employment, Interest and Money* was published in 1936. The following excerpt by Robert L. Heilbroner provides some insights into Keynes's life and work.

> It was the unemployment [of the Great Depression] that was hardest to bear. The jobless . . . were like an embolism in the nation's vital circulation; and while their indisputable existence argued more forcibly than any text that something was wrong with the system, the economists wrung their hands and racked their brains ... but could offer neither diagnosis nor remedy. Unemployment—this kind of unemployment—was simply not listed among the possible ills of the system: it was absurd, impossible, unreasonable, and paradoxical. But it was there.
>
> It would seem logical that the man who would seek to solve this impossible paradox of not enough production existing side by side with men fruitlessly seeking work would be a Left-

John Maynard Keynes.

winger, an economist with strong sympathies for the proletariat, an angry man. Nothing could be further from the fact. The man who tackled it was almost a dilettante with nothing like a chip on his shoulder. The simple truth was that his talents inclined in every direction. He had, for example, written a

most recondite book on mathematical probability, a book that Bertrand Russell had declared "impossible to praise too highly"; then he had gone on to match his skill in abstruse logic with a flair for making money— he accumulated a fortune of £500 000 by way of the most treacherous of all roads to riches: dealing in international currencies and commodities. More impressive yet, he had written his mathematics treatise on the side, as it were, while engaged in Government service, and he piled up his private wealth by applying himself for only half an hour a day while still abed.

But this is only a sample of his many-sidedness. He was an economist, of course—a Cambridge don with all the dignity and erudition that go with such an appointment. . . . He managed to be simultaneously the darling of the Bloomsbury set, the cluster of Britain's most avant-garde intellectual brilliants, and also the chairman of a life insurance company, a niche in life rarely noted for its

INFLATION

inflation *An increase in the overall price level.*

hyperinflation *A period of very rapid increases in the overall price level.*

Inflation is an increase in the overall price level. The reduction of inflation has long been a goal of government policy. Especially problematic are **hyperinflations**, or periods of very rapid increases in the overall price level.

Most Canadians are unaware of what life is like under very high inflation. In some countries, however, people are accustomed to prices rising by the day, by the hour, or even by the minute. During the hyperinflation in Bolivia in 1984 and 1985, for example, the price of one egg rose from 3000 pesos to 10 000 pesos in one week. In 1985, three bottles of aspirin sold for the same price as a luxury car had sold for in 1982. At the same time, the problem of handling money became quite burdensome. Banks stopped counting deposits—a deposit worth a few hundred Canadian dollars was equivalent to millions of pesos, and it just did not make sense to count a huge mail sack full of bills. Bolivia's currency, printed in West Germany and England, was the country's third biggest import in 1984, surpassed only by wheat and mining equipment.

Skyrocketing prices in Bolivia are a small part of the story. When inflation approaches 2000% per year, the economy, and indeed the whole organization, of a country begin to break down. Workers may go on strike to demand wage increases

intellectual abandon. He was a pillar of stability in delicate matters of international diplomacy, but his official correctness did not prevent him from acquiring a knowledge of other European politicians that included their ... neuroses and financial prejudices ... He ran a theater, and he came to be a Director of the Bank of England. He knew Roosevelt and Churchill and also Bernard Shaw and Pablo Picasso...

His name was John Maynard Keynes, an old British name (pronounced to rhyme with "rains") that could be traced back to one William de Cahagnes and 1066. Keynes was a traditionalist; he liked to think that greatness ran in families, and it is true that his own father was John Neville Keynes, an illustrious enough economist in his own right. But it took more than the ordinary gifts of heritage to account for the son; it was as if the talents that would have sufficed half a dozen men were by happy accident crowded into one person.

By a coincidence he was

The Prairies were particularly affected by the Depression, as it coincided with droughts that made much of the farmland unworkable. Pictured above is a Saskatchewan farm during the "Dirty Thirties."

born in 1883, in the very year that Karl Marx passed away. But the two economists who thus touched each other in time, although each was to exert the profoundest influence on the philosophy of the capitalist system, could hardly have differed from one another more. Marx was bitter, at bay, heavy and disappointed; as we know, he was the draftsman of Capitalism Doomed. Keynes loved life and sailed through it buoyant, at ease, and consummately successful to become the architect of Capitalism Viable.

Source: Robert L. Heilbroner, *The Worldly Philosophers* (New York: Simon & Schuster, 1961). Reprinted by permission.

in line with the high inflation rate, firms find it almost impossible to secure credit, and the economy grinds to a halt. Dramatic hyperinflations usually end very abruptly. In a few months, Bolivia went from having the highest inflation rate in the world to having one of the lowest inflation rates in the Western Hemisphere.

Luckily, hyperinflations are quite rare. Nonetheless, economists have devoted much effort to identifying (and disputing) the costs and consequences of even moderate inflation. What causes inflation? Who gains from inflation, and who loses? What costs does inflation impose on society, and how severe are they? We will focus on some of these questions in Chapters 8 and 14.

AGGREGATE OUTPUT, THE BUSINESS CYCLE, AND OUTPUT GROWTH

Rather than growing at an even rate at all times, economies tend to experience short-term ups and downs in their performance. The technical name for these ups and downs is the **business cycle**. The main measure of how an economy is doing is **aggregate output**, the total quantity of goods and services produced in the economy in a given period. Clearly, when less is produced (in other words, when aggregate output decreases), there are fewer goods and services to go around, and the

business cycle *The cycle of short-term ups and downs in the economy.*

aggregate output *The total quantity of goods and services produced in an economy in a given period.*

recession *A period during which aggregate output declines. Conventionally, a period in which aggregate output declines for two consecutive quarters.*

depression *A prolonged and deep recession.*

standard of living declines. When firms cut back on production, they also lay off workers, thus increasing the rate of unemployment.

Recessions are periods of time during which aggregate output declines. It has become conventional to classify an economic downturn as a "recession" when aggregate output declines for two consecutive quarters.[2] A prolonged and deep recession is called a **depression**, such as occurred in the 1930s. While, as mentioned previously, many definitions of recessions exist, by all definitions the Canadian economy experienced recessions in 1980/82 and in 1990/91, which coincided with recessions in the United States. But do not put too much stock in these formal classifications. For example, while the Canadian economy began to grow after the 1990/91 recession, the rate of growth was very slow and for some time unemployment continued to rise.

Devising explanations for and predicting the business cycle is one of the main concerns of macroeconomics. The key questions are: Why does the economy fluctuate so much, and why at times does it not seem to respond to the simple forces of supply and demand?

There is more to output than its up-and-down movements during business cycles. Over the long run, the overwhelming trend has been for output to increase. Between 1926 and 2000, the average growth rate in the Canadian economy was just under 4% per year. Because this is about twice the rate of average population growth over this period, there has been a growing amount of goods and services per person. While perhaps not all of this increase has led to a better quality of life, there are obvious benefits. Better access to nutrition and hygiene, and developments in medical care have extended life expectancy and reduced infant mortality. Television and the Internet have given more people access to events and information across the world. Improved, faster transportation has made travel to distant places affordable for most and brought more products from the rest of the world to Canada. In 1926 an orange was a luxury most Canadians could afford only on special occasions; now they are commonplace.

But the rate of output growth is not constant; for example, over the past 30 years it has been somewhat slower. Factors that affect a country's growth rate of output include (1) the growth in the number of workers and their abilities, (2) the growth in the stock of physical capital (that is, the amount and quality of equipment and factories), and (3) technological progress.

Considering each of these in turn, the number of workers depends on population growth from births and immigration. The size and quality of the workforce also depends on population health, education and training, and whether workers have the opportunity to be employed and choose to be employed given the opportunity. Trends to more labour force participation by married women with children, more part-time labour by students, and earlier retirement all affect the amount of available labour. The growth in physical capital depends upon new investment—not only in the private sector but also in the public sector, as roads and electricity generation plants clearly contribute to total production. Technological progress can make both labour and capital more productive and introduce new products and processes; the ongoing computer revolution is an obvious example.

Policy makers in Canada are concerned not only with the recessions of the business cycle but also with policies that might increase the long-run growth rate. Long-run growth issues, which affect almost all aspects of government policy we will discuss, are a particular focus of Chapter 19.

UNEMPLOYMENT

Even if you haven't been unemployed yourself, you probably know someone who has. So it is not surprising that the monthly unemployment data are widely reported. The **unemployment rate**—that is, the percentage of the labour force that is unemployed—is a key indicator of the economy's health.

FAST FACTS

A Canadian born in the 1920s had an average life expectancy of 59 years if male and 61 if female. Now the life expectancy at birth is estimated to be at least 75 for males and 81 for females.

unemployment rate *The percentage of the labour force that is unemployed.*

[2]*There are other, more complex definitions of recessions; for a survey of how some of these apply to Canada, see P. Cross, "Alternative Measures of Business Cycles in Canada: 1947–1992," Canadian Economic Observer, Statistics Canada, Cat. no. 11-010, February 1996.*

Although macroeconomists are interested in learning why the unemployment rate has risen or fallen in a given period, they also try to answer a more basic question: Why is there any unemployment at all? Of course, we do not expect to see zero unemployment. At any given time, some firms may go bankrupt due to competition from rival firms, bad management, or just bad luck. Employees of such firms typically are not able to find new jobs as soon as they have lost their old ones, and while they are looking for work, they will be counted as unemployed. Also, workers entering the labour market for the first time may require some time to find a job.

Graffiti sculpture? No, it's what remains of the Berlin Wall, which had separated the two halves of Berlin between 1961 and 1989, when the Wall was dismantled. Since then, the reunified Germany has faced many economic challenges. Macroeconomics studies not only what has happened in Germany since 1989, but also how economic events in Germany affect the rest of the world.

If we base our analysis on supply and demand, we would expect conditions to change in response to the existence of unemployed workers. Specifically, when there is unemployment beyond some minimum amount, there is an excess supply of workers—at the going wage rates, there are people who want to work who cannot find work. In microeconomic theory, the response to excess supply is a decrease in the price of the commodity in question and therefore an increase in the quantity demanded, a reduction in the quantity supplied, and the restoration of equilibrium. With the quantity supplied equal to the quantity demanded, the market clears.

The existence of unemployment seems to imply that the aggregate labour market is not in equilibrium—that something prevents the quantity supplied and the quantity demanded from equating. But why do labour markets not clear when so many other markets do? Or is it that labour markets are clearing and the unemployment data are reflecting something different? The implications of the unemployment data are a major puzzle in macroeconomics and a major focus of Chapters 8 and 15.

Government in the Macroeconomy

Much of our discussion of macroeconomics concerns the potential role of government in influencing the economy. There are three kinds of policy that the government has used to influence the macroeconomy:

Government Policies for Influencing the Macroeconomy:	1. Fiscal policy 2. Monetary policy 3. Growth or supply-side policy

■ **Fiscal Policy** One way in which the federal government affects the economy is through its tax and expenditure decisions, or **fiscal policy**. The federal government collects taxes from households and firms and spends these funds on various items ranging from naval ships to parks to social insurance payments to the Trans-Canada Highway. Both the magnitude and the composition of these taxes and expenditures have a major effect on the economy.

One of Keynes's main ideas in the 1930s was that fiscal policy could and should be used to stabilize the level of output and employment in the economy. More specifically, Keynes believed that the government should cut taxes and/or raise spending—so-called *expansionary fiscal policies*—to get the economy out of a slump. Conversely, he held that the government should raise taxes and/or cut spending—so-called *contractionary fiscal policies*—to bring the economy out of an inflation.

■ **Monetary Policy** Taxes and spending are not the only variables that the government controls. Through the Bank of Canada, the country's central bank, the

fiscal policy *Government policies regarding taxes and expenditures.*

government can influence the quantity of money in the economy. The effects and proper role of **monetary policy** are among the most hotly debated subjects in macroeconomics. Most economists agree that the quantity of money supplied affects the overall price level, interest rates and exchange rates, the unemployment rate, and the level of output. The main controversies arise regarding how monetary policy manifests itself and exactly how large its effects are.

■ **Growth Policies** Clearly, there are many government policies that might increase long-run growth. These include policies involving both government expenditure and revenue. The government might spend on education and training to improve the abilities and knowledge of the workforce (sometimes called human capital). Government expenditure on infrastructure such as roads, bridges, airports, and harbours may enhance productivity. Research financed by government may enhance technological progress, by means ranging from finding crop varieties more suited to the Canadian climate to finding better treatments for disease. With respect to government revenue, some economists worry that high taxes may discourage effort, saving, and investment, and hence, they advocate a less active and costly government so that tax rates can be lowered. But there is disagreement as to how large these disincentive effects are and hence how effective tax cuts may be.

The Components of the Macroeconomy

Macroeconomics focuses on four groups: *households* and *firms* (the private sector), the *government* (the public sector), and the *rest of the world* (the international sector). These four groups interact in a variety of ways, many of which involve either the receipt or the payment of income.

THE CIRCULAR FLOW DIAGRAM

A useful way of seeing the economic interactions among the four groups in the economy is to examine a **circular flow** diagram, which shows the income received and payments made by each sector. A simple circular flow diagram is pictured in Figure 6.1.

Let's walk through the circular flow step by step. Households work for firms and the government, and they receive wages for their work. Hence our diagram shows a flow of wages *into* the household sector as payment for those services. Households also receive interest on corporate and government bonds and dividends from firms. Many households receive other payments from the government, such as social insurance benefits, veterans' benefits, and welfare payments. Economists call these kinds of payments from the government (for which the recipients do not supply goods, services, or labour) **transfer payments**. Together, these receipts make up the total income received by the households.

Households spend by buying goods and services from firms and by paying taxes to the government. These items make up the total amount paid out by the households. The difference between the total receipts and the total payments of the households is the amount that the households save or dissave.[3] If households receive more than they spend, they *save* during the period. If they receive less than they spend, they *dissave*. A household can dissave by using up some of its previous savings or by borrowing. In the circular flow diagram, household spending is shown as a flow *out* of the household sector.

Firms sell goods and services to households and the government. These sales earn revenue, which shows up in the circular flow diagram as a flow of funds *into* the firm sector. Firms pay wages, interest, and dividends to households, and they pay taxes to the government. These payments are shown as flowing *out* of the firm sector.

The government collects taxes from households and firms. The government also makes payments. It buys goods and services from firms, pays wages and interest to

---

[3]*Saving by households is sometimes termed a "leakage" from the circular flow, because it withdraws income, or current purchasing power, from the system.*

households, and makes transfer payments to households. If the government's revenue is less than its payments, the government is dissaving.

Finally, households spend some of their income on *imports*—goods and services produced in the rest of the world. Similarly, people in foreign countries purchase *exports*—goods and services produced by domestic firms and sold to other countries.

One lesson of the circular flow diagram is that everyone's expenditure is someone else's receipt. If you buy computer software from Corel Corporation, you make a payment to Corel and Corel receives revenue. If Corel pays taxes to the government, it has made a payment and the government has received revenue.

> Everyone's expenditures go somewhere. It is impossible to sell something without there being a buyer, and it is impossible to make a payment without there being a recipient. Every transaction must have two sides.

THE THREE MARKET ARENAS

Another way of looking at the ways households, firms, the government, and the rest of the world relate to each other is to consider the markets in which they interact, as depicted in Figure 6.2.

FIGURE 6.1

The Circular Flow of Payments

Households receive income from firms and the government, purchase goods and services from firms, and pay taxes to the government. They also purchase foreign-made goods and services (imports). Firms receive payments from households and the government for goods and services; they pay wages, dividends, interest, and rents to households, and taxes to the government. The government receives taxes from both firms and households, pays both firms and households for goods and services—including wages to government workers—and pays interest and transfers to households. Finally, people in other countries purchase goods and services produced domestically (exports). *Note:* Though not shown in this diagram, firms and governments also purchase imports, firms purchase goods from each other, and firms may receive subsidies from government.

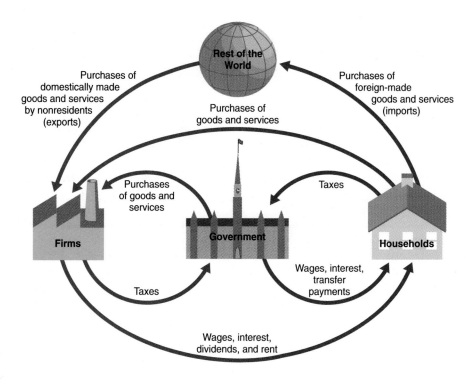

> The Three Market Arenas:
> 1. Goods-and-services market
> 2. Labour market
> 3. Money (financial) market

■ **Goods-and-Services Market** Households and the government purchase goods and services from firms in the *goods-and-services market*. In this market, firms also purchase goods and services from each other. For example, Bombardier buys steel from other firms to make its snowmobiles. In addition, firms buy capital goods from other firms. If Molson needs new equipment on its assembly lines, it will probably buy it from another firm rather than make it itself.

Firms *supply* to the goods-and-services market. Households, the government, and firms *demand* from this market. Finally, the rest of the world both buys from and sells to the goods-and-services market.

■ **Labour Market** Interaction in the *labour market* takes place when firms and the government purchase labour from households. In this market, households *supply* labour, and firms and the government *demand* labour. In the Canadian economy, firms are the largest demanders of labour, although the government is also a substantial employer. The total supply of labour in the economy depends on the sum of decisions made by households. Individuals must decide whether to enter the labour force (whether to look for a job at all) and how many hours to work.

■ **Money Market** In the *money market*—sometimes called the *financial market*—households purchase stocks and bonds from firms. Households *supply* funds to this market in the expectation of earning extra income in the form of dividends on stocks and interest on bonds. Households also *demand* (borrow) funds from this market to finance various purchases. Firms borrow to build new facilities in the hope of earning more in the future. The government borrows by issuing bonds. The rest of the world both borrows from and lends to the money market; every morning you can now hear reports on the radio about the U.S. and Japanese financial markets. Much of the borrowing and lending of households, firms, the government, and the international sector is coordinated by financial institutions—commercial banks, insurance companies, and the like. These institutions take deposits from one group and lend them to others.

When a firm, a household, or the government borrows to finance a purchase, it has an obligation to pay that loan back, usually at some specified time in the future. Most loans also involve payment of interest as a fee for the use of the

FIGURE 6.2

The Three Basic Markets

Households, firms, the government, and the rest of the world all interact in the goods-and-services, labour, and money markets.

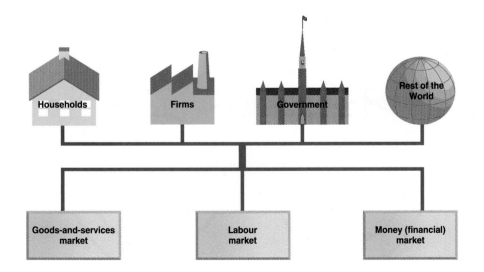

borrowed funds. When a loan is made, the borrower nearly always signs a "promise to repay," or *promissory note*, and gives it to the lender. When the federal government borrows, it issues "promises" called **government bonds**, **notes**, or **Treasury bills** in exchange for money. Corporations issue **corporate bonds**. A corporate bond might state, for example, "Nova Corporation agrees to pay $5000 to the holder of this bond on January 1, 2005, and interest thereon at 8.3% annually until that time."

Instead of issuing bonds to raise funds, firms can also issue shares of stock. A **share of stock** is a financial instrument that gives the holder a share in the firm's ownership and therefore the right to share in the firm's profits. If the firm does well, the value of the stock increases, and the stockholder receives a *capital gain*[4] on the initial purchase. In addition, the stock may pay **dividends**—that is, the firm may choose to return some of its profits directly to its stockholders, rather than retaining them internally to buy capital.

One of the critical variables in the money market is the *interest rate*. Interest rates will be a focus in later chapters.

government bonds, notes, and **Treasury bills** *Promissory notes issued by the federal government when it borrows money.*

corporate bonds *Promissory notes issued by corporations when they borrow money.*

shares of stock *Financial instruments that give to the holder a share in the firm's ownership and therefore the right to share in the firm's profits.*

dividends *The portion of a corporation's profits that the firm pays out every period to its shareholders.*

An Introduction to Aggregate Demand and Aggregate Supply

A main goal of our macroeconomic models is to explain business cycle fluctuations in output (and hence employment) and the price level. Our basic approach will be to analyze the behaviour of aggregate demand and aggregate supply. **Aggregate demand** is the total demand for goods and services in an economy. **Aggregate supply** is the total supply of goods and services in an economy.

Eventually (by Chapter 14) we will use these concepts in a model of both output and the price level. As it might help to see what this model will look like in diagram form, examine the *aggregate demand* and *aggregate supply* curves in Figure 6.3. Measured on the horizontal axis is aggregate output. Measured on the vertical axis is the *overall price level*, not the price of a particular good or service. (This is a very important point—be sure to keep it in mind.) The economy is in equilibrium at the point at which these curves intersect.

As you will discover, aggregate demand and supply curves are much more complicated than the simple demand and supply curves that we described in Chapters 4 and 5. The simple logic of supply, demand, and equilibrium in individual markets does not explain what is depicted in Figure 6.3. Indeed, it will take us the entire next chapter just to describe what is meant by "aggregate output" and the "overall price level." Furthermore, although we will look to the behaviour of households and firms in individual markets for clues about how to analyze aggregate behaviour, there are important differences when we move from the individual to the aggregate level.

However, the reason we are giving you this preview is so that you can begin to see how a model such as this might help distinguish between different types of macroeconomic events. Figure 6.4 illustrates a rightward shift in the aggregate demand curve, that is, an increase in the level of aggregate output demanded at every price level. As we will discuss in future chapters, this might be due to an expansionary fiscal policy such as an increase in government spending, or to an expansionary monetary policy that stimulated investment spending or export spending. The point for now is that you can see the extra spending has two effects: it increases aggregate output but the extra economic activity also puts upward pressure on the price level. How much output will increase and how much the price level will increase depends on such factors as the slope of the aggregate supply curve.

From about World War II to the early 1970s, most economists emphasized shifts in aggregate demand and felt that the policy choice was whether to pursue expansionary policies such as are illustrated in Figure 6.4. The choice then became

aggregate demand *The total demand for goods and services in an economy.*

aggregate supply *The total supply of goods and services in an economy.*

---

[4] A capital gain *occurs whenever the value of an asset increases. If you bought a stock for $1000 and it is now worth $1500, you have earned a capital gain of $500.*

FIGURE 6.3

The Aggregate Demand and Aggregate Supply Curves

A major theme in macroeconomics is the behaviour of aggregate demand and aggregate supply. Note the aggregate demand and aggregate supply curves are *not* the same as the simple demand and supply curves described in Chapters 4 and 5.

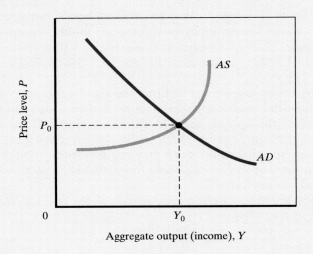

a tradeoff between the increase in output (reducing unemployment) and the increase in the price level that would boost inflation. But as we described earlier in this chapter, this view was shaken by the stagflation of the 1970s, when unemployment and inflation worsened simultaneously. Stagflation is represented as a leftward (or upward) shift of the aggregate supply curve, so that, at every given level of output, firms increase prices (and hence the price level increases). The result is an increase in price level plus a fall in output, as shown in Figure 6.5. One reason firms might have increased prices in this manner in the 1970s was the sharp increase in the world price of oil. We will study other possible reasons.

Growth policies such as those discussed earlier might tend to increase productivity, allowing firms to increase output at any given price level and hence shift the aggregate supply curve to the right. Such policies are sometimes called **supply-side policies.** But our aggregate demand/aggregate supply model is a short-run one, not fully suited to analyzing long-run growth, so we will postpone further discussion of this point until later chapters.

Because of the complexity of the aggregate demand and aggregate supply curves, we will need to build our analysis piece by piece. In Chapter 7, we discuss the methods of measuring economic activity and aggregate output. In Chapter 8, we describe the key macroeconomic problems of business cycles, inflation, and unemployment. Chapters 9 through 14 present the material we need to understand the equilibrium levels of aggregate output and the overall price level. In these chapters, we discuss the behaviour of households, firms, and the government in both the goods-and-services market and the money market. Chapter 15 brings the labour market into the picture. Later chapters elaborate on this material and discuss a number of important macroeconomic policy issues.

The Canadian Economy: Trends and Cycles

Macroeconomics is concerned both with long-run trends—Why has the Canadian economy done so well over the past 100 years while Great Britain's has done rather poorly?—and with short-run fluctuations in economic performance—Why did the world experience a severe recession in the early 1980s? Most of this part of the text focuses on short-run fluctuations because they are somewhat better understood. As we mentioned earlier in this chapter, these short-term ups and downs in the economy are known as the *business cycle*. A stylized business cycle is illustrated in Figure 6.6.

Because on average the Canadian economy grows over time, the business cycle in Figure 6.6 shows an overall positive trend—the *peak*, or the highest point, of a

supply-side policies
Government policies that focus on aggregate supply and increasing production rather than stimulating aggregate demand.

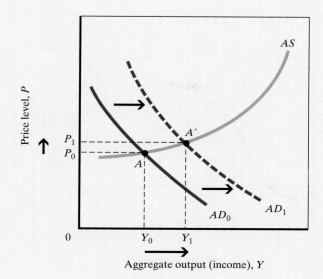

FIGURE 6.4

Shift of the Aggregate Demand Curve

A rightward shift of the aggregate demand curve will increase both equilibrium output and the equilibrium price level.

new business cycle is higher than the peak of the previous cycle. The period from a *trough*, or bottom of the cycle, to a peak is called an **expansion** or a **boom**. During an expansion, output and employment grow. The period from a peak to a trough is called a **contraction**, **recession**, or **slump**. During a recession, output and employment fall.

In judging whether an economy is expanding or contracting, it is important to note the difference between the level of economic activity and its rate of change. If, for example, the economy has just left a trough (point *A* in Figure 6.6), it will be growing (rate of change is positive), but its level of output will still be low. Conversely, if the economy has just started to decline from a peak (point *B* in Figure 6.6), it will be contracting (rate of change is negative), but its level of output will still be high.

expansion or **boom** *The period in the business cycle from a trough up to a peak, during which output and employment rise.*

contraction, **recession**, or **slump** *The period in the business cycle from a peak down to a trough, during which output and employment fall.*

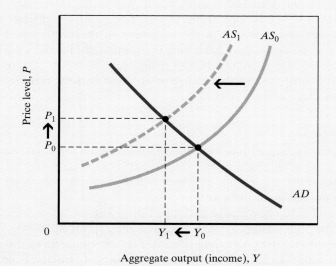

FIGURE 6.5

Shift of the Aggregate Supply Curve

A leftward shift of the aggregate supply curve will lead to a fall in equilibrium output and an increase in the equilibrium price level.

FIGURE 6.6

A Stylized Business Cycle

In this business cycle, the economy is expanding as it moves through point *A* from the trough to the peak. When the economy moves from a peak down to a trough, through point *B*, the economy is in recession.

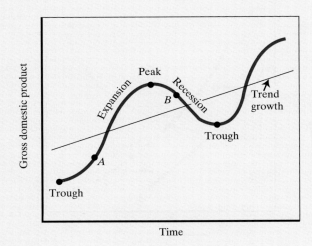

The business cycle in Figure 6.6 is symmetric, which means that the length of an expansion is the same as the length of a contraction. All business cycles are not symmetric, however. It is possible, for example, for the expansion phase to be longer than the contraction phase. When contraction comes, it may be fast and sharp, while expansion may be slow and gradual. Moreover, the economy is not nearly as regular as the business cycle in Figure 6.6 indicates. While there are ups and downs in the economy, they tend to be fairly erratic.

What do actual business cycles in Canada look like? You can see the answer to this question in Figure 6.7, where Canadian GDP per capita is plotted for the 1926–2000 period. (GDP, or gross domestic product, is a measure of national output). While the economy has obviously experienced tremendous growth over this period, the progression has not been smooth. The peaks and troughs of the business cycles are apparent, and each business cycle has been unique. The economy is not so simple that it has regular cycles.

The periods of the Great Depression and World War II are clearly the most striking points of Figure 6.7, although other contractions and expansions have taken place. In particular, the recessions at the beginning of the 1980s and 1990s are noteworthy. Some of the cycles have been long in duration, and some have been very short. You can see that the economy did not really come out of the Depression until World War II. It is also evident that the economy was slow to recover from the 1990–91 recession.

THE CANADIAN ECONOMY SINCE 1970

Since 1970, the Canadian economy has seen three recessions and large fluctuations in the rate of inflation. By analyzing how the various parts of the economy behaved during these hectic times, we can learn a lot about macroeconomic behaviour. The following chapters concentrate on these years.

Figures 6.8, 6.9, and 6.10 show the behaviour of three key variables during the period since 1970: GDP, the unemployment rate, and the rate of inflation. These graphs are based on quarterly data (i.e., data compiled for each quarter of the year) rather than on annual data. The first quarter of a year consists of January, February, and March; the second quarter consists of April, May, and June; and so on. The numerals I, II, III, and IV denote the four quarters. (For example, "1972 III" refers to the third quarter, or summer, of 1972.)

FIGURE 6.7

Real GDP per Capita, 1926–2000

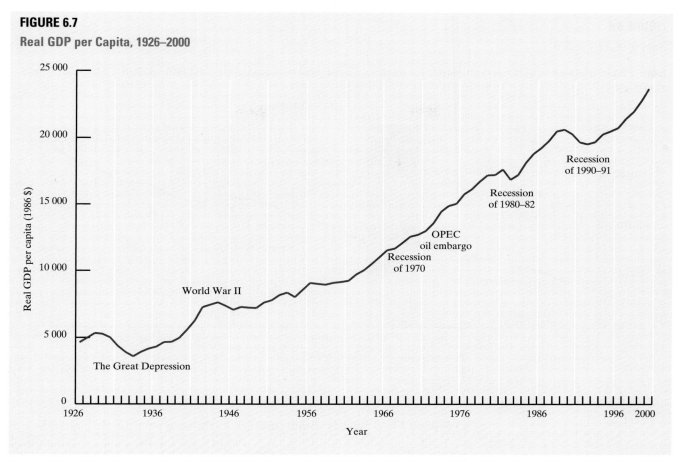

Source: Adapted from Statistics Canada, CANSIM database, Series D31248, D14442; *Bank of Canada Banking and Financial Statistics,* Table A2, June 2000; and B. G. Spencer, C. H. Feaver, and F. T. Denton, unpublished population estimates, McMaster University, January 2000. Data for 2000 based on first quarter.

Figure 6.8 plots GDP for the period 1970 I–2000 I. In the following chapters we will focus particularly on two recessionary periods within this period: 1980 II–1982 IV and 1990 II–1991 I. These periods make useful reference points when we examine how other variables behave during these periods.[5]

One concern of macroeconomics is unemployment. Unemployment generally rises during recessions and falls during expansions. This can be seen clearly in Figure 6.9, which plots the unemployment rate for the period 1970 I–2000 I. During the 1980–1982 recession, the unemployment rate reached a maximum of 12.6% in the fourth quarter of 1982. The unemployment rate continued to rise after the 1990–1991 recession and reached a peak of 11.6% in 1992 IV, falling more or less steadily after that.

Macroeconomics is also concerned with the inflation rate. A measure of the overall price level is the GDP deflator, an economy-wide price index. (The construction of the GDP deflator, also known as the GDP price deflator or GDP price index, is discussed in the next chapter. It is an index of prices of all domestically produced goods in the economy.) The percentage change in the GDP deflator provides one measure of the overall rate of inflation. Figure 6.10 plots the percentage change in the GDP deflator for the 1970 I–2000 I period.[6] For reference purposes,

---

[5]As Figure 6.8 shows, GDP rose in the fourth quarter of 1980 before falling again in the third quarter of 1981. Given this fact, one possibility would be to treat the 1980 II–1982 IV period as if it included two separate recessionary periods: 1980 II–1980 III and 1981 III–1982 IV. Because the expansion between these periods was so short-lived, however, they are generally considered a single recession.

[6]The percentage change in Figure 6.10 is the percentage change year-over-year. For example, the value for 1970 I is the percentage change from 1969 I, the value for 1970 II is the percentage change from 1969 II, and so on.

FIGURE 6.8

Real GDP, 1970 I–2000 I

Real GDP in Canada since 1970 has risen overall, but there have been three recessionary periods: 1970 I–1970 II, 1980 II–1982 IV, and 1990 II–1991 I.

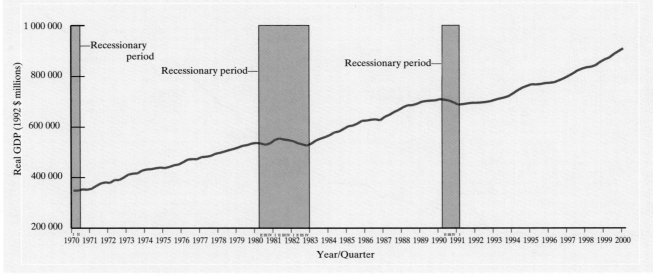

Source: Statistics Canada, CANSIM database, Series 14872.

we have picked two periods within this time as showing particularly high inflation: 1973 IV–1975 I and 1979 II–1981 IV. In the first period, the inflation rate peaked at 15.1% in the second quarter of 1974. In the second period, it peaked at 11.4% in the first quarter of 1981. Since 1983, the rate of inflation has been quite low by the standards of the 1970s and by this measure was even negative for a time in the late 1990s. In the first quarter of 2000 it was 3.3%.

Macroeconomics tries to explain the behaviour of and the connections among variables such as GDP, the unemployment rate, and the GDP deflator. In the next chapter we will begin by discussing the first variable, GDP, and how it is calculated.

FIGURE 6.9

Unemployment Rate, 1970 I–2000 I

The Canadian unemployment rate since 1970 shows wide variations. The1980/82 and 1990/91 recessionary periods show particularly large increases.

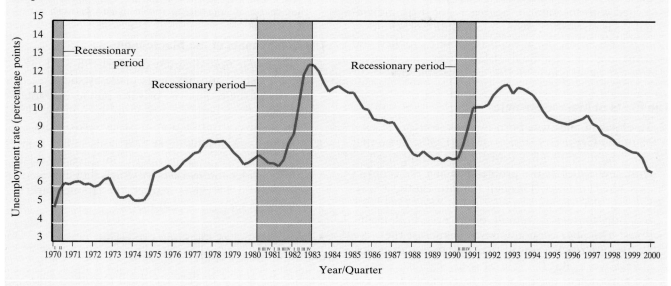

Source: 1970–1975: Adapted from Statistics Canada, *Historical Labour Force Statistics*, Cat. no. 71-201; 1976–1996: Adapted from Statistics Canada, CANSIM database, Series D767611; 1997–2000: Adapted from Statistics Canada, CANSIM database, Series D980745.

FIGURE 6.10

Percentage Change in the GDP Deflator (year-over-year, by quarter), 1970 I–2000 I

The percentage change in the GDP deflator measures the overall rate of inflation. Since 1970, inflation has been high in two periods: 1973 IV–1975 I and 1979 II–1981 IV. Inflation since 1983 has been moderate.

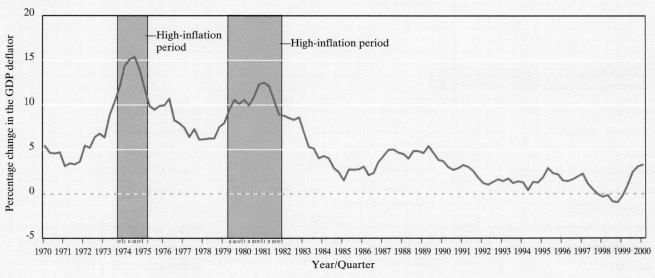

Source: Adapted from Statistics Canada, CANSIM database, Series D15612.

Summary

1. *Microeconomics* examines the functioning of individual industries and the behaviour of individual decision-making units. *Macroeconomics* is concerned with the sum, or aggregate, of these individual decisions—the consumption of *all* households in the economy, the amount of labour supplied and demanded by *all* individuals and firms, the total amount of *all* goods and services produced.

The Roots of Macroeconomics

2. Macroeconomics was born out of the effort to explain the *Great Depression* of the 1930s. Since that time, the discipline has evolved, concerning itself with new issues as the problems facing the economy have changed. Through the late 1960s, it was believed that the government could "fine tune" the economy to keep it running on an even keel at all times. The poor economic performance of the 1970s and 1980s showed that *fine tuning* does not always work. But the central issue remains: Can the government use its power to influence the level of economic activity (e.g., to reduce unemployment), and if so, how?

Macroeconomic Concerns

3. The three topics of primary concern to macroeconomists are increases in the overall price level, or *inflation*; the growth rate of aggregate output; and the level of employment.

Government in the Macroeconomy

4. Among the tools that governments have available to them for influencing the macroeconomy are *fiscal policy* (decisions on taxes and government spending); *monetary policy* (control of the money supply); and *growth* or *supply-side policies* (policies that focus on increasing the long-run growth rate).

The Components of the Macroeconomy

5. The *circular flow* diagram shows the flow of income received and payments made by the three sectors of the economy—private, public, and international. Everybody's expenditure is someone else's receipt—every transaction must have two sides.

6. Another way of looking at how households, firms, the government, and the international sector relate is to consider the markets in which they interact: the goods-and-services market, the labour market, and the money (financial) market.

An Introduction to Aggregate Demand and Aggregate Supply

7. A major theme in macroeconomics is the behaviour of *aggregate demand* and *aggregate supply*. The logic underlying the aggregate demand and supply curves is much more complex than the logic underlying simple individual market demand and supply curves.

The Canadian Economy: Trends and Cycles

8. Macroeconomics is concerned with both long-run trends and the short-run fluctuations that are part of the *business cycle*. Since 1970, the Canadian economy has seen three recessions and large fluctuations in the rate of *inflation*.

Review Terms and Concepts

aggregate behaviour 114

aggregate demand 123

aggregate output 117

aggregate supply 123

business cycle 117

circular flow 120

contraction, recession, or slump 125

corporate bonds 123

depression 118

dividends 123

expansion or boom 125

fine tuning 115

fiscal policy 119

government bonds, notes, and Treasury bills 123

Great Depression 114

hyperinflation 116

inflation 116

macroeconomics 113

microeconomics 113

monetary policy 120

recession 118

shares of stock 123

stagflation 115

sticky prices 114

supply-side policies 124

transfer payments 120

unemployment rate 118

1. The economy was one of the major issues during the 1993 federal election. Most people believed that the economy was in recession. However, a careful look at the data shows that GDP stopped falling and began growing in the spring of 1991. In other words, the recession ended well before the election. What was it about the economy that led the public to perceive things as so bad? (Hint: Think about the labour market.)

2. During the late 1990s, the economy continued to recover from the recession of the early 1990s. However, different regions of the economy were growing at very different rates.

   Describe the economy of your province. What is the most recently reported unemployment rate? How has the number of payroll jobs changed over the past three months? The past year? How does your region's performance compare to the Canadian economy's performance over the past year? What explanations have been offered in the press? How accurate are these?

3. Explain briefly how macroeconomics is different from microeconomics. How can macroeconomists use microeconomic theory to guide them in their work, and why might they wish to do so?

4. In 2000, a company paid its blue-collar employees $10 per hour but its white-collar employees only $8 per hour. It gave all employees a $1 raise in 2001, so that blue-collar employees were making $11 and white-collar employees $9 per hour. Yet the average wage paid to all employees in the company actually declined between 2000 and 2001. How is this possible? How does this question have anything to do with macroeconomics?

5. The federal budgets of 1994 and especially 1995 brought in large cuts in government spending at a time when the economy was recovering slowly from the 1990–1991 recession. These cuts were designed to reduce the federal deficit but some who opposed them argued that the government was pursuing contractionary fiscal policy at the wrong time. Explain their logic.

6. A major expansionary period in the Canadian economy occurred during World War II. The U.S. economy experienced expansion during the Korean and Vietnam wars. Why do you think expansion occurs during wartime?

7. "In the 1940s, one could buy a bottle of pop for 5 cents, eat dinner at a restaurant for less than a dollar, and purchase a house for $10 000. From this statement, it follows that consumers today are worse off than consumers in the 1940s." Comment.

*8. During the late 1980s, the Bank of Canada was increasingly concerned with inflation. As the economy grew more rapidly, the Bank acted to raise interest rates. This policy was designed to slow the rate of spending growth in the economy. How might higher interest rates be expected to slow the rate of spending growth? Give some examples.

9. The text mentions that during the hyperinflation in Bolivia, so much paper money was required for a transaction that it became burdensome. Clearly this problem could have been solved simply by issuing new bank notes with more zeroes, so that fewer notes denominated in millions or billions could have been used instead of a sackful of notes denominated in thousands. Think of other problems that a very rapid rate of inflation would cause and suggest possible full or partial solutions.

7

Measuring National Output, National Income, and the Price Level

Gross Domestic Product
"Final Goods and Services"

"Produced Within a Given Period of Time"

"By Factors of Production Located Within a Country"

Calculating GDP
The Expenditure Approach

The Income Approach

From GDP to Personal Income

Nominal Versus Real GDP
Calculating Real GDP

Measuring the Price Level
The GDP Deflator

The Consumer Price Index

Limitations of the GDP Concept
GDP and Social Welfare

The Underground Economy

Per Capita GDP/GNP

Looking Ahead

national income and expenditure accounts *Data collected and published by the government describing the various components of aggregate income and output in the economy.*

gross domestic product (*GDP*) *The total market value of all final goods and services produced within a given period by factors of production located within a country.*

Learning Objectives

1 Define *GDP*. Explain the difference between GDP and GNP.
2 Explain how to use the expenditure approach when calculating GDP. Define *value added*.
3 Explain how to use the income approach when calculating GDP.
4 Distinguish between real GDP and nominal GDP.
5 Explain how the GDP price deflator and the consumer price index are calculated.
6 Outline the shortcomings of per capita GDP as a measure of social well-being.

Macroeconomics relies on data, much of it collected by the government. To study the economy, we need data on total output, total income, total consumption, and the like. One of the main sources of these data are the **national income and expenditure accounts,** which describe the various components of aggregate income in the economy.

The national income and expenditure accounts do more than convey data about the performance of the economy. They also provide an important conceptual framework that macroeconomists use to think about how the various pieces of the economy fit together. When an economist thinks about the macroeconomy, the categories and vocabulary he or she uses come from the national income and expenditure accounts.

The national accounts can be compared to the mechanical or wiring diagrams for an automobile engine. The diagrams by themselves do not explain how an engine works, but they do identify and name the key parts of the engine and show how they are connected.

Gross Domestic Product

The key concept in the national income and expenditure accounts is **gross domestic product**, or **GDP**.

> GDP is the total market value of a country's output. It is the market value of all final goods and services produced within a given period of time by factors of production located within a country.

Canadian GDP—the value of all the output produced by factors of production in Canada—was about $1 trillion in 2000. Let us analyze the definition phrase by phrase.

"FINAL GOODS AND SERVICES"

Goods and services produced refers to **final goods and services**. Many goods are **intermediate goods**; they are produced by one firm for use in further processing by another firm. Steel sold to appliance manufacturers is an intermediate good. The value of intermediate goods is not counted in GDP.

Why aren't intermediate goods counted in GDP? Suppose that in producing a car GM pays $100 for tires. GM uses these tires (among other components) to assemble a car, which it then sells for $12 000. The value of the car (including its tires) is $12 000, not $12 000 + $100. In other words, the final price of the car already reflects the value of all its components. To count in GDP both the value of the tires sold to the automobile manufacturers and the value of the automobiles sold to the consumers would result in double-counting.

Double-counting can also be avoided by counting only the value added to a product by each firm in its production process. The **value added** during some stage of production is the difference between the value of goods as they leave that stage of production and the cost of the goods as they entered that stage. Value added is illustrated in Table 7.1. The four stages of the production of a litre of milk are (1) raw milk, (2) processing, (3) shipping, and (4) retail sale. In the first stage of production, value added is simply the value of sales. In the second stage, the dairy purchases the milk from the farmer, processes it, and sells it to the shipper. The dairy pays the farmer $0.70 per litre and charges the shipper $1. The value added by the dairy is thus $0.30 per litre. The shipper then sells the milk to retailers for $1.20. The value added in the third stage of production is thus $0.20. Finally, the retailer sells the milk to consumers for $1.50. The value added at the fourth stage is $0.30, and the total value added in the production process is $1.50, the same as the value of sales at the retail level. Adding the total values of sales at each stage of production ($0.70 + $1 + $1.20 + $1.50 = $4.40) would significantly overestimate the value of the litre of milk.

Hence the contribution to GDP from the litre of milk can be computed two equivalent ways: the $1.50 at the final stage as it is sold to the consumer or the total value added, also $1.50.

> In calculating GDP, we can either sum up the value added at each stage of production or take the value of final sales. We do not want to use the value of total sales in an economy to measure how much output has been produced.

"PRODUCED WITHIN A GIVEN PERIOD OF TIME"

GDP is concerned only with new, or current, production. Old output is not counted in current GDP because it was already counted at the time it was produced. It would be double-counting to count sales of used goods in current GDP. If someone sells a used car to you, the transaction is not counted in GDP, because no new production has taken place. Similarly, the cost of building a house is counted in GDP only at the time it is built, not each time it is resold. In short:

> GDP ignores all transactions in which money or goods change hands but in which no new goods and services are produced.

Sales of stocks and bonds are also not counted in GDP. These sales are merely exchanges of paper assets and do not correspond to current production. But what if I sell the stock or bond for more than I originally paid for it? Profits from the stock or bond market have nothing to do with current production, so they are not counted in GDP. However, if I pay a fee to a broker for selling a stock of mine to someone else, this fee is counted in GDP, because the broker is performing a service for me. This service is part of current production.

final goods and services *Goods and services produced for final use.*

intermediate goods *Goods that are produced by one firm for use in further processing by another firm.*

value added *The difference between the value of goods as they leave a stage of production and the cost of the goods as they entered that stage.*

Table 7.1	Value Added in the Production of a Litre of Milk (hypothetical numbers)	
Stage of Production	**Value of Sales**	**Value Added**
(1) Raw milk	$0.70	$0.70
(2) Processing	1.00	0.30
(3) Shipping	1.20	0.20
(4) Retail sale	1.50	0.30
Total value added		1.50

"BY FACTORS OF PRODUCTION LOCATED WITHIN A COUNTRY"

> GDP is the value of output produced by factors of production *located within a country.*

The three basic factors of production are land, labour, and capital. The labour of Canadian residents counts as a domestically owned factor of production for Canada. The output produced by Canadians abroad (for example, Canadians working for a foreign company) should *not* be counted in Canadian GDP, because the output is not produced within Canada. Likewise, profits earned abroad by Canadian companies should not be counted in Canadian GDP. However, profits earned in Canada by foreign-owned companies are counted in Canadian GDP.

It is sometimes useful to have a measure of the output produced by factors of production owned by a country's residents regardless of where the output is produced. This measure is called **gross national product,** or **GNP.** For most countries, including Canada, the difference between GDP and GNP is small.[1] In 1999, GNP for Canada was $919.4 billion, which is close to the $949.4 billion value for Canadian GDP.

GNP is calculated from GDP by adding in investment income paid by nonresidents to residents of Canada less investment income paid by residents of Canada to nonresidents. Canadian GNP is lower than Canadian GDP because more interest, profits, and dividends flow out of Canada than into Canada.

In principle, there should also be an adjustment for labour income. When a band from Newfoundland goes to New York to give a concert, in principle their payment should be part of Canadian GNP but not Canadian GDP, because it was earned by residents of Canada but not within Canada's borders. Similarly if a U.S. resident from Sweetgrass, Montana works as a mechanic just across the border in Coutts, Alberta, in principle the wage that person earns should be part of Canadian GDP but not part of Canadian GNP. However, Statistics Canada does not make these kinds of adjustments, because although the net adjustments would be small they would be difficult and expensive to calculate.

The distinction between GDP and GNP can be tricky. Consider the Honda plant in Alliston, Ontario. The plant is owned by the Honda Corporation, a Japanese firm, although most of the workers employed at the plant are Canadian workers. Although all of the output of the plant is included in Canadian GDP, only part of it is included in Canadian GNP. The wages paid to Canadian workers are part of Canadian GNP, while the profits from the plant are not. The profits from the plant are counted in Japanese GNP because this is output produced by Japanese-owned capital. The profits, however, are not counted in Japanese GDP because they were not earned in Japan.

gross national product (GNP)
The total market value of all final goods and services produced within a given period by factors of production owned by a country's residents, regardless of where the output is produced.

---

[1]*In a few countries, however, there is a large difference between GDP and GNP. For instance, the tiny country of Lesotho (surrounded entirely by South Africa) has an extremely poor and rudimentary domestic economy. Most residents of Lesotho earn their living by working in the mines and industries of neighbouring South Africa. These payments from abroad are not counted in GDP, although they are part of GNP. According to the International Financial Statistics published by the International Monetary Fund, Lesotho's GNP has exceeded its GDP by about 50% in recent years.*

The Honda plant in Alliston, Ontario is owned by a Japanese firm, though most of the plant's workers are Canadian residents. Thus all of the plant's output is included in Canadian GDP, but only part of it is included in Canadian GNP. The wages paid to Canadian workers are part of GNP, while the plant's profits are not. The plant's profits are part of Japanese GNP.

Calculating GDP

GDP can be computed in two ways. One way is to add up the amount spent on all final goods during a given period. This is the **expenditure approach** to calculating GDP. The other way is to add up the income—wages, rents, interest, and profits—received by all factors of production in producing final goods. This is the **income approach** to calculating GDP. These two methods of computation lead to the same value for GDP for the reason we discussed in the previous chapter: *every payment (expenditure) by a buyer is at the same time a receipt (income) for the seller.* We can measure either income received or expenditures made, and we will end up with the same total output.

Suppose that the economy is made up of just one firm and that the firm's total output this year sells for $1 million. Because the total amount spent on output this year is $1 million, this year's GDP is $1 million. Remember, the expenditure approach calculates GDP on the basis of total expenditures for final goods and services in the economy.

But *every one* of the million dollars of GDP is either paid to someone or remains with the owners of the firm as profit. Using the income approach, we add up the wages paid to employees of the firm, the interest paid to those who lent money to the firm, and the rents paid to those who leased land, buildings, or equipment to the firm. What is left over is profit, which is, of course, income to the owners of the firm. Thus, if we add up the incomes of all the factors of production, including profits to the owners, we get a GDP of $1 million.

THE EXPENDITURE APPROACH

Recall from Chapter 6 the four main groups in the economy: households, firms, the government, and the rest of the world. There are also four main categories of expenditure:

expenditure approach *A method of computing GDP that measures the amount spent on all final goods during a given period.*

income approach *A method of computing GDP that measures the income—wages, rents, interest, and profits—received by all factors of production in producing final goods.*

The expenditure approach calculates GDP by adding together these four components of spending. In equation form:

$$GDP = C + I + G + (EX - IM)$$

Canadian GDP was $949.4 billion in 1999. The four components of the expenditure approach are shown in Table 7.2, along with their various categories.

personal consumption expenditures (*C*) *A major component of GDP: expenditures by consumers on goods and services.*

durable goods *Goods that last a relatively long time, such as cars and household appliances.*

semidurable goods *Goods such as clothing that do not last as long as durable goods but that last longer than nondurable goods.*

nondurable goods *Goods that are used up fairly quickly, such as gasoline.*

services *The things we buy that are not classed as goods, such as legal and dental services.*

gross private investment (*I*) *The purchase of new capital by the private sector—housing, plants, equipment, and inventory.*

fixed capital formation *Investment in durable capital assets. Includes firms' purchases of machinery as well as individuals' purchases of new housing.*

change in business inventories *The amount by which firms' inventories change during a period. Inventories are the goods that firms produce now but intend to sell later.*

■ **Consumption (*C*)** A large part of GDP consists of **personal consumption expenditures (*C*)**. Table 7.2 shows that in 1999 the amount of personal consumption expenditures accounted for 58.3% of GDP. These are expenditures by consumers on goods and services.

There are four main categories of consumer expenditures: durable goods, semidurable goods, nondurable goods, and services. **Durable goods**, such as automobiles, furniture, and household appliances, are goods that last a relatively long time. Goods that do not last as long as durable goods but which may give some length of service are called **semidurable goods**. These include such items as clothing, footwear, and books. **Nondurable goods** are used up fairly quickly and include food for home consumption and gasoline. **Services** are almost anything else a consumer can purchase that can't be classified as a good. Expenditures for dental treatment or legal advice are considered services, as are restaurant meals. As Table 7.2 shows, in 1999 durable goods expenditures accounted for 8.0% of GDP, semidurables for 5.3%, nondurables for 13.7%, and services for 31.3%.

■ **Investment (*I*)** *Investment,* as we use it in economics, is the purchase of new capital—housing, plants, equipment, and inventory. The economic use of the term is in contrast to its everyday use, where *investment* often refers to purchases of common stocks, bonds, or mutual funds ("He *invested* in some 8% corporate bonds"). Two subjects that have always generated much interest, foreign investment in Canada and Canadian investment in other countries, are discussed in the Global Perspective box titled "Foreign Investment in Canada and Canadian Investment Abroad."

Total investment in the private sector is called **gross private investment (*I*)** or "business investment" by Statistics Canada. It has two components, **fixed capital formation** and **change in business inventories.** *Fixed capital formation* includes expenditures by firms for new machines, tools, plants, and so forth.[2] Because these items are goods that firms buy for their own final use, they are part of "final sales" in the economy and are therefore counted in GDP. Fixed capital formation also includes outlays on new residential construction by individuals.

Change in Business Inventories It is sometimes confusing that inventories are counted as part of capital and that changes in inventory are counted as part of investment. But conceptually it makes some sense. The inventory that a firm owns has a value, and it serves a purpose, or provides a service, to the firm. The fact that it has value is obvious. Just think of the inventory of a new car dealer or of a clothing store, or stocks of newly produced but as yet unsold computers awaiting shipment. All these have value.

---

[2]*The distinction between what is considered investment and what is considered consumption is sometimes fairly arbitrary. A firm's purchase of a car or a truck is counted as investment, but a household's purchase of a car or a truck is counted as consumption of durable goods. In general, expenditures by firms for items that last longer than a year are counted as investment expenditures. Expenditures for items that last less than a year are seen as purchases of intermediate goods.*

Table 7.2

Components of GDP, 1999: The Expenditure Approach

	Billions of Dollars	Percentage of GDP
Total Gross Domestic Product	949.4	100.0
Personal Consumption Expenditures (C)	553.6	58.3
Durable goods	76.2	8.0
Semidurable goods	50.2	5.3
Nondurable goods	130.2	13.7
Services	297.0	31.3
Gross Private Investment (I)	167.7	17.7
Fixed capital formation	163.4	17.2
Inventory change	4.3	0.5
Government Purchases (G)	200.0	21.1
Net Exports (EX – IM)	27.9	2.9

Note: Numbers may not add exactly due to rounding.

Source: Statistics Canada, *National Income and Expenditure Accounts*, Cat. no. 13-001.

But what *service* does inventory provide? Firms keep stocks of inventory for a number of reasons. One is to meet unforeseen demand. Firms are never sure how much they will sell from period to period. Sales go up and down. To maintain the goodwill of their customers, firms need to be able to respond to unforeseen increases in sales. The only way to do that is with inventory.

Some firms use inventory to provide direct services to customers. In fact, that is the main function of a retail store. A grocery store provides a service—convenience. The store itself doesn't produce any food at all. It simply assembles a wide variety of items and puts them on display so that consumers with widely varying tastes can come and shop in one place for what they want. The same is true for a clothing or hardware store. To provide their services, such stores need light fixtures, counters, cash registers, buildings, and lots of inventory.

Thus, capital stocks are made up of plant, equipment, and inventory; inventory accumulations are part of the change in capital stocks, or investment.

GDP is not the market value of total final *sales* during a period, but rather the market value of total *production*. The relationship between total production and total sales is this: total production (GDP) equals final sales of domestic goods plus the change in business inventories:

GDP = Final sales + Change in business inventories

In 1999, production exceeded sales by $4.3 billion. Thus, inventories at the end of 1999 were $4.3 billion more than they were at the beginning of 1999.

Gross Investment Versus Net Investment   During the process of production, capital (especially machinery and equipment) produced in previous periods gradually wears out. Thus, GDP does not give us a true picture of the real production of an economy. GDP includes newly produced capital goods but does not take account of capital goods that are "consumed" in the production process.

Capital assets decline in value over time. The amount by which an asset's value falls each period is called its **depreciation.** For example, a personal computer purchased by a business today may be expected to have a useful life of four years before becoming worn out or obsolete. Over that period of time, the computer steadily depreciates.

What is the relationship between gross private investment *(I)* and depreciation? **Gross investment** is the total value of all newly produced capital goods (plant, equipment, housing, and inventory) produced in a given period. It takes no account of the fact that some capital wears out and must be replaced. **Net investment** is equal to gross investment minus depreciation. Net investment is a measure of how much the stock of capital *changes* during a period. If net investment is positive, the capital stock has increased; if net investment is negative, the capital stock has

depreciation *The amount by which an asset's value falls in a given period.*

gross investment *The total value of all newly produced capital goods (plant, equipment, housing, and inventory) produced in a given period.*

net investment *Gross investment minus depreciation.*

Foreign Investment in Canada and Canadian Investment Abroad

Some Canadians worry that so many firms in Canada are not Canadian-owned. For example, the car-making industry in Canada consists entirely of subsidiaries of foreign-controlled multinationals, making Canada one of the few large industrial economies without a domestically owned automobile manufacturer. More generally, approximately 50% of the Canadian manufacturing and resource industries are owned by foreign interests.

Fear that such a large degree of foreign ownership would weaken Canadian sovereignty led the federal government to set up the Foreign Investment Review Agency (FIRA) in 1973 to monitor the acquisition of Canadian businesses. Another major intervention was the establishment in 1975 of Petro-Canada, a federal-government-owned oil refiner and distributor, which was intended to offset the very high degree of foreign ownership in that industry. However, in practice, FIRA approved nearly all applications presented to it. The agency was dismantled about ten years after its inception, to be replaced by Investment Canada, which had a mandate to encourage foreign investment. In 1991, Petro-Canada was privatized (although the government retains a holding as a passive investor) and has since sold or closed a number of its retail outlets.

Direct investment in a country means acquiring ownership and control of part of that country's capital stock. (Note that this is using the word investment in its everyday sense of purchasing assets; it is not necessarily related to capital formation.) It normally includes any investment made by a foreign investor in an enterprise in which the investor owns 10% of the equity, and hence is judged as having some measure of control.

Annual direct investment in other countries by Canadians is now greater than foreign direct investment in Canada. In 1966, Canadian direct investment abroad as a percentage of foreign direct investment in Canada stood at 20%. By 1999, that figure had grown to 107%. Perhaps this growth in Canadian investment abroad has been a factor in the decision by successive governments to be less concerned about restricting investment by others in Canada. Indeed the federal and provincial governments now strive to attract foreign investment as a spur to economic activity. Foreign investment helps develop the economy and create jobs, but naturally the return to this investment goes to the foreign investor.

Figure 1 illustrates the flow of direct investment in Canada from abroad and direct investment abroad by Canadians for 1999. In both cases, the United States and the United Kingdom are Canada's largest direct investment partners (and have traditionally been so). Other countries, such as Hong Kong, are newer entrants. While still a small fraction of the total, Canada's direct investments in Hong Kong rose 12-fold between 1985 and 1995, and Hong Kong's direct investments in Canada over the same period increased almost 20-fold.

The U.S. share of 72% of foreign direct investment in Canada can be compared to Canadian direct investment in the United States, which while being 52% of Canadian direct investment outside Canada, is only about 9% of all foreign direct investment in the United States. Japan, the United Kingdom, and the Netherlands all have a significantly larger share of foreign direct investment in the United States than does Canada.

FIGURE 1

Foreign Direct Investment in Canada and Canadian Direct Investment Abroad, 1999

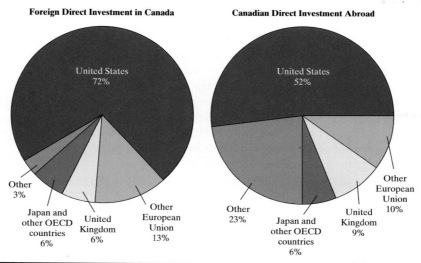

Source: Statistics Canada, *Canada's International Investment Position,* Cat. no. 67-202.

decreased. Put another way, the capital stock at the end of a period is equal to the capital stock that existed at the beginning of the period plus net investment.

Capital $_{\text{end of period}}$ = Capital $_{\text{beginning of period}}$ + Net investment

If we subtract depreciation from gross domestic product (to get a measure of production adjusted for "used up" capital), we obtain **net domestic product**.

net domestic product *GDP minus depreciation.*

■ **Government Purchases (G)** **Government purchases** represent the expenditures of all levels of government for final goods and services and include such diverse items as office supplies and the wages of government employees. Government purchases also include government purchases of fixed capital goods such as public buildings or highways. It is important to note that government purchases as counted in gross domestic product do not include transfer payments (such as welfare payments or seniors' benefits) or interest on the public debt, which is treated as a transfer because it is not a payment for current goods or services. Table 7.2 shows that government purchases accounted for 21.1% of GDP in 1999.

government purchases (G) *Expenditures by federal, provincial, and local governments for final goods and services.*

Note that goods and services produced by the government are typically not sold in any market and hence are valued at cost, although some Canadians would value them differently. (Consider different attitudes about national defence or public art galleries.)

■ **Net Exports (EX – IM)** The value of **net exports (EX – IM)** is the difference between *exports* (sales to foreigners of Canadian-produced goods and services) and *imports* (Canadian purchases of goods and services from abroad). This figure can be positive or negative. In 1999, Canada exported more than it imported; the level of net exports was thus positive ($27.9 billion).

net exports (EX – IM) *The difference between exports (sales to foreigners of Canadian-produced goods and services) and imports (Canadian purchases of goods and services from abroad). The figure can be positive or negative.*

The reason for including net exports in the definition of GDP is simple. Consumption, investment, and government spending (*C, I,* and *G*) include expenditures on goods produced both domestically and by foreigners. Therefore, *C + I + G* overstates domestic production because it contains expenditures on foreign-produced goods—that is, imports, which have to be subtracted out of GDP to obtain the correct figure. At the same time, *C + I + G* understates domestic production because some of what a country produces is sold abroad and is therefore not included in *C, I,* or *G*. Thus, exports (*EX*) have to be added in. If a Canadian firm produces newsprint and sells it in Germany, the newsprint is clearly part of Canadian production and should thus be counted as part of Canadian GDP.

THE INCOME APPROACH

Table 7.3 presents the income approach to calculating GDP, which looks at GDP in terms of who receives it as income, not who purchases it.

The income approach to GDP breaks down GDP into three components: net domestic income, depreciation (capital consumption), and indirect taxes less subsidies:

GDP = Net domestic income + Depreciation + (Indirect taxes – Subsidies)

net domestic income *The total income earned by the factors of production located in a country.*

As we examine each, keep in mind that total expenditures always equal total income.

labour income *Wages, salaries, and fringe benefits paid to households by firms and government.*

■ **Net Domestic Income** Net domestic income is the total income earned by factors of production located within a country. Table 7.3 shows that net domestic income is the sum of six items: (1) labour income, (2) corporate profits, (3) interest income, (4) farm income, (5) unincorporated business income, and (6) an inventory valuation adjustment.

Labour income is wages, salaries, and fringe benefits paid to households by firms and government. This is the largest item by far (52% of GDP). **Corporate profits** are the income of corporate businesses (either paid out as dividends or ploughed back into the firm as retained earnings) and are 10.7% of GDP.

corporate profits *The income of corporate businesses (either paid out as dividends or ploughed back into the firm as retained earnings).*

Interest income is the difference between the interest households receive and the interest they pay out (5.5% of GDP). It does not include interest paid on the public debt because, as mentioned, it is assumed such interest does not flow from the production of goods and services. **Farm income** is, not surprisingly, income earned by farms and was just 0.2% of GDP in 1999. **Unincorporated business income** is income earned by unincorporated businesses (which also includes most rental income). Finally, profits include gains from the holding of inventories that have increased in value during the year. As this gain does not correspond to production, we need to subtract out an **inventory valuation adjustment**.

■ **Depreciation** Recall from our discussion of net versus gross investment that when capital assets wear out or become obsolete, they decline in value. The measure of that decrease in value is called *depreciation*. This depreciation is a part of GDP in the income approach.

It may seem odd that we must *add* depreciation to net domestic income when we calculate GDP by the income approach. But remember that we want a measure of *all* income, including income that results from the replacement of existing plant and equipment. Because national income does not include depreciation,[3] to get to total income (gross domestic product) we need to add depreciation. In 1999, depreciation accounted for $119.0 billion, or 12.5% of GDP.

■ **Indirect Taxes Less Subsidies** The next income component in Table 7.3 is indirect taxes less subsidies. In calculating final sales on the expenditures side, **indirect taxes**—sales taxes, customs duties, and licence fees, for example—are included. These taxes must thus be accounted for on the income side.

To clarify this, suppose that the sales tax is 7% and that a firm sells 100 000 jellybeans for $100 plus tax. The total sales price is thus $107, and this is the value of output recorded in the expenditure approach to calculating GDP. Of this $107, $7 goes to pay the tax to the government, some goes to pay wages to the workers in the jellybean factory, and some goes to pay interest. The rest is the firm's profits plus depreciation.

To have the income and expenditure sides match, the sales tax must be recorded on the income side. If it were not included as part of income, then the basic rule that everyone's expenditure is someone else's income would be violated. Indirect taxes are an expenditure of the households or firms who buy things, but they are not income of firms that sell the products. (Thinking along these lines, indirect

Table 7.3	**Components of GDP, 1999: The Income Approach**	
	Billions of Dollars	**Percentage of GDP**
Gross Domestic Product	949.4	100.0
Net Domestic Income	706.4	74.4
Labour income	493.3	52.0
Corporate profits before taxes	101.4	10.7
Interest income	52.3	5.5
Farm income	2.3	0.2
Unincorporated business income	59.4	6.3
Inventory valuation adjustment	−2.2	−0.2
Depreciation	119.0	12.5
Indirect Taxes Less Subsidies	124.2	13.1

Note: Numbers may not add exactly due to rounding.

Source: Statistics Canada, *National Income and Expenditure Accounts,* Cat. no. 13-001.

---

[3]*The reason national income does not include depreciation is that depreciation has been subtracted from corporations' total revenue in computing the value of corporate profits, and the value of corporate profits is what is used in computing national income.*

taxes can be considered income of the government.) We must thus add indirect taxes on the income side to make things balance.

Subsidies are payments made by the government for which it receives no goods or services in return. These subsidies are subtracted from domestic income to get GDP. (Remember that in the definition of GDP above is indirect taxes *less* subsidies.) For example, farmers receive substantial subsidies from the government. Subsidy payments to farmers are income to farm proprietors and are thus part of domestic income, but they do not come from the sale of agricultural products and thus are not part of GDP. To balance the expenditure side with the income side, these subsidies must be subtracted on the income side.

Figure 7.1 summarizes what we know so far. Most importantly, it reminds us that GDP calculated by the income approach is the same as GDP calculated by the expenditure approach: in both cases $949.4 billion in 1999.

subsidies *Payments made by the government for which it receives no goods or services in return.*

From GDP to Personal Income

Although GDP is the most important item in national income accounting, some other concepts are also useful to know. For example, how much income do residents of Canada actually receive?

FIGURE 7.1

The Expenditure Approach and the Income Approach to Calculating GDP

Components are drawn to scale for 1999 values. See Tables 7.2 and 7.3 for exact numbers. Net exports can be negative but were positive in 1999 as shown. The inventory valuation adjustment is typically negative, as it was in 1999, and it is put in the "other" category only because it is typically small.

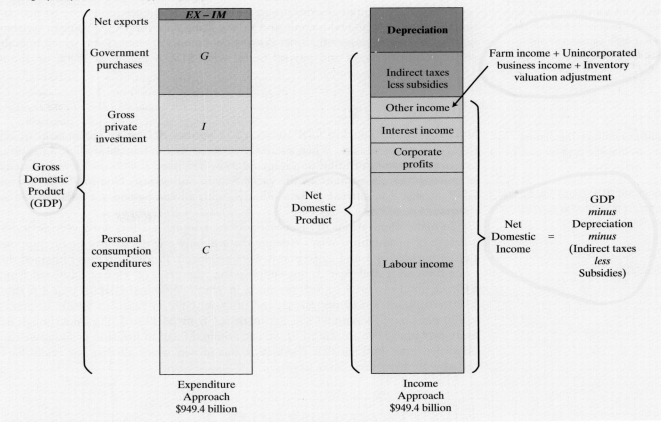

Source: Adapted from Statistics Canada, *National Income and Expenditure Accounts*, Cat. no. 13-001.

To study this question, we return to net domestic income from the previous section. Recall that it is the sum of labour income, corporate profits, and so forth. But some of this is investment income earned by nonresidents of Canada and there is other investment income, earned abroad by residents of Canada, that we have not yet included. We therefore define **net national income** as equal to net domestic income plus investment income from nonresidents minus investment income to nonresidents.[4]

To obtain **personal income**, that is, the total income of households, we have to add in the transfer payments that they have received (including the interest on the public debt) and subtract that portion of corporate profits that they did not receive, that is, retained earnings. To calculate **personal disposable income**, the income that households can potentially spend, we must subtract personal taxes.

Finally, what do households do with this income? Except for a couple of minor items (e.g., they may give some to nonresidents), there are two choices. They may consume it (as personal consumption expenditures, the C that we defined in the expenditure approach) or they may save it as **personal saving**. For example, if your monthly disposable income is $500 and you spend $450 of it, you have $50 left over at the end of the month. Your personal saving is thus $50 for the month. Your personal saving level can be negative: if you earn $500 and spend $600 during the month, you have *dissaved* $100. In order to spend $100 more than you earn, of course, you will either have to borrow the $100 from someone, take the $100 from your savings account, or sell an asset that you own.

The **personal saving rate** is the percentage of personal disposable income saved, an important indicator of household behaviour. A low saving rate means that households are spending a large amount of their income. A high saving rate means that households are cautious in their spending behaviour. The Canadian personal saving rate in 1999 was 1.4%, quite low by Canadian historical standards.

Figure 7.2 summarizes the progression from net domestic income to net national income to personal income and saving using data for 1999. You can see that personal income is larger than net domestic income. Personal taxes, which include personal income taxes and payroll taxes, were $189.6 billion in 1999, or about 25% of personal income.

Nominal Versus Real GDP

So far, we have looked at GDP measured in **current dollars,** or the current prices that one pays for things. When a variable is measured in current dollars (i.e., without an adjustment for inflation), it is said to be described in *nominal terms*. (If there is an adjustment for inflation, the variable is in *real terms*.) **Nominal GDP** is thus GDP measured in current dollars—that is, with all components of GDP valued at their current prices.

In many applications of macroeconomics, nominal GDP is not a very desirable measure of production. Why? Assume there is only one good—say pizza. Suppose that in both years 1 and 2, 10 pizzas were produced. Production thus remained the same for year 1 and year 2. But suppose that the price of a pizza increased from $10 per pizza in year 1 to $20 per pizza in year 2. Nominal GDP in year 1 is thus $100 (10 pizzas × $10 per pizza), and nominal GDP in year 2 is $200 (10 pizzas × $20 per pizza). Nominal GDP has increased from $100 to $200, even though no more pizza has been produced. If we use nominal GDP to measure growth, we can be misled into thinking that production has grown when all that has really happened is that the price level has risen.

---

[4]*Just as in the distinction between GNP and GDP, the adjustment is only for investment income and not other income. Also, just as we can start from net domestic income and obtain net domestic product and gross domestic product (as in Figure 7.1), we can begin with net national income and obtain net national product and gross national product:*

Net domestic income + (Indirect taxes − Subsidies) = Net domestic product
Net national income + (Indirect taxes − Subsidies) = Net national product
Net domestic product + Depreciation = Gross domestic product
Net national product + Depreciation = Gross national product.

FIGURE 7.2

The Progression from Net Domestic Income to Personal Income

The bar at the left represents net domestic income from Figure 7.1. We subtract net investment income outflows to obtain national income and then add transfer payments less retained earnings to get the middle bar, personal income. This is divided into the components of personal taxes (which includes transfers to government) and personal disposable income, the latter spent as shown in the bar on the right.

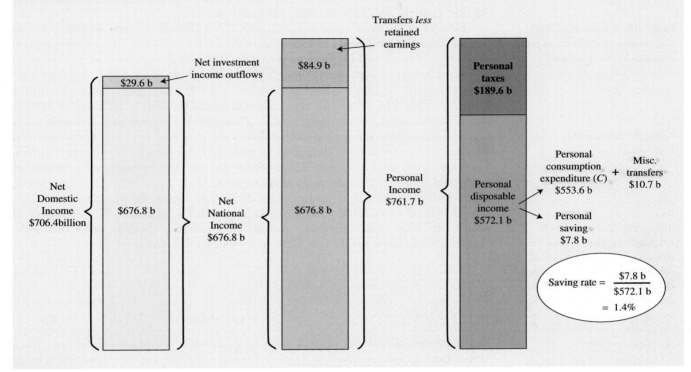

Source: Adapted from Statistics Canada, *National Income and Expenditure Accounts*, Cat. no. 13-001 and CANSIM matrix 6572.

Saving Rate = $\dfrac{\text{Personal Saving}}{(\text{Personal Consumption Expenditure} + \text{Misc. transfers})}$

If there were only one good in the economy—like pizza—it would be easy to measure production and compare one year's value to another. We would just add up all the pizzas produced each year. In the example in the previous paragraph, production is 10 pizzas in both years. If instead the number of pizzas had increased to 15 in year 2, we would simply say that production had increased by 5 pizzas, which is a 50% increase.

Now suppose there were a second good in our economy, say sunglasses. If pizza production has increased by 50% and sunglasses production has only increased by 20%, how much has total output increased? More generally, how do we add pizza and sunglasses quantities together to get a single measure for the total quantity of output? Nominal GDP adds pizzas and sunglasses together by adding their dollar values, but as we just saw some of the change in nominal GDP is price change not quantity change. The next section discusses a measure of the quantity of total output called real GDP. We will then consider the problem of overall price change. While we will focus on a simple example with a few goods, remember that Statistics Canada has to deal with thousands of goods, each of whose price is changing over time.

CALCULATING REAL GDP

Table 7.4 presents all the data we will need for a simple three-good economy. The table presents price (denoted *P*) and quantity (denoted *Q*) data for pizza, sunglasses, and T-shirts for year 1 and year 2.

The first thing to note from Table 7.4 is that *nominal output*—output in current dollars—in year 1 for pizzas is the price of pizza in year 1 ($10) times the number of units of pizza produced in year 1 (10), which is $100. Similarly, nominal output in year 1 is 5 × $50 = $250 for sunglasses and 10 × $15 = $150 for T-shirts. The sum of these three amounts, $500 in column 5, is nominal GDP in year 1 in this simple economy. Nominal GDP in year 2—calculated by using year 2's quantities and year 2's prices—is $800 (column 6). Nominal GDP has thus risen from $500 in year 1 to $800 in year 2, an increase of 60%.[5]

You can see from the table that the price of each good changed between year 1 and year 2—the prices of pizza and sunglasses rose and the price of T-shirts fell. How much of the change in nominal GDP between years 1 and 2 is due to production changes and how much to price changes?

First let us focus on production change. To do this define **real GDP** as GDP as if prices had not changed. For example, in column 7 of Table 7.4, we pretend as if year 1 prices were still in effect in year 2 so that pizza output would be valued at 15 pizzas (the year 2 quantity) times $10 (the year 1 price) or $150. Similarly sunglasses output would be valued at 6 × $50 = $300 and T-shirt output would be valued at 10 × $15 = $150 so that the total would be $600. This total of $600 is real GDP for year 2 using year 1 prices. The use of constant prices is sometimes described as measuring in **constant dollars**. We note that for year 1, the nominal GDP of $500 can also be described as real GDP for year 1 using year 1 prices. Therefore from year 1 to year 2, real GDP has increased from $500 to $600, or 20%, and that is our measure of real output growth. If we wanted a comparable figure for real GDP for a third or subsequent year, again we would measure outputs for those years using year 1 prices. We would refer to real GDP in terms of year 1 prices or "year 1 dollars" and say that year 1 is the **base year**. Currently, Statistics Canada publishes real GDP in terms of 1992 dollars.

Measuring the Price Level

THE GDP DEFLATOR

Real GDP is a measure of output. Now let us consider a measure of the price level. Going back to our example in Table 7.4, nominal GDP for year 2, which is what year 2 quantities (15 pizzas, 6 pairs of sunglasses, and 10 T-shirts) would actually cost altogether at year 2 prices, is $800. Year 2 real GDP, which is what those same quantities *would have cost* in total at year 1 prices, is $600. Hence, dividing nominal GDP of $800 by real GDP of $600 gives us a measure of price change. We call this measure the **GDP deflator** or some variation of this term, such as the GDP implicit price deflator or the GDP price index. Expressed as a percentage in this case, it is ($800/$600) × 100 = 133.3, which estimates the overall rate of price change as 33.3%. We call it a "deflator" because if we deflate nominal GDP by dividing it by 1.333 (to reflect that prices are 33.3% higher) we obtain $800/1.333 = $600 or real GDP.

real GDP *A measure of GDP that removes the effects of price changes from changes in nominal GDP.*

constant dollars *Measuring in constant prices.*

base year *The year which provides reference values. For example, in the calculation of real GDP, the year which provides the prices that are used to value the outputs of all other years.*

$$GDP\ deflator = \frac{nominal\ GDP}{real\ GDP}$$

GDP deflator *Current dollar (nominal) GDP divided by constant dollar (real) GDP, converted to a percentage by multiplying by 100. Also called the GDP implicit price deflator or the GDP price index.*

Table 7.4		A Three-Good Economy					
	(1)	(2)	(3)	(4)	(5) GDP in Year 1 in Year 1 Prices $P_1 \times Q_1$	(6) GDP in Year 2 in Year 2 Prices $P_2 \times Q_2$	(7) GDP in Year 2 in Year 1 Prices $P_1 \times Q_2$
	Production		Price per Unit				
	Year 1 Q_1	Year 2 Q_2	Year 1 P_1	Year 2 P_2			
Pizza	10	15	$10	$20	$100	$300	$150
Sunglasses	5	6	$50	$60	$250	$360	$300
T-shirts	10	10	$15	$14	$150	$140	$150
Total					$500	$800	$600

nominal GDP year 1

nominal GDP year 2

$$\%\ change = \frac{GDP\ year\ 2 - GDP\ year\ 1}{GDP\ year\ 1} \times 100\%$$

[5]*The percentage change is calculated as [(800 − 500)/500] × 100 = 0.6 × 100 = 60%.*

The GDP deflator for year 3 is year 3 nominal GDP divided by year 3 real GDP at year 1 prices. That is, we always compare what current quantities actually cost at current prices with what those same quantities would have cost at year 1 prices.

The GDP deflator for the base year will always have a value of 100. You can work this out in this case by finding that nominal GDP for year 1 is $500 and real GDP for year 1 (at year 1 prices) is also $500 and ($500/$500) × 100 = 100.

THE CONSUMER PRICE INDEX

Let us look at another measure of price change, besides the GDP deflator. The **consumer price index (CPI)** is the most well-known price index. It is calculated every month using the price of a fixed, standardized bundle of goods meant to represent the consumption of the average consumer.

As an example, Table 7.5 uses the same prices and quantities as Table 7.4. except now we view these goods from the perspective of consumption rather than production. We choose the fixed, standardized bundle of goods as the actual consumption quantities during year 1, that is, 10 pizzas, 5 pairs of sunglasses, and 10 T-shirts. The value of these quantities at year 1 prices is 10 × $10 + 5 × $50 + 10 × $15 = $500. The price of that same bundle at year 2 prices is 10 × $20 + 5 × $60 + 10 × $14 = $640. The value of the consumer price index, conventionally expressed as a percentage, is ($640/$500) × 100 = 128.0. According to the consumer price index, prices increased by 28% in this economy between year 1 and year 2.

It is very important to note that if we calculated this same price index for year 3 or any subsequent year, *we would still use the bundle of year 1 quantities*. Year 2, year 3, or subsequent quantities are never used. Because the standardized bundle of goods is based on the year 1 quantities, year 1 is called the *base year* for the consumer price index. Note that the value of the CPI in year 1 is ($500/$500) × 100 = 100—that is, the value of the bundle at year 1 prices, or $500, divided by the value of the bundle at base-year prices, also $500 because the base year is year 1 multiplied by 100.

The GDP deflator and the consumer price index are both methods of aggregating different prices into a single overall measure of the price level. Economists call the general problem of aggregating a number of variables into a single measure (of adding apples and oranges) the *index number problem* because they call a measure of a group of variables an index. In calculating an **index**, we denote the importance of each item by assigning it a **weight**.

As an example of the index number problem, suppose in an economics course there is an exam and a project. Suppose Chris gets 90% on the exam and 70% on the project while Ursula gets 70% on the exam and 90% on the project. Who will get the higher grade? We cannot say until we know the weights, which presumably reflect the importance the instructor has assigned to each component. If the instructor has assigned equal weight to the exam and the project, we can make the weights 0.5 and 0.5, and the two students will receive equal grades. But if the instructor has assigned three-quarters of the weight to the exam and one-quarter of the weight to the project, the weights can be 0.75 and 0.25 and Chris will get the higher grade.

The consumer price index "weights" the various prices by using the year 1 quantities. Returning to our example, we always price 10 pizzas, 5 pairs of sunglasses, and 10 T-shirts. On the other hand, the GDP deflator was based on year 2 quantities—that is, it weighted the prices using the year 2 quantities (15 pizzas, 6 pairs of s unglasses, and 10 T-shirts). The CPI estimated an overall price change of 28% while the GDP deflator, you will recall, estimated an overall price change of 33%. The different weights result in different estimates of price change, just as different weights on the economics course components would change the final grades received by Chris and Ursula.

A key difference between the consumer price index and the GDP deflator is that the CPI always uses the same bundle of goods, that is, it always weights the prices the same way. Hence, it is called a **fixed-weight price index**. The GDP deflator for year 3 would use year 3 quantities, for year 4 it would use year 4 quantities, and so on, so it is not a fixed-weight index.

consumer price index (CPI) *A price index calculated every month using the price of a standardized bundle of goods meant to represent the consumption of the average consumer.*

$$CPI = \frac{Q_1 \times P_1}{Q_2 \times P_1} \times 100\%$$

index *A measure of a group of variables.*

weight *The importance attached to an item within an index.*

fixed-weight price index *A price index calculated by pricing the same bundle of goods each period.*

	(1)	(2)	(3)	(4)	(5)	(6)
	Consumption		**Price per Unit**		**Value of Year 1 Quantities at Year 1 Prices**	**Value of Year 1 Quantities at Year 2 Prices**
	Year 1 Q_1	Year 2 Q_2	Year 1 P_1	Year 2 P_2	$P_1 \times Q_1$	$P_2 \times Q_1$
Pizza	10	15	$10	$20	$100	$200
Sunglasses	5	6	$50	$60	$250	$300
T-shirts	10	10	$15	$14	$150	$140
Total					$500	$640

Calculation steps for consumer price index:

First: Take bundle prices for both years, using bundle quantities for base year (year 1 in this case). Form an index for each year by dividing each year's bundle price by the base-year bundle price and multiplying by 100.

$$\text{Consumer price index in year 2} = \frac{\text{Price of year 1 bundle at year 2 prices}}{\text{Price of year 1 bundle at base-year prices}} \times 100$$

$$= \frac{\$640}{\$500} \times 100 = 128$$

$$\text{Consumer price index in year 1} = \frac{\text{Price of year 1 bundle at year 1 prices}}{\text{Price of year 1 bundle at base-year prices}} \times 100$$

$$= \frac{\$500}{\$500} \times 100 = 100$$

Second: Determine the percentage change in the price index from year 1 to year 2.

$$\text{Percentage change} = \frac{(\text{Year 2 index} - \text{Year 1 index})}{\text{Year 1 index}} \times 100$$

$$= \frac{(128 - 100)}{100} \times 100 = 28$$

The CPI is more widely used than the GDP deflator. In our example we included the same goods in both measures, but in practice the CPI only includes consumer goods while the GDP deflator includes all goods produced in the economy. In setting wage settlements or adjusting pensions for the cost of living, we most often want a measure of inflation for consumer prices, the focus of the CPI. We could use a GDP deflator just for consumption goods, but there is a second problem, one of time. National accounts are only published quarterly and with a lag of almost a quarter. Even then they are subsequently revised. The problem is that it is very difficult to obtain timely data on the quantities produced each quarter.

In contrast, all the quantities required to calculate the CPI are gathered in the base year. No new quantity information is required. So all that is needed for the CPI is price information, which can be obtained more quickly. For example, in pricing food for the CPI, Statistics Canada hires "shoppers" who go to dozens of food stores across the country and record the prices of a standard list of closely defined commodities, from four-litre bags of 2% milk to one-kilogram bunches of green seedless grapes. Some product prices, such as clothing, where the shoppers must scrutinize quality closely to make sure it is no better or no worse than the standardized item, are harder to measure than food. But the result is that Statistics Canada is able to produce the CPI for a given month within about three weeks after the month-end, much more quickly than would be feasible to produce any measure based on the national accounts.

When we discuss inflation in Chapter 8, we will discuss a few of the problems with the CPI. Many of these problems have the same root cause. As a fixed-weight index, the CPI does not automatically adjust for new products or improved products. Moreover when the price of one product increases, we might expect consumers to shift their consumption toward other goods and hence lessen the impact of the price increase on the cost of living. Because the CPI is fixed-weight, it does not adjust for this.

Limitations of the GDP Concept

We generally think of increases in GDP as good. But GDP is a measure of aggregate economic activity, not of happiness or well-being. Here are some of the limitations of the GDP concept as a measure of welfare.

GDP AND SOCIAL WELFARE

A decrease in crime clearly increases social welfare, but crime levels are not measured in GDP. If crime levels went down, society as a whole would be better off, but a decrease in crime is not an increase in output, and thus it is not reflected in GDP. Neither is an increase in leisure time. To the extent that households desire extra leisure time (rather than having it forced on them by a lack of jobs in the economy), an increase in leisure is also an increase in social welfare, even if GDP is reduced with less time spent on producing measurable output.

Most nonmarket and domestic activities such as housework are not counted in GDP even though they amount to real production. However, if I decide to hire someone to clean my house, GDP increases. The salaries of cleaning people are counted in GDP, but the time I spend doing the same things is not counted. In other words, a mere change of institutional arrangements, even though no more output is being produced, can show up as a change in GDP.

This may lead to biased measures of GDP growth. For example, perhaps partly due to the increase in the number of two-earner households, there has been a sharp decrease in the number of meals produced at home (value of preparation not counted in GDP) and a corresponding increase in the number of meals purchased away from home (counted in GDP). Statistics Canada has embarked on a research project that eventually may incorporate nonmarket activities in a set of national accounts.

Furthermore, GDP seldom reflects losses or social ills. GDP accounting rules do not adjust for production that pollutes the environment. The more production there is, the larger is GDP, regardless of how much pollution results in the process. GDP also makes no allowance for resource depletion. If, for example, a stand of timber is cut or a vein of nickel is mined, the entire value of new output is counted toward GDP and no allowance is made for the reduction in the value of timber available for cutting or of nickel available for mining.

GDP also has nothing to say about the distribution of output among individuals in a society. It does not distinguish, for example, between the case in which most output goes to a few people and the case in which output is evenly divided among all people. We cannot use GDP to measure the effects of redistributive policies (which take income from some people and give income to others). Such policies have no direct impact on GDP. GDP is also neutral about the kinds of goods that an economy produces. Symphony performances, cigarettes, professional hockey games, beer, milk, economics textbooks, and comic books all get counted, regardless of the different values that society might attach to them.

Despite these limitations, GDP is still a highly useful measure. The effects of some of its shortcomings do not change very much over time, and hence real GDP growth is a valuable measure of changes in economic activity, particularly over a short period. But in the short run and the long run, think of real GDP as a measure of aggregate economic activity, not as a direct measure of economic welfare.

THE UNDERGROUND ECONOMY

Many transactions in the economy are missed in the calculation of GDP, even though in principle they should be counted. Most illegal transactions are missed unless they are "laundered" back into legitimate business. Income that is earned but not reported as income for tax purposes is usually missed. The part of the economy that should be counted in GDP but is not is sometimes called the **underground economy.**

underground economy *The part of the economy in which transactions take place and in which income is generated that is unreported and therefore not counted in GDP.*

Table 7.6
Per Capita GNP for Selected Countries, 1998

Country	U.S. Dollars
Switzerland	39 980
Norway	34 310
Denmark	33 040
Japan	32 350
United States	29 240
Austria	26 830
Germany	26 570
Sweden	25 580
Finland	24 280
France	24 210
United Kingdom	21 410
Australia	20 640
Italy	20 090
Canada	**19 170**
Israel	16 180
Spain	14 100
Greece	11 740
Portugal	10 670
Chile	4 990
Mexico	3 840
Turkey	3 160
Botswana	3 070
Jamaica	1 740
Egypt	1 290
Jordan	1 150
Philippines	1 050
Bolivia	1 010
Indonesia	640
Mali	250
Mozambique	210

Source: World Bank, *World Development Indicators, 2000,* Table 1.1.

per capita GDP or GNP *A country's GDP or GNP divided by its population.*

Tax evasion is usually thought to be the major incentive for people to participate in the underground economy. A number of studies have attempted to estimate the size of the Canadian underground economy, with estimates ranging from 1% to 25% of GDP.[6] While these figures may seem quite dramatic, the estimated size of the Canadian underground economy is comparable to the size of the underground economy in the United States and in most European countries and is probably much smaller than the size of the underground economy in the Eastern European countries. Estimates of Italy's underground economy range from 10% to 35% of Italian GDP. At the lower end of the scale, estimates for Switzerland range from 3% to 5%.

Why should we care about the underground economy? To the extent that GDP reflects only a part of economic activity rather than being a complete measure of what the economy produces, it is obviously misleading. Unemployment rates, for example, may be lower than officially measured if people work in the underground economy without reporting this fact to the government.

Per Capita GDP/GNP

GDP and GNP are sometimes measured in per capita terms. **Per capita GDP or GNP** is simply a country's GDP or GNP divided by its population. It is a better measure of well-being for the average person than total GDP or GNP. Table 7.6 lists the per capita GNP of various countries for 1995. Switzerland is the country with the highest per capita GNP, followed by Norway, Denmark, and Japan.

Canada is fourteenth-ranked on this list. But while national accounting, despite its imperfection has some validity as a measure of a single nation's economic activity, international comparisons are far more controversial. As the underground economy example makes clear, the flaws in GDP and GNP may matter more in some countries than in others. Also, comparing the outputs of different countries simply by converting them to a single currency (by convention U.S. dollars) ignores the fact that a U.S. (or Canadian) dollar can often purchase much more in a country such as Mexico or Turkey than it can in the United States or Canada and much less in a country like Japan or Switzerland.

Part of the problem is that this kind of comparison is very sensitive to exchange rates. For example, if we used the exchange rates that prevailed in 1991 when the Canadian dollar had a higher value, we would find that the per capita GDP of Canada would be about equal to that of Sweden rather than significantly lower as in the table. A more sophisticated exercise is to convert the per capita GDPs using what are called *purchasing power parities*, which try to price equivalent goods and services across countries in equivalent terms. For example, the same restaurant meal that costs $50 in Vancouver might cost $500 in Tokyo but the purchasing power parity approach would count each as making the same contribution to this adjusted measure of GDP. While this lessens the problems in comparing per capita GDPs, it does not nearly eliminate them, partly because goods and services themselves are so different across countries. In any case, the 1998 comparisons using purchasing power parities would rank Canada seventh in the above table (at the equivalent of US$22 814) with the United States listed as first at US$29 240. But the important result is that using this measure, differences between countries tend to shrink. Mozambique, the lowest-ranked country in the table, would have a per capita GDP of US$740 on this basis.

There have been attempts to provide international comparisons of quality of life by developing more broadly based international indexes of welfare that put weight on infant mortality, health status, education levels, and the relative status of women, none of which figure directly in the national accounts. You probably know that one such index (the Index of Human Development) published by the United Nations often ranks Canada very highly, sometimes first. In considering this, however, you should bear in mind what you have learned in this chapter about

[6]*See Philip Smith, "Assessing the Size of the Underground Economy: The Statistics Canada Perspective," Canadian Economic Observer, Statistics Canada, Cat. no. 11-010, May 1994.*

index numbers. Not only are there difficulties in measuring the individual components, the resulting index values can be (and are) very sensitive to the chosen weights and hence the results are problematic.

Looking Ahead

This chapter has introduced you to many of the key variables that macroeconomists are interested in, including GDP and its components. There is, however, much more to be learned regarding the data that macroeconomists use. In the next chapter we discuss the data on employment, unemployment, and the labour force, and in Chapters 11 and 12 we discuss the data on money and interest rates. Finally, in Chapter 20 we discuss in more detail the data on the relationship between Canada and the rest of the world.

In some countries, the only way to purchase consumer goods may be the underground market. Here, Russian consumers buy appliances from the back of a truck.

1. One source of data on the key variables in the macroeconomy is the national income and expenditure accounts. These accounts provide an important conceptual framework that macroeconomists use to think about how the various pieces of the economy fit together.

Gross Domestic Product

2. *Gross domestic product (GDP)* is the key concept in national income accounting. GDP is the total market value of all final goods and services produced within a given period by factors of production located within a country. GDP excludes intermediate goods, because to include goods both when they are purchased as inputs and when they are sold as final products would be double-counting and thus an overstatement of the value of production.

3. GDP excludes all transactions in which money or goods change hands but in which no new goods and services are produced. GDP includes the profits that foreign companies earn in Canada. GDP excludes profits earned by Canadian companies in foreign countries.

4. *Gross national product (GNP)* is the market value of all final goods and services produced during a given period by factors of production owned by a country's residents.

Calculating GDP

5. The *expenditure approach* to computing GDP adds up the amount spent on all final goods and services during a given period. The four main categories of expenditures are *personal consumption expenditures (C), gross private investment (I), government purchases (G),* and *net exports (EX − IM)*. The sum of these four equals GDP.

6. The four main components of personal consumption expenditures (C) are *durable goods, semidurable goods, nondurable goods,* and *services.*

7. *Gross private investment (I)* is the total investment made by the private sector in a given period of time. Gross private investment includes *fixed capital formation* and *changes in business inventories.* Gross investment does not take *depreciation*—the decrease in the value of assets—into account. *Net investment* is equal to gross investment less depreciation.

8. *Government purchases (G)* include expenditures for final goods and services. The value of *net exports (EX − IM)* equals the difference between exports (sales abroad of Canadian-produced goods and services) and imports (Canadian purchases of goods and services from abroad).

9. Because every payment (expenditure) by a buyer is at the same time a receipt (income) for the seller, GDP can also be computed in terms of who receives it as income. This is the *income approach* to calculating gross domestic product. The GDP equation using the income approach is GDP = Net domestic income + Depreciation + (Indirect taxes − Subsidies).

From GDP to Personal Income

10. The *net domestic income* portion of GDP minus net investment income outflows gives *net national income.* Adding transfer payments to net national income gives *personal income. Personal income* is the total income of households. *Personal disposable income* is what households have to spend or save after paying their taxes. The *personal saving rate* is the percentage of personal disposable income that is saved rather than spent.

Nominal Versus Real GDP

11. GDP that is measured in current dollars (the current prices that one pays for goods) is called *nominal GDP.* If we use nominal GDP to measure growth, we can be misled into thinking that production has grown when all that has really happened is a rise in the price level, or inflation. A better measure of production is *real GDP,* which is nominal GDP adjusted for prices changes.

Measuring the Price Level

12. The GDP deflator is a measure of the overall price level. The consumer price index is a measure of the price level of consumer goods.

Limitations of the GDP Concept

13. We generally think of increases in GDP as good, but some problems arise when we try to use GDP as a measure of happiness or well-being. The peculiarities of GDP accounting mean that institutional changes can change the value of GDP even if real production has not changed. GDP ignores most social ills, such as pollution. Furthermore, GDP tells us nothing about what kinds of goods are being produced or how income is distributed across the population. GDP also ignores many transactions of the underground economy.

14. *Per capita GDP or GNP* is a country's GDP or GNP divided by its population. Per capita GDP or GNP is a better measure of well-being for the average person than is total GDP or GNP. International comparisons of per capita GDP or GNP are problematic, however.

Review Terms and Concepts

base year 144

change in business inventories 136

constant dollars 144

consumer price index (CPI) 145

corporate profits 139

current dollars 142

depreciation 137

durable goods 136

expenditure approach 135

farm income 140

final goods and services 133

fixed capital formation 136

fixed-weight price index 145

GDP deflator 144

government purchases (*G*) 139

gross domestic product (GDP) 132

gross investment 137

gross national product (GNP) 134

gross private investment (*I*) 136

income approach 135

index 145

indirect taxes 140

interest income 140

intermediate goods 133

inventory valuation adjustment 140

labour income 139

national income and expenditure accounts 132

net domestic income 139

net domestic product 139

net exports (*EX* − *IM*) 139

net investment 137

net national income 142

nominal GDP 142

nondurable goods 136

per capita GDP or GNP 148

personal consumption expenditures (*C*) 136

personal disposable income 142

personal income 142

personal saving 142

personal saving rate 142

real GDP 144

semidurable goods 136

services 136

subsidies 141

underground economy 147

unincorporated business income 140

value added 133

weight 145

Equations:

1. Expenditure approach to GDP: GDP = C + I + G + (EX − IM)

2. GDP = Final sales + Change in business inventories

3. Income approach to GDP: GDP = Net domestic income + Depreciation + (Indirect taxes − Subsidies)

Problem Set

1. From the table below, calculate the following:
   a. Gross private investment
   b. Net exports
   c. Gross domestic product
   d. Gross national product
   e. Net national product
   f. Net national income
   g. Personal income
   h. Personal disposable income

Transfer payments	50
Subsidies	5
Social insurance payments	35
Depreciation	50
Investment income from nonresidents	4
Government purchases	75
Imports	50
Investment income to nonresidents	5
Indirect taxes	20
Exports	60
Net private investment	100

Personal taxes	60
Corporate profits	45
Personal consumption expenditures	250
Dividends	4

2. Why should calculating GDP by the expenditure approach yield the same answer as calculating GDP by the income approach?

3. Why do we bother to construct real GDP if we already know nominal GDP?

4. Consider the following data for the country of Fruitland:

	Production (in number of units)		Price per Unit (in units of currency)	
	2000	2001	2000	2001
Apples	10	20	10	10
Oranges	5	8	10	12
Peaches	20	15	5	10

a. Calculate nominal GDP for 2000.
b. Calculate nominal GDP for 2001.
c. What is the percentage change in nominal GDP between 2000 and 2001?
d. Construct the GDP deflator for 2001 using 2000 as the base year. What is the percentage change in this price index from 2000 to 2001?

5. Explain what double-counting is and discuss why GDP is not equal to total sales.

6. If it were possible, would you include underground economic activity in GDP if you were using it as a measure of economic activity? If you were using it as a measure of economic welfare?

7. Which of the following transactions would not be counted in GDP? Explain your answers.
a. Molson issues new shares of stock to finance the construction of a plant.
b. Molson builds a new plant.
c. Company A successfully launches a hostile takeover of Company B, in which it purchases all the shares of Company B.
d. Your grandmother wins $10 million in Lotto 6/49.
e. You buy a new copy of this textbook.
f. You rent your copy of this textbook to your roommate for a term.
g. The government pays out seniors' benefits.
h. A public utility installs new antipollution equipment in its smokestacks.
i. Luigi's Pizza buys 15 kilograms of mozzarella cheese, holds it in inventory for one month, and then uses it to make pizza, which it sells.
j. You spend the entire weekend cleaning your apartment.
k. A drug dealer sells $500 worth of illegal drugs.

8. If you buy a new car, the entire purchase is counted as consumption in the year in which you make the transaction. Explain briefly why this is in one sense an "error" in national income accounting. (*Hint:* How is the purchase of a car different from the purchase of a pizza?) How might you correct this error?

9. Explain why imports are subtracted in the expenditure approach to calculating GDP.

10. GDP calculations do not directly include the economic costs of environmental damage (e.g., global warming, acid rain). Do you think these costs should be included in GDP? Why or why not? How could GDP be amended to include environmental damage costs?

11. In 2000, shares in Nortel constituted such a large part of the total value of shares on the Toronto Stock Exchange that it had a weight of one-third in the TSE 300 index. Given this, suppose the share values of all the other 299 companies in the TSE 300 index fell by 1% but the TSE 300 index was unchanged. By what percentage did Nortel shares increase?

12. In Spring 2000, two McGill University professors, Tom Velk and Al Riggs, published a grading of the economic performance of six prime ministers. They used ten indicators but here are just three:

	Inflation	Unemployment	Real GDP Growth
St. Laurent	A+ (5)	B (3)	A+ (5)
Diefenbaker	A (4)	C (2)	B (3)
Pearson	D (1)	B (3)	A (4)
Trudeau	D (1)	F (0)	C (2)
Mulroney	B (3)	A (4)	D (1)
Chretien	C (2)	A (4)	D (1)

The grades were calculated as rankings based on improvement in the indicator during time in office, with ties possible. Taking these as given, and assigning points such that an A+ is a 5, an A is a 4, a B is a 3, etc., calculate the grade point averages. (You should find that St. Laurent has the highest.) Using all ten indicators, Velk and Riggs concluded that Mulroney should receive the highest grade. Criticize this method of grading prime ministers, concentrating on the index number problem.

13. Every fall *Maclean's* publishes a ranking of Canadian universities based on a number of indicators including average class size, amount spent on student services, etc. Such a ranking faces the index number problem—that is, the result depends on the weights put on each indicator in calculating the overall index. Write a short explanation of this to someone who has not read this chapter, explaining how two people might agree on the indicators to be used in comparing universities X and Y and on the numerical values of those indicators, but still disagree on which university was better.

Macroeconomic Problems: Unemployment and Inflation

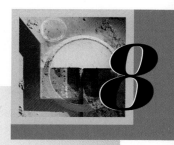

Learning Objectives

1 Explain how the unemployment rate is measured.

2 Distinguish among frictional, structural, and cyclical unemployment. Describe the economic and social costs of unemployment.

3 Define *inflation*. Outline the problems of price indexes such as the consumer price index.

4 Explain the differences between anticipated and unanticipated inflation. Define *real interest rate*. Indicate who gains and who loses from inflation.

Recessions, Depressions, and Unemployment

Defining and Measuring Unemployment

Components of the Unemployment Rate

The Costs of Unemployment

Other Consequences of Recessions

Inflation

Defining Inflation

Price Indexes

The Costs of Inflation

Inflation: Public Enemy Number One?

Global Unemployment Rates and Inflation

Looking Ahead

Sometime during 1990, total employment in Canada stopped growing and began to decline. In July of that year, total employment hit 13.7 million. By January 1991, more than a million people were unemployed. At the same time, after seven years of growth, real output declined in 1990 and again in 1991. For many, this recession was something to read about in the newspaper. After all, over 12 million workers still had jobs. But for the workers who had no jobs, unemployment was a painful reality. Ten years earlier, Canada had wrestled with high inflation. Consumer prices increased an average of 10% in 1980, 12.4% in 1981, and 10.9% in 1982. For those living on fixed incomes, such levels of inflation represented a substantial decrease in their economic well-being. Economists disagree as to how harmful inflation is more generally, although it is accepted that very high rates of inflation, experienced recently by countries such as Russia and Bolivia, are harmful to economic growth.

These "twin evils" of unemployment and inflation are concerns of macroeconomists. In this chapter we explore these concerns, describing the periodic ups and downs in the economy that we call the *business cycle*. Later chapters focus on the likely causes of *business cycles* and some of the things that government may do to prevent or minimize the damage they create. First, however, we need to know a little bit more about what the business cycle is. What are recessions and depressions? Who is hurt by them? What are the consequences of inflation? Who benefits and who loses when the price level rises rapidly? Why should policy makers in Ottawa be concerned about the business cycle?

Recessions, Depressions, and Unemployment

recession *Roughly, a period in which real GDP declines for at least two consecutive quarters.*

A **recession** is roughly a period in which real GDP declines for at least two consecutive quarters, whereas real GDP is a measure of the actual output of goods and services in the economy during a given period of time. Thus, when real GDP falls, less is being produced. When less output is produced, fewer inputs are used, employment declines, the unemployment rate rises, and a smaller percentage of the capital stock at our disposal is utilized (i.e., more plants and equipment are running at less than full capacity). When real output falls, real income declines.

depression *A prolonged and deep recession. The precise definitions of* prolonged *and* deep *are debatable.*

A **depression** is a prolonged and deep recession, although there is much disagreement over how severe and how prolonged a recession must be in order to be called a depression. Nearly everyone agrees that the Canadian economy experienced a depression between 1929 and the late 1930s. Recessions took place between 1980 and 1982, and 1990 and 1991, with the effects of the latter lingering well into the 1990s.

Table 8.1 summarizes some of the differences between these recessions and the early part of the Great Depression. Between 1929 and 1933, real GDP declined by almost 28%. In other words, in 1933 Canada produced 28% less than it had in 1929. While only 2.9% of the labour force was unemployed in 1929, 19.3% was unemployed in 1933. By contrast, during the recession of 1980–1982, the growth of real GDP was 1.8% and output fell 2% during the 1990–1991 recession. The table also shows unemployment rates were not as high as during the Great Depression. Clearly, although the more recent recessions were difficult periods, they did not come close to the severity of the Great Depression.

DEFINING AND MEASURING UNEMPLOYMENT

The most frequently discussed symptom of a recession is unemployment. In 1982, Canada's unemployment rate was over 10% for the first time since the 1930s. But although unemployment is widely discussed, most people are unaware of what unemployment statistics mean or how they are derived.

The unemployment statistics released every month are based on a survey of households—the Labour Force Survey—conducted by Statistics Canada. Every month Statistics Canada interviews a sample of 52 000 households. Each interviewed household answers questions regarding the work activity of household members 15 years of age or older during the calendar week that contains the fifteenth of the month.

employed *Any person 15 years old or older (1) who works for pay or profit, either for someone else or in his or her own business, (2) who works without pay in a family enterprise, or (3) who has a job but has been temporarily absent, with or without pay.*

If a household member 15 years of age or older did any work at all for pay or profit, either for someone else or in his or her own business or farm, that person is classified as **employed.** A household member is also considered employed if he or she worked without pay in a family enterprise. Finally, a household member is counted as employed if he or she held a job from which he or she was temporarily absent due to illness, bad weather, vacation, labour disputes, or personal reasons, whether that person was paid or not.

unemployed *A person 15 years old or older who is not working, is available for work, and generally has made specific efforts to find work.*

Those who are not employed fall into one of two categories: (1) unemployed or (2) not in the labour force. To be considered **unemployed,** a person must be available for work and generally have made specific efforts to find work. Individuals who have not searched for work but who expect to start work soon, including those on temporary layoff, are also counted as unemployed. Persons who are not looking for work, either because they do not want a job or because they have given up looking, are classified as **not in the labour force.**

not in the labour force *People who are not looking for work, either because they do not want a job or because they have given up looking.*

The total **labour force** in the economy is the number of people employed plus the number of unemployed:

labour force *The number of people employed plus the number of unemployed.*

$$\text{Labour force} = \text{Employed} + \text{Unemployed}$$

Table 8.1	Real GDP and Unemployment Rates 1929–1933, 1979–1982, and 1989–1991

THE EARLY PART OF THE GREAT DEPRESSION, 1929–1933

	Percentage Change in Real GDP	Unemployment Rate	Number of Unemployed (millions)
1929		2.9	0.1
1930	−3.3	9.1	0.4
1931	−11.2	11.6	0.5
1932	−9.3	17.6	0.7
1933	−7.2	19.3	0.8

Note: Percentage change in real GDP between 1929 and 1933 was −27.7%.

THE RECESSIONS OF 1980–1982 AND 1990–1991

	Percentage Change in Real GDP	Unemployment Rate	Number of Unemployed (millions)
1979		7.5	0.9
1980	1.5	7.5	0.9
1981	3.7	7.6	0.9
1982	−3.2	11.0	1.4
1989		7.5	1.1
1990	−0.2	8.1	1.2
1991	−1.9	10.4	1.5

Note: Percentage change in real GDP between 1979 and 1982 was 1.8%, and −2.0% between 1989 and 1991.

Source: Adapted from M. C. Urquhart and K.A.H. Buckley (eds.), *Historical Statistics of Canada,* 1st ed. (Toronto: Macmillan, 1965); Statistics Canada, *Labour Force Annual Averages,* Cat. no. 71-220; Statistics Canada, CANSIM database, Series D14442, D767286, and D767287.

The total population 15 years of age or older is equal to the number of people in the labour force plus the number not in the labour force:

Population = Labour force + Not in labour force

With these numbers, several ratios can be calculated. The **unemployment rate** is the ratio of the number of people unemployed to the total number of people in the labour force:

$$\text{Unemployment rate} = \frac{\text{Unemployed}}{\text{Employed} + \text{Unemployed}}$$

unemployment rate *The ratio of the number of people unemployed to the total number of people in the labour force.*

In April 2000, the labour force contained 15.942 million people, 14.863 million of whom were employed and 1.079 million of whom were looking for work. The unemployment rate was thus 6.8%:

$$\frac{1.079}{14.863 + 1.079} = 6.8\%$$

The ratio of the labour force to the population 15 years old or over is called the **labour-force participation rate:**

$$\text{Labour-force participation rate} = \frac{\text{Labour force}}{\text{Population}}$$

labour-force participation rate *The ratio of the labour force to the total population 15 years old or older.*

Table 8.2 shows the relationship among these numbers for selected years since 1950. The years 1982 and 1991 have been added to show the effects of these recessions. Although the unemployment rate has gone up and down, the labour-force participation rate grew fairly steadily from 1950 to 1990. Most of this increase was due to the growth in the participation rate of women. Recent declines in participation rates may be due to discouraged-worker effects, which we will discuss later in this chapter.

Column 3 in Table 8.2 shows how many new workers the Canadian economy has managed to absorb in recent years. The number of employed workers increased by 6 million between 1950 and 1982 and by about 3.5 million between 1982 and 1999.

COMPONENTS OF THE UNEMPLOYMENT RATE

The unemployment rate by itself conveys a limited amount of information. To understand the level of unemployment better, we must look at unemployment rates across groups of people, regions, and industries.

■ **Unemployment Rates for Different Demographic Groups**   Marked differences in rates of unemployment exist across demographic groups. Table 8.3 shows the unemployment rate for 1982, 1991 (both recession years), and for 1999, broken down by age and sex. Total unemployment came down gradually over that period, but the same patterns were not evident for men and women, or for older and younger labour force participants.

Men aged 25 and over had the lowest rate of unemployment in 1982, but the lowest rates in 1991 and 1999 were those of women aged 25 and over. Younger workers between age 15 and 24 fared much worse than the average in those three years. Within that group, men fared worse than women. Table 8.3 also provides data on unemployment rates by level of education. Note, unemployment is lower among those with more education. We provide the figures for those with university degrees, and it can be seen that unemployment is below the national average for all age groups. For those with other postsecondary certificates or diplomas, average unemployment rates are higher than for those with university degrees, but still below national averages by age. The main point of Table 8.3 is that an unemployment rate of 7.6% does not mean that every group in society has a 7.6% unemployment rate. As has been shown,

There are large differences in unemployment rates across demographic groups.

Table 8.2	Employed, Unemployed, and the Labour Force, 1950–2000					
	(1) Population 15 Years Old or Over (millions)	(2) Labour Force (millions)	(3) Employed (millions)	(4) Unemployed (millions)	(5) Labour-Force Participation Rate	(6) Unemployment Rate
1950	9.6	5.2	5.0	0.2	53.7	3.6
1960	11.8	6.4	6.0	0.4	54.2	7.0
1970	14.5	8.4	7.9	0.5	57.8	5.7
1980	18.6	12.0	11.1	0.9	64.6	7.5
1982	19.2	12.4	11.0	1.4	64.7	11.0
1990	21.3	14.3	13.2	1.2	67.3	8.1
1991	21.6	14.4	12.9	1.5	66.7	10.4
1999	24.0	15.7	14.5	1.2	65.6	7.6
2000 (April)	24.2	15.9	14.9	1.1	65.8	6.8

Source: Statistics Canada, *Historical Labour Force Statistics*, Cat. no. 71–201; *Labour Force Annual Averages*, Cat. no. 71-220; and *Labour Force Information*, Cat.no. 71–001. Columns 5 and 6 may not be calculated exactly from data in columns 1 to 4 due to considerable rounding.

■ **Unemployment Rates by Province** Unemployment rates vary by province or by region in Canada, as they do for many other countries. This is true for a variety of reasons. For one thing, different provinces have different combinations of industries, which do not all grow and decline at the same time and at the same rate. For another, the labour force is not completely mobile—that is, workers often cannot or do not want to pack up and move to take advantage of job opportunities in other parts of the country.

Figure 8.1 shows April 2000 unemployment rates by province. These range from a low of 4.8% in Saskatchewan to a high of 16.8% in Newfoundland. Even within provinces, there can be great variation by area. Ontario, for example, had an overall unemployment rate of 5.5% in April 2000. This rate in turn encompassed a rate of 8.5% in Sudbury and of 5.1% in Hamilton. Newfoundland's rate was 16.8% but in St. John's it was 9.7%. The important point here is that:

> The unemployment rate does not tell the whole story. A particular national or provincial rate of unemployment does not mean that the entire country or the entire province has the same rate.

In newspapers and the electronic media, both national and provincial unemployment rates are most commonly reported on a seasonally adjusted basis. **Seasonal adjustment** is a statistical process designed to remove the usual seasonal variations from a data series to give a better idea of the underlying trend. For example, in Canada, the unadjusted unemployment rate always increases from December to January, as winter deepens and the Christmas shopping rush is completed. Hence, the sharp increase in the unadjusted unemployment rate from 6.4% in December 1999 to 7.3% in January 2000 was consistent with the standard seasonal pattern. The seasonally adjusted rate for those two months was the same at 6.8%, indicating no unexpected change in labour market activity.

While this statistical device does help us look at overall trends, we should not forget that a person who is unemployed as part of a seasonal fluctuation is still unemployed. Moreover the severity of seasonality varies across provinces. For example, the January 1999 unemployment rate in Ontario was 6.6% on a seasonally adjusted basis, which was not much lower than the unadjusted figure of 7.0%. But in Nova Scotia, which has more seasonal industries, the seasonally adjusted unemployment rate was 9.5%, much less than the unadjusted rate of 10.2%. Concentrating only

Table 8.3

Unemployment Rates by Demographic Group, 1982, 1991, and 1999

	1982	1991	1999
Total	11.0	10.4	7.6
Men			
25+ years	8.2	9.2	6.4
15–24 years	20.9	18.8	15.3
Women			
25+ years	8.7	8.8	6.2
15–24 years	15.9	13.3	12.6
University Degree			
45+ years	3.0	4.1	3.7
25–44 years	4.9	5.1	4.3
15–24 years	10.3	7.6	7.6
Diploma			
45+ years	4.8	6.3	5.0
25–44 years	6.8	8.2	5.8
15–24 years	12.5	11.4	8.9

Source: Statistics Canada, *Labour Force Annual Averages,* Cat. no. 71-220, various issues; *Labour Force Historical Review* (CD–ROM); and CANSIM database, Series D980753 and D980760.

seasonal adjustment *A statistical process designed to remove usual seasonal variations from a data series.*

FIGURE 8.1

Provincial Unemployment Rates, April 2000

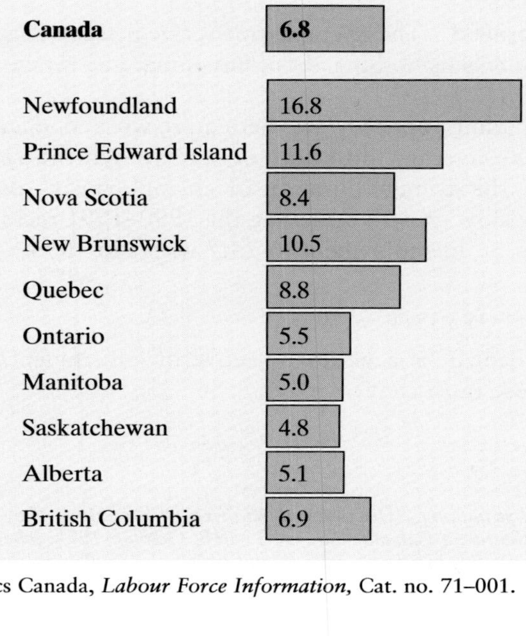

Canada	6.8
Newfoundland	16.8
Prince Edward Island	11.6
Nova Scotia	8.4
New Brunswick	10.5
Quebec	8.8
Ontario	5.5
Manitoba	5.0
Saskatchewan	4.8
Alberta	5.1
British Columbia	6.9

Source: Statistics Canada, *Labour Force Information,* Cat. no. 71–001.

FIGURE 8.2

Unemployment Rates in Different Industries, April 2000

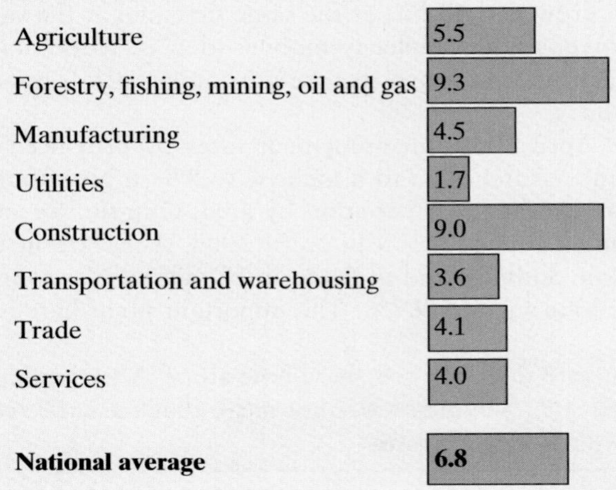

Agriculture	5.5
Forestry, fishing, mining, oil and gas	9.3
Manufacturing	4.5
Utilities	1.7
Construction	9.0
Transportation and warehousing	3.6
Trade	4.1
Services	4.0
National average	**6.8**

Source: Statistics Canada, CANSIM database, D968154–D968161.

on seasonally adjusted figures might lead you to miss the relative severity of seasonal unemployment in Nova Scotia.

■ **Unemployment Rates in Different Industries** Unemployment rates also differ from industry to industry. Figure 8.2 shows that in April 2000 workers in the construction industry experienced unemployment rates much higher (9.0%) than the national average. The lowest unemployment rate was in utilities (1.7%).

■ **Discouraged-Worker Effects** Remember that people who decide to stop looking for work are classified as having dropped out of the labour force rather than as being unemployed. During recessions people often become so discouraged about ever finding a job that they stop looking.[1] This actually lowers the unemployment rate, because those no longer looking for work are no longer counted as unemployed.

A simple example can demonstrate how this **discouraged-worker effect** lowers the unemployment rate. Suppose that there are 1 million unemployed out of a labour force of 10 million. This would mean an unemployment rate of $1/10 = 0.10$, or 10%. If 100 000 of these 1 million unemployed people simply stop looking for work and drop out of the labour force, there would be 0.9 million unemployed out of a labour force of 9.9 million. The unemployment rate would then drop to $0.9/9.9 = 0.091$, or 9.1%.

■ **The Duration of Unemployment** The unemployment rate measures unemployment at a given point in time. It tells us nothing about how long the average unemployed worker is out of work.

During recessionary periods, not only are there more workers unemployed, but as Figure 8.3 shows, the average duration of unemployment rises. In fact, between 1979 and 1983, the average duration of unemployment rose from 14.8 weeks to 21.8 weeks. The slow growth following the 1990–1991 recession resulted in an increase in duration of unemployment to 25.7 weeks in 1994.

THE COSTS OF UNEMPLOYMENT

Why should fuller employment be a policy objective of government? What costs does unemployment impose on society?

discouraged-worker effect
The decline in the measured unemployment rate that results when people who want to work but cannot find jobs grow discouraged and stop looking, thus dropping out of the ranks of the unemployed and the labour force.

---

[1]*See, for example, Ernest B. Akyeampong, "Discouraged Workers—Where Have They Gone?"* Canadian Economic Observer, *Statistics Canada, Cat. no. 11-010, October 1992, where it is reported that there was a significant rise in school, college, and university enrollment in Canada during the 1990–1991 recession.*

■ **Some Unemployment Is Inevitable** Before we discuss the costs of unemployment, it must be noted that some unemployment will always occur. Remember that to be classified as unemployed, a person must be looking for a job. Every year, thousands of people enter the labour force for the first time. Some have dropped out of high school, some are high school or university graduates, and still others are finishing graduate programs. At the same time, new firms are starting up and others are expanding and creating new jobs, while other firms are contracting or going out of business. In short, the economy is dynamic: people grow and acquire skills and the structure of the job market is continuously changing.

At any moment, there is a set of job seekers and a set of jobs that must be matched with one another. It is important that the right people end up in the right jobs. The right job for a person will depend on that person's skills, his or her preferences regarding work environment (large firm or small, formal or informal), where he or she lives, and his or her willingness to commute. At the same time, firms want workers who can meet the requirements of the job and grow with the company.

To make a good match, workers must acquire information on job availability, wage rates, location, and work environment. Firms must acquire information on worker availability and skills. This information-gathering process consumes time and resources. The search process may involve travel, interviews, preparation of a résumé, telephone calls, and hours spent going through the newspaper. But to the extent that these efforts lead to a better match of workers and jobs, they are well spent. As long as the gains to firms and workers exceed the costs of the search, the result is efficient.

■ **Frictional and Structural Unemployment** When Statistics Canada does its survey about work activity, it interviews many people who are involved in the normal search for work. Some of these people are entering the labour market or switching jobs. Such unemployment is necessary to the functioning of the labour market because it makes sense for individuals to invest some time looking for a job that matches their skills and preferences.

The portion of unemployment that is due to this "normal working of the labour market" is called **frictional unemployment**. The frictional unemployment rate is never zero. It may, however change over time. As jobs become more and more differentiated and the number of required skills increases, matching skills and jobs becomes more complex, and the frictional unemployment rate may rise. Programs that help the matching of workers and jobs, such as the computer listings maintained by Human Resources and Development Canada offices, both improve the efficiency of the labour market and reduce frictional unemployment.

The concept of frictional unemployment is imprecise, just as the phrase "the normal working of the labour market" is imprecise. But you can think of frictional unemployment as denoting short-run job and skill matching problems, problems that last a few weeks. Frictional unemployment refers to that portion of the unemployed who will soon fill a suitable, existing vacancy—it just has not happened yet.

Unemployment due to more serious matching problems because of structural changes in the economy is called **structural unemployment**. This includes unemployment due to the collapse of the northern cod fishery, technological change in the automotive industry, public sector reductions in administration or health care, or closure of plants due to demand reductions (e.g., distilleries) or international competition (e.g., textiles). It would also include unemployment due to the oversupply of new entrants for a small number of existing jobs (e.g., lawyers). There may be vacancies in other sectors (and perhaps in other parts of Canada), such as, for example, the financial service sector or high-tech industries. The problem is that the available jobs do not match the skills of the unemployed.

Structural unemployment is a consequence of long-run adjustment problems that may last for years. Policies that reduce structural unemployment may involve retraining or relocation. In some cases those unemployed by structural shifts in the economy may leave the labour force entirely, for example, through taking early retirement. Even if the overall level of economic activity is increased, it will not

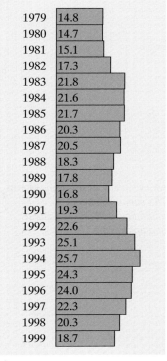

FIGURE 8.3

Average Duration of Unemployment (in weeks), 1979–1999

Year	Weeks
1979	14.8
1980	14.7
1981	15.1
1982	17.3
1983	21.8
1984	21.6
1985	21.7
1986	20.3
1987	20.5
1988	18.3
1989	17.8
1990	16.8
1991	19.3
1992	22.6
1993	25.1
1994	25.7
1995	24.3
1996	24.0
1997	22.3
1998	20.3
1999	18.7

Source: Statistics Canada, *Labour Force Annual Averages*, Cat. nos. 71-220 and 71-529; *Labour Force Historical Review* (CD-ROM).

frictional unemployment *The portion of unemployment that is due to the normal working of the labour market; used to denote short-run job and skill matching problems.*

structural unemployment *The portion of unemployment that is due to changes in the structure of the economy that result in a significant loss of jobs in certain industries.*

completely solve the problems of the structurally unemployed, because the expansion may be in a sector of the economy for which they are ill equipped. It may, however, increase opportunities for retraining and career changes.

Although structural unemployment is to be expected in a dynamic economy, it is no less painful to the workers who experience it. In some ways, those who lose their jobs because their skills are obsolete are the ones who experience the greatest pain. The fact that some structural unemployment is inevitable does not mean that it costs society nothing.

A central issue in macroeconomics is whether the government can influence the overall level of economic activity in order to achieve a more socially desirable outcome including a lower unemployment rate. Assuming that it can, it is important to determine how much unemployment can be attributed to frictional and structural factors. Attempts to reduce the unemployment rate below that level just by increasing the level of aggregate economic activity may not be sustainable, because the main problem is that the unemployed do not match the type of positions an expansion may create.

natural rate of unemployment *The sum of frictional unemployment and structural unemployment.*

We sometimes call the sum of frictional and structural unemployment rate the **natural rate of unemployment.** Many economists object to this term in that the word "natural" gives an impression of inevitability, or even of acceptability. Alternatively, it could be called the "target rate of unemployment," although that too has its shortcomings. Perhaps it might be a target if a government were attempting to stimulate overall economic activity. But remember there are other policies such as retraining or improving the availability of labour market information that may reduce unemployment by reducing the frictional or structural components. The natural rate could also be called the "full-employment unemployment rate," although again that seems to accept all structural unemployment as desirable. Many economists, on the basis of a model we shall discuss in Chapters 14 and 15 that suggests unemployment below the natural rate will add to inflation, use the term *NAIRU*, or "nonaccelerating inflation rate of unemployment." We will use the term "natural rate" because it is simple and it is widely used, but you should understand its deficiencies.

As controversial as the name is, estimates of the size of the natural rate are even more controversial and range from at least 4% to 8%. If it is indeed the target for a policy to stimulate economic activity, you can see how important such a large discrepancy is. Some economists argue that the natural rate is very unstable and hence not useful. This view goes hand-in-hand with the view that such concepts as structural unemployment are too imprecise. We have described structural unemployment as matching unemployment. But perhaps when the overall level of economic activity is low, employers will only hire an employee who is a near-perfect match, but during a boom, they will be much more accepting. We will discuss the natural rate and the labour market more extensively in Chapter 15.

■ **Cyclical Unemployment and Lost Output**   Output grows substantially in the long run (as, for example, was shown in Figures 6.6, 6.7, and 6.8 in Chapter 6) with changes in technology and increases in capital and the number of workers. But the pattern is not a smooth one, with output sometimes well below potential output, corresponding to an unemployment rate well above the natural rate. For example, from 1991 to 1994 unemployment averaged above 10%, and between 1992 and 1993 it averaged above 11%. We call such unemployment in excess of the natural rate **cyclical unemployment.** This unemployment can be attributed to recessions and periods of slow economic growth.

cyclical unemployment *The increase in unemployment that occurs during recessions and periods of slow economic growth. Cyclical unemployment + frictional unemployment + structural unemployment = the actual rate of unemployment.*

In one sense, an increase in unemployment during a recession is simply a manifestation of a more fundamental problem. The basic problem is that firms are producing less. Remember that a recession entails a decline in real GDP, or real output. When firms cut back and produce less, they employ fewer workers and less capital. Thus, the first and most direct cost of a recession is the loss of real goods and services that otherwise would have been produced.

Never was the loss of output more dramatic than during the Great Depression. In Table 8.1 you saw that real output fell about 28% between 1929 and 1933. It is, of course, the real output of the economy that matters most—the food we eat, the medical care we get, the cars we drive, the movies we watch, the new houses that are built, the pots we cook in, and the education that we receive. When output falls by 28%, life changes dramatically for a lot of people.

High unemployment at other times as well is associated with lost output. Pierre Fortin[2] of the University of Quebec at Montreal has estimated that high unemployment in the early and mid-1990s led to a gap of about 10% between actual and potential output, which he compares with estimates of 1.5% for the United States. Throughout the 1990s and into the new century, U.S. unemployment was persistently below Canadian unemployment, suggesting a continued output gap in Canada. While estimates of output gaps vary, they will include the loss in output associated with discouraged workers as well as underutilization of labour and capital. The losses are clearly substantial and permanent in the sense that society loses forever the output that someone could have produced in 2001 but didn't because he or she was unemployed.

■ **Social Consequences** The costs of recessions and depressions are neither evenly distributed across the population nor easily quantifiable. The social consequences of the depression of the 1930s are perhaps the hardest to comprehend. Most people who are alive today did not live through the Great Depression and can only read about it in books or hear stories told by parents and grandparents. Few emerged from this period unscathed. At the bottom were the poor and the fully unemployed, about 20% of the labour force. During the worst years of the Depression, about 12% of Canadians per year relied on emergency relief.[3] Farm incomes dropped as the world demand for Canada's agricultural products declined. Severe drought in the Prairies compounded the overall difficulties in the economy and forced many farmers off their land.

A collection of letters written to then Prime Minister R. B. Bennett records some of the misery. In one such letter in 1934, an Elizabeth McCrae writes, desperate for any kind of job anywhere in Canada:[4]

> I have applied for every position that I heard about but there were always so many girls who applied that it was impossible to get work. So time went on and my clothing became very shabby . . . Many prospective employers just glanced at my attire and shook their heads . . .
>
> First I ate three very light meals a day; then two and then one. During the past two weeks I have eaten only toast and drunk a cup of tea every other day. In the past fortnight I have lost 20 pounds and the result of this deprivation is that I am so very nervous that I could never stand a test [for stenographic work] along with one, two and three hundred girls . . .
>
> Day after day I pass a delicatessen and the food in the window looks oh, so good! So tempting and I'm so hungry! . . . I wouldn't mind if I could just lay down and die but to starve, oh it's terrible to think about.
>
> Mr. Bennett, even if you can do nothing for me I want to thank you for your kindness in reading this letter and if I were jobless and semi-hungry for a life-time I would still be a Conservative to the last, and fight for that Government.
>
> Thanking you again for your very kind attention, I am
>
> Your humble servant,
> (Miss) Elizabeth McCrae

The prime minister received many such letters and as a compassionate man of some means, often enclosed with his reply a few dollars from his own funds, not insignificant sums at the time. It is not known whether any money was sent to Elizabeth McCrae.

[2]Pierre Fortin, "A Strategy for Deficit Control Through Faster Growth," Canadian Business Economics, Fall 1994: 3–26.
[3]L. M. Grayson and Michael Bliss, eds., The Wretched of Canada (Toronto: University of Toronto Press, 1971), p. ix.
[4]Grayson and Bliss, pp. 83–85.

The Cheops pyramid consists of 2 300 000 blocks of stone of 2 tonnes each and is 140 metres high. As a way of visualizing the lost output due to high Canadian unemployment between 1990 and 1996, Professor Lars Osberg of Dalhousie University has estimated that if all unemployed workers in excess of an unemployment rate of 7.5% had built pyramids by hand using the same methods as the slaves of ancient Egypt, at least 1.2 pyramids like the Cheops pyramid could have been constructed every year.

Source: Lars Osberg, "The Great Pyramids of Canada", letter to Nature, December 12, 1996.

FIGURE 8.4

Inflation Rate in Canada (Percentage Change in CPI), 1970–1999

Year	Rate
1970	3.4
1971	2.9
1972	4.8
1973	7.7
1974	10.7
1975	10.9
1976	7.5
1977	7.8
1978	9.0
1979	9.2
1980	10.1
1981	12.4
1982	10.9
1983	5.8
1984	4.3
1985	4.0
1986	4.1
1987	4.4
1988	4.0
1989	5.0
1990	4.8
1991	5.6
1992	1.5
1993	1.8
1994	0.2
1995	2.2
1996	1.6
1997	1.6
1998	0.9
1999	1.7

Source: Adapted from Statistics Canada, CANSIM database, Series P200000.

Economic hardship accompanied the more recent recessions as well. One measure of how many people in Canada are facing economic difficulties is the percentage of individuals below the annual Statistics Canada definition of low income. This percentage rose from 14.7% of Canadians (3.5 million people) in 1981 to 17.3% (4.2 million people) in 1984.[5] The number of registered food banks in Canada jumped from just 1 in 1981 to 292 by 1991.[6] In addition to economic hardship, prolonged unemployment may also bring with it a number of social and personal ills: anxiety, depression, a deterioration of physical and psychological health, drug abuse (including alcoholism), and suicide.

■ **Lower Investment and Long-Term Growth**   In addition to lost output today and serious, immediate social consequences, recessions may lead to lost output in the future. When the economy experiences a recession, the level of investment tends to fall.

The production of capital—that is, *investment*—is one of the keys to future economic growth and progress. Thus, eliminating or reducing contractions in output could increase the level of investment and ultimately the rate of growth.

OTHER CONSEQUENCES OF RECESSIONS

Recessions are likely to slow down the rate of inflation. As Figure 8.4 shows, in 1980 inflation in Canada reached double-digit levels; by 1983, after the 1980–1982 recession, the inflation rate had been cut nearly in half. While rates of inflation prior to the 1990–1991 recession were not high compared to 1980 levels, the recession slowed them nonetheless. The inflation rate, which was 4% in 1988, was approaching 6% in 1991. After 1991, inflation dropped substantially and has remained low.

In short, it appears that recessions bring lower inflation, but much more analysis is needed before we can understand just why this is so. (We will do this analysis in Chapter 14.) The main point here is simply that:

> Inflation tends to fall during recessions.

Finally, some argue that recessions may increase efficiency by driving the least efficient firms in the economy out of business and forcing surviving firms to trim waste and manage their resources better.

Inflation

As can be seen in Figure 8.4, inflation rates differed during the expansionary periods prior to the recessions of 1980–1982 and 1990–1991. Inflation rates rose from 7.5% to 9.2% from 1976 to 1979. The period of growth from 1984 to 1988, however, did not seem to bring accelerating inflation with it.

Why is inflation a problem? If you understand that wages and salaries, as well as other forms of income, increase along with prices during periods of inflation,

---

[5]See Suzanne Methot, "Low Income in Canada," Canadian Social Trends, *Statistics Canada, Cat. no. 11-008, Spring 1987: 2–7.*
[6]See Jillian Oderkirk, "Food Banks," Canadian Social Trends, *Statistics Canada, Cat. no. 11-008, Spring 1992: 6–14.*

you will understand that this question is more subtle than you might think at first. If my income doubles and the prices of the things I buy double, am I any worse off? I can buy exactly the same things that I bought yesterday, so to the extent that my well-being depends on what I am able to buy, the answer is no.

However, incomes and prices do not all increase at the same rate during inflations. For some people, income increases faster than prices; for others, prices increase faster. Consequently, some people actually benefit from inflations, while others are hurt.

The remainder of this chapter focuses on the problem of inflation: its measurement, its costs, and the gains and losses experienced during inflationary periods.

DEFINING INFLATION

What is inflation? Clearly, not all price increases constitute an inflation. Prices of individual goods and services are determined in a number of ways. In competitive markets, the interaction of many buyers and many sellers—the operation of supply and demand—determines prices. In imperfectly competitive markets, prices are determined by producers' decisions. (This is the core of microeconomic theory.)

In any economy, prices are continuously changing as markets adjust to changing conditions. Lack of rain may dry up corn and wheat fields, thus reducing supply and pushing up the price of agricultural products. At the same time, low levels of production by oil producers may be driving up the price of oil and petroleum products. Simultaneously, major trade unions may be negotiating contracts with their employers that raise (or lower) wage rates.

When the price of one good rises, that price increase may or may not be part of a larger inflation. As we explained earlier, an **inflation** is an increase in the overall price level. It happens when many prices increase simultaneously. We measure inflation by looking at a large number of goods and services and calculating the average increase in their prices during some period of time. A **deflation** is a decrease in the overall price level. It occurs when many prices decrease simultaneously.

It is often useful to distinguish between a *one-time* increase in the overall price level and an increase in the overall price level that continues over a period of time. For example, the overall price level could rise 10% over a few months and then stop rising, or it could increase steadily over some years. Economists often use the term *inflation* to refer only to increases in the price level that continue over some significant period of time. We will refer to such periods as periods of **sustained inflation**.

PRICE INDEXES

Changes in the price level are measured using *price indexes*. In Chapter 7, we discussed exactly how to construct two measures of the price level, the GDP deflator and the **consumer price index (CPI)**. The values of the CPI (and the corresponding percentage changes) are given in Figure 8.5 for the period 1950–2000. The CPI is more widely used for most purposes, largely because it is available more quickly and on a monthly basis. The CPI measure of the change in the price level during April 1999 was available in May 1999 but the April 1999 GDP deflator, based on the national accounts, was not available until late 1999, and even then only a quarterly value was available.

Let us summarize from Chapter 7 how the CPI is calculated. The same standardized bundle of goods is priced each month. If the bundle cost $100 one month and $105 the next, we would say the price level had increased by 5%. The index is called a *fixed-weight index* because it always uses the same bundle (and hence the various prices always have the same weights in the index). See the Application box "The CPI Weights" for more information on this bundle.

The CPI has a number of problems, almost all related in some way to this fixed-weight aspect and most of which point to the CPI overstating inflation. One of these problems is called *substitution bias*. For example, if the price of a particular item, say beef, shoots up, people are likely to make substitutions, buying other meats or types of food. But because the CPI is based on the initial fixed bundle, the increase in the cost of living according to the CPI will be based on the assumption

inflation *An increase in the overall price level.*

deflation *A decrease in the overall price level.*

sustained inflation *An increase in the overall price level that continues over a significant period of time.*

consumer price index (CPI) *A price index calculated every month using the price of a standardized bundle of goods meant to represent the consumption of the average consumer.*

APPLICATION

The CPI Weights

As we have discussed in both this and the previous chapter, the CPI is based on the price of a particular bundle of goods, where that bundle is based on "average" consumption. The current CPI, while it is normally expressed as an index in which the 1992 value is set equal to 100, is in fact based on 1996 expenditure patterns. We do not usually describe the bundle in terms of how many litres of milk, how many loaves of bread, how many automobile tires, etc., it may contain. Instead we look at the overall shares of the expenditure made on various commodities or commodity groups. The data are presented in Figure 1.

As you would expect, the big items are shelter, food, and transportation. But remember these are average consumption expenditure shares for the country as a whole. For example, in terms of expenditure share, 3.4% of the bundle used in calculating the CPI is alcoholic beverages and tobacco products, yet some people do not smoke or drink at all, and others devote a much larger fraction of their total spending to these commodities.

This can make a difference. For example, Table 1 examines recent CPI inflation with and without the effects of changes in indirect taxes such as federal or provincial sales taxes. There are two big differences. First, in 1991 you can see that the CPI rate of inflation is 5.6% but only 3.4% after the effect of indirect taxes is removed. Of course the reason is that on January 1, 1991, the GST was introduced and that added about 2% to inflation as measured by the

FIGURE 1

Expenditure Patterns Underlying the Consumer Price Index

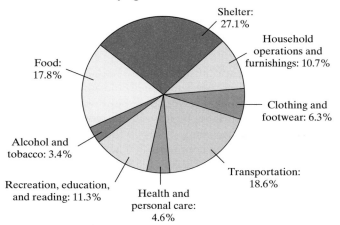

Source: Statistics Canada, *The Consumer Price Index*, Cat. no. 62-001, January 2000, p. 41. *Note:* Numbers may not add due to rounding.

CPI. Second, in 1994, CPI inflation was only 0.2%, but without the effects of indirect tax changes, it would have been 1.3%. That is because that year the federal government and some provincial governments lowered their cigarette taxes substantially to combat smuggling from the United States. Hence, if you had a cost-of-living provision in your wage contract that year and you were a non-smoker, you received an increase based on a CPI change of 0.2%, but in fact you did not benefit from the cut in taxes and hence your cost of living probably went up by more than that. Because the CPI is based on the average cigarette consumption, including nonsmokers, a heavy smoker may have had his or her cost of living fall but he or she would have received the same upward cost-of-living adjustment.

Table 1

Recent Behaviour of the CPI With and Without Indirect Taxes

Year	Percentage Change in CPI	Percentage Change in CPI Less Contribution of Indirect Taxes
1990	4.8	4.1
1991	5.6	3.4
1992	1.5	1.0
1993	1.8	1.7
1994	0.2	1.3
1995	2.2	2.2
1996	1.6	1.5
1997	1.6	1.6
1998	0.9	0.8
1999	1.7	1.8
2000 (Q1)	2.3	1.3

Source: Adapted from *Bank of Canada Banking and Financial Statistics* May 2000: Table H8. Figures for 2000 based on first quarter.

that individuals are still consuming the same amount of beef and hence, inflation will be overestimated.

Another problem is what is called *new goods bias*. While the CPI is fixed weight, nonetheless the base year and hence the weights are updated from time to time, and new products are added. But often the prices of new products (e.g., computers, cellular telephones) fall substantially in price soon after their introduction and before they are included in the CPI. Because the CPI inflation calculation does not include this sharp price fall, it may be biased upwards.

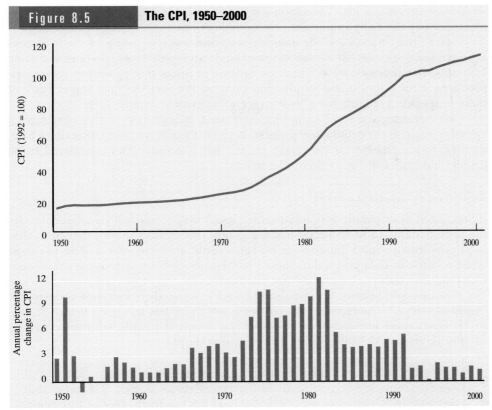

Figure 8.5   The CPI, 1950–2000

Source: Adapted from Statistics Canada, CANSIM database, Series P200000 and P119500. Data for 2000 based on first quarter.

Another aspect of the new goods problem is that sometimes new goods that are better than previous goods with the same function are introduced. Electronic calculators are clearly better than the mechanical adding machines they have replaced and most people would argue that CDs are better than vinyl records. Similarly there are quality improvements within the same good. A new laser printer may cost 10% more than the previous model, but that is not necessarily a price increase if it can print more quickly or with higher resolution. But adjusting for these quality improvements is a difficult task, and most economists think the Statistics Canada adjustments are insufficient. Hence this *quality bias* leads to another upward bias in the CPI inflation.

Finally, just as it tends to look at the same bundle of goods, Statistics Canada tends to survey prices in the same retail outlets. If there is a shift by consumers to lower-priced retailers, be they superstores or discount travel agents, this will lead to another upward bias, called *outlet substitution bias*.

The bottom line is:

> Changes in the consumer price index somewhat overstate changes in the cost of living.

How large is this effect? The Bank of Canada[7] has suggested the bias is up to 0.5% per year, so that if the rate of CPI inflation was 1.2%, true inflation could be as low as 0.7%. In the United States, some estimates suggest the bias may be higher, perhaps 1.0%. Particularly in the United States, there is now a policy debate about adjusting the CPI for these biases. If such an adjustment were made in either Canada or the United States, the result would be a lower official rate of inflation and hence every transfer payment or wage indexed to the rate of inflation

---

[7]Allan Crawford, *"Measurement Biases in the Canadian CPI: A Technical Note,"* Bank of Canada Review, *Summer 1993: 21–36.*

would not rise as quickly. Therefore, while the issue of CPI bias seems purely technical, it has potentially important policy implications.

Other price indexes include **industry price indexes,** consisting of the Industrial Product Price Indexes (IPPI) for finished and intermediate goods, and the Raw Material Price Index (RMPI). These are indexes of prices that producers receive for products at all stages in the production process, not just the final stage. Each of these indexes is available for a wide range of individual commodities.

One advantage of some of the industry price indexes is that they detect price increases early in the production process. Because their movements sometimes foreshadow future changes in consumer prices, they are sometimes considered to be leading indicators of future consumer prices.

THE COSTS OF INFLATION

If you asked most people why inflation is "bad," they would tell you that it lowers the overall standard of living by making goods and services more expensive. That is, it cuts into people's purchasing power. People are fond of recalling the days when a bottle of cola cost a dime and a hamburger cost a quarter. Just think what we could buy today if prices had not changed!

What people usually do not think about is what their incomes were in the "good old days." The fact that the cost of a soft drink has increased from 10 cents to 50 cents does not mean anything in real terms if people who once earned $5 000 now earn $25 000. Why? The reason is simple:

> People's income comes from wages and salaries, profits, interest and rent, and income from these sources increases during inflations as well. The wage rate is the price of labour, rent is the price of land, and so forth. During inflations, most prices—including input prices—tend to rise together, and input prices determine both the incomes of workers and the incomes of owners of capital and land.

■ **Inflation Changes the Distribution of Income**   Whether you gain or lose during a period of inflation depends on whether your income rises faster or slower than the prices of the things you buy. The group most often mentioned when the impact of inflation is discussed is the group of people living on fixed incomes. Clearly, if your income is fixed and prices rise, your ability to purchase goods and services falls proportionately. But who are the fixed-income earners?

Most people think of the elderly. Indeed, many retired workers living on private pensions receive monthly cheques that will never increase. Many pension plans, however, pay benefits that are indexed to inflation. The biggest source of income for many of the elderly is government benefits. These benefits are fully indexed.

Students from Toronto's Harbord Collegiate protest the increase in the price of chocolate bars from 5 cents to 8 cents in 1947. Since that time, the price level in Canada as measured by the CPI has increased by about a factor of nine.

real interest rate *The difference between the interest rate and the inflation rate.*

■ **Effects on Debtors and Creditors**   It is also commonly believed that debtors benefit at the expense of creditors during an inflation. Certainly, if I lend you $100 to be paid back in a year, and prices increase 10% in the meantime, I get back 10% less in real terms than what I lent you.

But suppose that we had both anticipated that prices would rise 10%. Of course, I would have taken this into consideration in the deal that I made with you. That is, I would charge you an interest rate high enough to cover the decrease in value due to the anticipated inflation. If, for example, we agree on a 15% interest rate, then you must pay me $115 at the end of a year. The difference between the interest rate and the inflation rate is referred to as the **real interest rate.** In our deal, I will earn a real interest rate of 5%. By charging a 15% interest rate, I have taken into account the anticipated 10% inflation rate. In this sense, I am not hurt by the inflation—I keep pace with inflation and earn a profit on my money, too—despite the fact that I am a creditor.

On the other hand, an unanticipated inflation—that is, an inflation that takes people by surprise—can hurt creditors. If the actual inflation rate during the period of my loan to you turns out to be 20%, then I as a creditor will be hurt. I charged you 15% interest, expecting to get a 5% real rate of return, when I needed to charge you 25% to get the same 5% real rate of return. Because inflation turned out to be higher than expected, I got a negative real return of 5%.

> Inflation that is higher than expected benefits debtors and inflation that is lower than expected benefits creditors.

■ **Administrative Costs and Inefficiencies**   There are, of course, costs associated even with anticipated inflation. One obvious cost is the administrative cost associated with simply keeping up. Store owners have to recalculate and re-post prices frequently, and this takes time that could be used more efficiently. During the rapid inflation in Israel in the early 1980s, a hotline was set up to give the hourly price index!

More frequent banking transactions may be required of people as well. For example, interest rates tend to rise with anticipated inflation. When interest rates are high, the opportunity costs of holding cash outside of banks is high. People therefore hold less cash and need to stop at the bank more often. (We discuss this phenomenon in more detail in the next part of this book.) In addition, if people are not fully informed, or if they do not understand what is happening to prices in general, they may make mistakes in their business dealings. These mistakes can lead to a misallocation of resources.

■ **Increased Risk and Slower Economic Growth**   When unanticipated inflation occurs regularly, the degree of risk associated with investments in the economy increases. Increases in uncertainty may make investors reluctant to invest in capital and to make long-term commitments. To the extent that the level of investment falls, the prospects for long-term economic growth are lessened.

INFLATION: PUBLIC ENEMY NUMBER ONE?

Economists have debated the seriousness of the costs of inflation for decades. There is wide agreement that very high inflation, such as in the Israeli example above, retards growth because substantial resources are spent in adjusting prices and in trying to adjust to the furious rate of price change. But there is substantial disagreement about the costs of low and moderate rates of inflation, particularly in comparison to the costs of a recession which some economists argue may be required to reduce inflation. As we also will discuss in subsequent chapters, it is sometimes argued that central banks can and have put economies into recessions in their attempts to curb moderate inflation. Can a lower inflation rate possibly be worth the costs of a recession?

Many of those who support a zero inflation target would agree that the costs of low and moderate inflation are not very high. However, they emphasize that the costs are incurred as long as the inflation continues. They sometimes also argue that there is a tendency for inflation to worsen over time. Hence, they claim, it is worthwhile to pay large once-and-for-all costs to obtain low inflation, which it is hoped will then last forever.

Your evaluation of these arguments may depend on your personal experience with unemployment and inflation as well as many other factors. Nevertheless, you need to understand more clearly the nature of the tradeoffs and the arguments concerning what kind of control governments have over the macroeconomy. These are the topics to which we turn in the coming chapters.

Global Unemployment Rates and Inflation

Unemployment and inflation are not just concerns of our own economy. Other countries at times experience high unemployment or high inflation (or both). The Great Depression of the 1930s was a worldwide phenomenon, and most countries, including Canada, experienced high rates of inflation in the 1970s after the OPEC oil price increases.

While unemployment rate comparisons across countries in part reflect differences in measurement methods, there have nonetheless been some important recent trends. The U. S. employment rate had exceeded 10% at times in the 1980s, but it fell steadily during the 1990s to about 4% by 2000. Unemployment in Europe also fell during this period, but on average more slowly, so that countries such as France, Germany, and Italy still had unemployment rates of about 10% at the turn of the century. In contrast, Japan's unemployment picture worsened during the 1990s, reflecting economic problems in Southeast Asia; the official unemployment rate had always been less than 3% in the 1980s, but by 2000 it was almost 5%.

Almost worldwide, inflation has recently been low. At the turn of the century, the inflation rate was well under 5% per year in all industrialized countries and in many developing economies as well, with China, for example, having almost zero inflation. The inflation change has been particularly dramatic in Eastern Europe. Russia, for instance, brought its inflation rate down from four-digit levels in 1992 to 90% in 1996 to less than 20% by the year 2000.

Looking Ahead

This ends our introduction to the basic concepts and problems of macroeconomics. The first chapter of this part introduced the field, the second discussed the measurement of the economy's output and income, and this chapter discussed two of the macroeconomy's major problems—unemployment and inflation—in detail.

Thus far, however, we have said nothing about what *determines* the level of output, the number of employed and unemployed workers, and the rate of inflation in an economy. The following chapters provide you with the background in macroeconomic theory you need to understand *how* the macroeconomy functions. With this knowledge, you will also be able to understand how the government can influence the economy through its taxing, spending, and monetary policies.

Summary

Recessions, Depressions, and Unemployment

1. A *recession* is a period in which real GDP declines for at least two consecutive quarters. When less output is produced, employment declines, the unemployment rate rises, and a smaller percentage of the capital stock is used. When real output falls, real income declines.

2. A *depression* is a prolonged and deep recession, although there is disagreement over how severe and how prolonged a recession must be in order to be called a depression.

3. The *unemployment rate* is the ratio of the number of unemployed people to the number of people in the labour force. To be considered unemployed and in the labour force, a person must generally be looking for work.

4. Marked differences in rates of unemployment exist across demographic groups, regions, and industries. Young people, for example, experience much higher unemployment rates than older workers.

5. When a person decides to stop looking for work, that person is considered to have dropped out of the labour force and is no longer classified as unemployed. People who stop looking because they are discouraged about ever finding a job are sometimes called *discouraged workers*.

6. Some unemployment is inevitable. Because new workers are continually entering the labour force, because industries and firms are continuously expanding and contracting, and because people switch jobs, there is a constant process of job search as workers and firms try to match the best people to the available jobs.

7. The unemployment that occurs because of short-run job and skill matching problems is called *frictional unemployment*. The unemployment that occurs because of longer-run structural changes in the economy is called *structural unemployment*. The *natural rate of unemployment* is the sum of the frictional rate and the structural rate. The increase in unemployment that occurs during recessions and depressions is called *cyclical unemployment*.

8. The major costs associated with recessions and unemployment are decreased real output, the damage done to the people who are unemployed, and lost output in the future. Recessions may reduce inflation.

Inflation

9. An *inflation* is an increase in the overall price level. It happens when many prices increase simultaneously. Inflation is measured by calculating the average increase in the prices of a large number of goods during some period of time. A *deflation* is a decrease in the overall price level. A *sustained inflation* is an increase in the overall price level that continues over a significant period of time.

10. A number of different indexes are used to measure the overall price level. Among them are the *GDP deflator, consumer price index (CPI)*, and *industry price indexes*.

11. Whether a person gains or loses during a period of inflation depends on whether his or her income rises faster or slower than the prices of the things he or she buys. The elderly may be insulated from inflation to some degree, because government benefits and many pensions are indexed to inflation.

12. Inflation that is higher than expected benefits debtors, and inflation that is lower than expected benefits creditors.

Global Unemployment Rates and Inflation

13. Unemployment rates and rates of inflation differ markedly across time and countries and can reach quite high levels.

Review Terms and Concepts

consumer price index (CPI) 163

cyclical unemployment 160

deflation 163

depression 154

discouraged-worker effect 158

employed 154

frictional unemployment 159

industry price indexes 166

inflation 163

labour force 154

labour-force participation rate 155

natural rate of unemployment 160

not in the labour force 154

real interest rate 166

recession 154

seasonal adjustment 157

structural unemployment 159

sustained inflation 163

unemployed 154

unemployment rate 155

Equations:

1. Labour force = Employed + Unemployed

2. Population = Labour force + Not in labour force

3. $\text{Unemployment rate} = \dfrac{\text{Unemployed}}{\text{Employed} + \text{Unemployed}}$

4. $\text{Labour-force participation rate} = \dfrac{\text{Labour force}}{\text{Population}}$

1. Between 1989 and 1990, total employment in Canada rose from 13 086 000 to 13 165 000, an increase of 79 000. At the same time, the number of unemployed rose from 1 065 000 to 1 164 000 and the unemployment rate rose from 7.5% to 8.1%.
   a. How can unemployment rise when the number of employed is also rising?
   b. From these numbers, calculate how large the labour force was in 1989 and 1990.

2. In 1989, economists were saying that the Canadian economy was close to full employment even though the unemployment rate was above 7%. How can they make this assertion?

3. Using the data in Table 8.2, calculate the changes in the unemployment rate and the labour-force participation rate that would occur if 200 000 unemployed persons dropped out of the labour force in April 2000.

4. "When an inefficient firm or a firm producing a product that people no longer want goes out of business, people are unemployed, but that's part of the normal process of economic growth and development; the unemployment is part of the natural rate and need not concern policy makers." Discuss this statement and its relevance to the economy today.

5. What is the unemployment rate in your province today? What was it in 1970, 1982, and 1991? How has your province done relative to the national average? Do you know, or can you determine, why?

6. Suppose that all wages, salaries, welfare benefits, and other sources of income were indexed to inflation. Would inflation still be considered a problem? Why or why not?

7. a. What do the CPI and industry price indexes measure? Why do we need all these price indexes? (Think about what purpose you would use each one for.)
   b. Consider an economy with two goods, gum and lemon drops. Suppose that, between year 1 and year 2, there is a downward shift in the supply schedule for gum and an upward shift in the supply schedule for lemon drops. Explain why the CPI for this two-good economy would overstate the increase in the cost of living.

8. Consider the following statements:
   a. "More people are employed in Tappania now than at any time in the past 50 years."
   b. "The unemployment rate in Tappania is higher now than it has been in 50 years."
   Can both of these statements be true at the same time? Explain.

9. If the interest rate is 7% and the inflation rate is, as expected, 3%, what is the real rate of interest?

10. Suppose that the interest rate is 6% but that recipients of interest must pay 50% of it as personal income tax. If the inflation rate is 1%, what is the real after-tax rate of interest to recipients of interest? What is the real after-tax rate of interest if the tax rate does not change, but the interest rate increases to 12% while the inflation rate increases to 7%?

11. Repeat question 10 assuming instead that the personal income tax rate is one-third.

Indexes of Economic Well-Being

One of the important lessons of Chapter 7 is that GDP per capita is a measure of economic activity or production but not a measure of economic well-being. In a paper presented to the meetings of the American Economic Association in Boston in January 2000, Lars Osberg of Dalhousie University and Andrew Sharpe of the Centre for the Study of Living Standards (Ottawa) propose well-being indexes for several countries based on four components: consumption, accumulation, inequality, and insecurity.

Ignoring measurement issues for the moment, the *consumption* component of the Osberg and Sharpe index, just like the consumption component of measured GDP, includes marketed goods and services but also includes nonmarket production not included in GDP such as household production

Consumption is only one component of measures of economic well-being.

(e.g., cooking, cleaning, and home repairs done by household members for themselves), volunteer work, underground-economy production, and leisure. They also include adjustments for life

FIGURE 1

Indexes of Economic Well-Being and Real GDP per Capita, Canada, 1980–1996.

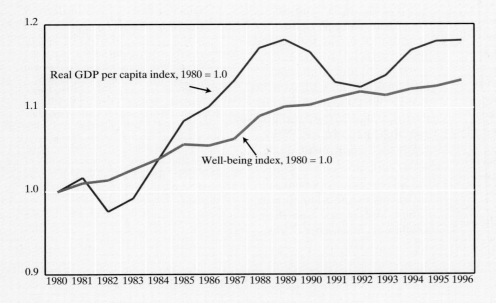

Source: Osberg and Sharpe, op. cit. (first)

expectancy and household size (e.g., two people may be able to enjoy a better lifestyle living together than apart because they can share items such as housing space). Government services are also included in this component.

The *accumulation* component is intended to reflect the fact that the current generation is made better off by knowing there will be income in the future, both for itself and for unborn generations. Therefore it includes contributions to that future income, including investment in plant, machinery, research, and residences, just as the investment component of GDP does. Unlike GDP (but like net domestic product), there is an allowance for depreciation of the existing stock of capital, and the Osberg and Sharpe measure also includes special treatment of research and development. There are also adjustments for depletion of natural resource stocks, environmental degradation, changes in the value of human capital (as education and on-the-job training can provide future income, just as an investment in physical capital can), and changes in foreign indebtedness.

The *inequality* component is based on measures of income inequality and poverty, including those that we discuss in Chapter 17 of the *Principles of Microeconomics* companion to this volume. For example, the Osberg and Sharpe well-being index will increase with decreases in the percentage of people who fall below the poverty line (defined, with some adjustments, as one-half the median after-tax family income) and with increases in the average income of those below the poverty line.

The *insecurity* component allows for effects from unemployment, illness, single-parent poverty, and old age poverty. These possibilities can all make individuals anxious about the future, so if the probability of such events can be reduced or their consequences lessened (e.g., by unemployment insurance, publicly provided health care, welfare payments, or old age pensions), well-being is increased.

The four components must be weighted to get a single index of economic well-being. As we discussed in the last two chapters, the result will depend on the weights. Osberg and Sharpe use weights of 0.4, 0.1, 0.25, and 0.25 for the four components in the order above (although they recognize that other observers could validly assign different weights). With the proviso that the results depend upon a number of data and measurement issues, Figure 1 shows their index for Canada since 1980. You can see it increases far more slowly than real GDP per capita, partly because of high unemployment and little change in income inequality over that period. Osberg and Sharpe's paper does not compare the levels of economic well-being directly across countries, but in other research they conclude that, by their measure, Canadian economic well-being exceeds that of the United States, in part due to the more equal income distribution in Canada.

Questions for Analytical Thinking

1. In some of their research, Osberg and Sharpe have made adjustments to the consumption component to remove the consumption of public transit and private vehicles involved in travelling to and from work. They make similar adjustments to take out the cost of burglar alarms, police forces, and pollution abatement devices. Why might such adjustments make sense?

2. The insecurity component is itself an index. In calculating it, Osberg and Sharpe base their weights on judgments of the proportions of the population "at risk." The weight is largest for ill health (everyone is at risk), second-largest for unemployment (working-age individuals at risk), third-largest for single-parent poverty (married women with children at risk), and smallest for old age poverty (weight calculated on the basis of individuals aged 45–64). If you were assigning weights, would your ranking from largest to smallest be the same? Why or why not?

3. The CBC video associated with this Case discusses a number of problems related to poverty, including child poverty. An address by Professor Shelley Phipps of Dalhousie University to the Canadian Economics Association meetings in May 1999 showed that little progress had been made in meeting the 1989 Canadian parliamentary resolution of eliminating child poverty by the year 2000. However, since 1975 poverty among seniors has declined dramatically, in large part due to the Canada/Quebec Pension Plan (a compulsory pension plan) and the Guaranteed Income Supplement (a transfer program to poor seniors). Discuss possible reasons why policy measures have not been enacted that would similarly reduce child poverty.

Sources: Lars Osberg and Andrew Sharpe, "International Comparisons of Trends in Economic Well-Being," Paper presented at the meetings of the American Economic Association, January 2000, Boston; Lars Osberg and Andrew Sharpe, "An Index of Economic Well-Being for Canada and the United States"—Both papers available at **www.csls.ca/**; Shelley Phipps, "Innis Lecture: Economics and the Well-Being of Canadian Children," *Canadian Journal of Economics*, November 1999: 1135–1163.

Video Resource: "Poverty," *The National*, November 23, 1999.

Web References for Part Two: Concepts and Problems in Macroeconomics

For more on the case study we just did on indexes of well-being, you can visit the Centre for the Study of Living Standards (www.csls.ca/). This is an Ottawa-based research group that has related research emphases on productivity and unemployment.

An alternative approach to comparing well-being across countries is contained in the the United Nations Index of Human Development, as mentioned at the end of Chapter 7. (In the year 2000, Canada was first, followed by Norway, the United States, Australia, and Iceland.) See the Web site of the United Nations Development Programme, Human Development Report (www.undp.org/hdro/). The site may require some navigation, but you can download the entire report for any year or just examine a press kit summary.

More generally for this Part, the main source for Canadian official statistics (on such matters as national accounting, unemployment, and inflation) is Statistics Canada (www.statcan.ca). While Statistics Canada makes most current data freely available, if you need a longer time series there may be a charge. However, most Canadian universities subscribe to the CANSIM service, which provides Statistics Canada free of charge. See datacentre.chass.utoronto.ca/datalist.html for information on how to access CANSIM data.

If you are looking for U.S. or international data, a useful general site, well maintained by Bill Goffe of the State University of New York at Oswego, is Resources for Economists on the Internet (rfe.org/). Click on "data" and you have a menu of choices. For many international comparisons, the best site to try for relatively developed countries is that of the Organisation for Economic Co-operation and Development (www.oecd.org/); for less developed countries, the United Nations site given above and the World Bank Group site (www.worldbank.org/) are recommended.

Aggregate Expenditure and Equilibrium Output

Aggregate Output and Aggregate Income (Y)

Income, Consumption, and Saving (Y, C, and S)

Explaining Spending Behaviour

Planned Investment (I)

Planned Aggregate Expenditure (AE)

Equilibrium Aggregate Output (Income)

The Saving/Investment Approach to Equilibrium

Adjustment to Equilibrium

The Multiplier

Looking Ahead: The Government and International Sectors

Appendix 9A: Deriving the Multiplier Algebraically

Learning Objectives

1 Explain why aggregate output is equal to aggregate income.

2 Define *marginal propensity to consume* and *marginal propensity to save*.

3 Define *investment*, as economists use the term. Distinguish *actual* and *planned investment*.

4 Describe equilibrium in the simple Keynesian model of national income determination. Explain the adjustment process if planned aggregate expenditure differs from aggregate output.

5 Analyze how a change in planned investment affects output in the model. Explain the concept of the spending multiplier.

6 *Appendix 9A*: Derive the multiplier algebraically.

We now begin our discussion of macroeconomic theory. We may know how to calculate GDP, but what factors *determine* GDP? We may know how to define and measure inflation and unemployment, but what circumstances *cause* inflation and unemployment? And what, if anything, can government do to reduce unemployment, inflation, and other macroeconomic maladies?

Analyzing the various components of the macroeconomy is a complex undertaking. The level of output and the overall price level—two of the chief concerns of macroeconomists—are influenced by events in three broadly defined "markets": goods-and-services markets, financial (money) markets, and labour markets. We will explore each of these markets, as well as the links between them and the corresponding markets in the rest of the world, in more detail in the chapters that follow.

■ **Macroeconomic Markets** Figure 9.1 presents the plan of the next seven chapters of this book, which form the core of macroeconomic theory. Our basic procedure is to build a simple model of the economy that can help us understand the real economy. In Chapters 9 and 10, we model the market for goods and services, often called simply the *goods market*. In Chapter 9, we explain several basic concepts and show how the equilibrium level of output is determined if there were no government and no imports or exports. In Chapter 10, we provide a more complete picture of the economy by adding government purchases, taxes, and net exports to the model.

FIGURE 9.1

Understanding Markets in the Macroeconomy

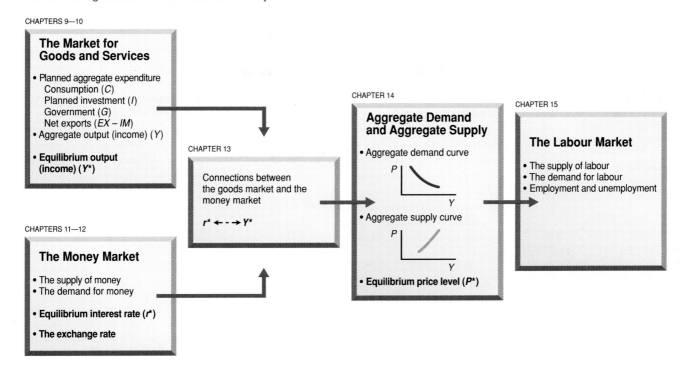

In Chapters 11 and 12, we model the *money market*. Chapter 11 introduces the money market and the banking system and discusses the way Canada's central bank (the Bank of Canada) controls the money supply. Chapter 12 analyzes the demand for money and the way interest rates are determined. Chapter 13 examines the relationship between the goods market and the money market. Chapter 14 then combines these elements to model aggregate demand and supply, first mentioned in Chapter 6. Chapter 14 also analyzes how the overall price level is determined, as well as the relationship between output and the price level. Finally, Chapter 15 discusses the supply of and demand for labour and the functioning of the labour market in the macroeconomy. This material is essential to an understanding of employment and unemployment.[1]

Before we begin our discussion of aggregate output and aggregate income, we need to stress that production, consumption, and the other activities that we will be discussing in this and the following chapters are ongoing activities. Nonetheless, it is helpful to think about these activities as if they took place in a series of *production periods*. During each period, some output is produced, income is generated, and spending takes place. At the end of each period we can examine the results. Was everything that was produced in the economy sold? What percentage of income was spent? What percentage was saved? Is output (income) likely to rise or fall in the next period? The answers to these questions help us to keep track of the economy's performance.

Aggregate Output and Aggregate Income (*Y*)

Each period, firms produce some aggregate quantity of goods and services, which we refer to as *aggregate output* (*Y*). In Chapter 7, we introduced the concept of

---

[1]*Throughout Chapters 9–15, we provide examples and policy applications relevant to our discussion in each chapter. In Chapter 16, we use everything we know about the three broadly defined markets to analyze such macroeconomic topics as stabilization policy and the federal budget balance.*

real gross domestic product as a measure of the quantity of output produced in the economy, Y. Output includes the production of services, consumer goods, and investment goods.

In Chapter 7 we showed that GDP (Y) can be calculated either in terms of income or in terms of expenditures. Because every dollar of expenditure is received by someone as income, we can compute total GDP (Y) either by adding up the total amount spent on all final goods during a period *or* by adding up all the income—wages, rents, interest, and profits—received by all the factors of production.

We will use the variable Y to refer to both **aggregate output** and **aggregate income** because, in fact, they are the same thing seen from two different points of view. When output increases, additional income is generated. More workers may be hired and paid; workers may put in, and be paid for, more hours; and owners may earn more profits. When output is cut, income falls, workers may be laid off or work fewer hours (and be paid less), and profits may fall. In sum:

> In any given period, there is an exact equality between aggregate output (production) and aggregate income. You should be reminded of this fact whenever you encounter the combined term **aggregate output (income)**.

Aggregate output can also be looked on as the aggregate quantity supplied, because it is the amount that firms are supplying (producing) during the period. In the discussions that follow, we use the phrase *aggregate output (income)*, rather than *aggregate quantity supplied*, but keep in mind that the two are equivalent.

■ **Think in Real Terms**   It is essential from the outset that you think in "real terms." For example, when we talk about output (Y), we mean real output, not nominal output. To help make things easier, we will frequently consider Y in terms of dollars, but think of this to be real GDP in constant dollars—a measure of the quantities of goods and services produced in the economy.

INCOME, CONSUMPTION, AND SAVING (Y, C, AND S)

■ **A Simple Economy**   The main goal of our model is to help understand short-run changes in output. Hence we will assume changes in the price level and interest rates can be ignored. For simplicity, we begin by assuming the economy has no government, exports, or imports. There is no economy actually like this, but keeping things simple will help us understand some important effects. We will show how to find equilibrium output in such an economy and that equilibrium output may be less than the level of potential output associated with full employment. This will allow us to consider, both in this chapter and in Chapter 10, government policies that in this model can increase economic activity and employment.

Each period (weeks, months, years, etc.), households receive some aggregate amount of income (Y). In a simple world with no government and no taxes, a household can do two, and only two, things with its income: it can buy goods and services—that is, it can consume—or it can save. The part of its income that a household does not consume in a given period is called **saving** (Figure 9.2). Thus, total household saving in the economy (represented by the letter S) is by definition equal to income minus consumption (represented by the letter C):

$$\text{Saving} \equiv \text{Income} - \text{Consumption}$$
$$S \equiv Y - C$$

The triple equal sign means that this equation is an **identity,** or something that is always true. ($S = 0$ would be an example of an equation that is not an identity because it is only true for some values of Y and C and not all the time.)

Remember that saving does *not* refer to the total savings that have been accumulated over time. Saving (without the final *s*) refers to the portion of a *single period's* income that is not spent in that period. Saving (S) is the amount that is added to (or subtracted from) *accumulated savings* in any given period. For example, if my income is $1000 per year and I spend $600, my saving is $400. If I started from nothing but did this for three years, my accumulated savings would be $1200.

---

aggregate output *The total quantity of goods and services produced (or supplied) in an economy in a given period.*

aggregate income *The total income received by all factors of production in a given period.*

aggregate output (income) (Y) *A combined term used to remind you of the exact equality between aggregate output and aggregate income.*

saving (S) *The part of its income that a household does not consume in a given period. Distinguished from savings, which is the current stock of accumulated saving.*

identity *Something that is true at all times.*

Part Three
Macroeconomic Principles
and Policy

176

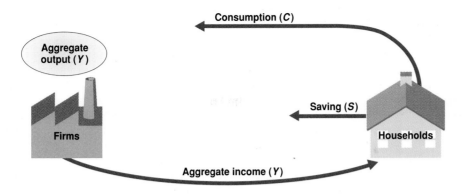

FIGURE 9.2

Saving ≡ Aggregate
Income − Consumption

All income is either spent on
consumption or saved in an
economy in which there is no
government. Thus, $S \equiv Y - C$.

EXPLAINING SPENDING BEHAVIOUR

■ **Household Consumption and Saving**   How do households decide how much to consume? In any given period, the amount of aggregate consumption in the economy depends on a number of factors, including:

Some *Determinants of* *Aggregate* *Consumption*:	1. Household income 2. Household wealth 3. Interest rates 4. Households' expectations about the future

That these factors work together to determine the spending and saving behaviour of households, both individually and in the aggregate, should not be surprising. Households with higher income and higher wealth are likely to spend more than households with less income and less wealth. Lower interest rates reduce the cost of borrowing, so lower interest rates are likely to stimulate spending. (The reverse is true for higher interest rates, which increase the cost of borrowing and are likely to decrease spending.) Finally, positive expectations about the future are likely to increase current spending, while uncertainty about the future is likely to decrease current spending.

While all these factors are important, we will concentrate for now on the relationship between income and consumption.[2] In *The General Theory*, Keynes argued that the amount of consumption undertaken by a household is directly related to its income. Thus:

The higher someone's income is, the higher his or her consumption is likely to be. Thus, people with more income tend to consume more than people with less income.

The relationship between consumption and income is called a **consumption function.** Figure 9.3 shows a hypothetical consumption function for an individual household. The curve is labelled $c(y)$, which is read "*c* as a function of *y*," or "consumption as a function of income." There are several things you should notice about the curve. First, it has a positive slope. In other words, as *y* increases, so does *c*. Second, the curve intersects the *c* axis above zero. This means that even at an income of zero, consumption is positive. Even if a household found itself with a zero income, it still must consume to survive. It would borrow or live off its savings, but its consumption could not be zero.

Keep in mind that Figure 9.3 shows the relationship between consumption and income for an individual household. But also remember that macroeconomics is concerned with aggregate consumption. Specifically, macroeconomists want to

consumption function *The relationship between consumption and income.*

---

[2]*The assumption that consumption is dependent solely on income is, of course, too simple. Nonetheless, many important insights about how the economy works can be obtained through this simplification. In Chapter 17, we relax this assumption and consider the behaviour of households and firms in the macroeconomy in more detail.*

FIGURE 9.3

A Consumption Function for a Household

A consumption function for an individual household shows the level of consumption at each level of household income. The lowercase letters c and y are used to emphasize that these are consumption and income for an individual household, not for the whole economy.

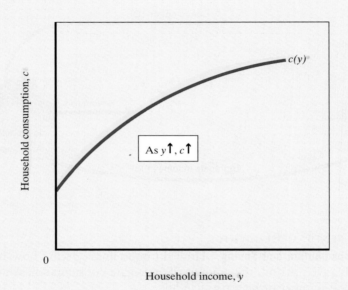

know how *aggregate* consumption (the total consumption of all households) is likely to respond to changes in *aggregate* income. If all individual households increase their consumption as income increases, and we assume that they do, it is reasonable to assume that a positive relationship exists between aggregate consumption (C) and aggregate income (Y).

For simplicity in our model, assume that points of aggregate consumption, when plotted against aggregate income, lie along a straight line, as in Figure 9.4. Because the aggregate consumption function is a straight line, we can write the following equation to describe it:

$$C = a + bY$$

Y represents aggregate output (income). C stands for aggregate consumption. The letter a is the point at which the consumption function intersects the C axis; it is a constant. The letter b is the slope of the line, in this case $\Delta C/\Delta Y$ (since consumption [C] is measured on the vertical axis, and income [Y] is measured on the horizontal axis).[3] Every time that income increases (say by ΔY), consumption increases by b times ΔY. Thus, $\Delta C = b \times \Delta Y$ and $\Delta C/\Delta Y = b$.

Suppose that the slope of the line in Figure 9.4 were 0.75 (that is, $b = 0.75$). An increase in income (ΔY) of \$100 would increase consumption by $b\Delta Y = 0.75 \times$ \$100, or \$75.

marginal propensity to consume (MPC) *That fraction of a change in income that is consumed, or spent.*

The **marginal propensity to consume (MPC)** is the fraction of a change in income that is consumed. In the consumption function above, b is the MPC. An MPC of 0.75 simply means that consumption changes by three-quarters (0.75) of the change in income. The slope of the consumption function is thus the MPC:

> Marginal propensity to consume $\equiv$ Slope of consumption function $= \dfrac{\Delta C}{\Delta Y}$

There are only two places income can go: consumption or saving. Thus, if \$0.75 of a \$1.00 increase in income goes to consumption, the remaining \$0.25 must go to saving. Likewise, if income decreases by \$1, consumption will decrease

[3]*The Greek letter Δ (delta) means "change in." For example, ΔY (read "delta Y") means the "change in income." If income (Y) in 2000 is \$100 and income in 2001 is \$110, then ΔY for this period is \$110 $-$ \$100 $=$ \$10. For a review of the concept of slope, see Appendix 1A to Chapter 1.*

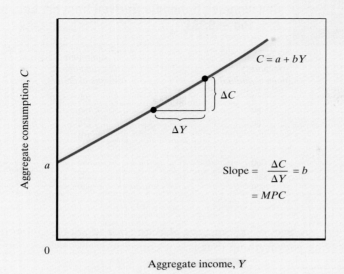

FIGURE 9.4

An Aggregate Consumption Function

The consumption function shows the level of consumption at every level of income. The upward slope indicates that higher levels of income lead to higher levels of consumption spending.

by $0.75 and saving will decrease by $0.25. The **marginal propensity to save (MPS)** is the fraction of a change in income that is saved: $\Delta S/\Delta Y$, where ΔS is the change in saving. Because everything not consumed is saved, the MPC and the MPS must add up to one:

marginal propensity to save (MPS) *That fraction of a change in income that is saved.*

$$MPC + MPS \equiv 1$$

Because the MPC and the MPS are such important concepts, it may help to review their definitions one more time:

The marginal propensity to consume (MPC) is the fraction of an increase in income that is consumed (or the fraction of a decrease in income that comes out of consumption). The marginal propensity to save (MPS) is the fraction of an increase in income that is saved (or the fraction of a decrease in income that comes out of saving).

Since C is aggregate consumption and Y is aggregate income, it follows that the MPC is *society's* marginal propensity to consume out of aggregate income and that the MPS is *society's* marginal propensity to save out of aggregate income.

■ **Numerical Example**   The numerical examples used in the rest of this chapter are based on the following consumption function:

$$C = \underbrace{100}_{a} + \underbrace{0.75}_{b}Y$$

This equation is simply an extension of the generic $C = a + bY$ consumption function we have been discussing. At an aggregate income of zero, consumption is $100 billion ($a$). As income rises, so does consumption. We will assume that for every $100 billion increase in income (ΔY), consumption rises by $75 billion ($\Delta C$). This means that the slope of the consumption function (b) is equal to $\Delta C/\Delta Y$, or $75 billion/$100 billion = 0.75. The marginal propensity to consume out of aggregate income is therefore 0.75; the marginal propensity to save is 0.25. Some numbers derived from this consumption function appear in Table 9.1 and are graphed in Figure 9.5.

Now consider saving. We already know that $Y \equiv C + S$. That is, income equals consumption plus saving. Therefore, once we know how much consumption will

Table 9.1	Consumption Schedule Derived from the Equation $C = 100 + 0.75Y$

Aggregate Income, Y (billions of dollars)	Aggregate Consumption, C (billions of dollars)
0	100
80	160
100	175
200	250
400	400
600	550
800	700
1000	850

result from a given level of income, we also know how much saving there will be. Recall that saving is everything that is not consumed:

$$S \equiv Y - C$$

From the numbers in Table 9.1, we can easily derive the saving schedule in Table 9.2. At an income of $200 billion, consumption is $250 billion; saving is thus a negative $50 billion ($S \equiv Y - C = \$200$ billion $- \$250$ billion $= -\$50$ billion). At an aggregate income of $400 billion, consumption is exactly $400 billion, and saving is zero. At $800 billion in income, saving is a positive $100 billion.

These numbers are graphed as a saving function in Figure 9.6. The 45° line, the solid black line in the top graph, provides a convenient way of comparing C and Y. (All the points along a 45° line are points at which the value on the horizontal axis equals the value on the vertical axis. Thus, the 45° line in Figure 9.6 represents all the points at which aggregate income equals aggregate consumption.) Where the consumption function is *above* the 45° line, consumption exceeds income, and saving is negative. Where the consumption function *crosses* the 45° line, consumption is equal to income, and saving is zero. Where the consumption function is *below* the 45° line, consumption is less than income, and saving is positive. Note that the slope of the saving function is $\Delta S / \Delta Y$, which is equal to the marginal propensity to save (*MPS*).

> The consumption function and the saving function are mirror images of one another. No information appears in one that does not also appear in the other. These functions tell us how households in the aggregate will divide income between consumption spending and saving at every possible income level.

PLANNED INVESTMENT (I)

Consumption, as we've seen, is the spending by households on goods and services. But what kind of spending do firms engage in? The answer is *investment*.

■ **What Is Investment?**   Let us begin with a brief review of terms and concepts. In everyday language, we use *investment* to refer to what we do with our savings: "I invested in a mutual fund and some Noranda stock." In the language of economics, however, *investment* refers to the creation of capital stock. To an economist, an investment is something that is used to create value in the future.

It is very important that you not confuse the two uses of the term. When a firm builds a new plant or adds new machinery to its current stock, it is investing. A restaurant owner who buys tables, chairs, cooking equipment, and silverware is investing. When a university builds a new sports centre, it is investing. From now on, we use the term **investment** in this sense, to refer to purchases by firms of new buildings and equipment and inventories, all of which add to firms' capital stocks.

investment *Purchases by firms of new buildings and equipment and additions to inventories, all of which add to firms' capital stock.*

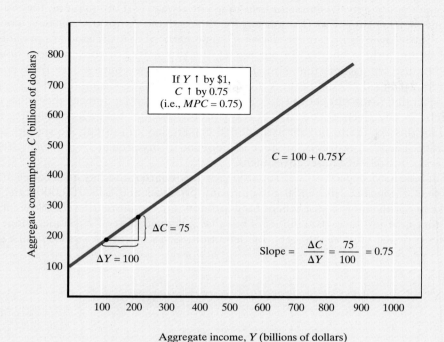

FIGURE 9.5

An Aggregate Consumption Function Derived from the Equation C = 100 + 0.75Y

In this simple consumption function, consumption is $100 billion at an income of zero. As income rises, so does consumption. For every $100 billion increase in income, consumption rises by $75 billion. The slope of the line is 0.75.

Recall that inventories are part of the capital stock. When firms add to their inventories, they are investing—they are buying something that creates value in the future. Most of the capital stock of a clothing store, for example, consists of its inventories of unsold clothes in its warehouses and on its racks and display shelves. The service provided by a grocery or department store is the convenience of having a large variety of commodities in inventory that are available for purchase at a single location.

Manufacturing firms generally have two kinds of inventories: *inputs,* or raw materials, and *final products.* An appliance manufacturer, for example, has stocks of rolled steel and electrical parts in inventory, all waiting to be used in producing new refrigerators and stoves. In addition, the manufacturer has an inventory of finished products awaiting shipment.

Investment is a flow variable; that is, it represents additions to capital stock in a specific period. A firm's decision on how much to invest each period is determined by many factors. For now, we will focus simply on the effects that given investment levels have on the rest of the economy.

Table 9.2	Deriving a Saving Schedule from a Consumption Schedule		
Y **Aggregate Income** (billions of dollars)	− C **Aggregate Consumption** (billions of dollars)	≡ S **Aggregate Saving** (billions of dollars)	
0	100	−100	
80	160	−80	
100	175	−75	
200	250	−50	
400	400	0	
600	550	50	
800	700	100	
1000	850	150	

Actual Versus Planned Investment   One of the most important insights of macroeconomics is deceptively simple: a firm may not always end up investing the exact amount that it planned to. The reason for this is that a firm does not have complete control over its investment decision; some parts of that decision are made by other actors in the economy. (In our model, this is not true of consumption, however. Because we assume that households have complete control over their consumption, planned consumption is always equal to actual consumption.)

Generally, firms can choose how much new plant and equipment they wish to purchase in any given period. If GM wants to buy a robot for its assembly line or Tim Hortons decides to buy an extra coffee-maker, they can usually do so without difficulty. There is, however, another component of investment over which firms have less control—inventory investment.

Suppose GM expects to sell 100 000 cars this quarter and has inventories at a level that it considers proper. If the company produces and sells 100 000 cars, it will keep its inventories just where they are now (at the desired level). Now suppose that GM produces 100 000 cars but that a sudden shift of consumer interest enables it to sell only 90 000 cars. By definition, GM's inventories of cars must go

FIGURE 9.6

Deriving a Saving Function from a Consumption Function

Since $S \equiv Y - C$, it is easy to derive a saving function from a consumption function. A 45° line drawn from the origin can be used as a convenient tool to compare consumption and income graphically. At $Y = 200$, consumption is 250. The 45° line shows us that consumption is larger than income by 50. Thus $S \equiv Y - C = -50$. At $Y = 800$, consumption is less than income by 100. Thus, $S = 100$ when $Y = 800$.

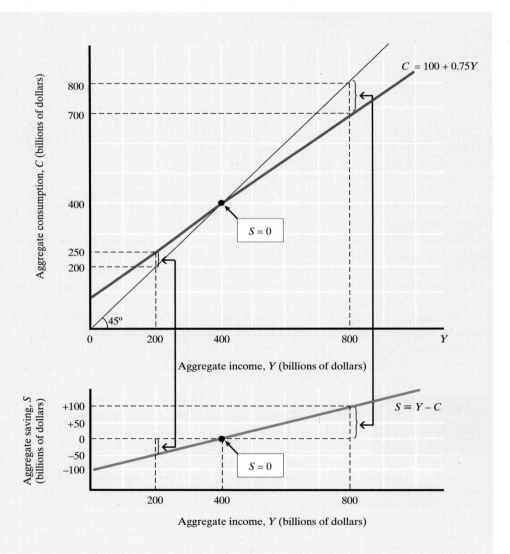

up by 10 000 cars. The firm's **change in inventory** is equal to production minus sales. The key point here is:

change in inventory *Production minus sales.*

> One component of investment—inventory change—is partly determined by how much households decide to buy, which is not under the complete control of firms. If households do not buy as much as firms expect them to, inventories will be higher than expected, and firms will have made an inventory investment that they did not plan to make.

Because involuntary inventory adjustments are neither desired nor planned, we need to distinguish between actual investment and **desired,** or **planned, investment.** In Chapter 7 we referred to all investment as I but from now on that symbol will refer to planned investment. (To use a special symbol would be tedious.) In other words, I will refer to planned purchases of plant and equipment and planned inventory changes. **Actual investment,** in contrast, is the *actual* amount of investment that takes place. If, for example, actual inventory investment turns out to be higher than firms planned, then actual investment is greater than I, planned investment.

desired, or **planned, investment (*I*)** *Those additions to capital stock and inventory that are planned by firms.*

actual investment *The actual amount of investment that takes place; it includes items such as unplanned changes in inventories.*

For the purposes of this chapter, we will model the amount of investment that firms plan to make each period (I) as fixed at some given level. We assume that this level does not vary with income. For purposes of the example that follows, we will assume that I = \$25 billion, regardless of income. As Figure 9.7 shows, this means that the planned investment function is simply a horizontal line.

PLANNED AGGREGATE EXPENDITURE (*AE*)

You may recall from Chapter 7 that the GDP measure of national output consists not only of consumption and investment, but also of government purchases (G) and exports (EX) minus imports (IM). Total **planned aggregate expenditure (*AE*)** is the total amount an economy plans to spend in a given period, and, similarly, is the sum of consumption, planned investment, government purchases, and exports minus imports.

planned aggregate expenditure (*AE*) *The total amount the economy plans to spend in a given period.*

> Planned aggregate expenditure $\equiv AE \equiv C + I + G + EX - IM$

For the moment, we are assuming there is no government, exports, or imports, so $G = 0$, $EX = 0$, and $IM = 0$:

$$AE \equiv C + I$$

We will now use the concept of planned aggregate expenditure to discuss the economy's equilibrium level of output.

Equilibrium Aggregate Output (Income)

Thus far, we have described the behaviour of firms and households. We now discuss the nature of equilibrium and explain how the economy achieves equilibrium.

A number of definitions of *equilibrium* are used in economics. However, they all refer to the idea that at equilibrium, there is no tendency for change. In microeconomics, equilibrium is said to exist in a particular market (for example, the market for bananas) at the price for which the quantity demanded is equal to the quantity supplied. The equilibrium price of a good is the price at which suppliers want to furnish the amount that demanders want to buy.

In macroeconomics, we define **equilibrium** in the goods market as that point at which planned aggregate expenditure is equal to aggregate output:

equilibrium *Occurs when there is no tendency for change. In the macroeconomic goods market, equilibrium occurs when planned aggregate expenditure is equal to aggregate output.*

> Aggregate output $\equiv Y$
> Planned aggregate expenditure $\equiv AE \equiv C + I$
> Equilibrium: $Y = AE$, or $Y = C + I$

This definition of equilibrium can hold if, and only if, planned investment and actual investment are equal. (Remember that we are assuming there is no unplanned consumption.)

To understand why this is true, consider the cases where Y does not equal AE. First, suppose that aggregate output is greater than planned aggregate expenditure:

$$Y > C + I$$

Aggregate output > Planned aggregate expenditure

When output is greater than planned spending, there is unplanned inventory investment. Firms planned to sell more of their goods than they did, and the difference shows up as an unplanned increase in inventories.

Next, suppose that planned aggregate expenditure is greater than aggregate output:

$$C + I > Y$$

Planned aggregate expenditure > Aggregate output

When planned spending exceeds output, firms have sold more than they planned to. Thus, inventory investment is smaller than planned. Again, planned and actual investment are not equal. Only when output is exactly matched by planned spending will there be no unplanned inventory investment.

> Equilibrium in the goods market is achieved only when aggregate output (Y) and planned aggregate expenditure ($C + I$) are equal, or when actual and planned investment are equal.

Table 9.3 derives a planned aggregate expenditure schedule and shows the point of equilibrium for our numerical example. (Remember, all our calculations are based on the equation $C = 100 + 0.75Y$.) To determine planned aggregate expenditure, we add consumption spending (C) to planned investment spending (I) at every level of income. Glancing down columns 1 and 4, we see one, and only one, level at which aggregate output and planned aggregate expenditure are equal: the point where $Y = 500$. We assume that the economy can produce these 500 units of output but note it is possible it could produce much more—equilibrium output could be well below the level of potential output associated with full employment.

Figure 9.8 illustrates the same equilibrium graphically. Figure 9.8a adds planned investment, constant at $25 billion, to consumption at every level of income. Since

FIGURE 9.7

The Planned Investment Function

For the time being, we will assume that planned investment is fixed. It does not change when income changes, so its graph is just a horizontal line.

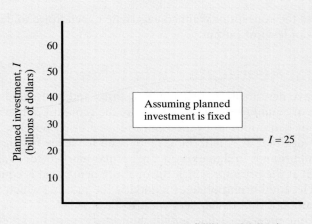

planned investment is a constant, the planned aggregate expenditure function is simply the consumption function displaced vertically by that constant amount. Figure 9.8b plots the planned aggregate expenditure function with the 45° line. The 45° line, which represents all points on the graph where the variables on the horizontal and vertical axes are equal, allows us to compare measurements along the two axes. The planned aggregate expenditure function crosses the 45° line at a single point, where $Y = \$500$ billion.[4] At that point, $Y = C + I$.

Now let's look at some other levels of aggregate output (income). First, consider $Y = \$800$ billion. Is this an equilibrium output? Clearly not. At $Y = \$800$ billion, planned aggregate expenditure is $725 billion. (See Table 9.3.) This amount is less than aggregate output, which is $800 billion. Because output is greater than planned spending, the difference ends up in inventory as unplanned inventory investment. In this case, unplanned inventory investment is $75 billion. Firms will respond by cutting output.

Next, consider $Y = \$200$ billion. Is this an equilibrium output? Again, clearly not. At $Y = \$200$ billion, planned aggregate expenditure is $275 billion. Thus, planned spending (AE) is greater than output (Y), and there is unplanned inventory disinvestment of $75 billion. Firms will respond by increasing output to rebuild inventories.

At $Y = \$200$ billion and $Y = 800$ billion, planned investment and actual investment are unequal. There is unplanned investment, and the system is out of balance. Only at $Y = \$500$ billion, where planned aggregate expenditure and aggregate output are equal, will planned investment equal actual investment.

Finally, let us find the equilibrium level of output (income) algebraically. Recall that we know the following:

(1) $Y = C + I$ (equilibrium)
(2) $C = 100 + 0.75Y$ (consumption function)
(3) $I = 25$ (planned investment)

Substituting (2) and (3) into (1) we get

$$Y = \underbrace{100 + 0.75Y}_{C} + \underbrace{25}_{I}$$

There is only one value of Y for which this statement is true, and we can find it by rearranging terms:

$$Y - 0.75Y = 100 + 25$$
$$Y - 0.75Y = 125$$
$$0.25Y = 125$$
$$Y = \frac{125}{0.25} = 500$$

The equilibrium level of output is thus 500, as we have already seen in Table 9.3 and Figure 9.8.

THE SAVING/INVESTMENT APPROACH TO EQUILIBRIUM

Because aggregate income must either be saved or spent, by definition, $Y \equiv C + S$, which is an identity. The equilibrium condition is $Y = C + I$, but this is not an identity because it does not hold when we are out of equilibrium.[5] Substituting $C + S$ for Y in the equilibrium condition, we can write:

---

[4]*The point at which the two lines cross is sometimes called the* Keynesian cross.
[5]*It would be an identity if* I *included unplanned inventory accumulations—in other words, if* I *were actual investment rather than planned investment.*

Table 9.3

**Deriving the Planned Aggregate Expenditure Schedule and Finding Equilibrium
(All Figures in Billions of Dollars)**

(1) Aggregate Output (income) (Y)	(2) Aggregate Consumption (C)	(3) Planned Investment (I)	(4) Planned Aggregate Expenditure (AE) C + I	(5) Unplanned Inventory Change Y − (C + I)	(6) Equilibrium? (Y = AE?)
100	175	25	200	−100	No
200	250	25	275	−75	No
400	400	25	425	−25	No
500	475	25	500	0	Yes
600	550	25	575	+25	No
800	700	25	725	+75	No
1000	850	25	875	+125	No

Note: The figures in column 2 are based on the equation $C = 100 + 0.75Y$.

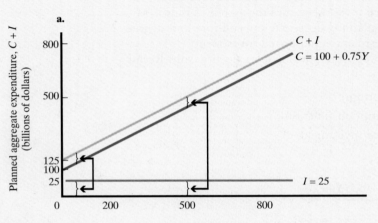

FIGURE 9.8

Equilibrium Aggregate Output

Equilibrium occurs when planned aggregate expenditure and aggregate output are equal. Planned aggregate expenditure is the sum of consumption spending and planned investment spending.

> Saving/investment approach to equilibrium: $C + S = C + I$
>
> Since we can subtract C from both sides of this equation, we are left with $S = I$. Thus, only when planned investment equals saving will there be equilibrium.

This saving/investment approach to equilibrium stands to reason intuitively if we recall two things: (1) output and income are equal and (2) saving is income that is not spent. Because it is not spent, saving is like a leakage out of the spending stream. Only if that leakage is counterbalanced by some other component of planned spending can the resulting planned aggregate expenditure equal aggregate output. This other component is planned investment (I).

This counterbalancing effect can be seen clearly in Figure 9.9. Aggregate income flows into the households, and consumption and saving flow out. The diagram shows saving flowing from households into the financial market. Firms use this saving to finance investment projects. If the planned investment of firms equals the saving of households, then planned aggregate expenditure ($AE \equiv C + I$) equals aggregate output (income) (Y), and there is equilibrium. In this case, the *leakage* out of the spending stream—saving—is matched by an equal *injection* of planned investment spending into the spending stream. For this reason, the saving/investment approach to equilibrium is also called the *leakages/injections approach* to equilibrium.

Figure 9.10 reproduces the saving schedule derived in Figure 9.6 and the horizontal investment function from Figure 9.7. Notice that S I at one, and only one, level of aggregate output, $Y = 500$. At $Y = 500$, $C = 475$ and $I = 25$. In other words, $Y = C + I$, and therefore equilibrium exists.

ADJUSTMENT TO EQUILIBRIUM

We have now defined equilibrium and learned how to find it, but we have said nothing about how firms might react to *disequilibrium*. Now let's consider the actions that firms might take when planned aggregate expenditure exceeds aggregate output (income).

We already know that the only way firms can sell more than they produce is by selling some inventory. This means that when planned aggregate expenditure exceeds aggregate output, unplanned inventory reductions have occurred. It seems reasonable to assume that firms will respond to unplanned inventory reductions by increasing output. If firms increase output, then income must also increase (since output and income are simply two ways of measuring the same thing). As General Motors builds more cars, for example, it hires more workers (or pays its existing workforce for working more hours), buys more steel, uses more electricity, and so on. These purchases by GM represent income for the producers of labour, steel, electricity, and so on. Therefore, if GM (and all other firms) try to keep their inventories intact by increasing production, they will generate more income in the economy as a whole. This in turn will lead to more consumption. Remember, when income rises, consumption also rises.

> The adjustment process will continue as long as output (income) is below planned aggregate expenditure. Thus, if firms react to unplanned inventory reductions by increasing output, an economy with planned spending greater than output will adjust to equilibrium, with Y higher than before. Similarly, if planned spending is less than output, there will be unplanned increases in inventories. In this case, firms will respond by reducing output. As output falls, income falls, consumption falls, and so forth, until equilibrium is restored, with Y lower than before.

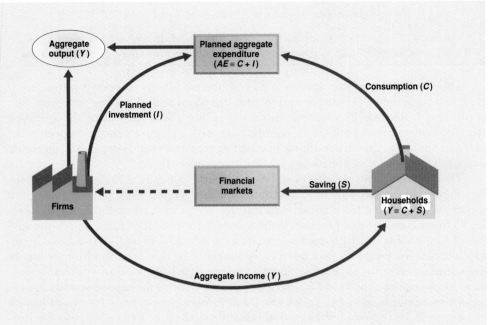

FIGURE 9.9

Planned Aggregate Expenditure and Aggregate Output (Income)

Saving is a leakage out of the spending stream. If planned investment is exactly equal to saving, then planned aggregate expenditure is exactly equal to aggregate output, and there is equilibrium.

As Figure 9.8 shows, at any level of output above $Y = 500$, such as $Y = 800$, output will fall until it reaches equilibrium at $Y = 500$, and at any level of output below $Y = 500$, such as $Y = 200$, output will rise until it reaches equilibrium at $Y = 500$.[6]

THE MULTIPLIER

Now that we know how the equilibrium value of income is determined, we need to ask: How does the equilibrium level of output change when planned investment changes? If there is a sudden change in planned investment, how will output respond, if it responds at all? As we will see, the change in equilibrium output is *greater* than the initial change in planned investment. Output changes by a multiple of the change in planned investment. Not surprisingly, this multiple is called the **multiplier.**

More formally, the multiplier is defined as the ratio of the change in the equilibrium level of output to a change in some autonomous variable. A variable is **autonomous** when it is assumed not to depend on the state of the economy—that is, when it is taken as given. For the purposes of this chapter we are taking planned investment to be autonomous; and if planned investment is the autonomous variable that is changing, we call the multiplier the *investment multiplier.* Another autonomous variable is the intercept of the consumption function, the a of $C = a + bY$. An increase in a would occur if there would be an increase in aggregate consumption at all levels of aggregate income, perhaps because of greater consumer confidence. Such an increase would also have a multiplier effect, and we could call the multiplier the *autonomous consumption multiplier.* In many models, including the one in this chapter, the autonomous consumption multiplier will equal the investment multiplier. Multipliers in these models are sometimes more fully called *spending multipliers.*

With planned investment taken as given, we can now ask the question of how much the equilibrium level of output changes when planned investment changes.

multiplier *The ratio of the change in the equilibrium level of output to a change in some autonomous variable.*

autonomous variable *A variable assumed not to depend on the state of the economy—that is, it is taken as given.*

---

[6]*In discussing simple supply and demand equilibrium in Chapters 4 and 5, we saw that when quantity supplied exceeds quantity demanded, the price falls and the quantity supplied declines. Similarly, when quantity demanded exceeds quantity supplied, the price rises and the quantity supplied increases. Remember, in the analysis here we are ignoring potential changes in prices or in the price level and focusing on changes in the level of real output (income). Later, after we have introduced money and the price level into the analysis, prices will be very important. At this stage, however, only aggregate output (income) (Y) adjusts when aggregate expenditure exceeds aggregate output (with inventory falling) or when aggregate output exceeds aggregate expenditure (with inventory rising).*

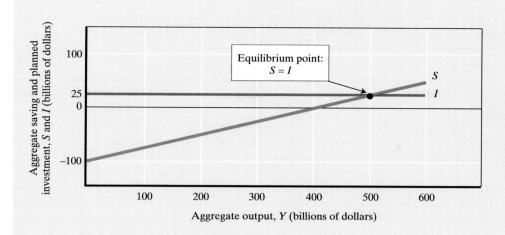

FIGURE 9.10

The *S* = *I* Approach to Equilibrium

Aggregate output will be equal to planned aggregate expenditure only when saving equals planned investment (*S* = *I*). Saving and planned investment are equal at *Y* = 500.

Remember that we are not trying here to explain *why* planned investment changes; we are simply asking how much the equilibrium level of output changes when (for whatever reason) planned investment changes.

Consider a sustained increase in planned investment of $25 billion—that is, suppose that *I* increases from $25 billion to $50 billion and stays at $50 billion. If equilibrium existed at *I* = $25 billion, an increase in planned investment of $25 billion will cause a disequilibrium, with planned aggregate expenditure greater than aggregate output by $25 billion. Firms immediately see unplanned reductions in their inventories, and, as a result, they begin to increase output.

Let's say that the increase in planned investment comes from an anticipated increase in travel that leads airlines to purchase more airplanes, car rental companies to increase purchases of automobiles, and bus companies to purchase more buses (all capital goods). The firms experiencing unplanned inventory declines will therefore be automobile manufacturers, bus producers, and aircraft producers. In response to declining inventories, these firms will increase output.

Now suppose that these firms raise output by the full $25 billion increase in planned investment. Does this restore equilibrium? No, because when output goes up, people earn more income and a part of that income will be spent. This increases planned aggregate expenditure even further. In other words, an increase in *I* also leads indirectly to an increase in *C*. To produce more cars, auto makers have to hire more workers or ask their existing employees to work more hours. They also must buy more steel, more tires, and so forth from other firms. Owners of these firms will earn more profits, produce more, hire more workers, and pay out more in wages and salaries.

This added income does not just vanish into thin air. It is paid to households that spend some of it and save the rest. The added production thus leads to added income, which leads to added consumption spending.

Therefore, if planned investment (*I*) goes up by $25 billion initially *and is sustained at this higher level,* an increase of output of $25 billion will *not* restore equilibrium, because it generates even more consumption spending (*C*). People buy more consumer goods. There are unplanned reductions of inventories of basic consumption items—washing machines, food, clothing, and so forth—and this prompts other firms to increase output. Thus, the cycle starts all over again.

Clearly, output and income can rise by significantly more than the initial increase in planned investment. But by how much? How large is the multiplier? This is answered graphically in Figure 9.11. Assume that the economy is in equilibrium at point *A*, where equilibrium output is 500. The increase in *I* of 25 shifts the *AE* ≡ *C* + *I* curve up by 25, because *I* is higher by 25 at every level of income. The new equilibrium occurs at point *B*, where the equilibrium level of output is 600. Like point *A*, point *B* is on the 45° line and is thus an equilibrium value. Output (*Y*) has thus increased by 100 (600 − 500), or four times the initial increase in planned investment of 25, between point *A* and point *B*. The multiplier in this example is therefore 4. At point *B*, aggregate spending is also higher by 100. If 25 of this additional 100 is investment (*I*), as we know it is, the remaining amount—75—is added consumption (*C*). From point *A* to point *B* then, Δ*Y* = 100, Δ*I* = 25, and Δ*C* = 75.

Why doesn't the multiplier process go on forever? Because only a fraction of the increase in income is consumed in each round. Successive increases in income become smaller and smaller in each round of the multiplier process until equilibrium is restored. In our example, for every $1 of new spending in the first round, the second round of spending is 0.75, the third round is 0.75 × 0.75 = 0.56, the fourth round is 0.75 × 0.75 × 0.75 = 0.42, and so on. As we discuss further in the appendix to this chapter, the sum of all these rounds of spending (i.e., 1 + 0.75 + 0.75^2 + 0.75^3 + ...) is 1/(1 − 0.75) = 4, which is of course the same as we calculated using the graph.

The size of the multiplier depends on the slope of the planned aggregate expenditure line. The steeper the slope of this line, the greater the change in output for a given change in investment. When planned investment is fixed, as it is in our example, the slope of the *AE* ≡ *C* + *I* line is just the marginal propensity to consume (Δ*C*/Δ*Y*). The greater the *MPC*, the greater the multiplier. This should not be surprising. A large *MPC* means that consumption increases a lot when income increases. The more consumption changes, the more output has to change to achieve equilibrium.

■ **The Multiplier Equation**   Is there a way to determine the size of the multiplier without using graphic analysis? The answer is yes.

Assume that the market is in equilibrium at an income level of *Y* = 500. Now suppose that planned investment (*I*), and thus planned aggregate expenditure (*AE*), increases and remains higher by $25 billion. Planned aggregate expenditure is thus greater than output, there is an unplanned inventory reduction, and firms respond by increasing output (income) (*Y*). This leads to a second round of increases, and so on.

What will restore equilibrium? Look back at Figure 9.10 and recall that planned aggregate expenditure (*AE* ≡ *C* + *I*) is not equal to aggregate output (*Y*) unless *S* = *I*; the leakage of saving must exactly match the injection of planned investment spending for the economy to be in equilibrium. Recall also that we assumed that planned investment jumps to a new higher level and stays there; it is a *sustained* increase of $25 billion in planned investment spending. As income rises, consumption rises and so does saving. Our *S* = *I* approach to equilibrium thus leads us to conclude that:

> Equilibrium will be restored only when saving has increased by exactly the amount of the initial increase in *I*.

Otherwise, *I* will continue to be greater than *S*, and *C* + *I* will continue to be greater than *Y*.[7]

It is possible to figure how much *Y* must increase in response to the additional planned investment before equilibrium will be restored. *Y* will rise, pulling *S* up with it until the change in saving is exactly equal to the change in planned investment—that is, until *S* is again equal to *I* at its new higher level. Since added saving is a *fraction* of added income (the *MPS*), the increase in *income* required to restore equilibrium must be *a multiple* of the increase in planned investment.

---

[7]*The* S = I *approach to equilibrium can be used to illustrate a property of this simple Keynesian model called the "paradox of thrift." If households attempt to reduce consumption to increase saving (i.e., become thriftier), they will be unable to increase aggregate saving as* S = I. *But the reduction in consumption will reduce planned aggregate expenditure (i.e., shift the* AE *line down in a diagram like Figure 9.11) and this will reduce output and income.*

Recall that the marginal propensity to save (MPS) is the fraction of a change in income that is saved. It is defined as the change in S (ΔS) over the change in income (ΔY):

$$MPS \equiv \frac{\Delta S}{\Delta Y}$$

Since ΔS must be equal to ΔI for equilibrium to be restored, we can substitute ΔI for ΔS and solve:

$$MPS = \frac{\Delta I}{\Delta Y}. \text{ Therefore, } \Delta Y = \Delta I \times \frac{1}{MPS}$$

As you can see, the change in equilibrium income (ΔY) is equal to the initial change in planned investment (ΔI) times $1/MPS$. The multiplier in this simple model is thus $1/MPS$:

$$\text{Multiplier} \equiv \frac{1}{MPS}$$

Because $MPS + MPC \equiv 1$, $MPS \equiv 1 - MPC$. It therefore follows that the multiplier is also equal to:

$$\text{Multiplier} \equiv \frac{1}{1 - MPC}$$

In our example, the MPC is 0.75, so the MPS must equal $1 - 0.75$, or 0.25. Thus, the multiplier is 1 divided by 0.25, or 4. The change in the equilibrium level of Y is thus $4 \times \$25$ billion, or $\$100$ billion. It is also important to note that the same analysis holds when planned investment falls. If planned investment falls by a certain amount and is sustained at this lower level, output will fall by a multiple of the reduction in I. As the initial shock is felt and firms cut output, they lay people off. The result: income, and subsequently consumption, fall.

■ **The Size of the Multiplier in the Real World** The multiplier derived in this chapter is based on a very simplified picture of the economy. The more realistic models we will consider include the effects of government, taxes, the international sector, interest rates, and price level changes. But it would be a mistake to move on from this chapter thinking that the real-world multiplier is as large as 4. Most estimates of the actual multiplier in Canada are less than 2, so a sustained increase in planned investment of $\$10$ billion would likely increase output by no more than $\$20$ billion. Even then, for reasons we shall discuss in later chapters, there may be circumstances in which the increase is not permanent.

■ **The Multiplier in Action: Recovering from the Great Depression** The Great Depression began in 1929 and lasted nearly a decade. Real output in 1938 was lower than real output in 1929. The unemployment rate was at double-digit levels for most of the 1930s. How is it possible that the economy got "stuck" at such a low level of income and a high level of unemployment? The essentially Keynesian model that we have analyzed in this chapter can help us to answer this question.

If firms do not wish to undertake much investment (I is low) or if consumers decide to increase their saving and cut back on consumption, then planned spending will be low. Firms do not want to produce more because, with many workers unemployed, households do not have the income to buy the extra output that firms might produce. And households, who would purchase more if they had more income, cannot find jobs that would enable them to earn additional income. The economy is thus caught in a vicious cycle.

How might such a cycle be broken? One possibility is for planned aggregate expenditure to increase, thereby increasing aggregate output via the multiplier ef-

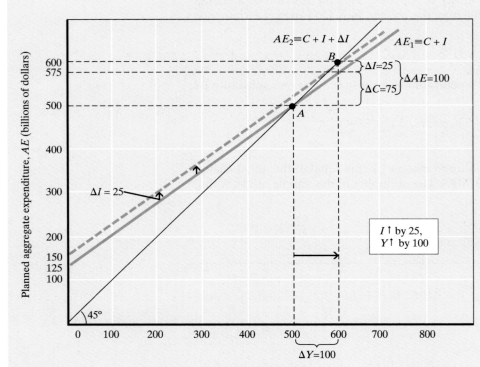

FIGURE 9.11

The Multiplier as Seen in the Planned Aggregate Expenditure Diagram

At point *A*, the economy is in equilibrium at *Y* = 500. When *I* increases by 25, planned aggregate expenditure is initially greater than aggregate output. As output rises in response, additional consumption is generated, pushing equilibrium output up by a multiple of the initial increase in *I*. The new equilibrium is found at point *B*, where *Y* = 600. Equilibrium output has thus increased by 100 (600 − 500), or four times the amount of the increase in planned investment.

fect. This increase in *AE* may occur naturally, or it may be caused by a change in government policy.

In the late 1930s, for example, the economy experienced a surge of investment primarily from the business sector. Between 1934 and 1939, total investment spending (in real terms) almost doubled. There can be no doubt that this increased investment had a multiplier effect. In just five years, employment increased by more than 400 000. As more workers were employed, more income was generated, and some of this added income was spent on consumption goods. Inventories declined and firms began to expand output. Between 1934 and 1939, real output (income) increased by one-third and the official unemployment rate dropped from 14.5% to 11.4%.

But 11.4% is still a very high rate of unemployment; the Depression was not yet over. Between 1939 and 1943, however, the Depression ended, with the unemployment rate dropping to 4.4% in 1941 and to 1.7% by 1943. This recovery was triggered by the mobilization for World War II and the significant increase in government purchases, which rose from $1.16 billion in 1939 to $2.5 billion in 1941 and to $5.2 billion in 1942. In the next chapter, we will explore this *government spending multiplier,* and you'll see how the government can help stimulate the economy by increasing its spending.

But even without considering government spending, the model of this chapter can be used to analyze the economy. See the Application box titled "The Multiplier in Practice."

Looking Ahead: The Government and International Sectors

In this chapter, we have taken the first important step in understanding how the economy works. We have described the behaviour of two sectors (household and firm) and have discussed how equilibrium is achieved in the market for goods and services. In the next chapter, we will relax some of the assumptions we have made and take into account the roles of government spending and net exports in the economy. This will give us a more realistic picture of how our complex economy works.

Sometimes we are interested in the effects of an increase in investment (or some other component of aggregate expenditure) on the entire macroeconomy. However, on other occasions we are interested only in the effects on particular communities, regions, or industries. For example, a politician might advocate public subsidization of a particular investment project, say the building of a bridge, not only because it will create 100 local jobs for a year in construction, but also because an additional 300 jobs will be created due to "spinoff" effects as the newly employed construction workers spend their wages throughout the community. The latter effect due to increased consumption is of course the multiplier.

An important point to bear in mind when considering the employment/multiplier arguments behind either a public project or public support of a private project is if the same funds could be used for alternative purposes: it may be that the multiplier effects will be at least as large. Hence in considering this kind of public policy, sufficient emphasis must also be given to the desirability and the usefulness of the project itself and not only to its job creation effects.

As an example, a new hydro megaproject can create jobs both directly and through multiplier effects. But spending on conservation projects can also create jobs directly and have multiplier effects as well. And if the conservation projects are successful and less is spent on electricity, funds not spent by consumers on electricity will likely be spent on other goods and again be respent through the economy in a multiplier process.

A hydro megaproject can create jobs but so can conservation projects, and in each case there are multiplier effects.

Similarly, professional sports teams are often said to create jobs in an area by multiplier-type spinoffs. But if the team were not there, it is likely that consumers would spend on other types of entertainment instead.

But while you should be careful in evaluating a multiplier-type argument for a particular project, the heart of the multiplier argument is easy to understand. When individuals become employed or increase their income in some other manner, they increase their spending and that can increase employment and incomes elsewhere in the economy. For example, in 1991, workers in Kapuskasing, Ontario bought the local pulp and paper mill to save it from closing. By 1997 the mill was so successful that the Quebec paper company Tembec in turn bought the mill from the workers. One millworker, for example, turned an initial investment of $26 000 into $260 000. Just as multiplier analysis would suggest, these sudden unexpected payments to workers had important effects on others in the community and more widely as the workers increased their spending. For example, the morning that the Tembec buyout was announced, a local appliance-store owner took a minute from an $8000 sale to tell *CBC National News* about his increase in business: "It's as if someone used a starter's pistol and then said the race was on." Multiplier analysis would further suggest both the appliance-store owner and some of the appliance suppliers might hire more workers, that the store owner and these new workers would increase their spending on the basis of their higher earnings, and so on, as the effects spread throughout the economy.

Source: *CBC National News* [television show], March 25, 1997.

Aggregate Output and Aggregate Income (Y)

1. Each period, firms produce an aggregate quantity of goods and services called *aggregate output* (Y). Because every dollar of expenditure is received by someone as income, aggregate output and aggregate income are the same thing.

2. The total amount of aggregate consumption that takes place in any given period of time depends on factors such as household income, household wealth, interest rates, and households' expectations about the future.

3. In an economy in which there are no imports or exports and no government, households can do only two things with their income: they can either spend on consumption or they can save. The letter C is used to refer to aggregate consumption by households. The letter S is used to refer to aggregate saving by households. By definition, saving equals income minus consumption: $S \equiv Y - C$.

4. The higher someone's income is, the higher his or her consumption is likely to be. This also holds true for the economy as a whole: there is a positive relationship between aggregate consumption (C) and aggregate income (Y).

5. The *marginal propensity to consume* (MPC) is the fraction of a change in income that is consumed, or spent. The *marginal propensity to save* (MPS) is the fraction of a change in income that is saved. Because all income must be either saved or spent, $MPS + MPC \equiv 1$.

6. The primary form of spending that firms engage in is investment. In economics, *investment* refers to the purchase by firms of new buildings and equipment and additions to inventories, all of which add to firms' capital stock.

7. *Actual investment* can differ from planned investment because changes in firms' inventories are part of actual investment and inventory changes are not under the complete control of firms. Inventory changes are partly determined by how much households decide to buy. The letter I is used to refer to planned investment only.

Equilibrium Aggregate Output (Income)

8. In an economy with no government, no imports, and no exports, *planned aggregate expenditure* (AE) equals consumption plus planned investment: $AE \equiv C + I$. *Equilibrium* in the goods market is achieved when planned aggregate expenditure equals aggregate output: $C + I = Y$. This holds if, and only if, planned investment and actual investment are equal. Equilibrium may occur well below full employment.

9. Because aggregate income must be saved or spent, the equilibrium condition $Y = C + I$ can be rewritten as $C + S = C + I$, or $S = I$. Thus, only when planned investment equals saving will there be equilibrium. This approach to equilibrium is called the *saving/investment approach* to equilibrium or the *leakages/injections approach* to equilibrium.

10. When aggregate expenditure exceeds aggregate output (income), there is an unplanned fall in inventories. Firms will therefore increase output. This increased output leads to increased income and even more consumption. This process will continue as long as output (income) is below planned aggregate expenditure. If firms react to unplanned inventory reductions by increasing output, an economy with planned spending greater than output will adjust to equilibrium, with Y higher than before.

11. Equilibrium output changes by a multiple of the change in planned investment or any other autonomous variable. In this simple model, the multiplier is equal to $1/MPS$.

actual investment 183

aggregate income 176

aggregate output 176

aggregate output (income) (*Y*) 176

autonomous variable 188

change in inventory 183

consumption function 177

desired, or planned, investment (*I*)
   183

equilibrium 183

identity 176

investment 180

marginal propensity to
   consume (*MPC*) 178

marginal propensity to save (*MPS*)
   179

multiplier 188

planned aggregate expenditure (*AE*)
   183

saving (*S*) 176

Equations:

1. $S \equiv Y - C$

2. $MPC \equiv$ Slope of consumption function $\equiv \dfrac{\Delta C}{\Delta Y}$

3. $MPC + MPS \equiv 1$

4. $AE \equiv C + I$

5. Equilibrium condition: $Y = AE$, or $Y = C + I$

6. Saving/investment approach to equilibrium: $S = I$

7. Multiplier $\equiv \dfrac{1}{MPS} \equiv \dfrac{1}{1 - MPC}$

1. Explain the multiplier intuitively. Why is it that an increase in planned investment of $100 raises equilibrium output by more than $100? Why is the effect on equilibrium output finite? How do we know that the multiplier is 1/*MPS*?

2. Explain how planned investment can differ from actual investment.

3. The following is the consumption schedule for the Republic of Nurd in 2001:

Y	50	60	70	80	90	100	110	120	130	140	150
C	52	62	71.5	80.5	89	97	104	110	115	119	122.5

   a. Construct a graph of the consumption function. (Assume that within each income range the slope of the consumption function is constant.)

   b. Compute the marginal propensity to consume over each income range. What is the geometrical meaning of the *MPC*? Explain why.

   c. Compute and graph the saving schedule (saving as a function of income, *Y*) for Nurd. Also compute the marginal propensity to save over each income range.

   d. Suppose that planned investment spending (*I*) is constant at $10. What is the equilibrium level of Nurd's gross domestic product (*Y*)? Graph the equilibrium level of income/output (*Y*) in two ways.

   e. Suppose that planned investment (*I*) in Nurd increases to $18 and remains at that level. What will Nurd's new equilibrium level of income/output (*Y*) be? Compute and show this equilibrium point graphically.

4. You are given the following data regarding Freedonia, a legendary country:

   (1) Consumption function: $C = 200 + 0.8Y$

   (2) Investment function: $I = 100$

   (3) $AE \equiv C + I$

   (4) $AE = Y$

   a. What is the marginal propensity to consume in Freedonia? The marginal propensity to save?

   b. Graph equations (3) and (4) and solve for equilibrium income.

   c. Suppose equation (2) were changed to: (2′) $I = 110$. What is the new equilibrium level of income? By how much does the $10 increase in planned investment change equilibrium income? What is the value of the multiplier?

   d. Calculate the saving function for Freedonia. Plot this saving function on a graph with equation (2). Explain why the equilibrium income in this graph must be the same as in part **b**.

5. If I decide to save an extra dollar, my saving goes up by that amount. But if everyone decides to save an extra dollar, income falls and saving does not rise. Explain.

6. You learned earlier that expenditures and income should always be equal. In this chapter, you've learned that *AE* and aggregate output (income) can be different. Is there an inconsistency here?

To begin, let us just work through the chapter's numerical example, concentrating on the algebra. Recall the consumption function is

$$C = 100 + 0.75Y$$

where 0.75 is the marginal propensity to consume. Planned investment $I = 25$. The solution method is always the same: write down the equilibrium condition, substitute in for the components and then solve. The equilibrium condition here is

$$Y = C + I$$

(remembering we are assuming no government purchases, exports, or imports). Substituting in $C = 100 + 0.75Y$ and $I = 25$,

$$Y = \underbrace{100 + 0.75Y}_{C} + 25$$

Rearranging to solve:

$$Y - 0.75Y = 100 + 25$$
$$Y(1 - 0.75) = 100 + 25$$

We can then solve for Y in terms of I by dividing through by $(1 - 0.75)$.

$$Y = (100 + 25)/(1 - 0.75) = 125/0.25 = 500$$

This solves for equilibrium Y. If we want to calculate the investment multiplier, one way is to increase I by 1 to 26, work through the whole calculation again, and find that Y will become 504. Hence an increase in I by 1 increases Y by 4: the multiplier is 4. But you could also see this by inspection of the last equation: an increase in I by 1, or an increase in autonomous consumption by 1 to 101, will clearly increase Y by the multiplier $1/(1 - 0.75) = 4$.

We can repeat this process for an algebraic example, assuming that instead of 100, autonomous consumption is a, the marginal propensity to consume is not 0.75 but b, and planned investment is not the specific value of 25 but just I. So we repeat the same steps as above with these replacements. Now our consumption function is

$$C = a + bY$$

where b is the marginal propensity to consume. In equilibrium,

$$Y = C + I$$

Now we solve these two equations for Y in terms of I. Substituting the first equation into the second, we get

$$Y = \underbrace{a + bY}_{C} + I$$

This equation can be rearranged to yield

$$Y - bY = a + I$$
$$Y(1 - b) = a + I$$

We can then solve for Y in terms of I by dividing through by $(1 - b)$:

$$Y = (a + I) \left(\frac{1}{1 - b}\right)$$

Now look carefully at this expression and think about increasing I by some amount, ΔI, with a held constant. If I increases by ΔI, income will increase by

$$\Delta Y = \Delta I \times \frac{1}{1 - b}$$

Since $b \equiv MPC$, the expression becomes

$$\Delta Y = \Delta I \times \frac{1}{1 - MPC}$$

The multiplier is thus

$$\frac{1}{1 - MPC}$$

Finally, since $MPS + MPC \equiv 1$, MPS is equal to $1 - MPC$, making the alternative expression for the multiplier $1/MPS$, just as we saw in the chapter.

Let's calculate this again by another method. Recall in the numerical example in the chapter that we stated that the multiplier would equal the sum of $1 + 0.75 + 0.75^2 + 0.75^3 + \ldots$, because the first-round dollar of spending is also a dollar of income to the recipient, which because the MPC is 0.75 induces an extra \$0.75 of second-round consumption spending, which is another \$0.75 of income, which induces an extra $0.75 \times 0.75 = 0.75^2$ of third-round consumption spending and so on. You could calculate this on your computer or calculator and find, for example, that after three rounds the total is $1 + 0.75 + 0.75^2 = 2.31$, after ten rounds the total is $1 + 0.75 + 0.75^2 + 0.75^3 + \ldots + 0.75^9 = 3.77$, and after twenty rounds the total is $1 + 0.75 + 0.75^2 + \ldots + 0.75^{19} = 3.99$, gradually getting closer and closer to 4.

The general formula for a sum of a series like $1 + b + b^2 + b^3 + \ldots$ is $1/(1 - b)$. Therefore the multiplier is:

$$\frac{1}{1 - b} = \frac{1}{1 - MPC}$$

just as in the chapter. Hence the sum of $1 + 0.75 + 0.75^2 + \ldots$ is $1/(1 - 0.75) = 4$ as above.

1. In the simple model of national income determination with no government, exports, or imports, assume that $C = 100 + 0.75Y$ but that planned investment depends on Y as well: $I = 20 + 0.15Y$. (Perhaps investors are more likely to invest when the economy is performing well.) The intercept 20 in the planned investment function could be called *autonomous planned investment*. Calculate equilibrium national output. Show that the multiplier for this example is 10. (This is not simply $1/(1 - MPC)$ because not just consumption but also planned investment depends on Y.)

2. Assume in this simple model of national income determination with no government, exports, or imports that $C = 100 + 0.8Y$ and $I = 50$. Solve for equilibrium national income and the multiplier. What would actual investment (not planned investment) be if actual output were 800?

3. Repeat question 2 with $C = 400 + 0.6Y$ and $I = 160$.

The Government and Fiscal Policy

Learning Objectives

1 Identify the tools of fiscal policy.

2 Describe how the inclusion of the government sector affects the aggregate expenditure model.

3 Derive the government spending multiplier, the tax multiplier, and the balanced-budget multiplier.

4 Analyze the effects of a change in government spending and/or a change in taxes on output.

5 Explain how the inclusion of the international sector in the model affects the aggregate expenditure model and the multiplier.

6 Describe the leakages/injections approach to equilibrium.

7 Define *full-employment budget*, *structural deficit*, and *cyclical deficit*.

8 *Appendix 10A*: Derive the fiscal policy multipliers algebraically.

9 *Appendix 10B*: Show algebraically how the fiscal policy multipliers are reduced when tax revenues depend on income.

10 *Appendix 10C*: Show algebraically how the fiscal policy multipliers are reduced when imports depend on income.

Government in the Economy
Government Purchases (G), Net Taxes (T), and Disposable Income (Y_d)
Finding Equilibrium Output

Fiscal Policy at Work: The Multiplier Effects
The Government Spending Multiplier
The Tax Multiplier
The Balanced-Budget Multiplier

More on the International Sector

The Federal Budget
An Overview of the Budget
The Federal Budget Balance and the Federal Debt
The Economy's Influence on the Budget Balance

Debts and Budget Balances in the Rest of the World

The Money Market and Monetary Policy: A Preview

Appendix 10A

Appendix 10B

Appendix 10C

Nothing in macroeconomics or microeconomics arouses as much controversy as the role of government in the economy. In microeconomics, the active presence of government in regulating competition, providing roads and education, and redistributing income is much applauded by those who believe that markets simply do not work well if left to their own devices. Opponents of government intervention argue that it is the government, not the market, that performs badly. They say bureaucracy and inefficiency could be eliminated or reduced if the government played a smaller role in the economy.

In macroeconomics, the debate over what the government can and should do has a similar flavour, although the issues are somewhat different. At one end of the spectrum are the Keynesians and their intellectual descendants, who believe that the macroeconomy fluctuates too much if left on its own and that the government should smooth out fluctuations in the business cycle. These ideas can be traced back to Keynes's analysis in *The General Theory*, which suggests that governments can use their taxing and spending powers to increase aggregate expenditure (and thereby stimulate aggregate output) in recessions or depressions. At the other end of the spectrum are those who claim that government spending is incapable of stabilizing the economy, or, worse, is destabilizing and harmful.

Perhaps the one thing most people can agree on is that, like it or not, governments are important actors in the economies of virtually all countries. On these grounds alone, it is worth our while to analyze the way in which the government influences the functioning of the macroeconomy.

fiscal policy *The government's spending and taxing policies.*

While the government has a wide variety of powers—including regulating firms' entry into and exit from an industry, setting standards for product quality, and setting minimum wage levels—in macroeconomics we study a government with general, but more limited, powers. Specifically, government can affect the macroeconomy through two policy channels: fiscal policy and monetary policy. **Fiscal policy,** the focus of this chapter, refers to the government's spending and taxing behaviour—in other words, its budget policy.[1] Fiscal policy is generally divided into three categories: (1) policies regarding government purchases of goods and services, (2) policies regarding taxes, and (3) policies regarding transfer payments (such as employment insurance, seniors' benefits, welfare payments, and veterans' benefits) to households. **Monetary policy,** the focus of the next two chapters, refers to the behaviour of the nation's central bank, the Bank of Canada, regarding the nation's money supply.

monetary policy *The behaviour of the Bank of Canada regarding the nation's money supply.*

Government in the Economy

Given the scope and power of local, provincial, and federal governments in the Canadian economy, it should be stressed that there are some matters over which these governments exert great control and some matters that are beyond their control. There is an important distinction between variables that a government controls directly and variables that are a consequence of government decisions *combined with the state of the economy.*

For example, tax rates are controlled by the government. By law, Parliament has the authority to decide who and what should be taxed and at what rate. Tax *revenue,* on the other hand, is not subject to complete control by the government. Revenue from the personal income tax system depends both on personal tax rates (which Parliament sets) *and* on the income of the household sector (which depends on many factors not under direct government control, such as how much households work). Revenue from the corporate profits tax depends both on corporate profits tax rates and on the size of corporate profits. The government can control corporate tax rates but not the size of corporate profits.

Government spending also depends both on government decisions and on the state of the economy. For example, in Canada the employment insurance program pays benefits to people who are unemployed. When the economy goes into a recession, the number of unemployed workers increases and so does the level of government employment insurance payments.

Because taxes and expenditures often go up or down in response to changes in the economy rather than as the result of deliberate decisions by policy makers, we will occasionally use the term **discretionary fiscal policy** to refer to changes in taxes or spending that are the result of deliberate changes in government policy.

discretionary fiscal policy *Changes in taxes or spending that are the result of deliberate changes in government policy.*

Government Purchases (G), Net Taxes (T), and Disposable Income (Y_d)

In Chapter 9, we explored the equilibrium level of national output and the multiplier in a simple economy with no government and no exports or imports. In this chapter we add government and international trade to the model. As we have mentioned, our purpose is to study the aggregate effects of government budgetary (fiscal) policy. In particular, we wish to consider how government policy might influence aggregate economic activity in this model, using the same kind of multiplier effects studied in Chapter 9.

[1]*The word* fiscal *comes from the root* fisc, *which refers to the "treasury" of a government.*

The basic idea behind the multiplier is that an increase in a spending component such as planned investment or government expenditure will increase output both initially and also by increasing income and hence inducing additional consumption expenditure. We can change the modelling of taxes or the trade sector and change the *numerical value* of the multiplier, but the idea behind it does not change.

We begin by adding a government sector that purchases goods and services (*G*) to this simple economy. But to make it as easy as possible to understand the basics of fiscal policy, we shall for the moment continue to assume there are no exports (*EX*) or imports (*IM*) in the economy; that is, we assume a "closed economy." Hence in Figure 10.1, begin by ignoring the links to the rest of the world. Trade is important to Canada and, as we shall see, trade effects change the size of the multiplier but they do not change the basic multiplier principle. Also to keep things simple, we will combine two major government activities—the collection of taxes and the payment of transfer payments—into a category we will call **net taxes (*T*)**. Specifically, net taxes are equal to the tax payments made to the government by firms and households minus transfer payments made to households by the government. Our model continues to ignore the effects of changes in the price level and interest rates.

Our earlier discussions of household consumption did not take taxes into account. We assumed that all the income generated in the economy was either spent or saved by households. However, when we take into account the role of government in the economy, as Figure 10.1 does, we see that as income (*Y*) flows toward households, the government takes income from households in the form of net taxes (*T*). The income that ultimately gets to households is called **disposable, or after-tax, income (*Y_d*)**:

net taxes (*T*) *Taxes paid by firms and households to the government minus transfer payments made to households by the government.*

disposable, or after-tax, income (*Y_d*) *Total income minus net taxes: Y − T.*

Disposable income = Total income − Net taxes
$$Y_d \equiv Y - T$$

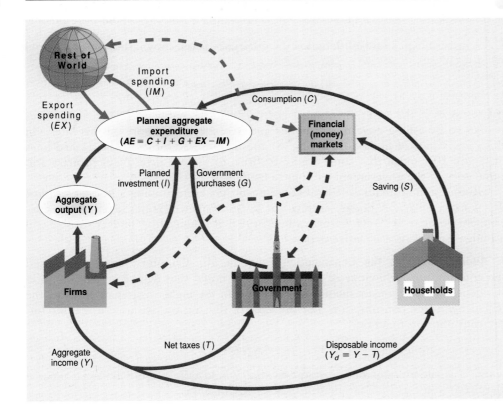

FIGURE 10.1

Adding Exports (*EX*), Imports (*IM*), Net Taxes (*T*), and Government Purchases (*G*) to the Circular Flow of Income

Rest of World

Import spending (*IM*)

Consumption (*C*)

Export spending (*EX*)

Planned aggregate expenditure (*AE ≡ C + I + G + EX − IM*)

Financial (money) markets

Planned investment (*I*)

Government purchases (*G*)

Saving (*S*)

Aggregate output (*Y*)

Firms

Government

Households

Aggregate income (*Y*)

Net taxes (*T*)

Disposable income (*$Y_d \equiv Y - T$*)

Y_d excludes taxes paid by households and includes transfer payments made to households by the government. Note that for now we are assuming that T does not depend on Y—that is, net taxes do not depend on income. This assumption is relaxed in Appendix 10B to this chapter. Taxes that do not depend on income are sometimes called *lump-sum taxes*.

As Figure 10.1 also shows, the disposable income (Y_d) of households must end up either as consumption (C) or saving (S). Thus, it follows that

$$Y_d \equiv C + S$$

Remember that the triple equal sign means that this equation is an identity, or something that is always true.

Because disposable income is aggregate income (Y) minus net taxes (T), we can write another identity:

$$Y - T \equiv C + S$$

Adding T to both sides:

$$Y \equiv C + S + T$$

This identity says that aggregate income gets cut into three pieces. Government takes a slice (net taxes, T), and then households divide the rest between consumption and saving (C and S).

Because governments spend money on goods and services, we also need to expand our definition of planned aggregate expenditure. With exports (EX) and imports (IM) both zero, planned aggregate expenditure (AE) is now equal to the sum of consumption spending by households (C), planned investment by business firms (I), *and* government purchases (G):

$$AE \equiv C + I + G$$

A government's **budget deficit** is the difference between what it spends (G) and what it collects in net taxes (T) in a given period:

$$\text{Budget deficit} \equiv G - T$$

budget deficit *The difference between what a government spends and what it collects in net taxes in a given period:* G − T.

If G exceeds T, the government must borrow from the public to finance the deficit. It does so by selling government bonds and Treasury bills (more on this later). In this case, a part of household saving (S) goes to the government. The dashed lines in Figure 10.1 mean that some S goes to firms to finance investment projects and some goes to the government to finance its deficit.

Recently the Canadian federal government has been running a **budget surplus:** T has exceeded G. A budget surplus (or budget balance) is net taxes minus government purchases: $T - G$. Clearly a budget deficit is a negative budget surplus and a budget surplus is a negative deficit.[2]

budget surplus *Net taxes minus government purchases:* T − G. *Also called the* budget balance.

■ **Adding Taxes to the Consumption Function**   In Chapter 9, we examined the consumption behaviour of households and noted that aggregate consumption (C) depends on aggregate income (Y): in general, the higher aggregate income, the higher aggregate consumption. For the sake of illustration, we used a specific linear consumption function:

$$C = a + bY$$

where a is the amount of consumption that would take place if national income were zero and b is the marginal propensity to consume.

[2]*A positive government surplus means the government is saving, in practice often by paying off government bond issues as they fall due (as opposed to paying off the old bonds with the proceeds from a new bond issue).*

We need to modify this consumption function now that we have added government to the economy. With taxes now a part of the picture, it makes sense to assume that disposable income (Y_d), rather than before-tax income (Y), determines consumption behaviour. If you earn a million dollars, but have to pay $950 000 in taxes, you have no more disposable income than someone who earns $50 000 but pays no taxes. What you have available for spending on current consumption is your disposable income, not your before-tax income.

To modify our aggregate consumption function to incorporate disposable income rather than before-tax income, instead of $C = a + bY$, we write

$$C = a + bY_d$$

or

$$C = a + b(Y - T)$$

Our new consumption function now has consumption depending on disposable income rather than on before-tax income.

■ **Investment**   What about investment? The government can have an important effect on investment behaviour through its tax treatment of depreciation and its other tax policies. Investment may also vary with economic conditions and interest rates, as we will see later. For our present purposes, however, we shall continue to assume that planned investment (I) is fixed.

FINDING EQUILIBRIUM OUTPUT

We know from Chapter 9 that equilibrium occurs where $Y = AE$—that is, where aggregate output equals planned aggregate expenditure. Remember that planned aggregate expenditure in a closed economy with a government is $AE \equiv C + I + G$. We can thus write the equilibrium condition as:

Equilibrium condition: $Y = C + I + G$

Much as in the previous chapter, this would be an identity (and hence true for all values of Y) if I represented actual investment. But remember that I represents *planned* investment so the equilibrium condition holds at the one value of Y where actual investment equals planned investment and there is no unplanned change in inventories. If output (Y) exceeds planned aggregate expenditure $(C + I + G)$, there will be an unplanned increase in inventories. In other words, actual investment will exceed planned investment. Conversely, if $C + I + G$ exceeds Y, there will be an unplanned decrease in inventories.

An example will illustrate the government's effect on the macroeconomy and the equilibrium condition. First, our specific consumption function, which was $C = 100 + 0.75Y$ before we introduced the government sector, now becomes

$$C = 100 + 0.75Y_d$$

or

$$C = 100 + 0.75(Y - T)$$

Second, we assume that the government is currently purchasing $100 billion of goods and services and collecting net taxes (T) of $100 billion.[3] In other words, the government is running a balanced budget, financing all of its spending with taxes. Third, we assume that planned investment (I) is $100 billion.

Table 10.1 calculates planned aggregate expenditure at several levels of disposable income. For example, at $Y = 500$, disposable income is $Y - T$, or 400. Therefore, $C = 100 + 0.75(400) = 400$. Assuming that I is fixed at $100 billion,

---

[3]*As we pointed out earlier, the government does not have complete control over tax revenues and transfer payments. We ignore this problem here, however, and set tax revenues minus transfers at a fixed amount. Things will become more realistic later in this chapter and in Appendix 10B.*

Table 10.1

Finding Equilibrium for *I* = 100, *G* = 100, and *T* = 100
(Assuming no Exports or Imports; All Figures in Billions of Dollars)

(1)	(2)	(3)	(4)	(5)	(6) Planned	(7)	(8) Planned	(9) Unplanned	(10) Adjust-
Output (Income) Y	Net Taxes T	Disposable Income $Y_d \equiv Y - T$	Consumption Spending $(C = 100 + 0.75\,Y_d)$	Saving S $(Y_d - C)$	Investment Spending I	Government Purchases G	Aggregate Expenditure C + I + G	Inventory Change Y − (C + I + G)	ment to Disequili- brium
300	100	200	250	−50	100	100	450	−150	Output↑
500	100	400	400	0	100	100	600	−100	Output↑
700	100	600	550	50	100	100	750	−50	Output↑
900	100	800	700	100	100	100	900	0	Equilibrium
1100	100	1000	850	150	100	100	1050	+50	Output↓
1300	100	1200	1000	200	100	100	1200	+100	Output↓
1500	100	1400	1150	250	100	100	1350	+150	Output↓

and assuming that *G* is fixed at $100 billion, planned aggregate expenditure is 600 (*C* + *I* + *G* = 400 + 100 + 100). Since output (*Y*) is only 500, planned spending is greater than output by 100. As a result, there is an unplanned inventory decrease of 100, giving firms an incentive to raise output. Thus, output of $500 billion is below equilibrium.

If *Y* = 1300, then Y_d = 1200, *C* = 1000, and planned aggregate expenditure is 1200. Here, planned spending is *less* than output, there will be an unplanned inventory increase of 100, and firms will have an incentive to cut back output. Thus, output of $1300 billion is above equilibrium. Only when output is 900 are output and planned aggregate expenditure equal, and only at *Y* = 900 does equilibrium exist.

In Figure 10.2 we derive the same equilibrium level of output graphically. First, the consumption function is drawn, taking into account the net taxes of 100. The old function was *C* = 100 + 0.75*Y*. The new function is *C* = 100 + 0.75 (*Y* − *T*) or *C* = 100 + 0.75 (*Y* − 100). This can be rewritten as *C* = 100 + 0.75*Y* − 75, or *C* = 25 + 0.75*Y*. The marginal propensity to consume has not changed—we assume that it remains 0.75. Thus, for example, consumption at an income of zero is $25 billion (*C* = 25 + 0.75*Y* = 25 + 0.75(0) = 25). Note that the consumption function in Figure 10.2 plots the points in columns 1 and 4 of Table 10.1.

Planned aggregate expenditure, you will recall, was arrived at by adding planned investment to consumption. But now, in addition to 100 in investment, we have government purchases of 100. Thus, because *I* and *G* are constant at 100 each at all levels of income, we add *I* + *G* = 200 to consumption at every level of income. The result is the new *AE* curve. This curve is just a plot of the points in columns 1 and 8 of Table 10.1. The 45° line helps us find the equilibrium level of real output, which, as we already know, is 900. If you examine any level of output above or below 900, you will find disequilibrium. Look, for example, at *Y* = 500 on the graph. At this level, planned aggregate expenditure is 600, but output is only 500. Inventories will fall below what was planned, and firms will have an incentive to increase output.

Fiscal Policy at Work: The Multiplier Effects

You can see from Figure 10.2 that if the government were able to change the levels of either *G* or *T*, it would be able to change the equilibrium level of output (income). At this point, we are assuming that the government does control *G* and *T*.

THE GOVERNMENT SPENDING MULTIPLIER

Suppose that you are an economic adviser to the finance minister and that the economy is sitting at the equilibrium output pictured in Figure 10.2. Output and income are being produced at a rate of $900 billion per year, and the government is currently buying $100 billion worth of goods and services each year and is financing

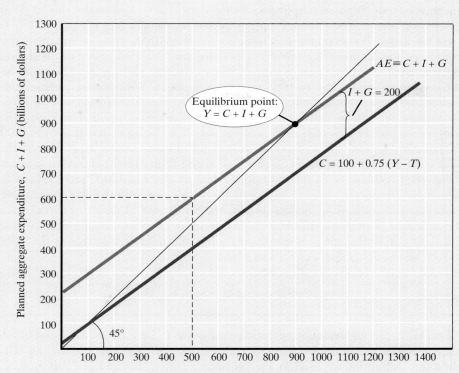

Since G and I are both fixed at $100 billion, the aggregate expenditure function is the new consumption function displaced upward by $I + G = 200$. Equilibrium occurs at $Y = C + I + G = $900 billion.

them with $100 billion in taxes. The budget is balanced. In addition, the private sector is investing (producing capital goods) at a rate of $100 billion per year.

The finance minister calls you and says, "Unemployment is too high. We need to lower unemployment by increasing output and income." After some research, you determine that an acceptable unemployment rate could be achieved only if aggregate output increases to $1100 billion.

The question you now need to answer is: how can the government use taxing and spending policy—fiscal policy—to increase the equilibrium level of national output? Suppose that the finance minister has let it be known that taxes must remain at present levels—Parliament has just passed a major tax reform package—so adjusting T is out of the question for several years. That leaves you with G. Your only option is to increase government spending while holding taxes constant.

To increase spending without raising taxes (which provides the government with revenue to spend), the government must borrow. When G is bigger than T, the government runs a deficit, and the difference between G and T must be borrowed. For the moment we will ignore the possible effect of the deficit and focus only on the effect of a higher G with T constant.

Meanwhile, the finance minister is awaiting your answer. How much of an increase in spending would be required to generate a $200 billion increase in the equilibrium level of output, pushing it from $900 billion up to $1100 billion and reducing unemployment to the finance minister's acceptable level?

You might be tempted to say that since we need to increase income by 200 (1100 − 900), we should increase government spending by the same amount.[4] But consider what would happen if we do. The increased government spending will throw the economy out of equilibrium. Since G is a component of aggregate spending, planned aggregate expenditure will increase by 200. Planned spending will be greater

---

[4]For the rest of this discussion, we will assume but not state that figures are in billions of dollars per year.

than output, inventories will be lower than planned, and firms will have an incentive to increase output. Suppose output rises by the desired 200. You might think, "Well, we increased spending by 200 and output by 200, so equilibrium is restored."

As we know, however, there is more to the story than this. The moment that output rises, the economy is generating more income. After all, this was the desired effect: the creation of more employment. Some of the newly employed workers become consumers and some of their income gets spent. With higher consumption spending, planned spending will be greater than output, inventories will be lower than planned, and firms will raise output, and thus income, again. This time firms are responding to the new consumption spending. Already, total income is over 1100.

This story should sound familiar. It is the multiplier in action. Although this time it is government spending (G) that is changed rather than planned investment (I), the effect is the same as the multiplier effect we described in Chapter 9. An increase in government spending has exactly the same impact on the equilibrium level of output and income as an increase in planned investment. A dollar of extra spending from either G or I is identical with respect to its impact on equilibrium output. Thus, the equation for the government spending multiplier is the same as the equation for the multiplier for a change in planned investment.[5]

$$\text{Government spending multiplier} \equiv \frac{1}{MPS}$$

government spending multiplier
The ratio of the change in the equilibrium level of output to a change in government spending.

Formally, the **government spending multiplier** is defined as the ratio of the change in the equilibrium level of output to a change in government spending. This is the same definition we used in the previous chapter, but now the autonomous variable is government spending rather than planned investment.

Remember that we were thinking of increasing government spending (G) by 200. We can use the multiplier analysis to see what the new equilibrium level of Y would be for an increase in G of 200. The multiplier in our example is 4. (Since b—the MPC—is 0.75, the MPS must be $1 - 0.75$, or 0.25. And $1/0.25 = 4$.) Thus, Y will increase by 800 (4×200). Since the initial level of Y was 900, the new equilibrium level of Y is $900 + 800 = 1700$ when G is increased by 200.

The level of 1700 is much larger than the level of 1100 that we calculated as necessary to lower unemployment to the desired level. Let us back up, then. If we want Y to increase by 200 and if the multiplier is 4, we need G to increase by only $200/4 = 50$. If G changes by 50, the equilibrium level of Y will change by 200, and the new value of Y will be 1100 ($900 + 200$), as desired.

Looking at Table 10.2, we can check our answer to be sure that it is an equilibrium. Look first at the old equilibrium of 900. When government purchases (G)

Table 10.2	Finding Equilibrium After a $50 Billion Government Spending Increase (Assuming no Exports or Imports; All Figures in Billions of Dollars; *G* Has Increased from 100 in Table 10.1 to 150 Here)								

(1)	(2)	(3)	(4)	(5)	(6)	(7)	(8)	(9)	(10)
Output (Income) Y	Net Taxes T	Disposable Income $Y_d \equiv Y - T$	Consumption Spending $(C = 100 + 0.75\,Y_d)$	Saving S $(Y_d - C)$	Planned Investment Spending I	Government Purchases G	Planned Aggregate Expenditure $C + I + G$	Unplanned Inventory Change $Y - (C + I + G)$	Adjustment to Disequilibrium
300	100	200	250	−50	100	150	500	−200	Output↑
500	100	400	400	0	100	150	650	−150	Output↑
700	100	600	550	50	100	150	800	−100	Output↑
900	100	800	700	100	100	150	950	−50	Output↑
1100	100	1000	850	150	100	150	1100	0	Equilibrium
1300	100	1200	1000	200	100	150	1250	+50	Output↓

[5] *We derive the government spending multiplier algebraically in Appendix 10A to this chapter.*

were 100, aggregate output (income) was equal to planned aggregate expenditure ($AE \equiv C + I + G$) at $Y = 900$. But now G has increased to 150. Thus, at $Y = 900$, ($C + I + G$) is greater than Y, there's an unplanned fall in inventories and output will rise. But by how much? The multiplier told us that equilibrium income would rise by four times the change in G, which was 50. Thus, Y should rise by $4 \times 50 = 200$, from 900 to 1100 before equilibrium is restored. Let's check. If $Y = 1100$, then consumption is $C = 100 + 0.75Y_d = 100 + 0.75(1000) = 850$. Since I equals 100 and G now equals 100 (the original level of G) + 50 (the additional G brought about by the fiscal policy change) = 150, then $C + I + G = 850 + 100 + 150 = 1100$. $Y = AE$, and the economy is in equilibrium.

The graphic solution to the finance minister's problem is presented in Figure 10.3. An increase in G of 50 shifts the planned aggregate expenditure function up by 50. The new equilibrium income occurs where the new AE line (AE_2) crosses the 45° line, which is at $Y = 1100$.

THE TAX MULTIPLIER

Remember that fiscal policy involves policies regarding government spending *and* policies regarding taxation. To see what effect a change in tax policy has on the economy, imagine the following. You are still an adviser to the finance minister, but now the finance minister instructs you to devise a plan to reduce unemployment to an acceptable level *without* increasing the level of government spending. In your plan, instead of increasing government spending (G), you decide to cut taxes and maintain the current level of spending. A tax cut increases disposable income, which is likely to lead to added consumption spending. (Remember our general rule that increased income leads to increased consumption.) Would the impact of a decrease in taxes on aggregate output (income) be the same as it would be for an increase in G?

Clearly, a decrease in taxes would increase income. The government spends no less than it did before the tax cut, and households find they have a larger after-tax,

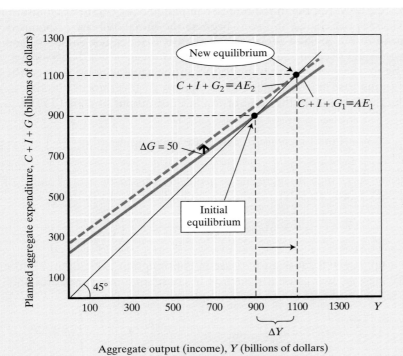

FIGURE 10.3

The Government Spending Multiplier in a Closed Economy

Increasing government spending by $50 billion shifts the *AE* function up by 50. As *Y* rises in response, additional consumption is generated. Overall, the equilibrium level of *Y* increases by 200, from 900 to 1100.

or disposable, income than they had before. This leads to an increase in consumption. Planned aggregate expenditure will increase, which will lead to inventories being lower than planned, which will lead to a rise in output. When output rises, more workers will be employed and more income will be generated, causing a second-round increase in consumption, and so on. Thus, income will increase by a multiple of the decrease in taxes. But there is a wrinkle:

> The multiplier for a change in taxes is *not the same* as the multiplier for a change in government spending.

tax multiplier *The ratio of change in the equilibrium level of output to a change in taxes.*

Why does the **tax multiplier**—that is, the ratio of change in the equilibrium level of output to a change in taxes—differ from the spending multiplier? To answer this question, it is helpful to compare the ways in which a tax cut and a spending increase work their way through the economy.

Look back at Figure 10.1. When the government increases its spending, there is an immediate and direct impact on the economy's *total* spending. Because G is a component of planned aggregate expenditure, an increase in G leads to a dollar-for-dollar increase in planned aggregate expenditure. When taxes are cut, however, there is no direct impact on spending. Taxes enter the picture only because they have an effect on the household's disposable income, which influences the household's consumption (which is part of total spending). As Figure 10.1 shows, the tax cut flows through households before affecting aggregate expenditure.

Let's assume that the government decides to cut taxes by $1. By how much would spending increase? We already know the answer. The marginal propensity to consume tells us how much consumption spending changes when disposable income changes. In the example we have been using throughout this chapter, the marginal propensity to consume out of disposable income is 0.75. This means that if households' after-tax incomes rise by $1, they will increase their consumption not by the full $1, but by only $0.75.[6]

To summarize: When government spending increases by $1, planned aggregate expenditure increases initially by the full amount of the rise in G, or $1. When taxes are cut, however, the initial increase in planned aggregate expenditure is only the *MPC* times the change in taxes. Because the initial increase in planned aggregate expenditure is smaller for a tax cut than it is for a government spending increase, the final effect on the equilibrium level of income will be smaller.

We figure the size of the tax multiplier in the same way we derived the multiplier for an increase in investment and an increase in government purchases. As you know, the final change in the equilibrium level of output (income) (Y) is

$$\Delta Y = (\text{Initial increase in aggregate expenditure}) \times \left(\frac{1}{MPS}\right)$$

Since the initial change in aggregate expenditure caused by a tax change of ΔT is $(-\Delta T \times MPC)$, we can solve for the tax multiplier by substitution:

$$\Delta Y = (-\Delta T \times MPC) \times \left(\frac{1}{MPS}\right) = -\Delta T \times \left(\frac{MPC}{MPS}\right)$$

Because a tax cut will cause an *increase* in consumption expenditures and output and a tax increase will cause a *reduction* in consumption expenditures and output, the tax multiplier is a negative multiplier:

> $$\text{Tax multiplier} \equiv -\left(\frac{MPC}{MPS}\right)$$

We derive the tax multiplier algebraically in Appendix 10A to this chapter.

---

[6]*What happens to the other $0.25? Remember that whatever households do not consume is, by definition, saved. The other $0.25 thus gets allocated to saving.*

If the *MPC* is 0.75, as in our example, the multiplier is $-0.75/0.25 = -3$. Hence a tax cut of $66.7 billion will increase the equilibrium level of output by $200 billion as $-66.7 \times -3 = 200$. Recall that the alternative was to increase G by $50 billion and use the government spending multiplier of 4.

THE BALANCED-BUDGET MULTIPLIER

We have now discussed (1) changing government spending with no change in taxes and (2) changing taxes with no change in government spending. But what if government spending and taxes are increased by the same amount? That is, what if the government decides to pay for its extra spending by increasing taxes by the same amount? Such a move would not change the government's budget surplus or deficit, since the increase in expenditures would be matched by an increase in tax income.

You might think in this case that equal increases in government spending and taxes have no effect on equilibrium income. After all, the extra government spending equals the extra amount of tax revenues collected by the government. But remember as we just discussed that the effect of a $1 increase in government spending (G) is larger than the effect of a $1 increase in taxes ($T$), because all of the $1 increase in G will be spent but the tax increase will reduce consumption by less than a dollar, $0.75 in our example, with the other $0.25 coming from saving.

So we know that a balanced-budget increase in G and T will raise output. But by how much? How large is this **balanced-budget multiplier**? The answer may surprise you. For this model, the:

> Balanced-budget multiplier $\equiv 1$

Let us combine what we know about the tax multiplier and the government spending multiplier to explain this. To find the final effect of a simultaneous increase in government spending and increase in net taxes, we need to add the multiplier effects of the two. The government spending multiplier is $1/MPS$. The tax multiplier is $-MPC/MPS$. The sum of the two is $(1/MPS) + (-MPC/MPS) \equiv (1 - MPC)/MPS$. Because $MPC + MPS \equiv 1$, then $1 - MPC \equiv MPS$. This means that $(1 - MPC)/MPS \equiv MPS/MPS \equiv 1$.[7]

Now let us work through a numerical example in which government spending increases by $40 billion and taxes are increased by $40 billion as well. Using the government spending multiplier, a $40 billion increase in G would *raise* output at equilibrium by $160 billion ($40 billion $\times$ the government spending multiplier of 4). Using the tax multiplier, we know that a $40 billion tax hike will *reduce* the equilibrium level of output by $120 billion ($40 billion $\times$ the tax multiplier of -3). The net effect is $160 billion minus $120 billion, or $40 billion. It should be clear, then, that the effect on equilibrium Y is equal to the balanced increase in G and T. In other words, the net increase in the equilibrium level of Y resulting from the change in G and the change in T is exactly the size of the initial change in G or T itself.

If the government wanted to raise Y by $200 billion without increasing a deficit, a simultaneous increase in G and T of $200 billion would do the trick. To see why, look at the numbers in Table 10.3. Back in Table 10.1, we discovered an equilibrium level of output of $900. With both G and T up by $200, the new equilibrium is $1100—higher by $200 billion. At no other level of Y do we find $(C + I + G) = Y$. In sum:

> An increase in government spending has a direct initial effect on planned aggregate expenditure; a tax increase does not. The initial effect of the tax increase is that households cut consumption by the *MPC* times the change in taxes. This change in consumption is less than the change in taxes, because the *MPC* is less than 1. The positive stimulus from the government spending increase is thus greater than the negative stimulus from the tax increase. The net effect is that the balanced-budget multiplier is 1.

balanced-budget multiplier
The ratio of change in the equilibrium level of output to a change in government spending where the change in government spending is balanced by a change in taxes so as not to change the surplus or deficit. The balanced-budget multiplier is equal to 1: the change in Y *resulting from the change in* G *and the equal change in* T *is exactly the same size as the initial change in* G *or* T *itself.*

---

[7]*We also derive the balanced-budget multiplier in Appendix 10A to this chapter.*

Table 10.3	Finding Equilibrium After a $200 Billion Balanced-Budget Increase in *G* and *T* (Assuming no Exports or Imports; All Figures in Billions of Dollars; Both *G* and *T* Have Increased from 100 in Table 10.1 to 300 Here)								
(1)	(2)	(3)	(4)	(5)	(6)	(7)	(8)	(9)
Output (Income) Y	Net Taxes T	Disposable Income $Y_d \equiv Y - T$	Consumption Spending $(C = 100 + 0.75 Y_d)$	Planned Investment Spending I	Government Purchases G	Planned Aggregate Expenditure $C + I + G$	Unplanned Inventory Change $Y - (C + I + G)$	Adjustment to Disequilibrium
500	300	200	250	100	300	650	−150	Output↑
700	300	400	400	100	300	800	−100	Output↑
900	300	600	550	100	300	950	−50	Output↑
1100	300	800	700	100	300	1100	0	Equilibrium
1300	300	1000	850	100	300	1250	+50	Output↓
1500	300	1200	1000	100	300	1400	+100	Output↓

Table 10.4 summarizes everything that we have said about fiscal policy multipliers for this model. If anything is still unclear, review the relevant discussions in this chapter.

■ **A Warning**   Although we have now added the role of government to our discussion, the story we have told about the multiplier is still incomplete and oversimplified. As noted at the end of the previous chapter, adding more realism to our story has the effect of reducing the size of the multiplier.

One example of this is the case in which taxes depend on income, which is the case in the "real world." For the sake of simplicity, we have been treating net taxes (*T*) as a lump-sum, fixed amount. Appendix 10B to this chapter shows that the size of the multiplier is reduced when we make the more realistic assumption that taxes depend on income. We continue to add more realism to our analysis in the next section and in the chapters that follow.

More on the International Sector

The Canadian economy does not operate in a vacuum. Rather, it influences and is influenced by the rest of the world. Up until this point, though, we have not taken into account the role of imports and exports in the macroeconomy; that is, our model has been of a closed economy, not an open economy.

Allowing for an open economy may change the value of the multiplier, but it does not change the basic analysis or idea. Essentially it adds a fourth component to planned aggregate expenditure—exports of goods and services, which we denote as *EX*. Exports are foreign purchases of goods and services produced in Canada. Opening the economy to the rest of the world also means that Canadian consumers and businesses have greater choice because they can decide to buy foreign-produced

Table 10.4	Summary of Fiscal Policy Multipliers			
		Policy Stimulus	Multiplier	Final Impact on Equilibrium Y
Government-spending multiplier		Increase or decrease in the level of government purchases: ΔG	$\dfrac{1}{MPS}$	$\Delta G \cdot \dfrac{1}{MPS}$
Tax multiplier		Increase or decrease in the level of net taxes: ΔT	$-\dfrac{MPC}{MPS}$	$\Delta T \cdot -\dfrac{MPC}{MPS}$
Balanced-budget multiplier		Simultaneous balanced-budget increase or decrease in the level of government purchases and net taxes: $\Delta G = \Delta T$	1	ΔG

goods and services (imports, or *IM*) in addition to domestically produced goods and services.

With imports and exports accounted for, the equilibrium condition for the economy becomes:

Open-economy equilibrium position: $Y = C + I + G + (EX - IM)$

Imports (*IM*) are subtracted to exclude those goods and services that are purchased from other economies, and hence are not part of domestic output. The expression (*EX − IM*) is referred to as **net exports.**

Consider the case where exports exactly equal imports so that net exports are zero. For that special case $EX - IM = 0$ and we can omit $EX - IM$ from the equilibrium equation above. Then everything in the early part of this chapter applies exactly. We would even have obtained the same results for the numerical example. When we were doing the tables we could have added an extra column for $EX - IM$ and on the graphs we could have marked $C + I + G + EX - IM$ instead of just $C + I + G$, but it would have made no difference at all because $EX - IM$ would have always been zero—the additional export spending would have been exactly balanced by a loss of spending on imports. Of course exports seldom equal imports exactly in a given year.

What might make net exports change? In later chapters we shall suggest that Canadian net exports might increase if the Canadian dollar falls in value relative to other currencies (making our exports cheaper and imports from other countries to Canada more expensive) or if Canada imposed an import tariff to restrict imports. In practice perhaps the most common reason for an increase in Canadian net exports is an increase in output and income in the United States, increasing Canadian sales to the United States of wood, newsprint, autos, auto parts, and other products. In any case, for the purposes of our numerical example, suppose net exports increase from 0 to 50. Because net exports is a component of planned aggregate expenditure just like planned investment (*I*) and government purchases (*G*), it should not surprise you that the multiplier effect is exactly as if planned investment had increased by 50 or government purchases had increased by 50. Hence if we start in the same situation depicted by Table 10.1 with no exports or imports but then we change exports and imports so that net exports become 50, output will increase by 200 to 1100 because the multiplier for that example is 4.

Note that an increase in exports is not necessarily a good thing just because it increases economic activity, because exports are goods Canada produces but others consume. As we discuss in Chapters 20 and 21, exports are the means by which Canada can import, now and in the future. But the Keynesian model of this chapter is a model of economic activity: it makes no prediction as to the effect of changes in exports and the other spending components on economic welfare, only that they affect economic activity.

We can consider more realistic models that involve the international sector. For example, rather than having net exports set at a specific number such as 50, we could allow the import component to depend on disposable income, just like consumption. (We study these kinds of models algebraically in Appendix 10C to this chapter.) This would lower the estimates of all the different multipliers because it recognizes that some of an increase in spending induced by an increase in income would "leak" out of the system as imports. For example, if there is an increase in planned investment through a major new tar sands project in Alberta, some of the extra dollars in construction workers' pockets might be used to purchase U.S.-made computers or Japanese-made stereo equipment, increasing spending in those countries but not in Canada.

■ **The Leakages/Injections Approach to Equilibrium**   As in Chapter 9, we can also examine equilibrium using the leakages/injections approach. Reexamine Figure 10.1, and now pay attention to the links with the rest of the world. You can see the leakages from the spending stream include saving (*S*) as in Chapter 9, but also net taxes (*T*), which the government takes out of the flow of income, and imports

net exports (*EX − IM*) An economy's total exports (*EX*) minus its total imports (IM).

FAST FACTS

In the first quarter of 2000, $Y = C + I + G + EX - IM = \$576 + \$183 + \$205 + \$454 - \$410 = \$1007$ (in billions and allowing for rounding and statistical discrepancy). Figures are on an annual basis, as if the quarterly flows were maintained for a year. The $1007 billion was the first time Canadian GDP (*Y*) exceeded $1 trillion.

(IM), which escape the flow of income to the rest of the world. (The imports leakage is drawn as escaping from total planned expenditure but would actually be the imported portion of consumption, planned investment, and government purchases.) The planned spending injections are investment (I) as before but now also government purchases (G) and exports (EX). If leakages ($S + T + IM$) equal planned injections ($I + G + EX$), there is equilibrium:

> **Leakages/injections approach to equilibrium: $S + T + IM = I + G + EX$**

This equilibrium condition is easy to derive.[8] We know in equilibrium that aggregate output (income) (Y) equals planned aggregate expenditure (AE). By definition, AE equals $C + I + G + EX - IM$, and by definition Y equals $C + S + T$. Therefore, at equilibrium

$$C + S + T = C + I + G + EX - IM$$

Subtracting C from both sides leaves

$$S + T = I + G + EX - IM$$

and adding IM to both sides leaves

$$S + T + IM = I + G + EX$$

Note that equilibrium does not require $G = T$ (a balanced government budget) or $EX = IM$ (a trade balance where exports equal imports) or saving to equal planned investment ($S = I$). It is only necessary that the sum of S, T, and IM equals the sum of I, G, and EX.

To verify this, let us go back to the numbers of Table 10.2 and assume as we did then that $EX = 0$ and IM also equals 0. Column 5 of Table 10.2 calculates saving by subtracting consumption from income at every level of disposable income ($S \equiv Y_d - C$). Since I and G are fixed and EX is assumed to be zero, $I + G + EX$ equals 250 at every level of income. Remembering that IM also is assumed to be zero, the table shows that $S + T + IM$ equals 250 only at $Y = 1100$. Thus the equilibrium level of output (income) is 1100, the same answer we arrived at through numerical and graphical analysis.

The Federal Budget

federal budget *The budget of the federal government.*

Because fiscal policy is the manipulation of items in the federal budget, we need to consider those aspects of the budget that are most relevant to our study of macroeconomics. The **federal budget** is an enormously complicated document, listing in great detail all the things the government plans to spend money on and all the sources of government revenues for the coming year. It is the product of a complex interplay of social, political, and economic forces.

In fact, "the budget" is really three different budgets. First, it is a *political document* that must pass Parliament and will be judged by the voting population at the next federal election. Second, it is a *reflection of certain goals* the government wants to achieve. For example, in addition to assisting the elderly, seniors' benefits could be viewed as helping to maintain the independence and dignity of the older population. Tax breaks for corporations engaging in research and development of new products are meant to encourage such research. Finally, the budget may be an *embodiment of some beliefs about how (if at all) the government should manage the macroeconomy.* The macroeconomic aspects of the budget are thus only a part of a more complicated story, a story that may at times be of more concern to political scientists than to economists.

---

[8]*A shortcoming in our model is that even though we have allowed for international trade, we have not allowed for international movements in capital and labour. Hence using the terminology of Chapter 7, we continue to assume that GDP, output produced within our economy, equals GNP, the output from the factors of production of our economy's residents. In Canada there is a net outflow of investment income so that GNP is less than GDP, recently by about 3%. However, GDP and GNP are still so highly correlated that there would be little gain to making our model more complex to correct this discrepancy.*

An Overview of the Budget

A highly condensed version of a federal budget is shown in Figure 10.4. In 1999/2000, the government estimated total receipts of $160 billion, largely from personal income taxes ($76.5 billion). Receipts from corporate taxes accounted for $22.5 billion, or only 14.1% of total receipts. Not everyone is aware of the fact that corporate taxes as a percentage of government receipts are quite small relative to personal taxes. (See also the Application box titled "Taxation in Canada" for an overview of the different types of taxes that have been used since Confederation and the importance of each as a source of federal government revenue.)

The federal government also budgeted $157 billion of expenditures in 1999/2000. Of this amount, $78.8 billion represented transfer payments.[9] Some of these were made directly to persons (as in the case of seniors' benefits) and some were paid to the provinces for their allocation (as for health care). Purchases of goods and services included $9.9 billion worth of defence spending. As you can see, interest payments on the federal debt accounted for 26.4% of government expenditure in 1999/2000, and were a greater expenditure than government purchases of goods and services.

The Federal Budget Balance and the Federal Debt

In 1999/2000, the federal government budgeted expenditures of $157 billion were less than the budgeted revenue of $160 billion. The budgeted surplus was therefore $3 billion although the actual surplus turned out to be somewhat higher. Other measures of the surplus, which are different because of such complexities as the method used for accounting the liabilities of the pension plan for government employees, were higher still. But during the 1970s, 1980s, and 1990s, the budget balance was much more typically negative as you can see from Figure 10.5, which gives the budget balance during 1970–1999 as a percentage of GDP.

How did such large deficits come about? In simplest terms, government inflows in the form of taxes were insufficient to cover outflows in the form of purchases of goods and services, transfer payments, and interest payments. When economic growth and hence revenue growth slowed in the mid-1970s, the government debt started to increase. The recession of 1980–1982 aggravated the situation further. As funds were borrowed to cover the shortfall, interest payments became an important factor, particularly with the higher interest rates of that time and the subsequent recession of the early 1990s. By the mid-1990s, the government budget

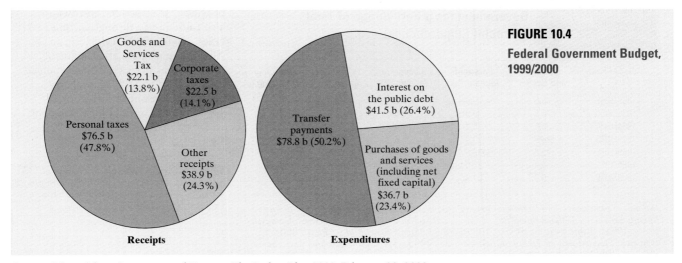

FIGURE 10.4

Federal Government Budget, 1999/2000

Source: Adapted from Department of Finance, *The Budget Plan 2000*, February 28, 2000.

---

[9]*Remember that there is an important difference between transfer payments and government purchases of goods and services. Much of the government budget goes for things that an economist would classify as transfers (payments that are grants or gifts) rather than purchases of goods and services. It is only the latter that are included in our variable G. Transfers are counted as part of net taxes.*

APPLICATION

Taxation in Canada

While taxation has been a part of Canadian life since the day the country began in 1867, the types of taxes used by governments to raise revenue have changed a great deal over the years. Table 1 gives some idea of these changes and shows the importance of some of the sources of federal government revenue as a percentage of the government's total financial requirements in each fiscal year.

At the time of Confederation, the principal source of revenue for the federal government was customs duties, that is, tariffs on imported goods. Also important were excise duties and taxes. Excise taxes were originally taxes on goods considered to be "luxury" items, and currently apply to products such as wine, tobacco, gasoline, jewellery, and automobile air conditioners. Excise duties are additional levies on tobacco, beer, and spirits. (Taxes that apply specifically to goods such as tobacco and alcohol are sometimes referred to as "sin taxes.")

Personal and corporate income taxes were introduced during World War I and provided much-needed revenue at a time of greatly increased government spending. Both taxes were originally imposed at rates of 4%, with surtaxes of 2% to 25% added to personal tax rates for higher levels of income. As can be seen in Table 1, the personal income tax as a percentage of the federal government's total financial requirements has increased greatly, while the share of the corporate income tax has generally fallen since 1950.

The first federal sales tax, introduced in 1920, was the Manufacturers' Sales Tax (MST) and, as the name implies, was collected directly from manufacturers. The cost of the MST was then incorporated into the retail price of the goods, and many consumers were unaware of its existence. As of January 1, 1991, the MST was abolished and replaced with the Goods and Services Tax (GST), collected from purchasers at the point of sale. Manufacturers as well as consumers pay the GST on their purchases, but manufacturers can claim refunds of the tax if the goods or services purchased are intermediate products used in their production processes.

The range of products subject to the federal sales tax is far wider under the GST than it was under the MST. Services, for example, were generally not included under the MST. However, the rate of tax is lower under the GST than under the MST. (In Quebec, Newfoundland, New Brunswick, and Nova Scotia, the GST has been combined with the provincial sales tax into a single sales tax.)

Deficit financing is not a tax, but is government borrowing to make up the revenue shortfall. (Because this increases government debt, it will increase future taxation.) Figures have been included here to show the varying role of taxation as a whole in financing a particular year's government expenditure. Deficit financing was used during the two World Wars and during the Great Depression; the federal government also borrowed steadily from the 1970s to the late 1990s.

While Table 1 shows the importance of various taxes as a share of what the government raised each year, remember that the amount the government raises in total has increased. In 1870 the federal government raised about 5% of GNP in taxes and borrowing. By 2000 this number had increased to about 17%. If we include provinces, who besides borrowing also raise money through income taxes, retail sales taxes (except in Alberta), and many other kinds of taxes such as licence fees, and municipalities, who mainly use property taxes, the consolidated total of all government taxes and borrowing was well over 40% of GNP.

Table 1	Selected Revenue Sources, Federal Government (as a Percentage of Total Financial Requirements)				
Fiscal Year	Customs and Excise	Personal Income Tax	Corporate Income Tax	Sales Tax	Deficit Financing
1867/1868	86.6	0.0	0.0	0.0	0.0
1899/1900	78.5	0.0	0.0	0.0	0.0
1934/1935	35.5	5.4	7.7	15.5	24.9
1949/1950	26.3	26.4	25.6	17.1	0.0
1969/1970	12.8	30.6	19.6	12.9	0.0
1989/1990	5.9	37.9	9.5	12.9	21.2
1999/2000	6.7	51.3	15.1	14.8	0.0

Sources: Fiscal years 1867/1868 to 1989/1990: W. Irwin Gillespie, *Tax, Borrow and Spend: Financing Federal Spending in Canada, 1867–1990* (Ottawa: Carleton University Press, 1991), Table B-3; Fiscal year 1999/2000: Adapted from *Budget Plan* 2000 (Ottawa: Department of Finance), February 28, 2000. (Methodologies and data may differ slightly between the two sources.)

Source: W. Irwin Gillespie, *Tax, Borrow and Spend: Financing Federal Spending in Canada, 1867–1990* (Ottawa: Carleton University Press, 1991).

FIGURE 10.5

The Federal Government Budget Balance as a Percentage of GDP, 1970–1999

The federal government experienced budget deficits for nearly all the 1970–1999 period. The deficits in the 1980s were particularly large by postwar standards.

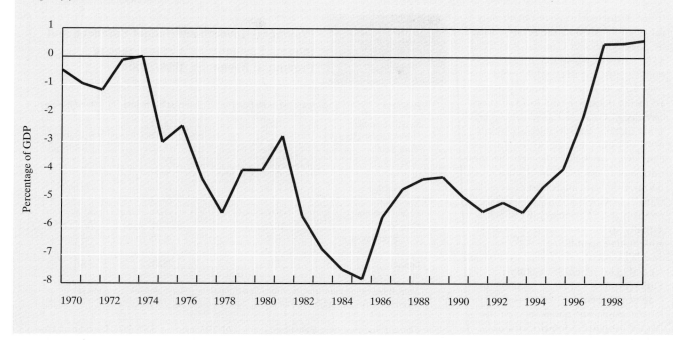

Source: Adapted from Statistics Canada, CANSIM database, Series D14816 (GDP), D15129 (budget balance).

would have been very strongly in surplus if not for the interest payments on past debt. Since 1997, the federal government has been running a surplus, and an important political issue has been whether the surpluses should be used to cut taxes, increase spending, or reduce the debt.

When the government runs a deficit, it must borrow to finance it. To borrow, the federal government sells government securities to the public. It issues pieces of paper promising to pay a certain amount, with interest, in the future. In return, it receives funds from the buyers of the paper and uses these funds to pay its bills. This borrowing increases the **federal debt,** the total amount owed by the federal government. The federal debt is the total of all accumulated deficits minus surpluses over time.

Given the large deficits that the federal government ran beginning in the mid-1970s, it should not be surprising that the federal debt rose sharply from then on. You can see this in Figure 10.6, where the federal debt as a percentage of GDP is plotted for 1946–1999. The debt to GDP ratio fell steadily from 1946 to 1974 then rose from about 15% of GDP in 1975 to about 70% in 1996. It has fallen slowly since then.

The importance of provincial government budgets is often underestimated. The Application box "Provincial Governments and Fiscal Policy" shows that as of 1999/2000 most provinces were running surpluses.

federal debt *The total amount owed by the federal government.*

THE ECONOMY'S INFLUENCE ON THE BUDGET BALANCE

The economic consequences of the government debt are discussed in detail in Chapter 16. We conclude this chapter with a discussion of the way the economy affects the budget balance.

■ **Tax Revenues Depend on the State of the Economy**   As we said earlier, some parts of the government's budget depend on the state of the economy, over which the government has no direct control. Consider the revenue side of the budget. The government passes laws that set tax rates and tax brackets, variables that the government does control. Tax revenue, on the other hand, depends on taxable income, and income depends on the state of the economy, which the government does *not*

In total, the federal government only raises about 50% of the revenue raised by governments in Canada. Provincial governments own-source revenue is only slightly less than 40%, while just over 10% is raised by municipal governments, largely in the form of property taxes. Provincial government personal income tax revenues are about 40% of total personal income tax revenue and provincial sales taxes in total raise more than the federal sales taxes. Because the provinces also receive transfer payments from the federal government, provincial governments actually spend more than the federal government spends.

Why then is the focus so often on federal government budgetary policy? One reason of course is because the federal government budget is the largest single budget, with even the largest province, Ontario, still only raising about one-third the revenue of the federal government. Also, in terms of fiscal policy, the provincial governments are unlikely to act in concert and have a fiscal policy effect like that of the federal government. In addition, unlike the federal government, provincial governments do not have access to monetary policy, which we will argue in the next two chapters is an important tool in influencing economic activity and which may be used to offset the effects of fiscal policy.

Table 1 presents data for the provincial and federal government finances for 1999/2000. It shows that New Brunswick has the largest deficit as a percentage of government revenue, followed by British Columbia, Manitoba,

Table 1	Provincial Government Budget Balances and Interest Payments as a Percentage of Provincial Revenues, 1999/2000

Province	Surplus (+) or Deficit (−)	Interest Payments	Bond Rating
Newfoundland	0.6%	15.3%	BBB
Prince Edward Island	0.1%	12.8%	BBB (high)
Nova Scotia	0.8%	18.5%	BBB (high)
New Brunswick	−15.0%	17.7%	A
Quebec	−0.9%	16.6%	A
Ontario	2.1%	15.1%	AA (low)
Manitoba	−1.8%	20.4%	A
Saskatchewan	6.0%	17.2%	A
Alberta	11.7%	8.3%	AA (high)
British Columbia	−6.6%	12.2%	AA (low)
Canada	**1.9%**	**25.9%**	**AAA**

Note: Bond ratings are from the Dominion Bond Rating Service. AAA is the top rating, followed by AA, A, and BBB. Adjectives high and low describe placement within a rating.

Sources: Adapted from Statistics Canada, CANSIM matrices 3777–3786; Department of Finance, *The Budget Plan 2000*, February 28, 2000; Dominion Bond Rating Service home page, July 20, 2000 (**www.dbrs.com**).

and Quebec. All the remaining provinces have surpluses.

While in most cases deficit problems are under control, past deficits have built large debts and all of the provinces make substantial interest payments. Even though the federal government has also eliminated its deficit, interest payments remain high because of past borrowing and are much higher as a percentage of revenue than for any of the provinces.

Nevertheless, the federal government bond rating remains better than that of any of the provinces. In principle the federal government can always pay off debt denominated in Canadian dollars by creating the Canadian dollars required (although the Bank of Canada must cooperate, as described in the next chapter). Economists call this "monetizing the debt." Provincial governments do not have this option, which at least partly accounts for their lower credit ratings.

control. The government can set a personal income tax rate of 20%, but the revenue that the tax brings in will depend on the average income earned by households. Clearly, the government will collect much more revenue when average income is $40 000 than it will when average income is $20 000.

■ **Some Government Expenditures Depend on the State of the Economy** Some items on the expenditure side of the government budget also depend on the state of the economy. As the economy expands, unemployment falls, and the result is a decrease in unemployment benefits. Welfare payments also decrease somewhat. Some of the people who receive these benefits during bad times are able to find jobs when the state of the economy improves, and they begin earning enough income that they no longer qualify. Transfer payments thus tend to go down automatically during an expansion. (The reverse is true in a slump. During a slump,

FIGURE 10.6

The Federal Government Debt as a Percentage of GDP, 1946–1999

The federal government debt increased dramatically in the 1980s as a result of the large deficits.

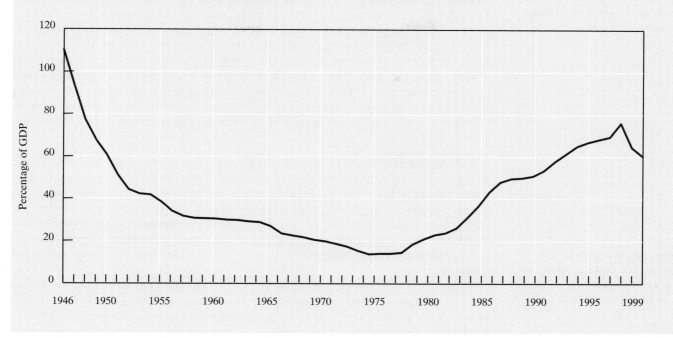

Source: Adapted from Statistics Canada, CANSIM database, Series D11000, D14816, and D469420.

transfer payments tend to increase because there are more people without jobs and more poor people generally.)

Another reason that government spending is not completely controllable is that inflation often picks up when the economy is expanding. This can lead the government to spend more than it had planned to spend. Suppose the government has ordered 20 planes at $2 million per plane and that inflation causes the actual price per plane to be higher than expected. If the government decides to go ahead and buy the planes anyway, it will be forced to increase its spending.

Finally, any change in the interest rate changes government interest payments. An increase in interest rates means that the government spends more in interest payments. When the government debt is relatively large, interest payments can be an important component of the total budget, as we saw in Figure 10.4.

■ **Automatic Stabilizers**   As the economy expands, the government's tax receipts increase. Also, transfer payments fall as the economy expands, which leads to a decrease in government expenditures. The revenue and expenditure items that change in response to changes in economic activity are known as **automatic stabilizers.** As the economy expands or contracts, "automatic" changes in government revenues and expenditures take place, and these tend to reduce the change in, or stabilize, GDP.

The fact that some revenues *automatically* tend to rise and some expenditures *automatically* tend to fall in an expansion means that the government surplus is larger, or the deficit is smaller, in an expansion than it otherwise would be. Suppose we wanted to assess whether a government is practising a policy designed to increase spending and income. If we looked only at the size of the government budget deficit, we might be fooled into thinking that the government is trying to stimulate the economy when, in fact, the real source of the deficit is a slump in the economy that caused revenues to fall and transfer payments to increase.

■ **Fiscal Drag**   If the economy is doing well, income will be high and so will tax revenue. Tax revenue rises with increases in income for two reasons. First, there is simply more income to be taxed when people are earning more. Second, as people

automatic stabilizers *Revenue and expenditure items in the federal budget that automatically change with the state of the economy in such a way as to stabilize GDP.*

earn more income, they move into higher tax brackets and the average tax rate that they pay increases. This type of increase in tax rates is sometimes called **fiscal drag,** because the increase in average tax rates that results when people move into higher brackets acts as a "drag" on the economy. As the economy expands and income increases, the automatic tax increase mechanism built into the system goes to work. Tax rates go up, reducing the after-tax wage, and this slows down the expansion.

Before 1974, people found themselves pushed into higher tax brackets by inflation alone. Suppose, for example, that my income rose 10% in 1973, but that the price level also rose by 10% in that year. My income did not increase at all in real terms, but since the tax brackets were not legislated in real terms, I ended up paying more taxes. In 1974, tax brackets and exemptions in the personal income tax system were indexed, that is, adjusted for inflation. In 1983, the government moved to a system of partial indexation, but returned to full indexation in the 2000 budget.

■ **Full-Employment Budget**   Because the condition of the economy affects the budget deficit so strongly, we cannot accurately judge either the intent or the success of fiscal policies just by looking at the deficit. Instead of looking simply at the size of the deficit, economists have developed an alternative way to measure how effective fiscal policy actually is. By examining what the budget would be like if the economy were producing at the full-employment level of output—the so-called **full-employment budget**—we can establish a benchmark for evaluating fiscal policy.

The distinction between the actual and full-employment deficits is an important one. Suppose that the economy is in a slump and that the deficit is $15 billion. Also suppose that if there were full employment, the deficit would fall to $5 billion. The $5 billion deficit that would remain even with full employment would be due to the structure of tax and spending programs rather than to the state of the economy. This deficit—the deficit that remains at full employment—is sometimes called the **structural deficit.** The structural deficit is the deficit of the full-employment budget. The $10 billion ($15 billion – $5 billion) part of the deficit that is caused by the fact the economy is in a slump is known as the **cyclical deficit.** The existence of the cyclical deficit depends on where the economy is in the business cycle, and it ceases to exist when full employment is reached. By definition, the cyclical deficit of the full-employment budget is zero.

Debt and Budget Balances in the Rest of the World

Table 10.5 shows the government budget balance and debt as a percentage of GDP for Canada and the six other major industrialized countries that make up the G-7 nations.[10] (The figures for Canada and the other countries have been adjusted by the International Monetary Fund to improve international comparability.) As can be seen, Canada's budget surplus as a percentage of GDP ranked us first in the G-7 in 1999. Canada had a debt-to-GDP ratio of about 57%, only slightly higher than that of the United States.

The Money Market and Monetary Policy: A Preview

We have now seen how households, firms, and the government interact in the goods market, how equilibrium output (income) is determined, and how the government uses fiscal policy to influence the economy. (We've also provided a brief introduction to the international sector's influence on aggregate expenditure and equilibrium output.) In the following two chapters, we analyze the money market and monetary policy—the government's other major tool for influencing the economy.

Table 10.5

Government Budget Balances and Debt as a Percentage of GDP, 1999, for G-7 Countries

	Budget Balance	Debt
Canada	2.8	56.7
France	−1.8	49.0
Germany	−1.1	52.4
Italy	−1.9	108.8
Japan	−7.1	37.7
United Kingdom	0.3	41.1
United States	0.5	50.6

Source: International Monetary Fund, *World Economic Outlook,* May 2000, Table 1.4.

---

[10]G-7 is short for "Group of Seven." Reference is often made as well to the G-5, which is the G-7 minus Canada and Italy. The United States is sometimes humorously referred to as the G-1.

1. The government can affect the macroeconomy through two specific policy channels. *Fiscal policy* refers to the government's taxing and spending behaviour. *Discretionary fiscal policy* refers to changes in taxes or spending that are the result of deliberate changes in government policy. *Monetary policy* refers to the behaviour of the Bank of Canada regarding the nation's money supply.

Government Participation in the Economy

2. The government does not have complete control over tax revenues and certain expenditures, which are partially dictated by the state of the economy.

3. As a participant in the economy, the government makes purchases of goods and services (G), collects taxes, and makes transfer payments to households. *Net taxes* (T) is equal to the tax payments made to the government by firms and households minus transfer payments made to households by the government.

4. *Disposable*, or *after-tax, income* (Y_d) is equal to the amount of income received by households after taxes: $Y_d \equiv Y - T$. After-tax income determines households' consumption behaviour.

5. The *budget deficit* is equal to the difference between what the government spends and what it collects in taxes: $G - T$. When G exceeds T, the government must borrow from the public to finance its deficit. The *budget surplus* or balance is $T - G$.

6. In an economy in which a government is a participant but in which there are no exports or imports (a "closed economy"), planned aggregate expenditure equals consumption spending by households (C) plus planned investment spending by firms (I) plus government spending on goods and services (G): $AE \equiv C + I + G$. Because the condition $Y = AE$ is necessary for the economy to be in equilibrium, it follows that $Y = C + I + G$ is the macroeconomic equilibrium condition.

Fiscal Policy at Work: The Multiplier Effects

7. Fiscal policy has a multiplier effect on the economy. A change in government spending gives rise to a multiplier equal to $1/MPS$. A change in taxation brings about a multiplier equal to $-MPC/MPS$. A simultaneous equal increase or decrease in government spending and taxes has a "balanced-budget" multiplier effect of 1.

More on the International Sector

8. Opening the economy to foreign trade adds two additional components to the equilibrium condition: exports (EX) and imports (IM). Exports are an injection into the circular flow; imports are a leakage from the circular flow. Thus the equilibrium condition for the economy becomes $Y = C + I + G + (EX - IM)$ when the international sector is taken into account. The expression ($EX - IM$) is referred to as *net exports*.

9. Another way of stating the equilibrium condition for the economy is that equilibrium occurs when leakages out of the system equal injections into the system. This occurs when saving plus net taxes plus imports (the leakages) equal planned investment plus government purchases plus exports (the injections): $S + T + IM = I + G + EX$.

The Federal Budget

10. The federal deficit was quite large during the 1980s, but began to fall during the 1990s and turned to surplus by 1997. Still, the debt (accumulated deficits less surpluses) remained about 60% of GDP as the last century closed.

11. *Automatic stabilizers* are revenue and expenditure items in the federal budget that automatically change with the state of the economy and thus tend to stabilize GDP. For example, during expansions the government automatically takes in more revenue, because people are making more money that is taxed. Higher income also means fewer transfer payments.

12. *Fiscal drag* is the negative effect on the economy that occurs when average tax rates increase because taxpayers have moved into higher income brackets during an expansion. These higher taxes reduce disposable income and slow down the expansion. Since 1974, tax brackets have been indexed to inflation to some degree.

13. The *full-employment budget* is an economist's construction of what the federal budget would be if the economy were producing at a full-employment level of output. A *structural deficit* is a federal deficit that remains even at full employment. *Cyclical deficits* occur when there is a downturn in the business cycle.

automatic stabilizers 217

balanced-budget multiplier 209

budget deficit 202

budget surplus 202

cyclical deficit 218

discretionary fiscal policy 200

disposable, or after-tax, income (Y_d) 201

federal budget 212

federal debt 215

fiscal drag 218

fiscal policy 200

full-employment budget 218

government spending multiplier 206

monetary policy 200

net exports ($EX - IM$) 211

net taxes (T) 201

structural deficit 218

tax multiplier 208

Equations:

1. Disposable income: $Y_d \equiv Y - T$

2. $AE \equiv C + I + G$ (assuming no exports or imports)

3. Government budget deficit $\equiv G - T$

4. Equilibrium in an economy with government: $Y = C + I + G$ (assuming no exports or imports)

5. Government spending multiplier $\equiv \dfrac{1}{MPS}$

6. Tax multiplier $\equiv -\left(\dfrac{MPC}{MPS}\right)$

7. Balanced-budget multiplier $\equiv 1$

8. Open-economy equilibrium position: $Y = C + I + G + (EX - IM)$

9. Leakages/injections approach to equilibrium in an open economy with government: $S + T + IM = I + G + EX$

Problem Set

1. Define *saving* and *investment*. Data for the simple closed economy of Newt show that saving exceeds investment and the government is running a balanced budget. What is likely to happen? What would happen if the government were instead running a deficit and saving were equal to investment?

2. Economists in the economy of Yuk estimate the following, assuming Yuk has no exports or imports:

Real output/income	1000 billion Yuks
Government purchases	200 billion Yuks
Total net taxes	200 billion Yuks
Investment spending (planned)	100 billion Yuks

Assume that Yukkers consume 75% of their disposable incomes and that they save 25%.

   a. You are asked by the business editor of the *Yuk Gazette* to predict the events of the next few months. Using the data above and the model of this chapter, can you make a forecast? (Assume that investment is constant.)

   b. If no changes were made, at what level of GDP (Y) would the economy of Yuk settle?

   c. Some local conservatives blame Yuk's problems on the size of the government sector. They suggest cutting government purchases by 25 billion Yuks. What effect would such cuts have on the economy? (Be specific.)

3. "A $1 increase in government spending will raise equilibrium income by more than a $1 tax cut, yet both have the same impact on a budget deficit. So if we care about a budget deficit, the best way to stimulate the economy is through increases in spending, not cuts in taxes." Comment.

4. Assume that the following situation prevails in the Republic of Nurd, a closed economy:

$Y = \$200$	$G = \$0$
$C = \$160$	$T = \$0$
$S = \$40$	
I (planned) $= \$30$	

Assume that households consume 80% of their income, that they save 20% of their income, that $MPC = 0.8$, and $MPS = 0.2$. That is, $C = 0.8Y_d$ and $S = 0.2Y_d$.

   a. Is the economy of Nurd in equilibrium? What is Nurd's equilibrium level of income? What is likely to happen in the coming months if the government takes no action?

   b. If $200 is the "full employment" level of Y, what fiscal policy might the government follow if its goal is full employment?

   c. If the full-employment level of Y is $250, what fiscal policy might the government follow?

   d. Suppose that $Y = \$200$, $C = \$160$, $S = \$40$, and $I = \$40$. Is Nurd's economy in equilibrium?

e. Starting with the situation in **d**, suppose that the government starts spending $30 each year with no taxation and continues to spend $30 every period. If I remains constant, what will happen to the equilibrium level of Nurd's domestic product (Y)? What will the new levels of C and S be?

f. Starting with the situation in **d**, suppose that the government starts taxing the population $30 every year without spending anything and continues to tax at that rate every period. If I remains constant, what will happen to the equilibrium level of Nurd's domestic product (Y)? What will be the new levels of C and S? How does your answer to **f** differ from your answer to **e**? Why?

5. Suppose that all tax collections are fixed (rather than dependent on income), and that all spending and transfer programs are also fixed (in the sense that they do not depend on the state of the economy, as, for example, employment benefits now do). If this were the case, would there be any automatic stabilizers in the government budget? Would there be any distinction between the full-employment deficit and the actual budget deficit? Explain.

6. Answer the following questions using the model in this chapter:

a. $MPS = 0.4$. What is the government spending multiplier?

b. $MPC = 0.9$. What is the government spending multiplier?

c. $MPS = 0.5$. What is the government spending multiplier?

d. $MPC = 0.75$. What is the tax multiplier?

e. $MPS = 0.1$. What is the tax multiplier?

f. If the government spending multiplier is 6, what is the tax multiplier?

g. If the tax multiplier is -2, what is the government spending multiplier?

h. If government purchases and taxes are both increased by $100 billion simultaneously, what will the effect be on equilibrium output (income)?

7. What is the relationship between the government budget deficit and the government debt? In a year in which Canada balances its budget, is there any effect on the size of the debt?

8. Go back to the initial set-up of question 4 and suppose that Nurd becomes an open economy, with exports (EX) 15 and imports (IM) 15. What is equilibrium output? What happens to equilibrium output if exports increase to 25?

| Appendix 10A | Deriving the Fiscal Policy Multipliers Algebraically (With Neither Taxes nor Imports Depending on Income) |

In this appendix we derive the fiscal policy multipliers, assuming that neither taxes nor imports depend on income. In Appendix 10B, we allow taxes but not imports to depend on income. In Appendix 10C, we focus on a numerical example and allow imports but not taxes to depend on income.

A Numerical Example

Let us first calculate the government spending, tax, and balanced-budget multipliers in the numerical example used in the chapter:

Consumption spending: $C = 100 + 0.75Y_d = 100 + 0.75(Y - T)$

Planned investment spending: $I = 100$

Government purchases: $G = 100$

Net exports: $EX - IM = 0$

Net taxes: $T = 100$

Y_d is disposable income, or income minus taxes: $Y_d = Y - T$. The solution method is always the same: write down the equation for planned aggregate expenditure,

substitute in for its components and then solve given the equilibrium condition that planned aggregate expenditure equals output. Hence

$$AE \equiv C + I + G + EX - IM$$
$$= 100 + 0.75(Y - T) + 100 + 100 + 0$$
$$= 100 + 0.75 (Y - 100) + 100 + 100 + 0$$

Note that we could simplify this to $AE = 225 + 0.75Y$ but we will leave the terms separate for now. Setting planned aggregate expenditure equal to output Y and solving:

$$Y = 100 + 0.75 (Y - 100) + 100 + 100 + 0$$
$$Y - 0.75Y = 100 - 0.75(100) + 100 + 100 + 0$$
$$(1 - 0.75)Y = 100 - 0.75(100) + 100 + 100 + 0$$

We can then solve for Y by dividing through by $(1 - 0.75)$:

$$Y = \frac{1}{1 - 0.75} [100 - 0.75(100) + 100 + 100 + 0]$$
$$= 4 \times 225$$
$$= 900$$

This solves for equilibrium $Y = 900$, just as in Table 10.1.

The Government Spending and Tax Multipliers

If we want to calculate the government spending multiplier, one way is to increase G by 1 to 101, work through the whole calculation again, and find that Y will become 904. Hence an increase in G by 1 increases Y by 4: the government spending multiplier is 4. But you could also see this by inspection of the last equation: an increase in G by 1 to 101, an increase in autonomous consumption (the part of consumption that does not depend on Y_d) by 1 to 101, an increase in planned investment spending I by 1 to 101, or an increase in net exports $EX - IM$ by 1 from 0 to 1 will all clearly increase Y by the multiplier $1/(1 - 0.75) = 4$.

The calculation is slightly different for an increase in net taxes. Again we could calculate the tax multiplier by increasing T by 1 to 101, working through the calculation and finding that Y will become 897 and hence an increase in T by 1 decreases Y by 3: the tax multiplier is −3. But you could also see this by inspection of the last equation: an increase in T by 1 will reduce output by $0.75/(1 - 0.75) = 3$.

For the balanced-budget multiplier we can work through the calculation if both G and T increase by 1 and find that output increases by 1 to 901. Hence if both G and T increase by 1, Y increases by 1 and the balanced-budget multiplier is 1. The balanced-budget multiplier is the sum of the government spending multiplier and the tax multiplier, or, here, $4 + (-3) = 1$.

Deriving the Multipliers

Now we will derive the government spending multiplier in general, so that instead of using particular numerical values we use algebraic expressions. But the procedure is exactly the same. We begin with the consumption function:

$$C = a + b(Y - T)$$

where b is the marginal propensity to consume. As you know, the equilibrium condition is

$$Y = C + I + G + EX - IM$$

Substituting for C, we get

$$Y = a + b(Y - T) + I + G + EX - IM$$

$$Y = a + bY - bT + I + G + EX - IM$$

This equation can be rearranged to yield

$$Y - bY = a + I + G - bT + EX - IM$$

$$Y(1 - b) = a + I + G - bT + EX - IM$$

We can then solve for Y by dividing through by $(1 - b)$:

$$Y = \frac{1}{(1 - b)} (a + I + G - bT + EX - IM)$$

We see from this last equation that if G increases by 1 with the other determinants of Y (a, I, T, and ($EX - IM$)) remaining constant, Y increases by $1/(1 - b)$. Thus, the multiplier is, as before, simply $1/(1 - b)$, where b is the marginal propensity to consume. And, of course, $1 - b$ equals the marginal propensity to save, so the government spending multiplier is $1/MPS$. In our numerical example, the marginal propensity to save was $1 - 0.75 = 0.25 =$ so $1/MPS = 1/0.25 = 4$.

We can also derive the tax multiplier. The last equation above says that when T increases by \$1, holding a, I, G and ($EX - IM$) constant, income decreases by $b/(1 - b)$ dollars. The tax multiplier is thus $-b/(1 - b)$, or $- MPC/(1 - MPC) = - MPC/MPS$. (Remember that we add the negative sign to the tax multiplier because the tax multiplier is a *negative* multiplier.) In the numerical example, $MPC = 0.75$ and $MPS = 0.25$ so $- MPC/MPS = -0.75/0.25 = -3$.

The Balanced-Budget Multiplier

The effect on Y of an increase in G is $\Delta G/(1 - b)$ and the effect on Y of an increase in T is $-b\Delta T/(1 - b)$. Adding these together gives:

$$\Delta Y = \frac{(\Delta G - b\Delta T)}{(1 - b)}$$

$$= \frac{(\Delta G - b\Delta G)}{(1 - b)} \quad \text{in the balanced-budget case where } \Delta G = \Delta T$$

$$= \frac{\Delta G(1 - b)}{(1 - b)}$$

$$= \Delta G$$

so the balanced-budget multiplier is 1. In other words, in this case the increase in output equals the increase in government purchases, which equals the increase in taxes.

In this model, the balanced-budget multiplier is 1, but in more complex models (such as those in Chapter 14), the balanced-budget multiplier is typically less than 1. The important point is that the government spending multiplier is larger than the tax multiplier and hence an increase in government purchases accompanied by an equal increase in taxes tends to have an expansionary effect on the economy.

Summary

1. In the simple model with neither taxes nor imports depending on income and where *MPC* is the marginal propensity to consume and 1 – *MPC* = *MPS* is the marginal propensity to save, it is possible to derive algebraically that the government spending multiplier is 1/*MPS*, the tax multiplier is –*MPC*/*MPS*, and the balanced-budget multiplier is 1.

Problem Set

1. What are equilibrium output, the government spending multiplier, and the tax multiplier for the numerical model in Appendix 10A except $C = 40 + 0.8Y_d$ and $T = 50$?

2. Repeat question 1 if $C = 200 + 0.6Y_d$ and $T = 150$.

Appendix 10B

The Case in Which Tax Revenues (But Not Imports) Depend on Income

In this chapter, we used the simplifying assumption that the government collects taxes in a lump sum. But now suppose that the government collects taxes not solely as a lump sum that is paid regardless of income, but also partly in the form of a proportional levy against income. As we noted in the chapter, this is clearly a more realistic assumption. Typically, tax collections are either based on income (as with the personal income tax) or they closely follow the ups and downs in the economy (as with sales taxes). Thus, instead of setting taxes equal to some fixed amount, let us say that tax revenues depend on income. If we call the amount of net taxes collected *T*, we can write: $T = T_0 + tY$.

This equation contains two parts. First, we note that net taxes (*T*) will be equal to an amount T_0 if income (*Y*) is zero. Second, the tax rate (*t*) indicates how much net taxes change as income changes. Suppose that T_0 is equal to –200 and *t* is 1/3. The resulting tax function is $T = -200 + 1/3Y$, which is graphed in Figure 10A.1. Note that when income is zero, the government collects "negative net taxes," which simply means that it makes transfer payments of 200. As income rises, tax collections increase because every extra dollar of income generates $0.33 in extra revenues for the government.

How do we incorporate this new tax function into our discussion? All we need to do is replace the old value of *T* (in the example in the chapter, *T* was set equal to 100) with the new value, –200 + 1/3*Y*. Instead of disposable income equalling *Y* – 100, the new equation for disposable income is

$$Y_d \equiv Y - T$$
$$Y_d \equiv Y - (-200 + 1/3Y)$$
$$Y_d \equiv Y + 200 - 1/3Y$$

Since consumption still depends on after-tax income, exactly as it did before, we have

$$C = 100 + 0.75Y_d$$
$$C = 100 + 0.75\,(Y + 200 - 1/3Y)$$

Figure 10A.1 The Tax Function

This graph shows net taxes (taxes minus transfer payments) as a function of aggregate income.

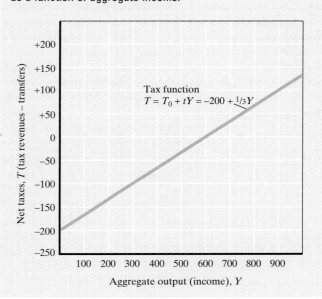

Tax function
$T = T_0 + tY = -200 + \frac{1}{3}Y$

Net taxes, *T* (tax revenues – transfers)

Aggregate output (income), *Y*

Nothing else needs to be changed. We solve for equilibrium income exactly as before, by setting planned aggregate expenditure equal to aggregate output. Recall that planned aggregate expenditure is $C + I + G + EX - IM$, and aggregate output is *Y*. If we assume, as before, that $I = 100$, $G = 100$, and $EX - IM = 0$, then planned aggregate expenditure is

$$AE \equiv C + I + G + EX - IM$$
$$= \underbrace{100 + 0.75(Y + 200 - 1/3Y)}_{C}$$

$$\underbrace{+ 100}_{I} \underbrace{+ 100}_{G} \underbrace{+ 0}_{EX - IM}$$

$$= 100 + 0.75Y + 150 - 0.25Y + 100 + 100 + 0$$

$$\text{or } AE = 450 + 0.5Y$$

Solving using the equilibrium condition that planned aggregate expenditure must equal output, that is, $AE = Y$,

$$Y = 450 + 0.5Y$$

$$\text{or } 0.5Y = 450$$

This means that $Y = 450/0.5 = 900$. The new equilibrium level of income is thus 900.

It is useful to consider the graphic analysis of this equation as shown in Figure 10A.2. AE_1 is the planned aggregate expenditure function when taxes are all lump-sum and equal to 100, as assumed in the main body of this chapter. (This planned aggregate expenditure function is calculated in Appendix 10A.) The most important thing you should note from Figure 10A.2 is that when we make taxes a function of income (instead of merely a lump-sum amount), the AE function becomes *flatter* than it was before (and hence the multiplier is smaller). Why is this so? When tax collections do not depend on income as in AE_1, an increase in income of $1 means that disposable income also increases by a dollar. Because taxes are a constant amount, adding more income does not raise the amount of taxes paid. Disposable income therefore changes dollar for dollar with any change in income. With the MPC of 0.75, the increase in consumption and hence in planned aggregate expenditure is $0.75 and the slope of AE_1 is 0.75.

When taxes depend on income, as in AE_2 a $1 increase in income does not increase disposable income by a full dollar, because some of the additional dollar must go to pay extra taxes. In our example, an extra dollar of income will increase disposable income by only $0.67, because $0.33 of the extra dollar goes to the government in the form of taxes. With the MPC of 0.75, the increase in consumption and hence in planned aggregate expenditure is $0.75 \times 0.67 = 0.50 and the slope of AE_2 is 0.5, less than the slope of AE_1.

The Government Spending and Tax Multipliers Algebraically

All of this means that if taxes are a function of income, the spending and tax multipliers are both less than they would be if taxes were a lump-sum amount. Using the same linear consumption function we used in the last two chapters, we can derive the multiplier:

When taxes are strictly lump sum ($T = 100$) and do not depend on income, the aggregate expenditure function is steeper than when taxes depend on income.

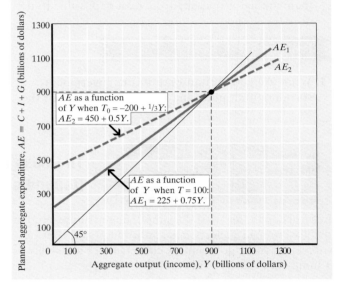

AE as a function of Y when $T_0 = -200 + \frac{1}{3}Y$: $AE_2 = 450 + 0.5Y$.

AE as a function of Y when $T = 100$: $AE_1 = 225 + 0.75Y$.

$$C = a + b (Y - T)$$
$$C = a + b (Y - T_0 - tY)$$
$$C = a + bY - bT_0 - btY$$

We know that $Y = C + I + G + EX - IM$. Through substitution we get:

$$Y = \underbrace{a + bY - bT_0 - btY}_{C} + I + G + EX - IM$$

Solving for Y:

$$Y = \frac{1}{(1 - b + bt)} (a + I + G - bT_0 + EX - IM)$$

This means that a $1 increase in G, I, a or $(EX - IM)$ will increase the equilibrium level of Y by:

$$\frac{1}{1 - b + bt}$$

Thus, if $b = MPC = 0.75$ and $t = 1/3$, as in our example, the spending multiplier is 2.0. (Compare this to 4, which would be the value of the spending multiplier if taxes were a lump sum—that is, if $t = 0$.)

A $1 lump-sum tax cut (a cut in T_0) will increase the equilibrium level of income by:

$$\frac{b}{1 - b + bt}$$

Thus, if $b = MPC = 0.75$ and $t = 1/3$, the tax multiplier is -1.5. (Compare this to -3, which would be the value of the tax multiplier if taxes were a lump sum.)

Summary

1. When taxes depend on income, a $1 increase in income does not increase disposable income by a full dollar, because some of the additional dollar must go to pay extra taxes. This means that if taxes are a function of income, both the government spending and tax multipliers are less than they would be if taxes were a lump-sum amount.

Problem Set

1. You are given the following model for the economy of a country:
   (i) Consumption function: $C = 85 + 0.5Y_d$
   (ii) Investment function: $I = 90$
   (iii) Government spending: $G = 60$
   (iv) Net taxes: $T = -40 + 0.25Y$
   (v) Disposable income: $Y_d \equiv Y - T$
   (vi) Net exports: $EX - IM = -5$
   (vii) Equilibrium: $Y = C + I + G + EX - IM$

   Solve for equilibrium income. How much does the government collect in net taxes when the economy is in equilibrium? What is the government's budget deficit or surplus?

Appendix 10C	The Case in Which Imports (But Not Tax Revenues) Depend on Income

It is logical to make imports depend on disposable income, because many imported goods are part of consumption and consumption depends on disposable income. We continue the numerical example from Chapter 10 but now we set exports to be 325 and imports equal to $25 + 0.25Y_d$. We could continue to have net taxes depend on income as in Appendix 10B, but leaving net taxes as a fixed 100 will avoid undue complication. Setting planned aggregate expenditure AE equal to output, our equilibrium condition is:

$$Y = C + I + G + EX - IM$$

and substituting for C, I, G, EX, and IM:

$$Y = 100 + 0.75Y_d + 100 + 100 + 325 - (25 + 0.25Y_d)$$
$$= 600 + 0.5Y_d$$
$$= 600 + 0.5(Y - T) \text{ (substituting for } Y_d)$$
$$= 600 + 0.5(Y - 100) \text{ (substituting for } T)$$
$$= 550 + 0.5Y$$

This implies $0.5Y = 550$ or $Y = (1/0.5) \times 550 = 1100$.

Note that the government spending multiplier is now $(1/0.5) = 2$, which is less than the multiplier of 4 in the original model. Allowing for imports to depend on income reduces the multiplier in the model because the extra spending from any increase in income will tend to leak to the rest of the world via imports. We can call the 0.25 in front of the Y_d in the import equation the "marginal propensity to import," which is abbreviated as MPM. It is the increase in spending on imports if disposable income increases by $1. We show in Chapter 21 that the government spending multiplier in a model like this is in general $1/(MPS + MPM)$, where the MPS is the marginal propensity to save. We can check that this works here because the $MPS = 1 - MPC = 0.25$ so that $1/(MPS + MPM) = 1/(0.25 + 0.25) = 2$, just as we obtained. You can see that if the MPM is larger, the leakage effect is greater and the multiplier is smaller.

There is one other thing we can check. If $Y = 1100$, then disposable income equals $Y - T = 1100 - 100 = 1000$ and imports equal $25 + 0.25Y_d = 25 + 0.25 \times 1000 = 275$. So the economy has positive net exports (a trade surplus) of $EX - IM = 325 - 275 = 50$. We can also work out that consumption $C = 100 + 0.75Y_d = 100 + 0.75 \times 1000 = 850$ so that saving $S = Y_d - C = 1000 - 850 = 150$ and therefore leakages $S + T + IM = 150 + 100 + 275 = 525$. Injections $I + G + EX = 100 + 100 + 325 = 525$ as well, so we confirm that leakages equal injections.

Summary

1. When imports depend on income, a $1 increase in income leads to an increase in imports as well as an increase in consumption. The increased spending on domestic goods is smaller as some of that spending leaks to the rest of the world. This reduces the multiplier.

1. a. In Appendix 10C we calculated that the multiplier was 2 when imports (but not tax revenue) depend on income, so that an increase in either I, G, or EX of 50 should increase output by 100. Confirm this by plugging in these values, one at a time, and working out the solution.

   b. Continuing with the same initial model, show that we also increase output by 100 if the consumption function $C = 100 + 0.75Y_d$ changes to $C = 150 + 0.75Y_d$. This shifts the whole consumption function up by 50 at every value of disposable income. Changing the constant part of the consumption function is sometimes called changing the level of "autonomous" consumption and you will see that it has the same multiplier effect as changing I, G, or $EX - IM$. You can also check that we would get the same effect by changing imports from $IM = 25 + 0.25Y_d$ to $IM = -25 + 0.25Y_d$, that is, shifting the import function down by 50.

   c. Now try increasing taxes by 50 to 150. You should be able to confirm that output falls by 50.

2. Consider an economy very similar to the one in Appendix 10C:

   Consumption spending: $C = 100 + 0.75Y_d = 100 + 0.75(Y - T)$
   Planned investment spending: $I = 100$
   Government purchases: $G = 100$
   Exports: $EX = 375$
   Imports: $IM = 25 + 0.25Y_d = 25 + 0.25(Y - T)$
   Net taxes: $T = -200 + 0.2Y$

where exports have been increased to 375 and now taxes depend upon income as discussed in Appendix 10B.

   a. Suppose firms produce output of 1000. What will the unplanned change in inventories be? What will investment spending (as distinct from planned investment spending) be?

   b. How much of a dollar of additional output (income) is spent on domestically produced goods and services in this economy?

   c. What will equilibrium output be? What will the unplanned change in inventories at that output be?

   d. Calculate saving, net taxes, and imports at equilibrium output (income). You should find that there is more saving than is necessary for investment spending. What happens to these extra funds?

   e. What is the government spending multiplier in this model? Explain why it is smaller than in the original model.

3. Repeat question 2 with the same consumption function but $I = 170$, $G = 250$, $EX = 30$, net taxes now fixed at $T = 100$, and a new import function $IM = 130 + 0.15Y_d = 130 + 0.15(Y - T)$.

   For part **d** now you should find that there is not enough domestic saving to cover investment spending and the government has a budget deficit, so the question is then where these extra funds come from. For part **e** calculate the tax multiplier and the government spending multiplier.

The Money Supply
and the Bank of Canada

Learning Objectives

1. Distinguish among the medium of exchange, store of value, and unit of account roles of money.
2. Distinguish between *commodity* and *fiat money*.
3. Define the alternative money supply measures M1 and M2.
4. List the four types of firms called the pillars of the Canadian financial system.
5. Define *desired reserve ratio*. Explain how the banking system creates money through deposit creation. Apply the deposit multiplier in numerical problems.
6. List the main functions of the Bank of Canada.
7. Identify the three main tools by which the Bank of Canada controls the money supply and explain how each tool works.
8. *Appendix 11A*: Derive the deposit and money multipliers algebraically.

An Overview of Money
What Is Money?
Commodity and Fiat Monies
Measuring the Supply of Money in Canada
The Canadian Financial System

How Banks Create Money
A Historical Perspective: Goldsmiths
The Modern Banking System

The Bank of Canada
The Bank of Canada's Balance Sheet

How the Bank of Canada Controls the Money Supply
Open Market Operations
Transfers of Government Deposits
The Bank Rate
The Supply Curve for Money

Looking Ahead

Appendix 11A: Deriving the Money Multiplier Algebraically

I n the last two chapters, we explored how consumers, firms, and the government interact in the goods market. We now turn to a discussion of the money market. This chapter and the next show how money markets work in the macroeconomy. We begin with an overview of what money is and the role it plays in the Canadian economy. We then discuss the forces that determine the supply of money and show how banks create money. Finally, we discuss the workings of the nation's central bank, the Bank of Canada, and the tools it has at its disposal to control the money supply.

An Overview of Money

You often hear people say things like "He makes a lot of money" (in other words, "He has a high income") or "She's worth a lot of money" (meaning "She is very wealthy"). It is true that your employer uses money to pay you your income, and your wealth may be accumulated in the form of money. But *money is not income, and money is not wealth*.

To see that money and income are not the same thing, think of a $20 bill. That single bill may pass through a thousand hands in a year, and it may never be used to pay anyone a salary. Suppose, for example, that I get a crisp, new $20 bill from an automatic teller machine, and I spend it on dinner. The restaurant puts that $20 bill in a bank in the next day's deposit. The bank gives it to a woman cashing a cheque the following day; she spends it at a movie that night. The bill has been through many hands but not as part of anyone's income.

WHAT IS MONEY?

We will soon get to a formal definition of money, but it is important that you start out with the right basic idea:

> Money is anything that is generally accepted as a medium of exchange.

Most people take the ability to obtain and use money for granted. When the whole monetary system works well, as it generally does in Canada, the basic mechanics of the system are virtually invisible. People simply take it for granted that they can walk into any store, restaurant, boutique, or gas station and buy whatever they want, as long as they have enough coloured pieces of paper.

The idea that you can buy things with money is so natural and obvious that it seems almost absurd to mention it. But stop and ask yourself the following questions: "How is it that a shop owner is willing to part with a steak and a loaf of bread that I can eat in exchange for some pieces of paper that are intrinsically worthless?" And why, on the other hand, are there times and places where it takes a shopping cart full of money to purchase a dozen eggs? The answers to these questions lie in what money is: a means of payment, a store of value, and a unit of account.

barter *The direct exchange of goods and services for other goods and services.*

■ **A Means of Payment, or Medium of Exchange** Money is vital to the working of a market economy. You can see why if you imagine what life would be like without it. The alternative to a monetary economy is **barter**, a process by which people exchange goods and services for other goods and services directly instead of exchanging via the medium of money.

How does a barter system work? Suppose you wake up in the morning and decide you want bacon, eggs, and orange juice for breakfast. Instead of going to the store and buying these things with money, you would have to find someone who has these items and is willing to trade them. You would also have to have something the bacon seller, the orange juice purveyor, and the egg vendor want. Having lots of pencils to trade will do you no good if the bacon, orange juice, and egg sellers do not want pencils.

A barter system requires a *double coincidence of wants* for trade to take place. That is, to effect a trade, I not only have to find someone who has what I want, but that person must also want what I have. Where the range of goods traded is small, as it is in relatively unsophisticated economies, it is not difficult to find someone to trade with, and barter is often used. In a complex society with many goods, however, barter exchanges involve an intolerable amount of effort. Imagine trying to find people who offer for sale all the things you buy in a typical trip to the grocery store, and who are willing to accept goods that you have to offer in exchange for their goods.

medium of exchange, or means of payment *What sellers generally accept and buyers generally use to pay for goods and services.*

Some agreed-upon **medium of exchange** (or, as it is sometimes called, **means of payment**) neatly eliminates the double-coincidence-of-wants problem. Under a monetary system, money is exchanged for goods or services when people buy things; goods or services are exchanged for money when people sell things. No one ever has to trade goods for other goods directly. Money is a lubricant in the functioning of a market economy.

store of value *An asset that can be used to transport purchasing power from one time period to another.*

■ **A Store of Value** Economists have identified other roles for money aside from its primary function as a medium of exchange. Money also serves as a **store of value**—that is, as an asset that can be used to transport purchasing power from one time period to another. If you raise chickens and at the end of the month sell them for more than the amount you want to consume immediately, you may decide to keep some of your earnings in the form of money that you will hold until the time you want to spend it.

There are many other stores of value besides money. You could have decided to hold your "surplus" earnings by buying such things as antique paintings, baseball cards, or diamonds, which you could sell later when you want to spend your earnings. Money has several important advantages over these other stores of value, however. First, it comes in convenient denominations and is easily portable. You don't have to worry about making change for a Renoir to buy a litre of gasoline. Second, because money is also a means of payment, it is easily exchanged for goods at all times. (A Renoir, of course, is not easily exchanged for other goods.) These two factors make up the **liquidity property of money.** Money is easily spent, flowing out of your hands like liquid. Renoirs and ancient Aztec statues are neither convenient nor portable and are not readily accepted as a means of payment.

The main disadvantage of using money as a store of value is that the value of money actually falls when the prices of goods and services rise. If, for example, the price of potato chips rises from $1 per bag to $2 per bag, the value of a dollar, in terms of potato chips, falls from one bag to half a bag. When this happens, it may be better to use potato chips (or perhaps antiques or real estate) as a store of value.

■ **A Unit of Account**   Finally, money also serves as a **unit of account**—that is, as a consistent way of quoting prices. All prices are quoted in monetary units. A textbook is quoted as costing $45, not 140 bananas or 4 videotapes, and a banana is quoted as costing 25¢, not 1.4 apples or 16 pages of a textbook.

Obviously, a standard unit of account is extremely useful when quoting prices for current or future payments. This function of money may have escaped your notice—after all, what else would people quote prices in except money?

COMMODITY AND FIAT MONIES

Introductory economics textbooks are full of stories about the various items that have been used as money by various cultures—candy bars, cigarettes (in World War II prisoner-of-war camps), huge wheels of carved stone (on the island of Yap in the South Pacific), cowrie shells (in West Africa), beads (among North American Native peoples), cattle (in southern Africa), small scraps of paper (in contemporary Canada). The list goes on and on. These various kinds of money are generally divided into two groups, commodity monies and fiat money.

Commodity monies are those items used as money that also have an intrinsic value in some other use. For example, prisoners of war made purchases with cigarettes, quoted prices in terms of cigarettes, and held their wealth in the form of accumulated cigarettes. Of course, cigarettes could also be smoked—they had an alternative use apart from serving as money. Gold represents another form of commodity money. For hundreds of years gold could be used directly to buy things, but it also had other uses, ranging from jewellery to dental fillings.

In Canada, commodity money has largely been replaced by fiat money. **Fiat money,** sometimes called **token money,** is money that is intrinsically worthless. The actual value of a five-, ten-, or fifty-dollar bill is basically zero; what other uses are there for a small piece of paper with some coloured ink on it?

Why would anyone agree to use worthless scraps of paper as money instead of something that has at least some value, such as gold, cigarettes, or cattle? If you think the answer is "Because the paper money is backed by gold or silver," you are wrong. True, there was a time when notes were convertible directly into gold. The government backed its notes in circulation by holding a certain amount of gold in its vaults. If the price of gold were $35 per ounce, for example, the government agreed to sell one ounce of gold for $35 worth of notes. But notes are no longer backed by any commodity—gold, silver, or anything else. They are exchangeable only for dimes, nickels, pennies, other notes, and so on.

The public accepts paper money as a means of payment and a store of value simply because the government has taken steps to ensure that its money is accepted. The government declares its paper money to be **legal tender.** That is, the government declares that its money can be used

Some of Yap's stone money wheels are so large that they are never moved.

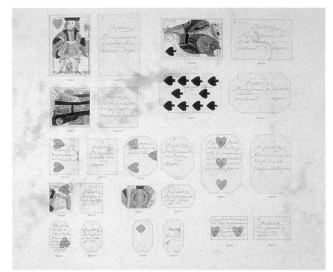

Upper: The first paper money in Canada was issued in Quebec (then New France) beginning in 1685. The representative of the King of France made it by signing playing cards, which sometimes had their corners cut off to indicate lower denominations. **Lower:** The modern Canadian currency bears the inscription "This note is legal tender," meaning that it can be used in settlement of debts. Previously the inscription was "will pay to bearer on demand," a carryover from the days when a bill could be exchanged for gold.

---

legal tender *Money that a government has required to be accepted in settlement of debts.*

currency debasement *The decrease in the value of money that occurs when its supply is increased rapidly.*

M1, or **narrow money** *Money that can be directly used for transactions. M1 equals currency held outside banks plus demand deposits.*

in settlement of debts. It does this by fiat (hence the term fiat money). It passes laws defining certain pieces of paper printed in certain inks on certain plates to be legal tender, and that is that. Printed on every Bank of Canada note in Canada is the phrase "This note is legal tender." Often, the government can get a start on gaining acceptance for its paper money by requiring that it be used to pay taxes. (Note that you cannot use chickens, baseball cards, or Renoir paintings to pay your taxes, only cheques or currency.)

Aside from declaring its currency legal tender, the government usually does one other thing to ensure that paper money will be accepted: it promises the public that it will not print paper money so fast that it loses its value. The practice of expanding the supply of currency so rapidly that it loses much of its value has been a problem throughout history and is known as **currency debasement.** (See the Application box titled "Debasement, Clipped Coins, and Counterfeiting" for a discussion of debasement before the era of paper currency.) Debasement of the currency has been a special problem of governments that lack the strength to take the politically unpopular step of raising taxes. Printing money to be used for government expenditures on goods and services can serve as a substitute for tax increases, and weak governments have often relied on the printing press to finance their expenditures. An example of this is Bulgaria, where the inflation rate hit a record of 1268% in 1997. We will discuss the links between money and inflation at great length in later chapters.

MEASURING THE SUPPLY OF MONEY IN CANADA

We now turn to a more detailed look at the various kinds of money in Canada. Recall that money possesses the following properties: it is used to buy things (a means of payment); it is used as a means of holding wealth (a store of value); and it is used to quote prices (a unit of account). Unfortunately, these characteristics apply to a broad range of assets in the Canadian economy. As we will see, it is not at all clear where we should draw the line and say, "Up to this is money, beyond this is something else."

To solve the problem of multiple monies, economists have given different names to different measures of money. The two most common measures of money are narrow money, called *M*1, and broad money, called *M*2.

■ **M1: Narrow Money** What should be counted as money? Clearly, coins and bills must be counted as money—they fit all the requirements. But what about chequing accounts? Cheques too can be used to buy things. Thus, your chequing account balance is virtually equivalent to bills in your wallet, and it should be included as part of the amount of money you hold. Chequing account deposits and other deposits that can be used directly for transactions are called *demand deposits* if depositors of such accounts have the right to cash in (demand) their entire balance at any time.

If we take the value of all currency (including coins) held outside of bank vaults and add to it the value of all demand deposits in chartered banks, we have defined **M1, or narrow money.** This is money that can be directly used for transactions—to buy things:

$$M1 \equiv \text{Currency held outside banks} + \text{Demand deposits}$$

APPLICATION

Debasement, Clipped Coins, and Counterfeiting

While it is unlikely to be sound monetary policy, a nation's government can always print more money if it needs it to pay its bills. Before the days of paper money, it was not quite so easy, but governments nonetheless used their ability to issue money as a means of finance.

From medieval to early modern times, silver was the monetary standard. (Hence the British "pound sterling" originally corresponded to a pound of silver.) Coins were supposed to contain sufficient metal to approximate their face value. But governments in financial difficulties still paid their bills by "debasement," that is, mixing in a cheaper metal such as copper with the silver so that more coins could be issued.

The public also played a part in reducing the value of money by "clipping" coins, shaving off small bits (to be remelted for bullion) before passing them off at face value. To discourage this practice, coins began to be marked or milled along the edges so it would be apparent if they had been altered. One of the chief duties of Sir Isaac Newton, Warden and later Master of the Mint in England in the late 1600s, was to prosecute clippers and counterfeiters on the state's behalf. These crimes were punishable by death.

In a world where some coins are obviously clipped or debased, there is a tendency for everyone to try to pay with devalued coins and to hoard any good coins that come along. This tendency "for bad money to drive out good" was described by Sir Thomas Gresham in the sixteenth century and is called *Gresham's Law*. As an example, in the late 1960s when the Canadian dollar was temporarily worth more than the U.S. dollar, more American coins began to circulate in

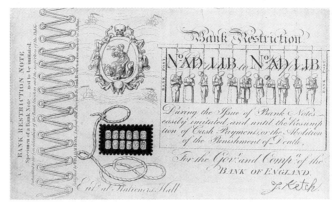

Designed to protest the number of forgery-related hangings in nineteenth-century England, this banknote depicts eleven corpses suspended from a scaffold.

Canada. Nowadays with the American dollar more valuable than the Canadian dollar, few American coins circulate in Canada because they are more valuable than Canadian coins and some individuals pick them out and save them.

The move to fiat money, where paper is substituted for metal, generates large savings in resources that would otherwise be expended for mining and melting metal. The Swedish Riksbank, the first central bank in the world, was the first to substitute bank notes for coin in 1668, largely because Sweden was using copper rather than silver coins, and (just like today), copper coins of any significant value were too bulky for convenience.

But paper money was tempting to counterfeit. During the Napoleonic Wars, Britain hanged nearly 400 men and women for passing forged notes. The Bank of England had a contest for "men of science and eminent artists" to design a note that could not be imitated. One entry was submitted to protest the hangings and de-

picted eleven corpses suspended from a scaffold (see photo).

Counterfeiting remains a problem today. In 1998 over $5 million worth of counterfeit Canadian notes were found in circulation. It is interesting that in most years, more U.S. than Canadian counterfeit money is seized in Canada. The most visible anticounterfeiting measure on Canadian currency is the Optical Security Device, a reflective rectangle in the upper left-hand corner of the $20, $50, and $100 notes. This changes colour from gold to green when tilted against the light. Further ways to discern genuine Canadian banknotes as well as statistics on counterfeiting in Canada are available from the RCMP Web site (**www.rcmp.ca**).

Sources: Bank of Canada Banking and Financial Statistics, February 2000; "British Illustrator Parodies Hangings," *Coin World*, August 13, 1996; Charles P. Kindleberger, *A Financial History of Western Europe* (London: George Allen & Unwin, 1985).

M1 in March 2000 was $98.9 billion, of which about 33% was currency. Notice that M1 is a stock measure. That is, it is measured at a point in time. Until now, we have considered supply as a flow—a variable with a time dimension: the quantity of wheat supplied *per year,* the quantity of automobiles supplied to the market *per year,* and so forth. M1 is a stock variable.

■ *M2: Broad Money* There are other measures of the money supply with which you should be familiar. Should savings accounts be considered money, for example? Personal savings deposits are a type of *notice deposit* because you may be required to give notice of a withdrawal. Many of these accounts cannot be used for transactions directly, but it is easy to convert them into cash or to transfer funds from a savings account into a chequing account. M1 plus notice deposits (the sum of personal savings deposits and nonpersonal notice deposits) in chartered banks yields **M2,** or **broad money.**

$$M2 \equiv M1 + \text{Notice deposits}$$

In March 2000, M2 was $476.4 billion, considerably larger than the total M1 of $98.9 billion.

■ Beyond *M*1 and *M*2   There are many alternative measures of the money supply. The Bank of Canada has recently featured three in its analysis, *Gross M*1, *M*1++, and *M*2++. While we didn't mention this detail in our initial definition, *M*1 excludes the private sector float of cheques and electronic orders in transit. *Gross M*1 is *M*1 plus the private sector float. *M*1++ is *Gross M*1 plus chequable deposits held at some "near banks" (trust companies, credit unions, caisses populaires, and mortgage loan companies) plus all nonchequable notice deposits at chartered banks and near banks. *M*2+ is *M*2 plus all deposits at near banks, and also includes life insurance company individual annuities, holdings of dollar money market mutual funds, and personal deposits at government-owned savings institutions. *M*2++ is *M*2+ plus Canada Savings Bonds and non-money-market mutual funds.

There are many technical details to calculating all these measures. However, the main point is that the narrower measures try to define a set of assets that can be used directly for transactions while the broader measures include more assets in the financial system that can be easily converted into a medium of exchange.

Chequing account balances are money, but not the cheques, credit cards, or debit cards that are used to transfer chequing account balances from payer to receiver. "Smart cards" with computer chips that are used to make small purchases are money ("digital money") because the balance is stored directly in the card.

Sometimes close substitutes for cash and chequing deposits such as term deposits are called **near monies** and, as noted, some of these are included in different definitions of the money supply. In our discussions of the money supply that follow, we will not assume any particular definition, but simply think of the money supply as the value of currency outside of banks plus deposits.

THE CANADIAN FINANCIAL SYSTEM

The Canadian financial system is often described as having four pillars: chartered banks, trust and mortgage loan companies, insurance companies, and securities firms. Originally, each type of institution had its own specific obligations and privileges in the Canadian financial system, enforced by federal government legislation that, for example, kept the banks out of other financial areas. These distinctions are now blurring as the regulatory legislation changes. Since 1987, chartered banks have been allowed to buy securities firms and these bank-affiliated firms now dominate the field: for example, the stock brokerage firm formerly known as McLeod Young Weir is now controlled by the Bank of Nova Scotia and is called ScotiaMcLeod. By a series of legislative changes in 1992 chartered banks can, through subsidiaries, enter the trust and insurance fields, so that, for example, since 2000, the Toronto-Dominion Bank has owned Canada Trust.

Presumably the goal of the restrictions is to try to reduce the dominance of the chartered banks within the financial system. Banks in Canada tend to be relatively large because Canada has what is known as a *branch* banking system. This means there are a relatively small number of institutions. (The largest six, in rough order from largest to smallest, are the Royal Bank, the Toronto-Dominion Bank, the Canadian Imperial Bank of Commerce, the Bank of Nova Scotia, the Bank of Montreal, and the National Bank of Canada, which among them have roughly 90% of the assets and the offices in the chartered banking system.) This type of system is in contrast to a *unit* banking system, such as existed for most of the twen-

near monies *Close substitutes for cash and chequing deposits.*

When Canadians talk of the "cash-less" society, they mean the growing use of cheques, credit cards, debit cards, and electronic bill-paying. Most people have access to cash; they just choose other forms of money for many transactions.

But when a society tries to get by without any form of money, not even cash, it reminds us what a valuable social invention money is. An example is the Russian economic crisis of the 1990s. Many firms were owned by the government and had no way to sell much of their output directly for money. The government itself was broke and provided no payment. Hence millions of workers of these firms were not paid money wages. How did they survive? The firms paid wages in kind, and work-ers had to devote much of their ef-fort to bartering these goods for what they needed.

The Russian-European Center for Economic Policy, a monitoring organization sponsored by the European Union, estimated that the proportion of industrial sales in Russia settled with barter rose from

In some parts of Russia, "cashless society" is literally what it says—no money. Without currency, workers might be paid in what they produce, such as the coffins "paid" to workers in Siberia in 1997.

about 10 percent in 1993 to 40 per-cent in 1996. One car company is said to have paid nine-tenths of its bills with finished automobiles.

Stories about individual house-hold transactions abound. Siberian workers in 1997 were paid in coffins; workers at a factory in Volgograd were paid in bras. In

Altai, Siberia, a local theatre charged two eggs for admission, and when eggs ran out, tickets became denominated in empty bottles.

Source: "The Cashless Society," *The Economist*, March 15, 1997.

---

tieth century in the United States, in which there are a relatively large number of independent institutions. The branch system, with its fewer, larger banks, is gener-ally regarded as a more stable arrangement. This was perhaps most evident during the Great Depression, when not a single bank in Canada failed but thousands in the United States did. In any case, as a result of legislative changes, branch bank-ing has grown over time in the United States, with most of the remaining restric-tions on nationwide banking lifted in 1997. It has been argued that gradually the U.S. system is becoming something more like the Canadian system.

In terms of deposit-taking institutions, the chartered banks in Canada have more than two-thirds of the assets. Other deposit-taking institutions include trust companies, credit unions, and caisses populaires. All these entities are called **financial intermediaries** because they "mediate," or act as a link, between people who have funds to lend and those who need to borrow. Financial intermediaries that do not take deposits include sales finance companies and life insurance com-panies. In the discussions that follow, when we refer to "banks" we mean "char-tered banks," but much of the same analysis will apply to other deposit-taking in-stitutions. Note, however, when we refer to "the Bank," with an uppercase B, we are referring to the Bank of Canada.

financial intermediaries *Banks and other institutions that act as a link between those who have money to lend and those who want to borrow money.*

How Banks Create Money

So far we have described the general way that money works and the way the supply of money may be measured in Canada. But how much money is there available at a given time? Who supplies it, and how does it get supplied? The time has now come to analyze these questions in detail. In particular, we want to explore a process that many find mysterious: the way that banks *create money*.

A HISTORICAL PERSPECTIVE: GOLDSMITHS

To begin to see how banks create money, consider the origins of the modern banking system. In the fifteenth and sixteenth centuries, citizens of many lands used gold as money, particularly for large transactions. Because gold is both inconvenient to carry around and susceptible to theft, people began to place their gold with goldsmiths for safekeeping. Upon receiving the gold, a goldsmith would issue a receipt to the depositor, charging a small fee for looking after the gold. After a time, these receipts themselves, rather than the gold that they represented, began to be traded for goods. The receipts thus became a form of paper money, making it unnecessary to go to the goldsmith to withdraw gold for a transaction.

At this point, all the receipts issued by goldsmiths were backed 100% by gold. If a goldsmith had 100 ounces of gold in his safe, he would issue receipts for only 100 ounces of gold, and no more. Goldsmiths thus functioned as mere warehouses where people stored gold for safekeeping. The goldsmiths found, however, that people did not come often to withdraw gold. Why should they, when paper receipts that could easily be converted to gold were "as good as gold"? (In fact, receipts were better than gold—more portable, safer from theft, and so on.) As a result, goldsmiths had a large stock of gold continuously on hand.

Since they had what amounted to "extra" gold sitting around, goldsmiths gradually realized that they could lend out some of this gold to would-be borrowers without any fear of running out of gold. Why would they do this? Quite simply, because it was to their advantage to do so—instead of just keeping their gold idly in their vaults, they earned interest on the loans they made. Something subtle, but dramatic, happened at this point. The goldsmiths changed from mere depositories for gold into banklike institutions that had the power to create money. This transformation occurred as soon as goldsmiths began making loans. Without adding any more real gold to the system, the goldsmiths increased the amount of money in circulation by creating additional claims to gold (i.e., receipts, which entitled the bearer to receive a certain number of ounces of gold on demand). There were thus more claims than there were ounces of gold.

A more detailed example may help to clarify this point. Suppose you go to a goldsmith who is functioning only as a depository, or warehouse, and ask for a loan to buy a plot of land that costs 20 ounces of gold. Also suppose that the goldsmith has 100 ounces of gold on deposit in his safe and receipts for exactly 100 ounces of gold out to the various people who deposited the gold. If the goldsmith decides he is tired of being a mere goldsmith and wants to become a real bank, he will lend you some gold. You don't want the gold itself, of course; rather, you want a slip of paper that represents 20 ounces of gold. The goldsmith in essence "creates" money for you by simply giving you a receipt for 20 ounces of gold (even though his entire supply of gold already belongs to various other people). When he does so, there will be receipts for 120 ounces of gold in circulation instead of the 100 ounces' worth of receipts before your loan, and the supply of money will have increased.

People think that the creation of money is mysterious. Far from it! The creation of money is simply an accounting procedure, among the most mundane of human endeavors. You may also suspect that the whole process is fundamentally unsound, or somehow dubious. After all, the banking system began when someone issued claims for gold that already belonged to someone else. Here you may be on slightly firmer ground.

Goldsmiths-turned-bankers did face certain problems. Once they started making loans, their receipts outstanding (claims on gold) were greater than the amount of gold they had in their vaults at any given moment. If the owners of the 120 ounces' worth of gold receipts all presented their receipts and demanded their gold at the same time, the goldsmith would find himself in trouble. With only 100 ounces of gold on hand, everyone could not get his or her gold at once.

In normal times, people would be quite happy to hold receipts instead of real gold, and this problem would never arise. If, however, people began to worry about the goldsmith's financial safety, they might begin to have doubts about whether their receipts really were as good as gold. Knowing that there were more receipts outstanding than there were ounces of gold in the goldsmith's vault, people might start to demand gold for receipts.

This situation leads to a paradox. It makes perfect sense to hold paper receipts (instead of gold) if you know you can always get gold for your paper. In normal times, goldsmiths could feel perfectly safe in lending out more gold than they actually had in their possession. But once you (and everyone else) start to doubt the safety of the goldsmith, then you (and everyone else) would be foolish not to demand your gold back from the vault.

A **run** on a goldsmith (or in our day, a **run on a bank**) occurs when many people present their claims at the same time. These runs tend to feed on themselves. If I see you going to the goldsmith to withdraw your gold, I may become nervous and decide to withdraw my gold as well. In fact, it is the *fear* of a run that usually causes the run to take place. Runs on a bank can be triggered by a variety of causes: rumours that an institution may have made loans to dubious borrowers who cannot repay them, wars, failures of other institutions that have borrowed money from the bank, and so on. Today's bankers differ from goldsmiths, in that today's banks and other deposit-taking institutions are highly regulated in Canada and most deposits are insured by the federally administered Canada Deposit Insurance Corporation.[1]

run on a bank *Occurs when many of those who have claims on a bank (deposits) present them at the same time.*

THE MODERN BANKING SYSTEM

To understand how the modern banking system works, you need to have a passing familiarity with some basic principles of accounting. Once you are comfortable with the way banks keep their books, the whole process of money creation will seem quite logical.

■ **A Brief Review of Accounting**   Central to accounting practices is the statement that "the books always balance." In practice, this means that if we take a snapshot of a firm—any firm, including a bank—at a particular moment in time, then by definition:

$$\text{Assets} - \text{Liabilities} \equiv \text{Capital (or Net worth), or}$$
$$\text{Assets} \equiv \text{Liabilities} + \text{Net worth}$$

Assets are things a firm owns that are worth something. For a bank, these assets include the bank building, its furniture, its holdings of government securities, cash in its vaults, bonds, stocks, and so forth. Most important among a bank's assets, for our purposes at least, are its *loans*. When a bank makes a loan, the borrower gives the bank an *IOU*, a promise to repay a certain sum of money on or by a certain date. This promise is an asset of the bank because it is worth something. The bank could (and sometimes does) sell the IOU to another bank for cash. Other bank assets include cash on hand (sometimes called *vault cash*) and deposits with the central bank—the **Bank of Canada**.

Bank of Canada *The central bank of Canada.*

---

[1]*The Canada Deposit Insurance Corporation (CDIC) insures deposits of up to $60 000 per depositor per member institution. Insurable deposits include savings and chequing accounts and term deposits of up to five years. If two depositors each have individual accounts as well as a joint account with each other, all three accounts are allowed $60 000 of coverage. Depositors are also allowed an additional $60 000 of coverage for registered retirement savings plan (RRSP) funds invested with member institutions in savings accounts or in term deposits of up to five years. The Quebec Deposit Insurance Board provides coverage to institutions incorporated in Quebec.*

FIGURE 11.1

Balance Sheet for a Hypothetical Bank (Billions of Dollars)

The balance sheet of a bank must always balance, so that the sum of assets (reserves and loans) equals the sum of liabilities (deposits and net worth).

	Assets		Liabilities	
Reserves	20	100	Deposits
Loans	90	10	Net worth
Total	110	110	Total

A firm's *liabilities* are simply its debts—what it owes. Stated another way, a bank's liabilities are the promises to pay, or IOUs, that it has issued. A bank's most important liabilities are its deposits. *Deposits* are debts owed to the depositors, because when you deposit money in your account, you are in essence making a loan to the bank.

The basic rule of accounting says that if we add up a firm's assets and then subtract the total amount it owes to all those who have lent it funds, the difference is the firm's net worth. *Net worth* represents the value of the firm to its stockholders or owners. How much would you pay for a firm that owns $200 000 of diamonds and had borrowed $150 000 from a bank to pay for them? Clearly, the firm is worth $50 000—the difference between what it owns and what it owes. If the price of diamonds were to fall, bringing their value down to only $150 000, the firm would be worth nothing.

We can keep track of a bank's financial position using a simplified balance sheet. The bank's assets are listed on the left-hand side, its liabilities and net worth on the right-hand side. By definition, the balance sheet always balances, so that the sum of the item(s) on the left side is exactly equal to the sum of the item(s) on the right side.

The balance sheet of a hypothetical bank is shown in Figure 11.1. The bank has $110 billion in *assets*, of which $20 billion are **reserves,** the deposits that the bank has made at the Bank of Canada and its cash on hand (coins and currency). Reserves are an asset to the bank because the bank can go to the Bank of Canada and get cash for them, just the way you can go to the bank and get cash for the amount in your savings account. Our bank's other asset is its loans, worth $90 billion.

Why do banks hold deposits with the Bank of Canada? It is because the Bank of Canada acts as a clearinghouse for all the transactions among the banks each day. For example, if you write a cheque to me on your account at the Bank of Nova Scotia and I deposit it in my account at the Bank of Montreal, the Bank of Montreal is owed $100 by the Bank of Nova Scotia. If I then write a cheque to my dentist for $50 and she deposits it in her account at the Royal Bank, the Bank of Montreal owes the Royal Bank $50. Such interinstitutional transactions are tallied and the banks are told what each owes or is owed each day. The deposits that each private bank holds with the Bank of Canada are used to pay what it owes the other private banks. Such deposits are known as settlement balances, because they are used to settle transactions between banks.

Until 1992, banks were required to set aside a prescribed fraction of their deposits in reserve, either as vault cash or as deposits with the Bank of Canada. Between 1992 and 1994, these *required* reserves were gradually eliminated.[2] Banks still set aside reserves, either as cash on hand or as settlement balances to clear their accounts with the Bank of Canada, but how much the banks set aside is decided by each bank rather than regulated by law. To simplify matters in the discussion that

reserves *The deposits that a bank has at the Bank of Canada plus its cash on hand.*

---

[2]*Because these required reserves did not earn interest, the elimination of the reserve requirement was to the banks' considerable financial advantage. (Trust companies, credit unions, etc., did not have to hold reserves.) Canada, Australia, and the United Kingdom are among the countries whose central banks do not impose required reserves. The Federal Reserve System (the "Fed") in the United States, however, still imposes required reserves on its banks.*

follows, we will assume that a bank will decide to keep a constant ratio of its deposits as reserves and that this desired **reserve ratio** is the same for all banks.

On the liabilities side of the balance sheet in Figure 11.1, the bank has taken deposits of $100 billion, so it owes this amount to its depositors. This means that the bank has a net worth of $10 billion to its owners ($110 billion in assets – $100 billion in liabilities = $10 billion net worth). The net worth of the bank is what "balances" the balance sheet. Remember:

> When some item on a bank's balance sheet changes, there must be at least one other change somewhere else to maintain balance.

For example, if a bank's reserves increase by $1, then one of the following must also be true: (1) its other assets (say, loans) decrease by $1; (2) its liabilities (deposits) increase by $1; or (3) its net worth increases by $1. Various fractional combinations of these are also possible.

■ **The Creation of Money**   Like the goldsmiths, today's bankers seek to earn income by lending money out at a higher interest rate than they pay depositors for use of their money.

Banks obviously prefer to make loans to customers rather than holding funds in their own vaults or at the central bank because they earn more income that way. Any funds a bank holds in its own vaults will pay no return and deposits at the central bank pay lower returns than would be obtainable elsewhere. Therefore:

> Banks usually make loans up to the point where they can just maintain their reserves to meet day-to-day needs.

A bank's desired amount of reserves is equal to its chosen reserve ratio times the total deposits in the bank. If, for example, a bank has deposits of $100 and its reserve ratio is 20%, the desired amount of reserves is $20. The difference between a bank's actual reserves and its desired reserves is its **excess reserves**:

> Excess reserves = Actual reserves – Desired reserves

We assume banks make loans up to the point where their excess reserves are zero.

Assume that there is only one private bank in the country, that the bank sets its desired reserve holdings as 20% of deposits, and that the bank starts off with nothing, as shown in panel 1 of Figure 11.2. Now suppose that currency is in circulation and that someone deposits $100 worth in the bank. The bank deposits the $100 with the central bank, so it now has $100 in reserves, as shown in panel 2. The bank now has assets (reserves) of $100 and liabilities (deposits) of $100. If the bank's reserve ratio is 20%, the bank has excess reserves of $80.

How much can the bank lend and still maintain its desired level of reserves? For the moment, let's suppose that anyone who gets a loan keeps the entire proceeds in the bank or pays them to someone else who does. Nothing is withdrawn as cash. In this case, the bank can lend $400 and still maintain its reserves, as you can see in panel 3 of Figure 11.2. With $80 of excess reserves, the bank can have up to $400 of additional deposits. The $100 in reserves plus $400 in loans (which are made as deposits) equal $500 in deposits. With $500 in deposits and a reserve ratio of 20%, the bank must have reserves of $100 (20% of $500)—and it does. The bank can lend no more than $400 because if it were to do so, it would require more than $100 in reserves in view of the higher deposits that would result, and it does not have more than $100 in reserves.

Remember, the money supply equals cash in circulation plus deposits. Before the initial deposit, the money supply was $100 ($100 cash and no deposits). After the deposit and the loans, the money supply is $500 (no cash outside of bank vaults and $500 in deposits).[3] It is clear, then, that when cash is converted into deposits, the supply of money can change.

---

[3]If banks create money when they make loans, does repaying a loan "destroy" money? The answer is yes.

reserve ratio *The percentage of its total deposits that a bank chooses to set aside as reserves.*

FIGURE 11.2

Balance Sheets of a Bank in a Single-Bank Economy

Panel 1

Assets	Liabilities
Reserves 0	0 Deposits

Panel 2

Assets	Liabilities
Reserves 100	100 Deposits

Panel 3

Assets	Liabilities
Reserves 100 Loans 400	500 Deposits

excess reserves *The difference between a bank's actual reserves and its desired reserves.*

FIGURE 11.3

The Creation of Money: Balance Sheets of Three Banks

	Panel 1 Eleanor deposits $100 in Bank 1.		**Panel 2** Sam has borrowed $80 from Bank 1 to pay Speedy; Speedy deposits the $80 in Bank 2.		**Panel 3** Wulong has borrowed $64 from Bank 2 to pay the bookstore; bookstore deposits the $64 in Bank 3.	
Bank 1	Reserves 100	100 Deposits	Reserves 20 Loans 80	100 Deposits	Reserves 20 Loans 80	100 Deposits
Bank 2	Reserves 0	0 Deposits	Reserves 80	80 Deposits	Reserves 16 Loans 64	80 Deposits
Bank 3	Reserves 0	0 Deposits	Reserves 0	0 Deposits	Reserves 64	64 Deposits

Bank 3 will lend out $51.20, which will eventually be deposited in a Bank 4, and so on.

Summary:	Deposits
Bank 1	100
Bank 2	80
Bank 3	64
Bank 4	51.20
⋮	⋮
Total	500.00

■ The Deposit Multiplier

In practice, however, there is more than one bank. However, this is not essential to the money creation process—it is still possible for an initial deposit of $100 in currency to result in an expansion of total bank deposits to $500, given all banks set their desired reserve ratios at 20%. For simplicity assume that we have a number of banks, all initially with no reserves, deposits, or net worth, and that Eleanor makes a deposit of $100 cash in Bank 1. (See panel 1 of Figure 11.3.) Bank 1 now has $100 of reserves. Suppose it lends $80 to Sam so that he can buy a new muffler from Speedy Muffler King. After Sam buys the muffler and Speedy has deposited Sam's cheque in Bank 2, the position is as in panel 2. Bank 1 has $20 reserves and its $80 in loans to Sam; its liabilities are Eleanor's $100 deposit. Bank 2 has Speedy's $80 deposit which so far it has kept entirely as reserves.

Suppose now Bank 2 keeps 20% of $80, or $16, as reserves, and lends out the remaining $64 to Wulong, who uses it to buy a new piece of software from his university bookstore. Panel 3 depicts the situation after the bookstore deposits Wulong's cheque in Bank 3. The position of Bank 1 has not changed. The assets of Bank 2 are now its $16 reserves and its $64 loan to Wulong; it still has Speedy's deposit of $80 as a liability. Bank 3 has the bookstore's $64 deposit which in panel 3 is still kept as reserves but its desired reserves are only 20% of that $64, or $12.80. So Bank 3 has excess of reserves of $51.20 which it will lend to someone who will eventually spend it and deposit it in a Bank 4. This process will continue over and over so that the total amount of deposits created will be $500, the sum of the deposits in each of the banks. Because the banking system can be looked at as one big bank, the outcome here for many banks is the same as the outcome in Figure 11.2 for one bank.

Of course, not every bank may have the same reserve ratio. Still the important point is:

deposit multiplier *The multiple by which deposits can increase for every dollar increase in new reserves; equal to 1 divided by the reserve ratio.*

An increase in new bank reserves leads to a greater than one-for-one increase in the money supply. Economists call the relationship between the final change in deposits and the change in reserves that caused this change the **deposit multiplier**. Stated somewhat differently, the deposit multiplier is the multiple by which deposits can increase for every dollar increase in new reserves.

Do not confuse the deposit multiplier with the spending multipliers we discussed in the last two chapters. They are not the same thing. The deposit multiplier describes the lending and re-lending of an addition to bank reserves, where much of the lending may be used to buy existing goods or financial assets. The spending multipliers describe how new income is spent and re-spent on new production throughout the economy.

In the example we just examined, reserves became $100 when the $100 in cash was deposited in a bank, and the amount of deposits increased by $500 ($100 from the initial deposit, $400 from the loans made by the various banks from their excess reserves). The deposit multiplier in this case is thus $500 ÷ $100 = 5, that is, 1 divided by the reserve ratio 0.2 (1 ÷ 0.2 = 5). Mathematically, as the reserve ratio is Reserves ÷ Deposits, and the deposit multiplier is Deposits ÷ Reserves, the deposit multiplier is just the reciprocal of the reserve ratio, or:

$$\text{Deposit multiplier} \equiv \frac{1}{\text{Reserve ratio}}$$

■ **The Money Multiplier**   In the simple example we have just covered, all cash ends up deposited in the banking system so that all money is in the form of bank deposits. Hence if we pretend that the $100 Eleanor initially deposited is newly printed by the Bank of Canada and given to her, the increase in the money supply is the increase in bank deposits of $500. Defining the **money multiplier** to be the increase in the total money supply (currency plus bank deposits) for each dollar of new reserves, the money multiplier in this simple case is exactly the same as the deposit multiplier.

In reality, at each stage of the deposit multiplier process there will be some leakage or "cash drain" as extra cash is taken to be held in wallets, in mattresses, or as deposits in foreign banks. This drain reduces the deposit multiplier because less cash is redeposited in the banking system at each stage of the deposit multiplier process. Also, because not all currency will end up as bank deposits, the increase in the money supply will be greater than the increase in bank deposits. The money multiplier will not be the same as the deposit multiplier, but it will be closely related, as shown algebraically in Appendix 11A to this chapter.

We have now seen how the private banking system creates money by making loans, and hence why in Canada, the amount of currency is only 33% of the money supply as measured by $M1$ and less than 7% of the money supply as measured by $M2$. We have also seen that the money supply depends on the desired reserve ratio, so that, for example, if banks become more cautious and increase their desired reserve ratio, the deposit and money multipliers will fall and the money supply will contract. In the next sections we examine the functions of the Bank of Canada, including its tools to control the money supply.

money multiplier *The multiple by which the total money supply (currency outside banks plus bank deposits) increases for each dollar increase in new reserves; equal to the deposit multiplier in the simple case where all money is held as bank deposits.*

The Bank of Canada

The country's central bank, the Bank of Canada, began operation in Ottawa in March 1935 as a private institution. It was converted to public ownership in 1938. The Bank is directed by a governor, a senior deputy governor, and a 12-member board of directors that meets at least four times per year. In February 2001, David Dodge was appointed governor for a seven-year term.

The Bank has four main functions.

1.   While it does not accept deposits from or make loans to the general public, it is a banker to the banks and other firms in the financial system. As we mentioned earlier, the deposits these institutions hold with the Bank are used in the clearinghouse as a means to settle the cheques their depositors write. In this function it also promotes stability, in particular serving as a lender of last resort so that fundamentally sound financial institutions do not collapse due to temporary difficulties.

The Bank of Canada in Ottawa.

2. It issues currency.

3. It is a banker to the federal government. The federal government has an account with the Bank of Canada and also collects any profits the Bank earns. The Bank will not simply print money to give to the government, but from time to time it may lend to the government by buying some portion of a new government bond issue, paying either by issuing currency or by crediting the government's account.

4. It tries to control the money supply, in ways that will be described.

The governor of the Bank of Canada is appointed by the federal government. He or she nonetheless has some degree of independence—an issue that has been repeatedly examined, especially during the recession of the 1990s, which was attributed by some to the tight monetary policy of the Bank. In 1961, the governor of the Bank of Canada, James Coyne, wished to pursue a tighter monetary policy than the government and was eventually forced to resign. Legislation in 1967 established a system in which the governor of the Bank (who is advised by a staff of economists and other professionals) continues to have much independence in directing the Bank's day-to-day operations. If a conflict arises between the governor of the Bank and the government of the day as to the conduct of Bank policy, the minister of finance may issue a written directive stating what policies should be enacted. If the governor feels unable to follow such a directive, the governor must resign. No such directive has ever been issued: it is sometimes argued that if the governor were forced to resign in such circumstances by a government anxious to expand the money supply, the result would be a financial crisis as international markets would lose confidence in the Canadian dollar and financial instruments.

THE BANK OF CANADA'S BALANCE SHEET

Although it is a special bank, the Bank of Canada is in some ways very similar to an ordinary private bank. Like an ordinary bank, the Bank of Canada has a balance sheet that records its asset and liability position at any moment in time. A simplified balance sheet for the Bank of Canada is presented in Table 11.1.

The largest of the Bank's assets by far consists of government securities: about $32 billion worth in March 2000. Government securities are obligations of the federal government, such as Treasury bills and government bonds, which the Bank has purchased over the years. The way in which these securities are acquired has important implications for the Bank's control of the money supply. (We return to this topic after our survey of the Bank's balance sheet.)

The bulk of the Bank's liabilities are currency notes. The five-dollar bill you carry in your pocket when you go to the store to buy milk is clearly an asset from your point of view—it is something you own that has value. But since every financial asset is by definition a liability of some other agent in the economy, whose liability is that five-dollar bill? Quite simply, that five-dollar bill, and bills of all other denominations in the economy, are a liability—an IOU—of the Bank of Canada. They are, of course, rather strange IOUs, because all they can be redeemed for are other IOUs of exactly the same type. They are, nonetheless, classified as liabilities of the Bank.[4]

The Bank's balance sheet also shows that, like an ordinary private bank, the Bank has accepted deposits. These deposits are recorded as liabilities. The bulk of the Bank's deposits come from private banks. Remember that private banks keep a certain share of their own deposits as deposits at the Bank of Canada. Since a private bank's deposits at the Bank of Canada are an asset from the private bank's point of view, those same reserves must be a liability from the Bank of Canada's point of view.

Table 11.1 also shows that the Bank of Canada holds deposits from the federal government. These deposits are an important instrument of monetary policy,

[4]*Because the Bank of Canada is not obliged to provide gold for currency, it can never go bankrupt. If depositors wish to withdraw their deposits, all they can get is paper currency.*

Table 11.1

Table 11.1	Assets and Liabilities of the Bank of Canada, March 2000 (Millions of Dollars)	

Assets		Liabilities	
Government of Canada securities	$31 693	Notes in circulation (currency)	$32 273
Other assets	2 713	Deposits:	
		Private banks	1 205
		Government of Canada	137
		Other	264
		Other liabilities (includes net worth)	527
Total	$34 405	Total	$34 405

Source: Bank of Canada Banking and Financial Statistics, May 2000, Table B2. Totals may not add due to rounding.

as you will see in the next section. Deposits that are not from the private banks or from the federal government (as given in the "Other" category of deposits) include deposits from the central banks of other countries.

How the Bank of Canada Controls the Money Supply

The Bank of Canada has at least three policy instruments to control the money supply: open market operations, transfers of government deposits, and the Bank rate.

OPEN MARKET OPERATIONS

We saw in Table 11.1 that the largest share of the Bank of Canada's assets was its holdings of Government of Canada securities. These, which include Treasury bills and government bonds, are the vehicles through which the government borrows money. When the Bank of Canada conducts **open market operations,** it buys or sells government securities in a public (or open) market.

When the Bank buys government securities, it takes its own funds (not part of the money supply) and gives them to whomever is selling the security (a member of the general public, for example) in exchange for the security. The funds are now in the hands of the seller, thus becoming part of the money supply. If the funds are then deposited in a bank, this will further increase the money supply by the money multiplier. (In our example in Figure 11.3, suppose Eleanor obtained her initial $100 to deposit by selling a government security.) The reverse occurs when the Bank sells government securities. This takes money away from the buyers of the securities and gives it to the Bank, decreasing the money supply. The Bank of Canada can thus expand the money supply by buying government securities from people who own them, and can reduce the money supply by selling these securities.

Table 11.2 illustrates as an example the *changes* in assets and liabilities of both the Bank of Canada and the private bank system when the Bank of Canada purchases $5 million of Government of Canada bonds on the open market with cheques drawn on itself. The recipients of the cheques deposit them in their private banks and the private banks in turn deposit these cheques in their accounts with the Bank of Canada. The Bank of Canada now has $5 million more in assets because of the increased holdings of government securities, but it also has $5 million more in liabilities because of the increased deposits it has. The private banks have $5 million more in deposits (held by the recipients of the original cheques) but, importantly, they also have $5 million more in their own deposits with the Bank of Canada, which means the private banks' reserves have increased by $5 million. This allows the private banks to increase their lending and hence the money supply will expand further through the money multiplier process as we have described.

While the term "open market operations" applies to transactions in government securities, with respect to the effect on the money supply, it does not matter what the Bank buys and sells. The Bank of Canada also manages the Department

open market operations *The purchase and sale by the Bank of Canada of government securities in the open market.*

Table 11.2

Balance Sheet *Changes* Caused by an Open Market Purchase by the Bank of Canada (Millions of Dollars)

BANK OF CANADA

Assets		Liabilities	
Government of Canada securities	+5	Deposits held by private banks	+5

PRIVATE BANKS

Assets		Liabilities	
Deposits at Bank of Canada (reserves)	+5	Deposits held by public	+5

Table 11.3

Balance Sheet *Changes* Caused by Transfers of Government Deposits from the Bank of Canada (Millions of Dollars)

BANK OF CANADA

Assets	Liabilities	
No change	Deposits held by private banks	+5
	Deposits held by Government of Canada	−5

PRIVATE BANKS

Assets		Liabilities	
Deposits at Bank of Canada (reserves)	+5	Deposits held by Government of Canada	+5

transfers of government deposits *The movement of government deposits between the Bank of Canada and private banks.*

Bank rate *The interest rate that private banks pay to borrow from the Bank of Canada.*

FAST FACTS

In December 2000, the Bank of Canada followed many other central banks and began a fixed-date policy for Bank rate changes, normally restricting changes to eight preannounced days per year.

of Finance's gold reserves (which are very small and in no sense "back" the currency) and foreign exchange account. The latter contains, for example, U.S. dollars and Japanese yen. If the Bank uses gold or, more commonly, foreign exchange, to buy Canadian dollars, it will decrease the money supply, just as above. Similarly, if the Bank purchases gold or foreign exchange using Canadian dollars, it will increase the money supply.

TRANSFERS OF GOVERNMENT DEPOSITS

The federal government holds deposits in the Bank of Canada and in the private banks. The Bank of Canada may make **transfers of government deposits** to the private banks, which are allocated among the banks according to a prescribed formula. This would give the private banks excess reserves, and the money supply would increase as the banks would be able to make new loans. Similarly, government funds may be transferred from the private banks to the Bank of Canada. This would decrease the money supply as the banks would then make fewer loans. In recent years, this method has been more commonly used than open market operations.

As an example, Table 11.3 illustrates the *changes* in assets and liabilities of both the Bank of Canada and the private bank system when the Bank of Canada transfers $5 million of Government of Canada deposits from itself to the private banks. Cheques written on the Government of Canada account with the Bank of Canada are deposited in the accounts of the private banks who in turn deposit these cheques into their own accounts at the Bank of Canada. As the Bank of Canada reduction in government deposits has been offset by an increase in private bank deposits, neither Bank of Canada assets nor total liabilities change. But the private banks have $5 million in new deposits from the Government of Canada and hence $5 million in new reserves (just as if they had new deposits from any other source). Again this allows the private banks to increase their lending and hence the money supply will expand.

THE BANK RATE

As we have noted, the private banks keep some of their reserves as deposits at the Bank of Canada; but sometimes they overdraw these accounts, so that instead of having deposits with the Bank, they have loans. The **Bank rate** is the interest rate the Bank of Canada *charges* on these loans (*negative reserves*). The Bank of Canada *pays* the Bank rate less 0.5% on deposits by the private banks (*positive reserves*).

Rather than borrowing and lending from the Bank of Canada, the private banks have the option of borrowing from each other at what is called the *overnight rate.*[5] Assume the Bank rate is 5.0%, so that the Bank of Canada is charging 5.0% on loans and paying 4.5% on deposits. You can see that the overnight rate is likely going to be below 5.0% because, if it were higher, a private bank would choose to borrow directly from the Bank of Canada instead of on the overnight market. You can also see that the overnight rate is likely going to be no less than 4.5% because, if it were lower, a private bank would choose to deposit funds in the Bank of Canada rather than lend them on the overnight market. Hence the overnight rate will normally be in what is called the "operating band" between the Bank rate and the Bank rate less 0.5%. As long as it is, the private banks will find it more attractive to borrow and lend from each other, rather than involve the Bank of Canada, and hence reserves with the Bank of Canada will be very close to zero (as there is no longer any legal requirement for them to keep such reserves).

It is normally Bank of Canada policy to keep the overnight rate well inside the operating band. If the overnight rate is at the edges of the band, the Bank of Canada will use its other monetary instruments, open market operations and transfers of government deposits, to move it toward the middle. Hence even though there is very little actual borrowing by the private banks from the Bank of Canada, the real importance of a change in the Bank rate is what it conveys about monetary policy more generally. Suppose the Bank announces an increase in the Bank rate. Private banks know that the overnight rate will increase. This will increase the cost of running short of reserves and being forced to borrow. Hence the private

---

[5]*See Appendix 12A for more detail on the Bank rate and the overnight rate.*

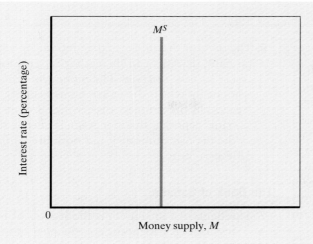

FIGURE 11.4

The Supply of Money

If the Bank of Canada sets the money supply curve at the same level regardless of the interest rate, the money supply curve is a vertical line.

banks will immediately increase their desired reserve ratio, reducing the money and deposit multipliers and tightening the money supply. Similarly a decrease in the Bank rate signifies an expansionary policy.

THE SUPPLY CURVE FOR MONEY

The main point of our discussion so far is that the Bank of Canada can influence the money supply by engaging in open market operations to buy and sell government securities, by effecting transfers of government deposits to and from the private banks, and by setting the Bank rate. In later chapters, we will use what is called a *money supply curve*, which has the money supply on the horizontal axis and the interest rate (the opportunity cost of holding money) on the vertical axis. If we assume that the Bank of Canada can set the money supply independently of interest rates and it chooses to do so, we can draw this money supply curve as a vertical line as in Figure 11.4. We will use the assumption of vertical money supply in most of our analysis in this book. If we make the more realistic assumption that the Bank of Canada has imperfect control over the money supply or that the Bank of Canada may change the money supply depending on the interest rate, the money supply curve would not be vertical, but this complication is not necessary for our understanding of monetary policy.

Looking Ahead

This chapter has discussed only the supply side of the money market. We have seen what money is, how banks create money by making loans, and how the Bank of Canada controls the money supply. In the next chapter we turn to the demand side of the money market. There we examine the demand for money and how the supply of and demand for money determine the equilibrium interest rate.

An Overview of Money

1. Money has three distinguishing characteristics. It is (1) a means of payment, or medium of exchange, (2) a store of value, and (3) a unit of account. The alternative to using money is a *barter* system, in which goods are exchanged directly for other goods. Barter is costly and inefficient in an economy with many different kinds of goods.

2. *Commodity monies* are those items used as money that also have an intrinsic value in some other use (for example, gold and cigarettes). *Fiat monies* are intrinsically worthless apart from their use as money. In order to ensure the acceptance of fiat monies, governments use their power to declare money *legal tender* and promise the public that they will not debase the currency by expanding its supply rapidly.

3. There are various definitions of money. Currency plus demand deposits comprise *M1*, or *narrow money*—money that can be used directly to buy things. The addition of notice deposits to *M1* gives *M2*, or *broad money*.

How Banks Create Money

4. The *reserve ratio* is the percentage of a bank's deposits that is kept as vault cash and as deposits at the nation's central bank, the Bank of Canada. Banks are free to choose their own level of reserves.

5. Banks create money by making loans. When a bank makes a loan to a customer, it simply creates a deposit in that customer's account. This deposit becomes part of the money supply. Banks can create money only when they have *excess reserves*—that is, reserves in excess of their *desired* reserves.

6. The *deposit multiplier* is the amount by which total bank deposits can increase for every dollar increase in new reserves. The *money multiplier* is the amount by which the entire money supply increases. In the simplest case, with all money held as bank deposits, the money multiplier is the same as the deposit multiplier and both are equal to 1/Reserve ratio.

The Bank of Canada

7. The Bank of Canada (1) is the banker of banks, acting as a clearinghouse for cheques and other transactions among private financial institutions and serving as a lender of last resort in emergencies, (2) issues currency, (3) is a banker for the federal government, and (4) controls the nation's money supply.

How the Bank of Canada Controls the Money Supply

8. The Bank of Canada has three tools at its disposal to control the money supply. It can (1) engage in open market operations to buy and sell government securities, (2) effect transfers of government deposits to and from private banks, and (3) set the Bank rate. *Buying* government securities, transferring government deposits *to* private banks, and *lowering* the Bank rate all increase the money supply. *Selling* government securities, transferring government deposits *from* private banks, and *increasing* the Bank rate all tighten the money supply.

9. If the Bank's money supply behaviour is not influenced by the interest rate, the supply curve for money is a vertical line.

Bank of Canada 235

Bank rate 242

barter 228

commodity monies 229

currency debasement 230

deposit multiplier 238

excess reserves 237

fiat, or token, money 229

financial intermediaries 233

legal tender 230

liquidity property of money 229

M1, or narrow money 230

M2, or broad money 232

medium of exchange, or means of payment 228

money multiplier 239

near monies 232

open market operations 241

reserve ratio 237

reserves 236

run on a bank 235

store of value 228

transfers of government deposits 242

unit of account 229

Equations:

1. $M1 \equiv$ Currency held outside banks + Demand deposits

2. $M2 \equiv M1$ + Notice deposits

3. Assets $\equiv$ Liabilities + Capital (or Net worth)

4. Excess reserves $\equiv$ Actual reserves – Desired reserves

5. Deposit multiplier $\equiv \dfrac{1}{\text{Reserve ratio}}$

1. In late 1996, a sluggish economy prompted the Bank of Canada to make several reductions in the Bank rate. Does this mean monetary policy was being tightened or loosened? Why?

2. Suppose there is a shift of funds in Canada away from term deposits and into chequing deposits. All other things being equal, what effect would such a shift have on the supply of broad money (M2)? What effect would it have on the supply of narrow money (M1)?

3. As King of Medivalia, you are constantly strapped for funds to pay your army. Your chief economic wizard suggests the following plan: "When you collect your tax payments from your subjects, insist on being paid in gold coins. Take these gold coins, melt them down, and then remint them with an extra 10% of brass thrown in. You will then have 10% more money than you started with." What do you think of the plan? Will it work?

4. M2 is sometimes thought to be a more stable measure of money than M1. Explain in your own words why this might be true, using the definitions of M1 and M2.

5. Do you agree or disagree with each of the following statements? Explain your answers.
   a. "Given that reserves held with the Bank of Canada did not pay interest, removing the requirement beginning in 1992 to hold a compulsory level of reserves was like removing a tax on banks: the removal was to the financial advantage of the banks and to the financial disadvantage of the government."
   b. "The money multiplier depends on the marginal propensity to save."
   c. "In 1996 the Bank of Canada lowered the Bank rate. This move was designed to expand the supply of money in circulation."

*6. When new money is added to the system through open market operations, some of this new money find its way out of the country into foreign banks or foreign investment funds. In addition, some portion ends up in people's pockets and mattresses rather than in bank deposits. Explain why these "leakages" reduce the deposit multiplier.

7. You are given the following simplified balance sheet for a bank:

ASSETS		LIABILITIES	
Reserves	$500	$3500	Deposits
Loans	3000		

The bank's reserve ratio is 10%.
   a. How much will the bank hold as reserves, given its deposits of $3500?
   b. How much are its excess reserves?
   c. By how much can the bank increase its loans?
   d. Suppose a depositor comes to the bank and withdraws $150 in cash. Show the bank's new balance sheet, assuming that the bank obtains the cash by drawing down its reserves. Does the bank now hold excess reserves?

8. A banking system has deposits of $100 billion. The desired reserve ratio is 25%, there are no excess reserves and there are no cash leakages: all cash is deposited in the banking system.
   a. What is the value of the deposit multiplier?
   b. If the desired reserve ratio is reduced to 20%, how much will deposits increase?
   c. Suppose the central bank wants the money supply to be $75 billion. What desired reserve ratio by the private banks will yield this money supply?

9. Repeat question 8 assuming that the banking system begins with deposits of $200 billion and a desired reserve ratio of 30%.

In the simple example in the chapter, we assumed that all money was held in bank deposits and hence the deposit multiplier was the same as the money multiplier. In this appendix we consider the more complicated case in which a fraction of bank deposits is held as currency. This makes the formula for the deposit multiplier more complex and makes it different from the money multiplier.

The Bank of Canada's liabilities include currency (CU) and private bank reserves (R) that are held as central bank deposits. As these influence the money supply, they are sometimes summed together and called "high-powered" money or monetary base (MB):

$$MB = CU + R$$

If we call the reserve ratio rr and deposits D,

$$R = rr \times D$$

Suppose we change our usual assumption that there are no cash leakages and assume instead that fraction c of deposits is held as currency. This means

$$CU = c \times D$$

so that

$$MB = CU + R$$
$$= c \times D + rr \times D$$
$$= (c + rr)D$$

or

$$D = MB/(c + rr)$$

The deposit multiplier is now defined as the ratio of deposits to the monetary base and is $1/(c + rr)$.

The total money supply (M^S) is the sum of deposits and currency. Hence

$$M^S = D + CU$$
$$= D + c \times D$$
$$= (1 + c)D$$
$$= MB(1 + c)/(c + rr)$$

The money multiplier is now the ratio of the money supply to the monetary base, that is, $(1 + c)/(c + rr)$. Note that if there is no cash drain as we assumed in the chapter, $c = 0$, all money is deposits, the money multiplier is equal to the deposit multiplier, and the formula for both the deposit multiplier and the money multiplier reduces to $1/rr$, the same formula as in the chapter.

Despite this more complex algebra, you should not lose sight of the main point. Bank reserves are part of the monetary base, and if bank reserves increase (due perhaps to open market operations or transfers of government deposits), the money supply will increase. The money supply will also increase if the desired reserve ratio falls, perhaps because the Bank rate decreases. Hence the Bank of Canada has some measure of control over the money supply using its instruments. The additional algebra also points out that the more currency the public wishes to hold (i.e., the higher c is), the smaller the money multiplier and the money supply will be. Changes in currency demand (such as occurred when currency demand increased with the Y2K scare) complicate the control of the money supply but they do not change the fundamental process.

Problem Set

1. What is the deposit multiplier if the reserve ratio is 25% and 15% of deposits are held as currency?

2. **a.** Prove algebraically that the money multiplier with a cash drain is less than the money multiplier without a cash drain.

   b. If the reserve ratio is 25% and 15% of deposits are held as currency, what is the money multiplier?

3. Repeat question 2, part **b** assuming the reserve ratio is 30% and 20% of deposits are held as currency.

Money Demand, Interest Rates, Exchange Rates, and Monetary Policy

Learning Objectives

1 List the determinants of the "demand for money."

2 Explain how the equilibrium interest rate is determined by supply and demand in the money market.

3 Explain how the Bank of Canada can influence the interest rate.

4 Define *fixed exchange rates* and *flexible exchange rates*. Explain how the distinction matters for monetary policy.

5 Contrast "tight" and "expansionary" monetary policies and their implications for the interest rate and the exchange rate.

6 *Appendix 12A:* Distinguish among the different types of interest rates and explain how monetary policy may affect them differently.

The Demand for Money

The Speculation Motive

The Transaction Motive

Transactions Volume, Output, and the Price Level

The Determinants of Money Demand (Review)

The Equilibrium Interest Rate

Supply and Demand in the Money Market

Shifts in the Money Demand Curve

The Bank of Canada: Changing the Money Supply to Affect the Interest Rate

Fixed Exchange Rates

Flexible Exchange Rates

Looking Ahead: Bank of Canada Behaviour and Monetary Policy

Appendix 12A: **The Various Interest Rates in the Canadian Economy**

Having discussed the *supply* of money in the last chapter, we now turn to a discussion of the *demand* for money. One of the main goals of this chapter and the previous chapter is to provide a theory of how the interest rate is determined in the macroeconomy. Once we have seen how the interest rate is determined, we can turn to the question of how the Bank of Canada affects the interest rate through **monetary policy**.

It is important that you understand exactly what the interest rate is. **Interest** is the fee that a borrower pays to a lender for the use of his or her funds. Firms and the government borrow funds by issuing bonds, and they pay interest to the firms and households (the lenders) that purchase those bonds. Households and firms that have borrowed from a bank must pay interest on those loans to the bank.

The **interest rate** is the annual interest payment on a loan expressed as a percentage of the loan. For example, a $1000 bond (representing a $1000 loan from a household to a firm) that pays $100 in interest per year has an interest rate of 10%. Note that the interest rate is expressed as an *annual* rate. It is the amount of interest received *per year* divided by the amount of the loan.

The interest rate for a short-term loan or bond, say for one year or less, may be much different from the interest rate on a long-term loan or bond, which perhaps will not be entirely repaid for five, ten, or even thirty years. To simplify, we will not worry about this distinction for now, and will simply refer to "the interest rate," but the model of this chapter is

monetary policy *The behaviour of the Bank of Canada regarding the money supply.*

interest *The fee that a borrower pays to a lender for the use of his or her funds.*

interest rate *The annual interest payment on a loan expressed as a percentage of the loan. Equal to the amount of interest received per year divided by the amount of the loan.*

really for short-term interest rates. Appendix 12A to this chapter provides a more detailed discussion of the effects of monetary policy on interest rates of different terms and also describes the various types of interest rates.

The Bank of Canada also may influence the **exchange rate** or the price of the Canadian dollar in terms of another currency, most typically in terms of the U.S. dollar. The value of the Canadian dollar affects how much Canadians pay for things purchased in the rest of the world, including bonds and securities in foreign financial markets and imported goods and services such as Japanese-made televisions or trips by Canadians to California. It also determines how much others pay for Canadian bonds and securities as well as for Canadian exported goods and services, such as Canadian aluminum or ski holidays by Germans in Banff.

The Demand for Money

What factors and forces determine the demand for money are central issues in macroeconomics. As we shall see, the interest rate, the level of aggregate income (*Y*), and the overall price level (which we will denote as *P* from now on) are important in determining how much money households and firms wish to hold.

Before we proceed, however, we must stress one point. When we speak of the demand for money, we are not asking "How much cash do you wish you could have?" or "How much income would you like to earn?" or "How much wealth would you like?" (The answer to these questions is presumably "as much as possible.") Rather, we are concerned with the question of how much of your financial assets you want to hold *in the form of money*, which does not earn interest, and how much you want to hold in interest-bearing securities, such as bonds. We take as given the *total* amount of financial assets that will be held in one of these two forms; our concern here is with how these assets are divided between money and interest-bearing securities.

THE SPECULATION MOTIVE

A number of theories have been offered to explain why the proportion of assets that households desire to hold as money may rise when interest rates fall, and fall when interest rates rise. One of these theories involves expectations and the relationship of interest rates to bond values.

First it is important to understand that the price of bonds is inversely related to the interest rate. Suppose, for example, that the one-year interest rate is 8% per annum and you are working for a company issuing a bond to borrow money for one year. You direct the printer to prepare a number of $1000 bonds that in one year will repay the principal of $1000. To cover the interest, each bond will have a coupon that in one year can be redeemed for $80.

Now suppose that by the time your company brings these bonds to the market, prevailing interest rates have gone up to 9%. Will you still be able to raise $1000 per bond? No. No one will pay $1000 for one of your 8% bonds because they can earn a better return on other bonds paying 9%. If you want to sell the bond issue, you will have to reduce your price. You should be able to sell each bond for about $991, because an individual who buys a bond for $991 and receives $1080 (principal plus coupon) in one year will earn $1080 − $991 = $89 interest, and $89 represents 9% interest on $991. The increase in the interest rate has made the price (or present value) of your bond fall until the effective rate of interest it pays (sometimes called the "yield") equals the market rate.

Suppose interest rates then suddenly fall to 7%. Holders of the bond will have an instant capital gain. The price of the bond will rise to about $1009, because a bond purchased at $1009 that will be worth $1080 a year later is paying an effective rate of interest of 7%. The fall in the interest rate has led to an increase in the price of the bond.

This inverse relationship between interest rates and the bond price will hold for any standard existing bond. (It will not hold for Canada Savings Bonds—this and more about bond pricing is covered in the Application box titled "Bonds and

Money Markets.") If we consider bonds with terms longer than one year, we can get larger swings in price for a given change in interest rates. For example, consider a bond that is 25 years from maturity, with annual coupons of $80 and a principal payment at maturity of $1000. If the 25-year interest rate is 8%, then the price of this bond will be $1000. If the 25-year rate of interest increases to 9%, the price of the bond falls to $902. If the 25-year rate of interest falls to 7%, the price of the bond increases to $1117.

While working out the exact values might require some work with a calculator or bond table, the key point here is simple:

> When interest rates fall, bond values rise; when interest rates rise, bond values fall.

The inverse relationship between interest rates and bond prices is as much a consequence of arithmetic as of theory and is demonstrated every day in every bond market in the world. However, it does lead to one theory of why individuals hold money. After all, why hold money, which pays little or no interest,[1] when the alternative is to hold assets such as bonds that pay higher rates of interest? Consider an investor who thinks that interest rates are about to increase. She will not want to hold bonds now because she knows that if interest rates go up, bond prices will fall and she will take a capital loss. Hence she will hold money now and if she is right and interest rates go up, she will then be able to purchase bonds more cheaply. Holding money in hope of rising interest rates is called the **speculation motive** for holding money.

It is sometimes argued that individuals will expect that if interest rates are particularly low, then interest rates are more likely to rise and that if interest rates are high, interest rates are more likely to fall. This would suggest that the speculation demand for money would be high when interest rates are low and the speculation demand for money would be low when interest rates are high. However most economists would argue that interest rates are not very predictable and thus may not be particularly likely to rise even when at historically low levels. Hence, while the speculation motive is clearly one reason money is held, we will not rely upon it to explain the relationship between the demand for money and the interest rate. We will examine this relationship further in the next section and describe a theory based on the role of money as a medium of exchange.

speculation motive *One reason for holding money instead of bonds. Because the market value of interest-bearing bonds is inversely related to the interest rate, investors may wish to hold money in anticipation that interest rates will increase so that bonds will be available at lower prices.*

THE TRANSACTION MOTIVE

When we discussed the speculation motive for holding money in the previous section, unless you speculate in financial markets you may have been thinking, "That's not why I hold money: I hold money to buy things." This is what is called the **transaction motive**. Not just individuals but firms such as your local supermarket or department store, and organizations such as your college or university all hold currency and bank deposits (particularly chequing accounts) for use as a medium of exchange.

But given the convenience of having money available for transactions (what economists call "liquidity"), why are not all assets held in this form? One reason is that there is an opportunity cost to holding money because there is forgone interest—the same assets would have earned a higher return if they had been held in some form of financial security, let us say a bond. This may not seem important if you have a relatively low level of assets. But for higher asset households, firms, and organizations, there are significant financial gains to keeping a minimum of money holdings, which pay no or little interest, and instead holding bonds, which have a much higher rate of expected return.

transaction motive *The main reason that households, firms, and other organizations hold money—for use as a medium of exchange.*

[1]*Remember that "money" includes some types of bank deposits that do pay interest, albeit at lower rates of interest than bonds. (If bond interest rates were not higher, no one would hold bonds, as they are less convenient than bank deposits.) When it comes to choosing whether to hold bonds or to hold money, it is the difference in the interest rates on the two that matters. With respect to money holding, a situation where bonds pay 8% and a bank deposit pays 3% is the same as one where bonds pay 5% and the bank deposit pays 0%. Therefore we can simplify our discussion by thinking of all money as paying zero interest.*

The primary motive for holding cash is to engage in transactions. Most people walk around with some money in their pockets and keep some money in their chequing accounts, but usually not huge amounts. The cost of holding money is forgone interest.

Hence the amount of assets held as money depends on the tradeoff between bond interest rates and convenience. The less money and the more bonds I hold, the more interest I will earn but the more likely I will run out of money and need to sell a bond. If I do that, I incur the extra inconvenience and costs of dealing with the bank and/or broker plus the sales commission. If interest rates are low, I am unlikely to risk these costs and I will want to hold more money and fewer bonds. But if interest rates are high, I will want to hold more bonds and less money.

If we assume that this inverse relationship between interest rates and holding money holds in aggregate, we can draw a demand curve for money as the curve labelled M^d in Figure 12.1. This looks like an ordinary demand curve where instead of price on the vertical axis, we have the interest rate, the opportunity cost of holding money. Summarizing this curve in words:

> At any given moment, there is a demand for money—for cash and chequing account balances. Although households and firms need to hold balances for everyday transactions, their demand has a limit. For both households and firms, the quantity of money demanded at any moment depends on the opportunity cost of holding money, a cost determined by the interest rate.

TRANSACTIONS VOLUME, OUTPUT, AND THE PRICE LEVEL

The money demand curve in Figure 12.1 is a function of the interest rate. There are other factors besides the interest rate that influence total desired money holdings. One is the dollar value of transactions made during a given period of time. The higher the total dollar value of transactions made in the economy, the more money is needed to make these transactions.

The total dollar volume of transactions in the economy depends on two things: the total *number* of transactions and the average transaction *amount*. A reasonable indicator of these is likely to be aggregate output (income) (Y). A rise in aggregate output—real GDP—means that there is more economic activity. Firms are producing and selling more output, more people are on payrolls, and household incomes are higher. In short, there are more transactions, and firms and households together will hold more money when they are engaging in more transactions. Thus, an increase in aggregate output (income) will increase the demand for money.

Figure 12.2 shows a shift of the money demand curve resulting from an increase in Y from Y_1 to Y_2:

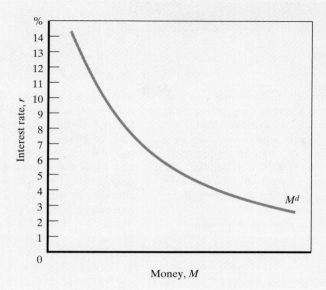

FIGURE 12.1

The Demand Curve for Money Balances

The quantity of money demanded (the amount of money households and firms wish to hold) is a function of the interest rate. Because the interest rate is the opportunity cost of holding money balances, increases in the interest rate will reduce the quantity of money that firms and households want to hold, and decreases in the interest rate will increase the quantity of money that firms and households want to hold.

> For a given interest rate, a higher level of output means an increase in the *number* of transactions and thus more demand for money. The money demand curve shifts to the right when Y rises. Similarly, a decrease in Y means a decrease in the number of transactions and a lower demand for money. The money demand curve shifts to the left when Y falls.

The amount of money needed by firms and households to facilitate their day-to-day transactions also depends on the average *dollar amount* of each transaction. In turn, the average amount of each transaction depends on prices, or rather, on the *price level (P)*. If all prices, including the price of labour (the wage rate) were to double, firms and households would need more money balances to carry out

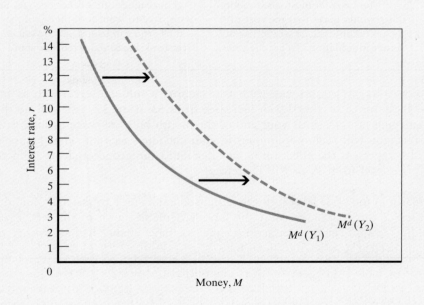

FIGURE 12.2

An Increase in Aggregate Output (Income) (Y) or Price Level (P) Will Shift the Money Demand Curve to the Right

An increase in Y means that there is more economic activity. There are thus more transactions, for which money is needed. As a result, both firms and households are likely to increase their holdings of money balances at a given interest rate.

While we have drawn this diagram for output increasing from Y_1 to Y_2, it would look very similar if instead the price level increased from P_1 to P_2.

Perpetuities

Let us first discuss a type of bond that is very rare, a "perpetuity" that pays interest forever and never repays the principal. For example, consider a bond that pays $80 interest per year forever. What would be the price of such a bond (i.e., its present value) if interest rates were 8% and not expected to change? The answer is $1000, because that is the sum that would have to be invested now at 8% to earn $80 per year every year in the future. More generally you can see that the annual payment from a perpetuity should equal the interest rate × the price of the perpetuity or:

The price of a perpetuity =
Annual payment ÷ Interest rate

We can verify the formula for our example because the price of the perpetuity $1000 = $80/0.08. If interest rates were instead 10%, the price of the perpetuity would be $80/0.1 = $800, which we can see is correct because at 10% interest, a sum of only $800 would be required to yield $80 per year.

Even though perpetuities are rare, thinking about them is useful for several reasons. First, they illustrate very well the inverse relation-

ship between interest rates and bond prices. As we just saw, for example, if interest rates increased from 8% to 10%, it was quick and easy to calculate that bond prices fell from $1000 to $800. But in addition, the concept of perpetuities may be helpful in valuing certain streams of costs and benefits.

As an example of the latter point, suppose there was a pollution source causing damages of $1 million per year. How much would it be worth paying to clean it up? While there are complex issues underlying every aspect of this kind of problem, the main point here is that it would be worth paying much more than $1 million. Many economists would get a quick idea of the amount by dividing $1 million by the rate of interest, just as in the formula above. In effect, they would be calculating the size of the perpetual bond that would be needed to cover the annual damage of the pollution, so that if interest rates were 8% and $1 million was needed to cover the annual costs, the price of such a perpetuity would be $1 million/0.08 = $12.5 million.

Moreover, in most cases economists would guess that the cost of the pollution damage would rise at least with inflation. To get the price

of a perpetuity that would pay one million inflation-adjusted or real dollars, we use the inflation-adjusted or real rate of interest (the ordinary or nominal rate of interest less inflation) and divide that into $1 million in our calculation. Most economists would consider the long-run real rate of interest to be between 3% and 6%. Let us use 5%. Hence a first approximation would be that it would be worth paying $1 million/0.05 = $20 million to clean up the pollution. A similar method could be used to value a resource such as a fish stock or a piece of parkland.

Canada Savings Bonds

The most familiar bond to most of us is the Canada Savings Bond or CSB. However, this is not the kind of bond that we were discussing when we were considering the speculation motive for money demand. A CSB cannot be sold in any market but must be redeemed at a bank or other financial services outlet.

Suppose you purchase a CSB and then interest rates go up. If you would like to switch to something with a higher rate of interest, you do not have to wait until the bond matures. You can simply go to your local bank branch and redeem your

their day-to-day transactions—each transaction would require twice as much money. If the price of your lunch increases from $3.50 to $7, you will no doubt begin carrying more cash. If your end-of-the-month bills are twice as high as they used to be, you will keep more money in your chequing account. Thus Figure 12.2 could also represent the effect on money demand from a once-and-for-all increase in the price level from P_1 to P_2. Therefore:

> Increases in the price level shift the money demand curve to the right, and decreases in the price level shift the money demand curve to the left. Even though the number of transactions may not have changed, the quantity of money needed to engage in them has.

THE DETERMINANTS OF MONEY DEMAND (REVIEW)

Figure 12.3 summarizes everything we have said about the demand for money. First, because the interest rate (r) is the opportunity cost of holding money balances for both firms and households, decreases in the interest rate will increase the quantity of money demanded. Thus, the quantity of money demanded is a negative function of the interest rate.

bond for face value plus any accumulated interest. You are at no risk of a capital loss. This is one reason why people buy CSBs even though they typically pay a lower rate of interest than other bonds. If after purchasing a CSB interest rates instead fall, your bond has increased in value, although there is no market in which to sell it to realize your capital gain.

The Money Market

In Appendix 12A to this chapter there is more discussion of the factors that affect interest rates, such as the length of time to maturity and the degree of risk. But let us close the discussion here by looking at some actual bond prices.

The illustration shows a fragment from the bond price listings in the *National Post* of June 9, 2000. The seventh row is for a bond from the Province of Quebec that had a coupon rate of 11% and matures in April 1, 2009. You can see that such a bond (or fraction of such a bond) with a face value of $100 had a bid price of $129.30. The price is more than $100 because prevailing interest rates in June 2000 were below the coupon rate set when the bond was originally issued in 1987. The market price of the bond had therefore

been bid up so that the purchaser would only earn the same yield on that bond as the prevailing interest rate paid on other, similar bonds.

Just below this listing there is another listing for another Province of Quebec bond that had a coupon rate of 5.5% with a maturity date of June 1, 2009. As you can see, the bid price is $93. It is less than $100 because by June 2000 interest rates were higher than the coupon rate set when the bond was issued in 1999. The price of the bond fell so that its effective yield matched the prevailing interest rate. The *National Post* conveniently gives the effective yield on both bonds, and even though their coupon rates are so different their effective yield is almost the same at just over 6.5%. This is as expected: both are from the same issuer and the maturity dates are very close. Hence the bond prices adjusted so that the effective yields were the same. If one bond were paying a higher effective yield, all buyers would choose that bond and its price would increase until its effective yield was the same as that on other, similar bonds.

If you study the clipping you may note a tendency for longer-term bonds to have a higher yield (as discussed further in Appendix 12A)

	Coupon	Mat. date	Bid $	Yld%
Quebec	10.250	Oct 15/01	105.00	6.28
Quebec	5.250	Apr 01/02	98.20	6.32
Quebec	7.500	Dec 01/03	103.41	6.39
Quebec	6.500	Dec 01/05	100.35	6.42
Quebec	7.750	Mar 30/06	106.20	6.45
Quebec	6.500	Oct 01/07	100.05	6.49
Quebec	11.000	Apr 01/09	129.30	6.56
Quebec	5.500	Jun 01/09	93.00	6.54
Quebec	8.500	Apr 01/26	122.90	6.63
Quebec	6.000	Oct 01/29	92.64	6.57
Saskat	6.125	Oct 10/01	99.82	6.26
Saskat	5.500	Jun 02/08	94.12	6.46
Saskat	8.750	May 30/25	127.93	6.48
Toronto	6.100	Aug 15/07	97.95	6.46
Toronto	6.100	Dec 12/17	94.53	6.63
Corporate				
AGT Lt	8.800	Sep 22/25	114.71	7.49
Air Ca	6.750	Feb 02/04	95.50	8.20
AssCap	5.400	Sep 04/01	98.53	6.66
Avco	5.750	Jun 02/03	97.38	6.74
Bell	6.500	May 09/05	99.79	6.55
Bell	6.150	Jun 15/09	96.78	6.63

Source: National Post, June 9, 2000, p. D12.

and that, at comparable terms to maturity, the yields for Saskatchewan bonds are a little less than those of Quebec bonds, suggesting bond purchasers thought the former were very slightly less risky. Yields for the corporate bonds are a bit higher, presumably reflecting greater perceived risk.

(In Chapter 17 there is an Application box titled "Reading the Stock Page" that you may wish to read.)

The demand for money also depends on the dollar volume of transactions in a given period. The dollar volume of transactions depends on both aggregate output (income), Y, and the price level, P. The relationship of money demand to Y and the relationship of money demand to P are both positive. Increases in Y or in P will shift the money demand curve to the right, and decreases in Y or P will shift the money demand curve to the left.

■ **Some Common Pitfalls** We need to consider several pitfalls in thinking about money demand. First, when we spoke in earlier chapters about the demand for goods and services, we were speaking of demand as a *flow variable*. A flow variable, you will recall, is measured over a period of time. For example, if you say that your demand for coffee is three cups, you need to specify whether you are talking about three cups per hour, three cups per day, three cups per week, and so forth. In macroeconomics, consumption and saving are flow variables. We consume and save continuously, but we express consumption and saving in time-period terms, such as $600 *per month*.

Money demand is *not* a flow measure. Rather it is a *stock variable*, measured at a given point in time. It answers the question: How much money do firms and households desire to hold at a specific point in time, given the current interest rate, volume of economic activity, and price level?

FIGURE 12.3

Determinants of Money Demand

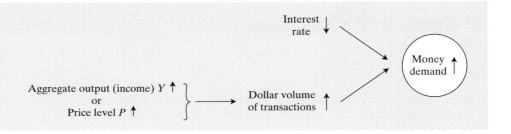

Second, many people think of money demand and saving as roughly the same thing, but they are not. Say that in a given year a household has income of $50 000 and expenses of $47 000. It has thus saved $3000 during the year. Say also that at the beginning of the year the household had no debt and $100 000 in assets. Since the household saved $3000 during the year, it has $103 000 in assets at the end of the year. Some of the $103 000 is held in stocks, some in bonds, some in other forms of securities, and some in money. How much the household chooses to hold in the form of money is its demand for money. Depending on the interest rate and the household's transactions, the amount of the $103 000 that it chooses to hold in the form of money could be anywhere from a few hundred dollars to many thousands. How much of its assets a household holds in the form of money is different from how much it spends during the year.

Finally, recall the difference between a shift in a demand curve and a movement along the curve. The money demand curve in Figure 12.1 shows optimal money balances as a function of the interest rate *ceteris paribus*, all else equal. Changes in the interest rate cause movements *along* the curve—*changes in the quantity of money demanded*. Changes in real GDP (Y) or in the price level (P) cause shifts of the curve as shown in Figure 12.2—*changes in demand*.

The Equilibrium Interest Rate

We are now in a position to consider one of the key questions in macroeconomics: How is the interest rate determined in the economy? We begin by focusing on the domestic rather than the international factors.

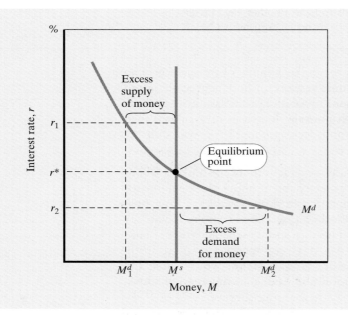

FIGURE 12.4

Adjustments in the Money Market

Equilibrium exists in the money market when the supply of money is equal to the demand for money: $M_d = M_s$. At r_1, the quantity of money supplied exceeds the quantity of money demanded, and the interest rate will fall. At r_2, the quantity demanded exceeds the quantity supplied, and the interest rate will rise. Only at r^* is equilibrium achieved.

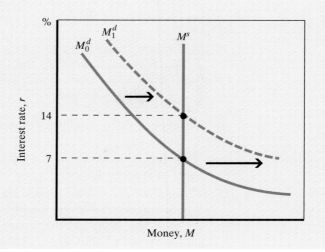

FIGURE 12.5

The Effect of an Increase in Income on the Interest Rate

An increase in aggregate output (income) shifts the money demand curve from M_0^d to M_1^d, which raises the equilibrium interest rate from 7% to 14%.

Financial markets (what we call the money market) almost always clear in Canada—that is, almost all financial markets reach an equilibrium where quantity demanded equals quantity supplied. Hence in our model of the money market,

> The point at which the quantity of money demanded equals the quantity of money supplied determines the equilibrium interest rate in the economy.

SUPPLY AND DEMAND IN THE MONEY MARKET

We saw in Chapter 11 that the Bank of Canada influences the money supply through its manipulation of the amount of reserves in the economy. Because we are assuming that the money supply does not depend on the interest rate, the money supply curve is simply a vertical line. (Review Figure 11.4.) In other words, we are assuming that the Bank uses its three tools (the Bank rate, transfers of government deposits, and open market operations) to set the money supply.

Figure 12.4 superimposes the vertical money supply curve on the downward-sloping money demand curve. Only at interest rate r^* is the quantity of money in circulation (the money supply) equal to the quantity of money demanded.

Why is r^* an equilibrium? First suppose the interest rate were at r_1, a higher rate of interest. As Figure 12.4 shows, at interest rate r_1 the quantity of money supplied exceeds the amount of money demanded. At such a high interest rate, the high opportunity cost of holding money will lead firms and households to attempt to reduce their money holdings by buying interest-bearing bonds. This increased demand to purchase bonds will increase the price of bonds, which as we learned earlier in the chapter, is the same as reducing the rate of interest. Excess supply in the supply and demand model always tends to reduce price. In this case the excess supply is of money and the price reduced is the rate of interest, the price of holding money.

Now suppose the interest rate was at r_2, below r^*. Again as Figure 12.4 shows, there is now excess demand for money. At such a low interest rate, firms and households would rather hold more money and hence they want to sell their bonds. This increased offering of bonds will tend to push down the price of bonds, which is the same as increasing the rate of interest. The excess demand for money will force up the rate of interest.

SHIFTS IN THE MONEY DEMAND CURVE

Shifts in the demand for money change interest rates. As we showed in Figure 12.2, an increase in either real aggregate output (Y) or the price level (P) will shift the money demand curve to the right. For example, in Figure 12.5, an increase in Y shifts the money demand from M_0^d to M_1^d. Interest rates increase from 7% before the increase in Y to 14% after the increase in Y. A reduction in aggregate output or the price level would shift the money demand curve to the left and lower interest rates. We conclude that

> An increase in aggregate output (Y) or the overall price level (P) will shift the money demand curve to the right and increase interest rates with a given money supply. Similarly a reduction in Y or P will reduce interest rates with a given money supply.

We explore this relationship in more detail in Chapter 14.

THE BANK OF CANADA: CHANGING THE MONEY SUPPLY TO AFFECT THE INTEREST RATE

Changes of the money supply affect the interest rate as well. Figure 12.6 shows how increasing the money supply from M_0^s to M_1^s will reduce the interest rate from 14% to 7%. If instead the money supply were reduced from M_0^s, the money supply curve would shift to the left and the new equilibrium interest rate would exceed 14%.

Recall from Chapter 11 that the Bank of Canada can increase or decrease the money supply by open market purchases or sales of securities, by transferring government deposits to or from private banks, and by lowering or raising the Bank rate. Moreover the Bank of Canada can get almost instant feedback on the effects of its policies by looking at the very-short-term interest rate, the overnight rate. If it is tightening the money supply and the money demand curve is stable, the overnight rate should rise. If it is expanding the money supply, the overnight rate should fall.

But monetary policy decisions involve more than just interest rates. In Chapter 11 we also mentioned that if the Bank of Canada used Canadian dollars to buy and sell foreign exchange such as U.S. dollars, this would have the same effects on the money supply as open market purchases and sales of securities. In the next two sections we begin our discussions of the interactions between the foreign exchange market and monetary policy.

FIXED EXCHANGE RATES

fixed exchange rate *A government policy that sets the exchange rate at a given level.*

A **fixed exchange rate** is a government policy that sets the exchange rate at a given level. While Canada has not had fixed exchange rates since 1970, understanding fixed exchange rates should help you understand the options for current exchange rate and monetary policy. We will continue to use the money demand and supply model we just developed.

As an example of fixed exchange rates, in 1962 the Canadian government fixed the value of the Canadian dollar at 92.5 cents American or US$0.925. This cannot be done simply by passing a law, for even if that could work within Canada, it could not prevent the Canadian dollar from being traded at other prices in the markets in other countries. Instead the government directed the Bank of Canada to buy and sell the Canadian dollar to keep the exchange rate at US$0.925.

In practice an approximate band around $0.925 was set, say between 92 cents and 93 cents American. No action was required of the Bank if the price of the dollar stayed within that range. But to set the upper limit, the Bank of Canada would always be prepared to sell the Canadian dollar at 93 cents American. This set a ceiling on the exchange rate because no one would pay more than 93 cents American for Canadian dollars if they were available from the Bank of Canada at that price. The Bank's role here was not operationally difficult, because the Bank of Canada can always issue more Canadian dollars to sell as many as required.

To fix the lower part of the band, the Bank of Canada also needed to be prepared to purchase the Canadian dollar at 92 cents American. This set a floor because no one would accept less than 92 cents American for a Canadian dollar knowing that the Bank of Canada would always buy at that price. Here the Bank's role could be more difficult as it needed enough U.S. dollars to make the required

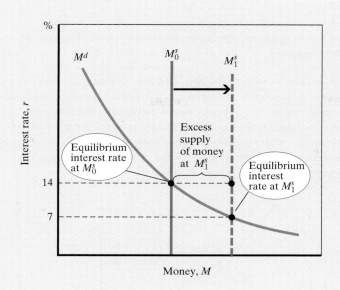

FIGURE 12.6

The Effect of an Increase in the Supply of Money on the Interest Rate

An increase in the supply of money from M_0^s to M_1^s lowers the rate of interest from 14% to 7%.

purchases and of course it cannot issue U.S. currency.[2] Some U.S. dollars are available in the Department of Finance's exchange fund account, which the Bank of Canada manages, and sometimes loans are available from other central banks. However, if the Bank of Canada had run out of foreign exchange, it would have had nothing with which to buy Canadian dollars and would have been unable to prevent the price of the Canadian dollar from falling.

From the above discussion you can see that the Bank must be prepared to alter the money supply in order to fix the exchange rate. Indeed, if the government decides to have fixed exchange rates, *that* is the monetary policy! Once the instruments of monetary policy are devoted to maintaining the exchange rate it is no longer possible, for example, to use monetary policy to influence interest rates.

We can see this in Figure 12.7, where we assume that U.S. interest rates are 7%. When discussing the effects of foreign interest rates in this book, we will assume that Canada is a small open economy. This means we are assuming that capital markets are open, that is, it is easy for those in Canada to purchase bonds in the rest of the world (such as in the United States) and easy for those outside of Canada to purchase Canadian bonds. It also means that Canada is assumed to be small enough so that events in Canada will not change U.S. interest rates.

Given these assumptions, let us consider the case where the Bank of Canada attempts *both* to pursue a fixed exchange rate policy *and* to set the money supply such that interest rates in Canada are 4%. How would you decide between purchasing a U.S. bond or a Canadian bond? Given that risk factors are comparable and you are convinced the exchange rate will stay fixed at its current level, you will buy the U.S. bond because it pays more interest. Everyone else will do that as well—no one will buy Canadian bonds. No one will wish to lend in Canada (that is buy Canadian bonds) because there is a higher available interest rate in the United States.

That may be enough to persuade you that the Bank of Canada's position would be untenable but we can explain further. With the higher U.S. interest rates available, firms and households will want to use their Canadian dollars to buy U.S. bonds. That is, firms and households will want to sell their Canadian dollars to purchase American dollars and then use those U.S. dollars to buy U.S. bonds. The increased supply of Canadian dollars will tend to drive down the value of the Canadian dollar. But under fixed exchange rates, the Bank of Canada cannot let that happen; the Bank will have to buy up the excess Canadian dollars and take them out of

---

[2]*Gold or other foreign currencies such as yen or British pounds can also be used to buy up excess Canadian dollars. But using Canadian dollars to buy U.S. dollars and then using the purchased U.S. dollars to buy back Canadian dollars obviously cannot reduce the excess supply of Canadian dollars.*

FIGURE 12.7

Under Fixed Exchange Rates, Canadian Interest Rates Will Not Remain Lower Than U.S. Interest Rates

Initially, the Canadian money supply is M_0^s. The Canadian money demand curve is M^d so Canadian interest rates are 4%, compared to U.S. interest rates of 7%. Bondholders try to shift from Canadian bonds to U.S. bonds, putting downward pressure on the Canadian dollar. Under fixed exchange rates, the Bank of Canada must support the exchange rate by purchasing Canadian dollars and hence reducing the money supply. This process continues until the money supply is reduced to M_1^s and Canadian interest rates are equal to U.S. interest rates at 7%.

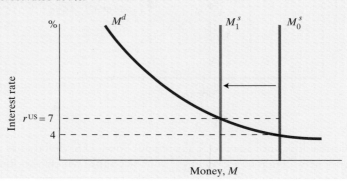

circulation, reducing the money supply. This process will continue until the money supply shifts to the left from M_0^s to M_1^s, at which point the Canadian interest rate also equals 7%, the U.S. interest rate.

In Figure 12.8 we assume that U.S. interest rates are still 7% but that Canadian interest rates are now 10%. Now bondholders want to shift their assets into Canada to take advantage of the higher interest rate. For example, some holders of U.S. bonds will want to sell these bonds for U.S. dollars, use those U.S. dollars to buy Canadian dollars and use the Canadian dollars to buy Canadian bonds. The increased demand for Canadian dollars on the foreign exchange market would tend to increase the value of the Canadian dollar. Again under fixed exchange rates, the Bank of Canada cannot let that happen and will respond by selling Canadian dollars, thus increasing the money supply. The process will continue until the money supply shifts to the right from M_0^s to M_1^s, at which point the Canadian interest rate equals the U.S. interest rate of 7%.

In practice, during the period of fixed exchange rates, Canadian interest rates were always somewhat above U.S. interest rates, partly because of transactions costs (the costs of buying and selling foreign exchange and bonds) and partly because the perceptions of foreign lenders that there was greater risk in Canada had to be offset by an interest premium. But this does not change the basic point:

> Under fixed exchange rates, the Bank of Canada must set the money supply to maintain the exchange rate and cannot use monetary policy to influence other economic variables. In particular, interest rates will be largely determined by U.S. interest rates.

FLEXIBLE EXCHANGE RATES

A **flexible (or floating) exchange rate** is an exchange rate that is not fixed by government policy. Under a **freely (or pure) floating exchange rate,** the central bank does not put any weight on the exchange rate in its conduct of monetary policy. Under a **managed (or dirty) floating exchange rate,** from time to time the central bank will buy and sell on exchange rate markets or use other monetary instruments to influence the value of its currency.

flexible (or floating) exchange rate *A government policy that does not fix the exchange rate.*

freely (or pure) floating exchange rate *A market-determined exchange rate policy in which no consideration is given to the level of the exchange rate in monetary policy decisions.*

managed (or dirty) floating exchange rate *A policy partway between fixed exchange rates and purely floating exchange rates in which the central bank may sometimes use its monetary instruments to influence the exchange rate but has no announced commitment to a specific level of the exchange rate.*

FIGURE 12.8

Under Fixed Exchange Rates, Canadian Interest Rates Will Not Remain Higher Than U.S. Interest Rates

Initially, the Canadian money supply is M_0^s. The Canadian money demand curve is M_d so Canadian interest rates are 10%, compared to U.S. interest rates of 7%. Bondholders try to shift from U.S. bonds to Canadian bonds, putting upward pressure on the Canadian dollar. Under fixed exchange rates, the Bank of Canada must prevent the exchange rate from rising by selling Canadian dollars and hence increasing the money supply. This process continues until the money supply is increased to M_1^s and Canadian interest rates are equal to U.S. interest rates at 7%. Note that this diagram and Figure 12.7 abstract from transactions costs and differences in perceived risk, which in practice led Canadian interest rates to be typically somewhat higher when Canada had fixed exchange rates before 1970.

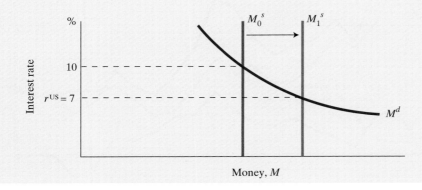

While the Canadian dollar has been floating since 1970, it has not been a pure floating exchange rate. For example, if you read on the business page that the Bank of Canada is "defending" the value of the Canadian dollar, that means the Bank is buying the Canadian dollar to support its price. This process is just as we described in the previous section on fixed exchange rates, except there is no hard and fast announced commitment to a given value for the dollar. One of the most important of the Bank of Canada's monetary policy decisions is the degree of attention it chooses to pay to the exchange rate.

Under flexible exchange rates, to the extent it allows free floating, the Bank of Canada can pursue an independent monetary policy by aiming its money supply tools at other goals besides a fixed exchange rate. Figure 12.9 shows that short-term interest rates in Canada still tend to move with short-term interest rates in the United States, but not always. So while there is clearly a relationship between interest rates in the two countries, there is also some degree of independence.[3]

However, a major difference between floating and fixed exchange rates is the obvious one—under floating exchange rates the value of the Canadian dollar can change. Figure 12.10 shows how wide the swings can be. For example, in 1991 the average value of the Canadian dollar was over 87 cents American, but by June 2000 its value was only about 68 cents American.

How do we explain such a large change? Remember from Figure 12.9 that the Canada-U.S. interest rate differential fell throughout the 1990s. This made Canadian bonds and securities relatively less attractive, so that some holders of Canadian bonds wanted to sell Canadian bonds for Canadian dollars, use those Canadian dollars to purchase U.S. dollars and then use U.S. dollars to buy U.S. bonds. This increased supply of the Canadian dollars on the exchange market reduced the value of the Canadian dollar.

---

[3]One reason for some of the correlation in interest rates is that the Bank of Canada is not following a purely floating exchange rate. Another reason is that just as explained in the previous section, there is a tendency for equalization in returns as bond purchasers seek the best interest rate. However, this equalization tendency is weaker with floating exchange rates than with fixed exchange rates. For example, I could decide to buy Canadian bonds paying 4% rather than U.S. bonds paying 7% because I expect the U.S. dollar to fall in value by 3% or more per year relative to the Canadian dollar. Hence the U.S.-dollar payments from the bond would be falling in terms of Canadian dollars and this loss would offset the higher U.S. rate of interest. We will discuss these matters more in Chapter 21, which concentrates on international aspects of the macroeconomy.

FIGURE 12.9

Canadian and U.S. Interest Rates, 1970–2000

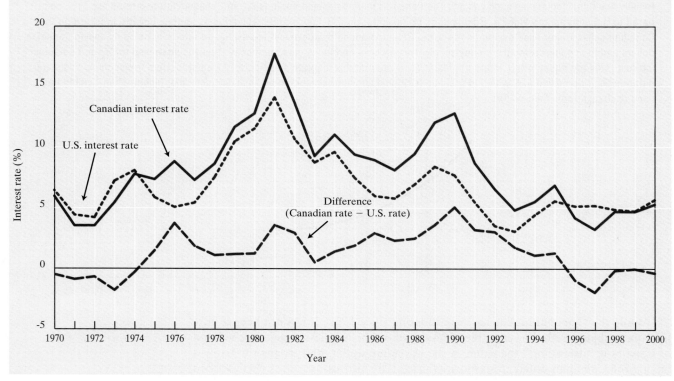

Source: Adapted from Statistics Canada, CANSIM database, Series B14007 and B54409. Rates are for three-month Treasury bills. Data for 2000 are for the first five months.

We can relate this to our discussion of fixed exchange rates. As noted, if interest rates are low relative to U.S. levels, bondholders want to shift out of Canadian bonds and into U.S. bonds, putting downward pressure on the value of the Canadian dollar. Under fixed exchange rates, the Bank of Canada intervenes by buying Canadian dollars (fixing the exchange rate by contracting the money supply) and the Canadian dollar is not allowed to fall in value. Under flexible exchange rates, there is no intervention and the value of the Canadian dollar falls.

Similarly, if interest rates in Canada are high relative to U.S. levels, there is a tendency for the Canadian dollar to increase in value. Under fixed exchange rates this is prevented by the Bank of Canada selling Canadian dollars (expanding the money supply), but under flexible exchange rates, the Canadian dollar is permitted to rise in value.

Before we conclude this section, let us introduce two terms. Canadian-dollar **appreciation** means an increase in the value of the Canadian dollar and **depreciation** means a decrease. If we say the Canadian dollar has appreciated against the U.S. dollar, the price of the Canadian dollar in terms of U.S. dollars has increased. Of course that also means that the U.S. dollar has fallen in value against the Canadian dollar, that is, the U.S. dollar has depreciated against the Canadian dollar.

Now let us summarize how interest rates and exchange rates move under floating exchange rates:

appreciation *An increase in value, for example, in the value of one currency relative to another.*

depreciation *A decrease in value, for example, in the value of one currency relative to another.*

> Unlike under fixed exchange rates, under floating exchange rates the Bank of Canada can attempt an independent monetary policy. Expanding the money supply will tend to reduce interest rates and depreciate the Canadian dollar. Restricting the money supply will tend to increase interest rates and appreciate the Canadian dollar.

FIGURE 12.10

Exchange Rate of Canadian Dollar in U.S. Funds, 1970–2000

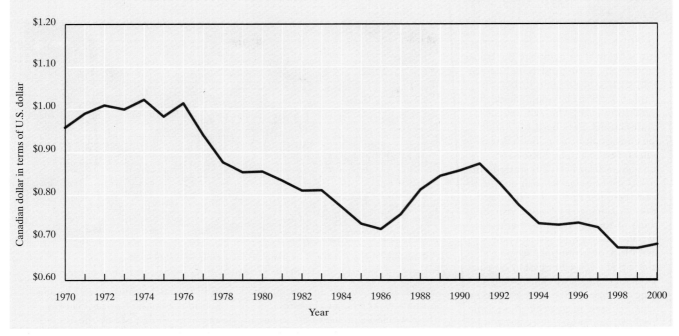

Source: Adapted from Statistics Canada, CANSIM database, Series B3400. Data for 2000 are for the first five months.

We can now see that, under floating exchange rates, the Bank of Canada has some choice over how it conducts monetary policy. The coming chapters will explain the various options and some of the controversies over what effects various choices have had and may have in the future.

Looking Ahead: Bank of Canada Behaviour and Monetary Policy

Chapter 10 began the discussion of government fiscal policy and the last two chapters have discussed the Bank of Canada and the role of monetary policy. We now know that under a fixed exchange rate policy, there is little scope for monetary policy to influence other economic variables. (Some have proposed that Canada return to a type of fixed exchange rate by forming a monetary union with the United States. See the Global Perspective box titled "Monetary Union.") However, under the floating exchange rate policy that has been in effect since 1970, the Bank can potentially influence other variables in the economy.

Suppose that under floating exchange rates the Bank pursues an **easy monetary policy** and increases the money supply. As we have discussed in this chapter, this will tend to reduce interest rates (see Figure 12.6, for example) and depreciate the Canadian dollar as firms and households try to shift out of Canadian bonds and into foreign bonds. The fall in interest rates will tend to stimulate output because lower interest rates will encourage spending, particularly investment spending.[4] The lower Canadian dollar will stimulate output by tending to increase net exports (by making Canadian exports cheaper on world markets and making imports to Canada more expensive). Both of these effects may work toward expanding output in Canada.

easy monetary policy *Central bank policies that expand the money supply.*

[4]*While it makes little difference to our main point, it is sometimes argued that the positive effect on spending comes not so much from a reduction in the interest rate and hence the cost of borrowing but from the increase in bank deposits and reserves associated with the monetary expansion. With more funds to lend, the banks can offer credit to individuals and firms who would not have received credit without the easier monetary policy, and the recipients of this credit use it to increase spending.*

A German Mint employee handles newly minted twenty-cent euro coins.

In 2002, eleven European countries are scheduled to complete the transition from having individual currencies such as the Italian lira or the French franc to having a single currency, the euro. This will reduce transactions costs both for major businesses and for individual travellers. For example, before the change, a traveller who started with 1000 deutschemarks cash and, without spending it, simply exchanged it and reexchanged it as she visited each of the 11 member countries, would have completed the journey with just over 600 deutschemarks if there were 4% commission on each exchange. But note that having a single currency, like having fixed exchange rates, means that there can only be one monetary policy (and one interest rate) for the entire area. This policy will be set by the European Central Bank (**www.ecb.int/**).

Thomas Courchene of Queen's University and Richard Harris of Simon Fraser University have argued that Canada should pursue a monetary union with the United States. They believe that the United States might agree if it were perceived as the first step to a monetary union of all North and South America, a countermove to the expanding reach of the euro. Under their proposal, Canada and the United States would issue a new currency (fixed in value to be equal to one U.S. dollar) and the new currency would circulate in Canada while the U.S. dollar would continue to circulate in the United States. Canada could no longer have an independent monetary policy, but Courchene and Harris argue that this could be an improvement, because it

would remove uncertainty facing importers, exporters, and investors, there would be an aggregate saving in the costs of currency conversion, and Canadian firms would increase their productivity growth because they no longer would be able to rely on the depreciating Canadian dollar to protect them from U.S. competition. They also argue that the Canadian economy may "dollarize" anyway—that is, more and more Canadian firms, and perhaps residents, will use U.S. dollars for their transactions in Canada. If this happens, Canada would lose complete control over its monetary policy. Under a monetary union, it might at least have some small input into the union's monetary policy.

Critics of this proposal argue that the loss of independent monetary policy will be particularly harmful to Canada, because Canada, unlike the United States, is a net exporter of commodities and hence is vulnerable in a different

way to shocks caused by changing world commodity prices. Thus a monetary policy set by the United States may often not be in the interests of Canada. These critics maintain that the fall in the Canadian dollar during the 1990s encouraged a Canadian export boom that was one of the few factors that prevented an even more serious period of low growth and high unemployment. Moreover, their view of the evidence is that Canadian productivity does not fall significantly as the Canadian dollar depreciates (i.e., "lazy firms" do not use the depreciating Canadian dollar as a shield). Finally, many argue that Canada is already excessively integrated with the United States.

Sources: Thomas Courchene and Richard Harris, "Canada and a North American Monetary Union," *Canadian Business Economics*, December 1999: 5–14; John Murray, "Going with the Flow: The Benefits of a Floating C$," *Canadian Business Economics*, December 1999: 15–24.

tight monetary policy *Central bank policies that restrict the money supply.*

Now consider the case where under floating exchange rates the Bank pursues a **tight monetary policy**. This will tend to increase interest rates, at least temporarily, and lead to a higher Canadian dollar. Reversing the arguments of the previous paragraph, both of these effects work toward restraining output. For example, critics of the Bank of Canada have argued that the significant tightening of monetary policy beginning in the late 1980s (with the rising interest rates as shown in Figure 12.9 and the appreciating Canadian dollar as shown in Figure 12.10) was a significant cause of the 1990–1991 recession, with persistent effects through the 1990s.

How does the Bank of Canada now conduct monetary policy? Its current central approach is to loosen or tighten its monetary position with the goal of keeping inflation within an announced range. The approach is discussed in more detail in the Application box titled "The Monetary Conditions Index."

APPLICATION

The Monetary Conditions Index

In the next few chapters we discuss how actions of the Bank of Canada might affect growth, employment, output, and inflation. As we will see, there are major controversies as to what monetary policy can and should do. However, the announced policy of the Bank of Canada has been clear since at least the mid-1980s. The Bank directs monetary policy toward price stability. The particular target over 1995 to 2001 was to keep a "core" price inflation rate within the range of 1% to 3% per year. The core inflation rate is measured by the CPI *excluding food and energy prices and indirect taxes* (as these are judged to be too volatile to give a clear signal of overall inflation). The inflation target range was jointly announced by the Bank and by the federal government—it was anticipated a new target would be announced sometime during 2001. You can read about current monetary policy either in the *Bank of*

Canada Review or on the Bank's Web site at **www.bankofcanada.ca**.

The Bank's announced rule for achieving its inflation target is quite simple. When it projects that inflation may be moving above the target range, it tightens monetary policy to try to reduce inflation. When it projects inflation is below its target range, it loosens monetary policy.

The problem is that it takes some time for the policies to affect inflation: according to Bank estimates, a period of about six to eight quarters. The Bank thus needs to have a more immediate measure of the effects of its policies. From our discussion of flexible exchange rates you know that changes in the money supply change short-term interest rates and the exchange rate. Hence it should not surprise you that the Bank of Canada measures the degree of monetary tightness using a Monetary Conditions Index (MCI), which de-

pends upon an interest rate (the 90-day commercial paper rate) and the exchange rate of the Canadian dollar in terms of U.S. dollars.

The actual index is calculated as: MCI = (Current interest rate − 1987 interest rate) + 1/3(Percentage exchange rate appreciation since 1987).

As you can see, 1987 has been chosen as the base year. The 1/3 in the expression lessens the weight on the exchange rate, which we have seen is more volatile than the interest rate. The Bank then uses its monetary instruments to try to move the MCI to the level its econometric models estimate is required to keep inflation within its target range over the projection period. From Figure 1 you can see that they have mostly been able to meet their targets of 1% to 3% CPI inflation. Critics have argued that the range was set too low (especially as the CPI probably overestimates inflation

We have now outlined the basics of fiscal and monetary policy. In the next three chapters we will elaborate on how these policies might work in stabilizing the economy and what the drawbacks may be.

Summary

1. *Interest* is the fee a borrower pays to a lender for the use of his or her funds. The *interest rate* is the annual interest payment on a loan expressed as a percentage of the loan; it is equal to the amount of interest received per year divided by the amount of the loan. Although there are many different interest rates in Canada, we focus on the short-term rate. This simplifies our analysis but still provides us with a valuable tool for understanding how the various parts of the macroeconomy relate to each other.

2. Monetary factors also influence the exchange rate, which is the price of one currency in terms of another.

The Demand for Money

3. The demand for money depends negatively on the interest rate. The higher the interest rate, the

higher the opportunity cost (more interest forgone) from holding money, and the less money people will want to hold. Thus, an increase in the interest rate reduces the demand for money, and the money demand curve slopes downward.

4. Increases in the volume of transactions in the economy increase money demand. The total dollar volume of transactions depends on both the total number of transactions and the average transaction amount.

5. A reasonable measure of the number of transactions in the economy is aggregate output (income) (*Y*). When *Y* rises, there is more economic activity, more is being produced and sold, and more people are on payrolls—in short, there are more transactions in the economy. Thus, an increase in *Y* causes the money demand curve to shift to the

as described in Chapter 8) and the result has been a tight monetary policy that was a major cause of high unemployment in the 1990s.

The Bank has other indicators of monetary tightness, for example the overnight interest rate discussed in the text. Sometimes it also pays more attention to the exchange rate than the MCI alone would suggest.

For example, in Spring 2000, the Federal Reserve Bank of the United States raised interest rates by 0.5%. As we have discussed, this would lead to a depreciation of the Canadian dollar as bondholders shifted toward higher-paying U.S. bonds. The Bank of Canada chose to prevent this depreciation by immediately raising the Bank rate by the same amount and tightening monetary policy.

Sources: Charles Freedman, "The Role of Monetary Conditions and the Monetary Conditions Index in the Conduct of Policy," *Bank of Canada Review,* Autumn 1995: 53–59; Bank of Canada Web site (**www.bankof canada.ca/**).

FIGURE 1

Percentage Change in CPI (All Items Less Food, Energy, and Indirect Taxes), January 1995–March 2000

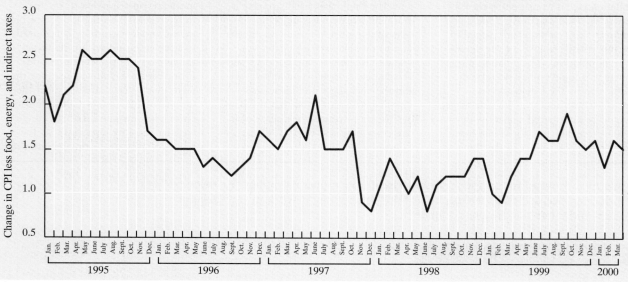

Source: *Bank of Canada Banking and Financial Statistics,* Table A1, various issues.

right. This follows because households and firms need more money when they are engaging in more transactions. A decrease in *Y* causes the money demand curve to shift left.

6. Changes in the price level affect the average dollar amount of each transaction. *Increases* in the price level will increase the demand for money (shift the money demand curve to the right) because households and firms will need more money for their expenditures. *Decreases* in the price level will decrease the demand for money (shift the money demand curve to the left).

The Equilibrium Interest Rate

7. The Bank of Canada can affect the equilibrium interest rate by changing the supply of money using one of its three tools—the Bank rate, transfers of government deposits, or open market operations.

8. The point at which the quantity of money supplied equals the quantity of money demanded determines the equilibrium interest rate in the economy. An excess supply of money will cause households and firms to attempt to buy more bonds and will drive the interest rate down. An excess demand for money will cause households and firms to attempt

to move out of bonds and will drive the interest rate up.

9. An increase in the price level is like an increase in Y in that both events cause an increase in money demand. The result is an increase in the equilibrium interest rate. A decrease in the price level leads to reduced money demand and a decrease in the equilibrium interest rate. An increase in money supply will reduce the equilibrium interest rate; a decrease in the money supply will increase the equilibrium interest rate.

Fixed Exchange Rates

10. Under a *fixed exchange rate* policy, the money supply must be adjusted to maintain the exchange rate and monetary policy cannot be used to influence other economic variables.

Flexible Exchange Rates

11. Since 1970 Canada has been under a *flexible exchange rate* policy, although it has been a *dirty float* under which the Bank of Canada on occasion attempts to affect the exchange rate by buying and selling Canadian dollars. Under flexible exchange rates, increases in the money supply tend to reduce interest rates and the value of the Canadian dollar and decreases in the money supply tend to increase interest rates and increase the value of the dollar.

Looking Ahead: Bank of Canada Behaviour and Monetary Policy

12. *Tight monetary policy* refers to Bank of Canada policies that restrict the money supply. *Easy monetary policy* refers to Bank policies that expand the money supply. Both policies may affect the economy by changing short-term interest rates and exchange rates.

Review Terms and Concepts

appreciation 260
depreciation 260
easy monetary policy 261
exchange rate 248
fixed exchange rate 256

freely (or pure) floating exchange rate 258
flexible (or floating) exchange rate 258
interest 247
interest rate 247

managed (or dirty) floating exchange rate 258
monetary policy 247
speculation motive 249
tight monetary policy 262
transaction motive 249

Problem Set

1. During 1999, real GDP (aggregate income) increased by 4.9% and the price level increased by 2.6%.
   a. Using money supply and money demand curves, show the effects of the increase in Y and P on interest rates assuming *no change* in the money supply.
   b. At the beginning of 1999, the prime interest rate (the interest rate that banks offer their best, least risky customers) stood at 6.75%. By the end of 1999, the prime rate had fallen to 6.50%. How does this differ from your answer in part **a**? Can you account for this difference using the money demand/money supply model?

2. The demand for money in a country with flexible exchange rates is given by the equation

$$M^d = 21\ 000 - 50\ 000r + 2Y$$

where M^d is money demand in dollars, r is the interest rate (a 5% interest rate means $r = 0.05$) and Y is

national income. Note that money demand will fall if the interest rate increases and increase if national income increases, just as we assumed in the chapter. We assume the price level is fixed, so we have not included that in our equation. Assume Y is initially equal to 10 000.
   a. If the money supply (M^s) is set by the central bank at $40 000, what is the equilibrium rate of interest?
   b. Suppose national income rises from $Y = 10\ 000$ to $Y = 11\ 000$. What happens to the equilibrium rate of interest if the central bank does not change the supply of money?
   c. Continuing from part **b**, how much does the central bank have to increase the money supply to restore the interest rate of part **a**?

3. Illustrate the following situations using supply and demand curves for money (under flexible exchange rates):

a. The Bank of Canada buys bonds in the open market during a recession.

b. During a period of sustained high inflation, the private banks increase their desired reserves.

c. The Bank of Canada acts to hold interest rates constant during a period of sustained high inflation.

d. During a period of no growth in GDP and zero inflation, the Bank of Canada lowers the Bank rate.

e. During a period of rapid real growth of GDP, the private banks increase their desired reserves.

4. During a recession, interest rates may fall even if the Bank of Canada takes no action to expand the money supply. Why is this true? Use a graph to explain your answer.

5. The demand for money in a country with flexible exchange rates is given by the equation

$$M^d = 10\,000 - 10\,000r + Y$$

where M^d is money demand in dollars, r is the interest rate (a 10% interest rate means $r = 0.1$), and Y is national income. Assume that Y is initially equal to 5000.

a. Graph the amount of money demanded (on the horizontal axis) against the interest rate (on the vertical axis).

b. Suppose the money supply (M^s) is set by the central bank at $10 000. On the same graph you drew for part **a**, add the money supply curve. What is the equilibrium rate of interest?

c. Suppose that income rises from $Y = 5000$ to $Y = 7500$. What happens to the money demand curve you drew in part **a**? Draw the new curve, if there is one. What happens to the equilibrium interest rate if the central bank doesn't change the supply of money?

d. If the central bank wants to keep the equilibrium interest rate at the same value as it was in part **b**, by how much should it increase or decrease the supply of money given the new level of national income?

6. We learned for the Keynesian cross model of Chapter 10 that, all else equal, an increase in government expenditure (G) or a decrease in taxes (T) would tend to stimulate output (Y). What would be the effects of such a stimulative fiscal policy on interest rates with floating exchange rates?

7. For each part of question 3, explain the effects on the exchange rate. Then redo each part assuming fixed exchange rates.

8. In the Application box "Bonds and Money Markets" earlier in the chapter, there was a discussion of evaluating a perpetual stream of benefits by comparison to a type of bond called a perpetuity. The same principle can be used for shorter horizons. Suppose you own a gold bar and you know you will sell it this year or next. Explain why the one-year interest rate (the return on a one-year bond) might be key to your decision.

| Appendix 12A | **The Various Interest Rates in the Canadian Economy** |

At the beginning of this chapter, we noted that there are many different interest rates in the economy. Although these different interest rates tend to move up or down with one another, it is useful to have some knowledge of their differences. In this appendix, we will first discuss the relationship between interest rates on securities with different *maturities,* or terms. We then discuss briefly some of the main interest rates in the Canadian economy.

The Term Structure of Interest Rates

The *term structure of interest rates* is the relationship between the interest rates offered on securities of different maturities. The key question here is: How are these different rates related? Does a two-year security (i.e., an IOU that promises to repay principal, plus interest, after two years) pay a lower annual rate than a one-year security (an IOU to be repaid, with interest, after one year)? What happens to the rate of interest offered on one-year securities if the rate of interest on two-year securities increases?

For the sake of example, assume that you want to invest some money for two years and that at the end of the two years you want it back. Assume also that you want to buy government securities. For the purposes of this analysis, we will restrict your choices to two: (1) you can buy a two-year security today and simply hold on to it for two years, at which time you cash it in (we will assume that the interest rate on the two-year security is 9% per year) or (2) you can buy a one-year security today. At the end of one year, you must cash this security in; you can then buy another one-year security. At the end of the second year, you will cash in the second security. We will assume that the interest rate on the first one-year security is 8%.

Which of these choices would you prefer? Currently, you don't have enough data to answer this question. To consider choice 2 sensibly, you need to know the interest rate on the one-year security that you intend to buy in the second year. This rate, however, will not be known until the second year. All you know now is the rate on the two-year security and the rate on the current one-year security. To decide what to do, you must form an *expectation* of the rate on the one-year security a year from now. If you expect the one-year rate (8%) to remain the same in the second year, you should obviously buy the two-year security. You would earn 9% per year on the two-year security but only 8% per year on the two one-year securities. If, on the other hand, you expect the one-year rate to rise to 12% a year from now, you should make the second choice. You would earn 8% in the first year, and you expect to earn 12% in the second year. The expected rate of return over the two years is thus about 10%, which is better than the 9% you can get on the two-year security. If you expected the one-year rate a year from now to be 10%, it would not matter very much which of the two choices you made. The rate of return over the two-year period would be roughly 9% for both choices.

We must now alter the focus of our discussion to get to the topic we are really interested in—how the two-year rate is determined. Let us assume that the one-year rate is 8% and that people expect the one-year rate a year from now to be 10%. What, then, is the two-year rate? According to a theory called the *expectations theory of the term structure of interest rates*, the two-year per annum interest rate is the rate that would give the same yield as a bond paying 8% the first year and 10% the second year. This will be very close to the average of the current one-year rate and the expected rate a year from now, or in this case 9%, the average of 8% and 10%.

If the two-year rate were lower than the average of the two one-year rates, people would not be indifferent as to which security they held. They would want to hold only the short-term, one-year securities. Thus, in order to find a buyer for a two-year security, the seller would be forced to increase the interest rate it offers on the two-year security until it is equal to the average of the current one-year rate and the expected one-year rate for next year. The interest rate on the two-year security will continue to rise until people are once again indifferent between one two-year security and two one-year securities.*

A shortcoming of this expectations theory is that it does not take into account that greater risk is associated with long-term bonds. Recall that if interest rates increase, bond prices fall and the price effect is larger for longer-term bonds (because the longer the term of the bond, the more interest will be paid and hence the more interest rates matter). While it is equally true that if interest rates fall, bond prices will rise, the upshot is that interest rate uncertainty makes long-term bonds riskier than short-term bonds. So even when interest rates are expected to remain unchanged, long-term bonds will have somewhat higher interest rates than short-term bonds. This is the typical pattern observed in the term structure.

Let us now consider the Bank of Canada's behaviour. We have seen that the Bank may affect the short-term interest rate by changing the money supply. What are the effects on long-term interest rates?

This turns out to be complicated. One effect is that, since the long-term interest rate is a sort of average that includes the short-term interest rate, if the short-term interest rate falls it may pull the long-term interest rate down a little bit. But there is another effect, and to understand it note the difference between the actual rate of interest that we have been modelling (sometimes also called the *market rate of interest* or the *nominal rate of interest*) and the *real* rate of interest which is the actual rate of interest less the rate of inflation. As an example, suppose you buy a bond for $1000 that will pay you $1070 in a year. This is an interest rate of 7%. But if there has been 2% inflation during the year, you do not have 7% more purchasing power, because goods that would have cost $1000 last year now cost $1020. Instead you have about 5% more purchasing power. The real rate of interest is a measure of that increase in purchasing power and equals the actual rate of interest less the rate of inflation or in this case 7% − 2% = 5%.

A simple model that works reasonably well is that the long-term real rate of interest is fairly constant, say 5%. Hence the long-term actual or nominal rate of interest is equal to 5% plus the expected rate of inflation. So under this theory, long-term interest rates change with the expected rate of inflation. As we will discuss in later chapters, an increase in the money supply that lowers the short-term interest rate may under some circumstances increase the inflation rate. Hence it may be that expansionary monetary policy will reduce the short-term interest rate but at the same time increase the long-term interest rate. Conversely a tightening of the money supply may increase the short-term interest rate but reduce the long-term rate.

This complication may not much matter for the effects of monetary policy on the economy. For example, an expansionary monetary policy under flexible exchange rates will tend to lower short-term interest rates, and that will lower short-term real interest rates as well (as the rate of inflation tends not to change very rap-

---

*For longer terms, additional future rates must be averaged in. For a three-year security, for example, the expected one-year rate a year from now and the expected one-year rate two years from now are added to the current one-year rate and averaged.

idly). Even if the long-term *nominal* interest rate increases, the long-term *real* rate of interest will be either constant or pulled down a bit. Hence if, as seems reasonable, it is the real rate of interest that matters for investment spending, investment spending will increase, just as was described at the end of Chapter 12 and will be further discussed in Chapter 13. By similar reasoning, a tighter monetary policy will tend to increase real interest rates, with a larger effect on short-term real interest rates, and investment spending will be reduced.

Types of Interest Rates

The following are some of the most widely followed interest rates in Canada.

■ **Bank Rate** The Bank rate is the rate the Bank of Canada charges on loans to private banks. The Bank rate was formerly tied to the three-month Treasury bill rate but now the Bank of Canada may set the Bank rate independently. The Bank rate is the rate charged on settlement balance deficits, but loans are rarely made at this rate as the private banks are usually able to obtain financing at lower rates in this situation. (See "Overnight Rate," below.)

■ **Overnight Rate** Private banks may borrow not only from the Bank of Canada but from each other and from other lenders as well. If, for example, one bank has excess settlement balances (for which it would receive a rate below the Bank rate from the Bank of Canada), it can lend funds to other banks experiencing settlement balance deficits (on which the Bank of Canada would charge the Bank rate). Since private banks always have the option of borrowing from the Bank of Canada at the Bank rate, the Bank rate acts as a upper bound on the overnight rate. Thus the overnight rate will be below the Bank rate.

The Bank of Canada announces the Bank rate as well as a target range below the Bank rate where it would like the overnight rate to be. However, it is not enough for the Bank simply to announce these rates. It also makes use of both transfers of government deposits (which give the banks more or less in their settlement balances) and of open market operations to keep the overnight rate in its desired range. Thus the Bank rate and the overnight rate are the interest rates most closely controlled by the Bank.

Borrowing and lending between the private banks, which takes place near the close of each working day, is generally for only a few days and often for only a single day, hence the name "overnight rate."

■ **Three-Month Treasury Bill Rate** Treasury bills are a type of short-term government security that matures in one year or less. Until 1996, the Bank rate was linked to the three-month Treasury bill rate. Although this is no longer the case, the three-month Treasury bill rate is still one of the most widely followed short-term interest rates.

■ **Government Bond Rate** Government bonds are a type of government security with terms of one year or more. There are one-year bonds, two-year bonds, and so on up to thirty-year bonds. Bonds of different terms have different interest rates. The relationship among the interest rates on the various maturities is the term structure of interest rates that we discussed in the first part of this appendix.

As noted in the Application box "Bonds and Money Markets," government bonds should not be confused with Canada Savings Bonds (CSBs). Ownership of government bonds may be transferred and thus there is a resale market for such securities. CSBs can be redeemed at any time but ownership may not be transferred.

■ **Commercial (or Corporate) Paper Rate** Firms have several alternatives for raising funds. They can sell stocks, issue bonds, or borrow from a bank. Large firms can also borrow directly from the public by issuing *commercial paper*, which are essentially short-term corporate IOUs that offer a designated rate of interest. The interest rate offered on commercial paper depends on the financial condition of the firm and the maturity date of the IOU.

■ **Prime Rate** Banks charge different interest rates to different customers. You would expect to pay a higher interest rate for a car loan than BC Telecom would pay for a $1 million loan to finance investment. Also, you would pay more interest for an unsecured loan, a "personal" loan, than for one that was secured by some asset, such as a house or car, to be used as collateral.

The *prime rate* is a benchmark that banks often use in quoting interest rates to their customers. A very low-risk corporation might be able to borrow at (or even below) the prime rate. A less well-known firm might be quoted a rate of "prime plus three-quarters," which means that if the prime rate is say, 10%, the firm would have to pay interest of 10.75%. Since the prime rate depends on the cost of funds to the bank, it moves up and down with changes in the economy.

■ **AAA Corporate Bond Rate** Corporations finance much of their investment by selling bonds to the public. Corporate bonds are classified by various bond dealers according to their degree of risk. Bonds differ from commercial paper in one important way: bonds have a longer maturity.

Bonds are graded in much the same way students are. The highest grade is AAA (or A++, depending on the rating agency), the next highest AA, and so on. The interest rate on bonds rated AAA is the *triple A corporate bond rate,* the rate that the least risky firms pay on the bonds that they issue.

1. The following table gives three key Canadian interest rates in April 1980 and again in April 1997:

	1980	1997
Three-month Treasury bills	15.05%	3.14%
Long-term government bonds	12.19%	7.18%
Prime rate	16.75%	4.75%

Source: Statistics Canada, CANSIM database, Series B14060, B14072, B14020.

Can you give an explanation for the extreme differences that you see? Specifically, comment on the following: (1) the fact that rates in 1980 were much higher than they were in 1997 and (2) the long-term rate was higher than the short-term rate in 1997 but below it in 1980.

The Asian Economic Crisis

After spectacular rates of economic growth since the 1960s, the Asian economies (including Hong Kong, Indonesia, Korea, Malaysia, Singapore, Thailand, and Taiwan) hit an economic crisis in 1997. For example, during an 18-month period in 1997/98, GDP in Indonesia fell by close to 20%. Its currency, the rupiah, depreciated about 85%, including a 33% depreciation over a two-day period. What was the cause, and what do our macroeconomic models suggest about policy responses?

Just about everything about the crisis is controversial, but almost everyone agrees that its principal causes were related to banking. State-run, private domestic, and private foreign banks alike lent too much on the basis of political connections and were often not aware of all the loans other banks had made to the same borrowers. In Korea, the *chaebol* (large conglomerates such as Hyundai, LG, Samsung, and Daewoo) were major borrowers from a banking system they helped control. International agencies such as the International Monetary Fund (IMF) had encouraged these economies to lift controls on foreign investment, and as a result large amounts of foreign money were used to finance a speculative boom in real estate. As it became clear that some of these loans were in trouble, particularly foreign banks stopped lending and tried to liquidate the loans they had, converting the proceeds into U.S. dollars. In the parlance of international finance markets, they "ran for the exits."

This put the domestic banks in a squeeze. Worried depositors withdrew their funds. As we studied in Chapter 11, banks do not have enough liquid assets to cover all deposits: they can only do that by calling in their loans, which takes time. Moreover, the collapse of business valuations and real estate prices as capital fled meant that many of these loans could not be repaid. Banks began to fail. A contributing factor was that so many of the banks were small: Indonesia, for example, started with close to 200 banks, almost half of them state banks. Banking and financial panics tend to be a vicious circle: they spread fear, which leads to the flight of capital as nervous depositors and investors react, which makes things worse, spreading still more fear.

While the crisis began in Thailand, it soon spread to Indonesia and Korea. The countries initially involved all had some form of fixed exchange rates. Thailand and its currency, the baht, were first hit. Before the crisis, the fixed exchange rate was just over 25 baht to the U.S. dollar. As you know from Chapter 12, this meant that the Thai central

Figure 1

The recalling of loans and collapse of some banks led to a leftward shift of the money supply curve. Tight money policy led to a further leftward shift, pushing interest rates still higher.

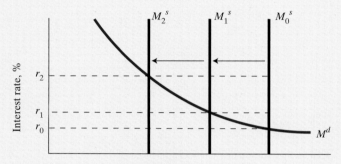

bank had to be prepared to purchase the baht using U.S. dollars or some other currency. Despite some help from Singapore, it was eventually unable to do this, and on July 2, 1997 it devalued by about 15%. Devaluations in the Malaysian ringgit, Philippines peso, and Indonesian rupiah followed, and most of these countries began floating their exchange rate, with substantial further exchange rate depreciation throughout 1997 and early 1998. Hong Kong was a notable exception, maintaining its fixed exchange rate, although in one two-hour period it spent US$1 billion defending the Hong Kong dollar.

To limit depreciation and help solve their banking problems,

South Korean stock investors contemplate in front of the electronic stock index board, at the Daeyu Security house in Seoul, Korea.

countries such as Thailand and Indonesia sought loans from the IMF. A condition of these loans was that the recipients had to pursue tight monetary and fiscal policies. These conditions have been sharply criticized by economists such as Joseph Stiglitz (former chief economist of the World Bank and now at Stanford University) and Paul Krugman (Princeton University). Let us use our analysis of the last four chapters to see why.

In terms of the money demand/money supply model of Chapters 11 and 12, the banking collapse can be somewhat crudely modelled as a leftward shift of the money supply curve, as in Figure 1 here. The main consequence was sharply higher interest rates. The imposed tight money policy moved the money supply curve still farther to the left with still higher interest rates.

The loss of confidence also reduced consumption and investment and, as in the Keynes cross model of Chapters 9 and 10 in Figure 2, multiplier effects reduced output still further. The effects were worsened by the tight monetary policy (increased interest rates reduce investment) and the tight fiscal policy prescribed by the IMF. In sum, the Asian countries experienced what has been described as the worst decline in output since the Great Depression.

Recovery began in 1999, South Korea in particular experiencing rapid growth. While there is also controversy about the causes of the turnaround, *The Economist* has argued that a principal factor was the relaxation of fiscal policy, so that by 1999 most of the countries were running government budget deficits designed to finance expansionary fiscal policies such as tax cuts and infrastructure projects. Another factor was clearly the export boom due to the exchange rate depreciations.

Hence the IMF's critics argue that its tight monetary and fiscal policies made the recession deeper and longer. The IMF's response is that these policies were necessary to prevent an exchange rate fall that would have made the situation still worse, particularly since many Southeast Asian firms had borrowed in U.S. dollars, and the greater the depreciation of the domestic currency the harder it would have been to repay these loans. In any case, domestic firms were hurt by the high interest rates associated with tight money. Possibly there were no good options, given that the IMF was unable to provide the truly massive support that would have been required to support the central banks (and indirectly the banking systems) of the affected countries.

Paul Krugman draws this lesson from the crisis: "… the essential truth of Keynes's big idea—that even the most productive economy can fail if consumers and investors spend too little, that the pursuit of sound money and balanced budgets is sometimes (not always!) folly rather than wisdom—is as evident in today's world as it was in the 1930s."

Questions for Analytical Thinking

1. The Asian economic crisis affected Canada to some degree, particularly the resource sector and particularly British Columbia. Explain why.

2. The IMF prescribed similar tight monetary and fiscal policy in the bailout of Mexico in 1996, yet Mexico recovered much more quickly from a similar recession and exchange rate collapse. This is generally attributed to the booming U.S. economy. Explain why, and why the slumping Japanese economy was a contributing factor in prolonging the Asian crisis.

3. A common investment forecast during the economic crisis was that companies that produced within Thailand and Indonesia but exported to world markets would do well. Explain the rationale behind such a forecast, emphasizing the importance of the exchange rate.

Sources: "On Their Feet Again?" *The Economist*, August 19, 1999, **www.econo mist.com/displayStory.cfm?Story_ID=23318 4CFID=753297CFTOEN=52069276**; Joseph Stiglitz, "What I Learned at the World Economic Crisis," *The New Republic*, April 17, 2000, **www.tnr.com/ 041700/stiglitz041700.html**; Paul Krugman, "Why Aren't We All Keynesians Yet?" *Fortune*, August 3, 1998, **web.mit.edu/krug man/www/keynes.html**; Paul Krugman, "Recovery? Don't Bet on It," The Unofficial Paul Krugman Web Page, **www.pkarchive. org/ crises/cover1.html**.

Video Resource: "Asian Economies: Toothless Tigers?" *News in Review*, February 1998.

Figure 2

The collapse in confidence led to a downward shift of the AE curve as consumption and investment fell. The higher interest rates from the tight monetary policy plus the reduction in government expenditure and increase in taxes from the tight fiscal policy led to a further downward shift in AE.

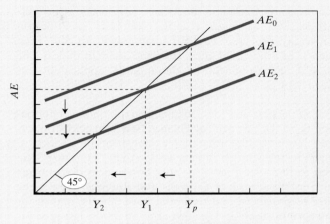

Aggregate output (income), Y

Web References for Part Three: Macroeconomic Principles and Policy

With respect to the Asian crisis and much else to do with the global macroeconomy, one of the best and most comprehensive sites is maintained by Columbia University professor Nouriel Roubini (**www.stern.nyu.edu/global macro/**). And as noted in the case, one of the most interesting commentators on the Asian crisis (which he predicted) as well as much else in economics is Princeton University professor Paul Krugman (**www.mit.edu/~krug man/**). As you would guess from the quote in the case, he is a noted proponent of the modern applicability of Keynesian ideas.

One of the best sites for Canadian macroeconomic information is the Department of Finance (**www.fin.gc.ca/**). It has the latest budget information plus statements on a variety of topics by the Minister of Finance. Go to its "HotLinks" section to find useful links to other government departments such as the Canadian Customs and Revenue Agency, the sites of provincial and territorial governments, and major financial institutions. One favourite site in the last group is the Toronto-Dominion Bank's economic reports (**www.tdbank.ca/**). Click on "Economic Reports" to find useful forecasts and economic commentary by province, for Canada as a whole and internationally.

The federal government's Policy Research Initiative site (**policyresearch.schoolnet.ca/**) is an excellent starting point for many policy-oriented searches. Click on "Links to Policy Research Organizations" to get a menu of many such groups and then click on "Canadian Policy Research Institutions" to get a variety of links from the Atlantic Provinces Economic Council to the Canada West Foundation, and from the Canadian Centre for Policy Alternatives (check out their "Alternative Federal Budget" for a left-of-centre economics perspective on federal budgetary policy) to the more conservative C. D. Howe Institute or Fraser Institute.

Bond ratings for the bonds of the federal government of Canada, as well as provincial and municipal governments and corporations, are available from the Dominion Bond Rating Service (**www.dbrs.com/**).

Another good site is operated by the Bank of Canada (**www.bankofcanada.ca/**). In the "English" section, click on "Monetary Policy" and then on "How Monetary Policy Works" for a graphical module consistent with our Chapter 11 and 12 analysis. (Remember, the Bank of Canada view is that to dampen inflation, spending must be reduced.) For other data sources, the Web addresses after Part Two also apply.

13

Money, the Interest Rate, and Output: Analysis and Policy

Learning Objectives

1 Outline how the interest rate affects investment in the goods market.

2 Describe how interest rate effects on the exchange rate affect net exports in the goods market.

3 Explain how aggregate output (income) affects the interest rate in the money market.

4 Distinguish between fiscal and monetary policy and expansionary and contractionary policy.

5 Describe crowding out.

6 List four main determinants of planned investment.

The Links Between the Goods Market and the Money Market

The Interest Rate and the Goods Market

Money Demand, Aggregate Output (Income), and the Money Market

Combining the Goods Market and the Money Market

Expansionary Policy Effects

Contractionary Policy Effects

The Macroeconomic Policy Mix

The Macroeconomic Policy Mix in Canada in the New Century

More on the Determinants of Planned Investment

Looking Ahead: The Price Level

I n Chapters 9 and 10, we discussed the market for goods and services—the **goods market**—without mentioning money, the money market, or the interest rate. We described how the equilibrium level of aggregate output (income) (Y) is determined in the goods market. At given levels of planned investment spending (I), government spending (G), exports (EX), imports (IM), and net taxes (T), we were able to determine the equilibrium level of output in the economy.

In Chapters 11 and 12, we discussed the financial market, or **money market**, with only passing references to the goods market, as we explained how the equilibrium level of the interest rate is determined in the money market and how this affects the exchange rate.

The goods market and the money market do not operate independently, however. Events in the money market have important effects on the goods market, and events in the goods market have important effects on the money market. Only by analyzing the two markets together can we determine the values of aggregate output (income) (Y) and the interest rate (r) that are consistent with the existence of equilibrium in *both* markets.

Looking at the two markets simultaneously also reveals how fiscal policy affects the money market and how monetary policy affects the goods market. This is our task in this chapter. By establishing how the markets affect each other, we will show how open market purchases of government securities (which expand the money supply) affect the equilibrium level of aggregate output and income. Similarly, we will show how fiscal policy measures (such as tax cuts) affect interest rates, exchange rates, investment

goods market *The market in which goods and services are exchanged and in which the equilibrium level of aggregate output is determined.*

money market *The market in which financial instruments are exchanged and in which the equilibrium level of the interest rate is determined.*

spending, and exports and imports. (We will assume that the exchange rate is flexible, as it is in Canada.) In this chapter, we will focus on output effects and assume no price-level effects; in the next chapter, we will include price-level effects.

The Links Between the Goods Market and the Money Market

There are two key *links* between the goods market and the money market.

■ **Link 1: Spending and Money Markets** The first link between the goods market and financial markets exists because some components of spending depend on prices in financial markets, in particular on interest rates and exchange rates. In Chapters 9 and 10 we assumed that planned investment spending (I) is fixed at a certain level, but we did so only to simplify our initial discussion. In practice, investment is not fixed and depends upon a number of variables, including the interest rate (r). The higher the interest rate, the lower the level of planned investment spending. (Interest rate increases may also dampen other types of spending such as consumption as we discuss in Chapter 17.)

There is another aspect to this link. As we just saw in the previous chapter, interest rates influence exchange rates. If Canadian interest rates rise relative to international interest rates, the Canadian dollar will appreciate and if Canadian interest rates fall relative to international interest rates, the Canadian dollar will tend to depreciate. These changes in the value of the Canadian dollar can affect exports (EX), imports (IM), and hence net exports ($EX - IM$).

Suppose the Canadian dollar appreciates in value and Canadian prices do not change. This means that Canadian exported goods and services become more expensive. Foreign buyers will buy fewer Canadian exports. Also, in Canada, the more valuable Canadian dollar makes imported goods cheaper and Canadians will buy more imported goods and services. Hence net exports (exports minus imports) will tend to fall if the Canadian dollar increases in value. Similarly, if the Canadian dollar depreciates, Canadian exports become cheaper on foreign markets and imports to Canada become more expensive. Net exports will tend to increase.

> The interest rate, which is determined in the money market, has important effects on planned investment. Changes in interest rates relative to international interest rates also affect the exchange rate, which affects net exports. Both planned investment and net exports are components of planned aggregate expenditure in the goods market.

■ **Link 2: Income and the Demand for Money** The second link between the goods market and the money market exists because the demand for money depends on income. As aggregate output (income) (Y) increases, the number of transactions requiring the use of money increases. (This point should also be fresh in your mind from the previous chapter.) Thus, an increase in output, with the interest rate held constant, leads to an increase in money demand. This leads us to conclude that:

> Income, which is determined in the goods market, has an important influence on the demand for money in the money market.

We examine these links in more detail in the sections that follow.

THE INTEREST RATE AND THE GOODS MARKET

It should come as no surprise that the relationship between the level of planned investment and the interest rate is a negative one.

> When the interest rate falls, planned investment rises.
> When the interest rate rises, planned investment falls.

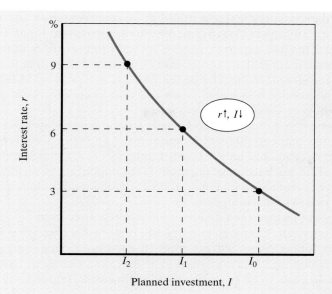

FIGURE 13.1

Planned Investment Schedule

Planned investment spending is a negative function of the interest rate.

To see why, recall that *investment* refers to the purchase of new capital—new machines and plants. Whether a firm decides to invest in a project depends upon whether the expected profits from the project justify its costs. One of the important costs of an investment project is the interest cost.

Consider a firm opening a new plant, or the investment required to open a new ice cream store. When a manufacturing firm builds a new plant, the contractor must be paid at the time the plant is built. When an entrepreneur decides to open a new ice cream parlour, she needs freezers, tables, chairs, light fixtures, and signs. These too must be paid for when they are installed.

The money needed to carry out such projects is generally borrowed and paid back over an extended period of time. Thus, the real cost of an investment project depends in part on the interest rate—the cost of borrowing. When the interest rate rises, it becomes more expensive to borrow, and fewer projects are likely to be undertaken;[1] increasing the interest rate, *ceteris paribus,* is likely to reduce the level of planned investment spending. Similarly, when the interest rate falls, it becomes less costly to borrow, and more investment projects are likely to be undertaken; reducing the interest rate, *ceteris paribus,* is likely to increase the level of planned investment spending.

The relationship between the interest rate and planned investment is illustrated by the downward-sloping demand curve in Figure 13.1. The higher the interest rate, the lower the level of planned investment. At an interest rate of 3%, planned investment is I_0. As the interest rate rises from 3% to 6% to 9%, planned investment falls from I_0 to I_1 to I_2. As the interest rate falls, however, more projects become profitable, so more investment is undertaken.

These direct effects of interest rates on planned investment would be sufficient for our discussion if the interest rate changes were "international," for example, if Canadian interest rates were changing along with U.S. interest rates. But if Canadian interest rates are changing independently (remembering from Chapter 12 that this is only possible with flexible and not fixed exchange rates), the Canadian dollar will change in value. As discussed in Chapter 12, an increase in Canadian interest rates relative to international interest rates will tend to appreciate the Canadian dollar and a decrease in Canadian interest rates relative to international interest rates will tend to depreciate the Canadian dollar. This will have effects on Canadian exports and imports.

---

[1] *Even if the firm has sufficient funds to pay for a project without borrowing, a higher interest rate means a higher opportunity cost of using those funds so that it may be more profitable to lend the money out or reduce existing debts rather than invest in the project.*

Suppose the Canadian dollar is priced at 75 cents American and it appreciates to par, that is, 100 cents American. Assuming Canadian-dollar prices do not change, every Canadian export now costs more in terms of U.S. currency. For example, a Canadian apple that cost 24 cents Canadian would cost $0.75 \times 24 = 18$ cents American before the appreciation but 24 cents American (= 24 cents Canadian) after the appreciation. These higher prices will discourage Americans and other foreigners from buying Canadian exports.

By the same token, imports into Canada will now be cheaper. For example, an American orange that cost 30 cents American will cost $30/0.75 = 40$ cents Canadian before the appreciation but only 30 cents Canadian (= 30 cents American) after the appreciation. This will encourage imports. As the appreciated Canadian dollar both decreases exports and increases imports, it clearly will tend to decrease net exports, which equal exports minus imports.

Now suppose instead the Canadian dollar depreciates from 75 cents American to 50 cents American. Canadian exports will now be cheaper. (Our Canadian apple price in the United States will fall from 18 cents to 12 cents American.) Imports to Canada will now be more expensive. (The American orange in Canada increases in price from 40 cents to 60 cents.) Exports will increase, imports will decrease and hence net exports will increase.

How do these effects of interest rate changes in turn affect aggregate output? Recall that planned aggregate expenditure (AE) is the sum of consumption (C), planned investment (I), government purchases (G), and net exports ($EX - IM$).

$$AE \equiv C + I + G + EX - IM$$

An increase in interest rates will reduce planned aggregate expenditure at least by reducing planned investment and (if Canadian interest rates are increasing relative to international interest rates so that the exchange rate appreciates) by reducing net exports. Similarly, a decrease in interest rates will tend to increase planned aggregate expenditure through some combination of increases in investment and net exports.

Figure 13.2 illustrates what might happen to planned aggregate expenditure in the Keynesian cross model of Chapter 10 when the interest rate rises from 3% to 6%. Because of the higher interest rates and the resulting reductions in planned investment and net exports, the planned aggregate expenditure schedule shifts downward. As you should recall for this model, a fall in any component of aggregate

FIGURE 13.2

The Effect of an Interest Rate Increase on Planned Aggregate Expenditure

An increase in the interest rate from 3% to 6% lowers planned aggregate expenditure and thus reduces equilibrium income from Y_0 to Y_1.

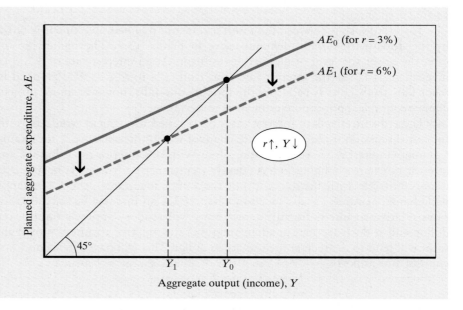

spending has a larger (or "multiplier") effect on equilibrium income (Y). Thus, the fall in equilibrium output (income) in this model will be larger than the downward shift in planned aggregate expenditure, that is, larger than the total fall in investment and net exports. In Figure 13.2, equilibrium Y falls from Y_0 to Y_1 when the interest rate rises.

We can summarize the effects of a change in the interest rate on the equilibrium level of output in this model:

> *Effects of a change in the Interest Rate:*
>
> ■ An increase in the interest rate (r) reduces planned investment (I) and, if the interest rate is rising relative to international interest rates, leads to an appreciation of the exchange rate, which reduces net exports ($EX - IM$).
> ■ Planned investment and net exports are part of planned aggregate expenditure (AE).
> ■ Thus, when the interest rate rises, planned aggregate expenditure (AE) at every level of income falls.
> ■ Finally, a decrease in planned aggregate expenditure lowers equilibrium output (income) (Y) by a multiple of the initial total decrease in planned investment and net exports.
>
> Using a convenient shorthand:
>
> $$r \uparrow \; \rightarrow I \downarrow, \; EX - IM \downarrow \; \rightarrow AE \downarrow \; \rightarrow Y \downarrow$$
>
> $$r \downarrow \; \rightarrow I \uparrow, \; EX - IM \uparrow \; \rightarrow AE \uparrow \; \rightarrow Y \uparrow$$
>
> In each case remember that the effect of r on $EX - IM$ comes through the exchange rate.

As you can see, the equilibrium level of output (Y) is not determined solely by events in the goods market, as we assumed in our earlier simplified discussions. The reason is that the money market affects the level of the interest rate, which then affects planned investment and net exports in the goods market. There is a different equilibrium level of Y for every possible level of the interest rate (r). The final level of equilibrium Y depends on what the interest rate turns out to be, which depends on events in the money market.

MONEY DEMAND, AGGREGATE OUTPUT (INCOME), AND THE MONEY MARKET

We have just seen how the interest rate—which is determined in the money market—influences the level of planned investment spending and thus the goods market. Now let us review the ways in which the goods market affects the money market.

In Chapter 12, we explored the demand for money by households and firms and explained why the demand for money depends negatively on the interest rate. An increase in the interest rate raises the opportunity cost of holding non-interest-bearing money (as compared to interest-bearing bonds), thus encouraging people to keep more of their funds in bonds and less of their funds in chequing account balances. The downward-sloping money demand curve (M^d) is shown in Figure 13.3.

We also saw in Chapter 12 that the demand for money depends on the level of income in the economy. More income means more transactions, and an increased volume of transactions implies a greater demand for money. With more people earning higher incomes and buying more goods and services, more money will be demanded to meet the increased volume of transactions. An increase in income therefore shifts the money demand curve to the right. (Review Figure 12.2 if necessary.)

FIGURE 13.3

Equilibrium in the Money Market

If the interest rate were 9%, the quantity of money in circulation would exceed the amount that households and firms want to hold. The excess money balances would cause the interest rate to drop as people try to shift their funds into interest-bearing bonds. At 3% the opposite is true. Excess demand for money balances would push interest rates up. Only at 6% would the actual quantity of money in circulation be equal to what the economy wants to hold in money balances.

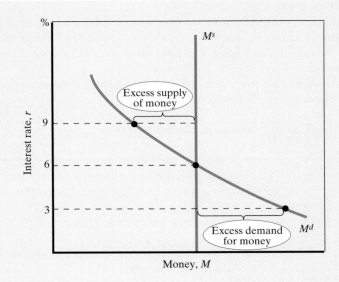

If, as we are assuming, the central bank's choice of the amount of money to supply does not depend on the interest rate, then the money supply curve is simply a vertical line. The equilibrium interest rate is the point at which the quantity of money demanded equals the quantity of money supplied. This equilibrium is shown at a 6% interest rate in Figure 13.3. If the amount of money demanded by households and firms is less than the amount in circulation as determined by the central bank, as it is at an interest rate of 9% in Figure 13.3, the interest rate will fall. If the amount of money demanded is greater than the amount in circulation, as it is at an interest rate of 3% in Figure 13.3, the interest rate will rise.

Now consider what will happen to the interest rate when there is an increase in aggregate output (income) (Y). This increase in Y will cause the money demand curve to shift to the right. This is illustrated in Figure 13.4, where an increase in income from Y_0 to Y_1 has shifted the money demand curve from M_0^d to M_1^d. At the initial interest rate of 6%, there is now excess demand for money, and the interest rate rises from 6% to 9%.

The equilibrium level of the interest rate is not determined exclusively in the money market. Changes in aggregate output (income) (Y), which take place in the goods market, shift the money demand curve and cause changes in the interest rate. With a given quantity of money supplied, higher levels of Y will lead to higher equilibrium levels of r. Lower levels of Y will lead to lower equilibrium levels of r. To use our convenient shorthand:

$$Y \uparrow \rightarrow M^d \uparrow \rightarrow r \uparrow$$

$$Y \downarrow \rightarrow M^d \downarrow \rightarrow r \downarrow$$

Combining the Goods Market and the Money Market

Now that we are aware of the links between the goods market and the money market, we can examine the two markets simultaneously. To see how the two markets

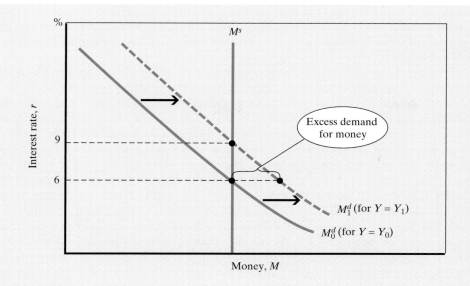

FIGURE 13.4

The Effect of an Increase in Income (Y) on the Interest Rate (r)

An increase in income from Y_0 to Y_1 shifts the M^d curve to the right. With a fixed supply of money, there is now an excess demand for money ($M^d > M^s$) at the initial interest rate of 6%. This causes the interest rate to rise. At an interest rate of 9% the money market is again in equilibrium with $M^s = M^d$, but at a higher interest rate than before the increase in income.

interact, it will be convenient to consider the effects of changes in fiscal and monetary policy on the economy. Specifically, we want to examine what happens to the equilibrium levels of aggregate output (income) (Y) and the interest rate (r) when certain key variables—notably government spending (G), net taxes (T), and the money supply (M^s)—increase or decrease.

EXPANSIONARY POLICY EFFECTS

Any government policy that would tend to stimulate aggregate output (income) (Y) is said to be expansionary. An **expansionary fiscal policy** is an increase in government spending (G) or a reduction in net taxes (T). An **expansionary monetary policy** is a policy to increase the money supply.

expansionary fiscal policy *An increase in government spending or a reduction in net taxes.*

expansionary monetary policy *A policy to increase the money supply.*

■ **Expansionary Fiscal Policy: An Increase in Government Purchases (G) or Decrease in Net Taxes (T)**   As you know from Chapter 10, government purchases (G) and net taxes (T) are the two tools of government fiscal policy. The government can stimulate the economy—that is, it can increase aggregate output (income) (Y)—either by *increasing* government purchases or by *reducing* net taxes. While the impact of a tax cut is somewhat smaller than the impact of an increase in G in the model of Chapter 10, both have a multiplier effect on the equilibrium level of Y.

Consider, for example, an increase in government purchases (G) of $10 billion. This increase in expenditure causes firms' inventories to be smaller than planned. Unplanned inventory reductions stimulate production, and firms increase output (Y). But because added output means added income, some of which is subsequently spent, consumption spending (C) also increases. Again, inventories will be smaller than planned and output will rise even further. The final equilibrium level of output is thus higher by a multiple of the initial increase in government purchases.

This multiplier story is incomplete, however, because we have not allowed for effects of changes in the interest rate, which we ignored in Chapter 10. As aggregate output (income) (Y) increases, an impact is felt in the money market. Specifically, the increase in income (Y) increases the demand for money (M^d). For a given money supply (M^s) this causes the interest rate (r) to rise[2] and hence planned investment (I) to fall. The rise in the interest rate also will lead to an appreciation in the exchange rate and hence cause net exports ($EX - IM$) to fall.

Hence an increase in government purchases (G) tends to reduce investment (I) and net exports ($EX - IM$). Because planned investment and net exports are components of planned aggregate expenditure ($AE = C + I + G + EX - IM$), the de-

---

[2]*A more commonsense version of this explanation, which nonetheless captures the essence, is that the money for the increase in government spending must be borrowed and that this increase in the rate of borrowing increases the demand for loans and hence increases interest rates.*

creases in I and $EX - IM$ work against the increase in G. The expansionary effect of the increase in government purchases on planned aggregate expenditure and aggregate output will tend to be partially offset by reductions in planned investment and net exports.

Perhaps because planned investment is so critical for long-term growth in the economy, many economists have concentrated on the tendency for increases in government spending to cause reductions in private investment spending, called the **crowding-out effect**. We illustrate it in Figure 13.5, *where to keep things simple, we do not include effects on net exports* (as if net exports happened not to be sensitive to changes in the exchange rate). An increase in government purchases from G_0 to G_1 shifts the planned aggregate expenditure curve ($C + I_0 + G_0 + EX - IM$) upward. The increase in (Y) from Y_0 to Y_1 causes the demand for money to rise, which results in a disequilibrium in the money market. The excess demand for money raises the interest rate (r) from r_0 to r_1, causing I to decrease from I_0 to I_1. The fall in I pulls the planned aggregate expenditure curve back down, which lowers the equilibrium level of income to Y^*. (Remember that equilibrium is achieved when $Y = AE$.) If net exports were sensitive to the exchange rate, the exchange rate appreciation that accompanies the higher interest rate would lead to a reduction in net exports and an additional downward shift of the planned aggregate expenditure line. The equilibrium output would be lower than Y^*, although not as low as Y_0.

The crowding-out effect depends on the **sensitivity** or **insensitivity of planned investment** spending to changes in the interest rate. Crowding out occurs because a higher interest rate reduces planned investment spending. Investment depends on factors other than the interest rate, however, and investment may at times be quite insensitive to changes in the interest rate. If planned investment does not fall when the interest rate rises, there is no investment crowding-out effect. For more details on one

crowding-out effect *The tendency for increases in government spending to cause reductions in private investment spending.*

interest sensitivity or **insensitivity of planned investment** *The responsiveness of planned investment spending to changes in the interest rate.* Interest sensitivity *means that planned investment spending changes a great deal in response to changes in the interest rate;* interest insensitivity *means little or no change in planned investment as a result of changes in the interest rate.*

FIGURE 13.5

The Crowding-Out Effect (Without Net Export Effects)

An increase in government spending G from G_0 to G_1 shifts the planned aggregate expenditure curve from 1 to 2. The crowding-out effect of the decrease in planned investment (brought about by the increased interest rate) then shifts the planned aggregate expenditure curve from 2 to 3.

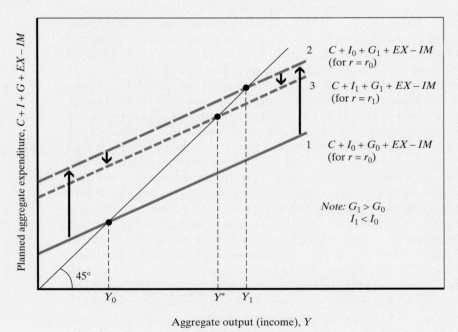

type of investment that is usually sensitive to interest-rate changes, see the Application box titled "How Interest Rates Affect Investment: The Case of New Housing."

Exactly the same reasoning holds for changes in net taxes. The ultimate effect of a tax cut on the equilibrium level of output depends on how the money market reacts. The expansion of Y that a tax cut brings about will lead to an increase in the interest rate and an appreciation of the Canadian dollar and thus a decrease in planned investment spending and net exports. The increase in Y will therefore be less than it would be if the interest rate did not rise.

To summarize the effects of an expansionary fiscal policy, we can write:

| Effects of an Expansionary Fiscal Policy: | $G \uparrow$ or $T \downarrow \rightarrow Y \uparrow \rightarrow M^d \uparrow \rightarrow r \uparrow \rightarrow I \downarrow, EX - IM \downarrow$
 $\rightarrow Y$ increases less than if r did not increase. |

■ Expansionary Monetary Policy: An Increase in the Money Supply

As has just been argued, under a flexible exchange rate regime such as Canada's, the effects of fiscal policy may be at least partially offset by reductions in planned investment and net exports. This may explain why much of the discussion (and criticism) of Canada's economic performance concentrates on monetary policy and the Bank of Canada. Note that, at least in our model so far, the Bank of Canada could prevent the rise in interest rates and the exchange rate (and the associated crowding-out effects) by expanding the money supply (M^s) to offset the increase in the demand for money (M^d) due to the fiscal expansion.[3]

What happens when, regardless of the current fiscal policy, the Bank of Canada decides to increase the supply of money through open market operations? At first, open market operations create excess reserves in the system and expand the quantity of money supplied (that is, the money supply curve shifts to the right). Because the quantity of money supplied is now greater than the amount households want to hold, the equilibrium rate of interest falls. Planned investment spending increases when the interest rate falls. If the fall in interest rates is relative to international interest rates, the Canadian dollar will depreciate and net exports will also increase. The increases in planned investment spending and net exports, in whatever combination, tend to increase output (Y). Hence an increase in the money supply tends to decrease the interest rate, depreciate the exchange rate, and increase output.[4]

If you review the sequence of events that follows the monetary expansion, you can see the links between the injection of excess reserves into the economy and the increase in output. First, the increase in the quantity of money supplied pushes down the interest rate. Second, the lower interest rate causes planned investment spending to rise and (through the exchange rate depreciation) net exports to rise as well. Third, the increase in these spending components means higher planned aggregate expenditure, which means increased output as firms react to unplanned decreases in inventories.

| Effects of an Expansionary Monetary Policy: | $M^s \uparrow \rightarrow r \downarrow \rightarrow I \uparrow, EX - IM \uparrow \rightarrow Y \uparrow$ |

It is worth reemphasizing here that the effects of r on $EX - IM$ come through an exchange rate depreciation.

The power of monetary policy depends on how much of a reaction occurs at each link of this chain. Perhaps most critically, it will matter how the monetary expansion

---

[3]Continuing our explanation from footnote 2, the Bank could in effect supply the money directly to the government to prevent government public borrowing from driving up interest rates.
[4]The increase in output (Y) will tend in turn to increase the demand for money and soften the effects on the exchange rate and the interest rate, but these complications are much less important than the main result for this model, that monetary expansion can expand output.

Recall from Chapter 7 that purchases of newly constructed houses are part of investment. This component of planned investment is one that is usually sensitive to changes in interest rates. House purchases are generally financed with a mortgage, a type of long-term loan. Thus part of the price of a house is the mortgage interest that must be paid.

Housing starts are a widely followed statistic in the Canadian economy. The number of housing starts in a given year is the number of residential units on which construction has begun in that year. Residential units include all types of dwellings, from single-family detached homes to row houses to apartment units.

The early 1980s were a time of very high interest rates by historical standards, largely because of tight monetary policy in Canada, echoing a similar tight money policy in the United States. Nominal mortgage rates increased from about 12% to about 18% from 1979 to 1982. The real mortgage rate (the nominal mortgage rate minus the inflation rate) rose from less than 4% to over 7% during the same period. It is not

When interest rates go down, it becomes less expensive to purchase a house. As a result, more new houses may be built and planned investment may increase.

surprising that such a large change in interest rates had an effect on housing starts, which declined by 36%. Starts of single-family detached homes declined by 46%. This decline was of course partially due to the 1980–1982 recession, but one reason for the recession was the high interest rates and their effect on interest-sensitive sectors such as construction.

By the mid-1990s, Canada was slowly coming out of the 1990–1991 recession. Between 1995 and 1996, the nominal mortgage

rate fell from about 9% to about 8%, reducing the real rate from about 7% to just over 6%. This was because of an easier monetary policy and the contractionary fiscal policy by all levels of government. (As discussed in this chapter, a contractionary fiscal policy involves less government borrowing and hence lower interest rates.) Housing starts rose by 10% and single-family detached-home starts increased by 27%. Lower interest rates helped stimulate housing investment.

affects interest rates and exchange rates and then how sensitive planned investment is to interest rates and how sensitive net exports are to exchange rate changes.

CONTRACTIONARY POLICY EFFECTS

Any government policy that would tend to reduce aggregate output (income) (Y) is said to be *contractionary*. Where expansionary policy is used to boost the economy, contractionary policy may be used to slow the economy. The effects of contractionary policy are just the reverse of those of expansionary policy: we go over them largely for review.

Why would the government adopt policies designed to reduce aggregate spending? As we will see in more detail in the next two chapters, one of the ways to fight inflation is to reduce aggregate spending. Thus, when the inflation rate is high, the government may feel compelled to use its powers to contract the economy. At other times, the government may have little choice but to pursue a contractionary policy. This would be the case when, for example, government spending must be reduced due to mounting debt.

contractionary fiscal policy
A decrease in government spending or an increase in net taxes.

■ **Contractionary Fiscal Policy: A Decrease in Government Spending (G) or an Increase in Net Taxes (T)** A **contractionary fiscal policy** is a decrease in government spending (G) or an increase in net taxes (T). The effects of this policy are the opposite of the effects of an expansionary fiscal policy.

A decrease in government purchases or an increase in net taxes leads to a decrease in aggregate output (income) (Y), a decrease in the demand for money (M^d), and a decrease in the interest rate (r). The decrease in Y that accompanies a contractionary fiscal policy is less than it would be if we did not take the money market into account because the decrease in r also causes planned investment (I) to *increase* and also leads to an exchange rate depreciation, which increases net exports ($EX - IM$). This offsets some of the decrease in planned aggregate expenditure brought about by the decrease in G or the increase in T.

Effects of a Contractionary Fiscal Policy:	$G \downarrow$ or $T \uparrow \rightarrow Y \downarrow \rightarrow M^d \downarrow \rightarrow r \downarrow \rightarrow I \uparrow, EX - IM \uparrow$ ⌐
	└→ Y decreases less than if r did not decrease.

■ **Contractionary Monetary Policy: A Decrease in the Money Supply**   A **contractionary monetary policy** is a policy to decrease the money supply. This decrease increases interest rates and leads to an appreciation of the exchange rate, reducing planned investment, net exports and hence output (income) (Y).

contractionary monetary policy *A policy to decrease the money supply.*

Effects of a Contractionary Monetary Policy:	$M^s \downarrow \rightarrow r \uparrow \rightarrow I \downarrow, EX - IM \downarrow \rightarrow Y \downarrow$

THE MACROECONOMIC POLICY MIX

Although we've been treating fiscal and monetary policy separately, it should be clear that fiscal and monetary policy can be used simultaneously. For example, both government purchases (G) and the money supply (M^s) can be increased at the same time. We have seen that an increase in G by itself raises both Y and r, while an increase in M^s by itself raises Y but lowers r. Therefore, if the government wanted to increase Y without changing r, it could do so by increasing both G and M^s by the appropriate amounts.

The term **policy mix** refers to the combination of monetary and fiscal policies in use at a given time. A policy mix that consists of a decrease in government spending and an increase in the money supply would favour investment spending over government spending. This is because both the increased money supply and the fall in government purchases would cause the interest rate to fall, which would lead to an increase in planned investment. The opposite is true for a mix that consists of an expansionary fiscal policy and a contractionary monetary policy. This mix favours government spending over investment spending. Such a policy will have the effect of increasing government spending and reducing the money supply. Tight money and expanded government spending would drive the interest rate up and planned investment down.

policy mix *The combination of monetary and fiscal policies in use at a given time.*

There is no hard-and-fast rule about what constitutes the "best" policy mix or the "best" composition of output. On this, as on many other issues, economists (and others) disagree. In part, one's preference for a certain composition of output—that is, the mix between private spending and government spending—depends on how one stands on such issues as the optimal role of government in the economy.

Table 13.1 summarizes the effects of various combinations of policies on several important macroeconomic variables in this model. If you can explain the reasoning underlying each of the effects shown in the table, you can be satisfied that you have a good understanding of the links between the goods market and the money market. (*Hint*: To determine interest rate effects, use the money supply/money demand diagram. Note that sometimes when both curves shift in the same direction, it cannot be determined whether interest rates increase, decrease, or stay the same. When the policies clash, that is, one is expansionary and the other is contractionary, it is straightforward to see that output can increase, decrease, or stay the same depending on the strength and extent of the policy measures.)

THE MACROECONOMIC POLICY MIX IN CANADA IN THE NEW CENTURY

Let us review the past 25 years of macroeconomic policy in Canada with a view to understanding the current position. In the late 1970s, mounting inflation led the U.S. central bank, the Federal Reserve, to pursue a tight monetary policy. (Chapter 14 discusses why a contractionary policy might reduce the rate of inflation.) U.S. interest rates increased; as we have seen, this puts downward pressure on the value of the Canadian dollar. Perhaps for this reason, the Bank of Canada largely followed the U.S. contractionary monetary policy and Canadian interest rates rose sharply as well. Just as described in this chapter, the high interest rates cut investment, particularly housing investment, and the economy suffered a sharp recession.

By 1982 the United States switched to an expansionary monetary policy, again largely followed by the Bank of Canada. The effects combined with expansionary fiscal policy and the benefits from increased exports to an expanding U.S. economy, and the Canadian economy began to grow steadily. However, there was a North American recession in the fall of 1990. This is sometimes partly attributed to a sharp drop in consumer confidence after Iraq's invasion of Kuwait in the summer of 1990. (In our model, this would be a downward shift of the consumption function.) The American recession was short-lived, and the United States began a steady expansion that continued through to this century, with the unemployment rate falling to the 4% range.

The Canadian recovery was much slower, because, in the view of many economists, the Bank of Canada stayed too long with a contractionary monetary policy to bring down inflation, which peaked at 5.6% in 1991. Government debt problems also led to higher taxes and cutbacks in government expenditure (contractionary fiscal policy) at both the federal and the provincial level. By the mid-1990s the Bank of Canada had moved toward a looser monetary policy; combined with the continued tight fiscal policy, this led to lower interest rates and depreciation of the Canadian dollar, just as our model would predict. The lower interest rates stimulated Canadian investment. The lower the value of the Canadian dollar, in combination with strong demand from the expanding U.S. economy, led to Canadian exports more than doubling in real terms during the 1990s. So the Canadian unemployment rate, which had peaked at over 11% in 1993, finally fell below 8% in 1999 and then below 7% as the new century began.

At the beginning of the new century, the Canadian macroeconomic policy mix included a mild tightening of monetary policy, with an increase in the Bank rate in the early part of the year 2000. Fiscal policy remained relatively tight: the overall government surplus of taxes over expenditure, at almost 3% of GDP, was the largest among the G-7 countries. (Contrast Japan, where government was running a *deficit* of almost 7% of GDP.) Much discussion centred on loosening fiscal policy, either by cutting taxes or by increasing expenditure on government programs.

More on the Determinants of Planned Investment

We have assumed in this chapter that planned investment depends only on the interest rate. Here we discuss some other factors and some complications.

■ **Real Interest Rates**   As we discussed in Chapter 8, the **real interest rate** is the interest rate minus the rate of inflation. In this chapter, we focused on output effects by assuming a constant price level and hence no inflation. But in the real world, where the price level can change, which should matter more for planned investment spending, the actual interest rate (sometimes called the **nominal interest rate**) or the real interest rate?

The answer is the real interest rate. To take an example, suppose Leon is considering investing in a new $1000 sign for his business either this year or next year. If he buys it this year he has to borrow the $1000; next year he will have sufficient funds to pay cash. The 8% rate of interest Leon will have to pay on the loan encourages him to postpone the purchase and save the $80 in interest. But then Leon takes the 3% inflation rate into account and recognizes that the sign will likely cost 3% more next year or $1030. So if he borrows he will pay $1080 next year, in-

real interest rate *The interest rate minus the inflation rate.*

nominal interest rate *Another name for the actual interest rate. The word "nominal" is added to the term to distinguish it from the real interest rate.*

Table 13.1	The Effects of the Macroeconomic Policy Mix		

		FISCAL	
		Expansionary ($\uparrow G$ OR $\downarrow T$)	**Contractionary** ($\downarrow G$ OR $\uparrow T$)
MONETARY	**Expansionary** ($\uparrow M^s$)	$Y\uparrow,r?,I?$ (EX–IM)?, C$\uparrow$	$Y?,r\downarrow,I\uparrow$ (EX – IM)$\uparrow$, C?
	Contractionary ($\downarrow M^s$)	$Y?,r\uparrow,I\downarrow$ (EX–IM)$\downarrow$, C?	$Y\downarrow,r?,I?$ (EX – IM)?, C$\downarrow$

Key

$\uparrow$: Variable increases.

$\downarrow$: Variable decreases.

? : Forces push the variable in different directions. Without additional information, we cannot specify which way the variable moves.

cluding the interest; if he does not borrow but waits, he will pay $1030. The difference is $1080 – $1030 = $50. Hence the real interest rate is $50 on $1000 or 5% (i.e., the actual interest rate of 8% minus the rate of inflation of 3%), and it is that rate of interest that should govern Leon's decision.

For the model of this chapter it is best to think of the interest rate as being for a short term, perhaps a year or less. As we discussed in Appendix 12A, the inflation rate typically does not change quickly, so if the short-term nominal interest rate falls, it is probable that short-term real interest rates will fall about as much, with similar, possibly smaller effects on interest rates for longer terms. So if short-term nominal interest rates fall, this will also tend to reduce real interest rates, especially short-term real interest rates, and hence increase planned investment spending. Similarly, if short-term nominal interest rates rise, this will also tend to increase real interest rates, especially short-term real interest rates, and hence planned investment spending will fall.

■ **Expectations and Animal Spirits**   Firms' expectations about their future sales play an important role in their investment decisions. When a firm invests, it adds to its capital stock, and capital is used in the production process. If a firm expects that its sales will increase in the future, it may begin to build up its capital stock (i.e., to invest) now so that it will be able to produce more in the future to meet the increased level of sales. The optimism or pessimism of entrepreneurs about the future course of the economy can thus have an important effect on current planned investment. Keynes used the phrase *animal spirits* to describe the feelings of entrepreneurs, and he argued that these feelings affect investment decisions.

■ **Capital Utilization Rates**   The degree of utilization of a firm's capital stock is also likely to affect planned investment. If the demand for a firm's output has been decreasing and the firm has been lowering output in response to this decline, the firm may have a low rate of capital utilization. For obvious reasons, firms tend to invest less in new capital when their capital utilization rates are low than when they are high.

■ **Relative Labour and Capital Costs**   The cost of capital (of which the interest rate is the main component) *relative* to the cost of labour can affect planned investment. If labour is expensive relative to capital (high wage rates), firms tend to substitute away from labour toward capital. They aim to hold more capital relative to labour when wage rates are high than when they are low.

To summarize:

The Determinants of Planned Investment:	■ The interest rate (especially the real interest rate) ■ Expectations of future sales ■ Capital utilization rates ■ Relative capital and labour costs

Looking Ahead: The Price Level

Our discussion of aggregate output (income) and the interest rate in the goods market and the money market is now complete. You should now have a good understanding of how the two markets work together. Thus far, however, we have not yet discussed the price level in any detail.

We cannot begin to understand the economic events of recent decades without an understanding of the aggregate price level. What causes the price level to change? Are there policies that might prevent large changes in the price level or stop them once they have started? Before we can answer such questions, we must understand the factors that affect the overall price level. That is the task of the next chapter. Up to this point we have essentially taken the price level as fixed, and now it is time to relax this assumption.

Summary

1. The *goods market* and the *money market* do not operate independently. Events in the money market have important effects on the goods market, and events in the goods market have important effects on the money market.

The Links Between the Goods Market and the Money Market

2. There are two important links between the goods market and the money market. First, the interest rate (*r*), which is determined in the money market, affects the level of planned investment spending in the goods market. If interest rates change in Canada relative to their international levels, this also affects exchange rates and hence net exports (exports minus imports), and this too affects the goods market. Second, the level of real output (income) (*Y*), which is determined in the goods market, determines the volume of transactions each period and thus affects the demand for money in the money market.

3. There is a negative relationship between planned investment and the interest rate because the interest rate determines the cost of investment projects. When the interest rate rises, planned investment will decrease; when the interest rate falls, planned investment will increase.

4. An increase in the interest rate relative to international interest rates also leads to an appreciation of the exchange rate, as explained in the previous chapter. A higher exchange rate means Canadian exports are more expensive to foreigners, and imports are less expensive to Canadians, and both factors tend to reduce net exports (exports minus imports). Similarly, a decrease in the interest rate relative to international levels leads to a depreciation of the exchange rate and an increase in net exports.

5. For every value of the interest rate, there is a different level of planned aggregate expenditure and a different equilibrium level of output. The final level of equilibrium output depends on what the interest rate turns out to be, which depends on events in the money market.

6. For a given quantity of money supplied, the interest rate depends on the demand for money. Money demand depends on the level of output (income). With a given money supply, then, increases and decreases in *Y* will affect money demand, which will affect the equilibrium interest rate.

Combining the Goods Market and the Money Market

7. An *expansionary fiscal policy* is an increase in government spending (*G*) or a reduction in net taxes (*T*). An expansionary fiscal policy based on increases in government spending tends to lead to a *crowding-out effect*: because increased government expenditures mean more transactions in the economy and thus an increased demand for money, the interest rate will rise. The decrease in planned investment spending that accompanies the higher interest rate will then partially offset (crowd out) the increase in aggregate expenditures brought about by the increase in *G*.

8. The increase in the interest rate associated with expansionary fiscal policy also tends to appreciate the exchange rate and reduce net exports, leading to a further type of "crowding out." Hence, increasing interest rates and appreciating exchange rates (and the resulting crowding-out effects) may tend to offset at least partially the effects of fiscal policy under flexible exchange rates.

9. An *expansionary monetary policy* is a policy to increase the money supply. An increase in the money supply leads to a lower interest rate, increased

planned investment and net exports, increased planned aggregate expenditure, and ultimately a higher equilibrium level of aggregate output (income) (Y).

10. A *contractionary fiscal policy* is a decrease in government spending or an increase in net taxes. A decrease in government spending or an increase in net taxes leads to a decrease in aggregate output (income) (Y), a decrease in the demand for money, and a decrease in the interest rate and hence in the exchange rate. However, the decrease in Y is somewhat offset by the additional planned investment that is undertaken as a result of the lower interest rate, and the additional net exports due to lower exchange rates.

11. A *contractionary monetary policy* is a policy to decrease the money supply. The higher interest rate brought about by the reduced money supply causes a decrease in planned investment spending as well as an exchange rate appreciation and hence

a fall in net exports. The result is a lower level of equilibrium output.

12. The *policy mix* is the combination of monetary and fiscal policies in use at a given time. There is no hard-and-fast rule about what constitutes the best policy mix or the best composition of output. In part, one's preference for a certain composition of output depends on one's stance regarding such issues as the optimal role of government in the economy.

More on the Determinants of Planned Investment

13. The real interest rate, that is, the interest rate less the inflation rate, matters more for planned investment spending than the actual interest rate. In addition, the level of planned investment in the economy also depends on expectations and animal spirits, capital utilization rates, and relative capital and labour costs.

Review Terms and Concepts

contractionary fiscal policy 282
contractionary monetary policy 283
crowding-out effect 280
expansionary fiscal policy 279

expansionary monetary policy 279
goods market 273
interest sensitivity or insensitivity of
    planned investment 280

money market 273
nominal interest rate 284
policy mix 283
real interest rate 284

Problem Set

1. Some economists argue that the "animal spirits" of investors are so important in determining the level of investment in the economy that interest rates don't matter at all. Suppose that this were true—that investment in no way depends on interest rates.
   a. How would Figure 13.1 be different?
   b. What would happen to the level of planned aggregate expenditures if the interest rate were to change?
   c. What would be different about the relative effectiveness of monetary and fiscal policy?

2. For each of the following, use the model of this chapter to predict the effects on the equilibrium levels of aggregate output (Y) and the interest rate (r):
   a. The government passes a major tax reduction bill and the central bank maintains a slow-growth policy (essentially holding M^s constant).
   b. The government raises taxes. At the same time, the central bank pursues an expansionary monetary policy.

   c. An international crisis leads to a sharp drop in consumer confidence and a drop in consumption. Assume that the central bank holds the money supply constant.
   d. The central bank attempts to increase the money supply to stimulate the economy, but plants are operating at 65% of their capacities and businesses are very pessimistic about the future.

3. Assume that the Bank of Canada is pursuing policies designed to keep the interest rate constant. In such a case, what actions would you expect to see the Bank take if the following were to occur? (In answering, indicate the effects of each set of events on $Y, C, S, I, EX – IM, M^s, M^d$, and r, assuming the model of this chapter.)
   a. There is an unexpected increase in investor confidence, leading to a sharp increase in orders for new plant and equipment.

b. A bank fails, causing a number of neurotic people (not trusting even the CDIC) to withdraw a substantial amount of cash from other banks and put it in their cookie jars.

4. Paranoia, the largest country in Central Antarctica, has an economy consistent with this chapter's model. It receives word of an imminent penguin attack. The news causes expectations about the future to be shaken. As a consequence, there is a sharp decline in investment spending plans.

  a. Explain in detail the effects of such an event on the economy of Paranoia, assuming no response on the part of the central bank or the government (M^s, T, and G all remain constant). Be sure to discuss the adjustments in the goods market and the money market.

  b. To counter the fall in investment, the king of Paranoia calls for a proposal to increase government spending. To finance the program, the chancellor of the exchequer has proposed three alternative options:

  (i) Finance the expenditures with an equal increase in taxes.

  (ii) Keep tax revenues constant and borrow the money from the public by issuing new government bonds.

  (iii) Keep taxes constant and finance the expenditures by printing new money.

Consider the three financing options and rank them from most expansionary to least expansionary. Explain your ranking.

5. Why might investment not respond positively to low interest rates during a recession? Why might investment not respond negatively to high interest rates during a boom?

6. In the early 1980s, the Bank of Canada was tightening the money supply in order to fight inflation. At the same time, government program spending was increasing. What would you expect the effects of this policy mix to be?

*7. The demand for money in a country with flexible exchange rates is given by the equation

$$M^d = 21\ 000 - 16\ 000r + 2Y$$

where M^d is money demand in dollars, r is the interest rate (a 5% interest rate means $r = 0.05$), and Y is national income. Note that money demand will fall if the interest rate increases and increase if national income increases, just as we assumed in the chapter. We assume the price level is fixed, so we have not included that in our equation. Assume that the money supply M^s is fixed at 22 000. Assume further that in this economy

Consumption:	$C = 100 + 0.075Y_d$
Planned investment:	$I = 200 - 500r$
Government purchases:	$G = 250$
Taxes:	$T = 400$
Net exports:	$EX - IM = 50$
Disposable income:	$Y_d = Y - T$

where it can be seen that it is assumed net exports do not depend on the exchange rate or the interest rate.

  a. Solve for output Y and the interest rate r.

  b. What is the effect of an increase in government purchases G by 1? (I.e., what is the government purchases multiplier?)

  c. Returning G to 250, what is the effect of changing the money supply to 23 000?

*8. Repeat question 7, with $M^d = 23\ 000 - 16\ 000r + 2Y$, $M^s = 24\ 000$, and $I = 235 - 1000r$.

Aggregate Demand, Aggregate Supply, and Inflation

The Aggregate Demand Curve

Deriving the Aggregate Demand Curve

The Aggregate Demand Curve: A Warning

Other Reasons for a Downward-Sloping Aggregate Demand Curve

Aggregate Expenditure and Aggregate Demand

Shifts of the Aggregate Demand Curve

The Aggregate Supply Curve

The Aggregate Supply Curve: A Warning

Aggregate Supply in the Short Run

Shifts of the Short-Run Aggregate Supply Curve

The Equilibrium Price Level

The Long-Run Aggregate Supply Curve

AD, AS, **and Monetary and Fiscal Policy**

Long-Run Aggregate Supply and Policy Effects

Causes of Inflation

Demand-Pull Inflation

Cost-Push, or Supply-Side, Inflation

Expectations and Inflation

Money and Inflation

Sustained Inflation as a Purely Monetary Phenomenon

Looking Ahead

Learning Objectives

1 Define *aggregate demand curve*. Explain why it slopes downward.

2 Identify how the aggregate demand curve shifts as monetary and fiscal policy changes.

3 Define *short-run aggregate supply curve*. Explain why it slopes upward and what factors will shift it.

4 Explain the distinction between the short-run aggregate supply and long-run aggregate supply curve and the implications for macroeconomic policy.

5 Outline the short-run and long-run effects on output and the price level of an expansionary or contractionary monetary or fiscal policy.

6 Distinguish demand-pull and cost-push inflation. Explain why sustained inflation is believed to be a purely monetary phenomenon.

One of the most important issues in macroeconomics is the determination of the overall price level. Recall that inflation—an increase in the overall price level—is one of the key concerns of macroeconomists and government policy makers. An understanding of the factors that affect the price level is essential to an understanding of macroeconomics.

In Chapter 8, we discussed how inflation is measured and the costs of inflation, but made no mention of the *causes* of inflation. For simplicity, the analysis we did in Chapters 9 through 13 generally took the price level as fixed. This allowed us to discuss the links between the goods market and the money market without the added complication of a changing price level. Having considered how the two markets work, we are now ready to take up the case of more flexible prices.

We begin this chapter by discussing the *aggregate demand curve* and the *aggregate supply curve*, introduced briefly in Chapter 6. We then put the two curves together and discuss how the equilibrium price level is determined in the economy. This analysis allows us to see how the price level affects the economy and how the economy affects the price level. Finally, we consider monetary and fiscal policy effects and the causes of inflation.

The Aggregate Demand Curve

The place to begin our exploration of the price level is the money market. As we saw in Chapter 12, people's demand for money depends on income (Y), the interest rate (r), and the price level (P).

It is not hard to understand why the price level affects the demand for money. Suppose you plan to purchase one bag of potato chips, a chocolate bar, and a doughnut. If these items cost $2, $1, and $0.50 respectively, you would need $3.50 in cash or in your chequing account to make your purchases. Suppose that the price of these goods doubles. To make the same purchases, you now need $7.

In general, the amount of money required to facilitate a given number of transactions depends directly and proportionately on the average price of those transactions. A doubling of the price level will double the demand for money. As prices and wages rise, households will want to keep more in their wallets and in their chequing accounts, firms will need more in their cash drawers, and so forth. If prices and wages are rising at 6% per year, for example, we can expect the demand for money to increase at about 6% per year, all other things equal.

> Money demand is a function of three variables: the interest rate (r), the level of real income (Y), and the price level (P). (Remember that Y is *real* output, or income. It measures the actual volume of output, without regard to changes in the price level.) Money demand will increase if the real level of output (income) increases, the price level increases, or the interest rate declines.

DERIVING THE AGGREGATE DEMAND CURVE

aggregate demand *The total demand for goods and services in the economy.*

Recall that **aggregate demand** is the total demand for goods and services in the economy. To derive the aggregate demand curve, we need to examine what happens to aggregate output (income) (Y) when the price level (P) changes. Does it increase, decrease, or remain constant when the price level increases? Our earlier discussions of the goods market and the money market provide us with the tools to answer this question.

The aggregate demand curve is derived assuming the fiscal policy variables [government purchases (G) and net taxes (T)] and the monetary policy variable (M^s) remain unchanged. In other words, it is assumed that the government does not take any action to affect the economy in response to changes in the price level.

As you know, an increase in the price level increases the demand for money and shifts the money demand curve to the right, as illustrated in Figure 14.1a. At the initial interest rate of 6%, an increase in the price level leads to an excess demand for money. Because of the higher price level, households and firms need to hold larger money balances than they did before. However, the quantity of money supplied remains the same. (Remember, we are assuming that the central bank takes no action to change the money supply.) The money market is now out of equilibrium. Equilibrium is reestablished at a higher interest rate, 9%.

The principal point of Chapter 13 was that this increase in interest rates would reduce planned aggregate expenditure. To summarize, there are two key reasons. First, higher interest rates will tend to make investment projects more costly and hence fewer will be desirable—*there will be less planned investment spending.* Second, if interest rates in Canada increase relative to interest rates elsewhere, bondholders will try to shift their assets into Canadian bonds, leading to an appreciation in the Canadian dollar as described in Chapter 12. Canadian exports will become more expensive on world markets and hence export volume will fall. The more valuable dollar will also reduce the price of imports to Canada and import volume will rise. Hence *net exports (exports minus imports) will also fall.* Both planned investment and net exports are components of planned aggregate expenditure ($AE \equiv C + I + G + EX - IM$) so AE will be lower.

This effect is shown in Figure 14.1b as a downward shift of the AE curve in the Keynesian cross diagram from Chapter 10. Lower AE in turn means that inventories are greater than planned, firms cut back on output, and Y falls from Y_0 to Y_1.

> An increase in the price level causes the level of aggregate output (income) to fall.

FIGURE 14.1

The Impact of an Increase in the Price Level on the Economy—Assuming No Changes in *G, T,* and M^s

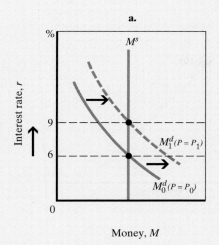

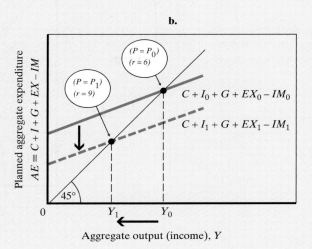

a. An increase in the price level from P_0 to P_1 increases the demand for money from M_0^d to M_1^d. With the supply of money unchanged, the interest rate increases from 6% to 9%.

b. The higher interest rate decreases planned investment and leads to an exchange rate appreciation, decreasing net exports. This reduces planned aggregate expenditure, causing equilibrium output (income) to fall from Y_0 to Y_1.

The situation is reversed when the price level declines. A lower price level causes money demand to fall, which leads to a lower interest rate. A lower interest rate stimulates planned investment spending and leads to a depreciation of the exchange rate, increasing net exports. This increases planned aggregate expenditure, which leads to an increase in Y.

> A decrease in the price level causes the level of aggregate output (income) to rise.

This negative relationship between aggregate output (income) and the price level is called the **aggregate demand (*AD*) curve**, shown in Figure 14.2.

Each point on the aggregate demand curve represents equilibrium in both the goods market *and* the money market. We have derived the *AD* curve by using the analysis we did in Chapter 13, in which the goods market and the money market were linked together. Therefore,

> Each pair of values of *P* and *Y* on the aggregate demand curve corresponds to a point at which both the goods market and the money market are in equilibrium.

aggregate demand (*AD*) curve
A curve that shows the negative relationship between aggregate output (income) and the price level. Each point on the AD curve is a point at which both the goods market and the money market are in equilibrium.

THE AGGREGATE DEMAND CURVE: A WARNING

It is important that you realize what the aggregate demand curve represents. As we pointed out in Chapter 6, the aggregate demand curve is much more complex than a simple individual or market demand curve. The *AD* curve is *not* a market demand curve, and it is *not* the sum of all market demand curves in the economy.

To understand why, recall the logic behind a simple downward-sloping household demand curve. A demand curve shows the quantity of output demanded (by an individual household or in a single market) at every possible price *ceteris paribus,* or all else equal. Thus, in drawing a simple demand curve, we are assuming that *other prices* and *income* are fixed. From these assumptions, it follows that

FIGURE 14.2

The Aggregate Demand (*AD*) Curve

At all points along the *AD* curve, both the goods market and the money market are in equilibrium.

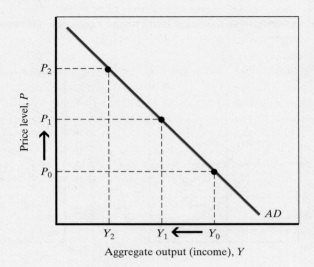

one of the reasons that the quantity demanded of a particular good falls when its price rises is that other prices do *not* rise. The good in question therefore becomes more expensive relative to other goods, which leads households to substitute other goods for the good whose price increased. In addition, if income does not rise when the price of a good does, real income falls. This may also lead to a lower quantity demanded of the good whose price has risen.

Things are different, however, when the *overall price level* rises. When the overall price level rises, many prices—including many wage rates (and thus many people's income)—rise together. For this reason, we cannot use the *ceteris paribus* assumption to draw the *AD* curve. Thus, the logic that explains why a simple demand curve slopes downward is not sufficient to explain why the *AD* curve also has a negative slope.

> Aggregate demand falls when the price level increases because the higher price level causes the demand for money (M^d) to rise. With the money supply constant, the interest rate will rise to reestablish equilibrium in the money market. *It is the higher interest rate that causes aggregate output to fall.*

You do not need to understand anything about the money market to understand a simple individual or market demand curve. However, to understand what the *aggregate* demand curve represents, you must understand the interaction between the goods market and the money market. Thus, the *AD* curve in Figure 14.2 embodies everything we have learned about the goods market and the money market up to now.

> The *AD* curve is *not* the sum of all the market demand curves in the economy. It is *not* a market demand curve.

OTHER REASONS FOR A DOWNWARD-SLOPING AGGREGATE DEMAND CURVE

The explanation so far for the downward sloping aggregate demand (*AD*) curve is that an increase in the price level will lead to an increase in money demand and higher interest rates, which both decrease investment and lead to an appreciation of the exchange rate and hence a fall in net exports. We might call this the *interest rate link*. There are at least two other factors that might lead to a downward slope of the *AD* curve: one that affects another component of aggregate output, consumption, and another that influences net exports.

■ **The Real Wealth/Consumption Link**   Consumption likely depends on wealth as well as income. Other things being equal, the more wealth households have, the more they consume. Wealth (or net worth) is not income but is the stock of accumulated assets (including, for example, holdings of money, shares of stock, bonds, and housing) minus any debts.

For some kinds of wealth, such as corporate bonds, an unexpected increase in the price level has no clear effect on consumption, because it hurts the lender but helps the borrower and any effects on consumption tend to offset each other. But an increase in the price level also reduces the value of wealth held as currency and government bonds and may reduce the consumption of holders while arguably having no effect on the expenditures of the issuing government. A change in consumption and hence planned aggregate expenditure due to a change in real wealth from a change in the price level is known as the **real wealth effect** or the **real balance effect** and is another reason for the negative relationship between the price level and output in the *AD* curve.

real wealth, or **real balance, effect** *The change in consumption brought about by a change in real wealth that results from a change in the price level.*

> An increase in the price level may decrease consumption by reducing the real value of some kinds of wealth.

■ **The Price/Net Exports Link**   We have already discussed the effect of any increase in the exchange rate on net exports. But even if the exchange rate did not change, an increase in the Canadian price level makes Canadian goods more expensive on foreign markets, reducing our exports. Similarly within Canada, imported goods and services will appear relatively cheap and imports will increase. (For example, more Canadians will travel to Florida or California instead of taking ski trips to British Columbia, given the increased prices in Canada.) Both of these effects will decrease net exports. In summary,

> Our final reason for the downward slope of the aggregate demand curve is that increases in the price level in Canada, even without changes in the exchange rate, make Canadian exports more expensive and Canadian imports cheaper, reducing net exports and hence output.

Finally, as an overall summary on the aggregate demand curve:

> The aggregate demand (*AD*) curve gives the values of the price level (*P*) and aggregate output (*Y*) at which both the goods market and the money market are in equilibrium. It slopes downward because increases in *P* increase money demand and hence increase interest rates, which in turn leads to an appreciation of the exchange rate. The higher interest rates reduce investment, the appreciated exchange rate and higher price level reduce net exports, and the higher price level reduces the real value of some kinds of wealth and hence consumption. All of these effects contribute to a reduction in *Y*.

AGGREGATE EXPENDITURE AND AGGREGATE DEMAND

Throughout our discussion of macroeconomics so far, we have referred to the total planned spending by households (*C*), firms (*I*), the government (*G*), and net exports (*EX* – *IM*) as planned aggregate expenditure. At equilibrium, planned aggregate expenditure ($AE \equiv C + I + G + EX - IM$) and aggregate output (*Y*) are equal:

$$\text{Equilibrium condition: } C + I + G + EX - IM = Y$$

How does planned aggregate expenditure relate to aggregate demand?

> At every point along the aggregate demand curve, the aggregate quantity demanded is exactly equal to planned aggregate expenditure, $C + I + G + EX - IM$.

You can see this in Figures 14.1 and 14.2. When the price level rises, it is planned aggregate expenditure that decreases, thus moving us up the aggregate demand curve.

But the aggregate demand curve represents more than just planned aggregate expenditure. Each point on the *AD* curve represents the *particular* level of planned aggregate expenditure that is consistent with equilibrium in the goods market and money market. Notice that the variable on the horizontal axis of the aggregate demand curve in Figure 14.2 is *Y*. At every point along the *AD* curve, $Y = C + I + G + EX - IM$.

SHIFTS OF THE AGGREGATE DEMAND CURVE

The aggregate demand curve in Figure 14.2 is based on the assumption that the government policy variables *G, T,* and M^s are fixed. If any of these variables changes, the aggregate demand curve will shift.

Consider an increase in the quantity of money supplied. If the quantity of money is expanded at any given price level, the interest rate will fall, causing planned aggregate expenditure to rise. The result is an increase in output at the given price level. Thus, as Figure 14.3 shows:

> An increase in the quantity of money supplied at a given price level shifts the aggregate demand curve to the right.

An increase in government purchases or a decrease in net taxes (or anything that increases aggregate output in the Keynesian cross model) increases aggregate output (income) at each possible price level. An increase in government purchases directly increases planned aggregate expenditure, which leads to an increase in output. A decrease in net taxes results in a rise in consumption, which increases planned aggregate expenditure, which also leads to an increase in output. Thus, as Figure 14.4 shows:

> An increase in government purchases or a decrease in net taxes shifts the aggregate demand curve to the right.

The same kind of reasoning applies to decreases in the quantity of money supplied, decreases in government purchases, and increases in net taxes. All of these shift the aggregate demand curve to the left.

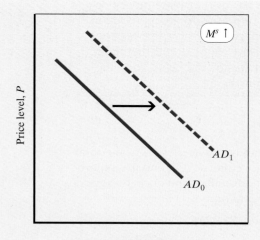

FIGURE 14.3

The Effect of an Increase in Money Supply on the *AD* Curve

An increase in the money supply (M^s) causes the aggregate demand curve to shift to the right, from AD_0 to AD_1. This shift occurs because the increase in M^s lowers the interest rate, which increases planned aggregate expenditure. The final result is an increase in output at each possible price level.

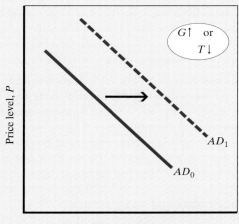

FIGURE 14.4

The Effect of an Increase in Government Purchases or a Decrease in Net Taxes on the AD Curve

An increase in government purchases (G) or a decrease in net taxes (T) causes the aggregate demand curve to shift to the right, from AD_0 to AD_1. The increase in G increases planned aggregate expenditure, which leads to an increase in output at each possible price level. A decrease in T causes consumption to rise. The higher consumption then increases planned aggregate expenditure, which leads to an increase in output at each possible price level.

Figure 14.5 summarizes the ways in which the aggregate demand curve shifts in response to changes in M^s, G, and T. To test your understanding of the AD curve, go through the figure piece by piece and explain each of its components.

The Aggregate Supply Curve

Aggregate supply is the total supply of goods and services in an economy. While there is little disagreement among economists about the logic behind the aggregate demand curve, there is a great deal of disagreement about the logic behind the aggregate supply curve. There is also disagreement about its shape.

aggregate supply *The total supply of all goods and services in an economy.*

THE AGGREGATE SUPPLY CURVE: A WARNING

The **aggregate supply (AS) curve** shows the relationship between the aggregate quantity of output supplied by all the firms in an economy and the overall price level. To understand the aggregate supply curve, we need to understand something about the behaviour of the individual firms that make up the economy.

Just as we warned that the aggregate demand curve is not the sum of individual demand curves, the aggregate supply curve is not the sum of individual supply curves. An individual supply curve for carrots has the quantity of carrots on its horizontal axis and the price of carrots on its vertical axis, and is drawn holding the prices of all other goods (inputs and outputs) constant. The aggregate supply curve has overall output (an aggregate of all outputs, including carrots) on the hor-

aggregate supply (AS) curve *A graph that shows the relationship between the aggregate quantity of output supplied by all firms in an economy and the overall price level.*

FIGURE 14.5

Shifts in the Aggregate Demand Curve: A Summary

Expansionary monetary policy	**Contractionary monetary policy**
$M^s \uparrow \rightarrow AD$ curve shifts to the right.	$M^s \downarrow \rightarrow AD$ curve shifts to the left.
Expansionary fiscal policy	**Contractionary fiscal policy**
$G \uparrow \rightarrow AD$ curve shifts to the right.	$G \downarrow \rightarrow AD$ curve shifts to the left.
$T \downarrow \rightarrow AD$ curve shifts to the right.	$T \uparrow \rightarrow AD$ curve shifts to the left.

izontal axis and the price *level* (an aggregate of all prices, including the price of carrots) on the vertical axis. Because it is the price *level* on the axis, the prices of many goods change as the economy moves along the curve.

AGGREGATE SUPPLY IN THE SHORT RUN

A short-run aggregate supply curve (*AS* curve) is shown in Figure 14.6. It is sometimes called a "price/output response curve" to emphasize that there are two ways to think about its slope. One way is to consider *output response*: the effect on aggregate output Y of an increase in the price level P. Suppose the price level increases by 10%, meaning firms' output prices have increased by 10%. Will firms change their level of output? It depends on input prices. As the price level increases, *some* input prices will increase automatically. For example, some wage and salary contracts have cost-of-living provisions that index them (in the short run) to changes in the price level. But not all wage and salary contracts are so indexed. Some wages, salaries, and other input prices may not change at all in the short run, sometimes because they are fixed by non-indexed contracts. So if output prices for firms increase by 10% but input prices only increase by 3% on average, firms will find it profitable to increase output and aggregate output Y will increase. So as P increases, Y increases and the *AS* curve slopes upward. Note that if all input prices increased by the same 10% as the increase in output prices, firms would not find it profitable to increase output and the *AS* curve would be vertical: increases in the price level P would not elicit increases in aggregate output Y.[1]

The second way to look at the slope of the *AS* curve is not so different, although we will not emphasize it as much. Instead of considering the effect of a change in P on Y, consider the *price level response*: the effect of a change in Y on the price level P. Many firms (some would argue most firms) do not simply respond to prices determined in the market but actually *set* prices. Only in perfectly competitive markets do firms simply react to prices determined by market forces. Firms in imperfectly competitive industries make both output *and* price decisions to maximize profits, on the basis of demand for their product and costs of production. As aggregate output increases (business is good) more and more such firms will find that the timing is right to increase output price as well as output, particularly as input prices begin to rise. Hence as Y increases, P increases and again the *AS* curve slopes upward.

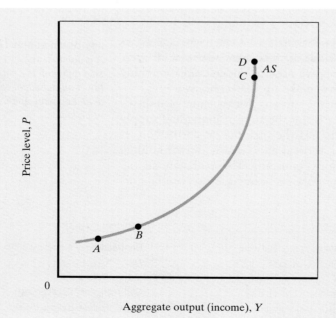

FIGURE 14.6

The Short-Run Aggregate Supply Curve

In the short run, the aggregate supply curve (the price/output response curve) has a positive slope. At low levels of aggregate output, the curve is fairly flat. As the economy approaches capacity, the curve becomes nearly vertical. At capacity, the curve is vertical.

[1]*All prices going up by the same percentage is analogous to changing the monetary unit of account from, say, old dollars to new dollars, where 1.1 new dollars equals one old dollar. A change in the monetary unit of account has no effect on the firms' profit-maximizing decisions. If the nominal values of all output and input prices increases by 10%, then nothing* real *happens. When all nominal values go up by 10%, firms' decisions regarding real output will not change.*

In Figure 14.6, at low levels of aggregate output Y (i.e., a recession) the AS curve has been drawn fairly flat. It becomes steeper as output increases. At low levels of aggregate output, most firms will have low levels of production, excess capacity, and often excess labour. Additional labour at existing wages will be easy to acquire by either recalling laid-off workers or hiring from the many unemployed. Hence the AS curve will be flat. Thinking in terms of output response, a small increase in the price a firm can obtain for its product will elicit a large increase in output, because the cost of extra units of production is low and stable. Thinking instead in terms of price-level response, at low levels of output as output increases firms are unlikely to raise prices very much for fear of losing the potential increase in sales to other firms who also have extra capacity. Thus, from either perspective,

> An increase in aggregate demand when the economy is operating at low levels of output is likely to result in an increase in output with little or no increase in the overall price level. That is, the aggregate supply (price/output response) curve is likely to be fairly flat at low levels of aggregate output.

Refer again to Figure 14.6. Aggregate output is considerably higher at point B than at point A, but the price level at point B is only slightly higher than it is at point A. The analysis in Chapters 9 through 13 mostly assumed a fixed price level as if the economy was operating on the flat part of the AS curve.

As output increases, the AS curve becomes steeper as firms' response to an increase in demand is likely to change from one of primarily increasing output to one of primarily increasing prices. Why? As firms increase their output, they will begin to bump into their short-run capacity constraints. In addition, unemployment will be falling as firms hire more workers to produce the increased output, so the economy as a whole will be approaching its capacity. Unable to produce much more, an increasing number of firms will take advantage of the increased demand by raising prices.

At some level of output, it is virtually impossible for firms to expand any further. At this level, all sectors are fully utilizing their existing factories and equipment. Plants are running double shifts, and many workers are on overtime. In addition, there is little or no cyclical unemployment in the economy. At this point, firms will respond to any further increases in demand only by raising prices.

> When the economy is producing at its maximum level of output—that is, at capacity—the aggregate supply curve becomes vertical.

Look again at Figure 14.6. Between points C and D, the AS curve is vertical. Moving from point C to point D results in no increase in aggregate output but only an increase in the price level.

To sum up:

> The short-run aggregate supply (AS) curve gives the responses by firms in terms of the price level and aggregate output as aggregate demand increases. The AS curve slopes upward because firms increase prices as they, and the economy as a whole, approach capacity constraints. The AS curve is not vertical as long as the economy is below full capacity and some input prices do not adjust completely in the short run. Therefore when the output price level (P) increases, input prices do not increase as much and firms find it profitable to increase output.

SHIFTS OF THE SHORT-RUN AGGREGATE SUPPLY CURVE

Just as the aggregate demand curve can shift, so too can the aggregate supply (price/output response) curve. Recall the individual firm behaviour that we have just considered in describing the shape of the short-run AS curve. Firms with the power to set prices choose the price/output combinations that maximize their profits. Firms in perfectly competitive industries choose the quantities of output to supply at given price levels. The *AS* curve traces out these price/output responses to economic conditions.

Anything that affects these individual firm decisions can shift the *AS* curve. Some of these factors include cost shocks, economic growth, stagnation, public policy, and natural disasters.

■ **Cost Shocks**   Firms' decisions are heavily influenced by costs. Some costs change at the same time that the overall price level changes, some costs lag behind changes in the price level, and some may not change at all. Changes in costs that occur at the same time that the price level changes are built into the shape of the short-run *AS* curve. However, there may be other cost changes that are *not* automatic responses to changes in the overall price level. These would include cost changes due to wage changes that are not due to cost-of-living clauses.

Another important example is changes in the cost of energy. During the fall of 1990, world crude oil prices doubled from about US$20 to US$40 a barrel. Once it became clear that the Persian Gulf War would not lead to the destruction of the Saudi Arabian oil fields, the price of crude oil on world markets fell back to below US$20 per barrel. In contrast, in 1973–1974 (due to war in the Middle East) and again in 1979 (due to revolution in Iran), the world price of oil increased substantially and remained at a higher level.[2] Oil is an important input in many firms and industries, and when the price of firms' inputs rises, firms respond by raising prices. At the aggregate level, this means that an increase in the price of oil (or a similar cost increase) *shifts* the *AS* curve to the left, as shown in Figure 14.7a. A leftward shift of the *AS* curve means a higher price level for a given level of output.

A decrease in costs shifts the *AS* curve to the right, as shown in Figure 14.7b. A rightward shift of the *AS* curve means a lower price level for a given level of output.

Shifts in the *AS* curve brought about by a change in costs are referred to as **cost shocks** or **supply shocks.**

■ **Economic Growth**   Economic growth, through increases in available factors of production or through technological advances, shifts the *AS* curve to the right. Recall that the vertical part of the short-run *AS* curve represents the economy's maximum (capacity) output. This maximum output is determined by the economy's existing resources and the current state of technology so that changes in these factors affect aggregate supply. For example, if the supply of labour increases, the *AS* curve will shift to the right. The labour force grows naturally with the population, but it can also increase for other reasons. Since the 1960s, for example, the percentage of women in the labour force has grown sharply. This increase in the supply of female workers has shifted the *AS* curve to the right.

Immigration can also shift the *AS* curve. During the 1970s, Germany, faced with a serious labour shortage, opened its borders to large numbers of "guest workers," largely from Turkey. Canada has seen large increases in immigration from time to time, with the most recent wave beginning in the late 1980s.

■ **Stagnation and Lack of Investment**   The opposite of economic growth is stagnation and decline. Over time, capital deteriorates and eventually wears out completely if it is not properly maintained. If an economy fails to invest in both public capital (sometimes called *infrastructure*) and private capital (plant and equipment) at a sufficient rate, the stock of capital will decline. If the stock of capital declines, the *AS* curve will shift to the left.

cost shock, or supply shock
A change in costs that shifts the aggregate supply (AS) curve.

---

[2]*The domestic price of oil in Canada during this period was regulated by the federal government. The bulk of Canadian oil at the time was produced in western Canada, particularly Alberta. The price of this oil when sold in Canada was allowed to rise, but was held below the world price. Oil not consumed in Canada was exported at the world price. However, the difference between the world price and the domestic price was taxed and the proceeds were used to subsidize the price of oil in Quebec and Atlantic Canada, which did not have access to western Canadian oil at its artificially low prices (because the pipeline did not extend that far). This restriction on oil prices, which has since been removed, was naturally a great source of conflict between the federal government and the oil-producing provinces.*

FIGURE 14.7

Shifts of the Aggregate Supply Curve

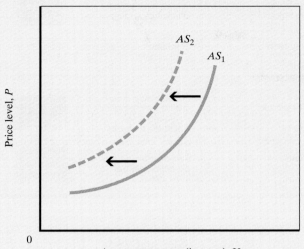

a. A decrease in aggregate supply

A leftward shift of the *AS* curve from AS_1 to AS_2 could be caused by an increase in costs (for example, an increase in wage rates or energy prices), natural disasters, capital deterioration, and the like.

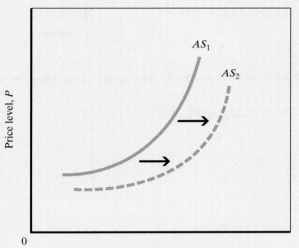

b. An increase in aggregate supply

A rightward shift of the *AS* curve from AS_1 to AS_2 could be caused by a decrease in costs, economic growth, public policy that stimulates supply, and the like.

■ **Public Policy**   Public policy may also shift the *AS* curve. In the 1980s, for example, the governments of Prime Minister Margaret Thatcher in the United Kingdom and President Ronald Reagan in the United States put into effect a form of public policy based on supply-side economics. Canada introduced some reductions in tax rates during this same period, but policy reform was by no means as sweeping as it had been in the United Kingdom and the United States. The idea behind these supply-side policies was to deregulate the economy and reduce taxes to increase the incentives to work, engage in entrepreneurial activity, and invest. The main purpose of these policies was to attempt to shift the *AS* curve to the right. It can be argued that the Goods and Services Tax, enacted January 1991, can be modelled as causing a leftward shift of the *AS* curve and hence worsened both inflation and the 1991 recession (although it may be that alternative taxes would have had much the same effect).

■ **Weather, Wars, and Natural Disasters**   Changes in weather can also shift the *AS* curve. A severe drought, for example, will reduce the supply of agricultural goods, while the perfect mix of sun and rain will produce a bountiful harvest. If an economy is damaged by war or natural disaster, the *AS* curve will shift to the left. Whenever part of the resource base of an economy is reduced or destroyed, the *AS* curve shifts to the left.

Figure 14.8 shows some of the factors that might cause the *AS* curve to shift.

The Equilibrium Price Level

The **equilibrium price level** in the economy occurs at the point at which the *AD* curve and the *AS* curve intersect. This equilibrium is shown in Figure 14.9, where the equilibrium price level is P_0 and the equilibrium level of aggregate output (income) is Y_0.

equilibrium price level *The point at which the aggregate demand and aggregate supply curves intersect.*

Chapter 14
Aggregate Demand, Aggregate
Supply, and Inflation

FIGURE 14.8

Factors That Shift the
Aggregate Supply Curve

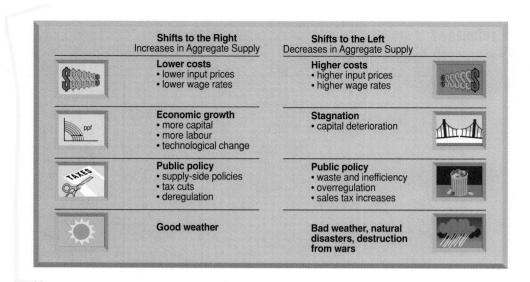

	Shifts to the Right Increases in Aggregate Supply	Shifts to the Left Decreases in Aggregate Supply	
	Lower costs • lower input prices • lower wage rates	**Higher costs** • higher input prices • higher wage rates	
	Economic growth • more capital • more labour • technological change	**Stagnation** • capital deterioration	
	Public policy • supply-side policies • tax cuts • deregulation	**Public policy** • waste and inefficiency • overregulation • sales tax increases	
	Good weather	**Bad weather, natural disasters, destruction from wars**	

Although Figure 14.9 looks simple, it is a powerful device for analyzing a number of important macroeconomic questions. Consider first what is true at the intersection of the *AS* and *AD* curves. Each point on the *AD* curve corresponds to equilibrium in both the goods market and the money market. Each point on the *AS* curve represents the price/output responses of all the firms in the economy. That means:

> The point at which the *AD* and *AS* curves intersect corresponds to an equilibrium in the goods and money markets and to the price/output decisions on the part of all the firms in the economy.

We will use this *AS/AD* framework to analyze the effects of monetary and fiscal policy on the economy and to analyze the causes of inflation. But first we need to return to the *AS* curve and discuss its shape in the long run.

The Long-Run Aggregate Supply Curve

While we have noted that the short-run *AS* curve becomes vertical at maximum capacity, it is doubtful that such a high level of output, with every factory working

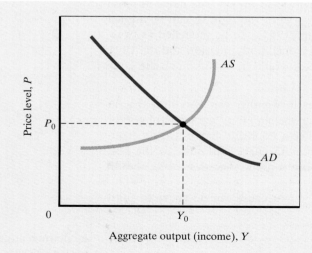

FIGURE 14.9

The Equilibrium Price Level

At each point along the *AD* curve, both the money market and the goods market are in equilibrium. Each point on the *AS* curve represents the price/output decisions of all the firms in the economy. P_0 and Y_0 correspond to equilibrium in the goods market and the money market and to the price/output decisions on the part of all the firms in the economy.

full-out and so many workers working overtime, can be sustained. The high demand for labour will lead to rising wages and costs, and this will tend to increase prices. Therefore many economists define **potential output** or **potential GDP**, to be the level of aggregate output that can be sustained in the long run without inflation, a level that is less than absolute capacity.

potential output, or **potential GDP** *The level of aggregate output that can be sustained in the long run without inflation.*

Let us examine this definition in the context of our model and Figure 14.10. Initially, the economy is in equilibrium at a price level of P_0 and aggregate output of Y_0 (the point at which AD_0 and AS_0 intersect). Let us suppose that this level of output happens also to be Y_p, potential output. If nothing further were to happen, the economy would remain at this level with a constant price level. Now imagine a shift of the AD curve to the right from AD_0 to AD_1. In response to this shift, both the price level and aggregate output rise in the short run, to P_1 and Y_1 respectively.

The *assumption* behind the definition of potential output (Y_p) is that if output exceeds Y_p, demand in input markets is sufficient that wages and other input costs will increase. For example, union wage contracts (or other wage and salary arrangements) without index clauses will come up for renewal and, with the increased demand for labour, will be renegotiated at higher wages to "catch up" with the price increase that has occurred. The lag until this occurs may be long or short, depending on the speed of adjustment in the economy. There may even be no lag if the price-level increase is *fully anticipated* so that the increase in the price level was expected and built into wage, salary, and other contracts. In any case, this increase in costs tends to push the AS curve up and to the left, from AS_0 to AS_1.

What will happen to output? Recall the assumption is that as long as output exceeds Y_p, increasing costs will continue. Hence as you can see in Figure 14.10, output will fall back from Y_1 to where it started, $Y_0 = Y_p$. But the price level will now be higher, at P_2.

Note that we have assumed that potential output, Y_p, does not depend on the price level so that potential output is the same at P_2 as it was at P_0. The reason that the increase in aggregate demand raised output in the short run (the reason that the short-run AS curve is not vertical) is that prices rose but some costs did not immediately adjust. If in the long run all prices and costs do adjust and rise by exactly the same percentage, aggregate output will be back at $Y_0 = Y_p$. Because in the model the economy will always return to Y_p, we call the vertical line through Y_p the long-run aggregate supply curve (*LRAS*). Thus,

> If wage rates and other costs fully adjust to changes in prices in the long run, then the long-run AS curve is vertical.

■ **Short-Run Equilibrium Below Potential GDP**   Thus far we have argued that if the short-run aggregate supply and aggregate demand curves intersect to the right of Y_0 in Figure 14.10, wages and other input prices will rise, causing the short-run AS curve to shift left and pushing GDP back down to Y_0. Although different economists have different opinions on how to determine whether an economy is operating at or above potential GDP, there is general agreement that there is a maximum level of output (below the vertical portion of the short-run aggregate supply curve) that can be sustained without inflation.

But what about short-run equilibria that occur to the *left* of Y_0? Suppose beginning from an equilibrium at price level P_0 and output Y_0, the AD curve now shifts to the left from AD_0 to AD_1, as in Figure 14.11. This might be due, for example, to contractionary fiscal or monetary policy. In response to this shift, both the price level and aggregate output fall in the short run, to P_1 and Y_1 respectively. Because output is below potential output (Y_p) and there is excess capacity and high unemployment, input prices (including wages) will *fall* and the aggregate supply curve will shift to the *right*, causing the price level to fall. Therefore, in the long run the level of real GDP will rise back to Y_p. But there is a great deal of disagreement among economists about how rapid this adjustment is, that is, how long it is to the "long run."

The "new classical" economics, which we discuss at length in Chapter 18, assumes that prices and wages are fully flexible and adjust very quickly to changing

FIGURE 14.10

The Long-Run Aggregate Supply Curve

When the *AD* curve shifts from AD_0 to AD_1, the equilibrium price level initially rises from P_0 to P_1 and output rises from Y_0 to Y_1. Costs respond in the longer run, shifting the *AS* curve from AS_0 to AS_1. Costs ultimately increase by the same percentage as the price level, and the quantity supplied ends up back at Y_0. $Y_0 = Y_p$ is sometimes called "potential GDP."

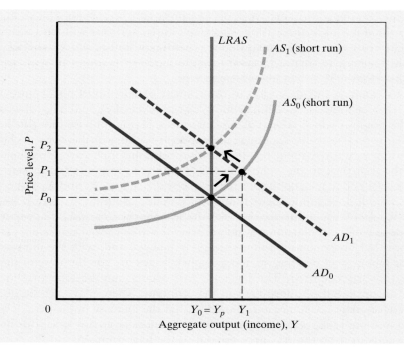

conditions. Hence the labour market adjusts or "clears" almost instantly so that the long run is attained very rapidly. For long-term contracts, adherents of this approach argue that workers and firms anticipate movements in the price level. As we noted above, if everyone fully anticipates the eventual price change and this is built into all contracts, cost increases do not lag price increases and the economy will always remain at potential output. Another possibility, discussed more fully in Chapter 18, is the *rational expectations* approach, which allows firms and workers to make mistakes in their anticipations, but maintains that they are just as likely to overestimate changes in the price level as to underestimate them. The result is that the economy may not be at potential output, but fluctuations will average to zero.

Other economists argue that even if the economy adjusts rapidly when it is above potential GDP, it adjusts slowly to long-run equilibrium when it is below potential GDP because there is resistance to cutting prices and wages. This could explain episodes such as the Great Depression. (Keynes made clear that he thought adjustment to full employment was slow by remarking that in the long run, we are all dead.)

FIGURE 14.11

A Leftward Shift of the Aggregate Demand Curve from an Initial Long-Run Equilibrium

When the *AD* curve shifts from AD_0 to AD_1, the equilibrium price level initially falls from P_0 to P_1 and output falls from Y_0 to Y_1. Costs begin to fall further after some delay, shifting the *AS* curve from AS_0 to AS_1. In the long run, costs ultimately fall by the same percentage as the price level, and the quantity supplied returns to $Y_0 = Y_p$.

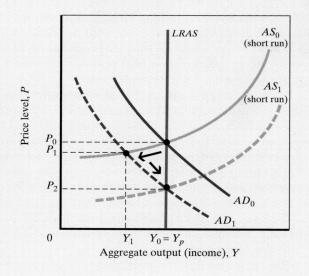

Figure 14.11 depicts a **deflation**, a decrease in the overall price level. As is implied by the diagram, deflation is typically accompanied by low or negative output growth and high and rising unemployment. Examples include the Great Depression and, more recently, Japan. In the latter case, the leftward aggregate demand shift was partly due to the fall in Japanese exports to the Southeast Asian countries experiencing their own economic crisis in the late 1990s. By early 2000, the Japanese price level was falling at a rate of about 1% per year, GDP growth was negative, and the official unemployment rate was almost 5%, very high by Japanese standards.

As a final point, our model has assumed that at potential output, inflation is zero. While it would add some complication and hence we will not model the extension formally, many of the results would hold if we instead assumed that there was some anticipated rate of inflation to which the economy had adjusted. Suppose, for example, that inflation was steady at 4% and the economy was at potential output. We would then interpret an increase in aggregate demand as likely to lead to additional inflation and a reduction in aggregate demand as leading to lower inflation. For example, during the Canadian recession of the early 1990s, with the leftward shift of the aggregate demand curve at least in part due to contractionary Bank of Canada monetary policy, inflation dropped from close to 5% to just over 1% (while unemployment rose from less than 8% to well over 11%). Similarly, while we have modelled Y_p as a constant, a more complete model would have it increasing over time as the economy grew, just as economic growth shifts the short-run aggregate supply curve to the right.

AD, AS, and Monetary and Fiscal Policy

We are now ready to use the *AS/AD* framework to consider the effects of monetary and fiscal policy. We will first consider the short-run effects.

Recall that the two fiscal policy variables are government purchases (G) and net taxes (T). The monetary policy variable is the quantity of money supplied (M^s). An *expansionary* policy will tend to stimulate the economy through an increase in G or M^s or a decrease in T. A *contractionary* policy will tend to slow the economy down through a decrease in G or M^s or an increase in T. (We discuss the controversy of contractionary monetary policy in Canada and its effect on the economy in the 1990s in the Issues and Controversies box titled "The Great Canadian Slump.") We saw earlier in this chapter that an expansionary policy shifts the AD curve to the right and that a contractionary policy shifts the AD curve to the left.

deflation *A decrease in the overall price level.*

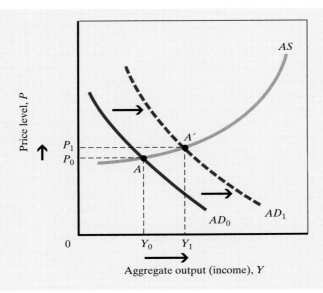

FIGURE 14.12

A Shift of the Aggregate Demand Curve When the Economy Is on the Nearly Flat Part of the *AS* Curve

Aggregate demand can shift to the right for a number of reasons, including an increase in the money supply, a tax cut, or an increase in government spending. If the shift occurs when the economy is on the nearly flat portion of the *AS* curve, the result will be an increase in output with little increase in the price level.

Japanese short-term interest rates were driven down in early 2000 to essentially zero (0.03%, in contrast to about 5.75% in Canada) as the Bank of Japan pursued expansionary monetary policy to combat deflation.

The Great Canadian Slump

As the new century began, the Canadian unemployment rate was well under 7%. It is easy to forget that the unemployment rate in 1992 was over 11% and was still over 8% in 1998. Many economists have blamed tight monetary policy by the Bank of Canada for the prolonged slump.

Professor Pierre Fortin of the University of Quebec at Montreal argues that the slump of the 1990s had by 1996 resulted in a cumulative loss of output of some $400 billion and that the loss in employment was greater than any since the Great Depression. To clarify his view that Bank policy was a principal cause of this problem, he begins by evaluating rival explanations.

For example, some have argued that globalization (and in particular free trade agreements with the United States) were responsible, but Professor Fortin emphasizes that Canada's exports surged during the 1990s, and in his view helped prevent Canada from sliding into outright depression. Technological change is also ruled out as an explanation, one reason being that the United States would likely experience the same technological forces, yet unemployment in the United States was in the 5% range during this period compared to Canadian unemployment of over 9%. He also eliminates political uncertainty due to constitutional problems as a potential cause because the employment situation in Quebec during this period, however bad, stayed steady relative to the Atlantic provinces and improved relative to Ontario. If political uncertainty were the problem, presumably Quebec would have been hit harder than surrounding provinces. Professor Fortin also presents evidence to suggest that little of the increased unemployment could be attributed to increases in minimum wages or payroll taxes.

After ruling out these other explanations, Professor Fortin turns to monetary policy. He points out that

An economic slump leads to high unemployment rates and increased business closures.

between 1981 and 1989, real short-term interest rates were about 1% higher in Canada than the United States; between 1990 and 1996 the gap rose to 3.6%. He attributes these high interest rates to the tight monetary policy that the Bank of Canada pursued to reduce the inflation rate. Professor Fortin argues this policy was followed with excessive zeal. For example, the Bank's 1989 goal of reducing inflation to below 2% by late 1995 was in fact achieved four years in advance. In addition, he supports a view of "inflation as lubricant," as also advanced by George Akerlof, William Dickens, and George Perry.

The idea of "inflation as lubricant" is that it is hard for an employer to cut nominal wages and maintain employee morale. However, it is possible for an employer, as an alternative to layoffs, to freeze nominal wages and allow inflation to erode real wages. Hence the view is that moderate inflation helps labour markets adjust and reduces unemployment.

It is not clear why employees would feel differently about real wage cuts, but perhaps they do. Would you

feel differently if your wage was frozen, but inflation was 4%, as opposed to receiving a 4% cut in the wage you received during a time of zero inflation? In any case, Professor Fortin provides evidence from a sample of wage settlements showing that during the period 1992–1994, a remarkable 47% of settlements were nominal wage freezes, which suggests that the nominal wage floor may well have been binding. Wayne Simpson, Norman Cameron, and Derek Hum of the University of Manitoba have estimated that this pay cut resistance effect may have increased unemployment at that time by as much as 2%. Fortin suggests that an inflation rate of about 3% be targeted, which would allow more firms to rely on real wage reductions over time rather than be forced to reduce their workforces.

As you can imagine, Professor Fortin has his critics, not least in the Bank of Canada. There are at least two strands of criticism. One concedes that the Bank of Canada tight monetary policy contributed to the slump, but argues that this was an unavoidable consequence of reducing inflation and that the long-run advantages of this will offset the costs of the slump. Another is that the Bank of Canada policy was not the major factor behind high Canadian interest rates; rather, the problem was the large and growing government debt. In any case much of the recent focus of the debate has switched from actual monetary policy to how monetary policy decisions are made, with the Bank's critics seeking a management structure that would concentrate less of the decision-making power in the hands of the Governor alone. It is felt this would reduce the likelihood of future episodes of such tight monetary policy.

Sources: Pierre Fortin, "The Great Canadian Slump," *Canadian Journal of Economics,* November 1996: 761–787; George A. Akerlof, William T. Dickens, and George L. Perry, "The Macroeconomics of Low Inflation," *Brookings Papers on Economic Activity* 1 (Washington, D.C.: Brookings Institution, 1996), pp. 1–59; Wayne Simpson, Norman Cameron, and Derek Hum, "Is Hypoinflation Good Policy?" *Canadian Public Policy,* September 1998: 291–308.

But how do these policies affect the equilibrium values of the price level (P) and the level of aggregate output (income)?

When considering the effects of a policy change, we must be careful to note where along the (short-run) AS curve the economy is at the time of the change. If the economy is initially on the flat portion of the AS curve, as shown by point A in Figure 14.12, then an expansionary policy, which shifts the AD curve to the right, results in a small price increase relative to the output increase: the increase in equilibrium Y (from Y_0 to Y_1) is much greater than the increase in equilibrium P (from P_0 to P_1). This is the case in which an expansionary policy works well. There is an increase in output with little increase in the price level.

However, if the economy is initially on the steep portion of the AS curve, as shown by point B in Figure 14.13, then an expansionary policy results in a small increase in equilibrium output (from Y_0 to Y_1) and a large increase in the equilibrium price level (from P_0 to P_1). In this case, an expansionary policy does not work well. It results in a much higher price level with little increase in output. The multiplier is therefore close to zero: output is initially close to capacity, and attempts to increase it further lead mostly to a higher price level.

Figures 14.12 and 14.13 show that it is important to know where the economy is *before* a policy change is put into effect. The economy is producing on the nearly flat part of the AS curve if most firms are producing well below capacity. When this is the case, firms will respond to an increase in demand by increasing output much more than they increase prices. The opposite is true if the economy is producing on the steep part of the AS curve. In this case, firms are close to capacity, and they will respond to an increase in demand by increasing prices much more than they increase output.

To see what happens when the economy is on the steep part of the AS curve, consider the effects of an increase in G with no change in the money supply. Why, when G is increased, will there be virtually no increase in Y? In other words, why will the expansionary fiscal policy fail to stimulate the economy?

Because firms are very close to capacity output when the economy is on the steep part of the AS curve, they cannot increase their output very much. The result, as Figure 14.13 shows, is a substantial increase in the price level. The increase in the price level increases the demand for money, which (with a fixed money supply) leads to an increase in the interest rate. As discussed in detail in Chapter 13, this reduces investment and (through exchange rate appreciation) reduces net exports. *There is nearly complete crowding out.* If firms are producing at capacity, prices and interest rates will continue to rise until the increase in G is completely matched by a decrease in planned investment and net exports, and there is complete crowding out.

LONG-RUN AGGREGATE SUPPLY AND POLICY EFFECTS

We have so far been considering monetary and fiscal policy effects in the short run. Regarding the long run, it is important to realize:

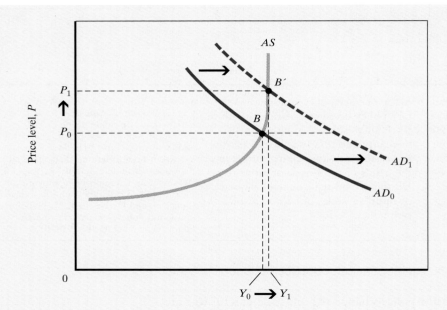

FIGURE 14.13

A Shift of the Aggregate Demand Curve When the Economy Is Operating at or near Maximum Capacity

If a shift of aggregate demand occurs while the economy is operating near full capacity, the result will be an increase in the price level with little increase in output.

> If the AS curve is vertical in the long run, and the economy is initially at potential output, neither monetary policy nor fiscal policy will have any effect on aggregate output in the long run.

Look back at Figures 14.10 and 14.11. Monetary and fiscal policy shift the AD curve. If the long-run AS curve is vertical, output always comes back to Y_p. In this case, policy affects *only* the price level in the long run, and the multiplier effect of a change in government spending on aggregate output in the long run is zero. Under the same circumstances, the tax multiplier is also zero.

This conclusion is sometimes interpreted as ruling out a role for aggregate demand policy but there is substantial disagreement. The controversy centres on two points. First, as we discussed, it is possible that if the economy is below potential GDP, wages and other input prices might *not* fall, or fall very slowly, and the economy can essentially get "stuck" in a position with high unemployment. In this case it may well be desirable to use monetary and fiscal policy to shift the AD curve to the right to restore full employment. Some economists would argue that this is essentially how the Great Depression ended—World War II can be interpreted as expansionary fiscal policy because the war effort entailed a huge increase in the level of government expenditure. (It is tragic that it was necessary to make these expenditures on weapons rather than in a socially productive direction.) Second, some economists argue that in some circumstances it may be useful to push the economy beyond potential output, or at least not to be too concerned about the possibility, because there will be some short-run gain in output and it is only in the long run that most of the increases in the price level will come.

For both these points, again the key question is how long is the long run? If it is one or two quarters or less, policy has little chance to affect output, but if the long run is three or four years, policy can have significant effects. Does the speed of adjustment depend on whether the economy is below potential output (and wages and prices must fall) or whether the economy is above potential output (where adjustment implies inflation)? It should not be surprising that a good deal of research in macroeconomics focuses on these questions. We shall return to this debate in Chapter 15.

Causes of Inflation

We now turn to the question of inflation and use the *AS/AD* framework to consider the causes of inflation.

■ **Inflation Versus Sustained Inflation: A Reminder**   Before we discuss the specific causes of inflation, recall the distinction we made in Chapter 8. **Inflation,** as you know, is an increase in the overall price level. Anything that shifts the *AD* curve to the right or the *AS* curve to the left causes inflation. But it is often useful to distinguish between a *one-time increase* in the price level (i.e., a one-time inflation) and an inflation that is sustained. A **sustained inflation** occurs when the overall price level continues to rise over some fairly long period of time.

It is generally accepted that there are many possible causes of a one-time increase in the price level. (We discuss the main causes next.) But for the price level to continue to increase period after period, most economists believe that it must be "accommodated" by an expanded money supply. This leads to the assertion that a sustained inflation, whatever the initial cause of the increase in the price level, is essentially a monetary phenomenon.

DEMAND-PULL INFLATION

Inflation that is initiated by an increase in aggregate demand is called **demand-pull inflation.** See Figures 14.12 and 14.13. Also see Figure 14.10, where an increase in aggregate demand increases aggregate output beyond potential output (Y_p) and, as illustrated, the high demand for labour and other inputs will increase costs and hence the price level until the economy returns to Y_p.

COST-PUSH, OR SUPPLY-SIDE, INFLATION

Inflation can also be caused by an increase in costs. Such inflation is referred to as **cost-push,** or **supply-side, inflation.** As we noted above, several times in the last few decades oil prices on world markets increased sharply. Because oil is used in virtually every line of business, costs increased.

An increase in costs (a cost shock) shifts the *AS* curve to the left, as Figure 14.14 shows. If we assume that the government does not react to this shift in *AS* by changing fiscal or monetary policy, the *AD* curve will not shift. The supply shift will cause the equilibrium price level to rise (from P_0 to P_1) and the level of aggregate output

inflation *An increase in the overall price level.*

sustained inflation *Occurs when the overall price level continues to rise over some fairly long period of time.*

demand-pull inflation *Inflation that is initiated by an increase in aggregate demand.*

cost-push, or **supply-side, inflation** *Inflation caused by an increase in costs.*

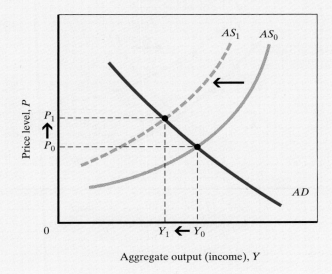

FIGURE 14.14

Cost-Push, or Supply-Side, Inflation

An increase in costs shifts the *AS* curve to the left. Assuming the government does not react to this shift so the *AD* curve does not shift, the price level rises and output falls.

stagflation *Occurs when output is falling at the same time that prices are rising.*

to decline (from Y_0 to Y_1). Recall from Chapter 6 that **stagflation** occurs when output is falling at the same time that prices are rising—in other words, when the economy is experiencing a contraction and an inflation simultaneously. Figure 14.14 shows that one possible cause of stagflation is an increase in costs.[3]

To return to monetary and fiscal policy for a moment, note from Figure 14.14 that the government could counteract reduction in output from the increase in costs (the cost shock) by engaging in an expansionary policy (an increase in G or M^s or a decrease in T). This would shift the AD curve to the right, and the new AD curve would intersect the new AS curve at a higher level of output. The problem with this policy, however, is that the intersection of the new AS and AD curves would take place at a price level even higher than P_1 in Figure 14.14. However those who believe that the economy does not adjust quickly when it is below potential output may accept the tradeoff of a higher price level in return for the more rapid reduction in unemployment.

> Cost shocks are bad news for policy makers. The only way they can counter the output loss brought about by a cost shock is by having the price level increase even more than it would without the policy action.

This situation is illustrated in Figure 14.15.

EXPECTATIONS AND INFLATION

When firms are making their price/output decisions, their *expectations* of future prices may affect their current decisions. If a firm expects that its competitors will raise their prices, it may raise its own price in anticipation of this.

Consider a firm that manufactures toasters. The toaster maker must decide what price to charge retail stores for its toaster. If it overestimates price and charges much more than other toaster manufacturers are charging, it will lose many customers. Conversely, if it underestimates price and charges much less than other toaster makers are charging, it will gain customers but at a considerable loss in revenue per sale. The firm's *optimum price*—the price that maximizes the firm's profits—is presumably not too far from the average of its competitors' prices. If it does not know its competitors' projected prices before it sets its own price, as is often

FIGURE 14.15

Cost Shocks Are Bad News for Policy Makers

A cost shock with no change in monetary or fiscal policy would shift the aggregate supply curve from AS_0 to AS_1, lower output from Y_0 to Y_1, and raise the price level from P_0 to P_1. Monetary or fiscal policy could be changed enough to have the AD curve shift from AD_0 to AD_1. This would return output to Y_0 but it would raise the price level further, to P_2.

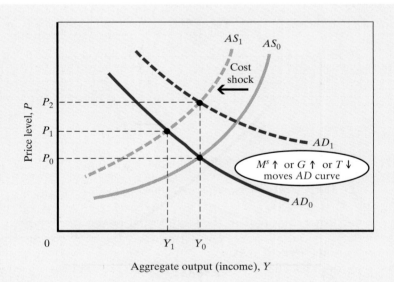

[3] *If the cost shock is an oil price increase, oil-producing regions within a country are not likely to share in the overall contraction and may well have a local boom. (That region's own* AD *curve has shifted to the right as its "exports" to other regions have increased in value.)*

the case, it must base its price on what it expects its competitors' prices to be.

Suppose that inflation has been running at about 10% per year. Our firm probably expects that its competitors will raise their prices about 10% this year, so it is likely to raise the price of its own toaster by about 10%. This is how expectations can get "built into the system." If every firm expects every other firm to raise prices by 10%, every firm will raise prices by about 10%. Thus, every firm ends up with the price increase it expected. And if workers gain wage increases to match price inflation, the spiral is reinforced.

The fact that expectations can affect the price level is vexing. Expectations can lead to an inertia that makes it difficult to stop an inflationary spiral. If prices have been rising, and if people's expectations are *adaptive*—that is, if they form their expectations on the basis of past pricing behaviour—then prices and wages may continue to rise even if demand is slowing or contracting.

Remember that the *AS* curve represents the price/output responses of firms. If firms increase their prices because of a change in inflationary expectations, the result is a leftward shift of the *AS* curve.

MONEY AND INFLATION

It is easy to see that an increase in the money supply can lead to an increase in the aggregate price level. As Figures 14.12 and 14.13 show, an increase in the money supply (M^s) shifts the *AD* curve to the right and results in a higher price level. This is simply a demand-pull inflation.

What would happen if the Bank of Canada kept trying to keep the economy above potential output by expanding the money supply more and more? The situation could lead to a **hyperinflation,** a period of very rapid increases in the price level. If no more output can be coaxed out of the economy and the *AD* curve shifts up and up, the price level will keep rising.

hyperinflation *A period of very rapid increases in the price level.*

SUSTAINED INFLATION AS A PURELY MONETARY PHENOMENON

Virtually all economists agree that an increase in the price level can be caused by anything that causes the *AD* curve to shift to the right or the *AS* curve to shift to the left. These include expansionary fiscal policy actions, monetary expansion, cost shocks, changes in expectations, and so forth. It is also generally agreed, however, that for a *sustained* inflation to occur, the central bank must accommodate it. In this sense, a sustained inflation can be thought of as a purely monetary phenomenon.

This argument has gained wide acceptance. It is easy to show, as we just did, how expanding the money supply can continuously shift the *AD* curve. It is not as easy to come up with other reasons for continued shifts of the *AD* curve if the money supply is constant. One possibility is for the government to increase spending continuously. But this process cannot continue forever—the economy would end up being all government, with no tax base or borrowing capacity to support it.

Looking Ahead

In Chapters 9 and 10, we discussed the concept of an equilibrium level of aggregate output and income, the idea of the multiplier, and the basics of fiscal policy. Those two chapters centred on the workings of the goods market alone.

In Chapters 11 and 12, we analyzed the money market by discussing the supply of money, the demand for money, the equilibrium interest rate, and the basics of monetary policy. Chapter 13 brought our analysis of the goods market together with our analysis of the money market.

In this chapter, we used everything learned so far to discuss the aggregate supply and aggregate demand curves, first mentioned in Chapter 6. Using aggregate supply and aggregate demand curves, we can determine the equilibrium price level in the economy and understand some of the causes of inflation.

We have said little about employment, unemployment, and the functioning of the labour market in the macroeconomy. The next chapter will link everything we have done so far to this third major market arena—the labour market—and to the problem of unemployment.

The Aggregate Demand Curve

1. Money demand is a function of three variables: (1) the interest rate (r); (2) the level of real income (Y); and (3) the price level (P). Money demand will increase if the real level of output (income) increases, the price level increases, or the interest rate declines.

2. *Aggregate demand* is the total demand for goods and services in the economy. The *aggregate demand (AD) curve* illustrates the negative relationship between aggregate output (income) and the price level. Each point on the *AD* curve is a point at which both the goods market and the money market are in equilibrium. The *AD* curve is *not* the sum of all the market demand curves in the economy.

3. At every point along the aggregate demand curve, the aggregate quantity demanded in the economy is exactly equal to planned aggregate expenditure.

4. The aggregate demand curve slopes downward because when the price level increases, households and firms want to hold larger money balances. If the money supply remains the same, this increased demand for money increases interest rates and reduces planned investment expenditure. Higher interest rates also lead to exchange rate appreciation and lower net exports. In consequence, planned aggregate expenditure will be lower, inventories will be greater than planned, firms will cut back on output and aggregate output (income) (Y) will fall. Conversely, a decrease in the price level will cause Y to rise.

5. An increase in the quantity of money supplied, an increase in government purchases, or a decrease in net taxes at a given price level shifts the aggregate demand curve to the right. A decrease in the quantity of money supplied, a decrease in government purchases, or an increase in net taxes shifts the aggregate demand curve to the left.

The Aggregate Supply Curve

6. *Aggregate supply* is the total supply of goods and services in an economy. The *aggregate supply (AS) curve* shows the relationship between the aggregate quantity of output supplied by all the firms in an economy and the overall price level. The *AS* curve is *not* a market supply curve, and it is *not* the simple sum of all the individual supply curves in the economy. For this reason, it is helpful to think of the *AS* curve as a "price/output response"

curve—that is, a curve that traces out the price decisions and output decisions of all the markets and firms in the economy under a given set of circumstances.

7. The shape of the short-run *AS* curve is a source of much controversy in macroeconomics. Many economists believe that at very low levels of aggregate output the *AS* curve is fairly flat, and at high levels of aggregate output the *AS* curve is vertical or nearly vertical. Thus, the *AS* curve slopes upward and becomes vertical when the economy reaches its capacity, or maximum, output.

8. Anything that affects individual firms' decisions can shift the *AS* curve. Some of these factors include cost shocks, economic growth, capital deterioration, public policy, and natural disasters.

The Equilibrium Price Level

9. The *equilibrium price level* in the economy occurs at the point at which the *AS* and *AD* curves intersect. The intersection of the *AS* and *AD* curves corresponds to equilibrium in the goods and money markets *and* to the price/output decisions on the part of all the firms in the economy.

The Long-Run Aggregate Supply Curve

10. For the *AS* curve to slope upward, some input prices must lag behind increases in the overall price level. If wage rates and other costs fully adjust to changes in prices in the long run, then the long-run *AS* curve is vertical.

11. The level of aggregate output that can be sustained in the long run without inflation is called *potential output* or *potential GDP*.

AD, AS, and Monetary and Fiscal Policy

12. If the economy is initially producing on the flat portion of the *AS* curve, an expansionary policy—which shifts the *AD* curve to the right—will result in a small increase in the equilibrium price level relative to the increase in equilibrium output. If the economy is initially producing on the steep portion of the *AS* curve, an expansionary policy results in a small increase in equilibrium output and a large increase in the equilibrium price level.

13. As the economy is always on the long-run aggregate supply curve in the long run, a great deal of controversy surrounds the length of the long run. Some economists argue, for example, that long-run

adjustment is particularly slow if the *AD* and *AS* curves intersect so that the economy is below potential output and the long-run adjustment will require wages and prices to fall. From this perspective, expansionary monetary and fiscal policy is viewed as a way to get back to potential output by shifting the aggregate demand curve to the right, albeit at the cost of some inflation.

Causes of Inflation

14. *Inflation* is an increase in the overall price level. A *sustained inflation* occurs when the overall price level continues to rise over some fairly long period of time. Most economists believe that sustained in-

flations can occur only if the central bank continuously increases the money supply.

15. *Demand-pull inflation* is inflation initiated by an increase in aggregate demand. *Cost-push*, or *supply-side*, *inflation* is inflation initiated by an increase in costs such as oil prices. An increase in costs may also lead to *stagflation*—the situation in which the economy is experiencing a contraction and an inflation simultaneously.

16. Inflation can become "built into the system" as a result of expectations. If prices have been rising and people form their expectations on the basis of past pricing behaviour, firms may continue raising prices even if demand is slowing or contracting.

Review Terms and Concepts

aggregate demand 290

aggregate demand (*AD*) curve 291

aggregate supply 295

aggregate supply (*AS*) curve 295

cost-push, or supply-side, inflation 307

cost shock, or supply shock 298

deflation 303

demand-pull inflation 307

equilibrium price level 299

hyperinflation 309

inflation 307

potential output, or potential GDP 301

real wealth, or real balance, effect 293

stagflation 308

sustained inflation 307

Problem Set

1. "The aggregate demand curve slopes downward, because when the price level is lower, people can afford to buy more, and aggregate demand rises. When prices rise, people can afford to buy less, and aggregate demand falls." Is this a good explanation of the shape of the *AD* curve? Why or why not?

2. Using aggregate supply and demand curves to illustrate your points, discuss the impacts of the following events on the price level and on equilibrium GDP (*Y*) in the *short run*:
   a. A tax cut holding government purchases constant with the economy operating at near full capacity.
   b. An increase in the money supply during a period of high unemployment and excess industrial capacity.
   c. An increase in the price of oil caused by a war in the Middle East, assuming that the central bank attempts to keep interest rates constant by expanding the money supply.
   d. An increase in taxes and a cut in government spending, supported by central bank actions to keep output from falling.

3. At the 1997 meetings of the Canadian Economics Association in St. John's, Newfoundland, leading

Canadian macroeconomists debated whether the Bank of Canada should conduct a more expansionary monetary policy. To frame the argument in terms of our model, some (call them the "activists") argued that the economy was well below potential output and that adjustment was far too slow. Others (call them the "monetary conservatives") opposed more expansionary monetary policy. They argued that while unemployment was high (the national unemployment rate was about 9.5%), the economy was in fact at potential output and that expansionary monetary policy would largely increase inflation (it was then about 1%, not far from zero). They felt the high unemployment was due to problems with labour market policy that macroeconomic policy could not fix.

Suppose that the Bank of Canada had then decided to pursue a more expansionary monetary policy. Use the *AD/AS* model of this chapter to explain what would happen to *Y* and *P* in the short run and long run if:
   a. The activists were right.
   b. The monetary conservatives were right.

4. Using aggregate supply and aggregate demand curves to illustrate, describe the effects of the following events on the price level and on equilib-

rium GDP in the *long run* assuming that input prices fully adjust to output prices after some lag:

   a. An increase in the money supply with GDP above potential GDP.
   b. A decrease in government spending and in the money supply with GDP above potential GDP.
   c. Starting with the economy at potential GDP, a war in the Middle East pushes up energy prices. The central bank expands the money supply to accommodate the inflation.

5. Two separate capacity constraints are discussed in this chapter: (1) the actual physical capacity of existing plants and equipment, shown as the vertical portion of the short-run *AS* curve and (2) potential GDP, leading to a vertical *LRAS* curve. Explain the difference between the two. Which is greater, full-capacity GDP or potential GDP? Why?

6. In country A, all wage contracts are indexed to inflation. That is, each month wages are adjusted to reflect increases in the cost of living as reflected in changes in the price level. In country B, there are no cost-of-living adjustments to wages, but the workforce is completely unionized. Unions negotiate three-year contracts. In which country is an expansionary monetary policy likely to have a larger effect on aggregate output? Explain your answer using aggregate supply and aggregate demand curves.

7. In 1994, cigarette taxes were cut sharply (by varying amounts in different provinces). Assuming the loss in government revenue from the cigarette tax cut was not replaced, illustrate both the short-run and the long-run effects on P and Y using an *AD/AS* diagram.

*8. (This Problem is especially difficult and long.) In an extension of question 8, Chapter 13, an economy with flexible exchange rates is described by the equations:

   (1) Money demand:
   $(M^d/P) = 23\ 000 - 16\ 000r + 2Y$
   (2) Money supply: $M^s = 24\ 000$
   (3) Consumption: $C = 100 + 0.75Y_d$
   (4) Planned investment: $I = 235 - 1000r$
   (5) Government purchases: $G = 250$
   (6) Taxes: $T = 400$
   (7) Net exports: $EX - IM = 50$
   (8) Disposable income: $Y_d = Y - T$

where M^d and M^s are money demand and money supply in dollars, P is the price level, r is the interest rate (a 5% interest rate means $r = 0.05$), and Y is national income. Note it is assumed that net exports do not depend on the exchange rate, the interest rate, or output.

   a. Using the goods market equilibrium condition $Y = C + I + G + EX - IM$, use equations (3)–(8) to solve for Y as a function of r, or equivalently r as a function of Y. This equation represents equilibrium in the goods market.
   b. Set money supply equal to money demand and solve for Y as a function of P and r. This equation represents equilibrium in the money market. Continue by substituting your expression for r from part **a** (the goods market equilibrium equation) into the money market equilibrium equation and solving for Y as a function of P. This is the equation of the aggregate demand (*AD*) curve and represents equilibrium in both the goods and the money market.
   c. Suppose the aggregate supply (*AS*) curve is vertical and is $Y = 1060$. Solve for the price level P where this *AS* curve intersects the *AD* curve from part **b**.
   d. Repeat parts **b** and **c** if the money supply is doubled. What happens to the price level?
   e. Now let us examine the government purchases multiplier, that is, the increase in output associated with an increase in government purchases ($\Delta Y/\Delta G$). Return the money supply to its original, undoubled value and suppose instead government purchases increase from 250 to 1176.25. Calculate the government purchases multiplier if
      (i) The *AS* curve is vertical at $Y = 1060$. (This should require no calculation.)
      (ii) The *AS* curve is horizontal at $P = 1$.
      (iii) The *AS* curve is $P = 940/(2000 - Y)$ (neither vertical nor horizontal).
      Which multiplier is the smallest and which the biggest?

*9. (This Problem is especially difficult and long.) Repeat question 8 with $(M^d/P) = 21\ 000 - 16\ 000r + 2Y$, an initial money supply $M^s = 22\ 000$, and $I = 200 - 500r$. For part **e**, G increases from 250 to 740.625.

The Labour Market, Unemployment, and Inflation

Learning Objectives

1 Explain the classical view of the labour market and its implications for the aggregate supply curve.

2 Explain how implicit or explicit contracts might prevent labour market clearing.

3 Outline efficiency wage theory and the possible effects of minimum wage laws.

4 Use the aggregate demand/aggregate supply model to explain the Phillips Curve and its shifts.

5 Explain why a vertical long-run Phillips curve implies a vertical long-run aggregate supply curve and describe the implications for monetary and fiscal policy.

The Classical View of the Labour Market

The Classical Labour Market and the *AS* Curve

Reconciling the Unemployment Rate to the Classical View

Explaining the Existence of Unemployment

Sticky Wages

Efficiency Wage Theory

Minimum Wage Laws

An Open Question

The Short-Run Relationship Between the Unemployment Rate and Inflation

The Phillips Curve: A Historical Perspective

AS/AD Analysis and the Phillips Curve

Expectations and the Phillips Curve

Is There a Short-Run Tradeoff Between Inflation and Unemployment?

The Long-Run *AS* Curve, Potential GDP, and the Natural Rate of Unemployment

Looking Ahead

I n Chapter 6, we stressed that there are three broadly defined markets in which households, firms, the government, and the rest of the world interact: (1) the goods market, which we discussed in Chapters 9 and 10, (2) the money market, which we discussed in Chapters 11 and 12, and (3) the labour market. In Chapter 8 we described some of the features of the Canadian labour market and explained how the unemployment rate is measured. Then, in Chapter 14, we considered the labour market briefly in our discussion of the aggregate supply curve. Because labour is an input, the workings of the labour market affect the shape of the *AS* curve. If wages and other input costs lag behind price increases, the *AS* curve will be upward-sloping; if wages and other input costs are completely flexible and rise at the same time as the overall price level, the *AS* curve will be vertical.

In this chapter we look further at the labour market's role in the macroeconomy. First, we consider what we call the classical view, which holds that wages always adjust to clear the labour market. We then consider why the labour market may not always clear and why unemployment may sometimes exist. Finally, we discuss the relationship between inflation and unemployment.

■ **The Labour Market: Basic Concepts** Let's review briefly what the unemployment rate measures. The **unemployment rate** is the number of people unemployed as a percentage of the labour force. To be unemployed, a person must be out of a job and actively looking for work. When a person stops looking for work, he or she is considered *out of the labour force* and is no longer counted as unemployed.

unemployment rate *The ratio of the number of people unemployed to the total number of people in the labour force.*

Chapter 15
The Labour Market,
Unemployment, and Inflation

It is important to realize that even if the economy is running at or near full capacity, the unemployment rate will never be zero. The economy is dynamic. Students graduate from schools and training programs; some businesses make profits and grow, while others suffer losses and go out of business; people move in and out of the labour force and change careers. It takes time for people to find the right job and for employers to match the right worker with the jobs they have to fill. This is **frictional** and **structural unemployment.** (Review Chapter 8 if these terms are unclear to you.)

In this chapter, we are concerned with **cyclical unemployment,** the increase in unemployment that occurs during recessions and periods of slow economic growth. When the economy contracts, the number of people unemployed and the unemployment rate rise. Canada has experienced several periods of high unemployment. During the Great Depression, the unemployment rate rose to nearly 20% in 1933 and stood at over 10% for most of the 1930s. In 1983, 1.5 million people were unemployed, putting the unemployment rate at 11.9%. The years 1992 and 1993 also saw unemployment rates above 11%.

In one sense, the reason that employment falls when the economy experiences a downturn is obvious. When firms cut back on production, they need fewer workers, so people get laid off.

> Employment tends to fall when aggregate output falls and rise when aggregate output rises.

But a decline in the demand for labour does not necessarily mean that unemployment will rise. If markets work as we described in Chapters 4 and 5, a decline in the demand for labour will initially create an excess supply of labour. As a result, the wage rate will fall until the quantity of labour supplied again equals the quantity of labour demanded, thus restoring equilibrium in the labour market. At the new lower wage rate, everyone who wants a job will have one.

If the quantity of labour demanded and the quantity of labour supplied are brought into equilibrium by rising and falling wage rates, there should be no persistent unemployment above the frictional and structural amount. Indeed, this was the view held by the classical economists who preceded Keynes, and it is still the view of a number of economists today.

The Classical View of the Labour Market

One view of the labour market, sometimes called the "classical" view, is illustrated in Figure 15.1. This approach assumes that the wage rate adjusts to equate the quantity of labour demanded with the quantity of labour supplied, thereby implying that unemployment does not exist. To see how this adjustment takes place, assume that there is a decrease in the demand for labour that shifts the demand curve in Figure 15.1 from D_0 to D_1. This decreased demand will cause the wage rate to fall from W_0 to W^* and the amount of labour demanded to fall from L_0 to L^*. The decrease in the quantity of labour supplied is a movement along the labour supply curve.

Each point on the **labour supply curve** in Figure 15.1 represents the amount of labour that households want to supply at the particular wage rate. Each household's decision regarding how much labour to supply is part of the overall consumer choice problem of a household. Each household member looks at the market wage rate, the prices of outputs, and the value of leisure time (including the value of staying at home and working in the yard or raising children) and chooses the amount of labour to supply (if any). If a household member is not in the labour force, it is because he or she has decided that his or her time is more valuable in nonmarket activities.

It is easy to see why this is so. If you choose to stay out of the labour force, it is because you (a member of society) place a higher value on the use of your time than society is currently placing on the product that you would produce if you were

frictional unemployment *The portion of unemployment that is due to the normal working of the labour market; used to denote short-run job/skill matching problems.*

structural unemployment *The portion of unemployment that is due to changes in the structure of the economy that result in a significant loss of jobs in certain industries.*

cyclical unemployment *The increase in unemployment that occurs during recessions and periods of slow economic growth. Cyclical unemployment + Frictional unemployment + Structural unemployment = Actual rate of unemployment*

labour supply curve *A graph that illustrates the amount of labour that households want to supply at the particular wage rate.*

employed. Consider, for example, households in less-developed countries. In many of these countries, the alternative to working for a wage is subsistence farming. If the wage rate in the labour market is very low, many will choose to farm for themselves. In this case, the value of what such workers produce in farming must be greater than the value that society currently places on what they would produce if they worked for a wage. If this were not true, wages would rise and more people would join the labour force.

Each point on the **labour demand curve** in Figure 15.1 represents the amount of labour that firms want to employ at the particular wage rate. Each firm's decision about how much labour to demand is part of its overall profit-maximizing decision. A firm makes a profit by selling output to households. It will hire workers if the value of its output is sufficient to justify the wage that is being paid. Thus, the amount of labour that a firm hires depends on the value of the output that workers produce.

The classical economists saw the workings of the labour market—the behaviour of labour supply and labour demand—as optimal from the standpoint of both individual households and firms and from the standpoint of society. If households want more output than is currently being produced, output demand will increase, output prices will rise, the demand for labour will increase, the wage rate will rise, and more workers will be drawn into the labour force. (I.e., some of those who preferred not to be a part of the labour force at the lower wage rate will be lured into the labour force at the higher wage rate.) At equilibrium, prices and wages reflect a tradeoff between the value that households place on outputs and the value of time spent in leisure and nonmarket work. At equilibrium, the people who are not working are those who have *chosen* not to work at that market wage. There is always *full employment* in this sense. Thus, the classical economists believed, the market will achieve the optimal result if left to its own devices, and there is nothing that the government can do to make things better.

labour demand curve *A graph that illustrates the amount of labour that firms want to employ at the particular wage rate.*

THE CLASSICAL LABOUR MARKET AND THE *AS* CURVE

Economists who hold the classical view of the labour market tend to believe the (short-run) *AS* curve is vertical. Recall from Chapter 14 that the *AS* curve is not

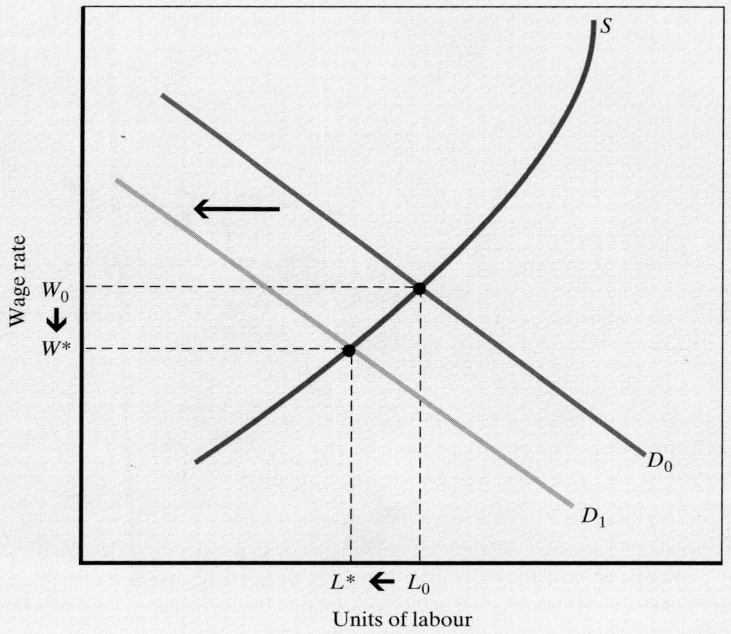

FIGURE 15.1

The Classical Labour Market

Classical economists believe that the labour market always clears. If the demand for labour shifts from D_0 to D_1, the equilibrium wage will fall from W_0 to W^*. Everyone who wants a job at W^* will have one.

vertical if, when the price level increases by 1%, not all wages and input prices immediately increase by 1%. In the long run there is complete adjustment as all wages and prices increase by 1% and output returns to its initial level: the long-run aggregate supply (*LRAS*) curve is vertical, as in Figure 14.10. It follows that those who believe that the wage rate adjusts quickly to clear the labour market are likely to believe that there will be no significant period in which wage changes will not have adjusted by the full 1% and hence *both* the short-run and long-run aggregate supply curves are vertical. Remember that if both the *AS* and *LRAS* curves are vertical, monetary and fiscal policy cannot affect the level of output and employment in the economy in either the short run or the long run.

RECONCILING THE UNEMPLOYMENT RATE TO THE CLASSICAL VIEW

If, as the classical economists assumed, the labour market works well, how can we account for the fact that the unemployment rate at times seems high? There seem to be times when over a million people who want jobs at prevailing wage rates cannot find them. How can we reconcile this situation with the classical assumption about the labour market?

Some economists answer this question by arguing that the unemployment rate is not a good measure of whether the labour market is working well. We know that the economy is dynamic and that at any given time some industries are expanding and some are contracting. We saw in Chapter 13, for example, that new house construction may be sensitive to changes in interest rates. Consider, then, a carpenter who is laid off because of a contraction in the construction industry. This person had probably developed specific skills related to the construction industry—skills that are not necessarily useful for jobs in other industries. If he were earning $30 000 per year as a carpenter, it may be that he could earn only $20 000 per year in another industry. He may eventually work his way back up to a salary of $30 000 in the new industry as he develops new skills, but this will take time. Will the carpenter take a job at $20 000? There are at least two reasons he may not. First, he may believe that the slump in the construction industry is temporary and that he will soon get his job back. Second, he may believe that he can earn more than $20 000 in another industry and will continue to look for a better job.

In January 1995, with an unemployment rate of 10.6% in Canada, 26 000 people responded to a call for applications by the General Motors of Canada plant in Oshawa, Ontario. The lineup began the day before applications were to be processed, in spite of freezing temperatures.

If our carpenter decides to continue looking for a job paying more than $20 000 per year, he will be considered unemployed because he is actively looking for work. This does not necessarily mean that the labour market is not working properly. The carpenter has *chosen* not to work for a wage of $20 000 per year, but if his value to any firm outside the construction industry is no more than $20 000 per year, we would not expect him to find a job paying more than $20 000. The unemployment rate as measured by the government is thus not necessarily an accurate indicator of whether the labour market is working properly.

If the degree to which industries are changing in the economy fluctuates over time, there will be more people like our carpenter at some times than at others. This will cause the measured unemployment rate to fluctuate. Thus, some economists argue, the measured unemployment rate may sometimes *seem* high even though the labour market is working well. The quantity of labour supplied at the current wage is equal to the quantity demanded at the current wage. The fact that there are people willing to work at a wage higher than the current wage does not mean that the labour market is not working. Whenever there is an upward-sloping supply curve in a market, the quantity supplied at a price higher than the equilibrium price is always greater than the quantity supplied at the equilibrium price.

Economists who view unemployment in this way do not see it as a major problem. Yet the images of the unemployed in the 1930s are still with us, and many find it difficult to believe that everything was optimal when over a million people were looking for work in 1982 and again in the 1990s. Not surprisingly, there are other views of unemployment, and to these we now turn.

Explaining the Existence of Unemployment

If unemployment is a major macroeconomic problem—and many economists believe that it is—then it is worthwhile to explore some of the reasons that have been suggested for its existence. Among these are sticky wages, efficiency wage theory, imperfect information, and minimum wage laws.

STICKY WAGES

One explanation for unemployment (above and beyond normal frictional and structural unemployment) is that wages are **sticky** on the downward side. That is, the equilibrium wage gets stuck at a particular level and does not fall when the demand for labour falls. This situation is illustrated in Figure 15.2, where the equilibrium wage gets stuck at W_0 (the original wage) and does not fall to W^* when demand decreases from D_0 to D_1. The result is unemployment of the amount $L_0 - L_1$, where L_0 is the quantity of labour that households want to supply at wage rate W_0 and L_1 is the amount of labour that firms want to hire at wage rate W_0. $L_0 - L_1$ is thus the number of workers who would like to work at wage rate W_0 but cannot find jobs.

sticky wages *The downward rigidity of wages as an explanation for the existence of unemployment.*

Unfortunately, the sticky wage explanation of unemployment begs the question. *Why* are wages sticky, if they are, and why do wages not fall to clear the labour market during periods of high unemployment? Many answers to this question have been proposed, but as yet no one answer has been agreed upon. The question is still very much open.

A soup kitchen during the Great Depression. The unemployment rate in 1933 was close to 20% in Canada and over 25% in the United States.

■ **Social, or Implicit, Contracts** One explanation for downwardly sticky wages is that firms enter into **social, or implicit, contracts** with workers not to cut wages. It seems that extreme events—such as a deep recession, or threat of bankruptcy—are necessary for firms to cut wages. Wage cuts did occur during the Great Depression. Even now workers will sometimes agree to wage cuts to keep a

social, or implicit, contracts *Unspoken agreements between workers and firms that firms will not cut wages.*

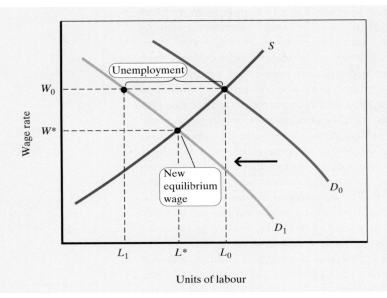

FIGURE 15.2

Sticky Wages

If wages "stick" at W_0 rather than fall to the new equilibrium wage of W^* following a shift of demand from D_0 to D_1, the result will be unemployment equal to $L_0 - L_1$.

firm from insolvency. (A recent example is Canadian Airlines, although the cuts did not save it from eventual takeover by Air Canada.) But naturally workers will be suspicious as to whether the firm really is in dire straits. Moreover firms may not even ask for wage cuts, thinking that the result will be an exodus of the better workers (who might find jobs elsewhere) and a reduction in morale and productivity that would more than offset the savings from the wage reduction. In any case, cutting wages seems close to being taboo.

■ **Explicit Contracts**   Many workers—in particular, unionized workers—sign one- to three-year employment contracts with firms. These contracts stipulate the workers' wages for each year of the contract. Thus, if the economy slows down and firms demand fewer workers, the wage will not fall. Rather, some workers will be laid off.

Although the existence of **explicit contracts** can explain why some wages are sticky, a deeper question must also be considered. Workers and firms surely know at the time a contract is signed that unforeseen events may cause the wages set by the contract to be too high or too low. Why, then, do firms and workers bind themselves in this way? One explanation is that negotiating wages is a costly process. Negotiations between unions and firms can take a considerable amount of time and it would be very costly to negotiate wages weekly or monthly. Contracts are a way of bearing these costs at no more than one-, two-, or three-year intervals. There is thus a tradeoff between the costs of locking workers and firms into contracts for long periods of time and the costs of wage negotiations. The length of contracts that minimizes negotiation costs seems to be (from what we observe in practice) between one and three years.

Some multiyear contracts adjust for unforeseen events by **cost-of-living adjustments (COLAs)** written into the contract. COLAs tie wages to changes in the cost of living: the greater the rate of inflation, the more wages are raised. COLAs thus protect workers from unexpected inflation. Not all contracts contain COLAs, however. Many contracts provide workers with little or no protection from unanticipated inflation, and many COLAs end up adjusting wages by a smaller percentage than the percentage increase in prices.

EFFICIENCY WAGE THEORY

Another explanation for unemployment centres on the **efficiency wage theory,** which holds that the productivity of workers increases with the wage rate. This could be due to lower turnover and improved morale. There may also be reduced "shirking" of work, because if a job pays well, an employee is less likely to risk losing it. If there is indeed such a productivity effect, firms may have an incentive

explicit contracts *Employment contracts that stipulate workers' wages, usually for a period of one to three years.*

cost-of-living adjustments (COLAs) *Contract provisions that tie wages to changes in the cost of living. The greater the inflation rate, the more wages are raised.*

efficiency wage theory *An explanation for unemployment that holds that the productivity of workers increases with the wage rate. If this is so, firms may have an incentive to pay wages above the market-clearing rate.*

to pay wages *above* the wage at which the quantity of labour supplied is equal to the quantity of labour demanded and there will be unemployment.

This view may be consistent with the reluctance by firms to cut wages during a recession. If the wage cut reduces morale sufficiently, the firms may lose more in productivity than they gain from the reduction in wages. But even though the efficiency wage theory predicts the existence of some unemployment, it is unlikely that the behaviour it is describing accounts for much of the observed large cyclical fluctuations in unemployment over time.

MINIMUM WAGE LAWS

The existence of **minimum wage laws** may explain at least a small fraction of unemployment. These laws set a floor for wage rates—a minimum hourly rate for any kind of labour. As of mid-2000, provincial and territorial minimum wages in Canada ranged from $5.50 per hour in Newfoundland to $7.20 per hour in the Yukon Territory. If the market-clearing wage for some groups of workers is below the minimum wage, this group will be unemployed. Refer again to Figure 15.2. If the minimum wage is W_0 and the market-clearing wage is W^*, then the number of unemployed will be $L_0 - L_1$.

Teenagers, who have relatively little job experience, are most likely to be hurt by minimum wage laws. If some teenagers can produce only $5 worth of output per hour, no firm would be willing to hire them in a province in which the minimum wage was $5.50. To do so would be to incur a loss of $0.50 per hour. In an unregulated market, these teenagers would be able to find work at the market-clearing wage of $5 per hour. If the minimum wage laws prevent the wage from falling below $5.50, however, these workers will not be able to find jobs, and they will be unemployed.

In response to this argument against the minimum wage, various jurisdictions in Canada once set lower minimum wages for younger employees. These youth rates have been eliminated in many cases, perhaps as a response to the age discrimination provisions of the 1982 Charter of Rights and Freedoms.

AN OPEN QUESTION

As we've seen, there are many explanations for why the labour market may not clear. The theories we have just set forth are not necessarily mutually exclusive, and there may be elements of truth in all of them. The aggregate labour market is very complicated, and there are no simple answers to the question of unemployment. Much current work in macroeconomics is concerned directly or indirectly with this question, and it is an exciting area of study. Which argument or arguments will win out in the end is an open question.

The Short-Run Relationship Between the Unemployment Rate and Inflation

The relationship between the unemployment rate and the inflation rate—two of the most important variables in macroeconomics—has been the subject of much debate. We now have enough knowledge of the macroeconomy to explore this relationship.

We must begin by considering the relationship between aggregate output (income) (Y) and the unemployment rate (U). An increase in Y means that firms are producing more output. To produce more output, more labour is needed in the production process. Therefore, an increase in Y leads to an increase in employment. An increase in employment means more people working (fewer people unemployed) and a lower unemployment rate. An increase in Y corresponds to a *decrease* in U. Thus U and Y are *negatively* related:

minimum wage laws *Laws that set a floor for wage rates—that is, a minimum hourly rate for any kind of labour.*

Table 15.1

Minimum Hourly Wages, July 2000

Newfoundland	$5.50
P.E.I.	5.60
Nova Scotia	5.60
New Brunswick	5.75
Quebec	6.90
Ontario	6.85
Manitoba	6.00
Saskatchewan	6.00
Alberta	5.90
British Columbia	7.15
Yukon	7.20
Northwest Territories	6.50
Nunavut	6.50

Note: There are also a number of special minimum wage rates. For details and updates see the Human Resources Development Canada Web site (**www.hrdc.gc.ca/**).

FAST FACTS

Until the early 1970s some provinces had separate minimum wages for men and women. For example in 1969, the P.E.I. minimum hourly wage was $0.95 for women, $1.25 for men.

Does the Minimum Wage Eliminate Jobs?

Many of you may work or will have worked for minimum wage and may well have been glad that the legislation prevented your employer from paying you still less. But does the minimum wage eliminate some potential jobs that you or others might otherwise obtain and hence contribute to unemployment? In a study instantly famous among economists, David Card (a Canadian) and Alan Krueger, both of Princeton University, found that when the state of New Jersey raised its minimum wage in 1992, contrary to standard economic theory, there appeared to be a small *increase* in fast-food restaurant employment relative to neighbouring Pennsylvania, where there had been no change in the minimum wage. While subsequent research showed that alternative methods of measurement might rather have indicated a small decrease in employment, nonetheless this evidence suggests that even in an industry where the minimum wage is important, moderate increases in the minimum wage may only have small employment effects.

In an article in the journal *Policy Options*, University of Toronto economist Dwayne Benjamin considers the relevance of the evidence for Canada (including his own research, some with co-authors Michael Baker and Shuchita Stanger). He points out that since 1975, largely because the minimum wage has

not kept pace with inflation, the average Canadian minimum wage has fallen from about 50% to well under 40% of the average manufacturing wage, and that Canadian minimum wages measured this way are comparable to U.S. minimum wages. (One conclusion we may draw is that the minimum wage is unlikely to be part of the explanation of worsening Canadian unemployment during this period or of higher unemployment in Canada relative to the United States.) It is estimated that roughly 5% of all jobs in Canada are paid at or below minimum wage.

Should those being paid the minimum wage want it to be increased? This is a tradeoff of course, because if it does eliminate jobs, it will be these individuals who suffer, but if their jobs are retained, they will benefit from the higher wages. Professor Benjamin points out that even though the long-run job elimination effects of a minimum wage increase are probably significantly larger than in the short run (as perhaps if minimum wages go up, in the long run some firms reconfigure their operations to save labour), it is likely that a rise in the minimum wage increases the total wage payments to minimum wage workers. (I.e., the increase in wages paid to those who retain their jobs will exceed the wages lost by those who lose their jobs.) So minimum

wage earners might well reasonably favour taking the chance on a minimum wage increase.

Will increasing the minimum wage significantly affect poverty? Perhaps not, because Professor Benjamin finds that the poorest 10% of households typically have no wage earners and cannot benefit from minimum wage changes. Only about 45% of the increase in minimum wages would accrue to the poorest 30% of individuals. One reason more of the benefit does not go to the poor is that about one-third of minimum wage workers are teenagers, many of whom come from middle-income and higher-income households. A study by Michael Shannon of Lakehead University and Charles Beach of Queen's University finds that an increase in the Ontario minimum wage of about 35% would have rather small effects on the overall poverty rate.

Sources: David Card and Alan B. Krueger, "Minimum Wages and Employment: A Case Study of the Fast-Food Industry in New Jersey and Pennsylvania," *American Economic Review*, vol. 84 September 1994: 772–793; Dwayne Benjamin, "Do Minimum Wages Really Matter?" *Policy Options*, July-August 1996: 37–41; Michael T. Shannon and Charles M. Beach, "Distributional Employment Effects of Ontario Minimum-Wage Proposals: A Microdata Approach," *Canadian Public Policy*, September 1995: 284–303.

When *Y* rises, the unemployment rate falls, and when *Y* falls, the unemployment rate rises.

Next consider an upward-sloping aggregate supply (*AS*) curve, as shown in Figure 15.3. This curve represents the relationship between *Y* and the overall price level (*P*). The relationship is a positive one: when *Y* increases, *P* increases, and when *Y* decreases, *P* decreases.

As is described in Chapter 14, the shape of the *AS* curve is determined by the behaviour of firms and how they react to an increase in demand. If aggregate demand shifts to the right and the economy is operating on the nearly flat part of the *AS* curve—far from capacity—output will increase but the price level will not change much. However, if the economy is operating on the steep part of the *AS* curve—close to capacity—an increase in demand will drive up the price level, but output will be constrained by capacity and will not increase much.

Think about what will happen following an event that leads to an increase in aggregate demand. First, firms experience an unanticipated decline in inventories. They respond by increasing output (*Y*) and hiring workers. Thus, the unemploy-

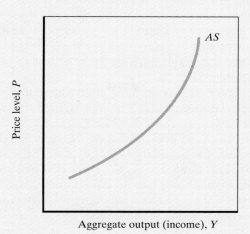

FIGURE 15.3

The Aggregate Supply Curve

The *AS* curve shows a positive relationship between the price level (*P*) and aggregate output (income) (*Y*).

ment rate falls. If the economy is not close to capacity, there will be little increase in the price level. But if aggregate demand continues to grow, the ability of the economy to increase output will eventually reach its limit. As aggregate demand shifts further and further to the right along the *AS* curve, the price level increases more and more, and output begins to reach its limit. At the point at which the *AS* curve becomes vertical, output cannot rise any further. If output cannot grow, the unemployment rate cannot be pushed any lower.

> Along the aggregate supply curve, there is a negative relationship between the unemployment rate and the price level. As the unemployment rate declines in response to the economy moving closer and closer to capacity output, the overall price level rises more and more, as shown in Figure 15.4.

The curve in Figure 15.4 has *not* been a major focus of attention in macro-economics. Rather, the curve that has been extensively studied is shown in Figure 15.5, which plots the inflation rate on the vertical axis and the unemployment rate on the horizontal axis. The **inflation rate** is the percentage change in the price level, not the price level itself.

inflation rate *The percentage change in the price level.*

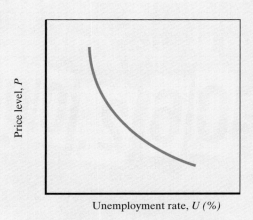

FIGURE 15.4

The Relationship Between the Price Level and the Unemployment Rate

Along the aggregate supply curve, there is a negative relationship between the price level (*P*) and the unemployment rate (*U*). As the unemployment rate declines in response to the economy's moving closer and closer to capacity output, the price level rises more and more.

The implications of Figures 15.4 and 15.5 are different. Figure 15.4 says that the *price level* remains the same if the unemployment rate remains unchanged. Figure 15.5 says that the *inflation rate* remains the same if the unemployment rate remains unchanged. The curve in Figure 15.5 is called the **Phillips Curve,** after A. W. Phillips, who first examined it using data for the United Kingdom. In simplest terms, the Phillips Curve is a graph showing the relationship between the inflation rate and the unemployment rate.

The rest of this chapter focuses on the Phillips Curve in Figure 15.5 because it is the macroeconomic relationship that has been studied the most. Keep in mind, however, that it is not easy to go from the *AS* curve to the Phillips Curve. We have moved from graphs in which the price level is on the vertical axis (Figures 15.3 and 15.4) to a graph in which the *percentage change* in the price level is on the vertical axis (Figure 15.5). Put another way, the theory behind the Phillips Curve is somewhat different from the theory behind the *AS* curve. Fortunately, most of the insights gained from the *AS/AD* analysis regarding the behaviour of the price level also apply to the behaviour of the inflation rate.

THE PHILLIPS CURVE: A HISTORICAL PERSPECTIVE

In the 1950s and 1960s, there was a fairly smooth relationship between the unemployment rate and the rate of inflation, as Figure 15.6 shows. As you can see, the data points suggest a downward-sloping curve; in general, the higher the unemployment rate, the lower the rate of inflation. The data in Figure 15.6 thus show a tradeoff between inflation and unemployment. To lower the inflation rate, we must accept a higher unemployment rate, and to lower the unemployment rate, we must accept a higher rate of inflation.

Textbooks written in the 1960s and early 1970s relied on the Phillips Curve as the main explanation of inflation. Things seemed simple—inflation appeared to respond in a fairly predictable way to changes in the unemployment rate. For this reason, policy discussions at that time revolved around the Phillips Curve. The role of the policy maker, it was thought, was to choose a point on the curve.

Life did not turn out to be quite so simple, however. The Phillips Curve broke down in the 1970s and 1980s. This is easily seen in Figure 15.7, which shows the unemployment rate and inflation rate for the period from 1970 to 2000. The points in Figure 15.7 show no particular relationship between inflation and unemployment.

Phillips Curve *A graph showing the relationship between the inflation rate and the unemployment rate.*

Londoners protest U.K. unemployment in excess of 3 million (about 10%) in 1993. British unemployment fell below 6% by 2000.

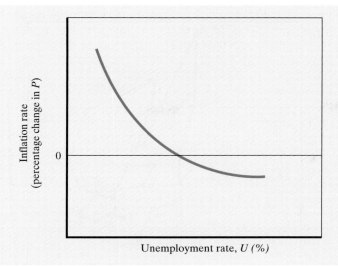

FIGURE 15.5

The Phillips Curve

The Phillips Curve shows the relationship between the inflation rate and the unemployment rate.

AS/AD ANALYSIS AND THE PHILLIPS CURVE

How can we explain the relative stability of the Phillips Curve in the 1950s and 1960s and the lack of stability after that? To answer this question, we need to return to *AS/AD* analysis.

If the *AD* curve shifts from year to year but the *AS* curve does not, the values of *P* and *Y* each year will lie along the *AS* curve (Figure 15.8a). The plot of the relationship between *P* and *Y* will be upward-sloping. Correspondingly, the plot of the relationship between the unemployment rate (which decreases with increased output) and the rate of inflation will be a curve that slopes downward. In other words, we would expect to see a negative relationship between the unemployment rate and the inflation rate.

But the relationship between the unemployment rate and the inflation rate will look different if the *AS* curve shifts from year to year but the *AD* curve does not. A leftward shift of the *AS* curve will cause an *increase* in the price level (*P*) and a

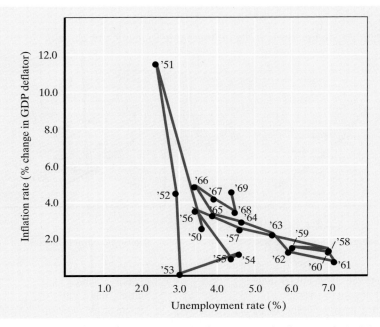

FIGURE 15.6

Unemployment and Inflation, 1950–1969

During the 1950s and 1960s there seemed to be an obvious tradeoff between inflation and unemployment. Policy debates revolved around this apparent tradeoff.

Sources: Inflation: Adapted from Statistics Canada, CANSIM database, Series D14476; Unemployment: Statistics Canada, *Labour Force Annual Averages*, Cat. no. 71-220.

FIGURE 15.7

Unemployment and Inflation, 1970–2000

During the 1970s and 1980s, it became clear that the relationship between unemployment and inflation was anything but simple.

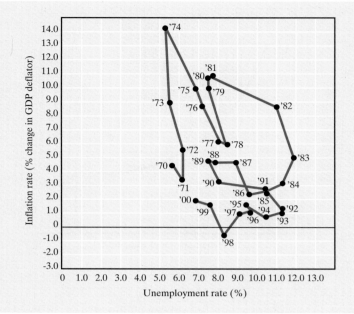

Sources: Inflation: Adapted from Statistics Canada, CANSIM database, Series D14476 and D15612; Unemployment: Statistics Canada, *Labour Force Annual Averages*, Cat. no. 71-220 and CANSIM database, Series D980745. Data for 2000 based on first quarter.

decrease in aggregate output (*Y*) (Figure 15.8b). Thus, when the *AS* curve shifts to the left, the economy experiences both inflation *and* an increase in the unemployment rate (because decreased output means increased unemployment). In other words, if the *AS* curve is shifting from year to year, we would expect to see a positive relationship between the unemployment rate and the inflation rate.

If the *AS* and the *AD* curves are shifting simultaneously, however, there is no systematic relationship between *P* and *Y* (Figure 15.8c) and thus no systematic relationship between the unemployment rate and the inflation rate.

FIGURE 15.8

Changes in the Price Level and Aggregate Output Depend on Both Shifts in Aggregate Demand and Shifts in Aggregate Supply

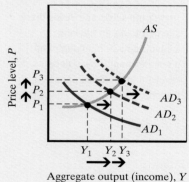

a.
AD shifts with no *AS* shifts trace out the *AS* curve (a positive relationship between *P* and *Y*).

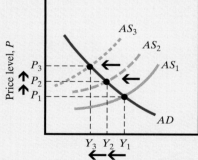

b.
AS shifts with no *AD* shifts trace out the *AD* curve (a negative relationship between *P* and *Y*).

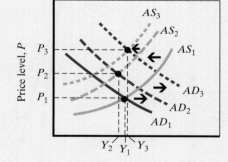

c.
If both *AD* and *AS* are shifting, there is no systematic relationship between *P* and *Y*.

■ The Role of Input Prices One of the main factors that causes the *AS* curve to shift is the price of inputs. One of the most important inputs in production is oil. The industrial product price index for the petroleum industry in Canada is plotted in Figure 15.9 for 1956 (the first year for which the index is available) to 2000. As you can see, the industry selling price of petroleum products changed very little through the 1950s and 1960s. There were thus no large shifts in the *AS* curve over that time due to changes in the price of oil. There were generally no other large changes in input prices in that same period, so overall the *AS* curve shifted very little. The main variation was in aggregate demand, so the shifting *AD* curve traced out points along the *AS* curve.

Figure 15.9 also shows that the price of oil increased dramatically in the 1970s. This led to large shifts in the *AS* curve during the decade. But the *AD* curve was also shifting throughout the 1970s. With both curves shifting, the data points for *P* and *Y* were scattered all over the graph, and the observed relationship between *P* and *Y* was not at all systematic.

This story about oil prices and the *AS* and *AD* curves in the 1960s and 1970s carries over to the Phillips Curve. The Phillips Curve was stable in the 1960s because the primary source of variation in the economy was demand, not costs. In the 1970s (and beyond), both demand *and* costs were varying, so no obvious relationship between the unemployment rate and the inflation rate was apparent.

Other factors that affect costs, such as changes in productivity, can shift the Phillips Curve. In the next section, however, we focus on a different type of reason for a Phillips Curve shift: a change in the expected rate of inflation.

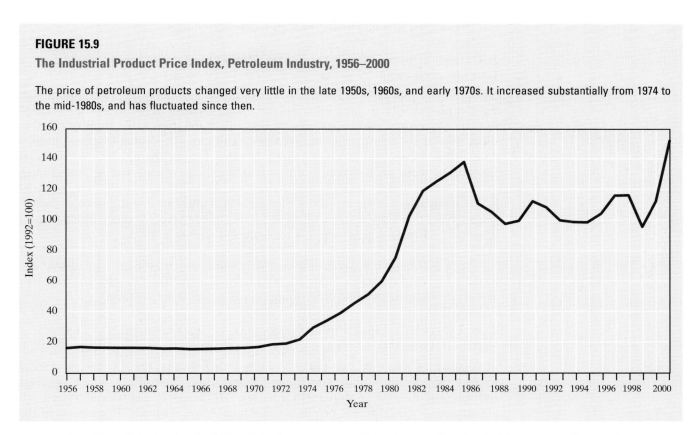

FIGURE 15.9

The Industrial Product Price Index, Petroleum Industry, 1956–2000

The price of petroleum products changed very little in the late 1950s, 1960s, and early 1970s. It increased substantially from 1974 to the mid-1980s, and has fluctuated since then.

Source: Adapted from Statistics Canada, CANSIM database, Series D694144 and P3275. Data for 2000 based on first five months.

EXPECTATIONS AND THE PHILLIPS CURVE

Another reason that the Phillips Curve is not stable concerns expectations. We saw in Chapter 14 that if a firm expects other firms to raise their prices, the firm may raise the price of its own product. If all firms are behaving in this way, then prices will rise because they are expected to rise. In this sense, expectations are self-fulfilling. Similarly, if inflation is expected to be high in the future, negotiated wages are likely to be higher than if inflation is expected to be low. Wage inflation is thus affected by expectations of future price inflation. Because wages are input costs, prices rise as firms respond to the higher wage costs. Thus, price expectations that affect wage contracts eventually affect prices themselves.

If the rate of inflation depends on expectations, then the Phillips Curve will shift as expectations change. For example, if inflationary expectations increase, the result will be an increase in the rate of inflation even though the unemployment rate may not have changed. In this case, the Phillips Curve will shift to the right. Conversely, if inflationary expectations decrease, the Phillips curve will shift to the left—there will be less inflation at any given level of the unemployment rate.

It so happened that inflationary expectations were quite stable in the 1950s and 1960s. The inflation rate was moderate during most of this period, and people expected it to remain moderate. With inflationary expectations not changing very much, there were no major shifts of the Phillips Curve, which helps explain its stability during the period.

Near the end of the 1960s, inflationary expectations began to increase, partly in response to the actual increase in inflation that was occurring because of the rapidly expanding U.S. economy caused by the U.S.-Vietnam War. (High aggregate output in the United States almost always stimulates the Canadian economy, primarily by increasing Canadian exports.) Inflationary expectations increased even further in the 1970s as a result of large oil price increases. These changing expectations also led to shifts of the Phillips Curve.

IS THERE A SHORT-RUN TRADEOFF BETWEEN INFLATION AND UNEMPLOYMENT?

Does the fact that the Phillips Curve broke down beginning the 1970s mean that there is no tradeoff between inflation and unemployment in the short run? Perhaps not. It may simply mean that other things affect inflation aside from unemployment. Just as the relationship between price and quantity demanded along a standard demand curve shifts when income or other factors change, so does the relationship between unemployment and inflation change when other factors change.

> There likely *is* a tradeoff between inflation and unemployment, but other factors besides unemployment affect inflation. Policy involves much more than simply choosing a point along a nice, smooth curve.

Back in Chapter 8, we mentioned that recessions may be the price that the economy pays to eliminate inflation. We can now understand this statement better. When unemployment rises, *other things being equal,* inflation falls.

THE LONG-RUN *AS* CURVE, POTENTIAL GDP, AND THE NATURAL RATE OF UNEMPLOYMENT

In Chapter 14 we noted that many economists believe that the *AS* curve is vertical in the long run. In the short run, we know that some input prices (which are costs to firms) lag increases in the overall price level. If the price level rises without a full adjustment of costs, firms' profits will be higher and output will increase. In the long run, however, input prices may catch up to output price increases. If input prices rise in subsequent periods, driving up costs, the short-run aggregate supply curve will shift to the left, and aggregate output will fall.

This situation is illustrated in Figure 15.10. Assume that the initial equilibrium is at the intersection of AD_0 and the long-run aggregate supply curve. Now con-

FIGURE 15.10

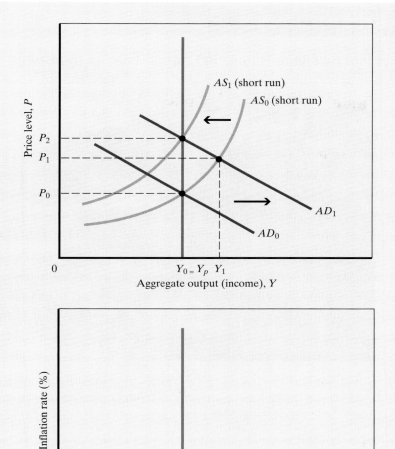

The Long-Run Phillips Curve: The Natural Rate of Unemployment

If the *AS* curve is vertical in the long run, so is the Phillips Curve. In the long run, the Phillips Curve corresponds to the natural rate of unemployment—that is, the unemployment rate that is consistent with the notion of a fixed long-run output at potential GDP.

sider a shift of the aggregate demand curve from AD_0 to AD_1. If input prices lag changes in the overall price level, aggregate output will rise from Y_0 to Y_1. (This is a movement along the short-run *AS* curve AS_0.) But in the longer run, input prices may catch up. For example, next year's labour contracts may make up for the fact that wage increases did not keep up with the cost of living this year. If input prices catch up in the longer run, the *AS* curve will shift from AS_0 to AS_1 and drive aggregate output back to Y_0. If input prices ultimately rise by exactly the same percentage as output prices, firms will produce the same level of output as they did before the increase in aggregate demand.

In Chapter 14, we noted that $Y_0 = Y_p$ is sometimes called *potential GDP*. Aggregate output can be pushed above Y_p in the short run. When aggregate output exceeds Y_p, however, there is upward pressure on input prices and costs. The unemployment rate is already quite low, firms are beginning to encounter the limits of their plant capacities, and so forth. At levels of aggregate output above Y_p, costs will rise, the *AS* curve will shift to the left, and the price level will rise. Thus potential GDP is the level of aggregate output that can be sustained in the long run without inflation.

This story is directly related to the Phillips Curve. Those who believe that the *AS* curve is vertical in the long run at potential GDP also believe that the Phillips Curve is vertical in the long run at some natural rate of unemployment. The **natural rate of unemployment** is the rate of unemployment that corresponds to fixed long-run output at potential GDP. The argument behind the vertical Phillips Curve is

natural rate of unemployment
A concept consistent with the notion of fixed long-run output at potential GDP. Generally considered the sum of the frictional and structural unemployment rates.

Why Is Unemployment So Much Higher in Canada Than in the United States?

During the 1950s, 1960s, and 1970s, the unemployment rates in Canada and the United States were very close, and the U.S. unemployment rate was often higher. But after the 1981–1982 recession, a gap appeared, and since then the Canadian unemployment rate has been higher, by as much as 4.5 percentage points when Canadian unemployment climbed to 11% in the early 1990s. Even by the year 2000 with improved economic conditions in Canada and an unemployment rate less than 7%, there was still a substantial gap with a U.S. unemployment rate of about 4%. What accounts for the difference?

This topic was addressed by Professor Craig Riddell of the University of British Columbia in his presidential address to the Canadian Economics Association in 1999. He points out that measurement issues are important. In Canada, someone who is searching for work by reading job ads—a "passive" method—is counted as unemployed, but in the United States such a person is counted as out of the labour force, unless there is also more "active" search such as contacting potential employers. Also, a much higher fraction of the U.S. population (almost 2% of adult males) is in prison. As inmates have a high unemployment rate when out of prison, the low U.S. unemployment rate may partly reflect that they are not included in the labour force while incarcerated. As an offsetting factor, Canadian unemployment statistics do not cover those living on Indian reserves (where unemployment is often high); the United States includes Indian reservation residents in its labour force statistics. But overall, Professor Riddell concludes that if both countries used the same measurement methods and an appropriate adjustment for differential incarceration rates were included, the "true" gap in the unemployment rate would be about one percentage point

narrower than the official gap.

Professor Riddell also examines another measure, concentrating on employment rather than unemployment. In 1989, even though the unemployment rate was more than 2 percentage points higher in Canada than in the United States, 62% of adults in Canada were employed, while in the United States the figure was almost the same at 63%. Looked at this way, the availability of jobs in the two economies was not so different. The key difference in unemployment rates during this period is that individuals who were not employed in Canada were much more likely to be searching for work and counted as unemployed while individuals not working in the United States were more likely not to be searching for work and hence counted neither as unemployed nor in the labour force. It may be argued that unemployment insurance, which is typically more generous and extensive in Canada, kept some individuals searching for work who would have otherwise left the labour force entirely.

But unemployment insurance is not a good explanation for the higher unemployment/lower employment

experienced by Canada during the 1990s, as the unemployment rate gap widened even as Canada drastically cut the program now called Employment Insurance. During the 1990s, the percentage of U.S. adults employed remained around 63% and even drifted a bit higher. But with the 1990–1991 recession, the comparable number in Canada dropped to 58%, although there was sharp improvement toward the end of the decade so that the rate was over 62% by mid-2000. Professor Riddell's view is that the Canada/U.S. difference in job availability during the 1990s was largely attributable to low aggregate demand resulting from the tight monetary policy in Canada that was aimed at pushing Canadian inflation below American inflation.

Source: W. Craig Riddell, "Presidential Address: Canadian Labour Market Performance in International Perspective," *Canadian Journal of Economics,* November 1999.

that whenever the unemployment rate is pushed below the natural rate, wages begin to rise, thus pushing up costs. This leads to a *lower* level of output, which pushes the unemployment rate back up to the natural rate. At the natural rate, the economy can be considered to be at full employment.

As noted in Chapter 8, even the term "natural rate" is controversial because it leaves the incorrect impression that much unemployment is acceptable, even desirable. Instead it is sometimes called the *nonaccelerating inflation rate of unemployment* or *NAIRU*. To understand this term, consider a version of the economy in Figure 15.10 in which there is some built-in level of inflation. If the *AD* and *AS* curves intersect to the right of Y_p as shown, the increase in the price level can be regarded as additional inflation (or an "acceleration" of inflation). If the *AD* and *AS* curves intersect to the left of Y_p, inflation would fall (negative acceleration or deceleration). Hence the rate of unemployment associated with Y_p is the rate associated with zero acceleration of inflation.

There are two types of government policy to be considered here. The first type includes the monetary and fiscal policies studied in Chapter 14 that are intended to stabilize output around Y_p; if successful these would stabilize unemployment at the natural rate without adding to inflation. A second type of policy might tend to lower the natural rate of unemployment (i.e., shift to the left the entire vertical long-run Phillips Curve in the bottom panel of Figure 15.10). These policies reduce frictional and structural unemployment by improving job search (e.g., by establishing Internet job listings) and by making potential employees better match available jobs (e.g., by retraining). But the natural rate can move for other reasons: for example, it appears to climb when for demographic reasons there are a disproportionate number of young people in the job market. Some economists argue the natural rate will tend to fall if the economy can be held close to full employment for some period, perhaps because employers themselves will invest in more training if skilled workers are harder to find.

Hence there are labour market policies to *lower* the natural rate of unemployment and monetary and fiscal policies to *attain* the natural rate. But because the natural rate can change, it must be treated cautiously as a guide to macroeconomic policy. Some economists estimated the natural rate for the United States in the early 1990s to be at least 6%. Yet the United States attained 4% unemployment by the late 1990s and early 2000s with no immediate inflation. Similarly the Canadian natural rate was estimated to be at least 7.5%, but unemployment in mid-2000 was 6.6%, again without much evidence that the underlying rate of inflation was increasing sharply. Hence there remains an important controversy as to the level of the natural rate. Nonetheless most economists agree that:

> There is a limit to how low the unemployment rate can be pushed without setting off a round of inflation.

Looking Ahead

This chapter concludes our basic analysis of how the macroeconomy works. In the preceding seven chapters, we have examined how households and firms behave in the three market arenas—the goods market, the money market, and the labour market. We have seen how aggregate output (income), the interest rate, and the price level are determined in the economy, and we have examined the relationship between two of the most important macroeconomic variables, the inflation rate and the unemployment rate. In Chapter 16, we use everything we have learned up to this point to examine a number of important policy issues.

Summary

1. Because the economy is dynamic, some *frictional* and *structural unemployment* is inevitable. Nonetheless, there are times of *cyclical unemployment* that concern macroeconomic policy makers.

2. In general, employment tends to fall when aggregate output falls and rise when aggregate output rises.

The Classical View of the Labour Market

3. Classical economists believe that the interaction of supply and demand in the labour market brings about equilibrium and that unemployment (beyond the frictional and structural amounts) does not exist.

4. The classical view of the labour market is consistent with the theory of a vertical aggregate supply curve.

Explaining the Existence of Unemployment

5. Some economists argue that the unemployment rate is not an accurate indicator of whether the labour market is working properly. Unemployed people who are considered part of the labour force may be offered jobs but may be unwilling to take those jobs at the offered salaries. Thus, some of the unemployed may have chosen not to work, but this does not mean that the labour market has malfunctioned.

6. Those who do not subscribe to the classical view of the labour market suggest several reasons why unemployment exists. Downwardly *sticky wages* may be brought about by *implicit* or *explicit contracts* not to cut wages. If the equilibrium wage rate falls but wages are prevented from falling also, the result will be unemployment.

7. *Efficiency wage theory* holds that the productivity of workers increases with the wage rate. If this is true, firms may have an incentive to pay wages above the wage at which the quantity of labour supplied is equal to the quantity of labour demanded. At all wages above the equilibrium, there will be an excess supply of labour and therefore unemployment.

8. *Minimum wage laws*, which set a floor for wage rates, may be one of the factors contributing to unemployment among teenagers. If the market-clearing wage for some groups of workers is below the minimum wage, some members of this group will be unemployed.

The Short-Run Relationship Between the Unemployment Rate and Inflation

9. There is a negative relationship between the unemployment rate (U) and aggregate output (income) (Y): when Y rises, U falls. When Y falls, U rises.

10. The relationship between the unemployment rate and the price level is negative. As the unemployment rate declines and the economy moves closer to capacity, the price level rises more and more.

11. The *Phillips Curve* is a graph illustrating the relationship between the *inflation rate* and the *unemployment rate*. During the 1950s and 1960s, this relationship was fairly stable, and there seemed to be a predictable tradeoff between inflation and unemployment. As a result of input price increases (which led to shifts in aggregate supply) and shifts in aggregate demand brought about partially by inflationary expectations, the relationship between the inflation rate and the unemployment rate since 1970 has been erratic. There likely *is* a short-run tradeoff between inflation and unemployment, but other things besides unemployment affect inflation.

12. Those who believe that the *AS* curve is vertical in the long run also believe that the Phillips Curve is vertical in the long run at the *natural rate of unemployment*. The natural rate is generally taken to be the sum of the frictional and structural rates. If government policy pushes the unemployment rate below the natural rate, inflation will result.

Review Terms and Concepts

cost-of-living adjustments (COLAs) 318

cyclical unemployment 314

efficiency wage theory 318

explicit contracts 318

frictional unemployment 314

inflation rate 321

labour demand curve 315

labour supply curve 314

minimum wage laws 319

natural rate of unemployment 327

Phillips Curve 322

social, or implicit, contracts 317

sticky wages 317

structural unemployment 314

unemployment rate 313

1. It is sometimes argued that Canada has a higher natural rate of unemployment than the United States because Canada has more complete employment insurance. Explain the argument.

2. Japan has traditionally had a substantially lower unemployment rate than Canada, at least since the 1960s. Japanese workers rarely move from one city to another and rarely switch employers, staying with one firm for their entire career. How, if at all, do these factors help to explain the difference in unemployment rates between the two countries?

3. In 2000, the imaginary country of Ruba was suffering a period of high unemployment. The king appointed as his minister of finance Jane Jones. Ms. Jones and her staff estimated the following supply and demand curves for labour from data obtained from the minister of labour, Steven Smith:

$$Q_D = 100 - 5W$$

$$Q_S = 10W - 20$$

where Q is the quantity of labour supplied/demanded in millions of workers and W is the wage rate in slugs, the currency of Ruba.

   a. Currently, the law in Ruba states that no worker shall be paid less than nine slugs per hour. Estimate the quantity of labour supplied, the number of unemployed, and the unemployment rate in Ruba.
   b. The king, over the objection of Minister Smith, has decreed that the law be changed to allow the wage rate to be determined in the market. If the market adjusted quickly, what would happen to total employment, the size of the labour force, and the unemployment rate? Show the results graphically.
   c. Do you think that the Rubanese labour market would adjust quickly to such a change in the law? Why or why not?

4. The following policies have at times been used or advocated for coping with the problem of unemployment. Briefly explain how each policy might work, and explain which type or types of unemployment (frictional, structural, or cyclical) the policy is designed to alter.

   a. Developing a computer list of job openings and a service that matches employees with job vacancies (sometimes called an "economic dating service").
   b. Lowering the minimum wage for teenagers.
   c. Retraining programs for workers who need to learn new skills in order to find employment.
   d. Public employment for people without jobs.
   e. Improving information about available jobs and current wage rates.
   f. A major public speech by the governor of the Bank of Canada in which he maintains that the inflation rate next year will be low.

5. Your boss offers you a wage increase of 10%. Is it possible that you are worse off, even with the wage increase, than you were before?

6. How would the following affect labour-force participation rates? Labour supply? Unemployment?

   a. Because the retired elderly are comprising a larger and larger fraction of the Canadian population, the government decides to raise employees' CPP contributions in order to continue paying CPP benefits to the elderly.
   b. A national child care program is enacted, requiring employers to provide free child care services.
   c. The Canadian government reduces restrictions on immigration into Canada.
   d. The welfare system is eliminated.
   e. The government subsidizes the purchase of new capital by firms (an investment tax credit).

7. Draw a graph to illustrate the following:

   a. A Phillips Curve based on the assumption of a vertical long-run aggregate supply curve
   b. The effect of accelerating inflationary expectations on a recently stable Phillips Curve
   c. Unemployment caused by a recently enacted minimum wage law

8. Suppose economists have predicted an upcoming recession. Also suppose that, as a result, firms plan to reduce workers' wages, but also expect the price level to fall (thus keeping the real wage constant). Would you expect to observe an increase in unemployment? Why or why not?

9. Obtain data on average hourly earnings of manufacturing workers and the unemployment rate for your province over a recent two-year period. Has unemployment increased or decreased? What has happened to wages? Does the pattern of unemployment help explain the movement of wages? Can you offer an explanation?

10. Suppose that the inflation-unemployment relationship depicted by the Phillips Curve was, in fact, stable. Do you think that the Canadian tradeoff and the Japanese tradeoff would be identical? If not, what kinds of factors might make the tradeoffs dissimilar?

16

The Debt and Stabilization Policy

The Federal Debt
The Burden of the Debt

Debt Management and Macropolicy
Economic Stability and Deficit Reduction

The Bank's Response to the State of the Economy

Lags in the Economy's Response to Monetary and Fiscal Policy
Recognition Lags
Implementation Lags
Response Lags

Learning Objectives

1 Explain the difference between the government deficit and the government debt.

2 Describe the impact of government debt on subsequent generations.

3 Explain how a commitment to a balanced government budget could destabilize output.

4 Explain why inflation targeting by the Bank of Canada may or may not stabilize output in the *AS/AD* model.

5 Outline the time lags of stabilization policy.

As we've noted throughout this book, macroeconomics is filled with important policy questions. Newspapers carry articles dealing with macroeconomic problems daily, and macroeconomic issues play an important role in many political campaigns. Using what we've learned about how the macroeconomy works, we can now examine some current issues and problems in greater depth.

In this chapter, we take up three key issues. First, perhaps the overriding macroeconomic policy of the last several years has been government debt and whether government surpluses should be used to pay it down or whether, instead, taxes should be cut or expenditures increased. Hence we explore the impact of the federal government debt on current and future generations. Second, if fiscal policies such as government purchases and net taxes are directed toward debt management, they cannot be used for other possible goals such as stabilizing the macroeconomy to prevent unnecessary unemployment and inflation. As a result we focus on the other main type of stabilization policy, monetary policy, and examine its role in this context. Third, we consider how long fiscal and monetary policies may take to affect the economy, an important factor in developing macroeconomic policy.

The Federal Debt

Recall that the **federal deficit** is the difference between what the federal government spends and what it collects in tax in a given period: $(G - T)$. In 1993, the deficit peaked at nearly \$40 billion but plunged sharply over the next four years and became a surplus by 1997. Recall also that the **federal debt** is the total of all accumulated federal deficits minus surpluses

federal deficit *The difference between what the federal government spends and what it collects in taxes in a given period (G − T).*

federal debt *The total of all accumulated federal deficits minus surpluses over time, or the total amount owed by the federal government.*

over time. We saw in Figure 10.6 how the federal debt as a percentage of GDP has grown in recent decades. The debt was about $575 billion or about $19 000 per Canadian in the year 2000. The government borrows to finance the debt primarily by issuing securities (such as bills, notes, and bonds).

THE BURDEN OF THE DEBT

It is easy to determine where the burden of a household's debt falls. When a family borrows to buy a house or a car, it takes out loans that must be paid off over time. Interest must be paid on these loans. The more a household must spend on principal and interest payments, the less it has to spend elsewhere.

In some respects, the federal government is like a household. In order to borrow, it must pay interest. In another sense, however, the federal government is different from a household. While most households pay off their debts at some point, the federal government has an infinite life. That is, there is no particular moment when the federal debt becomes due and must be paid off. Specific bills, notes, and bonds come due periodically, but the government can simply pay these off with the proceeds of another bill, note, or bond sale.

■ **Does the Debt Harm Subsequent Generations?**   This is one of those questions that has had a sequence of answers over time. Most federal government borrowing (about three-quarters) is from residents of Canada. One view once common was that there would be little burden because we "owe it to ourselves" (although of course the bondholders who receive the interest are not necessarily the same taxpayers who pay it).

This view, however, is incomplete. Even if all of the debt is owned by Canadians, there still may be a burden. In Chapter 13, we noted that a government deficit may tend to increase interest rates and this tends to crowd out either investment or (through exchange rate appreciation) net exports. If the economy is well below potential output and monetary policy is loose enough to limit interest rate increases, these effects may be small. *But if the economy is initially at potential output* and the long-run aggregate supply curve is vertical, the long-run crowding out is complete. For example, consider the long-run effect on the components of aggregate output (income) (Y) of an increase in government spending (G) of $100 financed by borrowing. With no increase in taxes and with no change in income, consumption will not change, at least in our model. As $Y = C + I + G + EX - IM$, if Y and C do not change and G is up by $100, then some combination of planned investment (I) and net exports ($EX - IM$) must fall by $100. The extra spending must come from somewhere.

These changes can hurt subsequent generations. A reduction in investment reduces the potential growth in the productive capacity of the economy. Subsequent generations will be worse off because there is a lower private sector capital stock than there would have been if the government had not run a deficit.

But what if there were no change in investment and all the crowding out were in net exports? How does this hurt future generations? Suppose that net exports were initially zero so that the crowding out effect reduces net exports to *negative* $100. This means that Canadians are buying $100 more of goods from nonresidents than they are selling to nonresidents. In other words, Canadians are spending $100 more than they produce. An individual who spends $100 more than he/she produces must either borrow $100 or use up $100 in assets. Similarly, if Canadians as a whole spend $100 more than they produce, they must be either borrowing the $100 from nonresidents or selling them $100 worth of assets. Hence a reduction in net exports implies that foreign ownership of Canadian assets and/or foreign indebtedness of Canadians will be higher than it otherwise would be. If Canadians currently spend more than they produce, in the future, Canadians will have to produce more than they consume. So while crowding out of net exports may not reduce future productive capacity as does a reduction of investment, it instead increases the fraction of returns from that future capacity that are transferred to nonresidents.

In summary:

> An increase in the government debt may crowd out some combination of investment and net exports. A reduction in investment means a lower level of future productivity capacity than would otherwise have occurred. A reduction in net exports means that either foreign ownership of Canadian assets or foreign indebtedness of residents of Canada will be higher than it would otherwise have been.

The burden of any debt will be considerably lessened if the economy continues to grow. It is at least possible that future generations will be considerably better off than we are. The Canadian government of the 1880s helped finance the national railway system by a combination of taxes and borrowing. Should Canadians of that time, who had short life spans, low nutrition levels, and little education by today's standards, have borrowed less and paid more taxes so that Canadians today could enjoy a more productive economy and a higher standard of living?

■ **Debt for the Finance of Capital Expenditures** To the extent that borrowing is done to finance the purchase of capital assets that will bring benefits over many years, borrowing money and issuing debt are perfectly logical and appropriate ways to finance acquisitions by households, firms, and governments. It makes sense to borrow if the return on the investment exceeds the borrowing rate.

Consider a household that borrows $100 000 to finance a home purchase. Because the house will bring benefits over many years, it is appropriate to pay for it out of future years' incomes by borrowing (signing a mortgage) and agreeing to pay back the loan over many years. When a large corporation decides to build a new production facility, it will more than likely borrow the money by issuing corporate bonds. Those bonds and the interest on them will be paid out of the company's future earnings. Students borrow to pay for education on the grounds that the future return on the acquired human capital will be sufficient to cover the interest expense.

The same logic can be applied to capital acquisitions made by the government. When the province of Saskatchewan builds a bridge, the benefits will be enjoyed by both future generations and people in the present. Most municipalities finance projects such as school buildings and roads by borrowing and issuing debt.[1] Imagine if Canada had tried to finance its part in World War II entirely with taxes and no borrowing. Tax rates would have been so high that it might have been difficult to convince the less patriotic that it was worth working. By borrowing, taxes over time could be "smoothed" so that later generations paid some of the debt as they benefited from the asset (the Allied victory) that was purchased.

Unfortunately, the federal government does not distinguish between capital expenditures and current spending in the budget process. Thus there is no precise way to know how much government borrowing can be justified as capital purchases that will bring benefits in the future. Some have called for the establishment of a federal capital budget so that "capital acquisition" would not be treated in the same manner as current expenditure.

■ **What Does a Deficit Measure?** Much of the concern over the federal debt centres on the fact that it represents a claim on the government in the future. However, a budget deficit may be a misleading indicator of the impact of the overall government budget. This is partly because of the treatment of capital expenditures just mentioned and also because some increases in future obligations are not considered. For example, a loan guarantee appears to cost nothing in terms of the current budget

---

[1]*Just as we argue that the debt may be offset by publicly owned assets (which in principle could include intangible assets such as "education," "health," or "peace"), the great English economist David Ricardo pointed out in the 1800s that the debt may also be offset to some extent by privately owned assets. In our model, consumption only depends on income and taxes. In a Ricardian model, consumers also respond directly to higher government borrowing by consuming less and saving more (in order to be able to pay the higher future taxes they expect will be required to service the increased debt). To the extent that these effects occur, they reduce the crowding out of investment and net exports.*

but may lead to a large expense in the future. Or consider a proposal for a one-time vaccination program. If the government does not fund the program, the current budget balance may look better but if in a number of years an epidemic occurs, the debt incurred to provide publicly funded medical care may be substantial.

Debt Management and Macropolicy

The size of the government debt has been of concern for many years. As we illustrated in Figure 10.6, the debt was very high as a percentage of GDP at the end of World War II and gradually declined until the early 1970s, largely because the growth of the debt in nominal terms was low and hence became a smaller and smaller fraction of more rapidly growing nominal GDP. But during an economic slowdown beginning in the mid-1970s (which continued partly because of the tight monetary policies that were part of the government's anti-inflationary position), the deficit rose to almost $4 billion. By the end of the 1970s, it had reached $10 billion (then about 3% of GDP).

As the debt rose, interest payments became part of the problem, although for several years (1977 to 1979, 1982 to 1985), the budget would not have been in surplus even if there had been no interest payments. So part of the problem was that noninterest government spending exceeded revenues. However, there were perhaps two key monetary events in the subsequent evolution of the debt.

First, in the early 1980s, Canada decided to follow the U.S. lead in pursuing a very tight monetary policy to curb inflation (which was 12.4% in 1981 as measured by the CPI). Interest rates in Canada rose sharply. (Treasury bill rates peaked at over 20%.) The economies of both Canada and the United States entered a deep recession. Largely because of the higher interest rates, interest payments on the government debt increased by $7 billion between 1980 and 1982, a major factor behind the jump in the deficit from $10.6 billion to over $20 billion. With the debt now growing rapidly, interest payments were close to $25 billion by 1985 as the deficit topped $30 billion (over 6% of GDP).

The second key event began in 1989. The economy had begun to grow after the 1980–1982 recession and the deficit had dropped substantially to about $20 billion (3% of GDP). However, monetary policy was tightened to deal with inflation. Three-month Treasury bill rates rose from an annual rate of 9.42% in 1988 to 12.80% in 1990. The increase in interest rates was once again an important factor behind the rise in the deficit: interest payments rose by about $10 billion between 1988 and 1990. As the recession continued, the deficit rose to $35 billion by 1993 (about 5% of GDP). By late 1997, while the deficit had been eliminated, the debt (the accumulated deficits) stood at about 70% of GDP.

Critics of the Bank of Canada argue that the tight monetary policy was therefore critical in the worsening of the federal debt and that the Canadian situation would have been much less serious had interest rates been kept down. Defenders argue that the problem was that government deficit spending both in the 1970s and the 1980s had made the government financial position vulnerable. They say the higher interest rates were necessary in 1981 to prevent a sharp exchange rate depreciation that would have proved inflationary. They credit the second period of higher interest rates in the late 1980s and early 1990s with the low inflation Canada experienced during the early and mid-1990s. The critics maintain that both episodes of tight money contributed to slow growth, harming the economy directly as well as contributing to deficit and debt problems.

In any case, in the mid-1990s the deficit began to fall. Between 1993 and 1997 the federal government significantly reduced spending (including transfers to the unemployed and to the provinces), but even these cuts only contributed about $6 billion to the over $30 billion reduction in the deficit. (It was, however, very important that federal government spending stopped increasing.) A main factor was a growth in tax revenues, which had not grown in real terms between 1989 and 1993 but grew by $25 billion (almost 15% in real terms) between 1993 and 1997. We will discuss this more in the next section.

FIGURE 16.1

Federal Government
Revenue, Expenditures,
and Interest Payments:
Real Percentage
Increases, 1975–2000

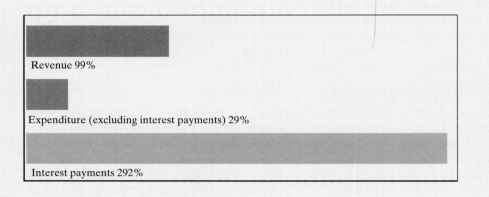

Source: Adapted from Statistics Canada, CANSIM database, Series D15088, D15103, D15115, D15652. Figures for 2000 based on first quarter at annual rates

FAST FACTS

The burden of the debt shrinks in a growing economy. If interest rates stay unchanged and there is always a zero federal budget balance, annual nominal GDP growth of 6% from 2000 to 2020 would bring the 2020 federal government debt-to-GDP ratio down from 58% to 18%. Interest payments would fall to only 8% of federal government revenues from about 26% in 2000: this "fiscal dividend" would free up roughly 18% of the budget (equal to about 40% of federal personal income tax revenues).

negative demand shock
Something that causes a negative shift in consumption or investment schedules or that leads to a decrease in net exports.

automatic stabilizers *Revenue and expenditure items in the federal budget that automatically change with the economy in such a way as to stabilize GDP.*

While interest payments continued to climb because of the accumulating debt, the rate of increase was held down by lower worldwide interest rates (and perhaps looser Bank of Canada monetary policy). For example, three-month Treasury bill annual rates averaged only 4.3% in 1996 and about 3% in the first half of 1997.

Figure 16.1 shows the real percentage increase in federal government revenues, expenditures (less interest payments), and interest payments from 1975 to 2000. Had it not been for "getting behind" and allowing the debt and hence interest payments to rise, government revenues would have more than covered government expenditures.

ECONOMIC STABILITY AND DEFICIT REDUCTION

As the federal government deficit and many of the provincial government deficits are now eliminated, should governments consider legislation to prevent future deficits? For example, in 1986, the United States Congress and President Ronald Reagan signed into law a bill known as the Gramm-Rudman-Hollings Bill, which set targets for reducing the federal deficit to zero in 1991. In a part that was ruled unconstitutional that same year by the U.S. Supreme Court, the bill proposed that if Congress did not subsequently meet these targets, spending cuts would be made automatically. The target dates were changed several times but were never achieved, although eventually a booming economy led to a roughly balanced U.S. budget by 1998.

The U.S. difficulty with this legislation illustrates problems that would be relevant for Canada as well. Parliament cannot pass laws that a subsequent Parliament cannot change. A constitutional provision might be possible, but Canada has had great difficulty changing its Constitution (just as attempts in the United States to introduce a "balanced budget amendment" in their Constitution have always failed).[2] But even if it were possible in political terms, would it be desirable? Should the government choose a target deficit, perhaps zero, and adjust government spending and taxes to achieve this target or should it decide how much to spend and tax and let the deficit adjust itself? The difference may be substantial. Consider a leftward shift of the *AD* curve caused by some negative demand shock. A **negative demand shock** is something that causes a negative shift in consumption or investment schedules or that leads to a decrease in net exports.

We know that a leftward shift of the *AD* curve lowers aggregate output (income), which causes the government deficit to increase. In a world without deficit targeting, the increase in the deficit during contractions provides an **automatic stabilizer** for the economy (described more fully in Chapter 10). The contraction-induced decrease in tax revenues and increase in transfer payments tends to boost

---

[2]*It can also be argued that a balanced-budget rule should not include capital expenditures on items such as roads, which provide benefits over the longer term. Sometimes governments have met tight budgetary targets by cutting capital expenditures and items such as maintenance, which may simply mean more costly projects and repairs in the future.*

consumer incomes and stimulate consumer spending at a time when spending would otherwise be weak. Thus, the decrease in aggregate output (income) caused by the negative demand shock is lessened somewhat by the growth of the deficit (Figure 16.2a).

In a world with deficit targeting, the deficit is not allowed to rise. Some combination of tax increases and government spending cuts would be needed to offset what would have otherwise been an increase in the deficit. We know that increases in taxes or cuts in spending are contractionary in themselves. The contraction in the economy will therefore be larger than it would have been without deficit targeting, because the initial effect of the negative demand shock is worsened by the rise in taxes or the cut in government spending required to keep the deficit from rising. As Figure 16.2b shows, deficit targeting acts as an **automatic destabilizer.** It requires taxes to be raised and government spending to be cut during a contraction. This reinforces, rather than counteracts, the shock that started the contraction.

To summarize:

> The current government budgetary system acts as an automatic stabilizer so that when output falls, tax revenues automatically decrease and government expenditures automatically rise, enhancing aggregate demand and hence cushioning the fall in output. Measures that set this deficit as zero eliminate this automatic stabilizer function.

The advantage of fixed deficit restrictions, however, would be that they ensure that long-term budgetary considerations are part of the political agenda, even in the short term when tax cuts or extra spending measures may be politically popular. The problem is how to preserve automatic stabilization and some degree of flexibility but prevent the serious government debt problems of the 1990s.

The Bank's Response to the State of the Economy

If the fiscal policies of government expenditure and taxes are directed toward either cutting the deficit or running surpluses to reduce the debt, that leaves monetary policy as the other possibility to stabilize aggregate demand and hence output. As we learned in Chapter 12, the Bank of Canada's current announced policy is inflation-targeting. When it believes inflation is moving toward the bottom of its target range (which was, for example, 1% to 3% in 2000), it will initiate more expansionary monetary policy. If inflation is moving toward the top of the target

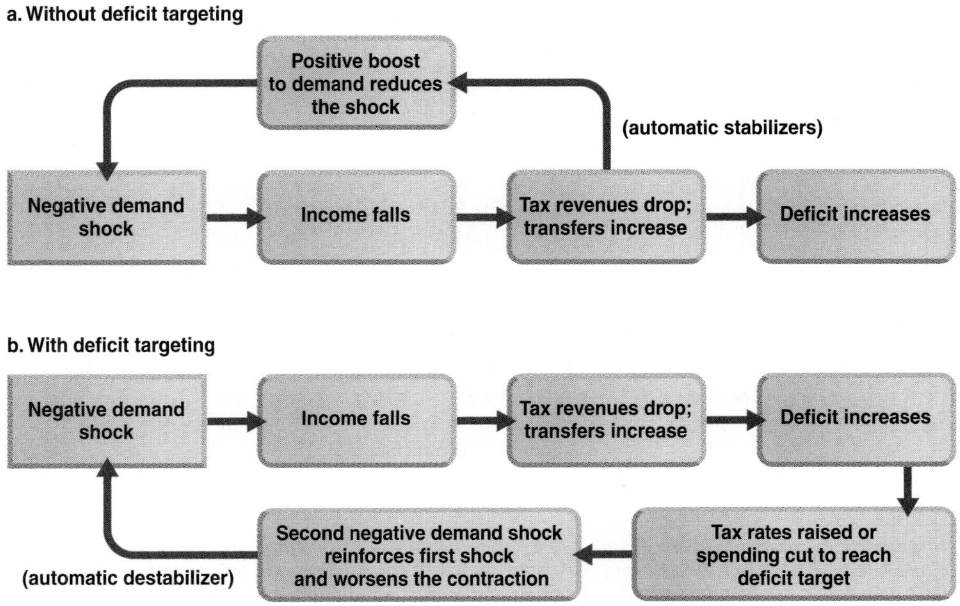

automatic destabilizers
Revenue and expenditure items in the federal budget that automatically change with the economy in such a way as to destabilize GDP.

FIGURE 16.2

Deficit Targeting as an Automatic Destabilizer

Deficit targeting changes the way the economy responds to negative demand shocks because it does not allow the deficit to increase. The result is a smaller deficit, but a larger decline in income than would have otherwise occurred.

a. Without deficit targeting

b. With deficit targeting

FIGURE 16.3

The Bank of Canada's Response to Low Inflation/Low Output

During periods of low inflation/low output, the Bank expands the money supply. This will shift the AD curve to the right, from AD_0 to AD_1, and lead to an increase in output. The economy moves toward potential output.

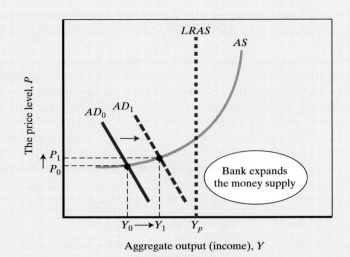

range, it will tighten monetary policy. Will this policy help keep the economy close to potential output without periods of high unemployment and high inflation?

The answer is often yes, *if the Bank of Canada's target range for inflation is consistent with potential output.* Let us see how this would work. In Figure 16.3, aggregate output is below potential output with high unemployment, perhaps because contractionary fiscal policy such as government cutting back expenditure has led to a low level of aggregate demand. But because the economy is below potential output, inflation is likely falling. If inflation reaches the low end of the target range, the Bank expands the money supply, shifting the AD curve to the right and increasing output and employment with some increase in the price level.

If despite the contractionary fiscal policy, aggregate demand is strong (say because of surging exports to a strong U.S. economy), inflation-targeting can still be appropriate. In Figure 16.4, aggregate output is above potential output and inflation is likely high. The Bank contracts the money supply, shifting the AD curve to the left, reducing output and the price level.[3]

FIGURE 16.4

The Bank of Canada's Response to High Inflation/High Output

During periods of high inflation/high output, the Bank contracts the money supply. This will shift the AD curve to the left, from AD_0 to AD_1, and lead to a decrease in the price level. The economy falls back toward potential output.

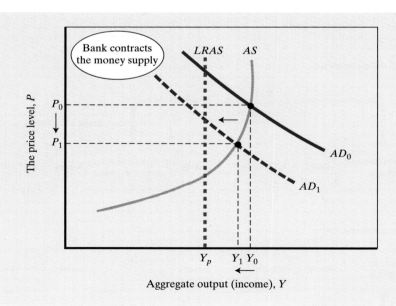

---

[3]*In practice, the price level rarely falls. As has been mentioned for example in Chapter 14, one can think of these changes in the price level as being added to the existing rate of inflation, so what the Bank actually achieves in this case is a decrease in the rate of inflation (i.e., in the percentage change in the price level), not a decrease in the price level itself.*

But such a policy will not always stabilize output in our model. Some economists think that in the early 1990s, inflation was above the Bank of Canada's target, yet output was below potential output. For example, as in Figure 16.5, there could have been a leftward shift in the aggregate supply (AS) curve, perhaps due to higher expectations of inflation affecting wage settlements and other input costs. But in this case the Bank would respond to the increase in inflation by cutting back on the money supply, shifting the aggregate demand curve to the left (from AD_0 to AD_2). Output will fall away from potential output, not move toward it.

Lags in the Economy's Response to Monetary and Fiscal Policy

As we have just discussed, one of the objectives of monetary and fiscal policy is stabilization of the economy. Consider the two possible time paths for aggregate output (income) (Y) shown in Figure 16.6. In path B (the dashed line), the fluctuations in GDP are smaller than those in path A (the solid line). One aim of **stabilization policy** is to smooth out fluctuations in output, to try to move the economy along a path like B instead of A. Stabilization policy is also concerned with the stability of prices. Here the goal is not to prevent the overall price level from rising at all but rather to achieve an inflation rate that is as low as possible given the government's other goals of high and stable levels of output and employment and managing its debt.

Stabilization goals are not easy to achieve. The existence of various kinds of **time lags,** or delays in the response of the economy to stabilization policies, can make the economy difficult to control. Economists generally recognize three kinds of time lags: recognition lags, implementation lags, and response lags. We will consider each, but it is useful to begin with an analogy.

■ **"The Fool in the Shower"**   Milton Friedman, the American Nobel prize–winning economist and a leading critic of stabilization policy, once likened government attempts to stabilize the economy to a "fool in the shower." The shower starts out too cold, because the pipes have not yet warmed up. So the fool turns up the hot water. Nothing happens right away, so he turns up the hot water a bit further. The hot water then comes on and scalds him. He immediately turns up the cold water. Again, nothing happens right away, so he turns up the cold still further. When the cold water finally starts to come up, he finds the shower too cold. And so it goes.

In Friedman's view, the government is constantly behaving like the fool in the shower, stimulating or contracting the economy at the wrong time. An example of

stabilization policy *Monetary and/or fiscal policy whose goals are to smooth out fluctuations in output and employment and keep prices as stable as possible.*

time lag *A delay in the economy's response to stabilization policies.*

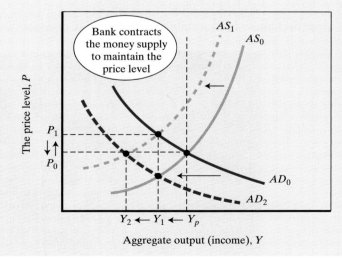

FIGURE 16.5

The Bank of Canada's Response to an Adverse Aggregate Supply Shock

The leftward shift of the aggregate supply curve (AS_0 to AS_1) moves output below potential output to Y_1 and increases the price level to P_1. The Bank responds to the increase in the price level with contractionary monetary policy, moving the price level back to P_0 but reducing output further to Y_2.

FIGURE 16.6

Two Time Paths for GDP

Path *A* is less stable—it varies more over time—than path *B*. Other things being equal, society prefers path *B* to path *A*.

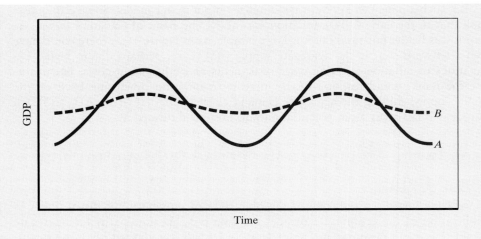

how this might happen is shown in Figure 16.7. Suppose the economy reaches a peak and begins to slide into recession at point *A* (at time t_0). Policy makers do not observe the decline in GDP until it has sunk to point *B* (at time t_1). By the time they have begun to stimulate the economy (point *C*, time t_2), the recession is well advanced and the economy has almost bottomed out. When the policies finally begin to take effect (point *D*, time t_3), the economy is already on its road to recovery. The policies thus push the economy to point *F'*—a much greater fluctuation than point *F*, which is where the economy would have been without the stabilization policy. Sometime after point *D*, policy makers may begin to realize that the economy is expanding too quickly. But by the time they have implemented contractionary policies and the policies have made their effects felt, the economy is starting to weaken. The contractionary policies therefore end up pushing GDP to point *G'* instead of point *G*.

Because of the various time lags, the expansionary policies that should have been instituted at time t_0 do not begin to have an effect until time t_3, when they are no longer needed. The dashed lines in Figure 16.7 show how the economy behaves as a result of the "stabilization" policies; the solid lines show the time path of GDP if the economy had been allowed to run its course and no stabilization policies had been attempted. In this case, stabilization policy makes income more erratic not less—the policy results in a peak income of *F'* as opposed to *F* and a trough income of *G'* instead of *G*.

Critics of stabilization policy argue that the situation in Figure 16.7 is typical of the interaction between the government and the rest of the economy. This is not necessarily true, however. We need to know more about the nature of the various kinds of lags before deciding whether stabilization policy is good or bad.

The government's attempts to stabilize the economy are like trying to get the water temperature just right in the shower, according to Milton Friedman.

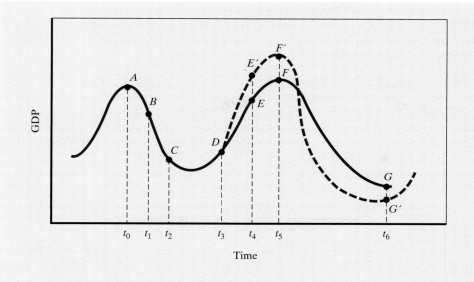

FIGURE 16.7

"The Fool in the Shower"— How Government Policy Can Make Matters Worse

Attempts to stabilize the economy can prove destabilizing because of time lags. An expansionary policy that should have begun to take effect at point *A* does not actually begin to have an impact until point *D*, when the economy is already on an upswing. Hence the policy pushes the economy to points *F'* and *G'* (rather than points *F* and *G*). Income varies more widely than it would have if no policy had been implemented.

RECOGNITION LAGS

It takes time for policy makers to recognize a boom or a slump. Many important data—those from the national accounts, for example—are available only quarterly. It usually takes several weeks to compile and prepare even the preliminary estimates for these figures. Thus, if the economy goes into a slump on January 1, the recession may not show up until the data for the first quarter are available in early June.

Moreover, the early national accounts data are only preliminary, based on an incomplete compilation of the various data sources. These estimates can, and often do, change as better data become available. This makes the interpretation of the initial estimates difficult, and **recognition lags** are the result.

recognition lag *The time it takes for policy makers to recognize the existence of a boom or a slump.*

IMPLEMENTATION LAGS

The problems that lags pose for stabilization policy do not end once economists and policy makers recognize that the economy is in a slump or a boom. Even if everyone knows that the economy needs to be stimulated or reined in, it takes time to put the desired policy into effect, especially for actions that involve fiscal policy. **Implementation lags** are the result.

The implementation lag for fiscal policy is long because it requires the government to bring a budget to Parliament (almost exclusively done in February or March) and for the budget to be passed.[4] Monetary policy can be changed much more quickly, upon the authority of the governor of the Bank of Canada. Therefore:

implementation lag *The time that it takes to put the desired policy into effect once economists and policy makers recognize that the economy is in a boom or a slump.*

> The implementation lag for monetary policy is generally much shorter than it is for fiscal policy.

RESPONSE LAGS

Even after a macroeconomic problem has been recognized and the appropriate policies to correct it have been implemented, there are **response lags**—the lags that occur because of the operation of the economy itself. Even after the government has formulated a policy and put it into place, the economy takes time to adjust to the new conditions.

response lag *The time that it takes for the economy to adjust to the new conditions after a new policy is implemented; the lag that occurs because of the operation of the economy itself.*

---

[4]*Don't forget, however, about the existence of automatic stabilizers. Many programs contain built-in countercyclical features that expand spending or cut tax collections automatically (without the need for government action) during a recession.*

Although monetary policy can be adjusted and implemented more quickly than fiscal policy, it may take longer to make its effect felt on the economy. What is most important is the total lag between the time a problem first occurs and the time the corrective policies are felt.

■ **Response Lags for Fiscal Policy** One way to think about the response lag in fiscal policy is through the government spending and tax multipliers. Remember that these multipliers measure the change in GDP caused by a given change in government spending or net taxes. It takes time for these multipliers to reach full value. There is thus a lag between the time a fiscal policy action is initiated and the time the full change in GDP is realized.

The reason for the response lag in fiscal policy—the delay in the multiplier process—is simple. During the first few months after an increase in government spending or a tax cut, there is not enough time for the firms or individuals who benefit directly from the extra government spending or the tax cut to increase their own spending.

Suppose that you are the owner of Transylvania Trucking, a small fleet of trucks. The government decides to increase its spending, and one of the things it spends more on is trucking services, including some extra purchases from your company. In the first months after you receive this extra business from the government, however, you are unlikely to increase your own purchases. Most of the things you buy—trucks, office furniture, stationery—are already contained in your inventories. It will generally take you some time before your own purchases are increased to reflect the extra income that you have received, and the multiplier effect of government spending will not be felt until this occurs.

> Neither individuals nor firms revise their spending plans instantaneously. Until they can make those revisions, extra government spending does not stimulate extra private spending.

Changes in government purchases are a component of aggregate expenditure. When *G* rises, aggregate expenditure increases directly; when *G* falls, aggregate expenditure decreases directly. When personal taxes are changed, however, an additional step intervenes, giving rise to another lag. Suppose that a tax cut has lowered personal income taxes across the board. Each household must decide what portion of its tax cut to spend and what portion to save. This decision is the extra step. Before the tax cut gets translated into extra spending, households must take the step of increasing their spending, which usually takes some time.

With a business tax cut, there is a further complication. Firms must decide what to do with their added after-tax profits. If they pay out their added profits to households as dividends, the result is the same as that of a personal tax cut. Households must decide whether to spend or to save the extra funds. Firms may also retain their added profits and use them for investment, but investment is a component of aggregate expenditure that requires planning and time.

In practice, it may take years for a change in taxes or in government spending to have its full effect on the economy. This means that if we increase spending to counteract a recession today, the full effects will not be felt for a substantial period. By that time, the state of the economy might be very different.

■ **Response Lags for Monetary Policy** As you know, monetary policy works by changing interest rates, which affect planned investment and also influence net exports through the channel of exchange rates. Interest rate changes may also have an impact upon consumption. For example, refrigerator sales may be affected directly by interest rates (for people who buy them "on time") but also indirectly, if interest rate changes change the rate of new house construction and if people tend to buy new refrigerators when they move into a new house.

But these things take time. If interest rates fall, it may make it affordable and desirable for me and others to buy new houses. But it will take some time for us to make the required financial arrangements and find the houses we want. Most of us will move into existing houses, but the larger effect on output will come from the building of new houses. It will take some time for builders to get the required approvals, plan the building, and do the building. Finally, only after we move in are we likely to buy any new carpets, draperies, and appliances so that the full effect of the initial change in interest rates will be felt.

Other channels will take varying lengths of time. The aluminum company Alcan may decide to take advantage of lower interest rates by building a new smelter but that will be a very long planning process, particularly with the required environmental approvals. However, some effects on output may be much quicker: GM may anticipate that a lower cost of borrowing will stimulate car sales and expand a shift in order to make sure inventory is sufficient. A fall in the Canadian dollar makes B.C. lumber more attractive on world markets and almost instantly stimulates sales and production.

While fiscal policy can be targeted by region (e.g., by the location choice for new government projects), there can only be one national monetary policy because the same interest rates and exchange rates will prevail across the country. Nonetheless, as the examples in the preceding paragraph make clear, the effects and lags of monetary policy changes can differ by region.

The lags in monetary policy are surely long and probably vary over time. One way to get an idea is to recall from Chapter 12 that the Bank of Canada's control of the money supply is based upon a model in which a current change in monetary policy is supposed to affect the inflation rate in about six quarters.

■ **Summary**   From this analysis it should be clear that stabilization is not easily achieved. It takes time for policy makers to recognize the existence of a problem, more time for them to implement a solution, and yet more time for firms and households to respond to the stabilization policies taken. Monetary policy can be adjusted more quickly and easily than taxes or government spending, and this makes it a useful instrument in stabilizing the economy. But the effects of both policies can be slow.

Summary

The Federal Debt

1. The *federal deficit* is the difference between what the federal government spends and what it collects in taxes ($G - T$). To finance the deficit, the federal government issues government securities (bills, notes, and bonds).

2. The *federal debt* is the total of all accumulated federal deficits minus surpluses over time. Because most of the federal debt is owned by Canadians, most interest payments on the federal debt are a transfer from one group (taxpayers) to another (bondholders).

3. An increase in the government debt may still be a burden on future generations because it can lead to higher interest rates, which crowd out investment. With lower investment, future capacity will be lower than it otherwise would have been. If the higher interest rates lead to exchange rate appreciation, there may be crowding out of net exports as well. Negative net exports correspond to Canadians spending more than they produce, which can only be financed by selling assets to nonresidents or by foreign borrowing. Therefore, if net exports fall, foreign ownership of Canadian assets and/or Canadian foreign indebtedness will rise. These in turn mean higher dividend and/or interest payments from Canada to nonresidents in the future. Canadians spending more than they produce now must be offset by future Canadians producing more than they spend.

4. Debt is not necessarily a bad thing. To the extent that borrowing is done to finance the purchase of capital assets that will bring benefits over many years, borrowing money and issuing debt are logical ways to finance acquisitions, whether by households, firms, or governments. Unfortunately, the federal government does not budget capital expenditures separately. There is thus no precise way to know how much government borrowing can be justified as capital purchases that will bring benefits in the future.

Debt Management and Macropolicy

5. The problem with federal government debt in Canada began in the mid-1970s, as the deficit increased as the economy slowed. Increases in interest payments started to become a significant factor and this was worsened by large interest rate increases in 1981–1982 and in 1989–1990. Critics of the Bank of Canada therefore blame the Bank in part for the increase in the debt. The reduction in the deficit in the mid-1990s was accomplished by some cuts in federal government spending, but also by much stronger growth in revenues than had been experienced in the early 1990s.

6. Deficit targeting measures that call for automatic spending cuts to eliminate or reduce the deficit may have the effect of destabilizing the economy because they prevent automatic stabilizers from working.

The Bank's Response to the State of the Economy

7. Because the Bank can control the money supply through open market operations, it has the ability to affect aggregate output (income) (Y), the interest rate, the exchange rate, and the price level. The Bank is likely to increase the money supply during times of low inflation and low output, and to decrease the money supply during periods of high inflation and high output. Attempts to reduce inflation when output is below potential output are likely to reduce output further.

Lags in the Economy's Response to Monetary and Fiscal Policy

8. *Stabilization policy* is an inclusive term used to describe both fiscal and monetary policy, the goals of which are to smooth out fluctuations in output and employment and to keep prices as stable as possible. Stabilization goals are not necessarily easy to achieve because of the existence of certain *time lags*, or delays in the response of the economy to macropolicies.

9. A *recognition lag* is the time it takes for policy makers to recognize the existence of a boom or slump. An *implementation lag* is the time it takes to put the desired policy into effect once economists and policy makers recognize that the economy is in a boom or a slump. A *response lag* is the time that it takes for the economy to adjust to the new conditions after a new policy is implemented—in other words, a lag that occurs because of the operation of the economy itself. Lags and effects will differ by sector and by region. In general, monetary policy can be implemented more rapidly than fiscal policy but both policies have long potential lags.

Review Terms and Concepts

automatic destabilizers 337	implementation lag 341	response lag 341
automatic stabilizers 336	negative demand shock 336	stabilization 339
federal debt 332	recognition lag 341	time lag 339
federal deficit 332		

Problem Set

1. Some people argue that the federal debt is not a problem because the country "owes the debt to itself." Who actually owns federal government securities? Does this mean that the debt is not a problem?

2. You are given the following information about the economy (all amounts are in billions of dollars):

(1) Consumption function: $C = 100 + (0.8 \times Y_d)$
(2) Taxes: $T = -150 + (0.25 \times Y)$
(3) Investment function: $I = 60$
(4) Disposable income: $Y_d = Y - T$
(5) Government spending: $G = 80$
(6) Net exports: $EX - IM = 0$
(7) Equilibrium: $Y = C + I + G + EX - IM$

Hint: Deficit is $D = G - T = G - [-150 + (0.25 \times Y)]$

a. Find equilibrium income. Show that the government budget deficit (the difference between government spending and tax revenues) is $5 billion.

b. The government passes a law that requires that the deficit be zero this year. If the budget adopted has a deficit that is larger than zero, the deficit target must be met by cutting spending. Suppose spending is cut by $5 billion (to $75 billion). What is the new value for equilibrium GDP? What is the new deficit? Explain carefully why the deficit is not zero.

c. Suppose that the new law was not in effect and that planned investment falls to $I = 55$.

What is the new value of GDP? What is the new government budget deficit? What happens to GDP if the law is in effect and spending is cut to reach the deficit target? (*Hint:* Spending must be cut by $21.666 billion to balance the budget.)

3. U.S. interest rates obviously affect Canadian monetary policy and Canada a great deal. In July 2000, the most important financial guessing game in the world was to guess whether the U.S. Federal Reserve, chaired by Alan Greenspan, would increase interest rates (which would probably have led to an increase in Canadian interest rates, given that the Bank of Canada at the time appeared unwilling to let the Canadian dollar fall below 67 cents U.S.). Unemployment was about 4.0% in the United States, well below what many economists thought was consistent with potential output. There were no signs of inflation and interest rates were not changed that July. Given what you know about subsequent changes in U.S. interest rates and inflation rates, did Greenspan make the correct decision? Using the concepts of recognition, implementation, and response lags, what were the risks?

4. Some U.S. states are required by law to balance their budgets. Is this measure stabilizing or destabilizing? Suppose all states were committed to a balanced-budget philosophy and the U.S. economy moved into a recession. What effects would this philosophy have on the size of the federal deficit?

5. Sometimes a central bank sets a policy called "leaning against the wind." Rather than targeting inflation, it reacts to real output changes. It responds to rapid real output growth by contracting the money supply and to slow or negative output growth by expanding the money supply. In an *AD/AS* framework, show that this is stabilizing in the face of both aggregate demand and aggregate supply shocks. Given what you know about recognition lags, why might inflation targeting nonetheless be preferred?

6. Explain why stabilization policy may be difficult to carry out. How is it possible that stabilization policies can actually be destabilizing?

7. It takes at least one year for the multiplier to reach its full value. How can you explain this phenomenon? Does this fact have any implications for fiscal policy?

*8. Rather than targeting inflation, as the Bank of Canada does, or targeting real output growth, as in question 5, some economists advocate targeting nominal output growth. Explain why this might be useful and what disadvantages it might have.

Household and Firm Behaviour in the Macroeconomy

Households: Consumption and Labour Supply Decisions

The Keynesian Theory of Consumption: A Review

The Life-Cycle Theory of Consumption

The Labour Supply Decision

Government Effects on Consumption and Labour Supply: Taxes and Transfers

Interest Rate Effects on Consumption

A Summary of Household Behaviour

Firms: Investment and Employment Decisions

Expectations and Animal Spirits

Excess Labour and Excess Capital Effects

Inventory Investment

A Summary of Firm Behaviour

Learning Objectives

1 Explain the life-cycle theory of consumption.

2 Explain how current and expected future real wage rates, employment constraints, and nonlabour income affect households' consumption and labour supply decisions.

3 Describe how changes in taxes and government transfer programs may affect consumption and labour supply.

4 Identify how interest rate and stock market changes may affect consumption spending.

5 Explain why expectations and adjustment costs are important for firms' employment and investment decisions.

6 Discuss the role of inventories in the output decision.

I n Chapters 9 through 15, we considered the interactions of house-holds, firms, the government, and the rest of the world in the goods, money, and labour markets. To keep our discussions as uncomplicated as possible, we have so far assumed fairly simple behaviour on the part of households and firms—the two basic decision-making units in the econ-omy. For example, we assumed that household consumption (C) depends only on income and that firms' planned investment (I) depends only on the interest rate. We did not consider the fact that households make con-sumption and labour supply decisions simultaneously and that firms make investment and employment decisions simultaneously.

Now that we understand the basic interactions in the economy, we must relax these assumptions. In the first part of this chapter, we present a more realistic picture of the influences on households' consumption and labour supply decisions. In the second part, we present a more detailed and realis-tic picture of the influences on firms' investment and employment decisions.

Households: Consumption and Labour Supply Decisions

Before discussing household behaviour, let's review what we have learned so far.

THE KEYNESIAN THEORY OF CONSUMPTION: A REVIEW

The assumption that consumption (C) depends on income, which we have used as the basis of our analysis so far, is one that Keynes stressed in his *General Theory of Employment, Interest and Money*. While Keynes believed that many factors, including interest rates and wealth, are likely to influence the level of consumption spending, he focused on current income:

> The amount of aggregate consumption depends mainly on the amount of aggregate income. The fundamental psychological law, upon which we are entitled to depend with great confidence both . . . from our knowledge of human nature and from the detailed facts of experience, is that men [and women, too] are disposed, as a rule and on average, to increase their consumption as their incomes increase, but not by as much as the increase in their income.[1]

Keynes is explaining the relationship between *aggregate* consumption and *aggregate* income by considering the behaviour of individual men and women, and arguing that at the individual level consumption is likely to increase with current income. Except for a few misers who save scraps of soap and bits of string despite million-dollar incomes, this makes sense. High-income people typically consume more than low-income people. In addition, Keynes is suggesting that, on average, individuals will only spend some fraction of any increase in income, that is, that the individual marginal propensity to consume (MPC) is less than 1.

Let us suppose we observe the annual consumption and income of one individual, Ellen. Suppose her behaviour is well approximated by:

$$\text{Ellen's consumption} = \$3000 + 0.8 \times (\text{Ellen's income})$$

where we are not concerning ourselves with changes in the tax system so you can think of "income" as disposable income. Of course this function is the same kind of linear function we have used in all our modelling of consumption, only this time we are approximating individual rather than aggregate behaviour. Ellen's behaviour obeys Keynes's "fundamental psychological law" in that her consumption increases with income and her MPC is 0.8, which is less than 1.

Economists call the proportion of income spent on consumption the **average propensity to consume (APC)**; it can be calculated by dividing consumption by income. Remember that the MPC is the increase in consumption divided by the increase in income. The APC is all consumption divided by all income. In further writing about the consumption function, Keynes suggested that the APC would likely fall with income, that is, the proportion of income spent on consumption falls. Ellen's consumption is consistent with this view. If her income is $20 000, her consumption is $3000 + 0.8 × $20 000 = $19 000 and her APC is $19 000/$20 000 = 0.95. If her income increases to $30 000, her consumption becomes $3000 + 0.8 × $30 000 = $27 000 and her APC falls to $27 000/$30 000 = 0.9.

average propensity to consume (APC) *The proportion of income households spend on consumption. Determined by dividing consumption by income.*

The average propensity to consume might vary for other reasons including age. At some ages many individuals will have APC values greater than one, as they borrow against future income or use up accumulated assets. At other ages, APC will commonly be less than one as people pay off past debts or save for the future. The next section looks at the effect of such life-cycle considerations upon consumption behaviour.

THE LIFE-CYCLE THEORY OF CONSUMPTION

The **life-cycle theory of consumption** is an extension of Keynes's theory. The idea of the life-cycle theory is that people make lifetime consumption plans. Realizing that they are likely to earn more in their prime working years than they earn earlier or later, they make consumption decisions based on their expectations of lifetime income. People tend to consume less than they earn during their main working years—that is, they *save* during those years—and they tend to consume more than they earn during their early and later years—that is, they *dissave*, or use up savings, during those years.

life-cycle theory of consumption *A theory of household consumption: households make lifetime consumption decisions based on their expectations of lifetime income.*

---

[1]John Maynard Keynes, The General Theory of Employment, Interest and Money (1936), *First Harbinger Ed. (New York: Harcourt Brace Jovanovich, 1964), p. 96.*

The lifetime income and consumption pattern of a representative individual is shown in Figure 17.1. As you can see, this person has a low income during the first part of her life, high income in the middle, and low income again in retirement. Her income in retirement is not zero because she has income from sources other than her own labour—pension payments, interest and dividends, and the like.

The consumption path as drawn in Figure 17.1 is constant over the person's life. This is an extreme assumption, but it illustrates the point, that the path of consumption over a lifetime is likely to be much more stable than the path of income. We may consume an amount greater than our incomes during our early working (and educational) careers. We do this by borrowing against future income, by taking out a car loan, a mortgage to buy a house, or a loan to pay for schooling. This debt is repaid when our incomes have risen and we can afford to use some of our income to pay off past borrowing without substantially lowering our consumption. The reverse is true for our retirement years. Here, too, our incomes are low. But if we consumed less than we earned during our prime working years, we have saved up a "nest egg" that allows us to maintain an acceptable standard of living during retirement.

Fluctuations in wealth are also an important component of the life-cycle story. Many young households borrow in anticipation of higher income in the future. Some households have *negative wealth*—the value of their assets is less than the debts they owe. A household in its prime working years saves to pay off debts and to build up assets for its later years, when income typically goes down. Households whose assets are greater than the debts they owe have *positive wealth*. With its wage earners retired, a household consumes its accumulated wealth. Generally speaking, wealth starts out negative, turns positive, and then falls near the end of life.

The key difference between the Keynesian theory of consumption and the life-cycle theory is that the life-cycle theory suggests that consumption and saving decisions are likely to be based not just on current income but on expectations of future income as well. The consumption behaviour of households immediately following World War II clearly supports the life-cycle story. Just after the war ended, Canadian GDP fell as wage earners moved out of war-related work. However, Canadian consumption spending did not fall as Keynesian theory would predict. People expected to find jobs in other sectors eventually, and they did not adjust their consumption spending to the temporarily lower incomes they were earning in the meantime.

permanent income
The average level of one's expected future income stream.

The phrase **permanent income** is sometimes used to refer to the average level of one's expected future income stream. If you expect that your income will be high in the future (even though it may not be high now), your permanent income is said

FIGURE 17.1

Life-Cycle Theory of Consumption

In their early working years, people consume more than they earn. This is also true in the retirement years. In between, people save (consume less than they earn) to pay off debts from borrowing and to accumulate savings for retirement.

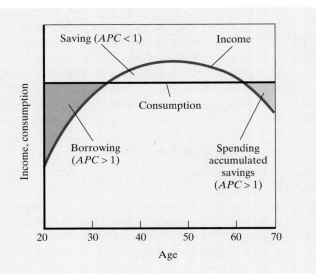

to be high. With this concept, we can sum up the life-cycle theory by saying that current consumption decisions are likely to be based on permanent income rather than on current income.[2]

But although this insight enriches our understanding of the consumption behaviour of households, the analysis is still missing something. What's missing is the other main decision of households: the labour supply decision.

THE LABOUR SUPPLY DECISION

Households decide not only how much to consume but also how much to work. These decisions are not made separately. Obviously,

> Households make consumption and labour supply decisions simultaneously. Consumption cannot be considered separately from labour supply, because it is precisely by selling one's labour that one earns the income that makes consumption possible.

While individuals do supply different amounts of labour at different times in the life cycle, there are other factors that will determine how much they want and are able to work.

■ **Wages** The opportunity cost of an hour of extra leisure is the forgone hourly wage and hence the extra consumption that wage would have bought. Hence the wage is the key variable in the tradeoff between consumption and leisure. While it is theoretically possible that an increase in the wage rate would lead to individuals feeling so much better off financially that they sacrifice some of the additional income and cut back on their hours worked, most economists read the evidence of various studies to suggest that increases in the wage rate have small but positive effects on both labour supply and consumption.

There are three important qualifications. First, distinguish between the **nominal wage rate**, the wage rate in current dollars, and the **real wage rate**, the wage rate that has been adjusted for inflation so that it measures the amount that wages can buy in terms of goods and services. Workers probably care more about the purchasing power of their wage, and therefore it is changes in the real wage that matter for labour supply and consumption.

nominal wage rate *The wage rate in current dollars.*

real wage rate *The amount that the nominal wage rate can buy in terms of goods and services.*

Second, because individuals at least to some extent plan over the life cycle, their expectations as to future real wages will matter for current labour supply and consumption decisions. The medical student who expects that his or her real wage will be higher in the future will be less likely to take a current part-time job and more likely to borrow to purchase a car.

Third, it does not matter what the wage rate is if you cannot find a job. Many households with employment would like to work more at the current wage but the work isn't available. An individual household constrained from working as much as it would like also cannot consume as much as it would like. As current aggregate income increases in the economy, more households are achieving their desired level of employment, and hence current aggregate consumption increases just as in the simple Keynesian consumption function. But again expectations for the future matter as households will probably not increase consumption as much if future employment prospects are poor.

To summarize:

> Households look at expected future real wage rates and employment prospects as well as the current real wage rate and employment status in making their current consumption and labour supply decisions.

---

[2]*The pioneering work on this topic was done by Milton Friedman; see* A Theory of the Consumption Function *(Princeton, N.J.: Princeton University Press, 1957). In the mid-1960s, Franco Modigliani did closely related work that included the formulation of the life-cycle theory.*

■ **Wealth and Nonlabour Income** Life-cycle theory holds that wealth fluctuates over the life cycle. Households accumulate wealth during their working years to pay off debts accumulated when they were young and to support themselves in retirement. This role of wealth is clear, but the existence of wealth also poses another question. Consider two households that are at the same stage in their life cycle and have pretty much the same expectations about future wage rates, prices, and so forth. They expect to live the same length of time, and both plan to leave the same amount to their children. They differ only in their wealth. Because of a past inheritance, household 1 has more wealth than household 2. Which household is likely to have a higher consumption path for the rest of its life? The answer should be obvious: household 1 would, because it has more wealth to spread out over the rest of its life.

> Holding everything else constant (including the stage in the life cycle), the more wealth a household has, the more it will consume, both now and in the future.

Now consider a household that has a sudden unexpected increase in wealth, perhaps an inheritance from a distant relative. How will the household's consumption pattern be affected? It should be obvious that the household will increase its consumption, both now and in the future, as it spends the inheritance over the course of the rest of its life.

An increase in wealth can also be looked upon as an increase in nonlabour income. **Nonlabour, or nonwage, income** is income that is received from sources other than working—inheritances, interest, dividends, and transfer payments such as welfare payments and social insurance benefits. As with wealth:

> An unexpected increase in nonlabour income will have a positive effect on a household's consumption.

But what about the effect of an increase in wealth or nonlabour income on labour supply? With the increase in wealth/nonlabour income, the recipient can consume more *and* have more leisure. He or she is likely not to want to work as hard. Hence:

> An unexpected increase in wealth or nonlabour income leads to a decrease in labour supply.

This point should be fairly obvious. If I suddenly win a million dollars in the lottery, I will probably work less in the future than I otherwise would have.

One major source of fluctuations in the wealth of the household sector is the stock market. Stock prices change considerably over time. Some households hold much of their wealth in stocks, and as stock prices rise or fall, so does household wealth. This is one of the ways in which the stock market affects the economy. By increasing or decreasing household wealth, the stock market influences how much households decide to spend and how much they decide to work. It has been argued that the personal saving rate in Canada has recently been very low (i.e., the average propensity to consume has been very high) because of the large run-up in stock prices in the 1990s. Households spent more because they had more stock-market wealth. (The Application box titled "Reading the Stock Page" discusses how to read stock market listings.)

GOVERNMENT EFFECTS ON CONSUMPTION AND LABOUR SUPPLY: TAXES AND TRANSFERS

When the government raises income tax rates, after-tax real wages decrease. This, in turn, lowers consumption. Conversely, when the government lowers tax rates, after-tax real wages increase. The result is an increase in consumption.

A change in tax rates also affects labour supply. We generally expect that an increase in tax rates, which lowers after-tax wages, will lower labour supply.

nonlabour, or nonwage, income *Any income that is received from sources other than working—inheritances, interest, dividends, transfer payments, and so on.*

Conversely, a decrease in tax rates will increase labour supply. The hope for an increase in labour supply was partly behind the Canadian federal tax reform of 1988, which cut the top marginal federal rate of tax on personal income from 34% to 29%. (Remember that there are separate provincial income tax systems, so that the top total marginal personal income tax rate is much higher, at 40% to 50% in most provinces.) But the evidence from Canada—and from the United States, where more dramatic personal income tax rate changes were made in the 1980s—suggests that the effect on labour supply may be fairly small.

Recall that *transfer payments* are payments such as social insurance benefits, veterans' benefits, and welfare benefits. An increase in transfer payments is an increase in nonlabour income, and we have seen that nonlabour income has a positive effect on consumption and a negative effect on labour supply. Increases in transfer payments thus increase consumption and decrease labour supply, while decreases in transfer payments decrease consumption and increase labour supply. Figure 17.2 summarizes these results.

Using this information, we can again come back to the life-cycle theory and the idea that people look ahead to make lifetime consumption decisions:

> If people look ahead, then changes in income tax rates that are expected to be permanent have a greater effect on current consumption than those that are expected to be temporary. If tax rates are lowered this year, but people expect them to go back up next year, the effect of the tax cut on current consumption is likely to be small.

Upper: Many households hold wealth in stock traded on exchanges such as the Toronto Stock Exchange (TSE). The value of such wealth fell when stock market values plunged sharply worldwide on "Black Monday," October 19, 1987, by more than $37 billion on the TSE alone.
Lower: A performance artist sets fire to some oversized bills in front of the New York Stock Exchange to symbolize all the money that went "up in smoke."

The United States has had clearly temporary income tax changes, for example the "surcharge" enacted in the late 1960s to help pay for its war against Vietnam. It also had an income tax rebate in 1975. The evidence suggests that these temporary income tax changes only had small effects. Canada's experience with temporary income tax changes has been limited: even the federal government's "temporary" surtax on personal income, first applied in 1985, was not removed until 2000.

Life-cycle theory also suggests that expectations of future transfer payments should matter for current behaviour. As an example, virtually all workers employed in Canada belong to the Canada Pension Plan (CPP) or the Quebec Pension Plan (QPP). Employees and employers are required to make annual contributions; a retired worker will receive a monthly CPP or QPP pension cheque for life. Some economists believe that the saving rate would be higher without the CPP/QPP system, as workers consume more and save less currently in expectation of the future CPP/QPP retirement benefits.

	Tax rates		Transfer payments	
	Increase	Decrease	Increase	Decrease
Effect on consumption	Negative	Positive	Positive	Negative
Effect on labour supply	Negative	Positive	Negative	Positive

FIGURE 17.2

Likely Effects of Government on Household Consumption and Labour Supply

APPLICATION

Reading the Stock Page

What Is a Stock?

In addition to issuing bonds, firms can finance investments by borrowing money directly from a bank or other lending institution. A third alternative is for firms to issue additional shares of stock. When a corporation issues new shares of stock, it does not add to its debt. Instead, it brings in additional "owners" of the firm, owners who agree to supply it with funds. The contributions of such owners are treated differently from loans made by outsiders, which are considered liabilities.

What is a share of stock, exactly? If you buy one share of Company QRS, and the firm has 1 million total shares outstanding, you have purchased a one-millionth ownership of the firm. You have a right—along with the owners of the other 999 999 shares—to select the management of the firm and to share in its profits. (This is not true of bondholders and other creditors of the firm, who have no say in its management.) Unlike bonds or direct borrowing, however, your stock does not promise a fixed annual payment. Rather, the returns you receive on your investment depend on how well Company QRS performs. If its profits are high, the firm may elect to pay dividends to its shareholders, although it is not required to do so. If the firm does well, you may also find that the price of QRS stock has gone up, in which case you could realize a *capital gain* by selling your

stock for more than you originally paid for it.

How to Read the Stock Page

In the Application box titled "Bonds and Money Markets" in Chapter 12, we discussed reading bond tables in the newspaper. Now let us discuss reading the stock page.

Figure 1 reproduces a fragment from the stock quotations for the Toronto Stock Exchange (TSE) that appeared in the *National Post* on July 18, 2000. (The TSE is by far the largest stock exchange in Canada.) These quotations report on trading from the previous day.

The *National Post* includes a legend every day to define the symbols used in their tables; not all newspapers have such detailed listings. Figure 1 explains the entry for the first stock listed, Imperial Oil. The fifth stock listed, IncoEpf, is an International Nickel "preferred share," meaning that it pays a preset dividend that does not vary with stock performance. This is much like a bond interest coupon, although bondholders get paid before preferred shareholders in case of financial trouble. The asterisk after the stock name denotes it is traded in U.S. dollars. The "u" by its dividend number indicates the dividend is paid in U.S. dollars.

Source: National Post, July 18, 2000, p. D8.

FIGURE 1

52W high	52W low	Stock	Ticker	Div.	Yield %	P/E	Vol 00s	High	Low	Close	Net Chg
39.55	26.50	ImpOil	IMO	0.78	2.1	19.6	945	37.00	36.30	37.00	+0.05
n2.75	1.26	ImpPlas	IPQ			20.6	1633	1.92	1.75	1.85	+0.14
36.65	21.50	Inco	N			25.3	6179	22.90	22.35	22.50	-0.05
14.50	6.15	IncoVBN					161	6.50	6.45	6.45	-0.10
43.00	37.00	IncoEpf*		u2.75	7.3		12	37.75	37.25	37.75	+0.50
25.75	19.50	IncmFnTr	INC	2.12	8.7		101	24.60	24.50	24.50	
n25.35	15.60	IndlAllia	IAG				50	24.85	24.50	24.60	-0.30
14.35	3.50	InexPhrm	IEX				79	7.10	6.65	7.00	-0.10
10.70	0.97	InflaZyme	IZP				408	4.50	4.39	4.45	+0.05
4.50	0.17	Infocorp	INP				103	1.85	1.60	1.70	-0.15
n13.60	1.50	InfIntAct	IIA				281	5.50	5.25	5.40	-0.05
n69.35	2.95	Infowave	IW				868	15.00	14.20	14.55	
3.35	1.95	Inmet♦	IMN			2.3	5	2.20	2.20	2.20	+0.01
0.19	0.02	Inmet wt					240	0.04	0.04	0.04	
1.20	0.30	Innova	IVO				109	0.84	0.80	0.80	-0.05
10.50	9.90	IntgrOil pf	ION	0.50	5.0		6	10.00	10.00	10.00	-0.05
23.50	15.25	IntgrOil		p0.01	0.1		23	23.00	22.85	23.00	+0.15
0.39	0.12	IntCurator	IC				z346	0.19	0.19	0.19	
7.45	0.35	IntData	IDC			95.5	59	1.95	1.85	1.91	+0.09
0.60	0.08	IntDatashr	IED				525	0.14	0.12	0.12	
6.70	3.50	IntFor A♦	IFP				396	3.65	3.50	3.50	-0.10
0.95	0.055	IntFreegld	ITF				210	0.25	0.22	0.22	-0.01

1. Stock issued by Imperial Oil (IMO). **2.** Over the past year sold at a high of $39.55, low of $26.50. **3.** Over past year paid dividend of 78¢ per share. **4.** Dividend as a percentage of stock's closing price (i.e., 2.1% of $37 = 78¢). **5.** Price-earnings ratio: Ratio of share price to the company's total earnings per share. **6.** Volume: On July 17, 2000, 94 500 shares were traded. **7.** On July 17, 2000, high price of $37, low price of $36.30. For untraded stocks, lowest asking price and highest bid price. **8.** IMO closed at $37, up $0.05 from the previous close.

Source: National Post, July 18, 2000, p. D8.

INTEREST RATE EFFECTS ON CONSUMPTION

Decreases in interest rates (especially decreases in real interest rates, where recall the real interest rate is the nominal interest rate minus the rate of inflation) may increase consumption by reducing the cost of borrowing to purchase a new car or appliance. However, the effect on aggregate consumption may not be that strong. Low real interest rates help borrowers, but they hurt lenders (such as retirees who are living off their savings), who may respond by reducing their consumption.

Because the effect of lower interest rates is to increase the consumption of some and reduce the consumption of others, the total effect is unclear, although most economists believe that for the economy as a whole, interest rate reductions tend to increase consumption, although perhaps by only a small amount. Conversely, interest rate increases will tend to reduce consumption somewhat.

This completes our discussion of household behaviour in the macroeconomy. Clearly, household consumption depends on more than current income. Households determine consumption and labour supply simultaneously, and they look ahead in making their decisions. To summarize:

> The following factors affect household consumption and labour supply decisions:
>
> - Current and expected future real wage rates
> - Current and expected future employment status
> - The initial value of wealth
> - Current and expected future nonlabour income
> - Current and expected future tax rates and transfer payments
> - Interest rates

Firms: Investment and Employment Decisions

Having taken a closer look at the behaviour of households in the macroeconomy, we now turn to a closer look at the behaviour of firms. In discussing firm behaviour earlier, we assumed that planned investment depends only on the interest rate. (Again we emphasize this is the *real* interest rate.) However, there are several other determinants of planned investment. We now turn to a discussion of these factors. We will also discuss the factors that affect firms' employment decisions.

■ **Investment Decisions** At any given time a firm has a certain stock of capital on hand. By *stock of capital* we mean the factories and buildings (sometimes called "plant") that firms own, the equipment they need to do business, and their inventories of partly or wholly finished goods. There are two basic ways that a firm can add to its capital stock. One way is to buy more machinery or build new factories or buildings. This kind of addition to the capital stock is called **plant and equipment investment.**

The other way for a firm to add to its capital stock is to increase its inventories. When a firm produces more than it sells in a given period, the firm's stock of inventories increases.[3] This type of addition to the capital stock is called **inventory investment.** Recall from Chapter 9 that unplanned inventory investment is quite different from planned inventory investment. When a firm sells less than it expected to, it experiences an unplanned increase in its inventories and is thus forced to invest more than it planned to. Unplanned increases in inventories result from factors beyond the firm's control.

While our focus will be on investment by firms, we should mention another investment decision made largely by households, residential construction. Because the decision to build a new house or apartment building is easily postponable, it depends strongly both on real interest rates and on the state of the economy. For example, residential construction fell by more than 25% during the 1990–1991 Canadian recession.

■ **Employment Decisions** In addition to investment decisions, firms also make *employment* decisions. At the beginning of each period, a firm has a certain number of workers on its payroll. On the basis of its current situation and its upcoming plans, the firm must decide whether it wants to hire additional workers, keep the same number of workers, or reduce its workforce by laying off some employees.

Until this point, our description of firm behaviour has been quite simple. In Chapter 9 we argued that firms increase production when they experience unplanned decreases in inventory and reduce production when they experience unplanned increases in inventory. We have also alluded to the fact that the demand

plant and equipment investment *Purchases by firms of additional machines, factories, or buildings within a given period.*

inventory investment *Occurs when a firm produces more output than it sells within a given period.*

---

[3]*The change in inventories is exactly equal to the difference between production and sales. If a firm sells 20 units more than it produces in the course of a month, its inventories fall by 20 units; if it produces 20 units more than it sells, its inventories rise by 20 units.*

for labour increases when output grows. In reality, the set of decisions facing firms is much more complex. A decision to produce additional output is likely to involve additional demand for both labour *and* capital.

■ **Decision-Making and Profit Maximization**   To understand the complex behaviour of firms in input markets, it is often assumed that firms make decisions to minimize their costs. In most cases, a firm must choose among alternative methods of production, or *technologies*. Different technologies generally require different combinations of capital and labour.

Consider a factory that manufactures shirts. Shirts can be made entirely by hand, with workers cutting the pieces of fabric and sewing them together. But shirts can also be made on huge, complex machines that cut and sew and produce shirts with very little human supervision. Between these two extremes are dozens of alternative technologies. For example, shirts can be partly hand-sewn, with the stitching done on electric sewing machines.

All of this is to say that firms' decisions regarding the amount of capital and labour that they will use in production are closely related. If firms maximize profits, they will choose the technology that minimizes the cost of production. That is, it is logical to assume that firms will choose the technology that is most efficient.

The most efficient technology depends on the relative prices of capital and labour. A shirt factory in the Philippines that decides to increase its production faces a large supply of relatively inexpensive labour. Wage rates in the Philippines are quite low. Capital equipment must be imported and is very expensive. A shirt factory in the Philippines is thus likely to choose a **labour-intensive technology**— that is, one that uses a large amount of labour relative to capital. When labour-intensive technologies are used, expansion is likely to increase the demand for labour substantially while increasing the demand for capital only modestly.

Conversely, a shirt factory in Germany that decides to expand production is likely to buy a large amount of capital equipment and to hire relatively few new workers. In other words, it will probably choose a **capital-intensive technology**— that is, a technique that uses a large amount of capital relative to labour. German wage rates are quite high relative to those in the Philippines. Capital, however, is in plentiful supply.

> Firms' decisions about labour demand and investment are likely to depend on the relative costs of labour and capital. The relative impact of an expansion of output on employment and on investment demand depends on the wage rate and the cost of capital.

EXPECTATIONS AND ANIMAL SPIRITS

In addition to the cost of capital and the cost of labour, firms' expectations about the future play an important role in investment and employment decisions.

Time is a key factor in investment decisions. Capital has a life that typically extends over many years. A developer who decides to build an office tower is making an investment that will be around (barring floods or other disasters) for several decades. In deciding where to build a plant, a manufacturing firm is committing a large amount of resources to purchase capital that will presumably yield services over a long period of time. Furthermore, the decision to build a building or to purchase a piece of large equipment must often be made years before the actual project is completed. While the acquisition of a small business computer may take only a few days, the planning process for downtown developments in large cities has been known to take decades.

For these reasons, investment decisions necessarily involve looking into the future and forming expectations about it. In forming their expectations, firms consider numerous factors. At a minimum, they usually gather information about the demand for their specific products, about what their competitors are planning, and about the macroeconomy's overall health. A firm is not likely to increase its production capacity if it does not expect to sell more of its product in the future. Canadian Pacific will not put up a new hotel if it does not expect to fill the rooms

labour-intensive technology
A production technique that uses a large amount of labour relative to capital.

capital-intensive technology
A production technique that uses a large amount of capital relative to labour.

at a profitable rate. Abitibi will not build a new plant if it expects the economy to enter a prolonged recession.

Of course, forecasting the future is fraught with dangers. Many events cannot be foreseen. Investments are therefore always made with imperfect knowledge. Keynes pointed this out in 1936:

> The outstanding fact is the extreme precariousness of the basis of knowledge on which our estimates of prospective yield have to be made. Our knowledge of the factors which will govern the yield of an investment some years hence is usually very slight and often negligible. If we speak frankly, we have to admit that our basis of knowledge for estimating the yield ten years hence of a railway, a copper mine, a textile factory, the goodwill of a patent medicine, an Atlantic liner, a building in the City of London amounts to little and sometimes nothing.

Keynes concludes from this that much investment activity depends on psychology and on what he calls the **animal spirits of entrepreneurs:**

animal spirits of entrepreneurs
A phrase coined by Keynes to describe investors' feelings.

> Our decisions . . . can only be taken as a result of animal spirits. In estimating the prospects of investment, we must have regard, therefore, to nerves and hysteria and even the digestions and reactions to the weather of those upon whose spontaneous activity it largely depends.[4]

Because expectations about the future are, as Keynes points out, subject to great uncertainty, they may change quite often. Thus animal spirits help to make investment a volatile component of GDP.

■ **The Accelerator Effect**   Expectations, at least in part, determine the level of planned investment spending. At any given interest rate, the level of investment is likely to be higher if businesses are optimistic. If businesses are pessimistic, the level of planned investment will be lower. But what determines expectations?

One possibility that seems to be borne out empirically is that expectations are optimistic when aggregate output (Y) is rising and pessimistic when aggregate output is falling.

> At any given level of the interest rate, expectations are likely to be more optimistic and planned investment is likely to be higher when output is growing rapidly than when it is growing slowly or falling.

It is easy to see why. If firms expect future output to grow, they must plan now to add productive capacity. One indicator of future prospects is the current growth rate.

If this is the case in reality, and the evidence indicates that it is, the ultimate result will be an **accelerator effect.** If aggregate output (income) (Y) is rising, investment will increase even though the level of Y may be low. Higher investment spending leads to an added increase in output, further "accelerating" the growth of aggregate output. Conversely, if Y is falling, expectations are dampened, and investment spending will be cut even though the level of Y may be high, thus accelerating the decline.

accelerator effect *The tendency for investment to increase when aggregate output increases and decrease when aggregate output decreases, thus accelerating the growth or decline of output.*

EXCESS LABOUR AND EXCESS CAPITAL EFFECTS

We need to make one further point about firms' investment and employment decisions: firms may sometimes choose to hold **excess labour** and/or **excess capital.** A firm holds excess labour (or capital) if it could reduce the amount of labour it employs (or capital it holds) and still produce the same amount of output.

Why would a firm ever want to employ more workers or have more capital on hand than it needs? After all, both labour and capital are costly—a firm has to pay wages to its workers, and it forgoes interest on its funds if they are tied up in machinery or buildings. Why would a firm want to incur costs that do not yield it anything in the way of revenue?

excess labour, excess capital
Labour and capital that are not needed to produce the firm's current level of output.

[4]*John Maynard Keynes,* The General Theory of Employment, Interest and Money *(1936),* First Harbinger Ed. *(New York: Harcourt Brace Jovanovich, 1964), pp. 149, 152.*

To see why, suppose that a firm suffers a sudden and fairly large decrease in sales, but that it expects the lower sales level to last only a few months, after which it believes that sales will pick up again. In this case, the firm is likely to lower production in response to the sales change in order to avoid too large an increase in its stock of inventories. This decrease in production means that the firm could get rid of some workers and some machines, because it now needs less labour and less capital to produce the now-lower level of output.

But things are not this simple. Decreasing its workforce and capital stock quickly can be quite costly for a firm. Abrupt cuts in the workforce hurt worker morale and may increase personnel administration costs, and abrupt reductions in capital stock may be disadvantageous because of the difficulty of selling used machines. These types of costs are sometimes called **adjustment costs** because they are the costs of adjusting to the new level of output. There are also adjustment costs to increasing output. For example, it is usually costly to recruit and train new workers.

Adjustment costs may be large enough that a firm chooses not to decrease its workforce and capital stock when production falls. In other words, the firm may at times choose to have more labour and capital on hand than it needs to produce its current amount of output, simply because it would be more costly to give them up than to keep them. In practice, excess capital takes the form of fully or partially idle machines. Excess labour may take the form of workers not working at their normal level of activity or at their normal tasks. The Application box titled "Slowdowns and Skilled Workers" shows how a Toronto office furniture manufacturer responded to economic slowdowns in the 1990s.

The existence of excess labour and capital at any given moment is likely to affect future employment and investment decisions. Suppose that a firm already has excess labour and capital due to a fall in its sales and production. When production picks up again, the firm will not need to hire as many new workers or acquire as much new capital as it otherwise would have. In general:

> The more excess capital a firm already has, the less likely it is to invest in new capital in the future. The more excess labour it has, the less likely it is to hire new workers in the future.

This has an implication for **productivity**, sometimes called **labour productivity**. Productivity is total output divided by the number of hours worked in the economy, that is, the output an average worker produces in one hour. As the economy contracts, often measured productivity falls, because firms keep some excess labour and do not cut back their workforce as much as their production. Similarly, as the economy expands, measured productivity often increases, because before hiring new workers, firms first utilize their existing workers more fully, producing more with the same labour. Hence short-term changes in measured productivity reflect the business cycle and typically do not imply anything about the potential of workers or management.

By similar reasoning, when output increases by 1%, the number of jobs will not rise by as much as 1%. As just discussed, when output increases, firms will first use their excess labour. They also may increase the hours per week their current labour force works. In addition, when firms do hire new workers, some jobs may be filled by people who were not counted as unemployed, perhaps because they already had part-time jobs. Also some individuals who were not previously searching for work may seek a job now that opportunities have improved. This increases the ranks of the officially unemployed, as individuals are only counted as unemployed when they are searching for work. **Okun's Law**, named for Arthur Okun, an American economist who first studied the relationship, summarized all these effects by stating that the unemployment rate decreases about one percentage point for every 2.5% increase in real GDP relative to potential GDP.

Further research has indicated that Okun's Law is not a "law" at all, as the relationship between output growth and unemployment is more complex. But the general idea is reflected in Table 17.1. When real output growth in Canada exceeds 2% (a rough estimate of the growth rate of potential GDP) the unemployment rate tends to fall, and when real output growth is less than 2% the unemployment rate

adjustment costs *The costs that a firm incurs when it changes its production level—for example, the administration costs of laying off employees or the training costs of hiring new workers.*

productivity, or **labour productivity** *Output per worker-hour; the amount of output produced by an average worker in one hour.*

Okun's Law *The theory, put forth by Arthur Okun, that the unemployment rate decreases about one percentage point for every 2.5% increase in real GDP relative to potential GDP. Later research and data have shown that the relationship between output and unemployment is not as stable as this "law" predicts.*

tends to rise. For example, the 5% increase in real GDP in 1988 was associated with a drop of 1.1 percentage points in the unemployment rate while the 1.8% drop in real GDP in 1991 corresponded to a 2.3-percentage-point jump in the unemployment rate. But the pattern is not uniform.

INVENTORY INVESTMENT

■ **The Role of Inventories**   Recall the distinction between a firm's sales and its output. If a firm can hold goods in inventory, which is usually the case unless the good is perishable or unless the firm produces services, then within a given period it can sell a quantity of goods that differs from the quantity of goods it produces during that period. When a firm sells more than it produces, its stock of inventories decreases; when it sells less than it produces, its stock of inventories increases. The following relationship thus holds:

> Stock of inventories (end of period) = Stock of inventories (beginning of period) + Production − Sales

For example, if a firm starts a period with 100 umbrellas in inventory, produces 15 umbrellas during the period, and sells 10 umbrellas in this same interval, it will have 105 umbrellas (100 + 15 − 10) left in inventory at the end of the period. A change in the stock of inventories is actually investment because inventories are counted as part of a firm's capital stock. In our example, inventory investment during the period is a positive number, 5 umbrellas (105 − 100). When the number of goods produced is less than the number of goods sold, inventory investment is negative.

■ **The Optimal Inventory Policy**   We can now consider firms' inventory decisions. Firms are concerned with what they are going to sell and produce in the future, as well as what they are selling and producing currently. At each point in time, a firm has some idea of how much it is going to sell in the current period and in future periods. Given these expectations and its knowledge of how much of its good it already has in stock, a firm must decide how much to produce in the current period.

Inventories are costly to a firm because they take up space and they tie up funds that could be earning interest. However, if a firm's stock of inventories gets too low, the firm may have difficulty meeting the demand for its product, especially if demand increases unexpectedly. The firm may lose sales as a result. The point between too low a stock of inventory and too high a stock of inventory is called the **desired,** or **optimal, level of inventories.** This is the level at which the extra cost (in lost sales) from decreasing inventories by a small amount is just equal to the extra gain (in interest revenue and decreased storage costs).

A firm that had no costs other than inventory costs would always aim to produce in a period exactly the volume of goods necessary to make its stock of inventories at the end of the period equal to the desired stock. If the stock of inventory fell lower than desired, the firm would produce more than it expected to sell to bring the stock up. If the stock of inventory grew above the desired level, the firm would produce less than it expected to sell in order to reduce the stock.

There are other costs to running a firm besides inventory costs, however. In particular, large and abrupt changes in production can be extremely costly because it is often disruptive to change a production process geared to a certain rate of output. If production is to be increased, there may be adjustment costs involved in hiring more labour and in increasing the capital stock. If production is to be decreased, there may be adjustment costs in laying off workers and decreasing the capital stock.

Because holding inventories and changing production levels are both costly, firms face a tradeoff between them. Because of adjustment costs, a firm is likely to smooth its production path relative to its sales path. This means that a firm is likely to have its production fluctuate less than its sales, with changes in inventories being used to absorb the difference each period. However, because there are incentives not to stray too far from the optimal level of inventories, fluctuations in production are

Table 17.1

The Relationship Between Output and Unemployment

Year	% Change in Real GDP	Change in Unemployment Rate
1980	1.5	0.0
1981	3.7	0.0
1982	−3.2	3.5
1983	3.2	0.8
1984	6.3	−0.5
1985	4.8	−0.8
1986	3.3	−0.9
1987	4.2	−0.7
1988	5.0	−1.1
1989	2.4	−0.3
1990	−0.2	0.6
1991	−1.8	2.3
1992	0.8	0.9
1993	2.2	−0.1
1994	4.1	−0.8
1995	2.3	−0.9
1996	1.5	0.2
1997	4.0	−0.5
1998	3.1	−0.8
1999	4.2	−0.7

Source: Adapted from the *Bank of Canada Review* (various issues), Tables A1 and A2.

desired, or **optimal, level of inventories** *The level of inventory at which the extra cost (in lost sales) from lowering inventories by a small amount is just equal to the extra gain (in interest revenue and decreased storage costs).*

Not every company lays off workers when business decreases. During the slump of the mid-1990s, the *Globe and Mail*'s *Report on Business Magazine* examined four businesses that confronted downturns without resorting to layoffs. Here is one of those stories.

Betting on a Full House
Teknion Furniture Systems

"The running joke here is that if you stand still for too long, you'll get painted," Frank Delfino, chief operating officer at Teknion Furniture Systems, a Toronto-based office furniture manufacturer, is describing his company's response to a current slowdown. To cope with a drop in sales, Teknion has put many of the 800 skilled tradespeople who work out of its suburban Toronto plant to work cleaning storage areas and painting machinery. ...

Teknion has faced its share of adversity. Like all Canadian furniture manufacturers, 14-year-old Teknion took a double hit in the late 1980s and early 1990s. The free trade agreement between Canada and the United States removed the 15% protective tariff that Canadian manufacturers had long enjoyed. The woes were com-pounded as the domestic economy tumbled into a recession in the early 1990s. ...

According to Delfino, the choice to turn a challenge into an opportunity is a reflection of the company's insistence on being a responsible employer, one that views layoffs as a strategy of last resort. "We know the damage that can be done," says Delfino. "People are not an expendable resource. When you lay off, you lose skill sets, morale and, most important, trust." In its entire history, no permanent employee has been laid off from Global [Teknion's parent company].

As well as asking people to clean house during slow periods, Teknion also strives to maintain staff numbers by opting for people over machines. Pointing to an idle automatic welding unit, Delfino says that "We think it is better to turn off a machine than to send someone home." The COO insists that the choice of people over technology makes economic as well as moral sense. "To turn on a giant, computerized piece of equipment for a short run is not always cost effective," he says.

Ushering a visitor through Teknion's spacious showroom, Delfino offers a last word about the company's people-focused, no-furlough culture. "Our philosophy is constant growth," he says. "To achieve growth, you need the resources and skills. If we were to lay off one-third of our workers—which would be an effective short term solution to our current situation—we would not have the people we needed two months from now when business gets better, which it will. To be prepared for that eventuality, we are willing to eat the cost of keeping our people at work today. In the long run, it's a strategy that works."

This illustrates two points of this chapter very well. The second-to-last paragraph makes it clear this firm considers the potential substitutions between labour and capital in its employment and investment decisions. And throughout the article it is obvious the firm is very concerned about the costs of labour turnover, and hence holds "excess" labour during times of downturn.

Source: Shona McKay, "You're (Still) Hired," *Report on Business Magazine*, December 1996, pp. 54–60.

not eliminated completely. Production is still likely to fluctuate somewhat, just not as much as sales fluctuate.

Two other points need to be made here. First, if a firm's stock of inventories is unusually or unexpectedly high, the firm is likely to produce less in the future than it otherwise would have, in order to decrease its high stock of inventories. In other words, although the stock of inventories fluctuates over time because production is smoothed relative to sales, at any point in time inventories may be unexpectedly high or low because sales have been unexpectedly low or high. An unexpectedly high stock will have a negative effect on production in the future, and an unexpectedly low stock will have a positive effect on production in the future.

> An unexpected increase in inventories has a negative effect on future production, and an unexpected decrease in inventories has a positive effect on future production.

Second, if a firm expects future sales to decrease, it is likely to respond by reducing production now to avoid accumulating inventory. So

FAST FACTS

Inventory investment typically drops sharply during a recession. In Canada, inventory investment in the first quarter of 1979 was at an annual rate of over 10 billion 1986 dollars. By the end of the 1980–1982 recession, it had fallen to *negative* 13 billion 1986 dollars.

Current production depends on expected future sales.

Because production is likely to depend on expectations of the future, animal spirits may once again play an important role. If firms become more optimistic about the future, they are likely to produce more now. Thus, Keynes's view that animal spirits affect investment is also likely to pertain to output.

A SUMMARY OF FIRM BEHAVIOUR

The following factors affect firms' investment and employment decisions:

- The wage rate and the cost of capital (An important component of the cost of capital is the interest rate)
- Firms' expectations of future output
- The amount of excess labour and excess capital on hand

The most important points to remember about the relationship between production, sales, and inventory investment are:

- Inventory investment (i.e., the change in the stock of inventories) equals production minus sales.
- An unexpected increase in the stock of inventories has a negative effect on future production.
- Current production depends on expected future sales.

Summary

Households: Consumption and Labour Supply Decisions

1. The Keynesian theory of consumption holds that household consumption is positively related to income: the higher income is, the higher consumption is. Keynes also believed that high-income households consume a smaller proportion of their income than do low-income households. The proportion of income that households spend on consumption is measured by the *average propensity to consume* (APC), which is equal to consumption divided by income.

2. The *life-cycle theory of consumption* holds that households make lifetime consumption decisions based on their expectations of lifetime income. Generally, households consume an amount less than their incomes during their prime working years and an amount greater than their incomes during their early working years and after they have retired.

3. Households make consumption and labour supply decisions simultaneously. Consumption cannot be considered separately from labour supply, because it is precisely by selling one's labour that one earns the income that makes consumption possible.

4. There is a tradeoff between the goods and services that wage income will buy and leisure or other nonmarket activities. The wage rate is the key variable that determines how a household re-

sponds to this tradeoff.

5. Economists generally presume that increases in the wage rate have small but positive effects on both labour supply and consumption.

6. The *nominal wage rate* is the wage rate in current dollars. The *real wage rate* is the amount that the nominal wage can buy in terms of goods and services. Households look at expected future real wage rates as well as the current real wage rate in making their consumption and labour supply decisions.

7. During times of unemployment, households' labour supply may be constrained. That is, households may wish to work a certain number of hours at current wage rates but may not be able to do so. Households consume less if they are constrained from working.

8. Holding all else constant (including the stage in the life cycle), the more wealth a household has, the more it will consume, both now and in the future.

9. An unexpected increase in *nonlabour income* (i.e., any income that is received from sources other than working, such as inheritances, interest, and dividends) will have a positive effect on a household's consumption and will lead to a decrease in labour supply.

10. The government influences household behaviour mainly through tax rates and transfer payments. An

increase in tax rates lowers after-tax income, decreases consumption, and is expected to decrease the labour supply; a decrease in tax rates raises after-tax income, increases consumption, and is expected to increase labour supply. Increases in transfer payments increase consumption and decrease labour supply, while decreases in transfer payments decrease consumption and increase labour supply.

11. Low interest rates tend to increase consumption for some, but may reduce the consumption of retirees for whom interest income is a significant portion of their income. Overall, most economists believe lower interest rates have at least a small stimulative overall effect on consumption.

Firms: Investment and Employment Decisions

12. Firms purchase inputs and turn them into outputs. Each period, firms must decide how much capital and labour (two major inputs) they wish to use in producing output. Firms can invest in plants and equipment or in inventory.

13. Because output can be produced using many different technologies, firms must make capital and labour decisions simultaneously. A *labour-intensive technique* is one that uses a large amount of labour relative to capital. A *capital-intensive technique* is one that uses a large amount of capital relative to labour. The ultimate decision of which technology to use depends on the wage rate and the cost of capital.

14. Expectations play an important role in investment and employment decisions. Keynes used the term *animal spirits of entrepreneurs* to refer to investors' feelings.

15. At any given level of the interest rate, expectations are likely to be more optimistic and planned investment is likely to be higher when output is growing rapidly than when it is growing slowly or falling. The ultimate result is an *accelerator effect* that can cause the economy to expand more rapidly during an expansion and contract more quickly during a recession.

16. *Excess labour and capital* are labour and capital that are not needed to produce a firm's current level of output. Holding excess labour and capital may be more efficient than laying off workers or selling used equipment. The more excess capital a firm already has, the less likely it is to invest in new capital in the future. The more excess labour it has, the less likely it is to hire new workers in the future.

17. *Productivity*, or *labour productivity*, is defined as output per worker. It is the amount of output produced by an average worker in one hour. Productivity fluctuates over the business cycle, tending to rise during expansions and fall during contractions. The fact that measured productivity falls during contractions does not mean that workers have less potential to produce output; it simply means that workers are not working at their capacity.

18. There is generally a negative relationship between output and unemployment: when output (Y) rises, the unemployment rate (U) falls, and when output falls, the unemployment rate rises. *Okun's Law* stated that the unemployment rate decreases about one percentage point for every 2.5% increase in GDP relative to potential GDP. However, Okun's Law is not a "law" at all—the economy is far too complex for there to be such a stable relationship between two macroeconomic variables.

19. Holding inventories is costly to a firm because they take up space and because they tie up funds that could be earning interest. However, not holding inventories can cause a firm to lose sales if demand increases. The *desired*, or *optimal*, *level of inventories* is the level at which the extra cost (in lost sales) from lowering inventories by a small amount is just equal to the extra gain (in interest revenue and decreased storage costs).

20. An unexpected increase in inventories has a negative effect on future production, and an unexpected decrease in inventories has a positive effect on future production.

21. The level of a firm's planned production path depends on the level of its expected future sales path. If a firm's expectations of its future sales path decrease, the firm is likely to decrease the level of its planned production path, including its actual production in the current period.

Review Terms and Concepts

accelerator effect 355

adjustment costs 356

animal spirits of entrepreneurs 355

average propensity to consume (*APC*) 347

capital-intensive technology 354

desired, or optimal, level of inventories 357

excess capital 355

excess labour 355

inventory investment 353

labour-intensive technology 354

life-cycle theory of consumption 347

nominal wage rate 349

nonlabour, or nonwage, income 350

Okun's Law 356

permanent income 348

plant and equipment investment 353

productivity, or labour productivity 356

real wage rate 349

1. During 1996 and 1997, interest rates declined fairly steadily in Canada, with the rate on a standard ten-year government bond falling from over 8% to less than 7%. Inflation was a steady 1.5%; assume inflation expectations did not change.

   a. How would you expect the lower interest rates to affect consumption and investment?

   b. One of the consequences of this was that the value of existing government bonds increased. (Recall from Chapter 11 that when the interest rates fall, bond prices increase.) How might this affect consumption and how would you expect this to affect aggregate demand?

2. Between 1995 and 1997, mortgage rates fell, with one-year mortgage rates falling three percentage points. During the 1997 federal election, the finance minister, Paul Martin, liked to point out that for a household with a $100 000 mortgage this was a saving of $3000 per year, larger than the value of the tax cut that some of the other parties were promising. Would these lower interest rates stimulate consumption as much as a tax cut? (In your answer, ignore the very small fall in inflation over this period.)

3. Graph the following two consumption functions:

   (i) $C = 300 + 0.5\,Y$

   (ii) $C = 0.5\,Y$

   a. For each function, calculate and graph the average propensity to consume (APC) when income is $100, $400, and $800.

   b. In both examples, what happens to the APC as income rises?

   c. In both examples, what is the relationship between the APC and the marginal propensity to consume?

   d. Under consumption function (i), a family with an income of $50 000 consumes a smaller proportion of its income than a family with an income of $20 000; yet if we take a dollar of income away from the rich family and give it to the poor family, total consumption by the two families does not change. Explain how this could be so.

4. During the late 1980s the price of houses increased dramatically across Canada. During the early 1990s home prices dropped. By 2000, house prices were generally rising again.

   What impact would you expect increases and decreases in home value to have on the consumption behaviour of home owners? Explain. In what ways might events in the housing market have in-fluenced the rest of the economy through their effects on consumption spending? Be specific.

5. Adam Smith is 45 years old. He has assets (wealth) of $20 000 and has no debts or liabilities. He knows he will work for 20 more years and that he will live 5 years after that, and during those 5 years he will earn nothing. His salary each year for the rest of his working career is $14 000. (There are no taxes.) He wants to distribute his consumption over the rest of his life in such a way that he consumes the same amount each year. Of course, he cannot consume in total more than his current wealth plus the sum of his income for the next 20 years. Assume that the rate of interest is zero and that Adam decides not to leave any inheritance to his children.

   a. How much will Adam consume this year? Next year? How did you arrive at your answer?

   b. Plot on a graph Adam's income, consumption, and wealth from the time he is 45 until the time he is 70 years old. What is the relationship between the annual increase in Adam's wealth and his annual saving (income minus consumption)? In what year does Adam's wealth start to decline? Why? How much wealth does he have when he dies?

   c. Suppose that Adam receives a pay raise of $100 per year, so that his income is $14 100 per year for the rest of his working career. By how much does his consumption increase this year? Next year?

   d. Now suppose that Adam receives a bequest this year of $100. That is, his income this year is $14 100, but in all succeeding years his income is back to $14 000. What happens to his consumption this year? In succeeding years?

6. Explain why a household's consumption and labour supply decisions are interdependent. What impact does this interdependence have on the way in which consumption and income are related?

7. Compile a list of factors that are important in determining how much labour you will supply during the summer. How might your list differ from that of a 40-year-old breadwinner?

8. Why do expectations play such an important role in investment demand? How, if at all, does this explain why investment is so volatile?

9. Explain why the size of its existing stock of inventories is negatively related to the amount of output a firm wishes to produce in a period.

10. How can a firm maintain a smooth production schedule even when sales are fluctuating? What are the benefits of a smooth production schedule? What are the costs?

11. Do you agree or disagree with the following statements? Explain your answers.
    a. "The primary reason productivity tends to increase during periods of increased output is that higher wages attract better workers into the labour force."

    b. "The distribution of current consumption levels by households within a society is likely to be less unequal than the distribution of current incomes."

12. If Canada has an unemployment rate of 9% and output grows by 3% over a year, what would Okun's Law predict the new unemployment rate to be? What if output grows by only 1%? (Continue to use our rough estimate that potential GDP grows by 2% per year.)

Web References for Part Four: Macroeconomic Analysis and Issues

For current data on the economies of Europe, Japan, North America, and other developed countries, a good source is the Organization for Economic Co-operation and Development site (**www.oecd.org/**). For other material on global labour markets, try the International Labour Organization (**www.ilo.org/**).

For information on Canadian federal government labour market programs (such as Employment Insurance), look at the Human Resources Development Canada site (**www.hrdc.gc.ca/**). The Centre for the Study of Living Standards (**csls.ca/**) also has a Canadian labour market focus.

Many of the sites listed in the Web References sections for Part Two and Part Three remain applicable, particularly the Statistics Canada and CANSIM sites for basic

Canadian data, and the ever-useful Department of Finance site, where budgetary information gives ongoing reports on the Canadian federal government surplus and the Canadian federal government debt. As was noted in the Part Three Web References, the Department of Finance site gives links to the sites of provincial and territorial governments where information on those governments' budgets is available, and to the sites of financial institutions where commentary on government financial performance is often found. And, again as noted in Part Three, the federal government's Policy Research Initiative site (**policyresearch.schoolnet.ca/**) is an excellent starting point for many policy-oriented searches, in part because of its link to so many independent think tanks.

Recovery in Europe and Deflation in Japan

One way to get a perspective on different types of macroeconomic policy is to compare Canada with other economies. Unemployment rates from different countries for Spring 2000 are presented in Figure 1, along with an arrow to indicate the direction of change since Spring 1997. It is clear that unemployment rates differ markedly across countries. It is also clear that over the 1997 to 2000 period, unemployment fell in Europe but rose in Japan. Why?

First let us consider the variation in unemployment rates. Compare to Canadian and U.S. unemployment rates of 6.8% and 4.0%, respectively, in Spring 2000, the unemployment rates of about 10% in France, Germany, and Italy appear high. But notice that not all Europe suffered from high unemployment rates: Britain had an unemployment rate of 5.6%, and a number of smaller countries, in

particular the Netherlands at 2.7%, had very low unemployment rates.

One explanation for the high overall European unemployment rate is that the macroeconomic slow-down of the 1990s (as most countries pursued contractionary policies in an attempt to reduce inflation) interacted with such programs as unemployment insurance. For example, in what is sometimes called the OECD model (OECD, 1994), the U.S./European unemployment differential (with Canada somewhere in between) is viewed as a result of the concentration of recent technological advance in such areas as computing. This has favoured the well-educated over the less-well-educated in both the United States and Europe. (One result is that there are more jobs in the financial sector but factory workers have been displaced by robot technology.) But low-skilled Europeans who, if they lived in the United States would be forced to

take low-paying "McJobs," have more access to public income support and hence can choose to remain unemployed for longer periods. Thus the United States has low unemployment but wider disparities among wage earners. Most European countries have high unemployment but less wage inequality.

Professor Steven Nickell of Oxford University has further analyzed these issues and argued that high levels of unemployment benefits need not cause high unemployment, provided the duration of benefits is limited and that there are resources for such programs as training, job search assistance, and subsidizing employment for the otherwise unemployable. Similarly, he argues that even though it might be thought that unionization contributes to wage rigidity, the evidence is that unionization does not contribute to unemployment if there are high levels of coordination

FIGURE 1

Unemployment Rates for Selected European Countries and Japan, 2000

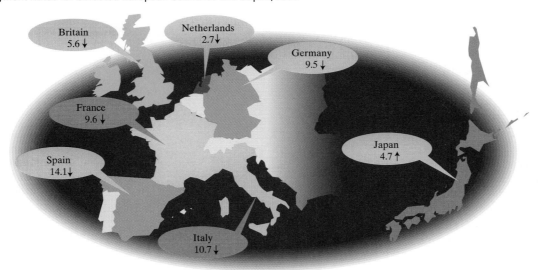

Britain 5.6 ↓
Netherlands 2.7 ↓
Germany 9.5 ↓
France 9.6 ↓
Japan 4.7 ↑
Spain 14.1 ↓
Italy 10.7 ↓

Source: "Economic Indicators," *The Economist,* July 12, 1997, p. 92 and August 19, 2000, p. 88. Arrows indicate direction of change since Spring 1997.

among unions, employers, and government in setting wages.

The Netherlands illustrates Professor Nickell's results, as it has a low rate of unemployment, even though unemployment benefits are high (replacing up to 70% of the wage rather than 38% as in Britain) and over 80% of Dutch workers are covered by union contracts (in contrast to less than 40% in Britain, about 35% in Canada, and about 15% in the United States). The Netherlands also has a system of centralized labour bargaining between employer groups and unions, with substantial government participation. This institutional setting appears to promote cooperation in improving productivity and reducing layoffs. In addition, the Netherlands is pursuing increasingly activist policies designed to get the long-term unemployed off government assistance and into employment.

Spain's unemployment rate is still the highest in Europe, but it fell the most over the three-year period, from 21.7% to 14.1%. It has been argued that high Spanish unemployment was in good part a matter of measurement, with perhaps half of Spanish unemployed actually working in the underground economy. One reason was laws that made it difficult to fire (and hence more risky to hire) permanent employees; an additional consequence was that in 1997 one-third of the employed in Spain were temporary/contract, in contrast to about one-tenth of the employed in Canada. These Spanish laws were weakened in 1997, and that may have helped reduce unemployment—although, as elsewhere in Europe, the primary factor was likely increased aggregate demand.

By Japanese standards, the unemployment rate of close to 5% is very high, compared to levels of just over 3% earlier in the 1990s and typically below that during the 1970s and 1980s. The rising unemployment is due to the Asian crisis

discussed in Case Study Three: Japanese exports to its neighbours have fallen and the Japanese have reacted to the uncertainty by reducing consumption and investment. The end result, as discussed in Chapter 14, is a leftward shift of the *AD* curve, falling output, rising unemployment, and falling prices. While the European countries were experiencing modest increases in inflation during this period, Japan's price level was falling as depicted in Figure 2.

Questions for Analytical Thinking

1. What kinds of fiscal and monetary policies would you propose in the case of Japan?

2. In Japan in the year 2000, two-year government bonds were paying 0.65% with a reasonable inflation forecast of –1%. Calculate the real rate of interest. Assume that nominal interest rates have been effectively driven to zero. What do you think the scope for monetary policy is? For fiscal policy?

3. In the Netherlands, what goals might the government have in its participation in the bargaining between employees and employers?

4. Nobel prize–winning economist Robert Solow has argued that much labour market deregulation in Europe has been accompanied

by higher rather than lower unemployment and argues that the prime reason for high unemployment in Europe is inadequate aggregate demand. Many European countries have adopted one currency and have agreed to meet certain common budget deficit goals. How does this limit fiscal and monetary policy? Explain the potential conflict within this group between, say, France, a high-unemployment country, and the Netherlands, a low-unemployment country.

Sources: Stephen Nickell, "Unemployment and Labor Market Rigidities: Europe Versus North America," *Journal of Economic Perspectives,* Summer 1997: 55–74; OECD, *Jobs Study: Evidence and Explanations* (Paris: Organization for Economic Cooperation and Development, 1994); "Economic Indicators," *The Economist,* July 12, 1997, p. 92 and August 19, 2000, p. 88; Robert Solow, "Unemployment in the United States and in Europe—A Contrast and Its Reasons," *CESifo Forum,* Spring 2000: 3–5; "Steep Drop in Spain's Unemployment," *CESifo Forum,* Spring 2000: 27.

Video Resource: "Deflation," *Venture,* January 20, 2000.

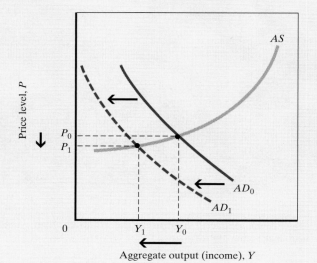

FIGURE 2

Deflation in Japan

Japan in the year 2000 was a classic case of deflation: falling aggregate demand led to falling output, rising unemployment, and a falling price level.

Issues in Macroeconomic Policy: Monetarism, New Classical Theory, and Supply-Side Economics

Learning Objectives

1 Outline the quantity theory of money.

2 Discuss the difference between monetarists and Keynesians in terms of policy recommendations.

3 Define *rational expectations*.

4 Describe the policy implications of the Lucas supply function.

5 Describe supply-side economics and the Laffer curve.

Keynesian Economics

Monetarism

The Velocity of Money

The Quantity Theory of Money

Inflation as a Purely Monetary Phenomenon

The Keynesian/Monetarist Debate

New Classical Macroeconomics

The Development of New Classical Macroeconomics

Rational Expectations

The Lucas Supply Function

Evaluating Rational-Expectations Theory

Real Business Cycle Theory

Supply-Side Economics

Evaluating Supply-Side Economics

Testing Alternative Macroeconomic Models

Throughout this book, we have noted that there are many disagreements and open questions in macroeconomics. For example, economists disagree on whether the aggregate supply curve is vertical, either in the short run or the long run. Some even doubt that the aggregate supply curve is a useful macroeconomic concept! There are different views on whether cyclical unemployment exists and, if it does, what causes it. Economists disagree about whether monetary and fiscal policies are effective at stabilizing the economy, and they support different views on the primary determinants of consumption and investment spending.

We discussed some of these disagreements in previous chapters, but only briefly. In this chapter, we discuss in more detail a number of alternative views of how the macroeconomy works.

Keynesian Economics

John Maynard Keynes's *General Theory of Employment, Interest and Money*, published in 1936, remains one of the most important works in the history of economics. While a great deal of the material in the previous nine chapters is drawn from modern research that postdates Keynes, much of it is built around a framework constructed by Keynes.

But what exactly is *Keynesian economics*? In one sense, it is the foundation of all of macroeconomics. Keynes was the first to stress aggregate demand and the links between the money market and the goods market. And it was Keynes who stressed the possible problem of sticky wages.

In fact, virtually all the debates that we discuss in this chapter can be understood in terms of the aggregate output/aggregate expenditure framework suggested by Keynes.

In recent years, the term "Keynesian" has been used more narrowly. Keynes believed in an activist federal government. That is, he believed that the government had an important role to play in fighting inflation and unemployment, and he argued that monetary and fiscal policy should be used to manage the macroeconomy. Thus, the term "Keynesian" is sometimes used to refer to economists who advocate active government intervention in the macroeconomy.

During the 1970s and 1980s, it became clear that managing the macroeconomy was more easily accomplished on paper than in practice. The inflation problems of the 1970s and early 1980s and the slowdowns of 1974–1975 and 1980–1982 led many economists to challenge the idea of active government intervention in the economy. Some of these challenges were simple attacks on the bureaucracy's ability to act in a timely manner. Others were theoretical assaults that claimed to show that monetary and fiscal policy could have *no effect whatsoever* on the economy, even if it were efficiently managed.

Two major schools of thought that are decidedly *against* government intervention have developed: monetarism and new classical economics. It is to these that we now turn.

Monetarism

The debate between "monetarist" and "Keynesian" economics is complicated by the fact that these terms mean different things to different people. If one takes the main monetarist message to be that "money matters," then almost all economists would agree. In the *AS/AD* story, for example, an increase in the money supply shifts the *AD* curve to the right, which leads to an increase in both aggregate output (*Y*) and the price level (*P*). Monetary policy thus has an effect on output and the price level. Monetarism, however, is usually considered to go beyond the notion that money matters.

THE VELOCITY OF MONEY

velocity of money *The number of times a dollar changes hands, on average, during a year; the ratio of nominal GDP to the stock of money.*

To understand monetarist reasoning, you must understand the **velocity of money**. You can think of velocity as the number of times a dollar changes hands, on average, during a year.

Suppose that in January you buy a new ballpoint pen with a $5 bill. The owner of the stationery store does not spend your $5 right away. She may hold on to it until, say, May, when she uses it to buy a dozen doughnuts. The doughnut store owner does not spend the $5 he receives until July, when he uses it (along with other cash) to buy 100 kilograms of coffee. The coffee distributor uses the bill to buy an engagement ring for his fiancée in September, but the $5 bill is not used again in the remaining three months of the year. Because this $5 bill has changed hands four times during the year, its velocity of circulation is 4. A velocity of 4 means that the $5 bill stays with each owner for an average of three months, or one-quarter of a year.

In practice, we use GDP, rather than the total value of all transactions in the economy, to measure velocity,[1] because GDP data are more readily available. The income velocity of money (*V*) is the ratio of nominal GDP to the stock of money (*M*):

$$V \equiv \frac{GDP}{M}$$

---

[1]*Recall that GDP does not include transactions in intermediate goods (such as the flour sold to a baker to be made into bread) or in existing assets (such as the sale of a used car). If these transactions are made using money, however, they do influence the number of times money changes hands during the course of a year. GDP is thus an imperfect measure of transactions to use in calculating the velocity of money.*

If $800 billion worth of final goods and services are produced in a year and if the money stock is $100 billion, then the velocity of money is $800 billion ÷ $100 billion, or 8.0.

We can expand this definition slightly by noting that nominal income (GDP) is equal to real output (income) (Y) times the overall price level (P):

$$GDP \equiv P \cdot Y$$

Through substitution, we can write

$$V \equiv \frac{P \cdot Y}{M}$$

or

$$M \cdot V \equiv P \cdot Y$$

At this point, it is worth pausing to ask if our definition has provided us with any insights into the workings of the economy. The answer is no. Because we defined V as the ratio of GDP to the money supply, the statement $M \cdot V = P \cdot Y$ is an identity—it is true by definition. It contains no more useful information than the statement "a bachelor is an unmarried man." The definition does not, for example, say anything about what will happen to $P \cdot Y$ when M changes. The final value of $P \cdot Y$ depends on what happens to V. If V falls when M increases, the product $M \cdot V$ could stay the same, in which case the change in M would have had no effect on nominal income. To give monetarism some economic content, we turn to a simple version of monetarism known as the **quantity theory of money.**

THE QUANTITY THEORY OF MONEY

The key assumption of the quantity theory of money is that the velocity of money is constant (or virtually constant) over time, an assumption that has a long history in economics. If we let $\overline{V}$ denote the constant value of V, the equation for the quantity theory can be written:

$$M \cdot \overline{V} = P \cdot Y$$

Note that the double equal sign has replaced the triple equal sign because the equation is no longer an identity. The equation is true if velocity is constant (and equal to $\overline{V}$), but not otherwise. If the equation is true, it provides an easy way to explain nominal GDP. Given M, which can be considered a policy variable set by the Bank of Canada, nominal GDP is just $M \cdot \overline{V}$ In this case, the effects of monetary policy are clear. Changes in M cause equal percentage changes in nominal GDP. For example, if the money supply doubles, nominal GDP also doubles. If the money supply remains unchanged, nominal GDP remains unchanged.

The key question is whether the velocity of money is really constant. Early economists believed that the velocity of money was determined largely by institutional considerations, such as how often people are paid and how the banking system clears transactions between banks. Because these factors change gradually, early economists believed that velocity was essentially constant.

If there is equilibrium in the money market, then the quantity of money supplied is equal to the quantity of money demanded. One can thus think about M in the quantity-theory equation as equalling both the quantity of money supplied and the quantity of money demanded. If the quantity-theory equation is looked upon as a demand-for-money equation, it says that the demand for money depends on nominal income (GDP, or $P \cdot Y$), but *not* on the interest rate. If the interest rate changes and nominal income does not, the equation says that the quantity of money demanded will not change. This is contrary to the theory of the demand for money in Chapter 12, which had the demand for money depending on both income and the interest rate.

■ **Testing the Quantity Theory of Money** One way to test the validity of the quantity theory of money is to look at the demand for money using recent data on the Canadian economy. The key question is: Does money demand depend on the interest rate? Most empirical work says yes. When demand-for-money equations are

quantity theory of money
The theory based on the identity $M \cdot V \equiv P \cdot Y$ and the assumption that the velocity of money (V) is constant (or virtually constant).

estimated (or "fit to the data"), the interest rate usually turns out to be an important explanatory factor. The demand for money does not appear to depend only on nominal income.

Another way of testing the quantity theory is to plot velocity over time and see how it behaves. Figure 18.1 plots the velocity of money for the 1961 I–2000 I period. The data in the figure clearly show that velocity is far from constant. In general, velocity rose from 1961 to 1990 and fell thereafter. Velocity was 7.3 in 1961 I, rose as high as 16.8 by 1990 III and dropped to 10.3 by 2000 I. You can see that there have also been fluctuations around these trends.

The debate over monetarist theories is more subtle than our discussion so far indicates, however. First, there are many definitions of the money supply. *M*1 is the money supply variable used for the graph in Figure 18.1, but there may be some other measure of the money supply that would lead to a smoother plot. Using a broader measure of the money supply, such as *M*2, may give a different view of trends in velocity. *M*2 velocity fell from about 3 in 1970 to about 2 in 2000. However, it still could be the case that a broad enough definition of *M* might show velocity to be constant.

Second, there may be a time lag between a change in the money supply and its effects on nominal GDP. Suppose that we experience a 10% increase in the money supply today, but that it takes one year for nominal GDP to increase by 10%. If we measured the ratio of today's money supply to today's GDP, it would seem that velocity had fallen by 10%. But if we measured today's money supply against GDP one year from now, when the increase in the supply of money had its full effect on income, then velocity would have been constant.

FIGURE 18.1

The Velocity of Money, 1961 I–2000 I (Annual Basis)

Velocity has not been constant over the period from 1961 to 2000. In general, velocity rose until 1990, and fell thereafter. There have also been fluctuations around these trends.

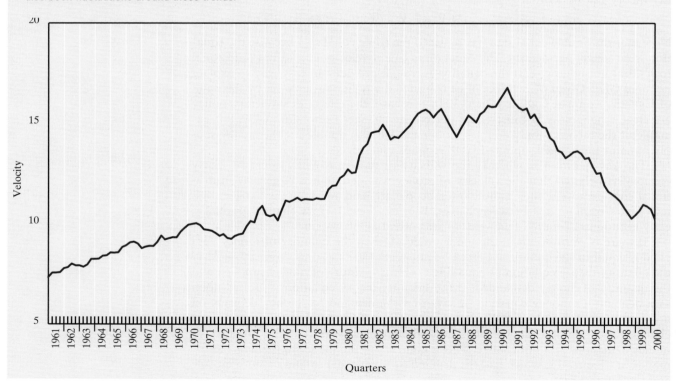

Source: Adapted from Statistics Canada, CANSIM database, Series D14840, B1627.

The debate over the usefulness of monetarist theory is primarily empirical. It is a debate that can be resolved by looking at facts about the real world and seeing whether they are in accord with the predictions of theory. Is there a measure of the money supply and a choice of the time lag between a change in the money supply and its effects on nominal GDP such that V is in effect constant? If so, then the monetarist theory is a useful approach to understanding how the macroeconomy works. If not, then some other theory is likely to be more appropriate. (We discuss the testing of alternative theories at the end of this chapter.)

INFLATION AS A PURELY MONETARY PHENOMENON

So far we have talked only about nominal output ($P \cdot Y$). We have said nothing about how a monetarist would break down a change in nominal output (due to a money-supply change) into a change in P and a change in Y. Here again it is not possible to make a general statement about what all monetarists believe. Some believe that all of the change occurs in P, and others believe that at least sometimes some of the change occurs in Y. If all of the change occurs in P, then there is a proportional relationship between changes in the money supply and changes in the price level. For example, a 10% change in M will lead to a 10% change in P if Y remains unchanged. We will call this view, that changes in M affect only P and not Y, the "strict monetarist" view.

There is considerable disagreement as to whether the strict monetarist view is a good approximation of reality. For example, the strict view is not compatible with a non-vertical AS curve in the AS/AD model in Chapter 14. In the case of a non-vertical AS curve, an increase in M, which shifts the AD curve to the right, increases both P and Y. (You may want to review why.)

Almost all economists would agree, however, that *sustained* inflation, which is inflation that continues over many periods, is a purely monetary phenomenon. As we pointed out in Chapter 14 in the context of the AS/AD framework, inflation cannot continue indefinitely unless the cental bank "accommodates" it by increasing the money supply.

Sustained inflation requires continuous increases in aggregate demand. But while a single shift in aggregate demand can easily result from an increase in government spending, it is hard to imagine this continuing forever. Eventually the public would not buy enough bonds to finance the continuously growing government deficit. Only if the Bank of Canada increases the money supply (i.e., buys some of the government bonds) can government spending (with its inflationary consequences) continue. In sum:

Inflation cannot continue indefinitely without increases in the money supply.

THE KEYNESIAN/MONETARIST DEBATE

The leading spokesperson for monetarism over the last few decades has been American economist Milton Friedman. Most monetarists, including Friedman, blame most of the instability in the economy on federal policies, arguing that the inflation encountered in many economies in the past could have been avoided if only the central banks had not expanded the money supply so rapidly.

Interestingly, most monetarists do not advocate an activist monetary stabilization policy. That is, they do not advocate expanding the money supply during bad times and slowing the growth of the money supply during good times. By and large, monetarists tend to be skeptical of the government's ability to "manage" the macroeconomy. The most common argument against such management is the one expressed in Chapter 16: that time lags make it likely that deliberate attempts to stimulate and contract the economy make the economy more, not less, unstable.

Friedman has for many years advocated a policy of steady and slow money growth. Specifically, he argues that the money supply should grow at a rate equal to the average growth of real output (income) (Y). That is, the central bank should pursue a constant policy that accommodates real growth but not inflation.

Keynesianism and monetarism are at odds with each other. Many Keynesians advocate the application of coordinated monetary and fiscal policy tools to reduce instability in the economy—that is, to fight inflation and unemployment. But not all Keynesians advocate an activist federal government. Some Keynesian economists believe that the best possible policy for government to pursue is basically noninterventionist.

Most Keynesians do agree that monetary and fiscal tools are not finely calibrated. The notion that monetary and fiscal expansions and contractions can "fine tune" the economy is not widely held. Still, many feel that the experiences of recent years also show that stabilization policies can help prevent even bigger economic disasters. Automatic stabilizers in particular, such as unemployment insurance, are viewed by many as having helped not only the unemployed but also the economy in general during economic downturns. In addition, Keynesian economists argue that the U.S. Federal Reserve's loosening of monetary policy in the early 1990s was a significant factor in ending the 1990–1991 recession in the United States and helped provide the necessary growth that reduced the U.S. unemployment rate to about 4% in 2000. They argue that one reason for the much higher Canadian unemployment rates (and the lower inflation) has been the tighter monetary policy pursued by the Bank of Canada.

In the 1960s, the debate between Keynesians and monetarists was the central controversy in macroeconomics. That controversy, while still alive today, is no longer at the forefront. Since the 1970s, the focus of thinking in macroeconomics has been on the new classical macroeconomics.

New Classical Macroeconomics

The key challenge to Keynesian and related theories has come from a school that is sometimes referred to as the *new classical macroeconomics*.[2] Like the terms "monetarism" and "Keynesianism," this term is somewhat vague. No two new classical macroeconomists think exactly alike, and no single model completely represents this school. The following discussion, however, conveys the general flavour of the new classical views.

THE DEVELOPMENT OF NEW CLASSICAL MACROECONOMICS

New classical macroeconomics has developed from two different, though related, sources. These sources are the theoretical and the empirical critiques of existing, or traditional, macroeconomics.

On the theoretical level, there has been growing dissatisfaction with the way traditional models treat expectations. Keynes himself recognized that expectations (in the form of "animal spirits") play an important role in economic behaviour. The problem is that traditional models have generally assumed that expectations are formed in rather naive ways. A common assumption, for example, is that people form their expectations of future inflation by assuming a continuation of present inflation. If they turn out to be wrong, they adjust their expectations by some fraction of the difference between their original forecast and the actual inflation rate. Suppose that I expect 10% inflation next year. When next year rolls around, the inflation rate turns out to be only 5%, so I have made an error of five percentage points. I might then predict an inflation rate for the following year of 7.5%, halfway between my earlier expectation (10%) and actual inflation last year (5%).

The problem with this traditional treatment of expectations is that it is not consistent with the assumptions of microeconomics. Specifically, it implies that people systematically overlook information that would allow them to make better forecasts, even though there are costs to being wrong. If, as microeconomic theory assumes, people are out to maximize their satisfaction and firms are out to maximize their profits, they should form their expectations in a smarter way. Instead of

[2]*The adjective "new classical" is used because many of the assumptions and conclusions of this group of economists resemble those of the classical economists—that is, those who wrote before Keynes.*

naively assuming that the future will be like the past, they should actively seek to forecast the future. Any other behaviour is not in keeping with the microeconomic view of the forward-looking, rational people who compose households and firms.

On the empirical level, there was stagflation in the Canadian and U.S. economies during the 1970s. Remember that stagflation is the simultaneous existence of high unemployment and rising prices. The Phillips Curve theory popular in the 1960s predicted that demand pressure pushes up prices, so that when demand is weak—in times of high unemployment, for example—prices should be stable (or perhaps even falling). The new classical theories were an attempt to explain the apparent breakdown in the 1970s of the simple inflation-unemployment tradeoff predicted by the Phillips Curve. Just as the Great Depression of the 1930s motivated the development of Keynesian economics, so the stagflation of the 1970s helped motivate the formulation of new classical economics.

RATIONAL EXPECTATIONS

In previous chapters, we stressed the importance of households' and firms' expectations about the future. A firm's decision to build a new plant depends on its expectations of future sales. The amount of saving a household undertakes today depends on its expectations about future interest rates, wages, and prices. The list of situations in which expectations come into play could be greatly expanded. As an example, see the Application box "Expectations and Financial Markets."

How are expectations formed? Do people simply assume that things will continue as they are at present? (This would be like predicting rain tomorrow because it is raining today.) What information do people use to make their guesses about the future? Questions like these have become central to current macroeconomic thinking and research. One theory, the **rational-expectations hypothesis,** offers a powerful way of thinking about expectations.

Suppose we want to forecast inflation. What does it mean to say that my expectations of inflation are "rational"? The rational-expectations hypothesis assumes that people know the "true model" that generates inflation—that is, they know how inflation is determined in the economy—and that they use this model to forecast future inflation rates. If there were no random, unpredictable events in the economy, and if people knew the true model generating inflation, then their forecasts of future inflation rates would be perfect. Because it is true, the model would not permit mistakes, and thus the people using it would not make mistakes either.

However, many events that affect the inflation rate are not predictable—they are random. By "true" model, then, we mean a model that is *on average* correct in forecasting inflation. Sometimes the random events have a positive effect on inflation, which means that the model underestimates the inflation rate, and sometimes they have a negative effect, which means that the model overestimates the inflation rate. On average, however, the model is correct. Therefore, rational expectations are correct on average, even though their predictions are not exactly right all the time.

A noneconomic example may help at this point. Over a number of rolls, the average roll of pair of fair dice will be close to seven. Suppose you have to predict what the roll of a pair of dice will be each time as they are rolled repeatedly. If you guess seven every time, you will be right sometimes but you should also find that you overpredict by about as much and as often as you underpredict. So while you won't be exactly right very often, *on average* you will be correct.

Sometimes people are said to have rational expectations if they use "all available information" in forming their expectations. This definition is somewhat vague, because it is not always clear what "all available information" means. The definition is precise, however, if by "all available information" we mean that people know and use the true model. One cannot have more or better information than the true model.

If information can be obtained at no cost, then someone is not behaving rationally if he or she fails to use all available information. Because there are almost always costs to making a wrong forecast, it is not rational to overlook information that could help improve the accuracy of a forecast as long as the costs of acquiring that information do not outweigh the benefits.

rational-expectations hypothesis *The hypothesis that people know the "true model" of the economy and that they use this model to form their expectations of the future.*

APPLICATION

Expectations and Financial Markets

Sometimes you might notice that a company announces a large increase in profits yet that same day its stock price falls. Why? Probably this is because investors were expecting an even bigger increase. An expected profit increase was built into market expectations and hence into the price of the stock. What matters for price movements when results become public is whether the results meet, exceed, or fall short of expectations.

Similarly, bad economic news may not always be associated with a decrease in stock market prices. For example, the announcement of an unexpectedly low level of housing starts in the United States in August 2000 was associated with a Wall Street rally that day. During this period the U.S. central bank (the Federal Reserve or "Fed") was considering raising interest rates. Higher interest rates tend to hurt stock prices, because individuals with new funds are more likely to purchase high-paying bonds. But the low level of housing starts made it less likely that the Fed would need to increase interest rates to cool the economy and hence reduced expectations of

The statements of Alan Greenspan, Chair of the United States Federal Reserve, are scrutinized closely for hints on the future direction of U.S. interest rates. Many think the "Chair of the Fed" is the second-most-powerful position in the United States government.

higher interest rates.

As a final example, announcements that inflation is higher than expected in Canada tend to lead to an appreciation of the Canadian dollar. Again the key is expectations. Investors expect that the Bank of Canada will increase interest rates to try to reduce inflation and, as you know, higher interest rates in Canada will tend to lead to an appreciated Canadian dollar. Investors buy the Canadian dollar immediately in hopes of cashing in on this appreciation and the dollar's value moves up because of this increase in demand. The expectation of a future increase in the price of the dollar translates into an immediate price increase.

■ **Rational Expectations and Wage/Price Adjustment** As was described in more detail in Chapter 14, the economy would stay at potential output if all prices and wages were fully flexible. The long run would be very short, in fact instantaneous, so that both the short-run and the long-run aggregate supply curves would be vertical. Changes in aggregate demand would rapidly lead to equal percentage increases in all prices and wages with no change in output.

Clearly, some prices and wages are not fully flexible because they are determined by long-term contracts. Hence it is argued that an increase in aggregate demand will increase output because firms can obtain higher prices for their products, without corresponding increases in all costs in the short run. Similarly, decreases in aggregate demand reduce output because firms receive lower prices without full cost adjustment. *But if all contracts fully anticipate and reflect changes in the price level,* there are no lags in cost adjustment—hence output would remain at potential output.

Do contracts fully anticipate changes in the price level? Under rational expectations, yes, except there may be random errors. Hence *if these mistakes were the only reason for GDP to deviate from potential output,* GDP would sometimes be above potential GDP and sometimes below, but on average, GDP would equal potential GDP. Changes in aggregate demand (such as those from fiscal or monetary policy) would affect the price level, not output. In the next section, we will examine a rational expectations model of output determination a bit more deeply and then we will revisit the implications for macroeconomic policy.

THE LUCAS SUPPLY FUNCTION

The **Lucas supply function,** named after American Nobel Prize–winning economist Robert E. Lucas, is an important part of a number of new classical macroeconomic theories. The function is deceptively simple. It says that the difference between real output (Y) and potential output (Y_p) depends on (is a function of) the difference between the actual price level (P) and the expected price level (P^e):

$$Y - Y_p = f(P - P^e)$$

The actual price level minus the expected price level ($P - P^e$) is the **price surprise.** If the price surprise is zero, it is assumed $Y = Y_p$. Before considering the policy implications of this function, we should look at the theory behind it.

Lucas begins by assuming that people and firms are specialists in production but generalists in consumption. If someone you know is a manual labourer, the chances are she sells only one thing—labour. If she is a lawyer, she sells only legal services. In contrast, people buy a large bundle of goods—ranging from gasoline to ice cream and pretzels—on a regular basis. The same is true for firms. Most companies tend to concentrate on producing a small range of products, but they typically buy a larger range of inputs—raw materials, labour, energy, capital. According to Lucas, this divergence between people's buying and selling experience creates an asymmetry. People know much more about the prices of the things they sell than they do about the prices of the things they buy.

At the beginning of each period, a firm has some expectation of the average price level for that period. If the actual price level turns out to be different, there is a price surprise. Say that the average price level is higher than expected. Because the firm learns about the actual price level slowly, some time goes by before it realizes that all prices have gone up. The firm does learn rather quickly, however, that the price of its *output* has gone up. The firm thus perceives—incorrectly, as it turns out—that its price has risen relative to other prices, and this leads it to produce more output.

A similar argument holds for workers. When there is a positive price surprise, workers at first believe that their "price"—their wage rate—has increased relative to other prices. In other words, workers believe that their real wage rate has risen. We know from theory that an increase in the real wage is likely to encourage workers to work more hours. The real wage has not actually risen, but it takes workers a while to figure this out. In the meantime, they supply more hours of work than they otherwise would have. This means that the economy will produce more output when prices are unexpectedly higher than when prices are at their expected level.

This is the rationale for the Lucas supply function. Unexpected increases in the price level can fool workers and firms into thinking that relative prices have changed, and this causes them to alter the amount of labour or goods they choose to supply.

■ **Policy Implications of the Lucas Supply Function**   If we assume that expectations are rational, the Lucas supply function implies that anticipated changes in aggregate demand have no effect on real output. This includes anticipated monetary and fiscal policies. Consider, for example, a change in monetary policy. In general, such a change will have some effect on the average price level. If the policy change is announced to the public, then people know what the effect on the price level will be, because they have rational expectations (and thus know the way that changes in mon-

Even though uncertainty exists, if you know the "model" generating the uncertainty, it is possible to have expectations about the future that are "on average" correct. Over a large number of rolls, the average roll of a pair of dice will be close to seven, so if you predict seven for any one roll, sometimes you will be too high, sometimes too low, and sometimes right on, but "on average" you will be right.

Lucas supply function *The supply function that embodies the idea that output (Y) depends on the difference between the actual price level and the expected price level.*

price surprise *The actual price level minus the expected price level.*

etary policy affect the price level). This means that the change in monetary policy affects both the actual price level and the expected price level in the same way. The new price level minus the new expected price level is thus zero—no price surprise. In such a case, there will be no change in real output, because the Lucas supply function states that real output can change from Y_p only if there is a price surprise.

The general conclusion is that *any* announced aggregate demand policy change that does not change potential output—in fiscal policy or any other policy—has no effect on real output, because the policy change affects both actual and expected price levels in the same way. If people have rational expectations, such policy changes can produce no price surprises and thus no increases in real output, and such a change in government policy can only affect real output if it is not generally known. Thus rational-expectations theory combined with the Lucas supply function proposes a very small role for government aggregate demand policy in the economy.

EVALUATING RATIONAL-EXPECTATIONS THEORY

If prices and wages adjust easily both upwards and downwards and price and wage contracts are set by firms and workers with rational expectations, output will always be determined by a vertical (both *short-run* and *long-run*) aggregate supply curve. Real output will always be either at potential output or, if there are significant expectational errors, real output will fluctuate randomly around potential output. Aggregate demand policy will have no effect.

The main argument in favour of rational expectations is that firms and workers making contracts, particularly big money contracts, will use the best information available. But perhaps obtaining the required information and modelling is too costly and difficult.

But even if the rational-expectations hypothesis is a good approximation to reality, it may be that the economy will not simply fluctuate around potential output. It may be that wages and prices, whether contracted or not, will not adjust. In particular, to many economists it seems that wages do not always fall in the face of high unemployment and that prices do not always fall in the face of high excess supply. This price and wage stickiness (sometimes called price and wage rigidity) might prevent rapid adjustment in the economy, even with rational expectations. Aggregate demand policy essentially overcomes these rigidities by increasing the price level.

Suppose, for example, that the wage that would clear a particular labour market is $10 per hour in 2000 dollars but the actual wage is sticky at $10.40 so that there is unemployment. Suppose further that expansionary aggregate demand increases the price level by 4% by 2001 and the actual wage in this market stays at $10.40. The 2001 wage is now $10 per hour in 2000 dollars, which is low enough to clear the labour market and the unemployment is removed.

Is there such stickiness in wages and prices? If so, why? These, along with whether rational expectations is a useful approximation, are among the central questions in macroeconomics. Economists who believe in a role for activist aggregate demand policy believe that there is such stickiness and that policy can help reduce its negative consequences. Economists opposed to activist aggregate demand policy are less convinced of the importance of stickiness and argue that, even if it exists, aggregate demand policy should not try to offset arrangements agreed to voluntarily by workers and firms. There are no conclusive results, but these are some of the questions that make macroeconomics an exciting area of research.

REAL BUSINESS CYCLE THEORY

As noted, the new classical macroeconomics assumes complete price and wage flexibility (market clearing) and rational expectations and hence a vertical aggregate supply (AS) curve. With a vertical AS curve, shifts in the aggregate demand (AD) curve cannot affect output. It seems unlikely that expectational errors alone can explain the degree of fluctuation and persistence of the business cycle of output.

Recent work that attempts to explain this cycle in terms of the new classical approach has come to be called **real business cycle theory**.

real business cycle theory
An attempt to explain business-cycle fluctuations under the assumptions of complete price and wage flexibility and rational expectations. It emphasizes shocks to technology and other shocks.

It is clear that if shifts of the *AD* curve cannot account for real output fluctuations (because the *AS* curve is vertical), then shifts of the *AS* curve must be responsible. However, the key task is to come up with convincing arguments as to what causes these shifts and why they persist over a number of periods. The problem is particularly difficult when it comes to the labour market. If prices and wages are completely flexible, then there is never any unemployment aside from frictional unemployment. For example, since the measured unemployment rate in Canada was less than 7% in 2000 but almost 10% in 1996, the puzzle is to explain why so many more people chose not to work in 1996 than in 2000.

Early real business cycle theorists emphasized shocks to the production technology. Say there is a negative shock in a given year that causes the marginal product of labour to decline. This leads to a fall in the real wage, which leads to a decrease in labour supply. People have been led to work less because the negative technology shock has led to a lower return from working. The opposite happens when there is a positive shock: the marginal product of labour rises, the real wage rises, and people choose to work more. This early work was not as successful as some had hoped because it required what seemed to be unrealistically large shocks to explain the observed movements in labour supply over time.

Since this initial work, different types of shocks have been introduced, and work is actively continuing in this area. To date, fluctuations of some variables, but not all of them, have been explained fairly well. Some argue that this work is doomed to failure because it is based on the unrealistic assumption of complete price and wage flexibility, while others hold more hope. Real business cycle theory is another example of the current state of flux in macroeconomics.

Supply-Side Economics

In our discussion of equilibrium in the goods market, beginning with the simple multiplier in Chapter 9 and continuing through Chapter 14, we have focused primarily on *demand*. Supply increases and decreases in response to changes in aggregate expenditure (which, as you recall, is closely linked to aggregate demand). Fiscal policy works by influencing aggregate expenditure through tax policy and government spending. Monetary policy works by influencing investment and consumption spending through increases and decreases in the interest rate. In essence, the theories we have been discussing are "demand-oriented."

As we have said a number of times, the 1970s were difficult times for the North American economy due to the presence of stagflation—high unemployment and inflation. In Canada, the unemployment rate in 1975 rose to 6.9%, rose again in 1976 to a then postwar high of 7.2% and climbed even higher by the end of the decade. Inflation reached double-digit levels by the mid-1970s and continued high into the 1980s. It seemed as if policy makers were incapable of controlling the business cycle.

As a result of these seeming failures, orthodox economics came under fire, particularly in the United States. One assault was from a group of economists who expounded what came to be called supply-side economics. The essential argument of the supply-siders was simple. Basically, they said, all the attention to demand in orthodox macro theory distracted attention from the real problem with the economy. The real problem, according to the supply-siders, was that high rates of taxation and heavy regulation had reduced the incentive to work, to save, and to invest. What was needed was not a demand stimulus but rather better incentives to stimulate *supply*.

If we cut taxes so that people take home more of their paycheques, the argument continued, they will work harder and save more. If businesses get to keep more of their profits and can get away from government regulations, they will invest more. This added labour supply and investment, or capital supply, will lead to an expansion of the supply of goods and services, which, in turn, will reduce inflation and unemployment at the same time. The ultimate solution to the economy's woes, the supply-siders concluded, was to be found on the *supply side* of the economy.

At their most extreme, supply-siders argued that the incentive effects of supply-side policies were likely to be so great that a major cut in tax rates would actually *increase* tax revenues. That is, even though tax *rates* would be lower, more people would be working and earning income and firms would earn more profits, so that the increases in the *tax bases* (profits, sales, and income) would outweigh the decreases in rates, resulting in increased government revenues.

■ **The Laffer Curve** Figure 18.2 presents a key diagram of supply-side economics. The tax rate is measured on the vertical axis, and tax revenue is measured on the horizontal axis. The assumption behind this curve is that there is some tax rate beyond which the supply response is large enough to lead to a decrease in tax revenue for further increases in the tax rate. At a tax rate of 0, work effort is high, but there is no tax revenue. At a tax rate of 100, the labour supply is presumably zero, since no one is allowed to keep any of his or her income. Somewhere in between 0 and 100 is the maximum-revenue rate.

The major debate in the 1980s, most prominently in the United States, was whether tax rates put the economy on the upper or lower part of the curve in Figure 18.2. The supply-side school claimed that the economy was at a point like *A* and that taxes should be cut. Others argued that the economy was at a point like *B* and that tax cuts would lead to lower tax revenue. The diagram in Figure 18.2 is called the **Laffer Curve,** after American economist Arthur Laffer, who, legend has it, first drew it on the back of a napkin at a cocktail party. The Laffer Curve influenced the reductions in personal and corporate tax rates introduced in the United States in 1981 under the Reagan administration.

EVALUATING SUPPLY-SIDE ECONOMICS

Supply-side economics has been criticized on a number of counts. Critics point out that it is unlikely that a tax cut would increase the supply of labour substantially.

As has been discussed in Chapter 14, there was little response in Canada to supply-side theories apart from some reductions in upper-bracket tax rates in 1988. In the United States, supporters of supply-side economics claim that Reagan's tax policies were successful in stimulating the economy. They point to the fact that almost immediately after the tax cuts of 1981 were put into place, the economy expanded and the recession of 1980–1982 came to an end. In addition, inflation rates fell sharply from the high rates of 1980 and 1981.

Laffer Curve *With the tax rate measured on the vertical axis and tax revenue measured on the horizontal axis, the Laffer Curve shows that there is some tax rate beyond which the supply response is large enough to lead to a decrease in tax revenue for further increases in the tax rate.*

FIGURE 18.2

The Laffer Curve

The Laffer Curve shows that the amount of revenue that the government collects is a function of the tax rate. It also shows that when tax rates are very high, an increase in the tax rate could cause tax revenues to fall. Similarly, under the same circumstances, a cut in the tax rate could generate enough additional economic activity to cause revenues to rise.

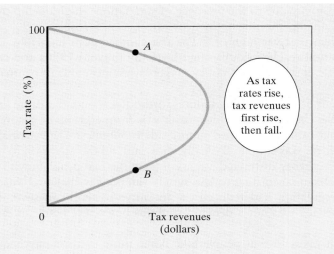

Critics of supply-side policies do not dispute these facts but offer an alternative explanation of how the economy recovered. The Reagan tax cuts were enacted just as the U.S. economy was in the middle of its deepest recession since the Great Depression. The unemployment rate stood at 10.8% in the fourth quarter of 1982. It was the recession, critics argue, that was responsible for the reduction in inflation—not the supply-side policies. Moreover, research done during the 1980s in the United States suggests that while the tax cuts did seem to increase the supply of labour somewhat, the increases were very modest.

But what about the recovery from the recession? Why did real output begin to grow rapidly in late 1982, precisely when the supply-side tax cuts were taking effect? Two reasons have been suggested. First, the supply-side tax cuts had large *demand*-side effects that stimulated the economy. Second, the U.S. central bank, the Federal Reserve, dramatically expanded the money supply and drove interest rates down at the same time that the tax cuts were being put into effect. The money supply expanded about 20% between 1981 and 1983, and interest rates dropped dramatically. In 1981, the average three-month U.S. Treasury bill paid 14% interest. In 1983, the figure had dropped to 8.6%.

Standard Keynesian approaches we have studied that emphasize the importance of aggregate demand also suggest that a huge tax cut will lead to an increase in output, particularly if the economy is initially below potential output and not growing rapidly. In addition, although an increase in planned investment (brought about by a lower interest rate) leads to added productive capacity and added supply in the long run, it also increases expenditures on capital goods (new plant and equipment investment) in the short run.

Whether the recovery from the 1980–1982 recession in the United States was the result of supply-side expansion or supply-side policies that had demand-side effects, one thing is clear: the extreme promises of the supply-siders did not materialize. President Reagan argued that because of the effect depicted in the Laffer Curve, the government could maintain expenditures (and even increase defence expenditures sharply), cut tax rates, *and* balance the budget. This was clearly not the case. Government revenues were below levels that would have been realized without the tax cuts. After 1982, the U.S. federal government ran huge deficits, with nearly $2 trillion added to the national debt between 1983 and 1992.

Testing Alternative Macroeconomic Models

You may wonder why there is so much disagreement in macroeconomics. Why cannot macroeconomists test their models against one another and see which one performs best?

One problem is that macroeconomic models differ in ways that are hard to standardize for. If, for example, one model takes the price level to be given, or not explained within the model, and another one does not, the model with the given price level may do better in, say, predicting output—not because it is a better model but simply because the errors in predicting prices have not been allowed to affect the predictions of output. The model that takes prices as given has a head start, so to speak.

Another problem arises in the testing of the rational-expectations assumption. Remember that if people have rational expectations, they are using the true model to form their expectations. Therefore, to test this assumption one needs the true model. One is never sure, of course, that whatever model is taken to be the true model is in fact the true one. Any test of the rational-expectations hypothesis is therefore a *joint* test (1) that expectations are formed rationally and (2) that the model that is being used is the true one. If the test rejects the hypothesis, it may be that the model is wrong rather than that expectations are not rational.

Another problem that macroeconomists have is that the amount of data available is fairly small. Most empirical work uses data beginning in about 1950, which in 2000 was about 50 years' (200 quarters') worth of data. While this may seem like a lot of data, it is not. Macroeconomic data are fairly "smooth," which means that a typical variable does not vary all that much from quarter to quarter or year to year.

To give an example of the problem of a small number of observations, consider trying to test the hypothesis that the price of oil affects investment. As we saw in Chapter 15, the price of oil changed very little in the 1950s and 1960s. Because of this, it would have been very difficult at the end of the 1960s to estimate the effect of the price of oil on investment. The variation in the price of oil was not great enough to show any effects. One cannot demonstrate that changes in the oil price explain changes in investment if the oil price does not change! The situation was different by the end of the 1970s, however, because by then the oil price had varied considerably. This kind of problem is encountered again and again in empirical macroeconomics. In many cases there are not enough observations for much to be said, and thus there is considerable room for disagreement.

We pointed out in Chapter 1 that it is difficult in economics to perform controlled experiments. Economists are for the most part at the mercy of the historical data. If we were able to perform experiments involving entire economies, we could probably learn more about the economy in a shorter time. Since this is not the case, we must wait. In time, the current range of disagreements in macroeconomics should be considerably narrowed.

Summary

Keynesian Economics

1. In a broad sense, Keynesian economics is the foundation of modern macroeconomics. In a narrower sense, the term *Keynesian* refers to economists who advocate active government intervention in the economy.

Monetarism

2. The monetarist analysis of the economy places a great deal of emphasis on the *velocity of money,* which is defined as the number of times a dollar changes hands, on average, during a year. The velocity of money is the ratio of nominal GDP to the stock of money, or $V \equiv GDP/M \equiv P \cdot Y/M$. Alternately, $M \cdot V \equiv P \cdot Y$.

3. The *quantity theory of money* assumes that velocity is constant (or virtually constant). This implies that changes in the supply of money will lead to equal percentage changes in nominal GDP. The quantity theory of money equation is $M \cdot \overline{V} = P \cdot Y$. The equation says that the demand for money does not depend on the interest rate.

4. Most economists believe that sustained inflation is a purely monetary phenomenon. Inflation cannot continue indefinitely unless the central bank "accommodates" it by expanding the money supply.

5. Most monetarists blame most of the instability in the economy on the federal government and are skeptical of the government's ability to manage the macroeconomy. They argue that the money supply should grow at a rate equal to the average growth of real output (income) (Y). That is, the central bank should expand the money supply to accommodate real growth but not inflation.

New Classical Macroeconomics

6. The *new classical macroeconomics* has developed from two different but related sources: the theoretical and the empirical critiques of traditional macroeconomics. On the theoretical level, there has been growing dissatisfaction with the way traditional models treat expectations. On the empirical level, stagflation during the 1970s caused many people to look for alternative theories to explain the breakdown of the Phillips Curve.

7. The *rational-expectations hypothesis* assumes people know the "true model" that generates economic variables. For example, rational expectations assumes that people know how inflation is determined in the economy and use this model to forecast future inflation rates.

8. The *Lucas supply function* assumes real output (Y) depends on the actual price level minus the expected price level, or the *price surprise*. This function in combination with the assumption that expectations are rational implies that anticipated policy changes have no effect on real output.

9. The combined assumptions of complete price and wage flexibility and rational expectations imply that the aggregate supply is vertical both in the short run and the long run and that aggregate demand policy cannot influence output.

10. *Real business cycle theory* is an attempt to explain business-cycle fluctuations under the assumptions

of complete price and wage flexibility and rational expectations. It emphasizes shocks to technology and other shocks.

Supply-Side Economics

11. *Supply-side economics* focuses on incentives to stimulate supply. Supply-side economists believe that if we lower taxes, workers will work harder and save more and firms will invest more and produce more. At their most extreme, supply-siders argue that incentive effects are likely to be so great that a major cut in taxes will actually increase tax revenues.

12. The *Laffer Curve* shows the relationship between tax rates and tax revenues. Supply-side econo-

mists use it to argue that it is possible to generate higher revenues by cutting tax rates, but evidence for the United States does not appear to support this proposition.

Testing Alternative Macroeconomic Models

13. Economists disagree about which macroeconomic model is best for several reasons: (1) macroeconomic models differ in ways that are hard to standardize for; (2) when testing the rational expectations assumption, one is never sure that whatever model is taken to be the true model is in fact the true one; (3) the amount of data available is fairly small.

Review Terms and Concepts

Laffer Curve 376
Lucas supply function 373
price surprise 373
quantity theory of money 367

rational-expectations
  hypothesis 371
real business cycle theory 375
velocity of money 366

Equations:

1. $V \equiv \dfrac{GDP}{M}$

2. $M \cdot V \equiv P \cdot Y$

3. $M \cdot \overline{V} = P \cdot Y$

Problem Set

1. The three diagrams in Figure 1 represent in a simplified way the predictions of the three theories presented in this chapter about the likely effects of a major tax cut.

   a. Match each of the following three theories with a graph: (1) Keynesian economics, (2) supply-side economics, (3) rational expectations/monetarism. Briefly explain the logic behind the three graphs.

   b. Which of the three theories do you find the most convincing? Explain your choice.

2. In the 1997 Canadian federal election, the four federalist parties had four main approaches in terms of macroeconomic policy. The Reform platform argued for sharp overall reductions in government transfers and purchases and, when the budget was balanced, tax cuts. The largest tax reductions came from increasing the basic tax credit all Canadians receive, as well as the spousal tax credit. (The current basic credit amounts to not charging the taxpayer the first $1000 of federal tax.) The Progressive Conservative platform also argued for sharp reductions in government spending and in addition advocated an immediate cut in tax rates of 10%, without waiting for a balanced

budget. The Liberal platform advocated no further cuts in government programs but no major new spending initiatives either; when the budget was balanced, half of any surplus would be in tax cuts, the other half in new programs. The NDP platform maintained that new government spending programs were necessary and that these would expand the economy; the programs would be paid for by revenues generated by the economic growth plus higher taxes on large corporations and high-income individuals.

   a. Analyze each of these positions from a Keynesian (aggregate-demand-oriented) perspective and from a supply-side perspective. Assume that the economy is below potential output.

   b. How would your answer change if the economy were at potential output?

3. A cornerstone of new classical economics is the notion that expectations are "rational." What do you think will happen to the prices of single-family homes in your community over the next several years? On what do you base your expectations? Is your thinking consistent with the notion of rational expectations? Explain.

Figure 1

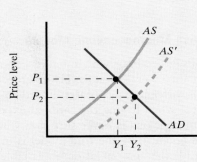

I.   II.   III.

4. You hold strict monetarist views, and you are given the following information. The money supply is $1000. The velocity of money is 5. What is nominal income? What is real income? What happens to nominal income if the money supply is doubled? What happens to real income?

5. "In an economy with reasonably flexible prices and wages, full employment is almost always maintained." Explain why this statement is true.

6. Supply-side advocates believe that governments can reduce tax rates and at the same time increase tax revenues. Others have called supply-side policies "voodoo economics." Explain the disagreement.

*7. Assume that in a hypothetical economy there is a simple proportional tax on wages imposed at a rate t. Suppose further that there are plenty of jobs around so that if people enter the labour force, they can find work. We define total government receipts from the tax as

$$T = t \cdot W \cdot L$$

where t = the tax rate, W = the gross wage rate, and L = the total supply of labour. The net wage rate is

$$W_n = (1 - t)W$$

The *elasticity* of labour supply (an indication of its responsiveness to changes in wages) is defined as

$$\frac{\text{Percentage change in } L}{\text{Percentage change in } W_n} = \frac{\Delta L/L}{\Delta W_n/W_n}$$

Suppose that t were cut from 0.25 to 0.20. For such a cut to *increase* total government receipts from the tax, how elastic must the supply of labour be? (Assume a constant gross wage.) What does your answer imply about the supply-side assertion that a cut in taxes can increase tax revenues?

Economic Growth and Productivity

Learning Objectives

1 Define *economic growth*.

2 Identify the sources of economic growth.

3 Define *aggregate production function* and explain the importance of diminishing returns.

4 Summarize the arguments for and against continued economic growth.

The Growth Process: From Agriculture to Industry

The Sources of Economic Growth
An Increase in Labour Supply
Increases in Physical Capital
Increases in Human Capital
Increases in Productivity

Growth and Productivity in the Canadian Economy
Growth in Canada Since Confederation
The Productivity "Problem"

Economic Growth and Public Policy
Growth Policy: A Long-Run Proposition

The Pros and Cons of Growth
The Pro-Growth Argument
The Anti-Growth Argument
Summary: No "Right Answer"

As you may recall from Chapter 1, **economic growth** occurs when an economy experiences an increase in total output. We call the period of sustained and rapid growth in the Western world that began in the Industrial Revolution and continues today the period of **modern economic growth**.

It is through economic growth that living standards improve. But growth also brings change. New things are produced, while others become obsolete. Some believe that growth is the fundamental objective of a society, because it lifts people out of poverty and enhances the quality of their lives. Others argue that economic growth erodes traditional values and leads to exploitation, environmental destruction, and corruption.

The first part of this chapter describes the economic growth process in some detail and identifies some sources of economic growth. After a review of the Canadian economy's growth record since Confederation, we turn to an examination of productivity measures in Canada and in other countries. The chapter concludes with a review of the debate over the benefits and costs of growth.

The Growth Process: From Agriculture to Industry

The easiest way to understand the growth process and to identify its causes is to think about a simple economy. In Chapter 2 we considered Colleen and Ivan, who were washed up on a deserted island. At first they had only a few simple tools and whatever human capital they brought with them to the island. They gathered nuts and berries and built a small cabin. Their "GDP" consisted of basic food and shelter.

economic growth *An increase in the total output of an economy. Defined by some economists as an increase of real GDP per capita.*

modern economic growth *The rapid and sustained increase in real output per capita that began in the Western world with the Industrial Revolution.*

Over time, things improved. The first year, they cleared some land and began to cultivate a few vegetables that they found growing on the island. They made some tools and dug a small reservoir to store rainwater. As their agricultural efforts became more efficient, they shifted their resources (i.e., their time) into building a larger, more comfortable home.

Colleen and Ivan were accumulating capital in two forms. First, they built *physical capital,* material things used in the production of goods and services—a better house, tools, and a water system. Second, they acquired more *human capital*—knowledge, skills, and talents. Through trial and error, they learned about the island, its soil and its climate, what worked and what didn't. Both kinds of capital made them more efficient and increased their productivity. Because it took less time to produce the food that they needed to survive, they could devote more energy to producing other things or to leisure.

At any given time, Colleen and Ivan faced limits on what they could produce. These limits were imposed by the existing state of their technical knowledge and the resources at their disposal. Over time, they expanded their possibilities, developed new technologies, accumulated capital, and made their labour more productive. In Chapter 2, we defined a society's *production possibility frontier (ppf),* which shows all possible combinations of output that can be produced given present technology and if all available resources are fully and efficiently employed. Economic growth expands those limits and shifts society's production possibility frontier out to the right, as Figure 19.1 shows.

■ **From Agriculture to Industry: The Industrial Revolution**   Before the Industrial Revolution in Great Britain, every society in the world was agrarian. Towns and cities existed here and there, but almost everyone lived in rural areas. People spent most of their time producing food and other basic subsistence goods. Then, beginning in England around 1750, technical change and capital accumulation increased productivity significantly in two important industries: agriculture and textiles. New and more efficient methods of farming were developed. New inventions and new machinery in spinning, weaving, and steel production meant that more could be produced with fewer resources. Just as new technology, capital equipment, and the resulting higher productivity made it possible for Colleen and Ivan to spend time working on other projects and new "products," the British turned from agricultural production to industrial production. In both cases, growth meant new products, more output, and wider choice.

FIGURE 19.1

Economic Growth Shifts Society's Production Possibility Frontier Up and to the Right

The production possibility frontier shows all the combinations of output that can be produced if all of society's scarce resources are fully and efficiently employed. Economic growth expands society's production possibility, shifting the ppf up and to the right.

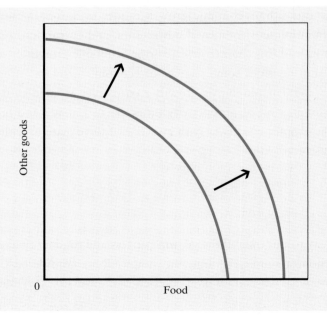

There was one major difference, however. Colleen and Ivan were fully in charge of their own lives. But peasants and workers in eighteenth-century England ended up with a very different set of choices. It was no longer possible to make a living as a peasant farmer. The cities offered the only real alternative for many, and a rural agrarian society was very quickly transformed into an urban industrial society.

■ **Growth in an Industrial Society** The process of economic growth in an industrial society such as Canada is more complex but follows the same steps we have just described for growth in an agrarian society.

Consider the development of the electronic calculator. Prior to 1970, calculators that could add, subtract, multiply, and divide weighed 20 kilograms, performed calculations very slowly, and were very expensive (a good calculator cost hundreds of dollars). Today, electronic calculators retail for as low as $3 or come free with a magazine subscription. Some are even small enough to fit into a wristwatch.

During the past 20 years, the growth of computer technology has changed the way we live and do business. Information transfer has been transformed by the Internet. Computers with Pentium processors and massive memory and storage capacity are selling for the price of small electronic calculators 25 years ago.

Technological change, innovation, and capital production (calculators, computers, and software) have increased productivity. If a diner spends less on accounting, its sandwiches will cost less. Sandwich buyers thus may go to see another movie or have another chocolate bar. The entertainment and confectionary sectors expand, and so on. That is economic growth.

The Sources of Economic Growth

Economic growth occurs either when (1) society acquires more resources or (2) society discovers ways of using available resources more efficiently. For economic growth to increase living standards, the rate of growth must exceed the rate of population increase. Thus, some economists define economic growth as *an increase in real GDP per capita.*

As we discuss the factors that contribute to economic growth, it will be helpful to think of an **aggregate production function.** An individual firm's production function is a mathematical representation of how a firm's output is determined by its inputs. In the aggregate production function, a country's output (Y, its gross domestic product) depends upon its inputs, that is the amount of labour (L) and the amount of capital (K) available in the economy (assuming the amount of land and natural resources is fixed).[1] The relationship between output and inputs may change as advances in technology and knowledge increase the amount that can be produced from each unit of input.

If you think of GDP as a function of both labour and capital, you can see that:

aggregate production function
The mathematical representation of the relationship between inputs and national output, or gross domestic product.

> An increase in GDP can come about through:
>
> 1. An increase in the labour supply
> 2. An increase in physical or human capital, or
> 3. An increase in productivity (the amount of product produced by each unit of capital or labour)

AN INCREASE IN LABOUR SUPPLY

An increasing labour supply can generate more output. Consider what would happen if another person joined Colleen and Ivan on the island. (Unlike the television show *Survivor*, we are *adding* people to the island!) She would join in the work and produce, and so GDP would rise. Or suppose that a person living in Canada who had not been a part of the labour force were to begin to work and use his time and energy to produce pottery. Real output would rise in this case also.

---

[1] *All the numbers in Tables 19.1 and 19.3 were derived from the simple production function:*
$Y = 3 \cdot K^{1/3}L^{2/3}$.

Table 19.1	Economic Growth from an Increase in Labour—More Output But Diminishing Returns and Lower Labour Productivity

Period	Quantity of Labour L (hours)	Quantity of Capital K (units)	Total Output Y (units)	Measured Labour Productivity Y/L
1	100	100	300	3.0
2	110	100	320	2.9
3	120	100	339	2.8
4	130	100	357	2.7

Whether output *per capita* rises when the labour supply increases is another matter. If the capital stock remains fixed while labour increases, the new labour will likely be less productive than the old labour. This phenomenon is called *diminishing returns,* and it worried Thomas Malthus, David Ricardo, and other early economists.

Malthus and Ricardo, who lived in England during the nineteenth century, were concerned that the fixed supply of land would ultimately lead to diminishing returns. With land in strictly limited supply, the ppf could be pushed out only so far as population increased. To increase agricultural output, people would be forced to farm less productive land or to farm land more intensively. In either case, the returns to successive increases in population would diminish. Both Malthus and Ricardo predicted a gloomy future as population outstripped the land's capacity to produce. What both economists left out of their calculations, however, was technological change and capital accumulation. New and better farming techniques have raised agricultural productivity so much that about 3% of the Canadian population now provides enough food for the entire country, with enough surplus to make Canada a net exporter of agricultural products.

Diminishing returns can also occur if a nation's capital stock grows more slowly than its workforce. Capital enhances workers' productivity. A person with a shovel digs a bigger hole than a person without one, and a person with a steam shovel outdoes them both. If a society's stock of plant and equipment does not grow and the technology of production does not change, additional workers will not be as productive, because they do not have machines to work with.

Table 19.1 illustrates how growth in the labour force, without a corresponding increase in the capital stock or technological change, might lead to growth of output but declining productivity and a lower standard of living. As labour increases, output rises from 300 units in period 1 to 320 in period 2, to 339 in period 3, and so forth, but **labour productivity** (output per worker-hour) falls. Output per worker-hour, Y/L, is a measure of labour's productivity.

The fear that new workers entering the labour force will displace existing workers and generate unemployment has been with us for a long time. New workers can come from many places. They might be immigrants, young people looking for their first jobs, or older people entering the labour force for the first time. Between 1946 and 1999, the number of women aged 25 and over in the labour force increased over tenfold, jumping from 585 000 to 6.0 million. Table 19.2 shows that in Canada since World War II, the population 15 years of age and over grew by 172.7% (or just over two-and-two-thirds times), while the labour force more than tripled. The Canadian economy, however, has shown a remarkable ability to expand right along with the labour force. The number of persons employed jumped by 9.8 million—more than tripling—during the same period.

labour productivity *Output per worker-hour; the amount of output produced by an average worker in one hour.*

As long as the economy and the capital stock are expanding rapidly enough, new entrants into the labour force do not displace other workers.

Table 19.2	Employment, Labour Force, and Population Growth, 1946–1999			
	Population 15 Years and Over (millions)	**LABOUR FORCE**		**Employment (millions)**
		Number (millions)	**Percentage of Population**	
1946	8.8*	4.8	54.5	4.7
1960	11.8*	6.4	54.2	6.0
1970	14.5	8.4	57.9	7.9
1980	18.6	12.0	64.5	11.1
1990	21.3	14.3	67.1	13.2
1999	24.0	15.7	65.4	14.5
Percentage change:				
1946–1999	172.7%	227.1%		208.5%
Annual rate	1.9%	2.3%		2.1%
1960–1999	103.4%	145.3%		141.7%
Annual rate	1.8%	2.3%		2.3%

Note: * indicates figures are for population age 14 years and over.

Sources: Adapted from Statistics Canada, *Labour Force Annual Averages*, Cat. no. 71-220 and *Historical Labour Force Statistics*, Cat. no. 71-201.

INCREASES IN PHYSICAL CAPITAL

An increase in the stock of capital can also increase output, even if it is not accompanied by an increase in the labour force. Physical capital both enhances the productivity of labour and provides valuable services directly.

It is easy to see how capital provides services directly. Consider what happened on Ivan and Colleen's island. In the first few years, they built a house, putting many hours of work into it that could have gone into producing other things for immediate consumption. With the house for shelter, Colleen and Ivan live in relative comfort and can thus spend time on other things. In the same way, capital equipment produced in one year can add to the value of a product over many years. For example, we still derive use and value from bridges and tunnels built decades ago.

It is also easy to see how capital used in production enhances the productivity of labour. Computers enable us to do almost instantly tasks that once were impossible or might have taken years to complete. An airplane with a relatively small crew can transport hundreds of people thousands of kilometres in a few hours. A bridge over a waterway at a critical location may save thousands of labour hours that would be spent transporting materials and people by other means. It is precisely this yield in the form of future valuable services that provides both private and public investors with the incentive to devote resources to capital production.

Table 19.3 shows how an increase in capital without a corresponding increase in labour might increase output. Several things about these numbers are notable. First, additional capital increases measured productivity: output per worker hour (Y/L) increases from 3.0 to 3.1, to 3.2, and finally to 3.3 as the quantity of capital

Opened in the spring of 1997, the Confederation Bridge provides the first fixed link between Prince Edward Island and the Canadian mainland. The development of such infrastructure plays an important role in economic growth.

Table 19.3	Economic Growth from an Increase in Capital—More Output, Diminishing Returns to Added Capital, Higher Measured Labour Productivity			
Period	**Quantity of Labour L (hours)**	**Quantity of Capital K (units)**	**Total Output Y (units)**	**Measured Labour Productivity Y/L**
1	100	100	300	3.0
2	100	110	310	3.1
3	100	120	319	3.2
4	100	130	327	3.3

Table 19.4	Fixed Nonresidential Capital Stock, All Industries, 1960–1999 (in Billions of 1992 Dollars)		
	Net Stock	**Equipment**	**Structures**
1960	191	36	155
1970	303	54	249
1980	429	92	337
1990	538	140	398
1999	596	180	416
Percentage change:			
1960–1999	212.0%	400.0%	168.4%
Annual rate	3.0%	4.2%	2.6%

Source: Adapted from Statistics Canada, CANSIM database, Series D993325–D993328.

(*K*) increases. Second, there are diminishing returns to capital. Increasing capital by 10 units first increases output by 10 units—from 300 in period 1 to 310 in period 2. But the second increase of 10 units yields only 9 units of output, and the third increase yields only 8.

Table 19.4 shows the real value of nonresidential capital stocks in Canada since 1960. The increase in capital stock is the difference between gross investment and depreciation. (Remember that some capital becomes obsolete and some wears out every year.) Since 1960, the capital stock has increased at a rate of 3.0% per year. The stock of equipment has increased faster than the stock of structures.

By comparing Tables 19.2 and 19.4, you can see that capital has been increasing faster than labour since 1960. In all economies experiencing modern economic growth, capital expands at a more rapid rate than labour. That is, the ratio of capital to labour (*K/L*) increases, and this too is a source of increasing productivity.

Increases in Human Capital

Investment in human capital is another source of economic growth. People in good health are more productive than people in poor health; people with skills are more productive than people without them.

Human capital can be produced in a number of ways. Individuals can invest in themselves by going to university, college, or vocational training programs. Firms can invest in human capital through on-the-job training. The government invests in human capital with programs to improve health, to provide schooling, and to provide job training.

Table 19.5 shows that the level of educational attainment has risen significantly since 1951. The percentage of the population over age 25 with no schooling or only an elementary-school level of education (0 to 8 years) has dropped dramatically from 55% in 1951 to just over 12% in 1999. The percentage of the over-25 population with a university degree has also seen striking changes. Moreover, the percentage of the population over 25 who had attended or completed some form of education beyond the high-school level was 54% in 1999, or more than double the 1980 level of 26%.

Increases in Productivity

Growth that cannot be explained by increases in the *quantity* of inputs can be explained only by an increase in the *productivity* of those inputs. In this case, each unit of input must be producing more output. The **productivity of an input** can be affected by factors including technological change and economies of scale.

■ **Technological Change** The Industrial Revolution was in part sparked by important new technological developments. New techniques of spinning and weaving—the invention of the "mule" and the "spinning jenny," for example—were critical.

productivity of an input *The amount of output produced per unit of an input.*

Table 19.5

Table 19.5 Highest Level of Schooling Attained by Persons Age 25 or Over, 1951–1999

	Percentage with 0–8 Years Only	Percentage with University Degree
1951*	55.0	NA
1961*	48.9	3.3
1975	33.2	8.2
1980	28.2	9.9
1990	16.8	12.5
1999	12.2	16.9

Note: * indicates figures are for persons age 25+ *not attending school; NA=not available.*

Sources: Adapted from Statistics Canada: 1951 Census (Cat. no. 92-000, Vol. II); 1961 Census, Vol. I, Part 3 (Cat. no. 92-557); *Labour Force Annual Averages* (Cat. no. 71-529); *Labour Force Historical Review* (CD-ROM).

The high-tech boom that swept the industrialized world in the early 1980s was driven by the rapid development and dissemination of semiconductor technology.

Technological change affects productivity in two stages. First, there is an advance in knowledge, or an **invention.** But knowledge by itself does nothing unless it is used. When new knowledge is used to produce a new product or to produce an existing product more efficiently, there is **innovation.**

invention *An advance in knowledge.*

Technological change cannot be measured directly. Some studies have presented data on "indicators" of the rate of technical change—the number of new patents, for example—but none is very satisfactory. Still, we know that technological changes that have improved productivity are all around us. Computer technology has revolutionized the office, hybrid seeds have dramatically increased the productivity of land, and more efficient and powerful aircraft have made air travel routine and relatively inexpensive.

innovation *The use of new knowledge to produce a new product or to produce an existing product more efficiently.*

The study of technological change is a central part of macroeconomics. As mentioned, the nineteenth-century English economists Malthus and Ricardo predicted that production, particularly food production, would not exceed the rate of population growth. This turned out to be wrong for at least the wealthier countries, because Malthus and Ricardo did not give sufficient role to technological change or capital accumulation. The focus of their approach, called *classical growth theory*, was on population growth and the diminishing returns to labour.

In contrast, *neoclassical growth theory*, as developed by the American economist Robert Solow and others, emphasizes capital accumulation (i.e., investment) and how that is determined by saving (if there are no foreign sources of capital) and the fact that saving depends on the total amount of output. Hence a technological advance will increase output which will stimulate saving. You might think there could be a virtuous circle, as the invested saving stimulates output, which would increase saving, which would increase output, etc. But unfortunately, diminishing returns to capital set in, making additional investment less and less effective and stopping the expansion. Technological progress is required for growth in this model, but there is no theory of technological progress: it is assumed to be determined by factors outside the model.

New growth theory emphasizes the determinants of technological progress. The rate of invention and innovation depends on how much is invested in research and development (R&D). This in turn depends on how profitable R&D is, and hence on government policies that protect or reward R&D (e.g., patents and government research contracts) and on the availability of an educated workforce that can be hired by innovative firms. Once a new discovery has been made, it does not need to be rediscovered by others and can spread throughout the economy without the use of additional resources. Proponents of new growth theory also sometimes downplay diminishing returns in capital, arguing that the productivity of new investment will not fall, because new investments will also tend to reflect the latest technological advances.

The productivity of the agricultural sector can be greatly affected by the weather. The flooding of the Red River in the spring of 1997 was the worst Manitobans had seen in the twentieth century. The flood meant losses of livestock, and delays in seeding. Ironically, Manitoba farmers faced droughts later that year.

Finally, note that technological change includes "managerial knowledge" such as improved personnel management techniques, account procedures, data management, and the like. As inventories are part of a firm's capital stock, reducing them by modern methods reduces costs and raises productivity: the "just-in-time" inventory method decreases stocks of assembly-line parts to what is needed over the next few hours. Inventory management systems are an example of a _capital-saving innovation_; an advance such as robotics is a _labour-saving_ innovation.

■ **Economies of Scale** _External economies of scale_ are cost savings that result from increases in the size of industries. The economies that accompany growth in size may arise from a variety of causes. For example, as firms in a growing industry build plants at new locations, they may have lower transport costs. There may also be some economies of scale associated with R&D spending and job-training programs.

■ **Other Influences on Productivity** In addition to technological change, other advances in knowledge, and economies of scale, other forces may affect productivity. During the 1970s and 1980s, for example, the government required many firms to reduce the air and water pollution they were producing. These requirements may have diverted capital and labour from the production of measured output and thus _reduced_ measured productivity. Similarly, occupational health and safety legislation such as the Canada Labour Code and its provincial counterparts require firms to protect workers from accidental injuries and potential health problems. These laws may also divert resources from measured output.

Negative effects such as these are more a problem of _measurement_ than of truly declining productivity. Legislation such as the Canadian Environmental Protection Act seeks to regulate air and water quality because clean air and water presumably have a value to society. Thus, the resources diverted to produce that value are not wasted. A perfect measure of output produced that is of value to society would include environmental quality and good health.

The list of factors that can affect productivity could include the ethics and values of the population, the number of entrepreneurs, sound monetary and financial institutions, the nature of property rights, the maintenance of law and order, political stability, and the provision of infrastructure by government. Weather can have an enormous impact on agricultural productivity. The droughts on the Prairies during the Depression are an example of this, as are the floods along the Red River in Manitoba in the spring of 1997 or the ice storm in eastern Canada in 1998.

Having presented the major factors that influence economic growth, we now turn to the growth record for Canada and to some estimates of the role these factors have played.

Growth and Productivity in the Canadian Economy

GROWTH IN CANADA SINCE CONFEDERATION

Economic growth in Canada in the years following Confederation in 1867 was quite strong. It has been estimated that from 1870 to 1910, growth in the Canadian economy was the most rapid of the industrial countries of the time.[2] As shown in Table 19.6, real growth averaged 3.3% annually from 1870 to 1885, 3.6% from 1885 to 1900, and 4.5% between 1900 and 1926. (This does not of course mean that the rate of growth was positive every year.) Among the notable events in Canada's economic history of this period were the completion of the Canadian Pacific Railway's transcontinental route in 1885 and the wheat boom from 1896 to 1913.

Table 19.6 shows that real growth from 1870 to 1999 is estimated to be about 3.9% per year on average. The per capita annual growth rate over the same period

[2]See Morris Altman, "Revised Real Canadian GNP Estimates and Canadian Economic Growth, 1870–1926," Review of Income and Wealth, _December 1992._

Table 19.6	Growth of Real Output in Canada, 1870–1999	
Period	**Average Output Growth Rate per Year (percent)**	**Average Output per Capita Growth Rate per Year (percent)**
1870–1885	3.3	1.8
1885–1900	3.6	2.5
1900–1926	4.5	2.2
1926–1939	1.9	0.5
1939–1950	5.8	4.0
1950–1960	4.6	1.8
1960–1970	5.2	3.3
1970–1980	4.6	3.1
1970–1973	6.4	4.4
1973–1980	3.8	2.5
1980–1990	2.9	1.7
1990–1999	2.3	1.3
1870–1999	3.9	2.2
1926–1999	3.9	2.2
1973–1999	3.0	1.8

Sources: From 1870–1926, output is real GNP: Adapted from Morris Altman, "Revised Real Canadian GNP Estimates and Canadian Economic Growth, 1870–1926," *Review of Income and Wealth,* December 1992; from 1926–1999, output is real GDP: Adapted from Statistics Canada, CANSIM database, Series D14442 and *Bank of Canada Banking and Financial Statistics,* Table A2; Population 1870–1900: Adapted from M. C. Urquhart and K.A.H. Buckley (eds.), *Historical Statistics of Canada,* 1st ed. (Toronto: Macmillan, 1965); Population 1926–1995: adapted from Statistics Canada, CANSIM database, Series D31248; Population 1996–1999: B. G. Spencer, C. H. Feaver, and F. T. Denton, unpublished population estimates, McMaster University, January 2000.

averaged 2.2%. Periods of low growth that stand out in the twentieth century are the period of the Great Depression and the 1990s.

THE PRODUCTIVITY "PROBLEM"

As was seen in Table 19.6, the rate of growth of the Canadian economy slowed after 1973. Since that time, the focus of much economic debate in Canada and elsewhere has been on the decrease in productivity growth rates that seem to be taking place. The productivity "problem" is a much discussed issue, and many explanations have been offered for it. Some economists have pointed to the rate of saving in Canada, which has not been as high as the rate in countries such as Japan. Others have blamed increased environmental and government regulation in the business sector. Still others have argued that the country is not spending as much on research and development as it should. Finally, some have suggested, high energy costs in the 1970s led to investment designed to save energy rather than to enhance productivity.

While some of these arguments may have some validity in explaining Canada's *relatively* low rates of productivity growth compared to other industrial countries, as can be seen in Table 19.7, declining rates of productivity growth after 1973 were a worldwide phenomenon. The table shows annual rates of productivity increases (or decreases in the case of negative entries) for all member countries of the OECD. In every country, the annual rate of change in total factor productivity slowed after 1973. In many countries, these annual rates slowed further after 1979.

One of the leading explanations for the decline in measures of productivity growth is that the nature of what is produced in today's advanced economies has changed so rapidly that we are no longer able to measure output as well as we once did. In the early years of national accounting, it was relatively easy to measure tonnes of wheat or metres of cloth. Today, however, an increasingly large fraction of output in many countries of the world is due to the service sector of their economies. It is not as easy to measure the output of a lawyer, a financial adviser, or a computer programmer. In addition, quality changes even in traditional products (better wheat, better cloth) are productivity improvements but are not reflected in traditional national accounting methods. These issues are discussed in more detail in the Issues and Controversies box titled "Can We Really Measure Productivity

Table 19.7	Productivity in the Business Sector, OECD Countries: Percentage Changes at Annual Rates

	Total Factor Productivity[a]			Labour Productivity[b]		
	1960–73[c]	1973–79	1979–97[d]	1960–73[c]	1973–79	1979–97[d]
G-7 Countries						
Canada	1.1	−0.1	−0.5	2.5	1.1	1.0
France	3.7	1.6	1.3	5.3	2.9	2.2
Germany[e]	2.6	1.8	1.2	4.5	3.1	2.2
Italy	4.4	2.0	1.1	6.4	2.8	2.0
Japan	4.9	0.7	0.9	8.4	2.8	2.3
United Kingdom	2.6	0.5	1.1	4.0	1.6	2.0
United States	1.9	0.1	0.7	2.6	0.3	0.9
Remaining OECD Countries						
Australia	2.0	1.0	0.9	3.0	2.5	1.5
Austria	3.3	1.1	0.9	5.9	3.1	2.3
Belgium	3.8	1.3	1.0	5.2	2.7	1.9
Denmark	2.1	0.6	1.2	3.9	2.3	2.1
Finland	4.0	1.9	2.6	5.0	3.2	3.5
Greece	2.7	0.8	−0.2	9.0	3.4	0.7
Ireland	4.5	3.8	3.7	4.8	4.3	4.1
Korea	NA	3.1	2.7	NA	6.6	5.6
Netherlands	3.5	1.7	1.0	4.8	2.6	1.5
New Zealand	1.3	−1.5	1.0	2.1	−1.1	1.3
Norway[f]	2.2	1.3	0.6	3.8	2.7	1.8
Portugal	2.6	−1.0	1.0	7.5	0.5	2.4
Spain	3.1	0.6	1.6	5.9	2.8	2.7
Sweden	1.9	0.0	1.1	3.7	1.4	2.0
Switzerland	1.5	−0.7	−0.1	3.3	0.8	0.6

NA=not available.

[a]Total factor productivity growth is equal to a weighted average of the growth in labour and capital productivity. The sample-period averages for capital and labour shares are used as weights.

[b]Output per employed person.

[c]Or earliest available year: 1961 for Greece, Ireland; 1962 for Japan, United Kingdom; 1964 for Austria; 1965 for France, Norway, Spain, Sweden; 1966 for Canada, Australia; 1967 for New Zealand; 1969 for the Netherlands; 1970 for Belgium; 1975 for Korea.

[d]Or latest available year: 1993 for Portugal; 1994 for Norway; 1995 for Australia, Austria, Korea, New Zealand, Switzerland; 1996 for Japan, Germany, France, Italy, the United Kingdom, Belgium, Denmark, Finland, Greece, Ireland, the Netherlands, Spain, Sweden.

[e]The two first averages are for West Germany. Percentage changes for 1979–1996 are calculated as the weighted averages of Western Germany productivity growth between 1979 and 1991 and total German productivity growth between 1991 and the latest year available.

[f]Mainland business sector (i.e., excluding shipping as well as crude petroleum and gas extraction).

Source: OECD, *Economic Outlook*, December 1998, No. 64, Annex Table 59. © OECD, 1998.

Changes?" The most important point to remember is that the productivity statistics we have been examining are widely debated.

Economic Growth and Public Policy

Whether or not the apparent decline in the rate of economic growth in Canada is in part measurement error, other nations have had much more rapid rates of growth than Canada in the past two or three decades. It often seems that a faster rate of economic growth might solve many Canadian problems (although see the next section for a discussion of opposing views). With increased growth, individuals and governments would have more resources to solve both individual and social problems.

An important part of economic growth is productivity growth. While recently Canadian productivity growth has been very similar to that of the United States, there is still a productivity gap of about 15% between Canada and the United States. While other major economies also trail the United States in productivity, Canada is one of the few for which the gap is not closing over time. In discussing public policies that might increase Canadian productivity, Professor Richard Harris of Simon Fraser University has suggested that of all the factors correlated with productivity growth, the "Big 3" are investment in machinery and equipment, education, and openness to trade and investment.[3] Let us first consider policies that might affect these.

■ **Policies to Stimulate Investment in Machinery and Equipment** Our discussion of growth theory emphasized capital accumulation and technological advance, so it is not surprising that some economists would argue for policies to stimulate new investment. New investment increases physical capital per worker and embodies new techniques and ideas, which diffuse throughout the economy and stimulate further growth. Many economists argue that monetary policies that keep interest rates down, plus tax incentives such as high depreciation allowances on new equipment, will therefore have important beneficial effects on growth. If monetary and fiscal policies can keep the economy at or near potential output, this will not only keep as many workers as possible in productive employment, but also stimulate further investment because firms will recognize that additional production is likely to find markets.

■ **Policies to Improve Education** As new growth theory in particular argues, policies that improve education may both increase invention and innovation by increasing the available pool of inventors, innovators, and researchers and provide an environment in which new ideas and techniques can spread. Public policies that promote education may also support a more equitable distribution of income.

It can be argued that there would be too little education without public subsidy. Think of individuals deciding whether to go for more schooling as making an investment decision, with the returns being at least partially in the form of higher incomes they may be able to earn. But because governments will tax these higher incomes, the individuals may tend to "under-invest" unless the government also pays some of the costs through subsidy. More generally, an educated population may make better citizens and be able to deal with problems more effectively and with less disruption.

■ **Openness to Trade and Investment** It has been argued that one difference between prosperous and poor countries has been openness, because exposure to other countries provides a source of ideas and innovations, and foreign producers provide additional competitive pressure on domestic producers to improve.[4] However, moves toward free trade in Canada in the late 1980s and the 1990s have not been accompanied by a resurgence of Canadian productivity growth. Some Canadian economists argue that the effects of free trade on productivity growth are important but have long lags so that net benefits are only starting to be experienced as the new century begins. The current decade will tell.

Besides the Big 3 of Professor Harris, pro-growth policies may focus on the related areas of saving or research and development. Let's consider each briefly.

■ **Policies to Increase the Saving Rate** As noted, growth theory emphasizes capital accumulation, which can be financed by saving. (Domestic investment can also be financed by foreign borrowing in an open economy). When the economy is below potential output, expansionary monetary and fiscal policies are designed at least partially to stimulate consumption, but not saving. But in the long run, particularly if the economy is at potential output, it is desirable if Canadians save. The more Canadians save, the more funds are available for investment by Canadians both in Canada and elsewhere. The returns to this investment will increase future potential output and incomes.

One of the factors that has affected national saving in Canada has been the "dissaving" by governments, particularly from the mid-1970s to the mid-1990s when the federal government and most provincial governments ran substantial deficits. As was discussed in more detail in Chapter 16, the government can promote growth by borrowing to invest in capital projects such as roads. One particular

---

[3] *See Richard G. Harris, "Determinants of Canadian Productivity Growth: Issues and Prospects,"* Industry Canada Research Publications Program Discussion Paper Number 8, *December 1999.*
[4] *See David S. Landes,* The Wealth and Poverty of Nations *(New York: Norton, 1998).*

When numbers like those presented in Table 19.7 are published, most people take them as "true." Even though we don't really know much about how they are constructed, we assume that they are the best measurements we can get.

Yet such data are often the source of great controversy. In fact, some have argued that the mix of products produced in the industrial countries and the increased pace of technological change in recent years have made it increasingly difficult to measure productivity changes accurately. The observed productivity decline in recent decades may thus simply be measurement error.

These arguments make a certain amount of sense at an intuitive level. Even in agriculture, where it is relatively easy to measure productivity growth, the possibility of mismeasurement exists. The output of a soybean farm can be measured in tonnes, and labour, capital, and land inputs present no serious measurement problems. So, over time, as farming techniques improved and farmers acquired new and better machinery, output per hectare and output per worker rose and have continued to rise. But today we have biotechnology. Genetic engineering now makes it possible to make soybeans higher in protein. Clearly, technology has improved and "output" has increased, but these increases do not show up in the data because of our relatively crude measures of output.

A similar problem exists with computers. If you simply counted the number of personal computers produced and measured the cost of the inputs used in their production, you would no doubt see some productivity advances. But computers produced for $1000 in 2001 contained processors capable of performing tasks literally thousands of times faster than computers produced a few years earlier. If we were to measure computer outputs not in terms of units produced but in terms of the actual "services" they provide to users, we would find massive productivity advances. The problem is that many of the products that we now use are qualitatively different than the comparable products that we used only a few years ago, and the standard measures of productivity miss many of these quality changes.

The problems are even greater in the service sector, where output is extremely difficult to measure. It is easy to understand the problem if you think of what information technology has done for legal services. As recently as ten years ago, a lawyer doing research to support a legal case might spend hundreds of hours looking through old cases and public documents. Today's lawyers can log on to a computer and in seconds do a keyword search on a massive legal database. Such time- and labour-saving productivity advances are not counted in the official data.

This brings us to what economists have called the "productivity paradox" or the "computer paradox." The number of computers used in the economy and the improvements in computer capabilities have both grown substantially since the 1970s. All of this new technology should be making the economy more productive, yet measured productivity growth has slowed.* Explanations for this seeming paradox are that most of the investment in computer technology has been in sectors in which it is difficult to measure output, or that possibly many of the gains are only now beginning to be realized.

*The issue of productivity measurement was the subject of Professor Zvi Griliches's Presidential Address to the American Economic Association in January 1994. The full text, entitled "Productivity, R&D, and the Data Constraint," appears in the *American Economic Review*, March 1994.

---

program whose financing has been criticized by some economists is the Canada Pension Plan (CPP), which has essentially transferred contributions from current workers to the currently retired, without building up an asset base (and hence without contributing to the national capital stock). In 1997, the federal government announced increases in contribution rates and other measures that will increase the plan's asset base. This change and the move to government surpluses has tended to offset the effects on national saving of recent declines in household saving rates.

■ **Policies to Increase Research and Development**   Considerable research on accounting for the sources of actual growth has consistently found that technological advance is important, just as the discussion in this chapter would suggest. Professor Jeffrey Bernstein of Carleton University has argued that one source of the Canada-U.S. productivity gap is that for much of the past 40 years, Canadian R&D expenditures have been roughly between 1.25% and 1.75% of GDP, in contrast to more than 2.5% of GDP in the United States. He argues that the benefits of increased and more complete R&D tax incentives greatly exceed their costs.[5]

Another obvious role for the government with respect to research and development is patent and copyright protection. Prospective inventors who knew that

[5]See Jeffrey I. Bernstein, "*Is the Labour Productivity Gap with the United States Made in Canada?*" Canadian Business Economics, *February 2000*.

the results of their expensive research could be copied at low cost by an outsider would not have much incentive to do the R&D in the first place. In Canada this issue has come to the fore with respect to pharmaceuticals. In the early 1990s, the federal government legislated more patent protection to international drug companies partially in return for promises to increase the percentage of pharmaceutical R&D performed within Canada. While at least on a worldwide scale, the tighter the patent protection the higher the price of new drugs, and the higher the price of new drugs the more incentive there is for development, the obvious disadvantage of keeping cheaper, generic substitutes out of the market is the higher prices faced by users of the drug.

Because patents do not provide perfect protection from imitators and because it may be desirable to develop new products without granting a monopoly to the developer, there may be a more direct role for government in R&D. An example of this would be Agriculture Canada, which over the years has developed new strains of many grains, vegetables, and fruits particularly suited to the Canadian climate. (One of Agriculture Canada's most notable developments is the now widely used oilseed canola.) Note that a private corporation would face the problem that, after it had invested in all the R&D, the purchaser of a single seed could then go into business by growing more seeds.

GROWTH POLICY: A LONG-RUN PROPOSITION

Suppose the government of Canada proposed a policy that would cost about $1 billion and would increase the average real growth rate permanently, say from 2.50% to 2.52%. Would such a small increase be worthwhile?

The answer is probably yes. In ten years, GDP would be almost $2 billion *per year* higher with the 2.52% growth rate than with the 2.50% rate and this increment would continue (and grow) every year. Yet the return in the first year would be less than the cost. One can imagine that a politician facing this choice in an election year might choose a program with a better short-term return, even at the expense of the longer term.

In any case, whether or not pro-growth policies work, are they worth pursuing? Not everyone agrees that the top priority in a developed economy should be continued growth. To close the chapter, we now turn to this debate.

The Pros and Cons of Growth

As we said at the beginning of this chapter, there are those who believe that growth should be the primary objective of any society and those who believe that the costs of growth are too great. It is worth reviewing the arguments on both sides.

THE PRO-GROWTH ARGUMENT

Advocates of growth argue that growth *is* progress. Resources in a market economy are used to produce what people want; if you produce something that people do not want, you are out of business. Even in a centrally planned economy, resources are targeted to fulfill needs and wants. If a society is able to produce those things more efficiently and at less cost, how can that be bad?

By applying new technologies and better production methods, resources are freed to produce new and better products. Certainly, for Colleen and Ivan accumulation of capital—a house, a water system, and so forth—and advancing knowledge were necessary to improve life on a formerly uninhabited island. In a modern industrial society as well, capital accumulation and new technology improve the quality of life.

One way to think about the benefits of growth is to compare two periods of time, say 1950 and 2000. In 2000, real GDP per capita was over three times what it was in 1950. This means that incomes have grown more than three times as fast as prices so that we can buy that much more.

While it is true that the things available in both time periods are not exactly the same, growth has given us *more choice,* not less. Consider transportation. In 1950, construction was just beginning on the Trans-Canada Highway. We had automobiles, but the highway system did not compare to what we have today. And even more significant advances have been made in air travel. Flying between cities was possible, but more costly, less comfortable, and slower in 1950 than it is today. It is now cheaper to get from Toronto to Vancouver than it was in the 1950s, and it takes a fraction of the time.

Do these changes improve the quality of life? Yes, because they give us more freedom. We can travel more frequently. I can see family and friends more often. I spend less time getting where I want to go so I can spend more time there. People are able to get to more places for less money.

What about consumer durables—dishwashers, microwave ovens, compact disc players, power lawnmowers, and so forth? Do they really enhance the quality of life? If they do not, why do we buy them? Few such things were around in the 1950s. In 1950, only a very few homes in Canada had dishwashers; today the figure is close to 50%. In 1950, less than half of all Canadian homes had gas or electric ranges; today virtually all homes do and, in addition, over 85% have microwave ovens.

What makes a dishwasher worthwhile? It saves the most valuable commodity of all: *time*. Many consumer durables have no intrinsic value—that is, they don't provide satisfaction directly. They do free us from tasks and chores that are not fun, however—no one really likes to wash clothes or dishes. If a product allows us to perform these tasks more easily and quickly, it gives us more time for other things.

And think of the improvement in the *quality* of those things that do yield satisfaction directly. Record players in the 1950s reproduced sound very imperfectly; high fidelity was just being developed, and stereo was in the future. Today you can get a compact disc player for your car. Small "boxes" available at discount stores for under $30 reproduce sound far better than the best machines available in the early 1950s. And the range of tapes and compact discs available is extraordinary.

Growth also makes it possible to improve conditions for the less fortunate in society. The logic is simple: when there is more to go around, the sacrifice required to help the needy is smaller. With higher incomes, we can better afford the sacrifices needed to help the poor. Growth also produces jobs. When population growth is not accompanied by growth in output, unemployment and poverty increase.

Those in advanced societies can be complacent about growth, or even critical of it, but leaders of developing countries understand its benefits well. When 75% of a country's population is poor, redistributing existing incomes may not do enough. The main hope for improvement in the long run is economic growth.

THE ANTI-GROWTH ARGUMENT

Those who argue against economic growth generally make four major points:

1. Any measure of output measures only the value of those things exchanged in the market. Many things that affect the quality of life are not traded in the market, and those things generally lose value when growth occurs.
2. For growth to occur, industry must cause consumers to develop new tastes and preferences. Therefore, we have no real need for many of the things we now consume. Wants are created, and consumers have become the servants, rather than the masters, of the economy.
3. The world has a finite quantity of resources, and rapid growth is consuming them at a rate that cannot continue. Because the available resources impose limits to growth, we should begin now to plan for the future, when growth will be impossible.
4. Growth may be associated with a less equitable distribution of income and is not necessarily associated with greater security from unemployment or ill health.

■ **Growth Has Negative Effects on the Quality of Life** Perhaps the most dramatic "unmeasurable" changes that affect the quality of life occur in the early stages of growth when societies become industrialized. More is produced: agricultural productivity is higher, more manufactured goods are available, and so forth. But most people are crowded into cities, and their lives change drastically.

Before industrialization, most people in the Western world lived in small towns in the country. Most were poor, and they worked long hours to produce enough food to survive. After industrialization and urbanization in eighteenth-century England, men, women, and children worked long hours at routine jobs in hot, crowded factories. They were paid low wages and had very little control over their lives.

Even today, growth continues to change the quality of life in ways that are observable but that are not taken into account when we calculate growth rates. Perhaps the most significant is environmental damage. As the industrial engine is fed, waste is produced. Often both the feeding and the waste cause massive environmental damage. A dramatic example is the strip-mining of coal that has ravaged many parts of North America. Another is the uncontrolled harvesting of forests. Modern growth requires paper and wood products, and large areas of timber have been cleared and never replanted. This may lead to environmental problems such as soil erosion and the endangering of wildlife habitats.

The disposal of industrial wastes has not begun to keep pace with industrial growth. It is now clear that growing and prosperous chemical companies have for decades been dumping hazardous, often carcinogenic, waste products into the soil and water. It is costing billions to clean them up. Those costs were never taken into account when the market was allocating resources to the growing chemical industry.

Growth-related problems are by no means confined to North America. Japan, for example, paid little attention to the environment during the early years of its rapid economic growth. Many of the results were disastrous. The best known of these results were the horrifying birth defects following the dumping of industrial mercury into the waters of Minamata Bay. In addition to birth defects, thousands of cases of "Minamata disease" in adults have been documented, and hundreds have died.

■ **Growth Encourages the Creation of Artificial Needs**   The nature of preferences has been debated within the economics profession for many years. The orthodox view, which lies at the heart of modern welfare economics, is that preferences exist among consumers and that the economy's purpose is to serve those needs. According to the notion of **consumer sovereignty**, people are free to choose, and things that people do not want will not sell. Thus, the consumer rules.

The opposite view is that preferences are formed within the economic system. To continue growing, firms need a continuously expanding set of demands. To ensure that demand grows, firms create it by managing our minds and manipulating our behaviour with elaborate advertising, fancy packaging, and other marketing techniques that persuade us to buy things for which we have no intrinsic need.

consumer sovereignty *The notion that people are free to choose, and that things that people do not want will not sell. Thus, "the customer rules."*

■ **Growth Means the Rapid Depletion of a Finite Quantity of Resources**   In 1972, the Club of Rome, a group of "concerned citizens," contracted with a group at MIT to do a study entitled *The Limits to Growth*.[6] The book-length final report presented the results of computer simulations that assumed present growth rates of population, food, industrial output, and resource exhaustion. According to these data, sometime after the year 2000 the limits will be reached, and the entire world economy will come crashing down:

> Collapse occurs because of nonrenewable resource depletion. The industrial capital stock grows to a level that requires an enormous input of resources. In the very process of that growth, it depletes a large fraction of the resource reserves available. As resource prices rise and mines are depleted, more and more capital must be used for obtaining resources, leaving less to be invested for future growth. Finally, investment cannot keep up with depreciation and the industrial base collapses, taking with it the service and agricultural systems, which have become dependent on industrial inputs (such as fertilizers, pesticides, hospital laboratories, computers, and especially energy for mechanization. … Population finally decreases when the death rate is driven upward by the lack of food and health services.[7]

This argument is similar to one offered almost 200 years ago by Thomas Malthus, whom we mentioned earlier in this chapter.

In the early 1970s, many thought that the Club of Rome's predictions had come true. It seemed as if the world were starting to run up against the limits of

[6]*Dennis L. Meadows et al.,* The Limits to Growth *(Washington: Potomac Associates, 1972).*
[7]*Meadows, pp. 131–132.*

world energy supplies; the prices of energy products shot up, and there were serious shortages. But dramatic changes have occurred in the years since. The higher prices encouraged new exploration for oil and gas, and new sources of energy have been developed, such as hydro projects in northern Quebec, oil sands projects in Alberta, the Sable Island gas development off Nova Scotia, Hibernia in Newfoundland, and a number of nuclear projects across the country. In addition, higher energy prices promote the development of new conservation measures. For example, automobile gas mileage has been pushed up to levels that were inconceivable in 1972. The resulting increases in supply and slowing of the rate of increase of demand have actually pushed energy prices down to levels that in real terms are about the same as they were before the oil price shocks of the 1970s.

■ **Growth and Income Distribution** Allowing innovators and the talented to keep all the returns generated by their ideas and abilities provides the maximum incentives for these key contributors to growth. Allowing savers to keep all the returns generated from their wealth provides the maximum incentive to save more capital. But taxing some of these returns for redistribution to the poor reduces inequality. Hence there may be a tradeoff between growth and equality in the distribution of income.

However, this is not clear. More equal distribution of income may itself provide political and social stability that promotes growth. Moreover, sometimes economic growth only seems to benefit the rich. If the benefits of growth trickle down to the poor, why are there more homeless today than there were 25 years ago?

SUMMARY: NO "RIGHT ANSWER"

We have presented the arguments for and against economic growth in simple terms. In reality, most acknowledge that there is no "right answer." To suggest that all economic growth is bad is wrong; to suggest that economic growth should run unchecked is equally wrong. The real question for society is: How can we derive the benefits of growth and at the same time minimize its undesirable consequences?

There are many tradeoffs. For example, perhaps we can grow faster if we pay less attention to environmental concerns. But how much environmental damage should we accept to get how much economic growth? Many argue that we can achieve a lower but acceptable level of economic growth *and* protect the environment at the same time.

As long as these tradeoffs exist, people will disagree. Much debate in contemporary politics is largely about the costs and benefits of shifting more effort toward the goal of economic growth and away from environmental and social welfare goals.

Summary

1. *Modern economic growth* is the rapid and sustained increase in real output per capita that began in the Western world with the Industrial Revolution.

The Growth Process: From Agriculture to Industry

2. All societies face limits imposed by the resources and technologies available to them. Economic growth expands these limits and shifts society's production possibility frontier up and to the right.

The Sources of Economic Growth

3. If growth in output outpaces growth in population, and if the economic system is producing what people want, growth will increase the standard of living. Growth occurs either when (1) society acquires more resources or (2) society discovers ways of using available resources more efficiently.

4. An *aggregate production function* embodies the relationship between inputs—the labour force and the stock of capital—and total national output.

5. A number of factors can contribute to an increase in GDP: (1) an increase in the labour supply; (2) an increase in physical capital—plant and equipment—and/or human capital—education, training, and health; (3) an increase in productivity brought about by technological change and/or economies of scale.

Growth and Productivity in the Canadian Economy

6. The annual rate of growth in real output in Canada averaged 3.9% from 1926 to 1999. Growth rates have slowed since 1973, and were as low as 2.3% on average between 1990 and 1999.

7. There has been much concern that the rate of growth in Canada is slowing. Productivity growth rates have declined since 1973, not only in Canada but in other industrialized nations as well.

Economic Growth and Public Policy

8. A number of public policies may be pursued with the aim of improving the growth of real output. These policies include efforts to improve education, to encourage saving, to stimulate investment, and to increase research and development.

The Pros and Cons of Growth

9. Advocates of growth argue that growth is progress. Growth gives us more freedom—that is, more choices. It saves time, improves the standard of living, and may be the only way to improve conditions for the poor. Growth creates jobs and increases income simply because there is more to go around.

10. Those who argue against growth generally make four major points. First, many things that affect the quality of life are not traded in the market, and these things generally lose value when there is growth. Second, to have growth, industry may cause consumers to develop new tastes and preferences for many things that they have no real need for. Third, the world has a finite quantity of resources, and rapid growth is eating them up at a rate that cannot continue. Fourth, growth may be associated with a less equitable distribution of income although it may alternatively be argued that a more equal distribution of income provides political and social stability that promotes growth.

Review Terms and Concepts

aggregate production function 383	innovation 387	modern economic growth 381
consumer sovereignty 395	invention 387	productivity of an input 386
economic growth 381	labour productivity 384	

Problem Set

1. Why can growth lead to a more unequal distribution of income? Assuming this is true, how is it possible for the poor to benefit from economic growth?

2. Tables 1, 2, and 3 present some data on three hypothetical economies. Complete the tables by figuring the measured productivity of labour and the rate of output growth. What do the data tell you about the causes of economic growth? (*Hint:* How fast are *L* and *K* growing?)

Table 1

Period	L	K	Y	Y/L	Growth Rate of Output
1	1052	3065	4506		
2	1105	3095	4674		
3	1160	3126	4842		
4	1218	3157	5019		

Table 2

Period	L	K	Y	Y/L	Growth Rate of Output
1	1052	3065	4506		
2	1062	3371	4683		
3	1073	3709	4866		
4	1084	4079	5055		

Table 3

Period	L	K	Y	Y/L	Growth Rate of Output
1	1052	3065	4506		
2	1062	3095	4731		
3	1073	3126	4967		
4	1084	3157	5216		

3. In earlier chapters, we studied models in which, depending upon the nature of aggregate supply, a reduction in the saving rate would increase consumption, stimulate aggregate demand, and increase output. In this chapter we have argued that a higher saving rate, even with lower consumption spending, is a key to long-run GDP growth. How can both of these arguments be correct?

4. Suppose that there is a bill before Parliament that would make major changes in tax policy. First, the corporate tax would be lowered substantially in an effort to stimulate investment. The bill contains a 15% investment tax credit—firms would be able to reduce their taxes by 15% of the value of investment projects that they undertake. To keep revenues constant, the bill would increase the GST by one percentage point, which would raise the price of consumer goods and reduce consumption. What tradeoffs do you see involved in this bill? What are the pros and cons?

5. If you wanted to measure productivity (output per worker) in the following sectors over time, how would you measure "output"? How easy is it to measure productivity in each of the sectors?
 a. Software
 b. Vegetable farming
 c. Education
 d. Airline transportation

6. Economists generally agree that high budget deficits today will reduce the growth rate of the economy in the future. Why is this the case? Do the reasons for the high budget deficit matter? In other words, does it matter whether the deficit is caused by lower taxes, increased spending, more job-training programs, and so on?

Web References for Part Five: Macroeconomics and Policy: A Closer Look

The main source for Canadian demographic data is Statistics Canada (**www.statcan.ca/**). If you encounter data series on the Statistics Canada site that are not free of charge, try the CANSIM site (**datacentre.chass. utoronto.ca/cansim/**). For a newcomer, this site is a little harder to navigate than the basic Statistics Canada site, but it is likely your university is a subscriber in which case there is no charge. For international demographic information, the Demography Department of the Australian National University (**demography.anu.edu.au/**) maintains a useful site with many links.

Besides the Statistics Canada site, information on economic growth is available at the Department of Finance site (**www.fin.gc.ca/**) that we have mentioned in other Web References sections, and also at the Industry Canada site (**www.ic.gc.ca/**). The Centre for the Study of Living Standards (**www.csls.ca/**) is an Ottawa-based research group that has a major research emphasis on productivity, particularly Canada-U.S. comparisons.

It is difficult to find a balanced source on the current debates in macroeconomics. The useful site of Professor Nouriel Roubini of Columbia University (**www.stern. nyu.edu/~nroubini/**) is recommended. Click on "Recent Macroeconomic Controversies and Policy."

Demography and Economic Growth

In Chapter 19, we concentrated on technological change and saving as factors influencing growth. While saving contributes to the growth of capital, what factors affect the growth of labour? After all, one simple reason why the Canadian economy produces so much more than it did 50 years ago is that there are roughly three times as many people in Canada. Population growth, labour-force participation rates, and the age structure of a society are all significant factors in determining how the economy will grow.

The study of how changes in population size and structure affect society is called *demography.* A useful tool in demography is a diagram called the "population pyramid," which shows the number of males and females by age. Figure 1 gives the population pyramid for Canada. Note the bulge in the 35–54 age group, which corresponds to the "baby boom" (those born in the late 1940s to the mid-1960s), and the subsequent "baby bust" with far fewer people in the 0–34 age group. This is because the total fertility rate peaked at close to four children per woman in the late 1950s but by 1995 was down to about 1.6 children per woman.

Because labour participation rates differ by age, this gives us a way to predict available labour supply in the future. The smaller proportion of young people shown by the population pyramid has led to a decline in labour force growth, from growth rates of close to 35% over the 1970s to about 10% over the 1990s. In a paper in the journal *Policy Options,* Professors Frank Denton and Byron Spencer of McMaster University consider the impact of such demographic trends on future economic growth.

Of course, labour force participation rates change over time. In

FIGURE 1 Canada's Population Pyramid, 2001

The pyramid shows the number of males and females in Canada for each age group. The baby boom is apparent in the 35–54 age groups.

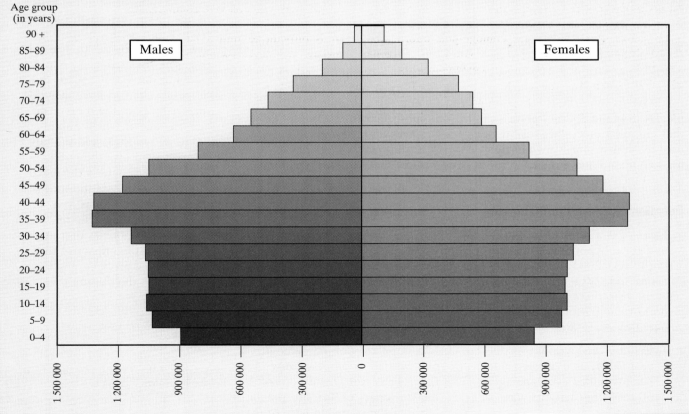

Source: F. T. Denton, C. H. Feaver, and B. G. Spencer, unpublished population forecast, McMaster University, 2000.

1951 about one-fifth of women aged 35 to 44 were in the labour force, but by 2000 it was about four-fifths. Male labour force participation has fallen, in part because younger men (like younger women) are on average pursuing more postsecondary education and in part because men aged 55 to 64 are leaving the labour force in increasing numbers in either voluntary or involuntary early retirement. Denton and Spencer conclude that because female participation rates are unlikely to increase much more, while the trend in male rates may continue, changes in participation rates will not be a source of much future labour force growth. When they incorporate assumptions such as constant fertility and immigration rates and modest falls in death rates, Denton and Spencer conclude that labour force growth will fall to about zero by 2016. If immigration fell to zero instead of being maintained at their assumed level of about 200 000 per year, both the population and labour force would decline at that point.

Even though total GDP depends strongly on these long-term labour force trends, GDP per capita is less sensitive. However, there are some issues for which total GDP is important. For example, Denton and Spencer point out that immigration could possibly be used as an instrument for raising total GDP and hence reducing the debt-to-GDP ratio.

Questions for Analytical Thinking

1. Figure 2 is a population pyramid for a hypothetical country in the year 2001 in which 100 males and 100 females are born every year, there is no immigration or emigration, and everyone dies at age 80.

   a. Redraw this pyramid for the year 2001, as if an epidemic has just killed everyone aged 50 to 60 but left everyone

FIGURE 2 Hypothetical Population Pyramid for Question 1

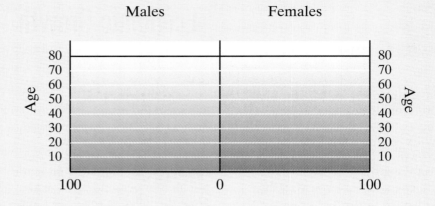

else untouched. Assuming the other assumptions do not change, redraw this pyramid again for the year 2011.

   b. Redraw this pyramid for the year 2011 if there is no epidemic but in the year 2001 a medical discovery is made so that only one-half of all males and one-quarter of all females die at age 80, and the remainder survive until 100.

   c. Returning to the original case with no epidemic or medical discovery, redraw the pyramid for 2001 if all males and females between 20 and 45 have just migrated elsewhere (and this continues, so that in subsequent years everyone leaves on their twentieth birthday). If we further assume that only people in that age group have children, so that fertility drops to zero in this country at that point, redraw the population pyramid for the year 2011.

2. Explain why Figure 1 is consistent with (i) a slightly higher number of boys being born than girls and (ii) a longer average life span for women.

3. In a popular book on demography entitled *Boom, Bust and Echo*, Professor David Foot of the University of Toronto points out that the changing pattern in demography has meant greater difficulty in job advancement for those born 1960 to 1966

(sometimes called "late boomers" or "Generation X"), falling crime rates, and an increased interest in gardening and birdwatching. Explain.

4. The video resource for this Case discusses the serious demographic problem facing Japan. The longest life span in the world combined with the low average birth rate of 1.4 babies per woman will mean that the number of individuals of age 65 and over will rise from 1 in 6 as this century began to 1 in 4 by 2020. The cost of caring for the elderly is projected to double. Proposed public policy changes have included increasing both the retirement age (the age at which public pensions are paid) and the rate of taxes paid into the public pension fund; but, as the video also makes clear, at the turn of the century Japan was in a serious macroeconomic slump. Explain how policies that might help reduce the impact of the demographic problem might also worsen the slump.

Sources: David K. Foot with Daniel Stoffman, *Boom, Bust and Echo* (Toronto: Macfarlane, Walter & Ross, 1996); Frank T. Denton and Byron G. Spencer, "Population, Labour Force, and Long-Term Economic Growth," *Policy Options*, January-February 1998: 3–9.

Video Resource: "Japan: Tarnished Miracle," *The National Magazine*, January 19, 1998.

International Trade, Comparative Advantage, and Protectionism

Learning Objectives

1 Define *trade surplus* and *trade deficit*.

2 Distinguish between absolute advantage and comparative advantage.

3 Explain how both countries in a trading relationship can gain from trade with appropriate terms of trade. Explain how with fixed money prices, exchange rates affect the terms of trade.

4 Outline the Heckscher-Ohlin Theorem.

5 Describe how economies of scale in production can lead to international trade.

6 Define *tariff, export subsidy,* and *quota.* Show how a tariff reduces the gains from trade and how the loss can be measured.

7 List the pros and cons of trade protection.

The International Economy: Trade Surpluses and Deficits

The Economic Basis for Trade: Comparative Advantage

Absolute Advantage Versus Comparative Advantage

Terms of Trade

Exchange Rates

The Sources of Comparative Advantage

The Heckscher-Ohlin Theorem

Other Explanations for Observed Trade Flows

Trade Barriers: Tariffs, Export Subsidies, and Quotas

Free Trade or Protection?

The Case for Free Trade

The Case for Protection

An Economic Consensus

I nternational trade is extremely important to the Canadian economy. Canada's imports of goods and services from the rest of the world have a value of about 40% of Canadian GDP and exports are about 43%. Canada's volume of trade (1999 exports and imports of $412 billion and $384 billion, respectively) ranks it among the ten largest trading countries in the world. Although the United States may be the world's largest trader, U.S. imports represent only about 13% of that country's GDP. This is one of the principal differences between the Canadian and U.S. economies.

Canada trades with virtually every country in the world. Our greatest volume of trade is with the United States, which has been the source of about three-quarters of Canada's goods imports since the end of World War II. Declining in importance over the years has been the United Kingdom, which furnished over 13% of Canada's goods and services imports in 1946 and only 3% in 1999. Canada's export markets have also changed substantially in the postwar period: in 1946, the United States purchased 40% of our goods exports and the United Kingdom 26%; in 1999, these figures stood at 86% and 1.5%, respectively. Japan is now Canada's second-largest trading partner, currently purchasing about 3% of Canadian goods exports and providing about 3% of our goods imports.

What types of goods and services is Canada trading? Table 20.1 lists some of the most important exports and imports in 1999 and shows the percentage of the total accounted for by each. It is probably not surprising that Canada exports lumber and imports coffee. What is perhaps less well known is the high volume of trade Canada has in motor vehicles and parts, both as exports and imports. This trade was promoted by the 1965 Canada–United States Automotive Products Trade Agreement (APTA), popularly known as the auto pact. The auto pact removed tariffs and other trade barriers on manufacturers' trade in motor vehicles and parts between the two countries to promote more efficient production on both sides of the border. But whether the trade be in auto parts with the United States, fruit with South America, grain with China, or financial services with the European Union, the inextricable connection of the economies of the world has had a profound impact on the discipline of economics and is the basis for one of its most important insights:

> All economies, regardless of their size, depend to some extent on other economies and are affected by events outside their borders.

To get you more fully acquainted with the international economy, this chapter discusses the economics of international trade. First, we examine Canada's trade surpluses and trade deficits. Next, we explore the basic logic of trade. Why should Canada or any other country engage in international trade? Finally, we address the controversial issue of protectionism. Should a country provide certain industries with protection in the form of import quotas, tariffs, or subsidies?

The International Economy: Trade Surpluses and Deficits

In recent years, Canada has exported more than it has imported. When a country exports more than it imports, it runs a **trade surplus.** When a country imports more than it exports, as Canada did in the early 1990s, it runs a **trade deficit.** Canada generally runs a trade surplus for goods and a trade deficit for services. Table 20.2 shows the Canadian balance of trade for goods and for goods and services combined for selected years since 1946.

Trade deficits can be a source of political controversy in countries that experience them. Especially in times of recession, when domestic jobs are being lost, the reaction against the importation of cheaper foreign-made goods can be quite severe. A natural response to try to protect domestic jobs is to call for governments to impose taxes and restrictions on imports (as Canada did on the importation of Japanese automobiles in the early 1980s) to make them more expensive and less

trade surplus *The situation when a country exports more than it imports.*

trade deficit *The situation when a country imports more than it exports.*

Table 20.1	Canada's Major Exports and Imports in 1999		
Major Goods Exports	*Percentage of Total Goods Exports*	*Major Goods Imports*	*Percentage of Total Goods Imports*
Automobiles	14.3	Motor vehicle parts	14.0
Motor vehicle parts	7.0	Automobiles	6.0
Trucks	5.4	Office machines and equipment	5.2
Lumber	3.6	Trucks	3.3
Natural gas	3.1	Crude petroleum	2.2
Wood pulp	1.9	Apparel and footwear	2.1
Newsprint	1.8	Fruits and vegetables	1.5
Wheat	0.9	Cocoa, coffee, and tea	0.9
Major Services Exports	*Percentage of Total Services Exports*	*Major Services Imports*	*Percentage of Total Services Imports*
Business services	50.7	Business services	48.8
Travel*	29.2	Travel*	29.2

*Note: Exports of travel services are the expenditures of nonresidents of Canada travelling in Canada; imports of travel services are the expenditures of Canadian residents travelling abroad.

Source: Adapted from Statistics Canada, CANSIM database, Series D59803–D59807, D59819–D59823, D397916–D397976, D399374–D399433.

available. As you might guess, this argument is not a new one. For hundreds of years, industries have petitioned governments for protection, and societies have debated the pros and cons of free and open trade. For the last century and a half, the principal argument used against protection has been the theory of comparative advantage, first discussed in Chapter 2.

The Economic Basis for Trade: Comparative Advantage

Perhaps the best-known debate on the issue of free trade took place in the British Parliament during the early years of the nineteenth century. At that time, the landed gentry—the landowners—controlled Parliament. For a number of years, imports and exports of grain had been subject to a set of tariffs, subsidies, and restrictions collectively called the **Corn Laws.** Designed to discourage imports of grain and encourage exports, the Corn Laws' purpose was to keep the price of food high. The landlords' incomes, of course, depended on the prices they got for what their land produced. The Corn Laws thus clearly worked to the advantage of those in power.

With the Industrial Revolution, a class of wealthy industrial capitalists began to emerge. The industrial sector had to pay workers at least enough to live on, and a living wage depended to a great extent on the price of food. Tariffs on grain imports and export subsidies that kept grain and food prices high increased the wages that capitalists had to pay, and these high wage payments cut into their profits. The political battle raged for years. But as time went by, the power of the landowners in the House of Lords was significantly reduced. When the conflict ended in 1846, the Corn Laws were repealed.

On the side of repeal was David Ricardo, a businessman, economist, member of Parliament, and one of the fathers of modern economics. Ricardo's principal work, *Principles of Political Economy and Taxation*, was published in 1817, two years before he entered Parliament. Ricardo's **theory of comparative advantage,** which he used to argue against the Corn Laws, claimed that trade enables countries to specialize in producing the products that they produce best. According to the theory:

> Specialization and free trade will benefit all trading partners (real wages will rise), even those that may be absolutely less efficient producers.

This basic argument remains at the heart of free trade debates even today.

■ **Specialization and Trade: The Two-Person Case**   The easiest way to understand the theory of comparative advantage is to examine a simple two-person society. Recall Ivan and Colleen, who were stranded on a deserted island in Chapter 2. Suppose that they have only two basic tasks to accomplish each week: gathering food to eat and cutting logs that will be used in constructing a house. If Colleen could cut more logs than Ivan in a day and Ivan could gather more berries and fruits, specialization would clearly benefit both of them.

But suppose that Ivan is slow and somewhat clumsy and that Colleen is better at both cutting logs *and* gathering food. Ricardo's point is that it still pays for them to specialize. They can produce more in total by specializing than they can by sharing the work equally. (It may be helpful to review the discussion of comparative advantage in Chapter 2 before proceeding.)

ABSOLUTE ADVANTAGE VERSUS COMPARATIVE ADVANTAGE

A country enjoys an **absolute advantage** over another country in the production of a product if it uses fewer resources to produce that product than the other country does. Suppose that country A and country B produce wheat, but that A's climate is more suited to wheat and its labour is more productive. Country A will therefore produce more wheat per hectare than country B and use less labour in growing it and bringing it to market. Country A thus enjoys an absolute advantage over country B in the production of wheat.

Table 20.2

Canada's Balance of Trade (Exports Minus Imports), 1946–1999 (Millions of Dollars)

	Goods	Goods and Services
1946	548	420
1956	−766	−1 327
1966	292	15
1976	1 524	−1 506
1986	9 977	4 333
1991	7 012	−4 408
1996	42 392	33 315
1997	23 793	14 437
1998	19 098	12 136
1999	33 788	27 718

Source: Adapted from Statistics Canada, CANSIM database, Series D59833 and D59834.

Corn Laws *The tariffs, subsidies, and restrictions enacted by the British Parliament in the early nineteenth century to discourage imports and encourage exports of grain.*

theory of comparative advantage *Ricardo's theory that specialization and free trade will benefit all trading partners (real wages will rise), even those that may be absolutely less efficient producers.*

absolute advantage *The advantage in the production of a product enjoyed by one country over another when it uses fewer resources to produce that product than the other country does.*

■ Gains from Mutual Absolute Advantage To illustrate Ricardo's logic in more detail, suppose that Australia and New Zealand each have a fixed amount of land and do not trade with the rest of the world. There are only two goods—wheat, used to produce bread, and cotton, used to produce clothing. This kind of two-country/two-good world does not exist, but its operations can be generalized to many countries and many goods.

To proceed, we have to make some assumptions about the preferences of the people living in New Zealand and those living in Australia. If the citizens of both countries go around naked, there is no need to produce cotton; all the land can be used to produce wheat. However, assume that people in both countries have similar preferences with respect to food and clothing: the populations of both countries use both cotton and wheat. We will also assume that preferences for food and clothing are such that both countries consume equal amounts of wheat and cotton.

Finally, we assume that each country has only 100 hectares of land for planting and that land yields are those given in Table 20.3. New Zealand can produce three times the wheat that Australia can on one hectare of land, and that Australia can produce three times the cotton that New Zealand can in the same space. New Zealand thus has an absolute advantage in the production of wheat, and Australia has an absolute advantage in the production of cotton. In cases like this, we say that the two countries have *mutual absolute advantage.*

If there is no trade and each country divides its land to obtain equal units of cotton and wheat production, each country produces 150 tonnes of wheat and 150 bales of cotton. New Zealand puts 75 hectares into cotton but only 25 hectares into wheat, while Australia does the reverse. (See Table 20.4.)

We can organize the same information in graphical form as production possibility frontiers for each country. In Figure 20.1, which presents the positions of the two countries before trade, each country is constrained by its own resources and productivity. If Australia put all its land into cotton, it would produce 600 bales of cotton (100 hectares × 6 bales/hectare) and no wheat; if it put all its land into wheat, it would produce 200 tonnes of wheat (100 hectares × 2 tonnes/hectare) and no cotton.

But let us consider some intermediate cases. Suppose Australia put 99 hectares into wheat and 1 hectare into cotton. It would produce 198 tonnes of wheat and 6 bales of cotton. Now suppose it switched another hectare from wheat to cotton so that it had 98 hectares of wheat and 2 hectares of cotton. You can see it would produce 196 tonnes of wheat and 12 bales of cotton. You can also see that Australia always faces a constant tradeoff in production: at any time, it can switch 1 hectare from wheat to cotton, and get 6 more bales of cotton but lose 2 tonnes of wheat. In terms of Figure 20.1, this is what makes the production possibility frontier a straight line. At any point on the frontier, 6 bales of cotton can be obtained for the sacrifice of 2 tonnes of wheat—this ratio never changes, so the slope never changes and the line is straight. (The constant slope of the curve is equal to the gain in cotton divided by the loss in wheat, which is 6 bales divided by −2 tonnes, which equals −3 bales/tonne.)

If you have any doubts about this, take a piece of paper and graph out Australia's production possibility curve to confirm the frontier is a straight line. The key reason the line is straight is that we are assuming that all land is the same and there is no land that is better for one crop or the other. Hence switching a hectare from one crop to the other always involves the same gains and losses.

Now turn to New Zealand. You should be able to see that New Zealand's maximum production of cotton is 200 bales, its maximum production of wheat is 600

Table 20.3	Yield per Hectare of Wheat and Cotton	
	New Zealand	*Australia*
Wheat	6 tonnes	2 tonnes
Cotton	2 bales	6 bales

Table 20.4	Total Production of Wheat and Cotton Assuming No Trade, Mutual Absolute Advantage, and 100 Available Hectares	
	New Zealand	**Australia**
Wheat	25 hectares × 6 tonnes/hectare 150 tonnes	75 hectares × 2 tonnes/hectare 150 tonnes
Cotton	75 hectares × 2 bales/hectare 150 bales	25 hectares × 6 bales/hectare 150 bales

tonnes and that again the production possibility frontier is a straight line, although this time with a slope of 1 bale divided by −3 tonnes, which equals −1/3 bales/tonne.

For both countries, the production possibility frontier represents all the combinations of goods that can be produced given the countries' resources and state of technology. Without trade, each country must pick a point along its own production possibility curve and both produce and consume at that point. We have assumed each country would consume 150 tonnes and 150 bales and have marked that point on the curves.

Because both countries have an absolute advantage in the production of one product, specialization and trade will benefit both. Australia should produce cotton and New Zealand should produce wheat. Transferring all land to wheat production in New Zealand yields a total of 600 tonnes; transferring all land to cotton production in Australia yields 600 bales. An agreement to trade 300 tonnes of wheat for 300 bales of cotton would double both wheat and cotton consumption in both countries. (Remember, before trade both countries produced 150 tonnes of wheat and 150 bales of cotton. After trade, each country will have 300 tonnes of wheat and 300 bales of cotton to consume. Final production and trade figures are in Figure 20.2 and Table 20.5.)

FIGURE 20.1

Production Possibility Frontiers for Australia and New Zealand Before Trade

Without trade, countries are constrained by their own resources and productivity.

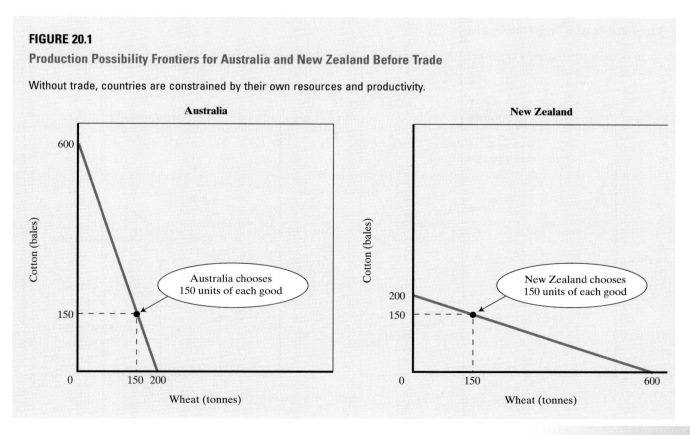

Table 20.5	Production and Consumption of Wheat and Cotton After Specialization					
	PRODUCTION				**CONSUMPTION**	
	New Zealand	**Australia**			**New Zealand**	**Australia**
Wheat	100 hectares × 6 tonnes/hectare 600 tonnes	0 hectares 0 tonnes		Wheat	300 tonnes	300 tonnes
Cotton	0 hectares 0 bales	100 hectares × 6 bales/hectare 600 bales		Cotton	300 bales	300 bales

> Trade enables both countries to move out beyond their previous resource and productivity constraints.

The advantages of specialization and trade seem obvious when one country is technologically superior at producing one product and another country is technologically superior at producing another product. But let us turn to the case in which one country has an absolute advantage in the production of *both* goods.

■ **Gains from Trade When One Country Has an Advantage in Both Goods**   Now suppose the yields changed to those given in Table 20.6. Now New Zealand has a considerable absolute advantage in the production of both cotton and wheat, with one hectare of land yielding six times as much wheat and twice as much cotton as one hectare in Australia. Ricardo would argue that *specialization and trade are still mutually beneficial.*

Again, preferences imply consumption of equal units of cotton and wheat in both countries. With no trade, New Zealand would divide its 100 available hectares

FIGURE 20.2

Expanded Possibilities After Trade

Trade enables both countries to move out beyond their own resource constraints—beyond their individual production possibility frontiers.

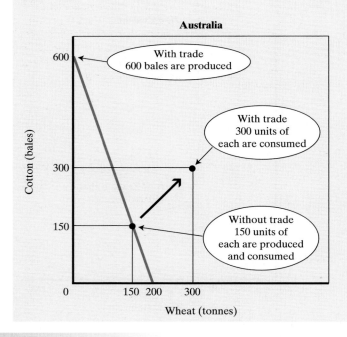

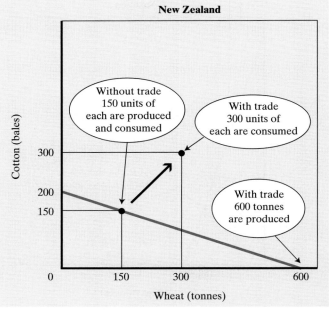

Table 20.6	Yield per Hectare of Wheat and Cotton		
		New Zealand	Australia
Wheat		6 tonnes	1 tonne
Cotton		6 bales	3 bales

evenly, or 50/50, between the two crops. The result would be 300 bales of cotton and 300 tonnes of wheat. Australia would divide its land into 75 hectares wheat and 25 hectares cotton. Table 20.7 shows that final production in Australia would be 75 bales of cotton and 75 tonnes of wheat. (Remember, we are assuming that, in each country, people consume equal amounts of cotton and wheat.) Again, before any trade takes place each country is constrained by its own domestic production possibility curve.

Now imagine that we are at a meeting of trade representatives of both countries. As a special adviser, David Ricardo is asked to demonstrate that trade can benefit both countries. He divides his demonstration into three stages, which you can follow in Table 20.8.

In stage 1, Australia transfers all its land into cotton production. When it does, it will have no wheat and 300 bales of cotton. New Zealand cannot completely specialize in wheat because it needs at least 300 bales of cotton and will not be able to get enough cotton from Australia. This is because we are assuming that each country wants to consume equal amounts of cotton and wheat. Thus, in stage 2, New Zealand transfers 25 hectares out of cotton and into wheat. Now New Zealand has 25 hectares in cotton that produce 150 bales and 75 hectares in wheat that produce 450 tonnes.

Finally, the two countries trade. We assume that New Zealand ships 100 tonnes of wheat to Australia in exchange for 200 bales of cotton. After the trade, New Zealand has 350 bales of cotton and 350 tonnes of wheat; Australia has 100 bales of cotton and 100 tonnes of wheat. Both countries are better off than they were before the trade (review Table 20.7), and both have moved beyond their own production possibility frontiers.

■ **Why Does Ricardo's Plan Work?** To understand why Ricardo's scheme works, first let us define comparative advantage. A country enjoys **comparative advantage** in the production of a good if that good can be produced at lower cost *in terms of other goods*. The real cost of producing cotton is the wheat that must be sacrificed to produce it. *When we think of cost this way, it is less costly to produce cotton in Australia than to produce it in New Zealand, even though a hectare of land produces more cotton in New Zealand.* Consider the "cost" of three bales of cotton in the two countries. In terms of opportunity cost, three bales of cotton in New Zealand cost three tonnes of wheat; in Australia, three bales of cotton cost only one tonne of wheat. Because three bales are produced by one hectare of Australian land, to get three bales an Australian must transfer one hectare of land from wheat to cotton production. And because a hectare of land produces a tonne of wheat, losing one hectare to cotton implies the loss of one tonne of wheat. Thus, *Australia has a comparative advantage in cotton production* because its opportunity cost, in terms of wheat, is lower than New Zealand's. This is illustrated in Figure 20.3.

comparative advantage *The advantage in the production of a product enjoyed by one country over another when that product can be produced at lower cost in terms of other goods than it could be in the other country.*

Table 20.7	Total Production of Wheat and Cotton Assuming No Trade and 100 Available Hectares	
	New Zealand	Australia
Wheat	50 hectares × 6 tonnes/hectare 300 tonnes	75 hectares × 1 tonne/hectare 75 tonnes
Cotton	50 hectares × 6 bales/hectare 300 bales	25 hectares × 3 bales/hectare 75 bales

	STAGE 1			STAGE 2	
	New Zealand	**Australia**		**New Zealand**	**Australia**
Wheat	50 hectares × 6 tonnes/hectare 300 tonnes	0 hectares 0 tonnes	Wheat	75 hectares × 6 tonnes/hectare 450 tonnes	0 hectares 0 tonnes
Cotton	50 hectares × 6 bales/hectare 300 bales	100 hectares × 3 bales/hectare 300 bales	Cotton	25 hectares × 6 bales/hectare 150 bales	100 hectares × 3 bales/hectare 300 bales

STAGE 3

	New Zealand		**Australia**
Wheat	350 tonnes	100 tonnes (trade) → (after trade)	100 tonnes
Cotton	350 bales	← 200 bales (trade) (after trade)	100 bales

Conversely, New Zealand has a comparative advantage in wheat production. A unit of wheat in New Zealand costs one unit of cotton; a unit of wheat in Australia costs three units of cotton.

> When countries specialize in producing those goods in which they have a comparative advantage, they maximize their combined output and allocate their resources more efficiently.

TERMS OF TRADE

Ricardo might suggest a number of options open to the trading partners. The one we just examined benefited both partners; in percentage terms, Australia made out slightly better. Other deals might have been more advantageous to New Zealand.

terms of trade *The ratio at which a country can trade domestic products for imported products.*

The ratio at which a country can trade domestic products for imported products is called the **terms of trade.** The terms of the trade determine how the gains from trade are distributed among the trading partners. In the case we just considered, the agreed-upon terms of trade were one tonne of wheat for two bales of cotton. Such terms of trade benefit New Zealand, which can now get two bales of cotton for each tonne of wheat. If it were to transfer its own land from wheat to cotton, it would get only one. The same terms of trade benefit Australia, which can now get one tonne of wheat for two bales of cotton. A direct transfer of its own land would force it to give up three bales of cotton for one tonne of wheat.

If the terms of trade changed to three bales of cotton for every tonne of wheat, only New Zealand would benefit. In fact, at those terms of trade *all* the gains from trade would flow to New Zealand. Such terms do not benefit Australia at all because the opportunity cost of producing wheat domestically is *exactly the same* as the trade cost: one tonne of wheat costs three bales of cotton. If the terms of trade went the other way—one bale of cotton for each tonne of wheat—only Australia would benefit. New Zealand gains nothing, because it can already substitute cotton for wheat at that ratio. To get a tonne of wheat domestically, however, Australia must give up three bales of cotton, and one-for-one terms of trade would make wheat much less costly for Australia.

Clearly, both parties must have something to gain for trade to take place. In this case, you can see that both Australia and New Zealand will gain when the terms of trade are set between 1:1 and 3:1, cotton to wheat.

EXCHANGE RATES

While the previous example makes most of our basic points, let us now take a few steps toward a more realistic model. First, we should remind ourselves that while

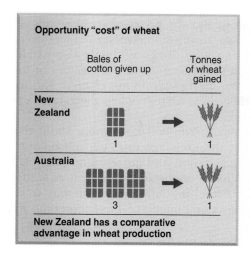

Opportunity "cost" of wheat

	Bales of cotton given up		Tonnes of wheat gained
New Zealand		→	
	1		1
Australia		→	
	3		1

New Zealand has a comparative advantage in wheat production

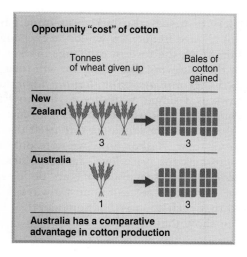

Opportunity "cost" of cotton

	Tonnes of wheat given up		Bales of cotton gained
New Zealand		→	
	3		3
Australia		→	
	1		3

Australia has a comparative advantage in cotton production

FIGURE 20.3

Comparative Advantage Means Lower Opportunity Cost

The real cost of cotton is the wheat that must be sacrificed to obtain it. The cost of three bales of cotton in New Zealand is three tonnes of wheat (one-half hectare of land must be transferred from wheat to cotton—refer to Table 20.6). But the cost of three bales of cotton in Australia is only one tonne of wheat (one hectare of land must be transferred). Thus, Australia has a comparative advantage over New Zealand in the production of cotton, and New Zealand has a comparative advantage over Australia in wheat production.

we discuss trade as if the country Australia trades with the country New Zealand, we do not mean that this is intergovernmental trade, but rather, that individual households and firms in one country trade with individual households and firms in the other. Private households decide whether to buy Toyotas or Chevrolets, and private firms decide whether to buy machine tools made in Canada or machine tools made in Taiwan, raw steel produced in Germany or raw steel produced in Hamilton.

> When trade is free (i.e., unimpeded by government-instituted barriers), patterns of trade and trade flows result from the independent decisions of thousands of importers and exporters and millions of private households and firms.

Second, we have assumed so far that production possibility frontiers are straight lines so that to produce three extra bales of cotton in Australia *always* means the sacrifice of one tonne of wheat. It would seem more likely that there is at least some land that is good for wheat and almost useless for cotton. Hence in a more realistic example, Australia probably would not specialize completely in cotton because that would involve growing cotton on land for which it is not well suited. More generally, it is unlikely a country will ever specialize completely in a single good. For the most part, we can just focus on the direction of trade and not concern ourselves with the degree of specialization.

Finally, in the Australia/New Zealand case, trade was by barter, cotton for wheat. In the real world, almost all goods are put on the market with money prices and these prices determine trade flows. Of course different money is used in different countries.

Before a resident of one country can buy a product made in, or sold by, someone in another country, a currency swap must take place. Consider Marc, who buys a Mazda from a dealer in Montreal. He pays in dollars, but the Japanese workers who made the car receive their salaries in yen. Somewhere between the buyer of the car and the producer, a currency exchange must be made. The regional distributor probably takes payment in dollars and converts them into yen before remitting the proceeds back to Japan.

To buy a foreign-produced good, then, I in effect have to buy foreign currency. The price of Marc's Mazda in dollars depends on both the price of the car stated in yen and the price of yen. You probably know the ins and outs of currency exchange very well if you have ever travelled in another country. In June 2000, a dollar exchanged for about 6 Mexican pesos. Now suppose that while in Mexico, you see a nice piece of jewellery for 180 pesos. How can you figure out whether to buy it? You calculate that 180 pesos is worth about $30. If the value of the peso fell so that a dollar was worth 10 pesos, that same piece of jewellery would cost only $18. The relative attractiveness of foreign goods to Canadian buyers, and of Canadian goods to foreign buyers, depends in part on **exchange rates**, the ratio at which two currencies are traded.

exchange rate *The ratio at which two currencies are traded. The price of one currency in terms of another.*

Of course the price of goods in domestic currency (e.g., the price of the jewellery in pesos) also influences trade patterns. But the prices of many goods do not change frequently, while the exchange rate for most currencies changes every minute on the foreign exchange market. So to keep things as simple as possible, in the following discussion we will focus on the impact of different values of the exchange rate *assuming that the domestic prices of goods do not change*. This allows us a simple way of studying how trade flows change when the rate of exchange between two countries' currencies changes.

How is the exchange rate itself determined? You will learn more about this in Chapter 21. For now, we note only that the exchange rates depend on such factors as the price level, interest rates, trade flows, and current and projected government fiscal and monetary policies. What is important to know here is that the exchange rate will almost always be at a level that allows for two-way trade so that each country has some level of exports and imports.[1] Here, however, we can show that:

> For any pair of countries, and given domestic prices, there is a range of exchange rates that can lead automatically to both countries realizing the gains from specialization and comparative advantage.

■ **Trade and Exchange Rates in a Two-Country/Two-Good World** First consider a new simple two-country/two-good example. Suppose that Canada and the United States produce only two goods—lumber and cloth. Table 20.9 gives the current prices of both goods as domestic buyers see them. In Canada both goods are C$5 per metre. In the United States, lumber is US$4 per metre, and the price of cloth is US$3 per metre.

Now suppose that Canadian and U.S. buyers have the option of buying at home or importing to meet their needs. The options they ultimately choose will depend on the exchange rate. For the time being, we will ignore transportation costs between countries and assume that Canadian and U.S. products are of equal quality.

Let us start with the assumption that the exchange rate is 1 Canadian dollar equals 50 U.S. cents, that is C$1 = US$0.50. Table 20.10 gives all the prices for lumber and cloth in Canadian dollars, using this exchange rate. As US$4 is worth C$8, the Canadian-dollar price of U.S. lumber is C$8 per metre and similarly U.S. cloth is C$6 per metre. Since both of these products cost only C$5 per metre in Canada, no Canadian will purchase the more expensive U.S. products. But note that Americans will also want to purchase from Canada. Since C$5 = US$2.50, the U.S.-dollar price of both Canadian products is US$2.50 per metre, a bargain compared to U.S. domestic prices of US$4 and US$3. American buyers will convert U.S. dollars to Canadian dollars and purchase both products from Canada. The United States will import both products and Canada will import nothing.

Now consider Table 20.11 in which the exchange rate is C$1 = US$1, or one-for-one. As US$4 now equals C$4 and US$3 now equals C$3, the Canadian-dollar prices of both goods are lower in the United States; so Canadian buyers will want to convert Canadian dollars into U.S. dollars and purchase from the United States. Americans will have no interest in Canadian products because at this exchange rate the U.S.-dollar prices of both Canadian products are US$5 and these exceed the U.S.-dollar prices of their own goods. At this exchange rate, Canada imports both goods.

It is easy to provide more examples at different exchange rates. So far we have shown that at C$1 = US$0.50 and C$1 = US$1, we get trade flowing in only one direction. In Table 20.12 we consider a case with an exchange rate in between: C$1

[1]*If Canada only exported, we would in effect be giving up goods in return for foreign currency. But we would expect that at least eventually this accumulated foreign currency would be used to import goods. Similarly, if Canada only imported, we would be acquiring goods by paying with Canadian currency. Eventually foreigners would want to use that currency to buy Canadian goods and Canada would export. Hence, at least in the long run, we cannot export without importing and we cannot import without exporting, and we can expect the exchange rate to adjust so that is so.*

Table 20.9

Domestic Prices of Lumber (per Metre) and Cloth (per Metre) in Canada and the United States

	Canada	United States
Lumber	C$5	US$4
Cloth	C$5	US$3

= US$0.80 (or equivalently US$1 = C$1.25). First notice that Canada will import cloth from the United States because the Canadian-dollar price of U.S. cloth is C$3.75 per metre, lower than the Canadian-dollar price of Canadian cloth. U.S. buyers will also find that American cloth is cheaper and not buy in Canada. At this same exchange rate, however, lumber is the same price in both countries and hence there likely will be no trade in lumber.

But suppose the exchange rate falls just slightly, so that the Canadian dollar is worth US$0.79. While U.S. cloth is still cheaper for both Canadians and Americans, U.S. lumber is now more expensive for Canadians. At this exchange rate, the U.S.-dollar price of $4 per metre converts to C$5.06 (4/0.79 is approximately 5.06). Since the domestic price in Canada is C$5 per metre, Canadians will buy Canadian lumber. But that price will also look good to U.S. buyers. In their currency, C$5 is now US$3.95 (5 × 0.79 = 3.95) and US$3.95 per metre is less than the U.S. price. Therefore, as the exchange rate falls from C$1 = US$0.80, trade begins to flow in both directions. The United States will import lumber and Canada will import cloth.

If you examine Table 20.13 carefully, you will see that in fact trade flows in both directions as long as the exchange rate for the Canadian dollar settles between US$0.60 and US$0.80. Stated the other way around, trade will flow in both directions as long as the price of a U.S. dollar is between C$1.25 and C$1.67.

■ **Exchange Rates and Comparative Advantage** Let us continue our example. If the Canadian dollar is between US$0.60 and US$0.80, the countries will automatically adjust and comparative advantage will be realized. At these exchange rates, Canadian buyers begin buying all their cloth in the United States. The Canadian cloth industry finds itself in trouble. Mills close and Canadian workers begin to lobby for tariff protection against American cloth. At the same time, the Canadian lumber industry does well, fuelled by strong export demand from the United States. Thus the lumber-producing sector expands. Resources, including capital and labour, are attracted into lumber production.

The opposite occurs in the United States. The U.S. lumber industry suffers losses as export demand dries up and Americans turn to cheaper Canadian imports. U.S. lumber companies turn to their government and ask for protection from cheap Canadian lumber. But cloth producers in the United States are happy. Not only are they supplying 100% of the domestically demanded cloth, but they are selling to Canadian buyers as well. Thus the cloth industry expands and the lumber industry contracts. Resources flow into cloth production.

With this expansion-and-contraction scenario in mind, let us look again at our original definition of comparative advantage. If we assume that prices reflect resource use and that resources can be transferred from sector to sector, we can calculate the opportunity cost of cloth and lumber in both countries. In Canada, the production of a metre of cloth consumes the same level of resources that the production of a metre of lumber consumes. Assuming that resources can be transferred, the opportunity cost of a metre of cloth is one metre of lumber. (Refer again to Table 20.9.) In the U.S., however, a metre of cloth uses resources costing US$3, while a metre of lumber costs US$4. Thus to produce a metre of cloth means the sacrifice of only three-quarters of a metre of lumber. Because the opportunity cost of a metre of cloth (in terms of lumber) is lower in the United States, we say that the U.S. has a comparative advantage in cloth production.

Conversely, consider the opportunity cost of lumber in the two countries. Increasing lumber production in the United States requires the sacrifice of four-thirds, or one and a third, metres of cloth for every metre of lumber—producing a metre of lumber uses US$4 worth of resources, while producing a metre of cloth requires only US$3 worth of resources. But each metre of lumber production in Canada requires the sacrifice of only one metre of cloth. Because the opportunity cost of lumber is lower in Canada, Canada has a comparative advantage in the production of lumber.

Table 20.10

Canadian-Dollar Prices of Lumber (per Metre) and Cloth (per Metre) in Canada and the United States If C$1 = US$0.50 (or US$1 = C$2)

	Canada	United States
Lumber	C$5	US$4 = C$8
Cloth	C$5	US$3 = C$6

Table 20.11

Canadian-Dollar Prices of Lumber (per Metre) and Cloth (per Metre) in Canada and the United States If C$1 = US$1

	Canada	United States
Lumber	C$5	US$4 = C$4
Cloth	C$5	US$3 = C$3

Table 20.12

Canadian-Dollar Prices of Lumber (per Metre) and Cloth (per Metre) in Canada and the United States If C$1 = US$0.80 (or US$1 = C$1.25)

	Canada	United States
Lumber	C$5	US$4 = C$5
Cloth	C$5	US$3 = C$3.75

Table 20.13	Trade Flows Determined by Exchange Rates	
Exchange Rate	**Price of US$**	**Result**
C$1 = US$1	C$1.00	Canada imports lumber and cloth
C$1 = US$0.80	C$1.25	Canada imports cloth
C$1 = US$0.79	C$1.27	Canada imports cloth; U.S. imports lumber
C$1 = US$0.61	C$1.64	Canada imports cloth; U.S. imports lumber
C$1 = US$0.60	C$1.67	U.S. imports lumber
C$1 = US$0.50	C$2.00	U.S. imports lumber and cloth

If exchange rates end up in the right ranges, the free market will drive each country to shift resources into those sectors in which it enjoys a comparative advantage. Only those products in which a country has a comparative advantage will be competitive in world markets.

The Sources of Comparative Advantage

Specialization and trade can benefit all trading partners, even those that may be inefficient producers in an absolute sense. If markets are competitive, and if foreign exchange markets are linked to goods-and-services exchange, countries will specialize in producing those products in which they have a comparative advantage.

So far, we have said nothing about the sources of comparative advantage. What determines whether a country has a comparative advantage in heavy manufacturing or in agriculture? What explains the actual trade flows observed around the world? Various theories and empirical work on international trade have provided some answers. Most economists look to **factor endowments**—the quantity and quality of labour, land, and natural resources—as the principal sources of comparative advantage. Factor endowments seem to explain a significant portion of actual world trade patterns.

factor endowments *The quantity and quality of labour, land, and natural resources of a country.*

THE HECKSCHER-OHLIN THEOREM

Eli Heckscher and Bertil Ohlin, two Swedish economists who wrote in the first half of the twentieth century, expanded and elaborated on Ricardo's theory of comparative advantage. The **Heckscher-Ohlin theorem** ties the theory of comparative advantage to factor endowments. It assumes that products can be produced using differing proportions of inputs and that inputs are mobile between sectors in each economy, but that factors are not mobile *between* economies. According to this theorem:

Heckscher-Ohlin theorem *A theory that explains the existence of a country's comparative advantage by its factor endowments: a country has a comparative advantage in the production of a product if that country is relatively well endowed with inputs used intensively in the production of that product.*

A country has a comparative advantage in the production of a product if that country is relatively well endowed with inputs used intensively in the production of that product.

This idea is simple. A country with a lot of good fertile land per person is likely to have a comparative advantage in agriculture. A country with a large amount of labour but little capital is likely to have a comparative advantage in labour-intensive goods.

OTHER EXPLANATIONS FOR OBSERVED TRADE FLOWS

Comparative advantage is not the only reason that countries trade, of course. It does not explain why many countries both import and export the same kinds of goods. Canada, for example, both exports and imports automobiles as we saw in Table 20.1.

And, just as industries within a country differentiate their products to capture a domestic market, so too do they differentiate their products to please the wide variety of tastes that exists worldwide. The Japanese automobile industry, for example, began producing small, fuel-efficient cars long before North American automobile makers did. In doing so, they developed expertise in creating products that attracted a devoted following and that elicited considerable brand loyalty. BMWs, made only in Germany, and Volvos, made only in Sweden, also have their champions in many countries. Just as product differentiation is a natural response to diverse preferences within an economy, it is also a natural response to diverse preferences across economies.

This idea is not inconsistent with the theory of comparative advantage. If the Japanese have developed skills and knowledge that gave them an edge in the production of fuel-efficient cars, that knowledge can be thought of as a very specific kind of capital not currently available to other producers. The Volvo company invested in a form of intangible capital that we call *goodwill*. That goodwill, which may come from establishing a reputation for safety and quality over the years, is one source of the comparative advantage that keeps Volvos selling on the international market. Some economists distinguish between gains from *acquired comparative advantages* and those from *natural comparative advantages*.

Acquired comparative advantage may in some cases require R&D expenditures that only make sense if the company is producing for the world market. This is one instance of an economy of scale. Relatively few countries make computer chips, for example. To illustrate another type of economy of scale: it may be cost-efficient to build a television plant big enough (and hence serve a market big enough) so that each size of television screen can have its own production line, thereby avoiding having to stop the line periodically to start making a different size. Hence economies of scale may be another source of the gains from specialization in trade.

Trade Barriers: Tariffs, Export Subsidies, and Quotas

Trade barriers—also called *obstacles to trade*—take many forms, the three most common of which are tariffs, export subsidies, and quotas. All of these are forms of **protection** by which some sector of the economy is shielded from foreign competition.

A **tariff** is a tax on imports. Tariffs vary by product and country of origin. According to the World Trade Organization, most Canadian import tariffs average about 4.9% on manufactured goods, 17.2% on clothing, and 31.5% on food, beverages, and tobacco. For some agricultural products such as milk, tariffs are over 200% for imports in excess of a quota. However, partly because Canada has many special trade arrangements such as those with the United States and Mexico, tariffs only represent in total about 1.1% of the cost of imports, and this percentage is expected to fall further.

Export subsidies—government payments made to domestic firms to encourage exports—can also act as a barrier to trade. One of the provisions of the Corn Laws that stimulated Ricardo's musings in the nineteenth century was an export subsidy that was automatically paid to farmers by the British government when the price of grain fell below a specified level. This subsidy tended to encourage British exports and to reduce the price of world grain. Foreign farmers who were not subsidized were driven out of the international marketplace by the artificially low prices.

Farm subsidies remain very much a part of the international trade landscape today. Many countries, especially those in Europe, continue to appease their farmers by heavily subsidizing exports of agricultural products. In fact, the political power of the farm lobby in many countries has had an important effect on international trade negotiations aimed at reducing trade barriers.

Closely related to subsidies is **dumping**. Dumping takes place when a firm or an industry sells products on the world market at prices *below* the cost of production. The charge has been levied against several specific Japanese industries, including automobiles, consumer electronics, and silicon computer chips.

Some dumping reflects subsidization by other countries. At other times it may be an attempt by an individual company to dominate a world market. After the lower prices of the dumped goods have succeeded in driving out all the competition, the dumping company can exploit its position by raising the price of its product. Many countries, including Canada, have trade laws that contain antidumping measures. The

protection *The practice of shielding a sector of the economy from foreign competition.*

tariff *A tax on imports.*

export subsidies *Government payments made to domestic firms to encourage exports.*

dumping *Takes place when a firm or industry sells products on the world market at prices below the cost of production.*

Canadian Anti-Dumping and Countervailing Directorate, a federal agency, examines many complaints of dumping every year and has the power to impose a duty on the good in question to raise its market price in Canada. In 1998 it ruled that fresh garlic was being dumped on the Canadian market by China, and set punitive duties that more than doubled the export price. Other recent cases have involved home appliances from the United States and cigarette tubes from France.

A **quota** is a limit on the quantity of imports. Quotas can be mandatory or voluntary, and they may be legislated or negotiated with foreign governments. In the best-known voluntary quota, or "voluntary restraint," negotiated with the Japanese government in 1981, Japan agreed to reduce the number of automobiles it exported to Canada. Other quotas in Canada apply primarily in the agricultural sector.

■ **World Trade and the World Trade Organization** Just as the British Corn Laws influenced the economies of the world in the nineteenth century, so in turn did the U.S. **Smoot-Hawley tariff** in the twentieth century. This piece of tariff legislation, which pushed the average tariff rate in the United States to 60%, was passed in 1930 and set off an international trade war when the United States' trading partners retaliated with tariffs of their own. For example, in the same year, Canada passed the (short-lived) Dunning tariff, which gave preferential treatment to Britain. Many economists point to the decline in trade that followed Smoot-Hawley as one of the causes of the worldwide depression of the 1930s.[2]

In 1947, Canada and 22 other countries agreed to reduce barriers to trade and established an organization to promote trade liberalization. The **General Agreement on Tariffs and Trade (GATT)** was first considered an interim arrangement, but it continued until 1995. The "Final Act" of the GATT was the Uruguay Round of multilateral trade negotiations that began in Punta del Este, Uruguay in 1986 and concluded on December 15, 1993. Negotiations took several years longer than anticipated when the United States and the European Union could not come to an agreement on agricultural policy.

The Uruguay Round involved over 100 countries, among them a huge number of developing countries. Previously, the GATT had been considered by many developing nations to be a "rich man's club." The Uruguay Round, with its broad involvement by so many countries, reflected a significant change in the world trade arena. Negotiations moved beyond the traditional GATT mandate of reducing tariffs and included reductions of nontariff barriers such as quotas. In addition, while the GATT had previously governed trade only in goods, the Final Act also covered trade in services, an increasingly large component of world trade. Finally, the Uruguay Round developed rules for trade-related intellectual property, such as patents, trademarks, and copyrights.

With so many sweeping changes, it was felt that the framework of the GATT had served its purpose, and it was time for an organizational restructuring. As a result, the GATT was abolished and the **World Trade Organization (WTO)** was established on January 1, 1995, the same day the Uruguay Round changes went into effect. As with the GATT, the WTO is headquartered in Geneva, Switzerland. Membership stands at over 130 countries, and several other countries have been granted observer status with a view to becoming full members in the future.

■ **Economic Integration: The European Union (EU)** **Economic integration** occurs when two or more countries join to form a free trade zone. In 1958, six European countries formed a customs union. Over the years, membership in the union grew, as did the economic ties among the countries. In 1991, the European Community (EC, or Common Market) went a step further and began the process of forming the largest free trade zone in the world. The economic integration process began in December of that year, when its 12 existing members (the United Kingdom, Belgium, France, Germany, Italy, the Netherlands, Luxembourg, Denmark, Greece, Ireland, Spain, and Portugal) signed the Maastricht Treaty. The treaty called for the end to

quota *A limit on the quantity of imports.*

Smoot-Hawley tariff *The U.S. tariff law of the 1930s that set the highest tariffs in U.S. history (60%). It set off an international trade war and caused the decline in trade that is often considered a cause of the worldwide depression of the 1930s.*

General Agreement on Tariffs and Trade (GATT) *An international agreement signed by Canada and 22 other countries in 1947 to promote the liberalization of foreign trade. Replaced by the World Trade Organization (WTO).*

World Trade Organization (WTO) *The body responsible for governing world trade. Entered into force January 1, 1995, replacing the General Agreement on Tariffs and Trade (GATT).*

economic integration *Occurs when two or more countries join to form a free trade zone.*

[2]*See especially Charles Kindleberger,* The World in Depression 1929–1939 *(London: Allen Lane, 1973).*

border controls, a common currency (to be called the *euro*), an end to all tariffs, and the coordination of monetary and even political affairs. In 1995, Austria, Finland, and Sweden became members of this **European Union (EU),** as the EC is now called, bringing the number of member countries to 15.

On January 1, 1993, all tariffs and trade barriers were dropped between the member countries. Border checkpoints were closed in early 1995. Citizens can now travel between member countries without passports. Eleven of the countries have adopted a common currency, the euro. Many economists believe that the advantages of free trade within the bloc, a reunited Germany, and the ability to work well as a bloc will make the EU one of the most powerful players in the international marketplace in the coming decades.

■ **Economic Integration: NAFTA** In 1988, Canada (under Prime Minister Brian Mulroney) and the United States (under President Ronald Reagan) signed the **Canada-U.S. Free Trade Agreement.** As of January 1, 1998, all industrial tariffs between Canada and the United States had been eliminated.

In addition, in 1992, Canada, the United States, and Mexico signed the **North American Free Trade Agreement (NAFTA),** in which the three countries agreed to establish all of North America as a free trade zone. NAFTA came into effect on January 1, 1994. The North American free trade area includes 360 million people and a total output of over $7 trillion—a larger output than that of the European Union. The agreement will eliminate all tariffs over a 10-to-15-year period and remove restrictions on most investments. (For more information, see the Global Perspective box titled "Free Trade in Canada.")

Free Trade or Protection?

One of the great economic debates of all time revolves around free trade versus protection. We briefly summarize the arguments in favour of each.

THE CASE FOR FREE TRADE

Let us begin with three short but powerful arguments in favour of free trade. First, international trade can improve the level of competition within an economy. For example, if automobile imports to North America were prohibited, many would guess that the prices of automobiles sold by the North American "Big Three" producers would increase.

Second, suppose Canada decided to put a new tariff on the imports of some product, say U.S. wine. It is probable that the United States would retaliate by putting a new tariff on Canadian beer. Canada could retaliate for the retaliation with a new tariff on U.S. strawberries, but soon there would be a U.S. tariff on Canadian apples in response. In short, even if protection were desirable, it is difficult to protect one's own industries without other countries protecting their industries. As Canada is both a relatively small economy (at least relative to its major trading partner) and a net exporter, it is hard to see it winning very many trade wars.

Third, there is a particular problem concerning tariffs on intermediate goods that are used as inputs for further manufacturing. For example, in the United States there is a substantial tariff on fine European cloth used in making expensive men's suits. Canadian manufacturers, primarily located in the Montreal area, do not pay such a tariff if the cloth is used in suits for export. Because such suits enter the United States without tariff under NAFTA, there has been a sharp increase in Canadian suit exports to the United States to the detriment of American manufacturers. A country's tariffs and quotas on intermediate goods may tend to hurt the domestic industries that use those goods.

Now let us consider the more intricate argument for free trade, that of comparative advantage. Trade has potential benefits for all countries. A good is not imported unless its net price to buyers is below that of the domestically produced alternative. When Americans in our earlier example found Canadian lumber less expensive than their own, they bought it, yet they continued to pay the same price for homemade cloth. Canadians bought less-expensive American cloth, but they

European Union (EU) *The European trading bloc composed of Austria, Belgium, Denmark, Finland, France, Germany, Greece, Ireland, Italy, Luxembourg, the Netherlands, Portugal, Spain, Sweden, and the United Kingdom.*

Canada-U.S. Free Trade Agreement *An agreement, which came into effect January 1, 1989, in which Canada and the United States agreed to eliminate all barriers to trade between the two countries over a ten-year period.*

North American Free Trade Agreement (NAFTA) *An agreement, which came into effect on January 1, 1994, signed by Canada, the United States, and Mexico, in which the three countries agreed to establish all of North America as a free trade zone.*

FAST FACTS

Canada is involved in two initiatives to develop still-bigger free trade areas. APEC (Asia-Pacific Economic Cooperation) is an organization of over 20 Pacific Rim countries that has announced the long-term goal of free trade. The Free Trade Area of the Americas is an initiative to bring free trade to North and South America.

The idea of free trade in Canada, especially with the United States, is not new. The Reciprocity Treaty of 1854–1866 allowed free trade in natural products between British North America and the United States and permitted each party to fish in the other's waters. More recently, the 1965 auto pact, mentioned earlier in this chapter, established free trade (for manufacturers satisfying certain conditions) in one sector of the economy.

The Canada-U.S. Free Trade Agreement, which came into effect January 1, 1989, was seen by many in Canada as a way of safeguarding access to U.S. markets. As Britain joined the other European countries in forming the European Union, and the United States (which was a large enough trader to stand on its own if it so chose) appeared to be growing more protectionist, Canada was finding itself increasingly alone.

Supporters of the trade agreement with the United States argued that a reduction in Canadian tariffs on American goods would allow Canadians to purchase lower-cost American goods more cheaply than domestically produced goods. Inefficient Canadian industries would be eliminated, allowing investment and resources to be concentrated in industries in which Canada could compete internationally, aided by the economies of scale achieved by building plants large enough to serve the combined Canadian and American market rather than the Canadian market alone. But there was nonetheless quite vocal opposition to the idea. Many Canadians argued that Canadian culture and political sovereignty would be imperilled by closer association with their powerful neighbour. Some felt that the deal as written did not provide sufficient guarantees for access to the American market. Most opposition, however, centred on the fear that those who lost jobs in the

President Carlos Salinas de Gortari of Mexico, President George Bush of the United States, and Prime Minister Brian Mulroney of Canada stand behind their respective chief trade negotiators, Jaime Serra Puche, Carla Hills, and Michael Wilson, at the signing of the NAFTA agreement in 1992.

eliminated industries would not easily, if ever, find jobs in the Canadian industries that were supposed to expand. (Some proponents of the agreement tried to assuage these fears by also supporting special adjustment assistance for those who lost jobs because of the deal. However, when the agreement was signed, no new assistance programs were implemented.) Despite the opposition, the Conservative government of Brian Mulroney, which supported the Canada-U.S. agreement, won reelection in 1988.

Subsequent proposals to include Mexico in the agreement were met with some reservation, both in Canada and in the United States. The economic recession in Canada that began in the early 1990s was blamed by many on the Canada-U.S. agreement, and there were those in both countries who argued that domestic jobs would be

lost to the much less expensive Mexican labour force. (You should think about these arguments in the light of what you have learned in this chapter.) As well, Canada seemed to have little economic reason for seeking a trade union with Mexico, as Canada-Mexico trade was very small. However, the two major U.S. presidential candidates in the campaign of 1992 supported the idea and the North American Free Trade Agreement (NAFTA) came into effect on January 1, 1994.

Canada's merchandise trade with Mexico doubled in the first five years of NAFTA. In addition, as part of a potential move toward free trade throughout the Americas, Canada and Chile implemented a free trade agreement in 1997, eliminating most industrial tariffs. Proposals were announced in 2000 for a possible free trade agreement with Costa Rica.

continued to buy domestic lumber at the same lower price. Under these conditions, *both Canadians and Americans ended up paying less and consuming more.*

At the same time, resources (including labour) move out of cloth production and into lumber production in Canada. In the United States, resources (including labour) move out of lumber production and into cloth production. Thus, the resources in both countries are more efficiently used. Tariffs, export subsidies, and quotas, which interfere with the free movement of goods and services around the world, reduce or eliminate the gains of comparative advantage.

We can use supply and demand curves to illustrate this point. We continue to use cloth, or more broadly textiles, in our example but make the more realistic assumption that instead of all Canadian cloth being produced at $5 per metre, different amounts of textiles will be produced, depending on the price. That is, we say there is a domestic supply curve for textiles. Suppose that Figure 20.4a shows such domestic supply along with domestic demand and we assume that in the absence of trade, the market clears at a price of $4.20 (now working entirely in Canadian dollars). At equilibrium, 450 million metres of textiles are produced and consumed.

We also change our previous two-country example to recognize that Canada imports not only from the United States but also, particularly for a product such as textiles, from other countries around the world, especially European and Asia-Pacific countries. The world market sets a world price. Because Canada is a small consumer and producer, Canadian demand and supply have essentially no effect on that price. Let us assume that the world price is $2 per metre. Assuming again no quality difference, no domestic producer will be able to charge more than $2. If there are no barriers to trade, the world price sets the price in Canada. As the price in Canada falls from $4.20 to $2, the quantity demanded by consumers increases

FIGURE 20.4

The Gains from Trade and Losses from the Imposition of a Tariff

A tariff of $1 per metre increases the market price facing consumers from $2 per metre to $3 per metre. The government collects revenues equal to the grey-shaded area. The loss of efficiency has two components. First, consumers must pay a higher price for goods that could be produced at lower cost. Second, marginal producers are drawn into textiles and away from other goods, resulting in inefficient domestic production.

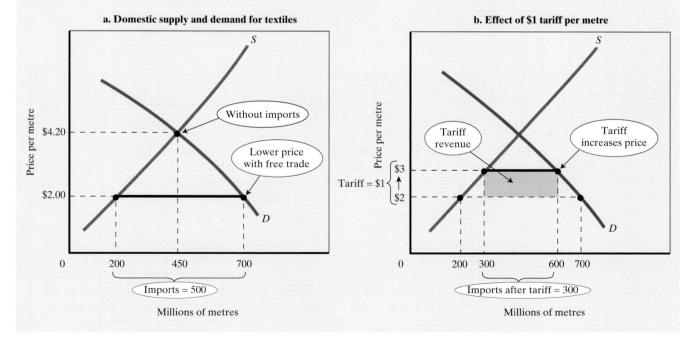

from 450 million metres to 700 million metres, but the quantity supplied by domestic producers drops from 450 million metres to 200 million metres. The difference, 500 million metres, is the quantity of textiles imported.

The argument for free trade holds that every country should specialize in producing the goods and services in which it enjoys a comparative advantage. Clearly, if foreign producers can produce textiles at a much lower price than domestic producers, they have a comparative advantage. As the world price of textiles falls to $2, domestic (Canadian) supply drops and resources are transferred to other sectors. These other sectors, which may be export industries or domestic industries, are not shown in Figure 20.4a. It is clear, however, that the allocation of resources is more efficient at a price of $2. Why should Canadians produce what foreign producers can produce at a lower cost? Canadian resources should move into the production of the things Canada produces best.

Now consider what happens to the domestic price of textiles when a trade barrier is imposed. Figure 20.4b shows the effect of a set tariff of $1 per metre imposed on imported textiles. The tariff raises the domestic price of textiles to $2 + $1 = $3. The result is that some of the gains from trade are lost. First, consumers are forced to pay a higher price for the same good; the quantity of textiles demanded drops from 700 million metres under free trade to 600 million metres because some consumers simply are not willing to pay the higher price.

At the same time, the higher price of textiles draws into textile production some marginal domestic producers who could not make a profit at $2. (Remember, domestic producers do not pay a tariff.) As the price rises to $3, the quantity supplied by producers rises from 200 million metres to 300 million metres. The overall result is a decrease in imports from 500 million metres to 300 million metres.

Finally, the imposition of the tariff means that the government collects revenue equal to the grey-shaded area in Figure 20.4b. This area is simply equal to the tariff rate per metre, ($1), times the number of metres that are imported after the tariff is in place (300 million metres). Thus, receipts from the tariff are $300 million.

What is the final result of the tariff? The answer should be clear. Domestic producers that were receiving revenues of only $2 per metre before the tariff was imposed now receive a higher price and earn higher profits. But these higher profits are achieved at a loss of efficiency. All of this leads us to conclude that:

> Trade barriers prevent a country from reaping the benefits of specialization, push it to adopt relatively inefficient production techniques, and force consumers to pay higher prices for protected products than they would otherwise pay.

THE CASE FOR PROTECTION

Arguments can also be made in favour of tariffs and quotas, of course. The most frequently heard of these are described below.

■ **Protection Saves Jobs**   The main argument for protection is that foreign competition costs Canadians their jobs. When Canadians buy Volvos, Canadian-made cars go unsold. This leads to layoffs in the domestic auto industry. When Canadians buy Japanese or German steel, steelworkers in Hamilton lose their jobs. When Canadians buy textiles from Korea or Taiwan, the millworkers in Quebec lose their jobs.

It is true that when we buy goods from foreign producers, domestic producers do suffer. But workers laid off in the contracting sectors may be ultimately reemployed in other expanding sectors. Foreign competition in textiles, for example, has clearly meant the loss of jobs in that industry. Many textile workers in Southern Ontario lost their jobs as the textile mills there closed down. But with the expansion of the high-tech computer industry in the Waterloo area as well as the opening of an automobile plant in the Cambridge region, many jobs have also been created in Southern Ontario.

Nevertheless, the adjustment process is far from costless. The knowledge that some other industry, perhaps in some other part of the country, may be expanding is of little comfort to the person whose skills become obsolete or whose pension benefits are lost when his or her company abruptly closes a plant or goes bankrupt. The social and personal problems brought about by industry-specific unemployment, obsolete skills, and bankruptcy as a result of foreign competition are significant.

This does reflect a real shortcoming in our model. We assumed full employment of resources. So, for example, we argued that the problem with putting a tariff on textiles was that it would draw firms and individuals into the textile industry to produce textiles at $3 per metre when others in the world could produce them for $2 per metre. The implication was that the workers in Canada would be better employed in some other industry, but what if the alternative is that they remain unemployed?

These problems can be addressed in two ways. (1) Canada could institute trade barriers. This would invite retaliation by other countries and cause the loss of the gains from free trade. Canadian consumers would then find themselves having to pay $3 per metre for textiles to save domestic jobs even though these textiles can be produced more efficiently at $2 per metre elsewhere. Or (2) Canada could take a long-term view and accept the transitional costs of unemployment in the textile industry and decide not to produce domestically something that can be produced more cheaply elsewhere. Perhaps the victims of free trade could be helped by retraining, or income or relocation assistance. Still, the costs of free trade are very likely to be borne disproportionately by the textile workers who lose their jobs. It is obvious that moves toward freer trade will have lower cost if the macroeconomy can otherwise be managed so that it is close to full employment.

Protected by the government, Japan's politically powerful farmers tie up very valuable land like these farms. Efficiency requires that land should be allocated to its most valuable use.

■ **Some Countries Engage in Unfair Trade Practices** Attempts by Canadian firms to monopolize an industry are illegal under the Competition Act. If a strong company decided to drive the competition out of the market by setting prices below cost, it would be aggressively prosecuted. But, the argument goes, if we won't allow a Canadian firm to engage in predatory pricing or monopolize an industry or market, can we stand by and let a German firm or a Japanese firm do so in the name of free trade? This is a legitimate argument and one that has gained significant favour in recent years. How should we respond when a large international company or a country behaves strategically against a domestic firm or industry? Free trade may be the best solution when everybody plays by the rules, but sometimes retaliation is necessary.

■ **Cheap Foreign Labour Makes Competition Unfair** Let us say that a particular country gained its "comparative advantage" in textiles by paying its workers low wages. How can Canadian domestic companies compete with foreign companies that pay wages that are less than a quarter of domestic wages?

First, we need to remember that while Canadian textile workers and companies may complain about competing with cheap foreign labour, other Canadians gain from being able to purchase cheaper foreign cloth. But, second, if Canadian firms cannot produce textiles as cheaply as foreign firms, this is a signal that labour and other resources are not being used efficiently. The reason that Canadian workers earn higher wages is that they are more productive: Canada has more capital per worker, and its workers are better trained. But the return to this higher productivity is only fully realized if workers are in industries in which they can produce

While there continues to be discussion of lowering barriers to interprovincial trade in Canada (barriers which, for example, have led the major brewers to locate breweries in almost every province rather than having more consolidated operations), the most recent evidence suggests that the effects of provincial borders are very low relative to the effects of national borders. Building on work by former Royal Bank of Canada economist and now MP John McCallum, John Helliwell of the University of British Columbia found that the even though Canada-U.S. trade barriers are not large, the Canada-U.S. border has nonetheless very large implications for trade.

To consider an example, Quebec is adjacent to both Ontario and the state of New York. In 1990 New York's GDP was two-and-one-half times greater than that of Ontario. If trade depended only upon provincial and state output levels and distances and national borders did not matter at all, you would expect Quebec to

have more than twice as much trade with New York as it did with Ontario. Yet Quebec had five times as much trade with Ontario as it did with New York. Similarly, the Californian economy is about 12 times larger than that of British Columbia and about the same distance from Ontario, yet Ontario has twice as much trade with British Columbia. And trade models without border effects predict that the Atlantic provinces would trade much more with the United States than with the rest of Canada, yet trade with the rest of Canada is considerably greater.

Professor Helliwell finds similar border effects in other industrial countries and even larger effects in developing countries. (Similarly, Daniel Trefler of the University of Toronto has found that models without border effects predict that there should be much *more* international trade than there actually is: apparently some international trade is replaced by domestic trade.)

Helliwell also finds other kinds of border effects: for example, investment capital is much more mobile across provinces than it is between Canada and other countries.

Are border effects simply due to trade barriers such as tariffs? Such tariffs have been largely eliminated by moves toward Canada-U.S. free trade, yet Professor Helliwell finds that the border effects, while lessened, still persist strongly. Even with free trade with the United States, interprovincial trade and other kinds of economic links between the Canadian provinces continue to be important. This suggests a continued important role for national economic policy, regardless of increased international trade and other types of "globalization."

Sources: John Helliwell, *How Much Do National Borders Matter?* (Washington, D.C.: Brookings Institution Press, 1998); Daniel Trefler, "The Case of the Missing Trade and Other Mysteries," *American Economic Review*, December 1995.

goods at a lower price than they can be produced in other countries. A low-wage country will never produce everything, but instead, wages and possibly exchange rates will adjust so that the low-wage country produces the goods in which it has a *comparative advantage* and Canada produces the goods in which it has a comparative advantage. We would expect the low-wage country to produce goods (e.g., cotton textiles) that require a lot of cheap, low-productivity labour and the natural resources available in those countries, and Canada to produce goods (e.g., computer software, nickel) that require high-productivity labour, more capital, and Canadian resources.

■ **Protection Safeguards National Independence and Security**   Beyond the argument of saving jobs, certain sectors of the economy may appeal for protection in the name of national independence and security. Many Canadians, remembering the rationing and food shortages during World War II, argue for the protection of the agricultural sector. In the event of war or other international disruptions, Canada would not want to depend on foreign countries for products as vital as food or energy. Some also argue that promoting east-west economic relations between Canadians, rather than north-south Canada-U.S. trade, helps protect Canada's sense of nationhood. (See the Global Perspective box titled "Trade and Borders.")

Closely related to the argument above is the claim that countries, particularly small or developing countries, may come to rely too heavily on one or more trading partners for many items. If Canada comes to rely on a major power for food or energy or some important raw material, it may be difficult for Canada to remain politically independent. Some critics of free trade argue that the developed countries have engaged in trade with the developing countries in a way that creates these kinds of dependencies.

■ Protection Safeguards Infant Industries Young industries in a given country may have a difficult time competing with established industries in other countries. And in a dynamic world, a protected **infant industry** might mature into a strong one worldwide because of an acquired, but real, comparative advantage. If such an industry is undercut and driven out of world markets at the beginning of its life, that comparative advantage might never develop.

Yet efforts to protect infant industries can backfire. Suppose that after protection has been imposed, it gradually becomes clear that such an industry will never be able to match world prices and withstand foreign competition. By that time, the industry might nonetheless have grown to employ a significant number of employees. Elimination of protection at that stage might cause great disruption. Indeed, it might be politically impossible to remove the protective measures. Even if the industry does achieve sufficient efficiency to stand on its own, its firms and workers may resist the elimination of protection, preferring instead to preserve high domestic prices and the resulting higher profits and/or wages. Real resources will be used up in lobbying for protection and real costs will be imposed upon the political system. Industry participants may never admit that the infant industry has grown up.

The infant-industry argument is one example of an argument for protection, sometimes called strategic trade policy, in which the government tries to pick successful industries and promote their development by protection or subsidy. Besides the attempt to acquire a comparative advantage by allowing time for the development of expertise and technology (sometimes called "learning by doing"), it is sometimes argued that in high fixed-cost industries in which ultimately there will be only a few highly profitable firms, a government subsidy may make the difference between success and failure, and a successful firm will be able to repay the subsidy.

The classic international example is probably the Japanese automobile industry, which received extensive tariff protection in its early years and has clearly been a success. More recently, the Japanese government provided developmental subsidies in a number of high-tech industries such as semiconductors, and it is less clear that the gains in terms of profits and employment will offset the costs. In Canada, federal government subsidies through Atomic Energy of Canada Limited have led to the development of the CANDU nuclear reactor, which is widely acknowledged as having some technological advantages over its competitors; but, nonetheless, the only international sales have been at extremely concessionary terms and the program has not come close to financial success. The basic problem is that picking winners is difficult.

> **infant industry** *A young industry that may need temporary protection from competition from the established industries of other countries in order to develop an acquired comparative advantage.*

An Economic Consensus

Critical to our study of international economics is the important debate between free traders and protectionists. On one side is the theory of comparative advantage, formalized by David Ricardo in the early part of the nineteenth century. According to this view, all countries benefit from specialization and trade. The gains from trade are real, and they can be large; free international trade raises real incomes and improves the standard of living.

On the other side of the debate are the protectionists, who point to the loss of jobs and argue for the protection of workers from foreign competition. But, although foreign competition can cause job loss in specific sectors, it is unlikely to cause net job loss in an economy, and workers may be absorbed over time into expanding sectors. This is particularly true in a net exporting country like Canada.

> Moves toward free trade will have victims, particularly in times of high unemployment. But while economists disagree about many things, the majority believe the long-term gains resulting from free trade offset the costs of transition.

1. All economies, regardless of their size, depend to some extent on other economies and are affected by events outside their borders.

The International Economy: Trade Surpluses and Deficits

2. Currently, Canada exports more than it imports—in other words, it runs a *trade surplus*. In the early 1990s, Canada imported more than it exported—a *trade deficit*.

The Economic Basis for Trade: Comparative Advantage

3. The *theory of comparative advantage*, dating to the writings of David Ricardo in the nineteenth century, holds that specialization and free trade will benefit all trading partners, even those that may be absolutely less efficient producers.

4. A country enjoys an *absolute advantage* over another country in the production of a product if it uses fewer resources to produce that product than the other country does. A country has a *comparative advantage* in the production of a product if that product can be produced at a lower cost in terms of other goods.

5. Trade enables countries to move out beyond their previous resource and productivity constraints. When countries specialize in producing those goods in which they have a comparative advantage, they maximize their combined output and allocate their resources more efficiently.

6. When trade is free, patterns of trade and trade flows result from the independent decisions of thousands of importers and exporters and millions of private households and firms.

7. The relative attractiveness of foreign goods to Canadian buyers and of Canadian goods to foreign buyers depends in part on *exchange rates*, the ratios at which two currencies are traded.

8. For any pair of countries, there is a range of exchange rates that will lead automatically to both countries realizing the gains from specialization and comparative advantage.

9. If exchange rates end up in the right range (i.e., in a range that facilitates the flow of goods between countries), the free market will drive each country to shift resources into those sectors in which it enjoys a comparative advantage. Only those products in which a country has a comparative advantage will be competitive in world markets.

The Sources of Comparative Advantage

10. The *Heckscher-Ohlin theorem* looks to relative *factor endowments* to explain comparative advantage and trade flows. According to the theorem, a country has a comparative advantage in the production of a product if that country is relatively well endowed with the inputs that are used intensively in the production of that product.

11. Some theories argue that comparative advantage can be acquired. Just as industries within a country differentiate their products to capture a domestic market, so too do they differentiate their products to please the wide variety of tastes that exists worldwide. This theory is not inconsistent with the theory of comparative advantage.

Trade Barriers: Tariffs, Export Subsidies, and Quotas

12. Trade barriers take many forms, the three most common of which are *tariffs, export subsidies*, and *quotas*. All of these are forms of *protection* by which some sector of the economy is shielded from foreign competition.

13. Although Canada historically has been a high-tariff country, the general movement is now away from tariffs and quotas. The World Trade Organization, of which Canada is a member, replaced the General Agreement on Tariffs and Trade (GATT) in 1995; its purpose is to reduce barriers to world trade and keep them down. Also important are the *Canada-U.S. Free Trade Agreement*, which came into effect January 1, 1989, and the *North American Free Trade Agreement*, signed by Canada, the United States, and Mexico, which came into effect on January 1, 1994.

14. The *European Union (EU)* is a free trade bloc composed of 15 countries: Austria, Belgium, Denmark, Finland, France, Germany, Greece, Ireland, Italy, Luxembourg, the Netherlands, Portugal, Spain, Sweden, and the United Kingdom. Many economists believe that the advantages of free trade within the bloc, a reunited Germany, and the ability to work well as a bloc will make the EU one of the most powerful players in the international marketplace in the coming decades.

Free Trade or Protection?

15. A country that follows a free trade policy will improve competition in its domestic markets, prevent

retaliatory trade restrictions by other countries, and help certain domestic industries by reducing the costs of their imported inputs. Moreover, trade barriers prevent a country from reaping the benefits of specialization, push it to adopt relatively inefficient production techniques, and force consumers to pay higher prices for protected products than they would otherwise pay.

16. The case for protection rests on a number of propositions, one of which is that foreign competition results in a loss of domestic jobs. But workers laid off in the contracting sectors may ultimately be reemployed in other expanding sectors. This adjustment process is far from costless, however.

17. Other arguments for protection hold that cheap foreign labour makes competition unfair; that some countries engage in unfair trade practices; that it safeguards national independence and security; and that it protects *infant industries*. Despite these arguments, however, most economists favour free trade.

Review Terms and Concepts

absolute advantage 403

Canada-U.S. Free Trade Agreement 415

comparative advantage 407

Corn Laws 403

dumping 413

economic integration 414

European Union (EU) 415

exchange rate 409

export subsidies 413

factor endowments 412

General Agreement on Tariffs and Trade (GATT) 414

Heckscher-Ohlin theorem 412

infant industry 421

North American Free Trade Agreement (NAFTA) 415

protection 413

quota 414

Smoot-Hawley tariff 414

tariff 413

terms of trade 408

theory of comparative advantage 403

trade deficit 402

trade surplus 402

World Trade Organization (WTO) 414

Problem Set

1. Canada imported $16.2 billion worth of "food, feeds, beverages and tobacco" in 1999 and exported $21.3 billion worth.

   a. Name some of the imported items that you are aware of in this category. Also name some of the exported items.

   b. Canada is said to have a comparative advantage in the production of agricultural goods. How would you go about testing this proposition? What data would you need?

   c. Are the numbers above consistent with the theory of comparative advantage? Suppose you had a more detailed breakdown of which items Canada imports and which it exports. What would you look for?

   d. What other theories of international trade might explain why the same goods are imported and exported?

2. The following table gives 1999 figures for tonne yield per hectare in Manitoba and Saskatchewan:

	Wheat	Canola
Manitoba	2.5	1.7
Saskatchewan	2.4	1.5

Source: Adapted from Statistics Canada, *Field Crop Reporting Series*, December 1999, Cat. no. 22-002.

   a. If we assume that farmers in Manitoba and Saskatchewan use the same amount of labour, capital, and fertilizer, which province has an absolute advantage in wheat production? Canola production?

   b. If we transfer land out of wheat into canola, how many tonnes of wheat do we give up in Manitoba per additional tonne of canola produced? In Saskatchewan?

   c. Which province has a comparative advantage in wheat production? In canola production?

The following table gives the distribution of land planted for each province in millions of hectares in 1999:

	Total Hectares Seeded	Wheat	Canola
Manitoba	5.0	1.3 (26%)	1.0 (20%)
Saskatchewan	19.0	5.9 (31%)	2.7 (14%)

Source: Adapted from Statistics Canada, *Field Crop Reporting Series*, December 1999, Cat. no. 22-002.

Are these data consistent with your answer to part **c**? Explain.

3. The North American Free Trade Agreement (NAFTA) took effect on January 1, 1994. The Final Act of the Uruguay Round of the General Agreement on Tariffs and Trade (GATT) took effect on January 1, 1995. Both were ratified over very strong political opposition from lobby groups. Using newspaper articles and periodicals at the time, write a short report about the opposition to each of these agreements. Who opposed them? Can you offer an explanation for their opposition? What logic did the Canadian government rely on in supporting these measures?

4. The provinces and territories of Canada may be viewed as separate economies, each specializing in the products it produces best and trading with each other.
   a. What product or products does your province or territory specialize in?
   b. Can you identify the source of the comparative advantage that lies behind the production of one or more of these products (a natural resource, plentiful cheap labour, a skilled labour force, etc.)?
   c. Do you think that the theory of comparative advantage and the Heckscher-Ohlin theorem help to explain why your region specializes in the way that it does?

5. Export subsidies have been proposed to prop up food prices and help struggling family farmers. Would you favour such subsidies?

6. New Zealand and Australia produce white and red wines. Current domestic prices for each are given in the following table:

	New Zealand	Australia
White wine	NZ$ 5	A$ 10
Red wine	NZ$ 10	A$ 15

Suppose that the exchange rate is NZ$1 = A$1.
   a. If the price ratios within each country reflect resource use, which country has a comparative advantage in the production of red wine? White wine?
   b. Will the current exchange rate lead to trade flows in both directions between the two countries?
   c. What range of exchange rates would lead to trade in both directions?

7. The goal of the European Union (EU) is to remove all trade barriers within its member countries and to become one "common market" with one uniform currency. Explain the likely benefits and costs to the EU's member countries. Should Canada be concerned about the EU? Why or why not?

8. Suppose one year of farm labour in Ontario can produce on average either 6 tonnes of beef or 30 kilolitres of milk, while one year of farm labour in Quebec can produce on average only 3 tonnes of beef or 24 kilolitres of milk.
   a. In terms of a kilolitre of milk, what is the opportunity cost of one tonne of beef in Ontario and Quebec?
   b. Assuming the price of milk is $1000 per kilolitre, find the range of prices for beef in which each province will specialize in one of these two products.

9. Repeat question 8 assuming that productivity improves in Quebec so that one year of farm labour in Quebec can produce on average 10 tonnes of beef or 60 kilolitres of milk.

10. A conservative columnist has written, "Canada is a future OPEC of water ... by 2010, Canada will be exporting large quantities of fresh water to the U.S. and more by tanker to parched nations all over the world." Can such trade be beneficial to Canada? Using the Internet for your research, describe a current proposal to sell bulk water (i.e., water by tanker or pipeline) outside Canada and explain the arguments for and against the project.

Open-Economy Macroeconomics: The Balance of Payments and Exchange Rates

Learning Objectives

1 Outline the components of the balance of payments. Distinguish between the current and capital accounts.

2 Explain why the sum of the trade balances for all nations is zero.

3 Derive the spending multiplier when imports depend on income.

4 Explain how net exports are affected by the Canadian price level, and explain the trade feedback effect.

5 Identify how the Canadian dollar exchange rate is determined.

6 Explain purchasing power parity and interest rate parity.

7 Describe the interactions between monetary and fiscal policy and the exchange rate.

8 Explain the "J-curve effect" of exchange rate changes on net exports.

The Balance of Payments

The Current Account

The Capital Account

The Global Balance of Payments

Equilibrium Output (Income) in an Open Economy

The International Sector and Planned Aggregate Expenditure

The Determinants of Exports and Imports

The Open Economy with Flexible Exchange Rates

The Market for Foreign Exchange

Factors That Affect Exchange Rates

Monetary and Fiscal Policy in the Open Economy

An Interdependent World Economy

The economies of the world have become increasingly interdependent over the past few decades. No economy operates in a vacuum, and economic events in one country can have repercussions on the economies of other countries.

International trade is a major part of today's world economy. Canada is one of the world's largest traders, and billions of dollars flow through the international capital market each day. In Chapter 20 we explored the main reasons for the existence of international exchange. Countries trade with each other to obtain goods and services they cannot produce themselves or because other nations can produce goods and services at a lower cost than they can. Foreign countries supply goods and services, labour, and capital to Canada, and Canada supplies goods and services, labour, and capital to the rest of the world.

From a macroeconomic point of view, the main difference between an international transaction and a domestic transaction concerns currency exchange:

When people in different countries buy from and sell to each other, an exchange of currencies must also take place.

Representatives of the 44 countries that met in Bretton Woods, New Hampshire in 1944 to allay the impending chaos in the international monetary system as World War II was ending.

Australian wine exporters, for example, cannot spend Canadian dollars in Australia—they need Australian dollars. Nor can a Canadian wheat exporter use Australian dollars to buy fertilizer from a Canadian company. Somehow, international exchange must be managed in a way that allows each partner in the transaction to wind up with his or her own currency.

As you know, trade between two countries depends on **exchange rates**—the price of one country's currency in terms of the other country's currency. If the British pound were very expensive, for example (thus making the dollar cheap), both Britons and Canadians would buy from Canadian producers. If the pound were very cheap (thus making the dollar expensive), both Britons and Canadians would buy from British producers. Within a certain range of exchange rates, trade flows in both directions, each country specializes in producing the goods in which it enjoys a comparative advantage, and trade is mutually beneficial.

Because exchange rates play such a major role in determining the flow of international trade, the way they are determined is very important. Since the turn of the century, the world monetary system has been changed on several occasions by international agreements and events. Until 1914, nearly all currencies were backed by gold. Their values were fixed in terms of a specific number of ounces of gold, which in turn determined their values in international trading (i.e., exchange rates).

The gold standard had three potential shortcomings. First, because a nation's money supply was fixed by its supply of gold, there was no possibility of active monetary policy. A nation that was experiencing an economic slump could not pursue expansionary monetary policy to try to speed adjustment to full employment. Second, there was a substantial resource cost: it seems expensive to mine gold with the sole purpose of keeping it in vaults. Third, the world money supply was governed by gold discoveries. For example, the Klondike gold rush in 1896 increased the world money supply but when no new gold was discovered, the money supply would tighten, perhaps causing slow growth and unemployment.

In any event, the gold standard did not survive the economic chaos of the world wars and the Great Depression. In 1944, as the end of World War II drew near, a large group of experts met in Bretton Woods, New Hampshire to set up a new system. The new system still had fixed exchange rates, but currencies were now fixed to the U.S. dollar, which was in turn fixed to gold at US$35 per ounce. Countries were to keep their currencies at the fixed exchange rates by buying and selling at the fixed rates (as discussed in Chapter 12), with the International Monetary Fund (IMF) created to lend to those countries who needed foreign exchange reserves to support their currency. But countries were allowed to change their exchange rates if they were clearly undervalued or overvalued. As someone once remarked, under the Bretton Woods system, exchange rates were "only fixed until further notice."

But suppose it was thought that the British pound was overvalued but no devaluation had yet occurred. Investors would sell British pounds. If the pound then was devalued, the pounds could be repurchased later at a lower price; if the pound was not devalued, the pounds could be repurchased at the same price with only the small loss of transactions costs. So one problem with the system was that since the fixed exchange rates could be changed, there was considerable speculative activity, perhaps forcing exchange rate changes that might have otherwise been unnecessary. The other key problem with the Bretton Woods system was that because the U.S. dollar was fixed to gold, there was no easy way to adjust its exchange rate: the United States would have to persuade all the other countries to change their values.

Canada first left the fixed exchange rate system from 1950 to 1962; it returned but left again in 1970. By 1971 most countries gave up trying to fix exchange rates formally and began allowing them to be determined essentially by supply and demand. For example, without government intervention in the marketplace, the price of British pounds in dollars is determined by the interaction of those who want to exchange dollars for pounds (those who "demand" pounds) and those who want to exchange pounds for dollars (those who "supply" pounds). If the quantity of pounds demanded exceeds the quantity of pounds supplied, the price of pounds will rise, just as the price of peanuts or paper clips would rise under similar circumstances. Much of Europe has moved toward a common currency, the euro, but the euro itself floats on world markets in the same manner.

If some of the above discussion sounds familiar, it should. Since Chapter 10, we have been introducing international factors in all of our modelling and discussion by considering the roles of both net exports and exchange rates. Part of the purpose of this chapter is to review and consolidate these topics. Then we will provide more detail and sketch for you some of the basics of more advanced models of what is called "open-economy macroeconomics." First, we discuss the *balance of payments*—the record of a nation's transactions with the rest of the world. Finally, we refine the international aspects of some of the analysis we have provided in our discussion of macroeconomics and macropolicy.

The Balance of Payments

We sometimes lump all foreign currencies—Swiss francs, Japanese yen, Brazilian cruzeiros, and so forth—together under the heading "foreign exchange." **Foreign exchange** is simply all currencies other than the domestic currency of a given country (in the case of Canada, the Canadian dollar). Canada's demand for foreign exchange arises because its residents want to buy things whose prices are quoted in other currencies, such as Australian jewellery, vacations in Europe, and bonds or stocks issued by Sony Corporation of Japan. Whenever Canadian residents make these purchases, Australians, Europeans, and Japanese gain Canadian dollars, which, from their point of view, are foreign exchange.

But where does the *supply* of foreign exchange come from? The answer is simple: Canada (actually, Canadian residents or firms) earns foreign exchange whenever it sells products, services, or assets to another country. Just as Switzerland earns foreign exchange when Canadian tourists go to visit Lake Geneva, Canada earns foreign exchange (in this case, Swiss francs) when Swiss tourists come to Canada to visit Niagara Falls. Similarly, American purchases of stock in Air Canada or Japanese purchases of real estate in Vancouver increase the Canadian supply of foreign exchange.

The record of a country's transactions in goods, services, and assets with the rest of the world is known as its **balance of payments.** The balance of payments is also the record of a country's sources (supply) and uses (demand) of foreign exchange.

Balance-of-payments accounting is quite straightforward if you remember the following simple rule:[1]

> Any transaction that brings in foreign exchange for a country is a credit (positive) item in that country's balance of payments; any transaction that causes a country to lose foreign exchange is a debit (negative) item.

foreign exchange *All currencies other than the domestic currency of a given country.*

balance of payments *The record of a country's transactions in goods, services, and assets with the rest of the world; also the record of a country's sources (supply) and uses (demand) of foreign exchange.*

---

[1]*Bear in mind the distinction between the balance of payments and a balance sheet. A balance sheet for a firm or a country measures that entity's stock of assets and liabilities at a moment in time. The* balance of payments, *by contrast, measures* flows, *usually over a period of a month, a quarter, or a year. Despite its name, the balance of payments is* not *a balance sheet.*

Table 21.1	Canadian Balance of Payments, 1999 (Billions of Dollars)

Current Account

Merchandise exports	360.6
Merchandise imports	−326.8
(1) Merchandise balance of trade	33.8
Exports of services	51.8
Imports of services	−57.8
(2) Net export of services	−6.0
Income received on investments	31.6
Income payments on investments	−63.8
(3) Net investment income	−32.2
(4) Net transfer payments	1.0
(5) Balance on current account (1 + 2 + 3 + 4)	−3.4

Capital Account

Change in official foreign exchange reserves (increase is −)	−8.8
Other financial assets (net flow) (increase is −)	−36.5
(6) Canadian financial assets (net flow) (increase is −)	−45.3
(7) Canadian financial liabilities to nonresidents (net flow)	33.9
(8) Capital transfers	5.1
(9) Balance on capital account (6 + 7 + 8)	−6.3
(10) Statistical discrepancy	9.7
(11) Balance of payments (5 + 9 + 10)	0

Note: All transactions that bring foreign exchange into Canada are credited (+) to the balance of payments; all transactions that cause Canada to lose foreign exchange are debited (−) to the balance of payments.

Source: Bank of Canada Banking and Financial Statistics, June 2000: Tables J1 and J2. The Bank of Canada now calls the capital account the "Capital and Financial Account."

Also keep in mind that the balance of payments is a record of all the ways a country earns foreign exchange and all the uses to which that foreign exchange is put.[2]

Let us now clarify one point. In the following discussion, it will be convenient to refer to Canada buying and selling goods, borrowing and lending funds, and so forth. This use of the word "Canada" does not mean just the government of Canada but also includes residents of Canada and firms in Canada. So when we say "Canada sells salmon to Japan" we do not mean to imply government involvement. Instead it implies that someone or some entity in Canada (most likely a resident or firm but conceivably a government of some level) has sold salmon to someone or some entity in Japan (again, conceivably a government of some level but more likely a resident or firm).

THE CURRENT ACCOUNT

The balance of payments is divided up into two major accounts, the *current account* and the *capital account*. These are shown in Table 21.1, which provides data on the Canadian balance of payments for 1999. We begin with the current account.

The first item in the current account is Canadian trade in merchandise. This category includes exports of newsprint, telecommunications equipment, and canola and imports of Scotch whisky, Japanese calculators, and German cars. Canada's merchandise exports *earn* foreign exchange for Canada and are thus a credit (+) item on the balance of payments. Canadian merchandise imports *use up* foreign exchange (it must surrender some of its holdings of foreign currencies to purchase foreign-produced goods and services) and are thus debit (−) items. The difference between a country's exports and its imports is its **balance of trade** and the difference between a country's merchandise exports and its merchandise imports is its

balance of trade *A country's exports minus its imports.*

[2]*As we shall see later, one of these uses is to add to existing stocks of foreign exchange. Thus, total uses of foreign exchange completely account for every unit of foreign exchange that is earned.*

merchandise balance of trade. If exports of goods are greater than imports, as was the case in 1999 in Canada, the merchandise balance of trade is positive.

The second item in the current account is services. Like most other countries, Canada buys services from and sells services to other countries. For example, a Canadian firm shipping wheat to England might purchase insurance from a British insurance company. A Dutch flower grower may fly her flowers to Canada aboard a Canadian airliner. In the first case, Canada is importing services and therefore using up foreign exchange; in the second, it is selling services to foreigners and earning foreign exchange. In 1999, Canada imported $6.0 billion more in services than it exported.

If a country's exports of goods and services are greater than its imports of goods and services, the country is said to run a **trade surplus**. If its exports of goods and services are less than its imports of goods and services, then the country has a **trade deficit**. You can calculate from Table 21.1 that Canada had a trade surplus of $27.8 billion in 1999 (a $33.8 billion surplus in goods and a $6.0 billion deficit in services).

The third item in the current account concerns *investment income*. Canadian residents hold foreign assets (stocks, bonds, and real assets like buildings and factories). Dividends, interest, rent, and profits paid to Canadian asset holders are a source of foreign exchange. Conversely, when residents of other countries earn dividends, interest, and profits on assets held in Canada, foreign exchange is used up. In 1999, investment income paid to nonresidents exceeded investment income received by Canada by $32.2 billion. This item reflects the return to foreign capital that was invested in developing Canadian resources and industry in the past.

The fourth item in Table 21.1 is *net transfer payments*. Transfer payments from Canada to nonresidents are another use of foreign exchange. Some of these transfer payments are from private Canadian residents and some are from the Canadian government. You may send a gift to your aunt in Spain or the government may send a veteran's pension cheque to a retiree living in Italy. Conversely, some nonresidents make transfer payments to Canada. "Net" refers to the difference between payments from Canada to nonresidents and payments from nonresidents to Canada. If we add the merchandise balance of trade, net export of services, net investment income, and net transfer payments we get the **balance on current account.**

The balance on current account shows how much a nation has spent on foreign goods, services, and transfers relative to how much it has earned from other countries. When the balance is negative, which it was for Canada in 1999, a nation has spent more on foreign products plus investment income and transfers paid than it has earned through the sales of its goods and services to the rest of the world plus investment income and transfers received. If a country has spent more abroad than it has earned, its net asset position vis-à-vis the rest of the world must decrease. By "net" we mean a nation's assets abroad minus its liabilities to the rest of the world. A country's liabilities to the rest of the world are assets of nonresidents. (A Japanese-owned building in Toronto, for example, can be thought of as a foreign liability of Canada and an asset of Japan.) Changes in a country's net asset position are recorded in the capital account.

THE CAPITAL ACCOUNT

The second major account in a country's balance of payments, the capital account, records the nation's capital inflows and outflows. Let us begin with item 6 in the capital account in Table 21.1. Governments and citizens around the world exchange title to physical assets (such as office buildings) and paper assets (such as stocks and bonds) across international boundaries. When a Canadian resident buys a U.S. bond or a Canadian firm purchases a factory in France, for example, foreign exchange is used up just as when a Canadian resident buys an American or French car. Domestic banks also make loans to foreign countries. When a Canadian bank makes loans abroad, the bank receives an IOU in exchange. Thus a loan made to Mexico (or any other country) is a *use* of foreign exchange also. If Canada increases its holdings of assets abroad, the figure recorded in the capital account is negative (a debit). In 1999, Canada increased its holdings abroad by $45.3 billion.

Foreign purchases of Canadian assets earn foreign exchange for Canada. Thus, when foreign countries increase their holdings of Canadian assets, the transactions are recorded in the capital account as positive figures (credits). As item 7 in Table 21.1 shows, foreign investment in Canada increased by $33.9 billion in 1999.

Finally, item 8, capital transfers, includes such transfers as the assets of new immigrants to Canada (less the assets of new emigrants from Canada) and inheritances received by Canadian residents from nonresidents less bequests from Canadian residents to nonresidents. The sum of items 6, 7, and 8 is the **balance on capital account**.

Every use of foreign exchange must have a source. That is, every bit of foreign exchange that a country uses to buy foreign goods, services, or assets must come from somewhere. Thus,

> The overall sum of all the entries in the balance of payments must be zero.

However, there are always measurement errors in compiling any set of aggregate accounts. Thus the statistical discrepancy term is used to correct for these errors so that the current account and the capital account will balance. If there were no errors in compiling the data, the statistical discrepancy would be zero.

Before we conclude our discussion of the current and capital accounts, let us reexamine part of item 6 in Table 21.1. The first of its two components, the change in official foreign exchange reserves, bears special mention. An increase in official foreign exchange reserves is a use of foreign exchange and is a negative item, while an outflow of reserves brings in foreign exchange to the market and is a positive item. From a balance of payments accounting perspective, it is as if the foreign exchange is given up when it is consigned to reserves and brought back when reserves are drawn down.

Changes in foreign exchange reserves reveal in part the extent to which the Bank of Canada deviates from a pure floating exchange rate. Under purely floating exchange rates, there would be no need for foreign exchange reserves or any purchases or sales by the Bank of Canada in foreign exchange markets. Under fixed exchange rates the Bank of Canada would have to buy any excess supply or sell any excess demand of Canadian dollars at the given exchange rate. As we have discussed in Chapter 12, the Canadian dollar exchange rate is floating but it is not a pure float as sometimes the Bank of Canada does intervene. An increase in foreign exchange reserves means that the government was a net seller of the Canadian dollar; a decrease in foreign exchange reserves means it was a net buyer.

THE GLOBAL BALANCE OF PAYMENTS

There is one final useful way of looking at the balance of payments. Let us begin by reconsidering Canada's 1999 merchandise balance of trade of $33.8 billion. What is the rest of the world's merchandise balance of trade with Canada? Clearly the answer is *negative* $33.8 billion. If Canada is selling $33.8 billion more worth of goods to the rest of the world than it is buying from the rest of the world, clearly the rest of the world is selling $33.8 billion less to Canada than it is buying from Canada.

If you think about this a bit more, you should come to two conclusions. First, if we take the balances of merchandise trade of all the countries in the world and add them up, the sum must be zero. At least until we start trading with Mars, one nation's export is another nation's import so the global balance of merchandise trade must be zero. Second, this same logic works for all the other balances. The net exports of services of all the nations of the world must sum to zero, the trade balances of the world must sum to zero, net investment income must sum to zero, net transfers must sum to zero, and all the capital accounts must sum to zero as well.

Perhaps the single most important consequence of this is that if one country runs a trade surplus, another runs a deficit. In our Keynesian models, it may appear attractive to increase aggregate demand by increasing net exports, for example, by instituting tariffs. But we should recall that for one country to increase net exports, others must reduce them and if those countries have insufficient aggregate demand, an increase in employment in one country may be matched by decreases elsewhere.

A policy that increases one nation's economic prospects at the expense of another's is sometimes called a *beggar-thy-neighbour* policy. One obvious drawback is that it invites tariff retaliation by the other countries. The result can be that no country increases its net exports but that there are great losses due to trade disruption.[3]

To sum up:

> Because one nation's export is another's import, all the trade balances of the world must add to zero.

Equilibrium Output (Income) in an Open Economy

It is now time to turn to an analysis of how all these trade and capital flows are determined, and what impacts they have on the economies of the countries involved.

THE INTERNATIONAL SECTOR AND PLANNED AGGREGATE EXPENDITURE

Recall that planned aggregate expenditure in an open economy is:

$$AE \equiv C + I + G + EX - IM$$

Remember also that if we look at the last two terms ($EX - IM$) together, we have the country's **net exports of goods and services.**

■ **Determining Import Levels**   Let us begin by considering the Keynesian cross model of Chapter 10. In that model we abstracted from the effects of the price level, of interest rates, and of exchange rates and, because we were focusing on the basic multiplier idea, we treated imports as given. But it seems natural that if Canadian income increases, Canadians will import more of everything, from U.S. oranges to Japanese stereo systems.

What if we make imports depend on income too? As we indicated in Chapter 10, imports are a "leakage" of aggregate expenditure. If this leakage increases with income, then clearly it will reduce the multiplier effect. If you studied Appendix 10C, you will have seen this shown with algebra and a numerical example. We shall show it again here using graphical methods. (This may also help you review the Keynesian cross model.)

A simple way to model imports as depending on income is to write:

$$IM = mY$$

where Y is income and m is some positive number.[4] Recall from Chapter 9 that the marginal propensity to consume (MPC) measures the change in consumption that results from a $1 change in income. Similarly, the **marginal propensity to import,** which we will abbreviate as MPM or m, is the change in imports caused by a $1 change in income. If $m = 0.2$, or 20%, and income is $1000, then imports, IM, are equal to $0.2 \times \$1000 = \$200$. If income rises by $100 to $1100, then the change in imports will be equal to $m \times$ (the change in income) $= 0.2 \times \$100 = \$20$.

■ **Solving for Equilibrium**   With all this in mind, we can now solve for equilibrium income. This procedure is illustrated in Figure 21.1. Starting from the blue line (the consumption function) in Figure 21.1a, we gradually build up the components of planned aggregate expenditure. Assuming for simplicity that planned investment, government purchases, and exports are all constant and do not depend on income, we move easily from the blue line to the brown line by adding the fixed amounts of I, G, and EX to consumption at every level of income. In this example, we take $I + G + EX$ to equal 80.

$C + I + G + EX$, however, includes spending on imports, which are not part of domestic production. To correct this, we must subtract the amount that is imported

net exports of goods and services ($EX - IM$) *The difference between a country's total exports and total imports.*

marginal propensity to import (MPM) *The change in imports caused by a $1 change in income.*

[3]*Retaliatory tariffs are often thought of as being a contributory factor in the Great Depression.*
[4]*We usually assume that $0 \leq m \leq MPC$. A $1 increase in income generates an increase in consumption measured by the* MPC *and some (conceivably all) of that increased consumption is imports.*

FIGURE 21.1

Determining Equilibrium Output in an Open Economy

In panel **a**, planned investment spending (*I*), government spending (*G*), and total exports (*EX*) are added to consumption (*C*). But *C* + *I* + *G* + *EX* includes spending on imports. In panel **b**, the amount that is imported at every level of income is subtracted to obtain planned aggregate expenditure. Equilibrium output occurs at $Y^* = 200$, the point at which planned domestic aggregate expenditure crosses the 45° line.

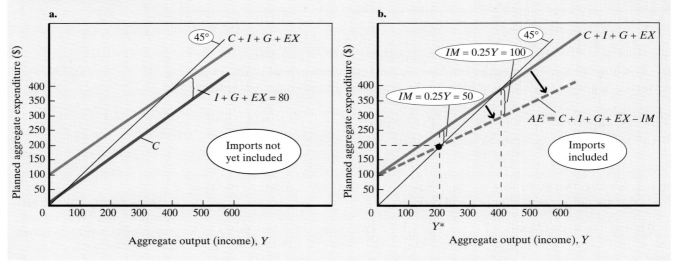

at each level of income. In Figure 21.1b, we assume that $m = 0.25$. That is, 25% of total income is spent on goods and services produced in foreign countries. Imports are a constant fraction of total income, and therefore at higher levels of income a larger amount is spent on foreign goods and services. For example, at $Y = 200$, $IM = 0.25Y$, or 50. Similarly, at $Y = 400$, $IM = 0.25Y$, or 100.

Remember that the *AE* function in Figure 21.1 must be planned aggregate expenditure on *domestically* produced goods and services. As income rises, some of the additional income is saved and the rest is spent. But not all of that added spending is on domestically produced goods and services. In fact, as income rises, some is saved and some is spent on imports. The dashed line in Figure 21.1b shows imports subtracted out of the *AE* function.

As before, equilibrium is reached when planned aggregate expenditure on domestic output is equal to aggregate domestic output (income). This is true at only one level of aggregate output, $Y^* = 200$, in Figure 21.1b. If *Y* were below Y^*, planned expenditure would exceed output, inventories would be lower than planned, and output would rise. At levels above Y^*, output would exceed planned expenditure, inventories would be larger than planned, and output would fall.

■ **The Open-Economy Multiplier** All of this has implications for the size of the multiplier, which we saw in Appendix 10C. We will now derive the open-economy government spending multiplier more formally.

Consider a sustained rise in government purchases (*G*). Initially, the increase in *G* will cause planned aggregate expenditure to be greater than aggregate output. Domestic firms will find their inventories to be lower than planned and thus will increase their output. But added output means more income. More workers are hired and profits are higher. Some of the added income is saved, and some is spent. The added consumption spending leads to a second round of inventories being lower than planned and raising output. Thus, equilibrium output rises by a multiple of the initial increase in government purchases. This is the multiplier.

In Chapters 9 and 10, we showed that the simple multiplier is equal to $1/(1 - MPC)$, or $(1/MPS)$. That is, a sustained increase in government purchases equal to ΔG will lead to an increase in aggregate output (income) of $\Delta G[1/(1 - MPC)]$. For example, if the *MPC* were 0.75 and government purchases rose by $10 billion, equilibrium income would rise by 4 × $10 billion, or $40 billion. The multiplier is [1/(1 − 0.75)] = [1/0.25] = 4.0.

In an open economy, however, some of the increase in income brought about by the increase in G is spent on imports rather than on domestically produced goods and services. The part of income that is spent on imports does not increase domestic income (Y) because imports are produced by foreigners. Thus, to compute the multiplier we need to know how much of the increased income is used to increase domestic consumption. (We are assuming here that all imports are consumption goods. In practice, some imports are investment goods and some are goods purchased by the government.) In other words, we need to know the marginal propensity to consume *domestic* goods. Domestic consumption is $C - IM$. So the marginal propensity to consume domestic goods is the marginal propensity to consume all goods (the MPC) minus the marginal propensity to import (the MPM). The marginal propensity to consume domestic goods is thus ($MPC - MPM$). Consequently,

$$\text{Open-economy multiplier} = \frac{1}{1 - (MPC - MPM)}$$

If the MPC is 0.75 and the MPM is 0.25, then the multiplier is 1/0.5, or 2.0. Note that this multiplier is smaller than the multiplier in which imports are not taken into account, which is 1/0.25, or 4.0.[5]

The major message of the open-economy multiplier model can be put quite succinctly:

> The effect of a sustained increase in government spending (or investment) on income—that is, the multiplier—is smaller in an open economy than in a closed economy. The reason is that when government spending (or investment) increases and income and consumption rise, some of the extra consumption spending that results is on foreign products and not on domestically produced goods and services.

THE DETERMINANTS OF EXPORTS AND IMPORTS

For simplicity, the model of this chapter has so far assumed that the level of imports depends only on income and the level of exports is fixed. In reality the amount of spending on imports depends on factors other than income and exports are not fixed. We have discussed this earlier in the text, in particular the effect of the exchange rate on net exports, but we will now consider the more complete picture.

■ **Export and Import Prices** We have made it clear earlier in the text that Canadian net exports depend on the relative price of Canadian goods compared to goods in the rest of the world. This relative price essentially depends on four things—the price level in Canada, the value of the Canadian dollar, the price level in other nations, and the nature of any import trade barriers such as tariffs. If Canadian prices rise, if the Canadian dollar appreciates, or if foreign goods become cheaper, Canadian goods will become more expensive relative to foreign goods. Canadian exports will tend to fall, Canadian imports will tend to rise and net exports will fall. Alternatively, if Canadian prices fall, if the Canadian dollar depreciates, or if foreign goods become more expensive, Canadian net exports will rise.

■ **Other Determinants of Imports** The same factors that affect households' consumption behaviour and firms' investment behaviour are likely to affect the demand for imports, because some imported goods are consumption goods and some are investment goods. For example, anything that increases consumption spending is likely to increase the demand for imports. As we discussed in more detail in Chapter 17, such factors as the after-tax real wage, after-tax nonlabour income,

---

[5]*The open-economy multiplier may also be expressed as* 1/(MPS + MPM), *where* MPS *is the marginal propensity to save.*

and interest rates affect consumption spending, and so these should also affect spending on imports. Trade restrictions such as quotas will also have an effect.

■ **Other Determinants of Exports** Let us now relax our assumption that exports are fixed. As we have noted, Canadian exports are other nations' imports. Germany imports goods, some of which are Canadian produced. So do France, Spain, and so on. Total expenditure on imports in Germany is a function of the factors we have just discussed, except that the variables are German variables rather than Canadian variables. This is true for all other countries as well. The demand for Canadian exports thus depends on economic activity in the rest of the world—rest-of-the-world real wages, wealth, nonlabour income, interest rates, and so on.

■ **The Trade Feedback Effect** We can now combine what we know about the demand for imports and the demand for exports to discuss the **trade feedback effect.** Suppose that Canada finds its exports increasing, perhaps because Americans suddenly decide they prefer Canadian beer to American beer. If Canadian exports to the United States rise by $100 million, will net Canadian exports (exports minus imports) increase by $100 million as well?

The answer is no. When Canadian exports increase, Canadian income rises, just as it would if consumption, investment, or government purchases were higher. This increase in Canadian income in turn increases Canadian demand for imports, so that some of the "extra" $100 million in export revenues goes to pay for additional purchases from abroad. For example, assume that a $1 increase in exports increases GDP by $1.40, and a $1 increase in income raises import spending by $0.15. In such a case, a $100 million increase in exports will raise imports by $21 million (or $100 million × 1.4 × 0.15). On balance, then, the $100 million in extra export revenues increases Canadian net exports by only $79 million, because $21 million of the $100 million is taken up by additional spending on imports.

But there is still more to the story. Because Canadian imports are somebody else's exports, the extra import demand from Canada raises the exports of the rest of the world. When other countries' exports to Canada go up, their output and incomes also rise, which in turn leads to an increase in the demand for imports from the rest of the world. Some of the extra imports demanded by the rest of the world come from Canada, so Canadian exports increase. The increase in Canadian exports stimulates Canadian economic activity even more, which leads to a further increase in the Canadian demand for imports, and so on. To summarize:

> An increase in Canadian economic activity leads to a worldwide increase in economic activity, which then "feeds back" to Canada. An increase in Canadian imports increases other countries' exports, which stimulates those countries' economies and increases their imports, which increases Canadian exports, which stimulates the Canadian economy and increases its imports, and so on. This is the trade feedback effect.

While Canada is a major trading country, the trade feedback effect is larger for bigger economies such as the United States or Japan. But the key point is that trade effects can lead to the spread of economic expansions (and contractions) across countries.

The Open Economy with Flexible Exchange Rates

We have now revisited the Keynesian cross model of Chapter 10, reminded ourselves that net exports are a component of planned aggregate expenditure, and shown how incorporating a marginal propensity to import in the model reduces the multiplier, but that the basic properties of the Keynesian cross model are retained. We have also revisited exchange rates as a factor influencing net exports. This should remind us of the work we have done in Chapter 12 and afterward, as we added a monetary sector to the basic model.

In Chapter 12 we drew the money market supply and demand diagram to show you the effects of changes in money demand and money supply on the interest rate.

trade feedback effect *The tendency for an increase in the economic activity of one country to lead to a worldwide increase in economic activity.*

We also referred to the foreign exchange market, which determines the price of the Canadian dollar in terms of another currency, say, the U.S. dollar. Given flexible exchange rates, we discussed that an increase in Canadian interest rates would increase the demand for Canadian dollars on the foreign exchange market and that would lead to an appreciation of the Canadian dollar. Let us now consider the issue slightly more formally, using a supply and demand diagram.

THE MARKET FOR FOREIGN EXCHANGE

In July 2000, the price of a Canadian dollar was about US$0.68, that is, 68 cents U.S. How was this determined? Most economists would use the framework of supply and demand. To explore this approach, we will assume there are just two countries, the United States and Canada. Most of the points we will make will still apply when considering many countries.

Exchange rates are posted daily at banks and other financial institutions. They are also available in newspapers, from electronic information services, and on the Internet. (One commercial provider, based in Ottawa, is at **www.accu-rate.ca/**.)

■ **The Supply and Demand for Canadian Dollars on the Foreign Exchange Market**
Governments, private citizens, and corporations exchange Canadian dollars for U.S. dollars every day. Those who *demand* Canadian dollars are holders of U.S. dollars who seek to exchange them for Canadian dollars. They may want these Canadian dollars in order to buy something produced in Canada (say, an aircraft component made near Winnipeg), to buy a service produced in Canada (such as a night in a hotel in Victoria), or to make a gift or transfer to a Canadian (the gift of C$20 to a Canadian from an American uncle). They may also wish to buy a Canadian stock, bond, or other asset, to invest in Canada (say, by building a factory), or they may be speculating that the Canadian dollar will rise relative to the U.S. dollar. The top panel of Table 21.2 reviews these reasons.

Table 21.2	Some Private Buyers and Sellers in International Exchange Markets: Canada and the United States

The Demand for Canadian Dollars (The Supply of U.S. Dollars)

1. Firms, households, or governments that import Canadian goods into the United States or wish to buy Canadian-made goods and services
2. Holders of U.S. dollars who wish to make a gift or transfer in Canadian dollars
3. Holders of U.S. dollars who want to buy Canadian stocks, bonds, or other financial instruments
4. U.S. companies that want to invest in Canada
5. Speculators who anticipate a rise in the value of the Canadian dollar

The Supply of Canadian Dollars (The Demand for U.S. Dollars)

1. Firms, households, or governments that import U.S. goods into Canada or wish to buy U.S.-made goods and services
2. Holders of Canadian dollars who wish to make a gift or transfer in U.S. dollars
3. Holders of Canadian dollars who want to buy stocks, bonds, or other financial instruments in the United States
4. Canadian companies that want to invest in the United States
5. Speculators who anticipate a rise in the value of the U.S. dollar

Note that anyone who buys Canadian dollars must buy them with something, in this case U.S. dollars. So the *demand* for Canadian dollars to this market is the *supply* of U.S. dollars.

Also, as shown in Figure 21.2, as the price of the Canadian dollar falls, Canadian goods, services, and assets are more attractive to holders of U.S. dollars who are more likely to want to trade those U.S. dollars for Canadian dollars (in order to buy Canadian goods, services, and assets). Hence the number of Canadian dollars demanded on the foreign exchange market increases.

Of course the same sort of factors that affect the demand for Canadian dollars affect the supply. Holders of Canadian dollars will want to trade them for U.S. dollars in order to buy U.S. goods, services, and assets. (See the bottom half of Table 21.2 for a more complete list.) And as shown in Figure 21.3, holders of Canadian dollars are more likely to want to trade them for U.S. dollars, the higher the value of the Canadian dollar (i.e., the cheaper the U.S. dollar). Hence the curve representing the supply of Canadian dollars in the foreign exchange market has a positive slope.

■ **The Equilibrium Exchange Rate**   When exchange rates are allowed to float, they are determined the same way that other prices are determined:

> The equilibrium exchange rate occurs at the point at which the quantity demanded of a foreign currency equals the quantity of that currency supplied.

This is illustrated in Figure 21.4. An excess demand for Canadian dollars will cause the Canadian dollar to appreciate. An excess supply of Canadian dollars will cause the Canadian dollar to depreciate.

We can connect the foreign exchange market to our earlier discussion of the balance of payments. Positive items correspond to the demand for Canadian dollars. For example, when a Japanese firm buys B.C. timber, that involves a purchase of Canadian dollars with Japanese yen. Similarly, negative items correspond to the supply of Canadian dollars. When we say the overall balance of payments must be zero, we are just saying the demand for Canadian dollars must equal the supply of Canadian dollars in the foreign exchange market.

FIGURE 21.2

The Demand for Canadian Dollars in the Foreign Exchange Market

When the price of Canadian dollars falls, Canadian goods, services, and assets become cheaper to U.S. buyers. U.S. buyers demand more Canadian dollars with which to buy Canadian goods, services, and assets.

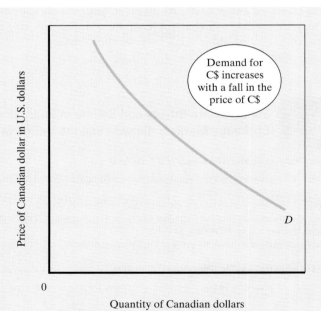

Demand for C$ increases with a fall in the price of C$

Price of Canadian dollar in U.S. dollars

D

0

Quantity of Canadian dollars

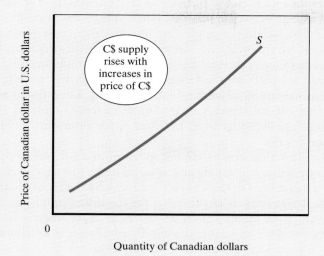

FIGURE 21.3

The Supply of Canadian Dollars in the Foreign Exchange Market

When the price of Canadian dollars rises, Canadians can obtain more U.S. dollars for each Canadian dollar. This means that U.S.-made goods and services appear less expensive to Canadian buyers. Thus, the quantity of Canadian dollars supplied is likely to rise with the exchange rate.

Because the overall balance of payments is always zero and hence not a very interesting indicator, some economists pay more attention to increases or decreases in the official foreign exchange reserves, sometimes also described as "the balance of payments" because it is the item left over after all the private transactions have been included. If foreign exchange reserves are falling, it would indicate that private supply of the Canadian dollar exceeded private demand and that the Bank of Canada was buying Canadian dollars, tending to support the exchange rate. Economists who use this terminology call this a *balance of payments deficit*; if private demand exceeded private supply, it would be called a *balance of payments surplus*. As we have noted, increases or decreases in foreign reserves indicate how much the Bank of Canada bought or sold in the foreign exchange market to peg the value of the Canadian dollar under fixed exchange rates or to influence the value of the dollar even if the exchange rate is floating.

If a central bank is having to support an exchange rate excessively under fixed exchange rates, economists call it a "balance of payments crisis." Hong Kong had such a crisis in late 1997. It was fixing its exchange rate against the U.S. dollar at

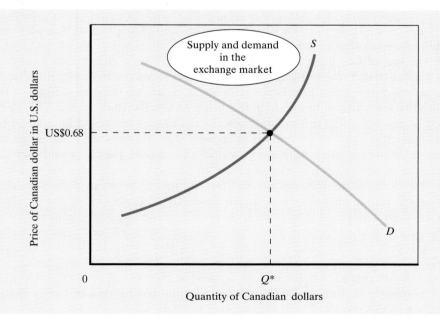

FIGURE 21.4

The Equilibrium Exchange Rate

When exchange rates are allowed to float, they are determined by the forces of supply and demand. All excess demand for Canadian dollars will cause the Canadian dollar to appreciate against the U.S. dollar. An excess supply of Canadian dollars will lead to a depreciating Canadian dollar.

a level that required support in the form of sizable purchases of Hong Kong dollars using official foreign exchange reserves. Given that it was virtually certain that the Hong Kong dollar would not appreciate but that there was some probability that it would depreciate (if authorities decided to reduce the drain on the reserves by devaluing to a lower peg against the U.S. dollar), speculators sold the Hong Kong dollar as well as shares on the Hong Kong stock market, leading to a stock market crash. The increase in private sales of the Hong Kong dollar necessitated the use of still more official reserves to buy up the excess supply of Hong Kong dollars and support the exchange rate, but there were sufficient reserves and the authorities did not devalue.

As a final point for this section, do not get confused between supply and demand in the money market and supply and demand in the foreign exchange market. In Chapter 12 and again later in this chapter, we focus on the money market, where the interest rate is determined. In that market the Canadian supply of money is all Canadian money currently in circulation. However, we have just discussed the foreign exchange market. In that market the supply of Canadian dollars is the number of Canadian dollars that holders *seek to exchange for U.S. dollars during a given time period*. As we have seen, supply and demand in that market determine the exchange rate.

FACTORS THAT AFFECT EXCHANGE RATES

In our analysis since Chapter 12, we have emphasized the role of interest rates on exchange rates, with increases in interest rates leading to exchange rate appreciation and decreases in interest rates leading to exchange rate depreciation. That will still be a very important part of our model but for the moment let us turn to price level effects.

■ **Purchasing Power Parity: The Law of One Price**   If the costs of transporting goods between two countries are small, we would expect the price of the same good in both countries to be roughly the same. The price of basketballs should be roughly the same in Canada and the United States, for example.

It is not hard to see why this is so. If the price of basketballs is cheaper in Canada, it will pay for someone to buy balls in Canada at a low price and sell them in the United States at a higher price. This decreases the supply and pushes up the price in Canada and increases the supply and pushes down the price in the United States. This process should continue as long as the price differential, and therefore the profit opportunity, persists. For a good with trivial transportation costs, therefore, we would expect this **law of one price** to hold. The price of a good should be the same regardless of where we buy it.

If the law of one price held for all goods, and if each country consumed the same market basket of goods, the exchange rate between the two currencies would be determined simply by the relative price levels in the two countries. Suppose that basketballs were the only good. If the price of a basketball were US$8 in the United States and C$10 in Canada, then the exchange rate would have to be one Canadian dollar equal to 80 cents U.S. because that equalizes the price in the two countries. If the exchange rate were instead one-to-one, people would buy basketballs in the United States and sell them in Canada at a profit. This would increase the demand for U.S. dollars and the supply of Canadian dollars until the price of the Canadian dollar was driven down to 80 cents U.S. If the rate were one Canadian dollar equals 50 cents U.S., people would buy basketballs in Canada and sell them in the U.S. at a profit, increasing the demand for Canadian dollars and the supply of U.S. dollars until the price of the Canadian dollar was driven up to 80 cents U.S.

The theory that exchange rates are set so that the price of similar goods in different countries is the same is known as the **purchasing power parity theory.** According to this theory, if it takes five times as many Mexican pesos to buy a kilogram of salt in Mexico as it takes Canadian dollars to buy a kilogram of salt in Canada, then the equilibrium exchange rate should be five pesos per dollar.

law of one price *If the costs of transportation are small, the price of the same good in different countries should be roughly the same.*

purchasing power parity theory *A theory of international exchange that holds that exchange rates are set so that the price of similar goods in different countries is the same.*

In practice, transportation costs for many goods are quite large, and the law of one price does not hold for these goods. (Haircuts are often cited as a good example. The transportation costs for a Canadian resident to get a French haircut are indeed large unless that person is an airline pilot.) Also, many products that are potential substitutes for each other are not precisely identical. For instance, a Jaguar and a Lexus are both cars, but there is no reason to expect the exchange rate between the British pound and the Japanese yen to be set so that the prices of the two are equalized. There are also trade barriers and differences in taxes. In addition, countries consume different market baskets of goods, so we would not expect the aggregate price levels to follow the law of one price.

Nevertheless, if the price level increases faster in the United States (i.e., there is higher inflation) than in Canada, we would expect that lower relative prices in Canada would lead to a higher demand for the Canadian dollar and a lower demand for the United States dollar. The U.S. dollar would depreciate and the Canadian dollar would appreciate. More generally,

> A high rate of inflation in one country relative to another puts pressure on the exchange rate between the two countries, and there is a general tendency for the currencies of relative high-inflation countries to depreciate. However, this adjustment is very imperfect so that relative prices between countries can change substantially over time.

Some further insight into purchasing power parity (and its imperfections) is provided by the Global Perspective box "McParity?"

Figure 21.5 shows the adjustments that might take place following an increase in the U.S. price level relative to the price level in Canada. This change in relative prices will affect residents of both countries. Higher prices in the United

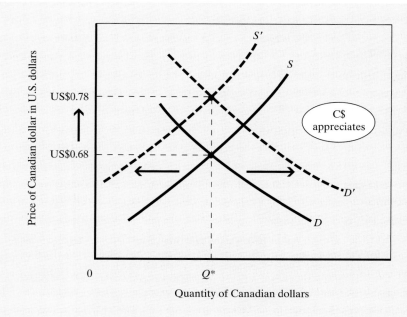

FIGURE 21.5

Exchange Rates Respond to Changes in Relative Prices

This figure shows the effects of an increase in the U.S. price level relative to the price level in Canada. The higher price level in the United States makes imports relatively less expensive. Thus, Americans are likely to increase their spending on imports from Canada, shifting the demand for Canadian dollars to the right, from *D* to *D*'. At the same time, Canadians see U.S. goods getting more expensive and reduce their demand for exports from the United States. Thus, the supply of Canadian dollars shifts to the left, from *S* to *S*'. The result is an increase in the price of Canadian dollars. The Canadian dollar appreciates and the U.S. dollar is worth less.

McParity?

Purchasing power parity theory argues that in the long run, exchange rates should adjust so that the price of the same basket of goods is the same everywhere, if measured in a common currency. Since 1986 *The Economist* magazine has been studying this proposition using a simple indicator, the price of a Big Mac. It was introduced for fun: as the magazine puts it, the exercise is not "intended as a precise predictor of exchange rates, but a tool to make economic theory more digestible."

Nonetheless, the Big Mac indicator has some advantages. Big Macs are available in about 120 countries and are pretty much the same everywhere. Moreover, there are economic studies that do suggest that on average and in the long term, the Big Mac index can be used to predict long-term currency movements.

In Table 1, we present the April 2000 prices of Big Macs in both local currency and in Canadian dollars, as adapted from *The Economist*. You can see the price in China was 9.90 yuan, which is only C$1.77, while in Switzerland it was 5.90 Swiss francs = C$5.13. If there is a tendency toward Big Mac purchasing power parity, there will be a tendency for the Canadian-dollar prices of the Big Macs in the two countries to converge, and hence a tendency for the Chinese currency to appreciate and for the Swiss franc to depreciate.

Deviations in worldwide Big Mac prices are large because Big Macs are not tradeable (they get cold) and there are barriers to trade for their components such as beef. There are also differences in taxes, with, for example, sales taxes in Canada and Europe much higher than those applied on a Japanese *Biggu Makku*.

Here is something you can check. According to the Big Mac Index in

Since 1986 *The Economist* has been tracking and comparing the prices of Big Macs wherever they are sold around the world. Although it is not a perfect indicator, some economic studies suggest that the Big Mac Index can predict long-term currency movement.

the table, the U.S. dollar was overvalued relative to the Canadian dollar in April 2000. Therefore the prediction was that the Canadian dollar would appreciate from the roughly 68 cents U.S. it was at that time. Has it?

Table 1	Price of a Big Mac in Various Countries, 2000		
Country	**Big Mac Price In Local Currency**	**Big Mac Price In Canadian Dollars**	***"Overvalued" or "Undervalued" Relative to C\$***
Canada	C$2.85	2.85	
Australia	A$2.59	2.27	Under
Britain	£1.90	4.42	Over
China	Yuan9.90	1.77	Under
France	FFr18.50	3.86	Over
Germany	DM4.99	3.49	Over
Italy	Lire4500	3.18	Over
Japan	¥294	4.10	Over
Mexico	Peso20.90	3.27	Over
New Zealand	NZ$3.40	2.49	Under
Russia	Ruble39.50	2.05	Under
Switzerland	SFr5.90	5.13	Over
United States	US$2.51	3.70	Over

*Big Mac prices are as of April 2000. A currency is "overvalued" using the Big Mac Index if the Big Mac price, converted to Canadian dollars, exceeds the Canadian price at that time of C$2.85. Purchasing power parity theory based on the Big Mac Index would predict that currencies listed as overvalued in column 4 would experience depreciations and currencies listed as undervalued would experience appreciations.

Sources: "Big MacCurrencies," *The Economist*, April 29, 2000, p. 75. The third and fourth columns of the table have been adapted from the original article using authors' calculations and data from *Bank of Canada Banking and Financial Statistics*, May 2000.

States make imports relatively less expensive. Thus, Americans are likely to increase their spending on imports from Canada, shifting the demand for Canadian dollars to the right, from D to D'. At the same time, Canadians see U.S. goods getting more expensive and reduce their demand for exports from the United States. Consequently, the supply of Canadian dollars shifts to the left, from S to S'. The result is an increase in the price of Canadian dollars. Before the change in relative prices, one Canadian dollar sold for US$0.68; after the change, one Canadian dollar costs US$0.78. The Canadian dollar appreciates and the U.S. dollar is worth less.

■ **Relative Interest Rates**   Now let us return to our emphasis on interest rates. You will have noted that when we listed the factors behind the demand and supply for Canadian dollars in Table 21.2, we included the demand to purchase financial assets. In the short run this is by far the most important factor. There are enormous pools of funds ("hot money") around the world, and its holders are always looking for the best possible interest rate. (It is estimated that $40 billion is traded every day in Canadian foreign exchange markets.) If interest rates increase in Canada, there will be an almost instant appreciation in the Canadian dollar due to the greater demand for Canadian interest-bearing securities.

Similarly, as shown in Figure 21.6, an increase in U.S. interest rates relative to Canadian rates will lead holders of Canadian securities to want to sell these securities for Canadian dollars, trade those Canadian dollars for U.S. dollars and buy U.S. securities. This will tend to shift the supply curve for Canadian dollars out, from S to S'. At the same time, there is less incentive for others to buy Canadian dollars in order to buy Canadian securities so this will tend to shift the demand curve for Canadian dollars down, from D to D'. The net result is a fall in the value of the Canadian dollar, from an initial value of US$0.87 to US$0.68. This roughly corresponds to the fall in the Canadian dollar during the 1990s as interest rates were lowered in Canada.

FIGURE 21.6

Exchange Rates Respond to Changes in Relative Interest Rates

If U.S. interest rates rise relative to Canadian interest rates, holders of Canadian dollars may be attracted into the U.S. securities market. To buy bonds in the United States, these buyers must exchange Canadian dollars for U.S. dollars. Thus, the supply of Canadian dollars shifts to the right, from S to S'. But others are also less likely to be interested in Canadian securities, because of the increased interest rates in the United States. Thus, the demand for Canadian dollars shifts to the left, from D to D'. The result is a depreciated Canadian dollar and an appreciated U.S. dollar.

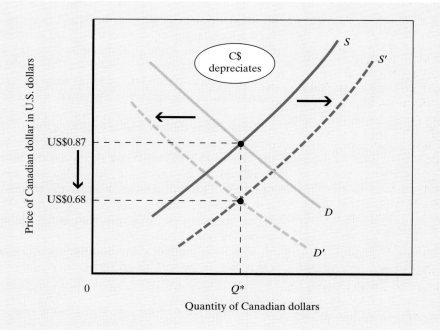

■ **Interest Rate Parity**   You may recall that under fixed exchange rates Canadian interest rates would be more or less fixed to a rate determined by world levels. For example, if Canadian interest rates fell from that world-determined rate (say, the U.S. interest rate), holders of Canadian securities would wish to sell their securities for Canadian dollars, then sell those Canadian dollars for U.S. dollars and buy the higher-interest U.S. securities. The Canadian dollar would depreciate. Under fixed exchange rates, the Bank of Canada would have to prevent that by using contractionary monetary policy to increase interest rates back to the world-determined level. Similarly, to prevent exchange rate appreciation, the Bank of Canada must be prepared to expand the money supply to keep interest rates down.

However, most of our policy discussion concentrated on the flexible exchange rate case, because Canada has not had fixed exchange rates since 1970. Under flexible exchange rates, interest rates in Canada can be freed from the world-determined level. Let us make sure we understand why that is so. Suppose per annum interest rates are 4% in Canada and 7% in the United States. If there is no difference in risk, then this means that the Canadian dollar must be expected to appreciate by 3%. A bondholder will be content with Canadian bonds paying the lower interest rate because of the extra bonus from the exchange rate appreciation. In general, assuming no risk premium:

> Canadian interest rate + Expected rate of appreciation of the Canadian dollar = U.S. interest rate

interest rate parity *The condition that, given equal risk, the interest rate paid on securities in country A will equal the interest rate paid on securities in country B plus the expected rate of appreciation of the currency of B relative to the currency of A.*

This condition is called **interest rate parity**.[6]

Monetary and Fiscal Policy in the Open Economy

Let us first consider the flexible exchange rate case. We have already considered monetary and fiscal policy with flexible exchange rates in the open economy in Chapters 12, 13, and 14. While completely exploring the implications of interest rate parity for this analysis is something to be left for more advanced courses, let us make one observation. If in equilibrium the exchange rate must be steady (neither appreciating or depreciating), then interest rate parity implies that interest rates will be the same in Canada as they are in the United States. So let us revisit the study of macropolicy under flexible exchange rates, still allowing for temporary differences in interest rates between the two countries, but now assuming that over time the interest rate differential will tend to be eliminated.

■ **Fiscal Policy Under Flexible Exchange Rates**   First let us review. Assume Canadian interest rates are initially at U.S. levels. (We will ignore any difference in risk for the rest of this chapter.) An expansionary fiscal policy will tend to increase some combination of aggregate output or the price level (an increase in aggregate demand). This will tend to increase the demand for money. If the money supply is not increased, interest rates will be higher. This will crowd out investment. The higher interest rates will also lead to an appreciation of the exchange rate and a crowding out of net exports.

We have made it clear that the crowding-out effect weakens the effects of fiscal policy. Now we can go further and argue that if the interest rate differential is

---

[6]*To make sure you understand the implications of interest rate parity, why will Ontario Hydro not necessarily borrow in Japan, just because interest rates are 3% there when they are 7% in Canada? The answer is that if there is such a differential in interest rates, the market must "expect" that the yen will appreciate relative to the Canadian dollar. Suppose Ontario Hydro borrows in yen and converts at 70 yen to the dollar. If by repayment time, the yen has appreciated so it is now at 60 yen to the dollar, it will take many more Canadian dollars to buy enough yen to pay off the loan than it would have had the initial exchange rate prevailed. The appreciation of the yen will add to the cost of the loan.*

eliminated over time, the effects of fiscal policy *under flexible exchange rates* may be *entirely* offset.

It may seem somewhat unusual but we will illustrate the effects of fiscal policy using the demand for money and supply of money graphs of Chapter 12. In Figure 21.7, the money market begins in equilibrium with Canadian interest rates equal to the "world-determined" U.S. rate of interest $r^{US} = 7\%$. The initial increase in aggregate demand from the expansionary fiscal policy shifts the money demand curve from M_0^d to M_1^d. There are higher interest rates that lead to an appreciation of the exchange rate. This leads to a reduction in net exports. Net exports are a component of planned aggregate expenditure so as net exports fall, aggregate demand falls and hence money demand falls. This process continues until aggregate demand (and hence money demand) is restored to its initial position with the differential in interest rates eliminated. In summary:

> An increase in aggregate demand from expansionary fiscal policy may in the end, under flexible exchange rates, have neither a permanent effect on aggregate demand nor change Canadian interest rates from their world-determined levels.

■ **Monetary Policy Under Flexible Exchange Rates**   Again this is partly review. In Figure 21.8, assume Canadian interest rates are initially equal to U.S. interest rates at 7%. The expansionary monetary policy (money supply curve from M_0^s to M_1^s) pushes interest rates down (in the diagram from 7% to 5%). But this leads to a depreciation of the Canadian dollar, increasing net exports and hence aggregate demand. This increases money demand (M_0^d to M_1^d) until the interest rate of 7% is restored. (Just as in the fiscal policy case, Canadian interest rates cannot be different from U.S. interest rates in equilibrium.) In sum:

> Expansionary monetary policy can increase aggregate demand under flexible exchange rates by depreciating the exchange rate.

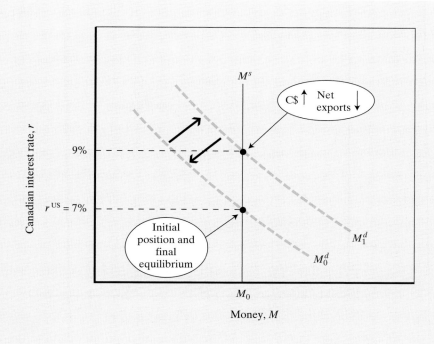

FIGURE 21.7

Fiscal Policy Has Only Temporary Aggregate Demand Effects Under Flexible Exchange Rates

The expansionary fiscal policy increases aggregate demand (aggregate output and/or the price level), which increases money demand. The higher interest rates of 9% lead to an appreciation of the Canadian dollar and net exports begin to fall until aggregate demand is restored to its initial level (and hence money demand is at its initial level). There is no permanent increase in aggregate demand and interest rates are restored to 7%.

■ Can Canadian Interest Rates Be Permanently Less Than U.S. Interest Rates? The model we have used rules out this possibility. (Incidentally, our model is based on what is called the Mundell-Fleming model. One of its inventors, Robert Mundell, who once taught at the University of Waterloo and now teaches at Columbia University, is a Canadian-born economist and winner of the 1999 Nobel Prize in economics.) But under different assumptions, Canadian interest rates could be lower. Canada could have a permanently lower rate of inflation than the United States. We noted when discussing purchasing power parity that this might lead to a depreciating U.S. dollar (an appreciating Canadian dollar). With a constantly appreciating Canadian dollar, the interest rate parity condition implies that interest rates in Canada can be permanently lower than in the United States. (Remember, the appreciation acts as a "bonus" that makes up for the lower rate of interest.)

However, as we also noted when discussing purchasing power parity, the effects of inflation differentials on exchange rate changes are problematic. For example, in the 1990s, Canada had a consistently lower inflation rate than the United States with no appreciation in the Canadian dollar. Some have argued that political uncertainty in Canada prevented this appreciation. In any case, the central insights of the Mundell-Fleming model are that under flexible exchange rates fiscal policy has relatively weak effects on aggregate demand while monetary policy has strong effects. These insights appear to be widely accepted.

■ Fixed Exchange Rates Even though the Canadian exchange rate has not been fixed since 1970, from time to time the Bank of Canada appears to act as if it is pegging it. A number of currencies (e.g., the Hong Kong dollar, the Argentina peso) are fixed against the U.S. dollar. The European Monetary Union in the year 2000 was a fixed-rate system with the goal of having a single currency, the euro, by 2002. In Chapter 12, we discussed how the central bank would fix the exchange rate. It must always be prepared to buy and sell its currency at the set rate. For example, if the Bank of Canada were fixing the exchange rate and if demand for the Canadian dollar exceeded supply so that the exchange rate would be about to appreciate, the Bank would have to sell extra Canadian dollars at the fixed exchange rate to meet the excess demand. If at the fixed exchange rate, supply of Canadian dollars

In 2002, the euro is scheduled to become the only currency in the European Monetary Union, and such currencies as French francs and German deutschemarks will no longer be legal tender.

FIGURE 21.8

Monetary Policy Has Permanent Aggregate Demand Effects Under Flexible Exchange Rates

The expansionary monetary policy pushes interest rates down to 5% and leads to a depreciation of the Canadian dollar. Net exports increase and this increases aggregate demand (and hence money demand) until interest rates are again 7%. Aggregate demand is permanently higher.

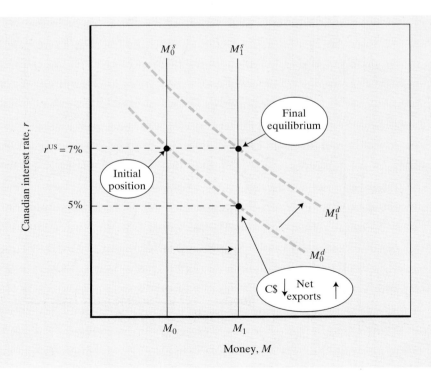

exceeded demand, the Bank of Canada would have to have enough foreign exchange (e.g., U.S. dollars) available to it to buy up the excess supply to prevent the exchange rate from depreciating.

■ **Fiscal Policy Under Fixed Exchange Rates**   In this case, there is no crowding out of the type we discussed in the fiscal policy/flexible exchange rate case. If there is expansionary fiscal policy, the central bank will have to expand the money supply to keep the interest rate at the world-determined level. Otherwise, the exchange rate would appreciate, which of course means it cannot be a fixed rate. (In terms of Figure 21.7, under fixed exchange rates the money supply would need to be increased to prevent interest rates from increasing from 7% to 9%.)

Hence under fixed exchange rates, an expansionary fiscal policy automatically induces an accommodating increase in the money supply. It will therefore tend to have a strong rather than a weak effect on aggregate demand. In short:

> If a small open economy like Canada had fixed exchange rates, interest rates would remain at levels essentially determined by international markets. With fixed exchange rates and interest rates, there is no crowding-out effect and fiscal policy can have strong effects on aggregate demand.

■ **Monetary Policy Under Fixed Exchange Rates**   Recall from Chapter 12 that having fixed exchange rates *is* a monetary policy. The central bank cannot use monetary policy for other goals (either to control inflation or to expand output) once it has decided to fix the exchange rate. For example, suppose the U.S. inflation rate is high and the rising price of imports from the United States is starting to put upward pressure on the Canadian inflation rate. With a fixed exchange rate, the Bank of Canada could not use contractionary monetary policy because that would tend to appreciate the exchange rate.[7]

> The decision to fix the exchange rate means that further monetary policy actions are not possible.

Now that we have completed our study of fiscal and monetary policy under flexible and fixed exchange rates, we summarize our conclusions in Table 21.3.

■ **Exchange Rates and the Balance of Trade: The J Curve**   As a matter of policy, sometimes a fixed exchange rate is changed to a new fixed exchange rate. If the exchange rate appreciates through this change, it is called a *revaluation*. If the exchange rate depreciates through this change, it is called a *devaluation*. The latter often occurs when there has been a trade deficit for some period of time. However, when there is a devaluation (or a depreciation under flexible exchange rates), it is unlikely that the trade balance will increase immediately. More likely the immediate effect will be to worsen it more and then the trade balance will improve over time. Let us conclude this chapter by examining this lag.

Assume Canada only trades in two goods and that the exchange rate is one Canadian dollar equals 80 cents U.S. Each month, Canada exports one million litres of maple syrup at C$5 per litre (US$4 per litre) and it imports five million litres of orange juice at C$1 per litre (US$0.80 per litre). As it happens, the value

Table 21.3	Summary of Effects of Fiscal and Monetary Policy Under Flexible and Fixed Exchange Rates	
	Flexible Exchange Rates	*Fixed Exchange Rates*
Fiscal policy	Weak	Strong
Monetary policy	Strong	Not applicable

---

[7]*This situation is sometimes described as Canada "importing" inflation under fixed exchange rates.*

of exports equals the value of imports, which equals C$5 million, so that net exports are precisely zero.

Now suppose the value of the Canadian dollar, which was initially 80 cents U.S., depreciates to 64 cents U.S. The instantaneous effect on exports is likely to be zero so exports are likely to remain at $5 million. While Canadian maple syrup is now cheaper to Americans, it will take some time before they respond and buy more. But the depreciation of the Canadian dollar is unlikely to change the U.S. price of orange juice from 80 cents U.S. per litre. However, 80 cents U.S. is now 80/64 = C$1.25, because of the 20% devaluation of the Canadian dollar. So if Canadians continue to import the five million litres of orange juice (perhaps complaining about the higher price, but not knowing what else to drink for breakfast), Canadian imports will now be C$1.25 × 5 million = C$6.25 million and net exports will be *negative* $1.25 million.

Over time, of course, Canadians will drink less of the now more expensive orange juice and Americans will buy more Canadian maple syrup, which is now less expensive to them. The general point is that the instantaneous effect of a depreciation is likely to be an initial *reduction* of the trade balance (perhaps for three or four quarters) because of the increased price of imports. This reduction will be followed by an increase as the price response effects kick in. (It is possible of course that the price responses will not be large enough to offset the initial decline, but it is widely accepted that they are.) The effect is drawn in Figure 21.9, and as the curve resembles the letter *J*, the movement in the balance of trade that it describes is sometimes called the **J-curve effect**.

J-curve effect *Following a currency depreciation, a country's balance of trade may get worse before it gets better. The graph showing this effect is shaped like the letter J, hence the name.*

An Interdependent World Economy

The economy of a small open country such as Canada is influenced to a great degree by economic events outside its borders. Policy makers face a sometimes difficult task in trying to regulate the Canadian economy in a world of much larger economic players. Canada is of course not the only country in the world in this situation. For example, just as the Canadian economy is highly dependent on the United States, so too are South Korea and Thailand very much dependent on Japan. In light of increasing levels of world trade, however, even powerful economies such as the United States and Japan are becoming more reliant on the rest of the world.

To this point, we have provided only the bare bones of open-market macroeconomics. If you continue your study of economics, as we hope you will, more will be added to the basic story we have presented.

FIGURE 21.9

The Effect of a Depreciation on the Balance of Trade (the J Curve)

Initially, a depreciation of a country's currency may worsen its balance of trade. The negative effect on the price of imports may initially dominate the positive effects of an increase in exports and a decrease in imports.

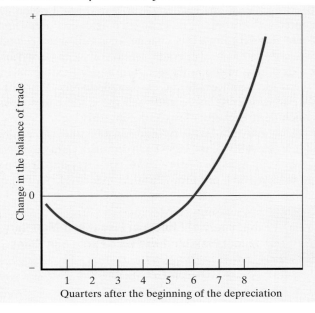

1. The main difference between an international transaction and a domestic transaction concerns currency exchange: when people in different countries buy from and sell to each other, an exchange of currencies must also take place.

2. The *exchange rate* is the price of one country's currency in terms of another country's currency.

The Balance of Payments

3. *Foreign exchange* is simply all currencies other than the domestic currency of a given country. The record of a nation's transactions in goods, services, and assets with the rest of the world is known as its *balance of payments*. The balance of payments is also the record of a country's sources (supply) and uses (demand) of foreign exchange.

Equilibrium Output (Income) in an Open Economy

4. In an open economy, the multiplier equals $1/1 - (MPC - MPM)$, where MPC is the marginal propensity to consume and MPM is the marginal propensity to import. The *marginal propensity to import* is the change in imports caused by a \$1 change in income.

5. In addition to income, other factors that affect the level of imports are the after-tax real wage rate, interest rates, and the relative prices of domestically produced and foreign-produced goods. The demand for exports is determined by economic activity in the rest of the world and by relative prices.

6. An increase in country A's economic activity tends to increase its imports, which helps to increase worldwide economic activity. This then "feeds back" to country A by stimulating its exports. This is the *trade feedback effect*.

The Open Economy with Flexible Exchange Rates

7. The equilibrium exchange rate occurs when the quantity demanded of a foreign currency in the foreign exchange market equals the quantity of that currency supplied in the foreign exchange market.

8. According to the *law of one price,* if the costs of transportation are small, the price of the same good in different countries should be roughly the same. The theory that exchange rates are set so that the price of similar goods in different countries is the same is known as *purchasing power parity theory*. In practice, transportation costs are significant for many goods, and the law of one price does not hold for these goods.

9. A high rate of inflation in one country relative to another puts pressure on the exchange rate between the two countries. There is a general tendency for the currencies of relatively high-inflation countries to depreciate. However, the depreciation often will not offset the differences in inflation so that relative prices between countries (that is, the price of one country's goods relative to those in the other, expressed in a common currency) can change substantially over time.

10. In the short term, changes in interest rates are probably the most important factor causing changes in exchange rates. For example, an increase in Canadian interest rates will lead holders of foreign securities to want to sell those securities for foreign currency, use that foreign currency to buy Canadian dollars and then use the Canadian dollars to buy Canadian interest-bearing securities. This involves an increase in demand for Canadian dollars and hence an appreciation of the Canadian dollar.

11. If we assume there is no difference in perceived risk, by the *interest rate parity condition*, the Canadian interest rate + Expected rate of appreciation of the Canadian dollar = U.S. interest rate. For example, Canadian interest rates can be less than U.S. interest rates as long as the Canadian dollar is expected to appreciate relative to the U.S. dollar, which acts as a "bonus" for holders of Canadian bonds and makes up for the lower interest rates.

Monetary and Fiscal Policy in the Open Economy

12. If in equilibrium the exchange rate is steady (neither appreciating nor depreciating), the interest rate parity condition implies that equilibrium Canadian interest rates will equal U.S. interest rates, even under flexible exchange rates.

13. Given this equilibrium equalization of interest rates, under flexible exchange rates, fiscal policy can only have temporary effects on aggregate demand. For example, the initial expansion due to an expansionary fiscal policy will tend to increase aggregate demand and hence money demand so that interest rates will increase given no additional money supply. The higher interest rates will lead to an appreciated exchange rate, which will lead to a reduction in net exports, reversing the expansion. Aggregate demand will return to its initial level and hence money demand and interest rates will also return to their initial levels.

14. Monetary policy under flexible exchange rates will have strong effects. For example, an expansionary monetary policy will depreciate the exchange rate and hence stimulate net exports and aggregate demand.

15. Under fixed exchange rates (that are expected to stay fixed), interest rates will also be effectively set at international levels because there are no exchange rate changes that can offset interest rate differentials. Accordingly, fiscal policy is likely to have strong effects on aggregate demand. For example, in a fiscal expansion there will be no "crowding-out" effects from higher interest rates or appreciated exchange rates.

16. Neither contractionary nor expansionary monetary policy is possible under fixed exchange rates. The money supply must be adjusted to maintain the exchange rate and hence cannot be used as a tool to achieve other objectives.

17. The initial effect of a devaluation from one fixed exchange rate to another (or a depreciation of the exchange rate under flexible exchange rates) is likely to be a decline in the trade balance. The immediate changes in the volumes of imports and exports are likely to be small but the amount paid for imports will increase because, after the depreciation, it will now take more of the devalued currency to buy the same volume. Hence net exports will decline. Over time, there will likely be increases in the volume of exports and reductions in the volume of imports because of the changes in prices due to the exchange rate changes and these will push net exports up. The initial decline in net exports followed by an increase is called the *J-curve effect*.

Review Terms and Concepts

balance of payments 427

balance of trade 428

balance on capital account 430

balance on current account 429

exchange rate 426

foreign exchange 427

interest rate parity 442

J-curve effect 446

law of one price 438

marginal propensity to import (*MPM*) 431

merchandise balance of trade 429

net exports of goods and services (*EX* – *IM*) 431

purchasing power parity theory 438

trade deficit 429

trade feedback effect 434

trade surplus 429

Equations:

1. Planned aggregate expenditure in an open economy:

$$AE \equiv C + I + G + EX - IM$$

2. Open-economy multiplier:

$$\frac{1}{1 - (MPC - MPM)}$$

Problem Set

1. List the balance-of-payments account (current or capital) under which each of the following transactions would be classified and explain whether the item represents a credit or debit entry in the Canadian balance of payments.

   a. You go on vacation to Mexico and spend $300 there on a hotel room, food, transportation, and so forth.

   b. You bring back an Oriental carpet that you bought on a trip to the Middle East. The carpet is worth $10 000.

   c. You buy a new Toyota (made in Japan) for $15 000.

   d. You send your cousin in England a birthday present worth $50.

   e. Volkswagen Inc. of Germany buys a factory in Canada for $100 million.

   f. A company in Japan buys 10% of all the shares in Domtar.

   g. You lend your uncle in Florida $5000.

   h. Your uncle pays you $500 in interest on the money you previously lent him. He also repays $1000 of the principal.

2. Suppose that the following situation prevails on the British pound/Canadian dollar foreign exchange market with floating exchange rates:

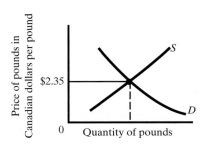

a. Name three phenomena that might shift the demand curve to the right.

b. Which, if any, of these three might cause a simultaneous shift of the supply curve to the left?

c. What effects might the three phenomena have on the balance of payments if the exchange rate floats? On the balance of trade?

3. In 1981 and 1982, central banks in both Canada and the United States pursued a tight money policy that sent interest rates up dramatically to over 20% (ultimately putting both economies in a deep recession, but lowering the inflation rate).

a. Explain how the Bank of Canada's tight monetary policy prevented a more substantial depreciation of the Canadian dollar. (As it was, the Canadian dollar depreciated from about 86 cents U.S. to about 81 cents U.S. from 1980 to 1982.)

b. The exchange rates of both countries tended to appreciate during this period relative to other countries with lower interest rates. For example, the Canadian dollar appreciated from about 1.5 German marks to almost 2 German marks between 1980 and 1982, and there were similar appreciations with respect to other currencies. Explain why.

c. From 1980 to 1982, Canada's merchandise trade balance with United States rose from about $1.6 billion in 1980 to about $11 billion in 1982 while there was a decline in the merchandise trade balance with the rest of the world from $7.1 billion to about $6.6 billion over the same period, with more substantial declines to follow. Explain this using the information in parts **a** and **b**.

4. Probably the two most important economies in the world are the United States and Japan, and trade disputes and policies between those countries affect other countries as well. The exchange rate between the U.S. dollar and the yen floats freely with relatively little intervention by the two central banks. Suppose that because of a large trade deficit with Japan, the United States decides to impose quotas on certain Japanese products imported into the United States and, as a result, the value of these imports falls.

a. The decrease in spending on Japanese products increases spending on U.S.-made goods. Why? What effect will this have on U.S. output and employment? On Japanese output and employment? On Canadian output and employment?

b. What happens to U.S. imports from Japan when U.S. output (or income) rises? If the quotas initially reduce imports from Japan by US$25 billion, why is the final reduction in imports likely to be less than US$25 billion? Explain in terms of the trade feedback effect.

c. Suppose that the quotas do succeed in reducing U.S. imports from Japan by US$15 billion. What will happen to the demand for yen? Why?

d. Assuming no change in interest rates or other factors, what will happen to the U.S. dollar/yen exchange rate, and why? (*Hint:* There is an excess supply of yen, or an excess demand for U.S. dollars.) What effects will the change in the value of each currency have on employment and output in Canada? On the balance of payments? (You can ignore complications such as the J curve.)

e. Considering the macroeconomic effects of a quota on Japanese imports, could a quota actually reduce employment and output in the United States, or have no effect at all? Explain.

5. What effect will each of the following events have on the balance of payments and the exchange rate if the exchange rate is fixed? If it is floating?

a. The Canadian government cuts taxes, and income rises.

b. The Canadian inflation rate increases, and prices in Canada rise faster than those in the countries with which Canada trades.

c. Canada adopts an expansionary monetary policy. Interest rates fall (and are now lower than those in other countries), and income rises.

d. A "Buy Canadian" advertising campaign is successful, and Canadian consumers switch from purchasing imported products to those made in Canada.

6. This question is also similar to the analysis of Appendix 10C. Consider the following model, which describes the economy of Hypothetica.

(1) Consumption function: $C = 100 + 0.8Y_d$

(2) Planned investment: $I = 38$

(3) Government spending: $G = 75$

(4) Exports: $EX = 25$

(5) Imports: $IM = 0.05Y_d$

(6) Disposable income: $Y_d \equiv Y - T$

(7) Taxes: $T = 40$

(8) Planned aggregate expenditure: $AE \equiv C + I + G + (EX - IM)$

(9) Definition of equilibrium income: $Y = AE$

a. What is equilibrium income in Hypothetica? What is the government deficit? What is the current account balance?

b. If government spending is increased to $G = 80$, what happens to equilibrium income? Explain, using the government spending multiplier. What happens to imports?

Now suppose that the amount of imports is limited to $IM = 40$ by a quota on imports. If government spending is again increased from 75 to 80, what happens to equilibrium income? Explain why the same increase in G has a bigger effect on income in the second case. What is it about the presence of imports that changes the value of the multiplier?

c. If exports are fixed at $EX = 25$, what must income be in order to ensure a current account balance of zero? (*Hint:* Imports depend on income, so what must income be for imports to be equal to exports?) By how much must we cut government spending to balance the current account? (*Hint:* Use your answer to the first part of this question to determine how much of a decrease in income is needed. Then use the multiplier to calculate the decrease in G needed to reduce income by that amount.)

7. The table below shows that the Canadian dollar/pound sterling rate in April 2000 is about the same as it was in 1981. However, since 1981 the Canadian dollar has depreciated sharply against the yen. Explain why this might be so.

Price of Canadian Dollar In:	1981	2000 (April)
Pound sterling	£0.41	£0.43
Yen	¥183	¥72

Source: Bank of Canada Review, May 1992; *Bank of Canada Banking and Financial Statistics,* May 2000.

(*Note:* All exchange rates can be quoted two ways, so that while it is most common for Canadians to think of the exchange rate as the value of one Canadian dollar, say one Canadian dollar = 68 cents U.S., that same exchange rate can be quoted as one U.S. dollar = 1/0.68 = C$1.47. In Canada, the British pound is usually quoted as the Canadian dollar price of a pound. So while the exchange rates in the table tell us that in April 2000 one Canadian dollar could be exchanged for 43p [1£ = 100p] in British currency, it is more usual to write that exchange rate as 1£ =1/0.43 = C$2.32.)

Economic Growth in Developing Countries

Learning Objectives

1 Distinguish between economic growth and economic development.

2 Describe the role of capital, human capital, and social overhead capital in economic growth and development.

3 Describe three tradeoffs affecting strategies for economic development.

4 Outline how rapid population growth affects economic development.

5 Outline the main agricultural policy issues in less developed economies.

6 Explain why the Third World debt is of global concern.

7 *Appendix 22A:* List six basic terms in Marxian economics. Define *tragedy of the commons* and explain its implications for an economy with collective ownership.

Life in the Developing Countries: Population and Poverty

Economic Development: Sources and Strategies

The Sources of Economic Development

Strategies for Economic Development

Growth Versus Development: The Policy Cycle

Issues in Economic Development

Population Growth

Food Shortages: Acts of Nature or Human Mistakes?

Agricultural Output and Pricing Policies

Third World Debt

Appendix 22A: **Marxian Economics**

Our primary focus in this text has been on economic issues facing Canada. Cuts to social programs, slow economic growth in recent years, and worries about the debt are familiar to Canadians. But the economics we have been studying also applies to other countries. Welfare reform is a big issue in the United States, Japan is facing major fiscal deficits, and the European central bank has been wrestling with the tradeoff between economic growth and potential inflation. We can analyze these and other issues in the United States, Japan, and Europe with some confidence because they have so much in common with Canada. In spite of differences in languages and cultures, all these countries have modern industrialized economies that rely heavily on markets to allocate resources. But what about the economic problems facing Somalia or Haiti? Can we apply the same economic principles that we have been studying to these less developed countries (sometimes called LDCs)?

Many economists think that the answer is yes. All economic analysis deals with the basic problem of making choices under conditions of scarcity, and the problem of satisfying their citizens' wants and needs is certainly as real for Somalia and Haiti as it is for the United States, Europe, and Japan. The universality of scarcity is what makes economic analysis relevant to all nations, regardless of their level of material well-being or ruling political ideology.

The basic tools of supply and demand, theories about consumers and firms, and theories about the structure of markets all contribute to an understanding of the economic problems confronting the world's developing nations. However, these nations often face economic problems quite different from those faced by richer, more developed countries. In the developing nations, the economist may have to worry about chronic food shortages, explosive population growth, and hyperinflations that reach triple, and even quadruple, digits. Canada and other industrialized economies rarely encounter such difficulties.

The instruments of economic management also vary from country to country. Canada has well-developed financial market institutions and a strong central bank (the Bank of Canada) through which the government can control the macroeconomy to some extent. But even limited intervention is impossible in some of the developing countries. In Canada, tax laws can be changed to stimulate saving, to encourage particular kinds of investments, or to redistribute income. In most developing countries, there are neither meaningful personal income taxes nor effective tax policies.

But even though economic problems and the policy instruments available to tackle them vary across countries, economic thinking about these problems can often be transferred quite easily from one setting to another. In this chapter we discuss several of the economic problems specific to developing countries in an attempt to capture some of the insights that economic analysis can offer.

Life in the Developing Countries: Population and Poverty

By the year 2015, the population of the world will reach over 7.1 billion people. Most of the world's more than 200 countries belong to the developing world, in which about three-quarters of the world's population lives.

In the early 1960s, the countries of the world could be assigned rather easily to categories. The *developed countries* included most of Europe, North America, Japan, Australia, and New Zealand; the *developing countries* included the rest of the world. The developing nations were often referred to as the "Third World" to distinguish them from the Western industrialized nations (the "First World") and the former socialist bloc of Eastern European nations (the "Second World").

Today, however, the world does not divide into three neat parts. Rapid economic progress has brought some developing nations closer to developed economies. Countries such as Argentina and Korea, while still considered to be "developing," are often referred to as middle-income, or newly industrialized, countries. Meanwhile, other countries, such as much of sub-Saharan Africa and some of South Asia, have stagnated and fallen so far behind the economic advances of the rest of the world that a new designation, the "Fourth World," has been coined. It is not clear yet where the republics of the former Soviet Union and other formerly Communist countries of Eastern Europe will end up. Production has fallen sharply in many of them. For example, between 1990 and 1997, real GDP fell by over 50% in Russia and Central Asia, and one estimate puts per capita GDP in Russia at around US$2500. Some of the new republics now have more in common with developing countries than with developed countries.

While the countries of the developing world exhibit considerable diversity, both in their standards of living and in their particular experiences of growth, marked differences continue to separate them from the developed countries. The developed countries have a higher average level of material well-being. By material well-being, we mean the amounts of food, clothing, shelter, and other commodities consumed by the average person. One very crude way to illustrate these differences across countries is to compare gross national product (GNP) per capita. (GNP is very much like GDP, but it is usually used for these kinds of comparisons because it only includes the production of a country's residents and not that of foreign factors of production.)

Other characteristics of economic development we can examine include improvements in basic health and education. The degree of political and economic freedom enjoyed by individual citizens might also be part of a comprehensive definition of what it means to be a developed nation. Some of these criteria are easier to quantify than others; Table 22.1 presents data for different types of economies according to some of the more easily measured indexes of development. As you can see, high-income economies enjoy higher standards of living according to whatever indicator of development is chosen.

Behind these statistics lies the reality of the very difficult life facing the people of the developing world. For most, meagre incomes provide only the basic necessities of life. Most meals are the same, consisting of the region's food staple—typically rice, wheat, or corn. Shelter is primitive. Many people share a small room, usually with an earthen floor and no sanitary facilities. The great majority of the population lives in rural areas where agricultural work is hard

Civil wars in the African nation of Angola have posed major obstacles to economic development. Homes and other valuable capital in that country are constantly being damaged or destroyed by wartime activities.

and extremely time-consuming. Productivity (output produced per worker) is low because household plots are small and only the crudest of farm implements are available. Low productivity means that farm output per person is at levels barely sufficient to feed a farmer's own family, with nothing left over to sell to others. School-age children may receive some formal education, but illiteracy remains chronic for young and old alike. Infant mortality runs 10 times higher than in high-income

Table 22.1	Indicators of Economic Development				
Country Group	Range of GNP per Capita in Country Group, 1998 (US$)	Life Expectancy, 1998 (years)	Infant Mortality, 1998 (deaths before age one per 1000 births)	Secondary School Enrollment, 1997 (number enrolled as percentage of relevant age group)	Percentage of Population in Urban Areas, 1998
Low-income (e.g., China, Ethiopia, Haiti, India)	760 or less	63	68	59	30
Lower middle-income (e.g., Guatemala, Latvia, Philippines, South Africa)	761–3030	68	35	73	58
Upper middle-income (e.g., Argentina, Brazil, Mexico, Poland)	3031–9360	71	26	71	77
High-income (e.g., Canada, Germany, New Zealand, United States)	9361 or greater	78	6	96	77

Source: World Bank, *World Development Indicators, 2000.* Note that all numbers, except for "Range of GNP per Capita," refer to weighted averages for each country group, where the weights equal the populations of each country in a specific country group.

countries. Although parasitic infections are common and debilitating, there is only one physician per 5000 people. In addition, many developing countries are engaged in civil and external warfare.

Life in the developing nations is a continual struggle against the circumstances of poverty, and prospects for dramatic improvements in living standards for most people are dim. However, as with all generalizations, there are important exceptions. Some countries are better off than others, and in any given country an elite group always lives in considerable luxury. Just as in any advanced economy, income is distributed in a fashion that allows a small percentage of households to consume a disproportionately large share of national income. Income distribution in developing countries is often so skewed that the richest households surpass the living standards of many high-income families in the advanced economies. Table 22.2 presents some data on the distribution of income in some developing countries. We can see that in Kenya, for example, the poorest one-fifth of the population (bottom 20%) gets 5.0% of total Kenyan income, but the richest one-fifth (top 20%) gets 50.2%.

Clearly, poverty—not affluence—dominates the developing world. Recent studies suggest that 40% of the people of the developing nations have annual incomes insufficient to provide for adequate nutrition.

> While the developed countries account for only about one-quarter of the world's population, they are estimated to consume three-quarters of the world's output. This leaves the developing countries with about three-fourths of the world's people, but only one-quarter of the world's income. The simple result is that most of our planet's population is poor.

In Canada, the poorest one-fifth (bottom 20%) of families receives 7.5% of total income, while the richest one-fifth receives about 39% of the income. But the inequality in the world distribution of income is much greater. When we look at the population of the world, the poorest one-fifth of families receives 1.4% of the total world income and the richest one-fifth receives 85% of world income!

Economic Development: Sources and Strategies

Economists have been trying to understand the process of economic growth and development since the days of Adam Smith and David Ricardo in the eighteenth and nineteenth centuries, but the study of development economics as it applies to the developing countries has a much shorter history. The geopolitical struggles that followed World War II brought increased attention to the developing countries and their economic problems. During this period, the central question of the new field of development economics was simply, why are some countries poor and others rich? If economists could understand the barriers to economic growth that prevent countries from developing and the prerequisites that would

Table 22.2	Income Distribution in Canada and in Some Developing Countries					
	Canada	*Sri Lanka*	*Kenya*	*Brazil*	*Pakistan*	*Indonesia*
Per capita GNP 1998	US$19 170	US$810	US$350	US$4630	US$470	US$640
Bottom 20%	7.5	8.0	5.0	2.5	9.5	8.0
Second 20%	12.9	11.8	9.7	5.5	12.9	11.3
Third 20%	17.2	15.8	14.2	10.0	16.0	15.1
Fourth 20%	23.0	21.5	20.9	18.3	20.5	20.8
Top 20%	39.3	42.8	50.2	63.8	41.1	44.9

Source: World Bank, *World Development Indicators, 2000,* Tables 1.1 and 2.8.

help them to develop, then they could prescribe suitable strategies for achieving economic advancement.

THE SOURCES OF ECONOMIC DEVELOPMENT

While a general theory of economic development applicable to all countries has not emerged and probably never will, some basic factors that limit a poor country's economic growth have been suggested. These include insufficient capital formation, a shortage of human resources and entrepreneurial ability, and a lack of social overhead capital.

■ **Capital Formation** One explanation for low levels of output in developing countries is the absence of sufficient quantities of necessary inputs. Developing countries have diverse resource endowments—Congo, for instance, is abundant in natural resources, while Bangladesh is resource poor. Almost all developing nations have a scarcity of physical capital relative to other resources, especially labour. The small stock of physical capital (including factories, machinery, farm equipment, and other types of productive capital) constrains labour's productivity and holds back national output.

But citing capital shortages as the cause of low productivity does not really explain much. To get to the heart of the matter, we need to know why capital is in such short supply in developing countries. Many explanations have been offered. One, the **vicious-circle-of-poverty hypothesis,** suggests that a poor country must consume most of its income just to maintain its already low standard of living. Just like a poor family, a poor nation finds that the opportunity cost of forgoing current consumption (i.e., saving instead of consuming) is too high. Consuming most of national income implies limited saving, and this in turn implies low levels of investment. Without investment, the capital stock does not grow, income remains low, and the vicious circle is complete. Poverty becomes self-perpetuating.

The difficulty with the vicious-circle argument is that if it were true, no country could ever develop. For example, Japanese GDP per capita at the turn of the century was well below that of many of today's developing nations. If the vicious-circle explanation were completely correct, Japan could never have grown into the industrial power it is today. The vicious-circle argument fails to recognize that every country has some surplus above consumption needs that is available for investment. Often this surplus is most visible in the conspicuous-consumption habits of the nation's richest families.

> Poverty alone cannot explain capital shortages, nor is poverty necessarily self-perpetuating.

In a developing economy, scarcity of capital may have more to do with a lack of incentives for citizens to save and invest productively than with any absolute scarcity of income available for capital accumulation. The inherent riskiness and uncertainty that surround a developing country's economy and its political system (including the frequency of internal war) tend to reduce incentives to invest in any activity, especially those that require long periods of time to yield a return. Many of the rich in developing countries take their savings and invest them in developed countries rather than risk holding them in what is often an unstable political climate (itself often due to the social and economic divisions within the country). Savings transferred to the developed countries do not lead to physical capital growth in the developing countries. The term **capital flight** is often used to refer to the fact that capital (domestic savings) often leaves developing countries in search of higher rates of return elsewhere. In addition, a range of government policies in the developing nations—including price ceilings, import controls, and even outright appropriation of private property—tend to discourage investment. In many cases, governments are controlled by an elite often involving the military and are unlikely to set policies in the broader social interest.

vicious-circle-of-poverty hypothesis *Suggests that poverty is self-perpetuating because poor countries are unable to save and invest enough to accumulate the capital stock that would help them grow.*

capital flight *The tendency for capital to leave developing countries in search of higher rates of return elsewhere.*

Whatever the causes of capital shortages, it is clear that the absence of productive capital prevents income from rising in any economy. The availability of capital is a necessary, but not a *sufficient*, condition for economic growth. The Third World landscape is littered with idle factories and abandoned machinery. Clearly, other ingredients are required to achieve economic progress.

■ **Human Resources and Entrepreneurial Ability** Capital is not the only factor of production required to produce output. Labour is an equally important input. But the quantity of available labour rarely constrains a developing economy. In most developing countries, rapid population growth for several decades has resulted in rapidly expanding labour supplies. The *quality* of available labour, however, may pose a serious constraint on the growth of income. Or, to put it another way, the shortage of *human capital*—the stock of knowledge and skill embodied in the workforce—may act as a barrier to economic growth.

Human capital may be developed in a number of ways. Because malnutrition and the lack of basic health care can substantially reduce labour productivity, programs to improve nutrition and health represent one kind of human capital investment that can lead to increased productivity and higher incomes. The more familiar forms of human capital investment, including formal education and on-the-job training, may also play an important role. Basic literacy, as well as specialized training in farm management, for example, can yield high returns to both the individual worker and the economy. Education has grown to become the largest category of government expenditure in many developing nations, in part because of the belief that human resources are the ultimate determinant of economic advance.

Just as financial capital seeks the highest and safest return, so does human capital. Students from developing countries, many of whom were supported by their governments, graduate every year from North American and European colleges and universities as engineers, doctors, scientists, economists, and the like. After graduation, these people face a difficult choice: to remain in North America or Europe and earn a high salary or to return home and accept a job at a much lower salary. Many people choose not to return home. This **brain drain** siphons off many of the most talented minds from developing countries.[1] But the brain drain is in part just a consequence of extending somewhat more equal opportunity to some of the world's poor. In any case, arguments about the brain drain are not very relevant to the consideration of basic literacy and skills programs.

Innovative entrepreneurs who are willing to take risks are an essential human resource in any economy. In a developing country, new techniques of production rarely need to be invented, since they can usually be adapted from the technology already developed by the technologically advanced countries. But entrepreneurs who are willing and able to organize and carry out economic activity appear to be in short supply. Family and political ties often seem to be more important than ability when it comes to securing positions of authority. Whatever the explanation:

> Development cannot proceed without human resources capable of initiating and managing economic activity.

■ **Social Overhead Capital** Anyone who has spent time in a developing nation knows how difficult it can be to send a letter, make a local phone call, or travel within the country itself. Add to this list of obstacles problems with water supplies, frequent electrical power outages—in areas where electricity is available at all—and often ineffective mosquito and pest control, and you soon realize how deficient even the simplest, most basic government-provided goods and services can be. In politically unstable areas, military spending is often high, to the detriment of spending on basic health and education.

In any economy, Third World or otherwise, the government has considerable opportunity and responsibility for involvement where conditions encourage

[1]*It is sometimes argued that there is also a brain drain from Canada to the United States, or between regions of Canada.*

FAST FACTS

In 2000 about 24 million sub-Saharan Africans were infected with AIDS, about 70% of the global total. There are forecasts that by 2010, average life expectancy will fall to close to age 30 in the worst-hit countries.

brain drain *The tendency for talented people from developing countries to become educated in a developed country and remain there after graduation.*

natural monopoly (as in the utilities industries) and where public goods (such as roads and pest control) must be provided. In a developing economy, the government must place particular emphasis on creating a basic infrastructure—roads, power generation, irrigation systems. There are often good reasons why such projects, referred to as **social overhead capital,** cannot successfully be undertaken by the private sector. First, many of these projects operate with economies of scale, which means that they can be efficient only if they are very large. In that case, they may be simply too large for any private company or group of such companies to carry out.

Second, many socially useful projects cannot be undertaken by the private sector because there is no way for private agents to capture enough of the returns to make such projects profitable. For example, consider the control of malaria by draining swamps. A private firm that tried to enter the business and charge neighbouring individuals might find a reluctance to pay, the so-called free-rider problem. Why should I pay if your purchase will also protect me? Why should you pay if my purchase will also protect you?

> The governments of developing countries can do important and useful things to encourage development, but many of their efforts must be concentrated in areas that the private sector would never touch. If government action in these realms is not forthcoming, economic development may be curtailed by a lack of social overhead capital.

STRATEGIES FOR ECONOMIC DEVELOPMENT

Just as no single theory appears to explain lack of economic advancement, so too is it unlikely that one development strategy will succeed in all countries. In fact, many alternative development strategies have been proposed over the past 30 or 40 years. Although these strategies have been very different, they all share the recognition that a developing economy faces certain basic tradeoffs. An insufficient amount of both human and physical resources dictates that choices must be made. Some of the basic tradeoffs that underlie any development strategy include those between agriculture and industry, exports and import substitution, and central planning and free markets.

■ **Agriculture or Industry?** Most Third World countries began to gain political independence just after World War II. The tradition of promoting industrialization as the solution to the problems of the developing world dates from this time. The early five-year development plans of India called for promoting manufacturing; the current government in Ethiopia (an extremely poor country) has similar intentions.

Industry has several apparent attractions over agriculture. Perhaps most important, one of the primary characteristics of more developed economies is their structural transition away from agriculture. As Table 22.3 shows, agriculture's share in GDP declines substantially as per capita incomes increase.

Many countries have pursued industry at the expense of agriculture. In many cases, however, industrialization has not brought the benefits that were expected. Experience suggests that simply trying to replicate the structure of developed economies does not in itself guarantee, or even promote, successful development.

Since the early 1970s, the agricultural sector has received considerably more attention. Agricultural strategies have had numerous benefits. Although some agricultural projects (such as the building of major dams and irrigation networks) are very capital intensive, many others (such as services to help teach better farming techniques and small-scale fertilizer programs) have low capital and import requirements. Programs like these can affect large numbers of households, and because their benefits are directed at rural areas, they are most likely to help a country's poorest families.

Experience over the last three decades suggests that some balance between these approaches leads to the best outcome—that is, it is important and effective

social overhead capital *Basic infrastructure projects such as roads, power generation, and irrigation systems.*

Table 22.3	The Share of Agriculture in Selected Developing Economies, 1998	
Country	**Per Capita Income (US$)**	**Agriculture (as a percentage of gross domestic product)**
Uganda	$310	45
Pakistan	$470	26
China	$750	18
Ukraine	$980	14
Thailand	$2160	11
South Africa	$3310	4

Source: World Bank, *World Development Indicators, 2000*, Tables 1.1 and 4.2.

to pay attention to both industry and agriculture. The Chinese have referred to this dual approach to development as "walking on two legs."

■ **Exports or Import Substitution?**   As developing countries expand their industrial activities, they must decide what type of trade strategy to pursue. The choice usually boils down to one of two major alternatives: import substitution or export promotion.

Import substitution is an industrial trade strategy that favours developing local industries that can manufacture goods to replace imports. For example, if fertilizer is currently imported, import substitution calls for establishment of a domestic fertilizer industry to produce replacements for fertilizer imports. This strategy gained prominence throughout South America in the 1950s. At that time, most developing countries exported agricultural and mineral products, goods that faced uncertain and often unstable international markets. Furthermore, the *terms of trade* for these nations—the ratio of export to import prices—seemed to be on a long-run decline.[2] A decline in a country's terms of trade means that its imports of manufactured goods become relatively expensive in the domestic market, while its exports—mostly primary goods such as rubber, grains, and oil—become relatively inexpensive in the world market.

Under these conditions, the call for import-substitution policies was understandable. Special government actions, including tariff and quota protection and subsidized imports of machinery, were set up to encourage new domestic industries. Multinational corporations were also invited into many countries to begin domestic operations.

Most economists believe that import-substitution strategies have failed almost everywhere they have been tried. With domestic industries sheltered from international competition by high tariffs (often as high as 200%), major economic inefficiencies were created. For example, Peru has a population of about 24 million, only a tiny fraction of whom could ever afford to buy an automobile. Yet at one time the country had five different automobile manufacturers, each of which produced only a few thousand cars per year. Since there are substantial economies of scale in automobile production, the cost per car was much higher than it needed to be, and valuable resources that could have been devoted to higher productivity activities were squandered producing cars.

Furthermore, policies designed to promote import substitution often encouraged capital-intensive production methods, which limited the creation of jobs and hurt export activities. Obviously, a country like Peru could not export automobiles, since it could produce them only at a cost far greater than their price on the world market. Worse still, import-substitution policies encouraged the use of expensive domestic products, such as tractors and fertilizer, instead of lower-cost

import substitution *An industrial trade strategy that favours developing local industries that can manufacture goods to replace imports.*

_____

[2]*It now appears that the terms of trade for Third World countries as a group were not actually on a long-run decline. Of course, the prices of commodities have changed, with some doing very well and others doing quite poorly. During the 1950s, however, many policy makers believed that the purchasing power of developing-country exports was in a permanent slump.*

imports. These policies thus served to tax the very sectors that might have successfully competed in world markets. To the extent that the Peruvian sugar industry had to rely on domestically produced, high-cost fertilizer, for example, its ability to compete in international markets was reduced, because its production costs were artificially raised.

As an alternative to import substitution, some nations have pursued strategies of export promotion. **Export promotion** is simply the policy of encouraging exports. As an industrial market economy, Japan is a striking example to the developing world of the long-term growth that exports can provide. With an average annual per capita real GDP growth rate of roughly 6% per year since 1960, Japan's achievements are in part based on industrial production oriented toward foreign consumers.

Several countries in the developing world have attempted to emulate Japan's success. Starting around 1970, Hong Kong, Singapore, Korea, and Taiwan (sometimes called the "four little dragons" between the two big dragons, China and Japan) all began to pursue export promotion of manufactured goods. Today their long-run growth rates have surpassed even Japan's. Other nations, including Brazil, Colombia, and Turkey, have also had some success at pursuing a more outward-looking trade policy.

export promotion *A trade policy designed to encourage exports.*

■ Central Planning or the Market?

As part of its strategy for achieving economic development, a country must decide how its economy will be directed. Its basic choices lie between a market-oriented economic system and a centrally planned one.

In the 1950s and into the 1960s, development strategies that called for national planning commanded wide support. The rapid economic growth of the Soviet Union, a centrally planned economy, provided a historical example of the speed with which a less developed agrarian country could be transformed into a modern industrial power. (The often appalling costs of this strategy—namely violation of human rights and environmental damage—were less widely known.) In addition, the underdevelopment of many commodity and asset markets in the Third World led many experts to believe that market forces could not direct an economy reliably and that major government intervention was therefore necessary.

FAST FACTS

Largely centrally planned economies increasingly have free-market aspects. A recent example is the introduction of a stock market in Vietnam in 2000, although initially there were only two companies listed.

Today, planning takes many forms in the developing countries. In a few extreme cases, central planning has replaced market-based outcomes with direct, administratively determined controls over such economic variables as prices, output, and employment. In other situations, national planning amounts to little more than the formulation of general 5- or 10-year goals that serve as rough blueprints for a nation's economic future.

The economic appeal of planning lies theoretically in its ability to channel savings into productive investment and to coordinate economic activities that private actors in the economy might not otherwise undertake. The reality of central planning, however, is that it is technically difficult, highly politicized, and a nightmare to administer. Given the scarcity of human resources and the unstable political environment in many developing countries, planning itself—let alone the execution of the plan—becomes a formidable task.

The failure of many central planning efforts has brought increasing calls for less government intervention and more market orientation in developing economies. The elimination of price controls, privatization of state-run enterprises, and reductions in import restraints are examples of market-oriented reforms that are frequently recommended by such international agencies as the **International Monetary Fund,** whose primary goals are to stabilize international exchange rates and to lend money to countries that have problems financing their international transactions, and the **World Bank,** which lends money to individual countries for projects that promote economic development.

Members' contributions to both organizations are determined by the size of their economies. Only 20% of the World Bank's funding comes from contributions; the other 80% comes from retained earnings and investments in capital markets. Throughout the developing world, a recognition of the value of market forces in determining the allocation of scarce resources appears to be increasing. Nonetheless, government still has a major role to play. In the decades

International Monetary Fund *An international agency whose primary goals are to stabilize international exchange rates and to lend money to countries that have problems financing their international transactions.*

World Bank *An international agency that lends money to individual countries for projects that promote economic development.*

ahead, the governments of developing countries will need to determine those situations in which planning is superior to the market and those in which the market is superior to planning.

GROWTH VERSUS DEVELOPMENT: THE POLICY CYCLE

Until now, we have used the words "growth" and "development" as though they meant essentially the same thing. But this may not always be the case. One can easily imagine instances in which a country has achieved higher levels of income (growth) with little or no benefit accruing to most of its citizens (development). Thus, one central question in evaluating alternative strategies for achieving economic development is whether economic growth necessarily brings about economic development.

In the past, most development strategies were aimed at increasing the growth rate of income per capita. Many still are, based on the theory that benefits of economic growth will "trickle down" to all members of society. If this theory is correct, then growth should promote development.

A World Bank study in 1974 indicated that increases in GDP per capita did not guarantee significant improvements in such development indicators as nutrition, health, and education. Although GDP per capita did indeed rise, its benefits trickled down to only a small minority of the population. This perspective, since rejected by a year 2000 World Bank study that concluded growth does in fact help the poorest, led to new development strategies that would directly address the problems of poverty. Such strategies favoured agriculture over industry, called for domestic redistribution of income and wealth (especially land), and encouraged programs to satisfy such basic needs as food and shelter.

In the late 1970s and early 1980s, the international macroeconomic crises of high oil prices, worldwide recession, and Third World debt forced attention away from programs designed to eliminate poverty directly. Then, during the 1980s and 1990s, the World Bank began demanding "structural adjustment" in the developing countries as a prerequisite for sending aid to them. **Structural adjustment** programs entail reducing the size of the public sector through privatization and/or expenditure reductions, substantially cutting budget deficits, reining in inflation, and encouraging private saving and investment with tax reforms. The hope was that saving and investment would increase enough to increase growth more than cuts in education and social overhead capital would reduce it. In any case, distributional consequences took a back seat.

Aid from the developed to the developing countries has become increasingly problematic, especially as the countries of the developed world struggle with their own economies. For example, in recent years, Canada has been reducing its level of aid to other countries. How much foreign aid does Canada provide and how is it used? For the answers to these questions, see the Global Perspective box titled "Canadian Foreign Aid."

structural adjustment *A series of programs in developing countries designed to (1) reduce the size of their public sectors through privatization and/or expenditure reductions, (2) decrease their budget deficits, (3) control inflation, and (4) encourage private saving and investment through tax reform.*

Issues in Economic Development

Every developing country has a cultural, political, and economic history all its own and therefore confronts a unique set of problems. Still, it is possible to discuss common economic issues that each nation must face in its own particular way. These issues include rapid population growth, food shortages, agricultural output and pricing policies, and the Third World debt problem.

POPULATION GROWTH

The populations of the developing countries are estimated to be growing at a rate of about 1.7% per year. (Compare this with a population growth rate of only 0.5% per year in the industrial market economies.) If the Third World's population growth rate remains at 1.7%, it will take only 41 years for the population of the Third World to double from its 1990 level of 4.1 billion to over 8 billion by the year 2031. It will take the industrialized countries 139 years to double their populations. What is so immediately alarming about these numbers is that, given the developing countries' current economic problems, it is hard to imagine how they can possibly absorb so many more people in such a relatively short period.

Concern over world population growth is not new. The Reverend Thomas Malthus (who would one day become England's first professor of political economy) expressed his fears about the population increases he observed 200 years ago. Malthus believed that populations grow geometrically (that is, at a constant growth rate; thus the absolute size of the increase each year gets larger and larger), but that food supplies grow much more slowly because of the diminishing marginal productivity of land.[3] These two phenomena led Malthus to predict the increasing impoverishment of the world's people unless population growth could be slowed.

Malthus's fears for Europe and America proved unfounded, because he anticipated neither the technological changes that revolutionized agricultural productivity nor the eventual decrease in population growth rates in Europe and North America. But Malthus's prediction may have been right, only premature. Do the circumstances in the developing world now fit his predictions? While some contemporary observers believe that the Malthusian view is correct and that the earth's population will eventually grow to a level that the world's resources will be unable to support, others argue that technological change and demographic transitions (to slower population growth rates) will permit further increases in global welfare.

■ **The Consequences of Rapid Population Growth**   We know far less about the economic consequences of rapid population growth than you might expect. Conventional wisdom warns of dire economic consequences from the developing countries' "population explosion," but these predictions are difficult to substantiate with the available evidence. The rapid economic growth of North America, for example, was accompanied by relatively rapid population growth by historical standards. Nor has any slowing of population growth been necessary for the economic progress achieved by many of the newly industrialized countries. Nonetheless, population expansion in many of today's poorest nations is of a magnitude unprecedented in world history, as Figure 22.1 clearly shows. From the year 1 A.D., until the mid-1600s, populations grew slowly, at rates of only about 0.04% per year. Since then, and especially since 1950, rates have skyrocketed. Today, populations are growing at rates of over 3% per year in parts of the developing world.

Because growth rates like these have never occurred before the twentieth century, no one knows what impact they will have on future economic development. But a basic economic concern is that such rapid population growth may limit investment and restrain increases in labour productivity and income. Rapid population growth changes the age composition of a population, generating many dependent children relative to the number of productive working adults. Such a situation may diminish saving rates, and hence investment, as the immediate consumption needs of the young take priority over saving for the future.

Even if low saving rates are not a necessary consequence of rapid population growth, other economic problems remain. The ability to improve human capital through a broad range of programs, from infant nutrition to formal secondary education, may be severely limited if the population explosion continues. Such programs are most often the responsibility of the state, and governments that are already weak cannot be expected to improve their services under the burden of population pressures that rapidly increase demands for all kinds of public goods and services.

For example, the population growth rate of the northwest African country of Mali is projected by the World Bank to be 2.7% from 1998 to 2015. This is one

---

[3]*The law of diminishing marginal productivity says that with a fixed amount of some resource (land), additions of more and more of a variable resource (labour) will produce smaller and smaller gains in output.*

FIGURE 22.1

The Growth of World Population, Projected to 2020 A.D.

For thousands of years, population grew slowly. From 1 A.D. until the mid-1600s, population grew at about 0.04% per year. Since the Industrial Revolution, population growth has occurred at an unprecedented rate.

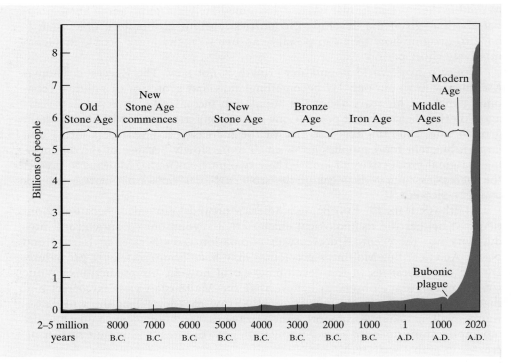

of the highest growth rates in the world, and it means that Mali's 1998 population of 10.6 million will grow to 16.7 million by 2015, nearly a 60% increase in only 17 years. This is a daunting prospect, and it is hard to imagine how in so little time Mali will be able to provide its population with the physical and human capital needed to maintain, let alone improve, already low standards of living.

■ **Causes of Rapid Population Growth**   Population growth is determined by the relationship between births and deaths—that is, between **fertility rates** and **mortality rates.** The **natural rate of population increase** is defined as the difference between the birth rate and the death rate. If the birth rate is 4%, for example, and the death rate is 3%, the population is growing at a rate of 1% per year.

Historically, low rates of population growth were maintained because of high mortality rates despite high levels of fertility. That is, families had many children, but average life expectancies were low, and many children died young. In Europe and North America, improvements in nutrition, in public health programs (especially those concerned with drinking water and sanitation services), and in medical practices have led to a drop in the mortality rate and hence to more rapid population growth. Eventually fertility rates also fell, returning population growth to a low and stable rate.

Public health programs and improved nutrition over the past 30 years have brought about precipitous declines in mortality rates in the developing nations also, the current AIDS epidemic in parts of Africa being a tragic exception. But fertility rates have not declined as quickly, and the result has been high natural rates of population growth. Reduced population growth depends to some extent on decreased birth rates, but attempts to lower fertility rates must take account of how different cultures feel and behave with regard to fertility.

Family planning and modern forms of birth control are important mechanisms for decreasing fertility, but by themselves such programs have had rather limited success in most countries where they have been tried. If family planning strategies are to be successful, they must make sense to the people who are supposed to benefit from them. The planners of such strategies must therefore understand why families in developing countries have so many children.

To a great extent, in developing countries people want large families because they believe they need them. Economists have attempted to understand fertility patterns in the developing countries by focusing on the determinants of the demand for children.

fertility rate *The birth rate. Equal to the number of births per year divided by the population multiplied by 100.*

mortality rate *The death rate. Equal to the number of deaths per year divided by the population multiplied by 100.*

natural rate of population increase *The difference between the birth rate and the death rate. It does not take migration into account.*

Canadian Foreign Aid

On a per capita basis, Canada is one of the more generous foreign aid donors among the G-7 countries, ranking well ahead of the United States for example. However, while Canada is part of a multi-country agreement with the United Nations that sets a target for government-provided donations at 0.7% of GNP, currently only about half that level of funding is being provided. Only four donor countries have recently been meeting this target: Denmark, the Netherlands, Norway, and Sweden.

The government funds provided through the Canadian International Development Agency (CIDA) have been used for projects from assistance for earthquake victims to the provision of vitamin A capsules to prevent child mortality and blindness. Many CIDA projects involve the education of children, in particular assuring equal access for boys and girls. In Upper Egypt, for example, Canada has been part of a project to set up

According to the Canadian International Development Agency, 113 million children in developing economies have never seen the inside of a school. Two-thirds of these are girls.

"girl-friendly" schools in 200 rural communities, as there are cultural barriers to girls attending school outside their own villages.

Sources: Canadian International Development Agency, "1998–99 Estimates"; "1999–00 Estimates"; "CIDA and Basic Education: A Priority (Backgrounder)" (All at **www.acdi-cida.gc.ca/**).

In agrarian societies, children are important sources of farm labour, and they may thus make significant contributions to household income. In societies without public old age support programs, children may also provide a vital source of income for parents when they become too old to support themselves. With the high value of children enhanced by high rates of infant mortality, it is no wonder that families try to have many children to ensure that a sufficient number will survive into adulthood.

Cultural and religious values also affect the number of children families want to have, but the economic incentives to have large families are extremely powerful. Only when the relationship between the costs and benefits of having children changes will fertility rates decline. Expanding the opportunities for women in an economy increases the opportunity costs of child-rearing (by giving women a more highly valued alternative to raising children) and often leads to lower birth rates. Government incentives for smaller families, such as subsidized education for families with fewer than three children, can have a similar effect. In general, rising incomes appear to decrease fertility rates, indicating that economic development itself reduces population growth rates.

Economic theories of population growth suggest that fertility decisions made by poor families should not be viewed as uninformed and uncontrolled. An individual family may find that having many children is a rational strategy for economic survival given the conditions in which it finds itself. This does not mean, however, that having many children is a net benefit to society as a whole. When a family decides to have a large number of children, it imposes costs on the rest of society; the children must be educated, their health provided for, and so forth. In other words, what makes sense for an individual household may create negative effects for the country as a whole.

> Any country that wants to slow its rate of population growth will probably find it necessary to have in place economic incentives for fewer children (perhaps by expanding the economic opportunities for women) as well as family planning programs.

FOOD SHORTAGES: ACTS OF NATURE OR HUMAN MISTAKES?

Television footage and newspaper photos portraying victims of famines in developing countries burn indelible images of starving people into the minds of the rest of the world. Such events forcefully dramatize the ongoing food crisis in many of the developing nations. The famines that have struck various parts of Africa and Asia in this century represent the most acute form of the chronic food shortage confronting the developing nations.

Pictures of parched fields might lead a casual observer to conclude that famines are ultimately acts of nature. After all, if the rains do not come or the locusts do, human beings can do little but sit and wait. But this simplistic view of food shortages fails to recognize the extent to which contemporary food crises are the result of human behaviour. Even such natural events as severe flooding can often be traced to the overharvesting of firewood, which denudes the landscape, increases soil erosion, and exacerbates spring floods.

Human behaviour is indeed a very strong factor in the inadequate distribution of available food to those who need it. India now grows enough grain to feed its vast population, for example, but malnutrition remains widespread because many people cannot afford to buy it. Other parts of the distribution problem involve poor storage facilities and transportation and communication barriers that prevent supplies from reaching those in need. World and domestic politics also heavily influence where, how, and whether food is available. War between the Hutu and the Tutsis in Rwanda in 1994 led to a mass exodus, loss of crops, and starvation. In the late 1990s, an inability to resolve its political and security disputes with Japan, South Korea, and the United States slowed food aid to a starving North Korea.

While severe food shortages are recognized chronic problems, developing countries often pursue farm policies that actually discourage agricultural production. Agricultural production in sub-Saharan Africa today is lower than it was 20 years ago. Economists believe that misguided agricultural policies are responsible for much of this decline.

AGRICULTURAL OUTPUT AND PRICING POLICIES

Few governments in either industrialized or developing countries have permitted market forces alone to determine agricultural prices. In Canada, the United States, and much of Europe, farm subsidies often encourage production that results in food surpluses rather than shortages. Some developing countries follow similar policies, maintaining high farm prices both to increase agricultural production and to maintain farm incomes. However, many developing countries follow a different route, offering farmers low prices for their output.

To appreciate the motives behind different pricing policies, you need to understand several things about the structure of agricultural markets in many developing countries. Often the government is the primary purchaser of both basic foodstuffs and export crops. The governments of some developing countries buy farm output and sell it to urban residents at government-controlled prices. By setting the prices they pay to farmers at low levels, the government can afford to sell basic foodstuffs to urban consumers at low prices. Governments often find this an attractive course of action because the direct political influence of the relatively small urban population typically far outweighs the influence of the majority who live in the countryside. Because most city dwellers spend about half their incomes on food, low consumer prices bolster the real incomes of the urban residents and help keep them content. Urban food riots have been common in developing nations over the years, and whether a government is allowed to exist may hinge on its food-pricing strategy.

Several African nations have come to rely on foreign support to help provide food for their people. Here, you see grain received from the French Red Cross by people in Rwanda.

While we can easily appreciate the political motives behind food pricing, policies that set artificially low prices have significant pitfalls. Farmers react to these prices—often set so low that farmers cannot cover their production costs—by reducing the amount of output they produce. In the city, meanwhile, excess demand for food at the artificially low ceiling prices imposed by the government may promote the emergence of black markets.

Many developing economies that have followed low agricultural pricing policies have experienced exactly these results. Until recently, for example, Mexico kept corn prices low in order to hold down the price of tortillas, the staple in the diet of much of Mexico's urban population. As a result, corn production fell as farmers switched to crops whose prices the government did not control. Domestic corn shortages became widespread, and corn had to be imported to meet urban demand.

■ **Agricultural Output: The Supply Side**   About 3% of Canada's population lives on farms. Yet this small fraction of the population is able to produce enough food for Canada's own needs and have enough left over to make Canada a substantial net exporter of agricultural products. In most developing economies, a single farmer can provide barely enough food to feed his or her own family. While differences in agricultural pricing policies account for a part of this gap, other factors are also at work. The problem is a shortage of inputs, including land, fertilizer, irrigation, machinery, new seed varieties, and agricultural extension services (which provide credit and technical advice to farmers).

Modern agricultural science has created a so-called **Green Revolution** (not to be confused with the "environmental revolution") based on new, high-yield varieties of wheat, rice, and other crops. Using new, faster-growing varieties instead of the single-crop plants they have relied upon for centuries, some farmers can now grow three crops of rice a year. In Mexico, under ideal conditions, "miracle" wheat has produced over seven tonnes per hectare, compared with traditional varieties that yield less than one tonne per hectare.

If the Green Revolution suggests that science can, in principle, solve world food shortages, the often disappointing history of developing countries' experiments with scientific agriculture offers a less optimistic outlook. Economic factors have greatly limited the adoption of Green Revolution techniques in developing countries. New seeds are expensive, and their cultivation requires the presence of many complementary inputs, including fertilizers and irrigation. With poorly developed rural credit markets, farmers often face interest rates so high that new technologies, regardless of their promise of higher crop yields, are out of reach or ultimately unprofitable. Given the costs and benefits of new inputs and the inherent riskiness of any new method of cultivation, it is not surprising that it has been difficult to get farmers in the developing countries to accept the advances of the Green Revolution.

Farmers in developing countries are also constrained by the amount of land they have to work. In some countries, high population density in the rural areas requires highly labour-intensive cultivation. In other countries, poor distribution of land decreases agricultural output. Throughout Latin America, for example, it is estimated that less than 2% of all landowners control almost 75% of the land under cultivation. Improved crop yields often follow land reforms that redistribute holdings, because owner households are often more productive than tenant farmers. Land reform has had positive effects on output in countries with economic systems as diverse as those of South Korea and the People's Republic of China.

Green Revolution *The agricultural breakthroughs of modern science, such as the development of new, high-yield crop varieties.*

Although acts of nature will always threaten agricultural production, human actions, especially policies designed to support the agricultural sector, can have a major impact on reducing the food problems of the developing world.

THIRD WORLD DEBT

In the 1970s, development experts worried about many crises facing the developing world, but the debt crisis was not among them. Within a decade, this situation

Chapter 22
Economic Growth in
Developing Countries

465

changed dramatically. The financial plight of countries such as Brazil, Mexico, and the Philippines had become front-page news. What alarmed those familiar with the debt situation was not only its potential impact on the developing countries, but a belief that it threatened the economic welfare of the developed countries as well.

Between 1970 and 1984, developing countries' combined debt increased by 1000%, to almost US$700 billion. As recession took hold in the economically advanced countries during the early 1980s, growth in the exports of the debtor countries slowed, and many found they could no longer pay back the money they owed. Part of the problem was that some of the borrowing had not been for sound investment with economic returns but instead had been for ill-advised megaprojects or military spending. Also, interest rates rose sharply during the early 1980s, largely due to tight monetary policy in the United States.

As the situation continued to deteriorate, many feared that debtor nations might simply repudiate their debts outright and default on their outstanding loans. When *default* (nonpayment) occurs with domestic loans, some collateral is usually available to cover all or part of the remaining debt. For loans to a country, however, such collateral is virtually impossible to secure. Given their extensive involvement with Third World borrowers, Western banks did not want to set in motion a pattern of international default. Nor did borrowers want to default. Leaders of the developing countries recognized that to default might result in the denial of access to developed-country banking facilities and to markets in the industrial countries. Such results would likely pose major obstacles to further development efforts.

Various countries rescheduled their debt as an interim solution. Under a **debt rescheduling** agreement, banks and borrowers negotiate a new schedule for the repayment of existing debt, often with some of the debt written off and with repayment periods extended. In return, borrowing countries are expected to sign an agreement with the International Monetary Fund to revamp their economic policies to provide incentives for higher export earnings and lower imports. This kind of agreement is often referred to as a **stabilization program,** and it usually requires painful austerity measures such as currency devaluations, a reduction in government expenditures, and an increase in tax revenues.

By the early 1990s, the debt crisis had lessened somewhat, largely as a result of reduced interest rates. The international economy subsequently revived somewhat, helping some countries to increase their export earnings. Other countries have benefited from new domestic policies. Still other countries, however, continue to face debt burdens that are unmanageable in the short run. Table 22.4 presents figures for a selected group of countries in 1998.

While there has perhaps been some improvement, the debt situation contributed to the two great economic crises of the 1990s. First in early 1995, the Mexican peso collapsed and Mexico was on the brink of defaulting on its obligations. Then beginning in 1997, a number of East Asian countries (including

debt rescheduling *An agreement between banks and borrowers through which a new schedule of repayments of the debt is negotiated; often some of the debt is written off and the repayment period is extended.*

stabilization program *An agreement between a borrower country and the International Monetary Fund in which the country agrees to revamp its economic policies to provide incentives for higher export earnings and lower imports.*

FAST FACTS

In the first six months of the East Asian economic crisis of 1997, the Indonesian rupiah depreciated by 80% against the Canadian dollar.

Table 22.4	**Total (Public and Private) External Debt for Selected Countries, 1998 (Billions of U.S. Dollars)**	
Country	**Total External Debt**	**Total External Debt as a Percentage of GNP**
Brazil	232.0	29
Russian Federation	183.6	62
Mexico	160.0	41
Indonesia	150.9	169
India	98.2	20
Thailand	86.2	76
Poland	47.7	28
Peru	32.4	55
Sudan	16.8	172
Nicaragua	6.0	295

Source: World Bank, *World Development Indicators, 2000,* Tables 4.18 and 4.19.

Thailand, Indonesia, and Korea) suffered huge capital outflows and very large reductions in the values of their currencies. In each case an international effort headed by the International Monetary Fund provided loans to the affected countries. As usual, the IMF loans came with strings, requiring structural adjustment policies that enforced government austerity. Perhaps there was an argument for such policies in the case of Mexico, as there had been substantial government borrowing. However, many leading economists thought that austerity was overdone in East Asia; many of the governments of the affected countries had been running a fiscally sound budget policy and, it was argued, the cutbacks required by the IMF deepened the impact of the crisis.

One economic lesson of recent years is that proper management of foreign capital in developing countries is essential. Much foreign borrowing was wasted on projects that had little chance of generating the returns necessary to pay back their initial costs. In other cases, domestic policies that used debt as a substitute for adjusting to new economic circumstances proved to be harmful in the long run. And, overall, much of the optimism about the prospects of the developing economies was inappropriate. Whatever else we may have learned from these mistakes, the debt crisis underscored the growing interdependence of all economies—rich and poor, large and small.

Summary

1. The economic problems facing the developing countries are often quite different from those confronting industrialized nations. The policy options available to governments may also differ. Nonetheless, the tools of economic analysis are as useful in understanding the economies of less developed countries as in understanding the Canadian economy.

Life in the Developing Countries: Population and Poverty

2. The central reality of life in the developing countries is poverty. Although there is considerable diversity across the developing nations, most of the people in most developing countries are extremely poor by Canadian standards.

Economic Development: Sources and Strategies

3. Almost all developing countries have a scarcity of physical capital relative to other resources, especially labour. The *vicious-circle-of-poverty hypothesis* argues that poor countries cannot escape from poverty because they cannot afford to postpone consumption (that is, to save) in order to make investments. In its crude form, the hypothesis is wrong inasmuch as some prosperous countries were at one time poorer than many developing countries are today. However, it is often difficult to mobilize savings efficiently in many developing nations.

4. Human capital—the stock of education and skills embodied in the workforce—plays a vital role in economic development.

5. Developing countries are often burdened by inadequate *social overhead capital,* ranging from poor public health and sanitation facilities to inadequate roads, telephones, and court systems. Such social overhead capital is often expensive to provide, and many governments are simply not in a position to undertake many useful projects because they are too costly.

6. Because developed economies are characterized by a large share of output and employment in the industrial sector, many developing countries seem to believe that development and industrialization are synonymous. In many cases, developing countries have pursued industry at the expense of agriculture, with mixed results. Recent evidence suggests that some balance between industry and agriculture leads to the best outcome.

7. *Import substitution* policies, a trade strategy that favours developing local industries that can manufacture goods to replace imports, were once very common in the developing countries. In general, such policies have not succeeded as well as those promoting open, export-oriented economies.

8. The failure of many central planning efforts has brought increasing calls for less government intervention and more market orientation in developing economies.

Issues in Economic Development

9. Rapid population growth is characteristic of many developing countries. Large families can be economically rational for parents who need support in

their old age, or because children offer an important source of labour. But the fact that parents find it in their interests to have large families does not mean that having many children is a net benefit to society as a whole. Rapid population growth can put a strain on already overburdened public services, such as education and health.

10. Food shortages in developing countries are not simply the result of bad weather. Public policies that depress the prices of agricultural goods, thereby lowering farmers' incentives to produce, are common throughout the developing countries, and human behaviour is very much behind the inadequate distribution of available food to those who need it. While acts of nature will always

threaten agricultural production, human actions, especially policies designed to support the agricultural sector, can have a major impact on reducing the food problems of the developing world.

11. Between 1970 and 1984 the debts of the developing countries grew tenfold. As recession took hold in the advanced countries during the early 1980s, growth in the exports of the debtor countries slowed, and many found they could no longer pay back money they owed. The prospect of loan defaults by Third World nations threatened the entire international financial system and transformed the debt crisis into a global problem. While Third World debt has not been in the press as much lately, the problem is still serious in many countries.

Review Terms and Concepts

brain drain 456

capital flight 455

debt rescheduling 466

export promotion 459

fertility rate 462

Green Revolution 465

import substitution 458

International Monetary Fund 459

mortality rate 462

natural rate of population increase 462

social overhead capital 457

stabilization program 466

structural adjustment 460

vicious-circle-of-poverty hypothesis 455

World Bank 459

Problem Set

1. Suppose you were a member of a citizen advisory panel to the Canadian International Development Agency and the agency was considering the following programs for a poor agricultural country. What questions would you ask about each project?

   a. A multi-year program that will distribute wheat made from Canadian flour, free of charge, to all citizens

   b. A program to sell farmers' output for them in the main city without charge, even for transport

   c. A program to provide free agricultural machineries (e.g., combines) to farmers

   d. A program to build rural schools

   e. A program to provide money to the country's university so that students would be able to attend without paying fees

   f. A program to improve the rural telephone system

2. The GDP of any country can be divided into two kinds of goods: capital goods and consumption goods. The proportion of national output devoted

to capital goods determines, to some extent, the nation's growth rate.

   a. Explain how capital accumulation leads to economic growth.

   b. Briefly describe how a market economy determines how much investment will be undertaken each period.

   c. "Consumption versus investment is a more painful conflict to resolve for developing countries." Comment.

   d. If you were the benevolent dictator of a developing country, what plans would you implement to increase per capita GDP?

3. "The main reason developing countries are poor is that they don't have enough capital. If we give them machinery, or build factories for them, we can greatly improve their situation." Comment.

4. "Poor countries are trapped in a vicious circle of poverty. For output to grow, they must accumulate capital. To accumulate capital, they must save (consume less than they produce). But because they are poor, they have little or no extra output

available for savings—it must all go to feed and clothe the present generation. Thus they are doomed to stay poor forever." Comment on each step in this argument.

5. If children are an "investment in the future," why do some developing countries offer incentives to households that limit the size of their families? Why are these incentives often ignored?

6. If you were in charge of economic policy for a developing country and wanted to promote rapid economic growth, would you choose to favour industry over agriculture? What about exports versus import substitution? In each case, briefly explain your reasoning. How do you explain the fact that many countries choose industry and a protectionist import-substitution policy?

7. "All we need to do is to promote rapid growth of per capita incomes in the developing countries and the poverty problems will take care of themselves." Comment.

8. "Famines are acts of God, resulting from bad weather or other natural disasters. There is nothing we can do about them except to send food relief after they occur." Explain why this position is inaccurate. Concentrate on agricultural pricing policies and distributional issues.

Appendix 22A	**Marxian Economics**

The People's Republic of China, Cuba, North Korea, and Vietnam are all examples of countries that have pursued a non-market-oriented approach toward development through a system sometimes called **communism**. Historically, "communism" has referred to an economic system in which the people control the means of production (capital and land) directly, without the intervention of a government or state. In the countries above, however, the government controls the means of production, so the system is more properly called "centrally planned socialism," wherein central planning refers to the way government manages the economy. A **socialist economy** is one in which most capital is owned by the government rather than by private citizens. A **capitalist economy** is one in which most capital is privately owned. Actual economies are never pure capitalist or pure socialist but somewhere in between.

The economic collapses of the former Soviet Union and the planned socialist systems of the Eastern European countries have convinced many that centrally planned economies do not perform well enough to be sustainable. Be that as it may, a socialist ideology was dominant in these countries for over 70 years during the twentieth century, and there remain a number of important developing economies committed to such a system—although often with more and more experimentation with markets.

The intellectual roots of the centrally planned system lie with Karl Marx. Here we briefly mention some of his most basic concepts. This does not pretend to be a complete introduction to his ideas (which would take a book in itself); it is only intended to help you understand some of the key terms. The definitions of those terms, which appear in bold type in this Appendix, will be found in the glossary below.

■ **Marxian Economics: An Overview** Stated simply, Marxian economic analysis concludes that the capitalist system is morally wrong and doomed to ultimate failure. Marx's work does not contain a blueprint for the operation of a socialist or communist economy. In fact, Marx did not write much about socialism; he wrote about capitalism. Published mostly after his death in 1883, his major work, the three-volume *Das Kapital*, is an extensive analysis of how capitalist economies function and how they are likely to develop over time. *The Communist Manifesto* (written with Friedrich Engels and published in 1848) and his other writings contain only a rough sketch of the socialist and communist societies that Marx predicted would ultimately replace capitalism.

Ironically, Marx's economics is based on the work of Adam Smith and David Ricardo, two economists who were staunch defenders of capitalism. But Marx uses the economics of Smith and Ricardo in a novel way. Instead of looking at capitalism from the perspective of human beings as consumers, Marx adopts the perspective of human beings as workers. Work, according to Marx, is the creative activity of humankind which allows human beings to reach their full potential. But under a capitalist system work becomes a means to an end: a source of profit to employers and a source of consumer goods for workers. One of Marx's main ethical objections to capitalism is that it degrades work and prevents people from realizing their full potential.

■ **Asymmetries of Power in Marx's Economic Theory** In contrast to the theory advanced in the rest of this text, Marx's theory claims that the capitalists and workers do not meet in the labour market as equals. This claim is based on two arguments. First, capitalists enjoy access to wealth through ownership of society's **means of**

production, Marx's term for land and capital. But individual workers have no way to make a living except by selling their labour power. Thus workers are forced to sell their capacity to work to capitalists if they are to survive. Capitalists, on the other hand, can survive by consuming their wealth. Second, Marx argues that unemployment is endemic to capitalism. This further strengthens the hand of the capitalist since the workers' choice is not between work and leisure but between work and unemployment. Thus Marx argues that there is an asymmetry of power in the labour market which allows capitalists to keep wages lower than they otherwise would be and to impose dehumanizing working conditions.

In the theory adopted in the rest of this text, competition may result in some equalization of power in the labour market. Capitalists compete for workers who can choose to work for the capitalist who offers the best terms and conditions of employment. According to this theory, competition results in improved wages and working conditions. In contrast, Marx's theory suggests that the existence of unemployment allows capitalists to compete by reorganizing production processes to get the maximum work from workers at the lowest wage. Thus the very process that results in lower prices for consumers also results, according to Marx, in deteriorating working conditions and worker alienation. **Alienation** is a term used by Marx to describe a condition of workers under capitalism in which they lose a sense of meaning or purpose in life because their main life activity—work—is under the control of their employer.

■ The Nature of Profit: The Marxian View

Like the theories of his predecessors Smith and Ricardo, Marx begins his treatment of profit by focusing on the ability of capitalist society to produce a **surplus** of goods and services above and beyond what is needed to keep the labour force clothed and fed at at least a subsistence level and beyond what is needed to replace capital goods and services consumed in the production process. This surplus can provide profits for the capitalists or improve the living standards of the workers. The distribution of surplus—and thus the share of this surplus which ends up as profit—depends, in Marx's theory, on the relative strengths of workers and capitalists.

Marx argues that unemployment keeps the workers in a weak bargaining position and thus allows capitalists to claim a relatively large share of the surplus as profit. Marx admits that in periods of rapid economic growth, labour demand grows faster than labour supply, increasing the wages of workers and reducing profits. But he argues that this trend will not persist indefinitely. Capitalists will respond to higher wages by replacing workers with capital and to lower profits by reducing levels of production and labour demand. Thus unemployment rises, restoring the bargaining strength of capitalists.

In summary, Marx sees profit as determined by the ability of a society to produce a surplus (which is based on the skills and knowledge of workers and the nature of the means of production with which they work) and the ability of those who own the means of production to capture part of that surplus. Unemployment keeps workers from acquiring the bargaining strength needed to capture the entire surplus. Moreover, implicit in Marx is the view that profit is unjust since profit is claimed by the capitalist based on ownership of capital goods and services and not on the basis of any real contribution of the capitalist to the production of surplus.

■ The Nature of Profit: The Neoclassical View

The bulk of this text has presented mainstream, or neoclassical, economic theory. At this point we should reflect briefly on the nature of profit in that model, because it is so different from the Marxian notion of profit.

Neoclassical economics views both capital and labour as productive factors of production that are bought and sold in perfectly competitive markets. If you have one worker digging a hole and you want a bigger hole faster, you can accomplish your goal by hiring a second worker or by giving the first worker a better shovel. Add labour and you get more product; add capital and you also get more product. According to neoclassical theory, every factor of production in a competitive market economy ends up being paid in accordance with the market value of its product. Profit-maximizing firms hire labour and capital as long as both contribute more to the final value of a product than they cost.

In sum, neoclassical theory views profit as the legitimate return to capital. Marx, however, saw profit as unjustly expropriated by nonproductive capitalists who own the means of production and thus are able to exploit labour.

■ Marx's Predictions

Marx concluded that capitalism was doomed. The essence of his argument was that the rate of profit has a natural tendency to fall over time. With the rate of profit falling, capitalists increase their exploitation of workers, pushing them deeper and deeper into misery. At the same time, the ups and downs of business cycles become more and more extreme. Ultimately, Marx believed, workers would rise up and overthrow the repressive capitalist system.

The theory that capitalism would ultimately collapse under its own weight was part of Marx's longer view of history. Capitalism had emerged naturally from a previous stage (*feudalism*) that had emerged from an even earlier stage (*ancient slavery*), and so forth. In the economic evolutionary process, Marx believed, capitalism would come to be replaced by socialism, which ultimately would be replaced by communism.

At each stage of economic evolution, Marx said, a

set of rules called the *social relations of production* defines the economic system. Contradictions and conflicts inevitably arise at each stage, and these problems are ultimately resolved in the establishment of a new set of social relations. The conflicts in capitalism include alienation, increasing exploitation, misery (or, as Marx called it, "emiserization"), and deeper and deeper business cycles.

It is clear that Marx was eager for the demise of capitalism. He advocated strong and powerful labour unions for two reasons. First, unions would push wages above subsistence and transfer some surplus value back to workers. Second, unions were a way of raising the consciousness of workers about their condition. Only through class consciousness, Marx believed, would workers be empowered to throw off the shackles of capitalism.

At the heart of Marx's ideas is the argument that private ownership and profit are unfair and unethical. Even if it could be demonstrated that the incentives provided by the institution of private property result in faster economic growth or improved material living standards, one still could reject capitalism on moral grounds, on ideological grounds, or on both.

Modern Marxian analysts do not necessarily agree with everything that Marx wrote, just as analysts who favour market-oriented capitalism do not agree with every writing of Adam Smith. But Marxian analysts are more skeptical of the value of the market and particularly large corporations in both developed and less-developed economies, and are especially concerned about the links between governments and corporations and the influence this relationship has upon the allocation of economic resources and power.

■ **Collapse of Centrally Planned Economies** Whatever one's ideology, it is difficult to disagree with the observation that centrally planned socialist economies have not performed as well as market-oriented capitalist ones. While many would argue, with justification, that these economies were not run according to Marxist ideals, some observers believe they see a connection to some aspects of Marx's thinking. Marx famously wrote, "From each according to his abilities, to each according to his needs." While this may be attractive in many ways, a system in which earnings are not strongly connected to individual work, innovation, and saving may not provide enough incentives for such activities.

A term used to describe this, in both Marxian and non-Marxian contexts, is the **tragedy of the commons**. In places where the land is held in common, there may be an incentive for each farmer to overgraze his or her animals, reaping the full benefits from the additional grazing while the costs are borne collectively. Similarly, accommodation that is rented may not be cared for as well as homes that are owned, and some people may litter or pollute because the gains are individual and the costs collective. In the context of collective ownership, an individual may not have incentive to work, innovate, or save sufficiently, because the gains from these activities will be dispersed across the population.

Countries such as China have decided to try to provide these kinds of incentives by using markets to an increasing degree so that individuals can increase their earnings by working more or through entrepreneurship; it remains to be seen whether this trend can be consistent with maintaining an overall socialist system.

Glossary

alienation A term used by Marx to describe a condition of workers under capitalism in which they lose a sense of meaning or purpose in life, because their main life activity—work—is under the control of their employer. 470

capitalist economy An economy in which most capital is privately owned. 469

communism An economic system in which the people control the means of production (capital and land) directly, without the intervention of a government or state. 469

means of production Marx's term for land and capital. 469

socialist economy An economy in which most capital is owned by the government rather than by private citizens. Also called *social ownership*. 469

surplus In the Marxian sense, the output of goods and services in excess of what is necessary to: (1) keep the labour force clothed and fed at at least a subsistence level and (2) replace capital goods and services consumed in the production process. 470

tragedy of the commons The idea that collective ownership may not provide the proper private incentives for efficiency because individuals do not bear the full costs of their own decisions but do enjoy the full benefits. 471

1. What is the "tragedy of the commons"? Suppose that all workers in a factory are paid the same wage and have no chance of being fired. Use the logic of the "tragedy of the commons" to predict the result. How would you expect workers to behave?

2. "The difference between Canada and the Soviet Union is that Canada has a capitalist economic system and the Soviet Union had a totalitarian government." Explain how this comparison confuses the economic and political aspects of the two societies. What words describe the former economic system of the Soviet Union?

3. Explain why Karl Marx thought profit was unjustified. Contrast the Marxian view with the neoclassical view of profit.

4. "There is no doubt that a centrally planned socialist system has the potential to grow faster than a market-oriented capitalist system." Do you agree or disagree?

International Trade Negotiations

International trade negotiations are difficult to understand using only the theory of international trade we have studied. The standard argument for free trade suggests that, regardless of what other countries do, Canada should want to reduce trade barriers of imports into Canada so that Canadian consumers will be able to buy goods as cheaply as possible and Canadian resources will be used most efficiently. (This is sometimes called the "Adam Smith principle": Never make at home something you can purchase more cheaply elsewhere.) But in trade negotiations Canada tries to protect its own trade barriers (e.g., tariffs and quotas on imports) while trying to get other countries to lower their trade barriers. Other countries behave similarly.

To understand this, suppose Canada decides to increase its import quota on shoes. Allowing more imported shoes will reduce the Canadian price of shoes, making shoe consumers better off. But those involved in producing Canadian shoes will be worse off. While in theory the gainers (consumers) could fully compensate the losers (workers in the shoe industry), that seldom happens. Moreover, each gainer gains a little (somewhat cheaper shoes) but while there are fewer losers, each loser can lose a lot (a job, for example). So a political party that removes a particular trade barrier may find that it loses all the votes of those who are harmed but doesn't gain many votes from those who have gained, because the gain per consumer is small.

Since governments do not like to lose votes, one way they respond is to try to negotiate deals with other countries in which there

Protesters at the WTO meeting in Seattle in 1999 succeeded in delaying the trade negotiations.

are also immediate gains to Canadian producers, so there are vote gains as well as vote losses. For example, at international trade negotiations Canada might be prepared to loosen its import quotas on shoes and textiles in order to preserve or enhance its markets for the goods it exports, from wheat to commuter jets.

A well-known example of a major trade negotiation was the Third Ministerial meeting of the World Trade Organization (WTO) held in Seattle, Washington in November 1999. In the so-called "Battle of Seattle," 50 000 protesters succeeded in delaying the start of the meetings by over a day; in trying to disperse them, the police used tear gas and arrested hundreds. Different protesters had different causes: some were protesting potential trade liberalization that would threaten some U.S. jobs, some were protesting labour conditions and environmental practices in plants owned by multinationals in devel-

oping countries, and others were protesting the fall in incomes of North American farmers because of European agricultural subsidies. However they were unified in the view that trade negotiators were moving toward "globalization" while ignoring their concerns and giving undue influence to the governments of large, developed countries and large corporations.

When the negotiations themselves got under way, there were two broad groups of issues. First, there were conflicts between the developed and the developing economies—what are sometimes called "North-South" issues, because most of the world's developed economies are in the northern hemisphere. There had already been disagreement over who would be the new WTO director-general, resolved in a compromise whereby the developed countries' candidate Michael Moore of New Zealand would hold the position until 2002 followed by Thailand's Supachai Panitchpakdi until 2005. Of the actual issues, one of the most important was the demand by developing countries for faster implementation of the developed countries' pledge to eliminate trade restrictions on textile imports.

The second main group of issues was agricultural, and it included the Canadian government's key concern, agricultural subsidies. For example it has been estimated that Canadian subsidies to wheat are about $12 per tonne, in contrast to $89 per tonne in the United States and over $200 per tonne in the European Union. The high foreign subsidies have driven down the price of wheat on world markets, and Canada's wheat farmers have seen their incomes collapse. Canada wants such subsidies eliminated.

The Seattle meetings ended without achieving its goal of an agenda that would lead to resolution of these issues. But trade agreements continue to be made, and naturally disputes continue to arise. Here are some examples:

- The WTO concluded that its rules prohibit Canada's admission of imported vehicles by the makers associated with the auto pact (Ford, General Motors, and DaimlerChrysler) without duty while charging a duty of 6.1% on imports from Japan and Europe. Canada complied by allowing the auto pact to expire and charging the duty on all imports, increasing the Canadian prices of cars made by Mercedes Benz (owned by DaimlerChrysler) and Jaguar (owned by Ford).
- The United States has long maintained that Canadian provinces sell timber rights to their producers at below-market prices. Under the threat of U.S. trade sanctions, Canada imposes an export tax on softwood lumber and the United States imposes high tariffs on amounts in excess of a given quota. It has been estimated that U.S. consumers pay 25% more for their lumber because of these restrictions.
- The WTO allowed Canada to impose $2 billion in trade sanctions against Brazil because of the latter's subsidies to its jet maker Embraer, a competitor of Canada's Bombardier. Such sanctions are the main enforcement mechanism behind the WTO, but their effect is limited in many cases. For example, while the ruling allows Canada to put huge tariffs on Brazilian shoes and fruit juice, that may simply mean Brazilian producers of those items switch to only slightly less attractive markets elsewhere; the sanctions do not hit the Brazilian jet industry at all, because Canada does not import Brazilian jets.

Questions for Analytical Thinking

1. One of the big issues at Seattle was the attempt by the United States to require employment standards (e.g., maximum workdays, workplace safety rules, and possibly minimum wages) on plants in developing countries that export to the United States. Explain the following statements:

   a. "The U.S. position could be driven as much by protectionist as humanitarian concerns."

   b. "The developing countries' resistance to employment standards does not necessarily show disregard for the welfare of their own citizens."

   c. "The real tragedy behind bad working conditions in many factories exporting from the developing to the developed world is that the alternatives available to the workers are probably worse."

2. The Treaty of Westphalia of the seventeenth century articulated a not-always-honoured principle that nations should not be subject to international interference in internal matters. If the principle were followed, under what circumstances might it be consistent for Canada to ban imports from another country because of that country's low employment standards or its low environmental standards?

Sources: Ian Jack, "EU, Japan Gang Up on Canada," *National Post*, August 12, 2000; Janet McFarland, "Negotiated Settlement Still Best Route for Canada, Brazil," *Globe and Mail*, August 24, 2000; Peter Morton, "U.S. Think-Tank Steps into Lumber Fray, Calls Pact 'Boondoggle,'" *National Post*, July 10, 2000; Scott Sinclair, "The WTO: What Happened in Seattle? What's Next in Geneva?" *Canadian Centre for Policy Alternatives Briefing Paper Series: Trade and Investment*, February 7, 2000.

Video Resource: "World Trade: The Subsidy War," *News in Review*, February 2000.

A major site for discussions of global trade issues is run by the Center of International Development at Harvard University (www.cid.harvard.edu/cidtrade/). The World Trade Organization's site (www.wto.org/) gives the perspective of that important body. For a Canadian federal government perspective, see the site of the Department of Foreign Affairs and International Trade (www.dfait-maeci.gc.ca/). Critical commentary can often be found at the Canadian Centre for Policy Alternatives site (www.policy alternatives.ca/). Articles supporting free trade can often be found at the Fraser Institute site (www.fraserinstitute.ca/).

The site of Bloomberg.com (www.bloomberg.com/) is a good place for international financial information including currencies, international interest rates, and the performance of stock markets around the world.

One place for collected statistics on world development is the Web site of the United Nations Development Programme Human Development Report (www.undp.org/hdro/indicators.html). The site does change somewhat from year to year, but a good place to start is with the latest Human Development Report, which is full of interesting comparisons across and within countries. There is much more, including commentary on the statistics and other documents such as the Universal Declaration of Human Rights.

Concise Dictionary of Economic Terminology

absolute advantage The advantage in the production of a product enjoyed by one country over another when it uses fewer resources to produce that product than the other country does.

accelerator effect The tendency for investment to increase when aggregate output increases and decrease when aggregate output decreases, thus accelerating the growth or decline of output.

actual investment The actual amount of investment that takes place; it includes items such as unplanned changes in inventories.

adjustment costs The costs that a firm incurs when it changes its production level—for example, the administration costs of laying off employees or the training costs of hiring new workers.

aggregate behaviour The behaviour of all households and firms taken together.

aggregate demand The total demand for goods and services in the economy.

aggregate demand (*AD*) curve A curve that shows the negative relationship between aggregate output (income) and the price level. Each point on the *AD* curve is a point at which both the goods market and the money market are in equilibrium.

aggregate income The total income received by all factors of production in a given period.

aggregate output The total quantity of goods and services produced (or supplied) in an economy in a given period.

aggregate output (income) (*Y*) A combined term used to remind you of the exact equality between aggregate output and aggregate income.

aggregate production function The mathematical representation of the relationship between inputs and national output, or gross domestic product.

aggregate supply The total supply of all goods and services in an economy.

aggregate supply (*AS*) curve A graph that shows the relationship between the aggregate quantity of output supplied by all firms in an economy and the overall price level.

animal spirits of entrepreneurs A phrase coined by Keynes to describe investors' feelings.

appreciation An increase in value, for example, in the value of one currency relative to another.

automatic destabilizers Revenue and expenditure items in the federal budget that automatically change with the economy in such a way as to destabilize GDP.

automatic stabilizers Revenue and expenditure items in the federal budget that automatically change with the state of the economy in such a way as to stabilize GDP.

autonomous variable A variable that is assumed not to depend on the state of the economy—that is, it is taken as given.

average propensity to consume (*APC*) The proportion of income households spend on consumption. Determined by dividing consumption by income.

balance of payments The record of a country's transactions in goods, services, and assets with the rest of the world; also the record of a country's sources (supply) and uses (demand) of foreign exchange.

balance of trade A country's exports minus its imports.

balance on capital account The sum of the net flow of Canadian claims on nonresidents and the net flow of Canadian liabilities to nonresidents, measured in a given period.

balance on current account The merchandise balance of trade plus net exports of services, plus net investment income, plus net transfer payments.

balanced-budget multiplier The ratio of change in the equilibrium level of output to a change in government spending where the change in government spending is balanced by a change in taxes so as not to change the surplus or deficit. The balanced-budget multiplier is equal to 1: the change in *Y* resulting from the change in *G* and the equal change in *T* is exactly the same size as the initial change in *G* or *T* itself.

Bank of Canada The central bank of Canada.

Bank rate The interest rate that private banks pay to borrow from the Bank of Canada.

barter The direct exchange of goods and services for other goods and services.

base year The year which provides reference values. For example, in the calculation of real GDP, the year which provides the prices that are used to value the outputs of all other years.

black market A market in which illegal trading takes place at market-determined prices.

brain drain The tendency for talented people from developing countries to become educated in a developed country and remain there after graduation.

budget deficit The difference between what a government spends and what it collects in net taxes in a given period: $G - T$.

budget surplus Net taxes minus government purchases. $T - G$. Also called the *budget balance*.

business cycle The cycle of short-term ups and downs in the economy.

Canada-U.S. Free Trade Agreement An agreement, which came into effect January 1, 1989, in which Canada and the United States agreed to eliminate all barriers to trade between the two countries over a ten-year period.

capital Things that have already been produced that are in turn used to produce other goods and services.

capital flight The tendency for capital to leave developing countries in search of higher rates of return elsewhere.

capital market The input/factor market in which households supply their savings, for interest or for claims to future profits, to firms that demand funds in order to buy capital goods.

capital-intensive technology Technology that relies heavily on capital rather than human labour.

ceteris paribus Literally, "other things being equal." Used to analyze the relationship between two variables while the values of other variables are held unchanged.

change in business inventories The amount by which firms' inventories change during a period. Inventories are the goods that firms produce now but intend to sell later.

change in inventory Production minus sales.

circular flow A diagram showing the income received and payments made by each sector of the economy.

command economy An economy in which a central authority or agency draws up a plan that establishes what will be produced and when, sets production goals, and makes rules for distribution.

commodity monies Items used as money that also have intrinsic value in some other use.

comparative advantage The advantage in the production of a product enjoyed by one country over another when that product can be produced at lower cost in terms of other goods than it could be in the other country.

complements, complementary goods Goods that "go together"; a decrease in the price of one results in an increase in demand for the other, and vice versa.

constant dollars Measuring in constant prices.

consumer goods Goods produced for present consumption.

consumer price index (CPI) A price index calculated every month using the price of a standardized bundle of goods meant to represent the consumption of the average consumer.

consumer sovereignty The idea that consumers ultimately dictate what will be produced (or not produced) by choosing what to purchase (and what not to purchase).

consumption function The relationship between consumption and income.

contraction, recession, or slump The period in the business cycle from a peak down to a trough, during which output and employment fall.

contractionary fiscal policy A decrease in government spending or an increase in net taxes.

contractionary monetary policy A policy to decrease the money supply.

Corn Laws The tariffs, subsidies, and restrictions enacted by the British Parliament in the early nineteenth century to discourage imports and encourage exports of grain.

corporate bonds Promissory notes issued by corporations when they borrow money.

corporate income taxes Taxes levied on the net incomes of corporations.

corporate profits The income of corporate businesses (either paid out as dividends or ploughed back into the firm as retained earnings).

corporation A form of business organization resting on a legal charter that establishes the corporation as an entity separate from its owners. Owners hold shares and are liable for the firm's debts only up to the limit of their investment, or share, in the firm.

cost shock, or supply shock A change in costs that shifts the aggregate supply (*AS*) curve.

cost-of-living adjustments (COLAs) Contract provisions that tie wages to changes in the cost of living. The greater the inflation rate, the more wages are raised.

cost-push, or supply-side, inflation Inflation caused by an increase in costs.

crowding-out effect The tendency for increases in government spending to cause reductions in private investment spending.

currency debasement The decrease in the value of money that occurs when its supply is increased rapidly.

current dollars The current prices that one pays for goods and services.

cyclical deficit The deficit that occurs because of a downturn in the business cycle.

cyclical unemployment The increase in unemployment that occurs during recessions and periods of slow economic growth. Cyclical unemployment + Frictional unemployment + Structural unemployment = Actual rate of unemployment.

debt rescheduling An agreement between banks and borrowers through which a new schedule of repayments of the debt is negotiated; often some of the debt is written off and the repayment period is extended.

deflation A decrease in the overall price level.

demand curve A graph illustrating how much of a given product a household would be willing to buy at different prices.

demand schedule A table showing how much of a given product a household would be willing to buy at different prices.

demand-pull inflation Inflation that is initiated by an increase in aggregate demand.

deposit multiplier The multiple by which deposits can increase for every dollar increase in new reserves equal to 1 divided by the reserve ratio.

depreciation A decrease in value, for example, in the value of one currency relative to another.

depreciation The amount by which an asset's value falls in a given period.

depression A prolonged and deep recession. The precise definitions of prolonged and deep are debatable.

descriptive economics The compilation of data that describe phenomena and facts.

desired, or planned, investment Those additions to capital stock and inventory that are planned by firms.

desired, or optimal, level of inventories The level of inventory at which the extra cost (in lost sales) from lowering inventories by a small amount is just equal to the extra gain (in interest revenue and decreased storage costs).

discouraged-worker effect The decline in the measured unemployment rate that results when people who want to work but cannot find jobs grow discouraged and stop looking, thus dropping out of the ranks of the unemployed and the labour force.

discretionary fiscal policy Changes in taxes or spending that are the result of deliberate changes in government policy.

disposable, or after-tax, income (Y_d) Total income minus net taxes: $Y - T$.

dividends The portion of a corporation's profits that the firm pays out each period to shareholders. Also called *distributed profits*.

dumping Takes place when a firm or industry sells products on the world market at prices below the cost of production.

durable goods Goods that last a relatively long time, such as cars and household appliances.

easy monetary policy Central bank policies that expand the money supply.

economic growth An increase in the total output of an economy. It occurs when a society acquires new resources or when it learns to produce more using existing resources. Defined by some economists as an increase of real GDP per capita.

economic integration Occurs when two or more countries join to form a free trade zone.

economic problem Given scarce resources, how exactly do large, complex societies go about answering the three basic economic questions?

economic theory A statement or set of related statements about cause and effect, action and reaction.

economics The study of how individuals and societies choose to use the scarce resources that nature and previous generations have provided.

efficiency Allocative efficiency—the condition in which the economy is producing what people want at the least possible cost.

efficiency wage theory An explanation for unemployment that holds that the productivity of workers increases with the wage rate. If this is so, firms may have an incentive to pay wages above the market-clearing rate.

empirical economics The collection and use of data to test economic theories.

employed Any person 15 years old or older (1) who works for pay or profit, either for someone else or in his or her own business, (2) who works without pay in a family enterprise, or (3) who has a job but has been temporarily absent, with or without pay.

entrepreneur A person who organizes, manages, and assumes the risks of a firm, taking a new idea or a new product and turning it into a successful business.

equilibrium The condition that exists when quantity supplied and quantity demanded are equal. At equilibrium, there is no tendency for price to change. In the macroeconomic goods market, equilibrium occurs when planned aggregate expenditure is equal to aggregate output.

equilibrium price level The point at which the aggregate demand and aggregate supply curves intersect.

equity Fairness.

European Union (EU) The European trading bloc composed of Austria, Belgium, Denmark, Finland, France, Germany, Greece, Ireland, Italy, Luxembourg, the Netherlands, Portugal, Spain, Sweden, and the United Kingdom.

excess demand The condition that exists when quantity demanded exceeds quantity supplied at the current price.

excess capital Capital not needed to produce the firm's current level of output.

excess labour Labour not needed to produce the firm's current level of output.

excess reserves The difference between a bank's actual reserves and its desired reserves.

excess supply The condition that exists when quantity supplied exceeds quantity demanded at the current price.

exchange rate The price of one country's currency in terms of another currency.

excise taxes Taxes on specific commodities.

expansion or boom The period in the business cycle from a trough up to a peak, during which output and employment rise.

expansionary fiscal policy An increase in government spending or a reduction in net taxes.

expansionary monetary policy A policy to increase the money supply.

expenditure approach A method of computing GDP that measures the amount spent on all final goods during a given period.

explicit contracts Employment contracts that stipulate workers' wages, usually for a period of one to three years.

export promotion A trade policy designed to encourage exports.

export subsidies Government payments made to domestic firms to encourage exports.

factor endowments The quantity and quality of labour, land, and natural resources of a country.

factors of production The inputs into the production process. Land, labour, and capital are the three key factors of production.

fallacy of composition The belief that what is true for a part is necessarily true for the whole.

farm income Income earned by farms.

favoured customers Those who receive special treatment from dealers during crises.

federal budget The budget of the federal government.

federal debt The total of all accumulated federal deficits minus surpluses over time, or the total amount owed by the federal government.

federal deficit The difference between what the federal government spends and what it collects in taxes in a given period ($G - T$)

fertility rate The birth rate. Equal to the number of births per year divided by the population multiplied by 100.

fiat, or token, money Items designated as money that are intrinsically worthless.

final goods and services Goods and services produced for final use.

financial intermediaries Banks and other institutions that act as a link between those who have money to lend and those who want to borrow money.

fine tuning A phrase that refers to the government's role in regulating inflation and unemployment.

firm An organization that transforms resources (inputs) into products (outputs). Firms are the primary producing units in a market economy.

fiscal drag The negative effect on the economy that occurs when average tax rates increase because taxpayers have moved into higher income brackets during an expansion.

fiscal policy The spending and taxing policies used by the government to influence the economy.

fixed capital formation Investment in durable capital assets. Includes firms' purchases of machinery as well as individuals' purchases of new housing.

fixed exchange rate A government policy that sets the exchange rate at a given level.

fixed-weight price index A price index calculated by pricing the same bundle of goods each period.

flexible (or floating) exchange rate A government policy that does not fix the exchange rate.

foreign exchange All currencies other than the domestic currency of a given country.

freely (or pure) floating exchange rate A market-determined exchange rate policy in which no consideration is given to the level of the exchange rate in monetary policy decisions.

frictional unemployment The portion of unemployment that is due to the normal working of the labour market; used to denote short-run job/skill matching problems.

full employment A condition in which all resources available for use are being used.

full-employment budget What the federal budget would be if the economy were producing at a full-employment level of output.

GDP deflator Current dollar (nominal) GDP divided by constant dollar (real) GDP, converted to a percentage by multiplying by 100. Also called the GDP implicit price deflator or the GDP price index.

General Agreement on Tariffs and Trade (GATT) An international agreement signed by Canada and 22 other countries in 1947 to promote the liberalization of foreign trade. Replaced by the World Trade Organization (WTO).

goods market The market in which goods and services are exchanged and in which the equilibrium level of aggregate output is determined.

government bonds, notes, and Treasury bills Promissory notes issued by the federal government when it borrows money.

government interest payments Cash payments made by the government to those who own government bonds.

government purchases of goods and services (G) Expenditures by federal, provincial, and local governments for final goods and services.

government spending multiplier The ratio of the change in the equilibrium level of output to a change in government spending.

government transfer payments Cash payments made by the government directly to households for which no current services are received. They include old age security benefits, employment insurance, and welfare payments.

Great Depression The period of severe economic contraction and high unemployment that began in 1929 and continued throughout the 1930s.

Green Revolution The agricultural breakthroughs of modern science, such as the development of new, high-yield crop varieties.

gross domestic product (GDP) The total market value of all final goods and services produced within a given period by factors of production located within a country.

gross investment The total value of all newly produced capital goods (plant, equipment, housing, and inventory) produced in a given period.

gross national product (GNP) The total market value of all final goods and services produced within a given period by factors of production owned by a country's residents, regardless of where the output is produced.

gross private investment (I) The purchase of new capital by the private sector—housing, plants, equipment, and inventory.

Heckscher-Ohlin theorem A theory that explains the existence of a country's comparative advantage by its factor endowments: a country has a comparative advantage in the production of a product if that country is relatively well endowed with inputs used intensively in the production of that product.

households The consuming units in an economy.

hyperinflation A period of very rapid increases in the overall price level.

identity Something that is true at all times.

implementation lag The time that it takes to put the desired policy into effect once economists and policy makers recognize that the economy is in a boom or a slump.

import substitution An industrial trade strategy that favours developing local industries that can manufacture goods to replace imports.

income The sum of all a household's wages, salaries, profits, interest payments, rents, and other forms of earnings in a given period of time. It is a flow measure.

income approach A method of computing GDP that measures the income—wages, rents, interest, and profits—received by all factors of production in producing final goods.

index A measure of a group of variables.

indirect taxes Taxes like sales taxes, customs duties, and licence fees.

inductive reasoning The process of observing regular patterns from raw data and drawing generalizations from them.

Industrial Revolution The period in England during the late eighteenth and early nineteenth centuries in which new manufacturing technologies and improved transportation gave rise to the modern factory system and a massive movement of the population from the countryside to the cities.

industry All the firms that produce a similar product. The boundaries of a "product" can be drawn very widely ("agricultural products"), less widely ("dairy products"), or very narrowly ("cheese"). The term *industry* can be used interchangeably with the term *market*.

industry price indexes Measures of prices that producers receive for products at all stages in the production process.

infant industry A young industry which may need temporary protection from competition from the established industries of other countries in order to develop an acquired comparative advantage.

inferior goods Goods for which demand falls when income rises.

inflation An increase in the overall price level.

inflation rate The percentage change in the price level.

innovation The use of new knowledge to produce a new product or to produce an existing product more efficiently.

input or factor markets The markets in which the resources used to produce products are exchanged.

interest The fee that a borrower pays to a lender for the use of his or her funds. Almost always expressed as an annual rate.

interest income The difference between the interest households receive (not including interest on the public debt) and the interest households pay out.

interest rate The annual interest payment on a loan expressed as a percentage of the loan. Equal to the amount of interest received per year divided by the amount of the loan.

interest rate parity The condition that, given equal risk, the interest rate paid on securities in country A will equal the interest rate paid on securities in country B plus the expected rate of appreciation of the currency of B relative to the currency of A.

interest sensitivity or insensitivity of planned investment The responsiveness of planned investment spending to changes in the interest rate. *Interest sensitivity* means that planned investment spending changes a great deal in response to changes in the interest rate; *interest insensitivity* means little or no change in planned investment as a result of changes in the interest rate.

intermediate goods Goods that are produced by one firm for use in further processing by another firm.

International Monetary Fund An international agency whose primary goals are to stabilize international exchange rates and to lend money to countries that have problems financing their international transactions.

international sector From any one country's perspective, the economies of the rest of the world.

invention An advance in knowledge.

inventory investment Occurs when a firm produces more output than it sells within a given period.

inventory valuation adjustment The increase in the value of inventories during the year, subtracted in the calculation of net domestic income because it is included in profits, but does not correspond to new production.

investment Purchases by firms of new buildings and equipment and additions to inventories, all of which adds to firms' capital stock.

J-curve effect Following a currency depreciation, a country's balance of trade may decline before it increases. The graph showing this effect is shaped like the letter *J*, hence the name "J-curve effect."

labour demand curve A graph that illustrates the amount of labour that firms want to employ at the particular wage rate.

labour force The number of people employed plus the number of unemployed.

labour income Wages, salaries, and fringe benefits paid to households by firms and government.

labour market The input/factor market in which households supply work for wages to firms that demand labour.

labour productivity Output per worker-hour; the amount of output produced by an average worker in one hour.

labour supply curve A graph that illustrates the amount of labour that households want to supply at the particular wage rate.

labour-force participation rate The ratio of the labour force to the total population 15 years. old or older.

labour-intensive technology Technology that relies heavily on human labour rather than capital.

Laffer Curve The graph, named after Arthur Laffer, with the tax rate measured on the vertical axis and tax revenue measured on the horizontal axis. The Laffer Curve shows that there is some tax rate beyond which the supply response is large enough to lead to a decrease in tax revenue for further increases in the tax rate.

laissez-faire economy Literally from the French: "allow [them] to do." An economy in which individual people and firms pursue their own self-interests without any central direction or regulation.

land market The input/factor market in which households supply land or other real property in exchange for rent.

law of demand The negative relationship between price and quantity demanded. As price rises, quantity demanded decreases. As price falls, quantity demanded increases.

law of one price If the costs of transportation are small, the price of the same good in different countries should be roughly the same.

law of supply The positive relationship between price and quantity of a good supplied. An increase in market price will lead to an increase in quantity supplied, and a decrease in market price will lead to a decrease in quantity supplied.

legal tender Money that a government has required to be accepted in settlement of debts.

life-cycle theory of consumption A theory of household consumption: households make lifetime consumption decisions based on their expectations of lifetime income.

liquidity property of money The property of money that makes it a good medium of exchange as well as a store of value. It is portable and readily accepted and thus easily exchanged for goods.

Lucas supply function The supply function, named after Robert Lucas, that embodies the idea that output (Y) depends on the difference between the actual price level and the expected price level.

M1, or narrow money Money that can be directly used for transactions. M1 equals currency held outside banks plus demand deposits.

M2, or broad money M1 plus notice deposits.

macroeconomics The branch of economics that examines the economic behaviour of aggregates — income, employment, output, and so on — on a national scale and the effects of government economic policy on these aggregates.

managed (or dirty) floating exchange rate A policy part way between fixed exchange rates and purely floating exchange rates in which the central bank may sometimes use its monetary instruments to influence the exchange rate but has no announced commitment to a specific level of the exchange rate.

marginal propensity to consume (MPC) That fraction of a change in income that is consumed, or spent.

marginal propensity to import (MPM) The change in imports caused by a $1 change in income.

marginal propensity to save (MPS) That fraction of a change in income that is saved.

market The institution through which buyers and sellers interact and engage in exchange.

market demand The sum of all the quantities of a good or service demanded per period by all the households buying in the market for that good or service.

market organization The way an industry is structured. Structure is defined by how many firms there are in an industry, whether products are differentiated or are virtually the same, whether or not firms in the industry can control prices or wages, and whether or not competing firms can enter and leave the industry freely.

market supply The sum of all that is supplied each period by all producers of a single product.

means of production Marx's term for land and capital.

medium of exchange, or means of payment What sellers generally accept and buyers generally use to pay for goods and services.

merchandise balance of trade A country's merchandise exports minus its merchandise imports.

microeconomics The branch of economics that examines the functioning of individual industries and the behaviour of individual decision-making units—business firms and households — and the effects of government economic policy on these units.

minimum wage laws Laws that set a floor for wage rates—that is, a minimum hourly rate for any kind of labour.

model A formal statement of a theory. Usually a mathematical statement of a presumed relationship between two or more variables.

modern economic growth The rapid and sustained increase in real output per capita that began in the Western world with the Industrial Revolution.

monetary policy The behaviour of the Bank of Canada regarding the money supply.

money market The market in which financial instruments are exchanged and in which the equilibrium level of the interest rate is determined.

money multiplier The multiple by which the total money supply (currency outside banks plus bank deposits) increases for each dollar increase in new reserves; equal to the deposit multiplier in the simple case where all money is held as bank deposits.

monopolistic competition An industry structure (or market organization) in which many firms compete, producing similar but slightly differentiated products. There are close substitutes for the product of any given firm. Monopolistic competitors have some control over price. Price and quality competition follow from product differentiation. Entry and exit are relatively easy, and success invites new competitors.

monopoly An industry structure (or market organization) in which there is only one large firm that produces a product for which there are no close substitutes. Monopolists can set prices but are subject to market discipline. For a monopoly to continue to exist, something must prevent potential competitors from entering the industry and competing for profits.

mortality rate The death rate. Equal to the number of deaths per year divided by the population multiplied by 100.

movement along a demand curve What happens when a change in price causes quantity demanded to change.

multiplier The ratio of the change in the equilibrium level of output to a change in some autonomous variable.

national income and expenditure accounts Data collected and published by the government describing the various components of aggregate income and output in the economy.

natural rate of population increase The difference between the birth rate and the death rate. It does not take migration into account.

natural rate of unemployment The sum of frictional unemployment and structural unemployment.

near monies Close substitutes for cash and chequing deposits.

negative demand shock Something that causes a negative shift in consumption or investment schedules or that leads to a decrease in net exports.

net domestic income The total income earned by the factors of production located in a country.

net domestic product GDP minus depreciation.

net exports (EX − IM) The difference between exports (sales to foreigners of Canadian-produced goods and services) and imports (Canadian purchases of goods and services from abroad). The figure can be positive or negative.

net exports of goods and services (EX − IM) The difference between a country's total exports and total imports.

net income The profits of a firm.

net investment Gross investment minus depreciation.

net national income Net domestic income plus investment income from nonresidents minus investment income to nonresidents.

net taxes (T) Taxes paid by firms and households to the government minus transfer payments made to households by the government.

nominal GDP Gross domestic product measured in current dollars.

nominal interest rate Another name for the actual interest rate. The word "nominal" is added to the term to distinguish it from the real interest rate.

nominal wage rate The wage rate in current dollars.

nondurable goods Goods that are used up fairly quickly, such as gasoline.

nonlabour, or nonwage, income Any income that is received from sources other than working—inheritances, interest, dividends, transfer payments, and so on.

normal goods Goods for which demand goes up when income is higher and for which demand goes down when income is lower.

normative economics An approach to economics that analyzes outcomes of economic behaviour, evaluates them as good or bad, and may prescribe courses of action.

North American Free Trade Agreement (NAFTA) An agreement signed by Canada, the United States, and Mexico in which the three countries agreed to establish all of North America as a free trade zone.

not in the labour force People who are not looking for work, either because they do not want a job or because they have given up looking.

Ockham's razor The principle that irrelevant detail should be cut away.

Okun's Law The theory, put forth by Arthur Okun, that the unemployment rate decreases about one percentage point for every 2.5% increase in real GDP relative to potential GDP. Later research and data have shown that the relationship between output and unemployment is not as stable as Okun's "law" predicts.

oligopoly An industry structure (or market organization) with a small number of (usually) large firms producing products that range from highly differentiated (automobiles) to standardized (steel). In general, entry of new firms into an oligopolistic industry is difficult but possible.

open market operations The purchase and sale by the Bank of Canada of government securities in the open market.

opportunity cost That which we forgo, or give up, when we make a choice or a decision.

outputs Usable products.

partnership A form of business organization in which there is more than one proprietor. The owners are responsible jointly and separately for the firm's obligations.

payroll taxes Taxes levied at a flat rate on wages and salaries. Proceeds support various government-administrated social-benefit programs, including the social insurance system and the unemployment benefits system.

per capita GDP or GNP A country's GDP or GNP divided by its population.

perfect competition An industry structure (or market organization) in which there are many firms, each small relative to the industry, producing virtually identical products and in which no firm is large enough to have any control over prices. In perfectly competitive industries, new competitors can freely enter and exit the market.

perfect substitutes Identical products.

permanent income The average level of one's expected future income stream.

personal consumption expenditures (C) A major component of GDP: expenditures by consumers on goods and services.

personal disposable income Personal income minus personal taxes.

personal income The total income of households, calculated as net national income plus transfers to households less retained earnings.

personal saving The amount of disposable income that is left after total personal spending in a given period.

personal saving rate The percentage of personal disposable income that is saved. If the personal saving rate is low, households are spending a large amount relative to their incomes; if it is high, households are spending cautiously.

Phillips Curve A graph showing the relationship between the inflation rate and the unemployment rate.

planned aggregate expenditure (*AE*) The total amount the economy plans to spend in a given period. Equal to consumption plus planned investment: $AE \equiv C + I$.

plant and equipment investment Purchases by firms of additional machines, factories, or buildings within a given period.

policy mix The combination of monetary and fiscal policies in use at a given time.

positive economics An approach to economics that seeks to understand behaviour and the operation of systems without making judgments. It describes what exists and how it works.

post hoc, ergo propter hoc Literally, "after this (in time), therefore because of this." A common error made in thinking about causation: if event A happens before event B happens, it is not necessarily true that A caused B.

potential output, or potential GDP The level of aggregate output that can be sustained in the long run without inflation.

price The amount that a product sells for per unit. It reflects what society is willing to pay.

price ceiling A maximum price that sellers may charge for a good, usually set by government.

price rationing The process by which the market system allocates goods and services to consumers when quantity demanded exceeds quantity supplied.

price stability A condition in which there is little inflation in prices.

price surprise The actual price level minus the expected price level.

private sector Includes all independently owned profit-making firms, nonprofit organizations, and households; all the decision-making units in the economy that are not part of the government.

producers Those people or groups of people, whether private or public, who transform resources into usable products.

product or output markets The markets in which goods and services are exchanged.

production The process by which resources are transformed into useful forms.

production possibility frontier (*ppf*) A graph that shows all the combinations of goods and services that can be produced if all of society's resources are used efficiently.

productivity, or labour productivity Output per worker hour; the amount of output produced by an average worker in one hour.

productivity of an input The amount of output produced per unit of an input.

profit The difference between revenues and costs.

proprietorship A form of business organization in which a person simply sets up to provide goods or services at a profit. In a proprietorship, the proprietor (or owner) is the firm. The assets and liabilities of the firm are the owner's assets and liabilities.

protection The practice of shielding a sector of the economy from foreign competition.

public, or social, goods Goods or services whose benefits are social, or collective.

public sector Includes all agencies at all levels of government—federal, provincial, and local.

purchasing power parity theory A theory of international exchange that holds that exchange rates are set so that the price of similar goods in different countries is the same.

quantity demanded The amount (number of units) of a product that a household would buy in a given period if it could buy all it wanted at the current market price.

quantity supplied The amount of a particular product that a firm would be willing and able to offer for sale at a particular price during a given time period.

quantity theory of money The theory based on the identity $M \cdot V \equiv P \cdot Y$ and the assumption that the velocity of money (*V*) is constant (or virtually constant).

queuing A nonprice rationing mechanism that uses waiting in line as a means of distributing goods and services.

quota A limit on the quantity of imports.

ration coupons Tickets or coupons that entitle individual persons to purchase a certain amount of a given product per month.

rational-expectations hypothesis The hypothesis that people know the "true model" of the economy and that they use this model to form their expectations of the future.

real business cycle theory An attempt to explain business-cycle fluctuations under the assumptions of complete price and wage flexibility and rational expectations. It emphasizes shocks to technology and other shocks.

real GDP A measure of GDP that removes the effects of price changes from changes in nominal GDP.

real interest rate The difference between the interest rate and the inflation rate.

real wage rate The amount that the nominal wage rate can buy in terms of goods and services.

real wealth, or real balance, effect The change in consumption brought about by a change in real wealth that results from a change in the price level.

recession Roughly, a period in which real GDP declines for at least two consecutive quarters.

recognition lag The time it takes for policy makers to recognize the existence of a boom or a slump.

reserve ratio The percentage of its total deposits that a bank chooses to set aside as reserves.

reserves The deposits that a bank has at the Bank of Canada plus its cash on hand.

resources or inputs Anything provided by nature or previous generations that can be used directly or indirectly to satisfy human wants.

response lag The time that it takes for the economy to adjust to the new conditions after a new policy is implemented; the lag that occurs because of the operation of the economy itself.

retained earnings The profits that a corporation keeps, usually for the purchase of capital assets. Also called *undistributed profits*.

run on a bank Occurs when many of those who have claims on a bank (deposits) present them at the same time.

saving (*S*) The part of its income that a household does not consume in a given period. Distinguished from *savings*, which is the current stock of accumulated saving.

seasonal adjustment A statistical process designed to remove usual seasonal variations from a data series.

semidurable goods Goods such as clothing that do not last as long as durable goods but that last longer than nondurable goods.

services The things we buy that are not classed as goods, such as legal and dental services.

share of stock A certificate of partial ownership of a corporation that entitles the holder to a portion of the corporation's profits.

shift of a demand curve The change that takes place in a demand curve when a new relationship between quantity demanded of a good and the price of that good is brought about by a change in the original conditions.

Smoot-Hawley tariff The U.S. tariff law of the 1930s, which set the highest tariffs in U.S. history (60%). It set off an international trade war and caused the decline in trade that is often considered a cause of the worldwide depression of the 1930s.

social, or implicit, contracts Unspoken agreements between workers and firms that firms will not cut wages.

social overhead capital Basic infrastructure projects such as roads, power generation, and irrigation systems.

socialist economy An economy in which most capital is owned by the government rather than by private citizens. Also called *social ownership*.

speculation motive One reason for holding money instead of bonds. Because the market value of interest-bearing bonds is inversely related to the interest rate, investors may wish to hold money in anticipation that interest rates will increase so that bonds will be available at lower prices.

stabilization policy A term used to describe both monetary and fiscal policy, the goals of which are to smooth out fluctuations in output and employment and to keep prices as stable as possible.

stabilization program An agreement between a borrower country and the International Monetary Fund in which the country agrees to revamp its economic policies to provide incentives for higher export earnings and lower imports.

stagflation Occurs when the overall price level rises rapidly (inflation) during periods of recession or high and persistent unemployment (stagnation).

sticky prices Prices that do not always adjust rapidly to maintain equality between quantity supplied and quantity demanded.

sticky wages The downward rigidity of wages as an explanation for the existence of unemployment.

store of value An asset that can be used to transport purchasing power from one time period to another.

structural adjustment A series of programs in developing countries designed to (1) reduce the size of their public sectors through privatization and/or expenditure reductions, (2) decrease their budget deficits, (3) control inflation, and (4) encourage private saving and investment through tax reform.

structural deficit The deficit that remains at full employment.

structural unemployment The portion of unemployment that is due to changes in the structure of the economy that result in a significant loss of jobs in certain industries.

subsidies   Payments made by the government for which it receives no goods or services in return.

substitutes   Goods that can serve as replacements for one another; when the price of one increases, demand for the other goes up.

sunk costs   Costs that cannot be avoided, regardless of what is done in the future, because they have already been incurred.

supply curve   A graph illustrating how much of a product a firm will supply at different prices.

supply schedule   A table showing how much of a product firms will supply at different prices.

supply-side policies   Government policies that focus on aggregate supply and increasing production rather than stimulating aggregate demand.

sustained inflation   Occurs when the overall price level continues to rise over some fairly long period of time.

tariff   A tax on imports.

tax multiplier   The ratio of change in the equilibrium level of output to a change in taxes.

terms of trade   The ratio at which a country can trade domestic products for imported products.

theory of comparative advantage   Ricardo's theory that specialization and free trade will benefit all trading parties, even those that may be absolutely more efficient producers.

three basic questions   The questions that all societies must answer: (1) What will be produced? (2) How will it be produced? (3) Who will get what is produced?

tight monetary policy   Central bank policies that restrict the money supply.

time lag   A delay in the economy's response to stabilization policies.

trade deficit   Occurs when a country's exports of goods and services are less than its imports of goods and services in a given period.

trade feedback effect   The tendency for an increase in the economic activity of one country to lead to a worldwide increase in economic activity.

trade surplus   Occurs when a country's exports of goods and services are greater than its imports of goods and services in a given period.

transaction motive   The main reason that households, firms, and other organizations hold money—for use as a medium of exchange.

transfer payments (to households)   Cash payments made by the government to people who do not supply goods, services, or labour in exchange for these payments. They include social insurance benefits, veterans' benefits, and welfare payments.

transfers of government deposits   The movement of government deposits between the Bank of Canada and private banks.

underground economy   The part of the economy in which transactions take place and in which income is generated that is unreported and therefore not counted in GDP.

unemployed   A person 15 years old or older who is not working, is available for work, and generally has made specific efforts to find work.

unemployment rate   The ratio of the number of people unemployed to the total number of people in the labour force.

unincorporated business income   Income earned by unincorporated businesses (which also includes most rental income).

unit of account   A standard unit that provides a consistent way of quoting prices.

value added   The difference between the value of goods as they leave a stage of production and the cost of the goods as they entered that stage.

variable   A measure that can change from time to time or from observation to observation.

velocity of money   The number of times a dollar changes hands, on average, during the course of a year; the ratio of nominal GDP to the stock of money.

vicious-circle-of-poverty hypothesis   Suggests that poverty is self-perpetuating because poor countries are unable to save and invest enough to accumulate the capital stock that would help them grow.

wealth or net worth   The total value of what a household owns minus what it owes. It is a stock measure.

weight   The importance attached to an item within an index.

World Bank   An international agency that lends money to individual countries for projects that promote economic development.

World Trade Organization (WTO)   The body responsible for governing world trade. Entered into force January 1, 1995, replacing the General Agreement on Tariffs and Trade (GATT).

Solutions to Even-Numbered Problems

Chapter 1:

2. a, c, and f are examples of positive economics. b, d, and e are examples of normative economics because they make value judgments about the outcomes.

4. Total tax if 200 students are used = 200 students × 10 days × 5 hours per day × $5 per hour = $50 000. This would mean a tax of $5 per person ($50 000 ÷ 10 000 citizens).

    Total tax if 400 students are used = 400 students × 10 days × 5 hours per day × $5 per hour = $100 000. This would mean a tax of $10 per person.

    By paying an additional $5 in tax (i.e., $10 instead of $5), people avoid standing in line for an hour. If time is valued at $10 per hour, every citizen gains value of $5 when the waiting time is eliminated ($10 in benefits from reduced waiting time minus $5 in additional taxes). Moving from 200 to 400 students makes all citizens better off, and since the students are willing to work for $5, no one is worse off! Thus, switching to 400 students from 200 students would be efficient. One could argue that it is also fair because everyone is paying an equal amount, and because everyone gains from the higher tax in proportion to what he or she pays.

6. Equity is "fairness" in distributing burdens and benefits. Building the bridge would certainly be fair if those who used it and gained from its existence also paid the cost of building it.

8. a. Assuming the worker works an eight-hour day, the opportunity cost will be lost wages of $34 per day ($8.50 × 8 × 0.5) plus the cost of tuition, books, and other expenses incurred to attend classes and that would not be incurred if working.

b. The cost of gasoline, wear and tear on the automobile, and other travel expenses plus the value of the time spent travelling if used in the "next-best" way.

c. The difference between the grade Tom would have received if he had studied and the grade he actually received as a result of staying out all night partying.

d. The next-best thing Tova could have purchased with the $200.

e. The next-best thing the $1 million could have purchased plus the cost of tying up the money for ten years. Note that purchasing a bond with the $1 million was an option. The purchase of a bond would have yielded interest for ten years and the $1 million would have been returned to the lender.

f. The value of Alex's time in the next-best use.

Appendix 1A:

2. The slopes are as follows:

    a. −2

    b. −4

    c. 6

    d. −1/500 or −0.002

Chapter 2:

2. Both land and capital are inputs, but capital is something that is produced by human beings. Trees growing wild are like land; they are not produced by human beings. However, an orchard that is planted by human beings can be classified as capital. It took time, labour, and perhaps machinery to plant the orchard and to prune the trees.

4. a. A straight-line ppf curve intersecting the Y axis at 1000 units of luxury goods and intersecting the X axis at 500 units of necessity goods. These are the limits of production if all resources are used to produce only one good.

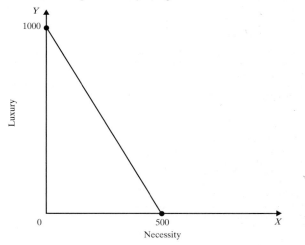

b. Unemployment or underemployment of labour would put the society inside the ppf. Full employment would move the society to some point on the ppf.

c. Answers will vary, but the decision should be based on the relative value of necessities and luxuries, and the degree of concern that all fellow citizens have enough necessities.

d. If left to the free market, prices would (at least ideally) be determined by market forces; incomes would be determined by a combination of ability, effort, and inheritance. It would be up to each individual to find a job and determine how to spend the income.

6. Answers will vary.

8. a. Figure c

    b. Figures a, d, e, f

    c. Clearly Figure d, probably Figure e

    d. Figure e

    e. All but Figure a

    f. Figure b

Chapter 3:

2. a. This, along with a variety of other information, can be found in the *Canada Yearbook*, an annual publication of Statistics Canada. It will be in your library.

b. The biggest functions of local government are education, police, sewers and sanitation, roads, and fire protection.

c. People in different places may have different preferences or demands for assigning a function to local government as opposed to provincial or federal government.

4. Unions and Canadian nationalists were the key opponents to NAFTA. Unions feared job losses since it would be cheaper to produce goods in Mexico. Canadian nationalists lamented the loss of political sovereignty and the reduction in our ability to use tariffs to pursue Canadian political objectives. Advocates of

NAFTA argued that prices of goods and services in Canada would fall (benefiting Canadian consumers) as a result of specialization according to comparative advantage (see Chapter 2), exploitation of economies of scale (Chapter 9), and reductions in monopoly power (Chapters 13 and 14).

6. Government expenditure as a percentage of GDP increased between 1980 and 1994. Government purchases of goods and services have fallen as a percentage of GDP in the two decades since 1970.

8. Disagree. Change the word "corporations" to "sole proprietorships" and the statement is true.

10. Large firms have a hierarchical structure with many levels of managers who try to organize work and motivate workers. Decisions are not made democratically but instead ultimately come from the "boss." Moreover, every firm has an elaborate system of incentives (rewards for good work), punishment (discipline for the failure to perform, including firing), and ideology (team spirit, loyalty to the firm) in place to motivate workers and assure coordination. A command economy has a similar system. Nonetheless, although firms do much planning and final decisions are made by the "boss," they must still ultimately respond to the consumers. Workers also have choices (they can choose to work for another firm) not available in a pure command economy. However, in conditions of high unemployment the firm may be able to coerce workers into doing what the firm wants.

12. Government spending could increase while taxes are decreasing due to deficit spending (borrowing). Government spending could increase while government employment is decreasing if government is purchasing goods and services from the private sector that it formerly produced itself.

Chapter 4:

2. a. A simple demand shift: same diagram for both cities.

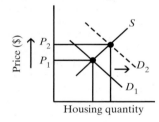

b. Rightward shift of supply with new development; leftward shift of demand with falling incomes: same diagram for both cities.

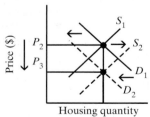

4. a. This sequence confuses changes in demand (shifts of the demand curve) with changes in quantity demanded (movements along a demand curve). First, a demand *shift* does cause price to rise. As price rises, the *quantity supplied* increases along the supply curve, and the *quantity demanded* declines along the demand curve as the market moves to reestablish equilibrium. Nothing here suggests that demand shifts back down.

b. This sequence confuses a change in price (per unit) with a change in total spending on meat. When price falls, the *quantity demanded* increases along the demand curve. Thus, the total amount spent (price × quantity demanded) depends on whether quantity demanded goes up by more than price per

unit falls. Total spending could increase if demand responds strongly to the lower price.

6. The advertising campaign, if successful, will result in a reduction in demand (a shift in the demand curve to the left). The impact, other things being equal, will be to lower tobacco sales and lower tobacco prices. This is shown in the diagram below as a new equilibrium at point B.

The marketing board fixes the amount of tobacco grown at a level below that which would be grown if tobacco growers were free from the marketing board restrictions. The fixed supply is shown by the new supply curve S_2 in the diagram below. The impact of the marketing board, other things held unchanged, is to reduce tobacco sales and increase prices. This is shown by the new equilibrium at point C. (Note that the change identified is from point A, where there is no marketing board and no advertising campaign, to point C, where there is a marketing board and no advertising campaign.)

In combination, the two policies reduce tobacco consumption, but it is impossible to predict whether tobacco prices will rise, fall, or remain constant. The combined impact of the policies is captured by the equilibrium point D. Notice that tobacco prices are the same as at point A, thus this is just one possible outcome. Try to identify conditions required for tobacco prices to rise and to fall.

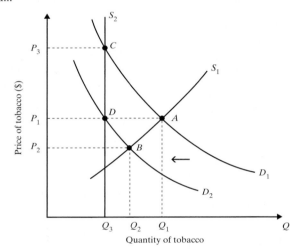

Appendix 4A:

2. a.

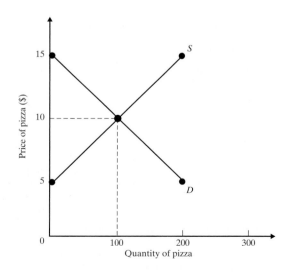

b. $Q_d = Q_s \rightarrow 300 - 20P = 20P - 100 \rightarrow P = \$10$. Substitute $P = \$10$ into either the demand or supply equation to get $Q = 100$.

c. With $P = \$15$, producers would want to supply $20(15) - 100 = 200$ pizzas, but consumers would want to buy $300 - 20(15) = 0$ pizzas. There would be an excess supply of pizzas, which would bring the price down. As the price decreased, quantity supplied would decrease while quantity demanded would increase until both were equal at a price of $10 and quantity of 100.

d. The new market demand for pizzas would be $Q_d = 600 - 40P$.

e. $Q_d = Q_s \rightarrow 600 - 40P = 20P - 100 \rightarrow P = 700/60 = \$11.66$. Substitute $P = \$11.67$ into either the demand or supply equation to get $Q = 133.2$.

Chapter 5:

2. Answers will vary. But scalping—regardless of its morality—helps to eliminate shortages by creating a "market" where the price can rise to its equilibrium value. Anyone willing to pay the equilibrium price should be able to obtain a ticket. Also, by allowing price rationing to work somewhat, scalping reduces the need for waiting in line, and so results in less wasted time.

4. Absolutely not. This statement confuses a shift of demand with change in quantity demanded along a demand curve. The demand for blue jeans shifted up, causing price to rise.

Chapter 6:

2. Answers will vary.

4. This could occur if relatively more blue-collar employees were laid off, so that the proportion of (lower-paid) white-collar employees in the company's workforce actually increased. This example points out how looking only at broad macroeconomic aggregates can be misleading.

6. Wars result in high levels of government spending, which helps to increase total spending in the economy.

*8. When demand shifts to the right in a market, prices tend to rise. Higher interest rates make buying a car or a home more expensive to those who must borrow to finance those items. Thus, high interest rates tend to shift demand curves back to the left, taking pressure off prices.

Chapter 7:

2. Every payment made by a buyer becomes income for the seller. Thus, the dollar value of the purchases of new goods and services in a year must be the dollar value of the income generated in that year.

4. a. Nominal GDP in 2000 = 250.

b. Nominal GDP in 2001 = 446.

c. Nominal GDP has increased 78.4%.

d. The GDP deflator equals 100 for 2000 and 125.6 for 2001. Therefore, prices have risen 25.6%.

6. Because goods and services produced in the underground economy are valued and paid for by individuals, they clearly belong in a measure of economic activity such as GDP. However, it is essentially a matter of personal choice if we are searching for a measure of economic welfare, particularly when considering illegal activities. Compare counting the sale of a beer at an unlicensed residence party to the sale of a package of marijuana to the sale of a package of heroin. Different individuals would include and not include different activities just as a pacifist might want to subtract defence expenditures from conventional GDP to use it as a measure of economic welfare.

8. The pizza is entirely consumed in the year it was produced, while the car will last many years. To correct for this, we could count just the value of the services provided by the car *each year*. For example, if the car lasts five years, then 20% of its value could be counted in each year's GDP.

10. There is no right or wrong answer here. But counting environmental damage requires a dollar estimate of this damage, about which there will be little consensus.

12. With these three indicators, we can see that St. Laurent gets a grade point average of 4.3, Diefenbaker a grade point average of 3, Pearson, Mulroney, and Chretien are all tied with 2.7, and Trudeau only gets 1. But the fact that Velk and Riggs get a much different answer when they use all ten indicators highlights the index number problem. Which is right, to use three indicators or ten? Or twelve or twenty? And should all the indicators get the same weighting, as in their grade point method, or should (for example) unemployment be regarded as more important than inflation and hence get a higher weighting? Other problems include the fact that the ranking method they use does not reflect how much better the top performer did than the second performer: the top performer will still get an A+ at best, the second performer will get an A, the third a B, etc. Finally, while Velk and Riggs try to make adjustments for this, much economic performance is beyond the control of the prime minister and depends particularly on U.S. economic events. And naturally, the economy is only one of many issues facing any prime minister.

Chapter 8:

2. "Full employment" is another term for the natural rate of unemployment. The idea behind this terminology is that if the only unemployment in the economy is the unemployment that comes about as the result of the normal working of the labour market, then there is no "unnecessary" unemployment. Labour is being "fully" utilized because the only unemployment that exists is the natural consequence of an efficiently working market. Thus, the economy can be at full employment with a 7% unemployment rate, provided that the 7% unemployment is frictional and structural only as these economists must have been asserting.

4. This is structural unemployment, which can sometimes exist for long periods, especially when workers must learn new skills to find jobs. The social costs of this unemployment might be greater than the costs of retraining these workers, providing some justification for government assistance.

6. Yes, inflation would still be a problem. There are other costs of inflation besides the redistribution of income that occurs when incomes are not indexed. These include the waste of time and resources spent coping with inflation, and the higher risk on financial assets in an inflationary environment. See the section on "Administrative Costs and Inefficiencies" under the heading "The Costs of Inflation."

8. Yes, both statements can be true. The labour force of Tappania may have grown faster than the number of employed, implying an increase in the number who are looking for work but not working, and an increase in the unemployment rate.

10. If the recipient receives 50% of the interest after tax, the recipient's after-tax interest rate is 50% of 6% or 3%. The real after-tax rate of interest is therefore 3% − 1% = 2%. Note that the ordinary real rate of interest is 6% − 1% = 5% and that it does not change as the interest rate increases to 12% while the inflation rate increases to 7% (as 12% − 7% = 5%). But the after-tax interest rate becomes 50% of 12% or 6%. Subtracting the new rate of inflation, the after-tax real rate of interest becomes 6% − 7% = −1%. However, note that the negative after-tax real rate of interest does not mean the lender (the interest recipient) would necessarily have been better off not lending. If she doesn't lend and just holds the money, she will lose 7% per year in purchasing power because of the inflation.

Chapter 9:

2. Actual investment includes unplanned changes in inventories that occur when sales fall short of firms' expectations.

4. a. $MPC = 0.8$; $MPS = 0.2$

b.

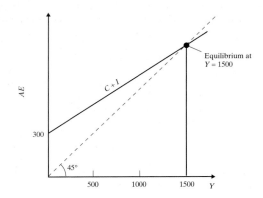

c. $\Delta Y = (1/MPS)\ \Delta I$. Multiplier $= 1/MPS = 1/0.2 = 5$. In this case, with the multiplier equal to 5 and an increase in investment of 10, $\Delta Y = (5)(10) = 50$. Equilibrium Y increases from 1500 to 1550.

d. $S = Y - C$
   $= Y - (200 + 0.8Y)$
   $= -200 + 0.2Y$

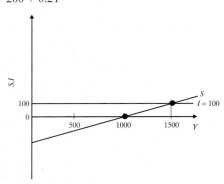

The equilibrium must be the same in both graphs because $Y = C + I$ and $S = I$ are the same condition. To see this, remember that $Y = C + S$ always. Substitute $C + S$ for Y in the equilibrium condition $Y = C + I$ to obtain $C + S = C + I$, which simplifies to $S = I$.

6. No. *AE* is *planned* aggregate expenditure. If you add unplanned changes in inventory to it, the sum equals aggregate output (income).

Appendix 9A:

2. $Y = C + I$ with no government, exports or imports
   $= 100 + 0.8Y + 50$

Rearranging to solve:

   $Y - 0.8Y = 150$
   $0.2Y = 150$ or equilibrium output $Y = (1/0.2) \times 150 = 750$

The multiplier is the expression in brackets that multiplies the sum of autonomous consumption and planned investment (which does not depend on Y and hence is autonomous in this example) to produce equilibrium output. In this case the multiplier is $(1/0.2) = 5$. If Y were 800, $C = 100 + 0.8(800) = 740$ so planned aggregate expenditure $AE \equiv C + I = 740 + 50 = 790$. Therefore actual output exceeeds planned aggregate expenditure and unplanned inventory accumulation $= 800 - 790 = 10$. Acutal investment is planned investment of 50 plus unplanned investment of $10 = 60$. With the unplanned inventory accumulation, producers will cut back production, pushing the economy back toward equilibrium output of 750.

Chapter 10:

2. a. $Y = 1000$, $Y_d = 800$, $C = 600$, $S = 200$, $I = 100$, $G = 200$.
   Since in a closed economy total spending $= C + I + G = 600 +$

$100 + 200 = 900$ is less than total output of 1000, one would predict that inventories will pile up, and firms will decide to reduce output.

b. Y would settle at 600. At this level of output, we would have $C = 300$, $I = 100$, and $G = 200$ so that $Y = C + I + G = 600$.

c. Cutting government purchases in this economy would make the fall in output worse! In particular, a cut of 25 would cause equilibrium Y to decline by $25(1/MPS) = (25)(4) = 100$. This would mean Y would decline to 500 instead of 600.

4. a. Equilibrium with government in a closed economy requires that output = spending, or that $Y = C + I + G$. Since we know that $Y = C + S + T$ by definition, then equilibrium also requires that $I + G = S + T$. To see if $Y = 200$ is an equilibrium, add $C + I + G$ to obtain $160 + 30 + 0 = 190$. This is *not* an equilibrium, because spending (190) is less than output (200). Alternatively, saving + taxes $= 40 + 0 = 40$, while investment + government spending $= 30 + 0 = 30$. Thus, $S + T$ is not equal to $I + G$.

In the coming months, we can expect output (Y) to decline and workers to be laid off. Equilibrium $Y = 150$. At $Y = 150$, $C + I + G = 0.8(150) + 30 + 0 = 150$.

b. Set $G = 10$ with taxes $= 0$. In this case, we would have $Y = C + I + G$ or $200 = 160 + 30 + 10$. (Note: There are other combinations of G and T that will bring equilibrium Y to 200, such as $G = 26$ and $T = 20$.)

c. Set $G = 20$ with taxes $= 0$. In this case, we would have $Y = C + I + G$ or $250 = 200 + 30 + 20$. Other combinations that would accomplish the same result include $G = 60$ and $T = 50$ or $G = 44$ and $T = 30$.

d. Yes. $Y = C + I + G$ ($200 = 160 + 40 + 0$). Also, $S + T = I + G$ ($40 + 0 = 40 + 0$).

e. We can get the answer directly from the multiplier:
   $\Delta Y = \Delta G(1/MPS)$
   $\Delta Y = (30)(5)$
   $\Delta Y = 150$
   The new level of Y is therefore $200 + 150 = 350$. C will be equal to $(0.8)(350) = 280$, while $S = (0.2)(350) = 70$.

f. Once again, we can get the answer directly from the tax multiplier:
   $\Delta Y = \Delta T(-MPC/MPS)$
   $\Delta Y = 30(-4)$
   $\Delta Y = -120$. Y falls by 120. The new level of Y is therefore $200 - 120 = 80$. Disposable income is $80 - 30 = 50$, so $C = (0.8)50 = 40$, while $S = (0.2)50 = 10$. The change in Y is larger when government spending changes by 30 than when taxes change by 30. This reflects the fact that the government spending multiplier is larger than the tax multiplier. A change in government spending affects output directly, while a change in taxes affects output indirectly, by a smaller amount, because households will reduce their spending by only a fraction of the tax change.

6. a. Government spending multiplier $= 1/0.4 = 2.5$.

b. Government spending multiplier $= 1/(1 - 0.9) = 10$.

c. Government spending multiplier $= 1/(1 - 0.5) = 2$.

d. Tax multiplier $= -0.75/(1 - 0.75) = -3$.

e. Tax multiplier $= -0.9/(1 - 0.9) = -9$.

f. *MPC* must be 0.833. Tax multiplier $= -0.833/(1 - 0.833) = -5.0$.

g. *MPC* must be 0.666. Government spending multiplier $= 1/(1 - 0.666) = 3.0$.

h. Output will increase by $100 billion (use the balanced-budget multiplier, which has a value of 1).

8. The quickest way to do this is to recall from our answer to question 4 that equilibrium output was 150 and to note that as equal amounts of exports and imports are added, we have not changed the leakages/injections balance and hence output will not change. As the export spending multiplier is the same multiplier as for government purchases (i.e., 5), an increase in exports by 10 will increase output by 50 to 200.

Now let us work it out in full for illustration. The steps are (a) to write down the equilibrium condition, (b) substitute, and (c) solve.

The equilibrium condition is
$$Y = AE = C + I + G + EX - IM$$
Substituting:
$$Y = 0.8Y_d + 30 + 0 + 15 - 15$$
$$Y = 0.8(Y - 0) + 30$$
And solving:
$$Y = 0.8Y + 30$$
$$0.2Y = 30$$
$$Y = (1/0.2) \times 30 = 150$$

If we repeat these same steps with EX changed to 25, $Y = 200$. Note the $(1/0.2) = 5$ in the last expression before the multiplication sign is the multiplier.

Appendix 10A:

2. The equilibrium condition is

$$Y = C + I + G + EX - IM$$
$$= 200 + 0.6(Y - T) + 100 + 100 + 0$$
$$= 400 + 0.6(Y - 150)$$
$$= 310 + 0.6Y$$

Solving:

$Y = 310 + 0.6Y$ or $0.4Y = 310$ or $Y = (1/0.4)310 = 2.5 \times 310 = 775$. The government spending multiplier is $(1/0.4) = 2.5$. The tax multiplier can be calculated by increasing taxes by 1 to 151 and re-solving to obtain output of 773.5, a reduction of 1.5 which implies a tax multiplier of -1.5. Note that the government spending multiplier is 2.5 and the tax multiplier is -1.5, so that their sum, the balanced-budget multiplier, is $2.5 + (-1.5) = 1$.

Appendix 10C:

2. a. Begin by writing down the expression for planned aggregate expenditure and substituting:

$$AE \equiv C + I + G + EX - IM$$
$$= 100 + 0.75(Y - T) + 100 + 100 + 375 - [25 + 0.25(Y - T)]$$
$$= 650 + 0.5 [Y - (-200 + 0.2Y)]$$
$$= 650 + 0.5(Y + 200 - 0.2Y)$$
$$= 650 + 0.5Y + 100 - 0.1Y$$
$$= 750 + 0.4Y$$

If $Y = 1000$, planned aggregate expenditure is $750 + 0.4(1000) = 1150$. Firms will find that they have an unplanned change of inventory of $1000 - 1150 = -150$. Actual investment spending will be planned investment spending plus the unplanned inventory change $= 100 - 150 = -50$.

b. From the slope of the planned aggregate expenditure function, 40 cents of every dollar of output (income) will be spent on domestically produced goods and services.

c. Equilibrium output will be where Y equals planned aggregate expenditure AE and there are no unplanned changes in inventories:

$$Y = 750 + 0.4Y$$
$$Y - 0.4Y = 750$$
$$0.6Y = 750$$
$$Y = (1/0.6)750 = 1.67 \times 750 = 1250$$

d. Net taxes are $-200 + 0.2(1250) = 50$. Hence disposable income $Y_d = Y - T = 1250 - 50 = 1200$, consumption $C = 100 + 0.75(1200) = 1000$ and saving $S = Y_d - C = 1200 - 1000 = 200$. Imports $IM = 25 + 0.25(1200) = 325$. Note that leakages $S + T + IM = 200 + 50 + 325 = 575$ equal injections $I + G + EX = 100 + 100 + 375 = 575$.

As given in the question, in equilibrium saving exceeds investment spending by 100. Of the extra saving, 50 goes to fund the government deficit, because G exceeds T by 50. That leaves 50 which must be saved internationally. This is the same 50 by which exports exceed imports. It is exactly as though you sell (earn) $50 per year more than you buy: you are saving $50 per year. In the international context, suppose everyone pays for exports and imports with IOUs. This economy will have IOUs of 375 from exporting: it can use 325 of them to pay off its import bill, and after all its imports are paid for it will still have 50 IOUs from other economies left over. These IOUs can be exchanged for bonds or stocks formerly owned by residents of other economies, but the principle is the same. The increase in the economy's assets and/or the decrease in its international debts will sum to 50.

e. From part **c** the multiplier is clearly 1.67, which is less than the 4 in the original model because any expansion automatically increases imports and taxes (because both now depend upon income) and that dampens the multiplier effect.

Chapter 11:

2. Term deposits are not included in $M1$, so $M1$ would increase. $M2$ includes both term and chequing deposits, so it is unaffected. If desired reserve ratios in the banking system are different for $M1$ than for $M2$, then there might be changes in desired reserves, which would further affect the overall supply of money.

4. $M2$ includes everything in $M1$, plus notice deposits in chartered banks. A shift of funds between, say, savings accounts and chequing accounts in chartered banks will affect $M1$ but not $M2$, because both savings accounts and chequing accounts are part of $M2$.

*6. Money injected through open market operations results in a multiple expansion of the money supply only if it leads to loans, and loans can be made only if the new money ends up in banks as deposits. If the Bank of Canada buys a bond from John Doe, who immediately deposits the proceeds into a dollar-denominated Swiss bank account, the Canadian money supply won't expand at all. If the money ends up in his pockets or in his mattress, the expansion of the money supply will stop right there. If he had deposited the proceeds in a Canadian bank, excess reserves would have been created, stimulating lending and further money creation.

8. a. Deposit multiplier $= 1/(\text{reserve ratio}) = 1/.25 = 4$. If there is one dollar of new money available for reserves, and the ratio of new reserves to new deposits is 0.25, there must be $4 of new deposits, as $0.25 \times \$4 = 1$.

There is another way to see this for those who are familiar with the kind of math we used in Appendix 10A, where we studied a very different type of multiplier, the spending multiplier in the Keynesian model. At each stage, 75% of new deposits is re-lent, because 25% is kept for reserves. So an extra dollar of new deposits will correspond (as money is lent, redeposited, and then re-lent after reserves are set aside) to an increase in the total money supply of $1 + 0.75 + 0.75^2 + \ldots = 1/(1 - 0.75) = 4$, because a sum of any series of the form $1 + x + x^2 + \ldots$ for $-1 < x < 1$ is $1/(1 - x)$ with $x = 0.75$ in this case.

b. With a reserve ratio of 0.25 and no excess reserves, $100 billion of deposits implies there are $25 billion of reserves. With that same $25 billion of reserves and a reserve ratio of 0.2, there will now be $5 \times \$25$ billion $= \$125$ billion of deposits, because the deposit multiplier is $1/0.2 = 5$.

c. With no cash leakages, the money supply is the same as the volume of deposits. $25 billion of reserves will support $75 billion if the reserve ratio is 1/3.

Appendix 11A:

*2. a. Money multiplier without cash drain – Money multiplier with cash drain $= 1/rr - (1 + c)/(c + rr) = [(c + rr) - rr(1 + c)]/[rr \times (c + rr)] = [c \times (1 - rr)]/[rr \times (c + rr)] > 0$ for all $0 < rr < 1$.

Therefore the money multiplier is smaller if there is a cash drain.

b. $(1+c)/(c + rr) = (1 + 0.15)/(0.15 + 0.25) = 2.875$. Note this is smaller than the money multiplier of 4 that would hold if there were no cash drain and $c = 0$.

Chapter 12:

2. a. Letting money supply equal to money demand, 40 000 = 21 000 − 50 000r + 2(10 000) or, solving, $r = 0.02$ or 2%.

b. Letting money supply equal to money demand, 40 000 = 21 000 − 50 000r + 2(11 000) or, solving, $r = 0.06$ or 6%.

c. Required money supply $M^s = 21\ 000 - 50\ 000(0.02) + 2(11\ 000)$ = 42 000.

4. A recession is a decline in real GDP. When output falls, there is less economic activity and fewer transactions. Fewer transactions means that (*ceteris paribus*) money demand will fall. This will cause a leftward shift in the M^d curve, which results in a lower equilibrium interest rate (assuming that the money supply remains fixed).

6. Increasing T and lowering G would reduce the equilibrium level of Y (real GDP). Thus, such contractionary fiscal policy would lower interest rates.

8. You should sell the gold bar this year if you think the price of gold will not increase by at least the return on a one-year bond.

Chapter 13:

2. a. The tax cut causes disposable income to rise and C to rise. C + I + G + EX − IM > Y, so inventories fall and output (Y) begins to rise. Increasing Y causes money demand to rise, putting upward pressure on r. Since the central bank does not accommodate, we get a higher Y but also a higher r, which causes I to fall, partially offsetting the effect of the tax cut on Y. (Final result: higher Y, higher r.)

b. The tax increase reduces disposable income and thus consumption. C + I + G + EX − IM < Y, so inventories build and output falls. A lower Y means lower money demand. At the same time the central bank is increasing the money supply. Interest rates will fall sharply, causing I to rise, perhaps offsetting the effects of the initial tax increase on Y. (Final result: ambiguous Y, lower r.)

c. Similar to **b.** The drop in consumption cuts aggregate expenditure: C + I + G + EX − IM < Y, so inventories rise and Y falls. As Y falls, money demand drops. If the central bank holds M^s constant, r will fall. Here again, the lower r may stimulate I, causing I to rise and partially offsetting the initial decline in Y. (Final result: lower Y, lower r.)

d. The central bank expands the money supply. $M^s > M^d$, so r falls. Normally, the lower r might be expected to cause I to rise, but gloomy expectations and no need for new plant and equipment keep I low. Thus the link to the goods market is broken, and the monetary policy doesn't have much impact. (Final result: lower r, little or no change in Y.)

4. a. The decline in investment would be a reduction in aggregate expenditure, causing equilibrium output (income) to decrease in the goods market. In the money market, the drop in income would decrease the demand for money (shift the M^d curve to the left), causing the interest rate to fall and investment spending to rise back up somewhat. If Paranoia trades with the outside world, the fall in the interest rate would also lead to an exchange rate depreciation and hence some increase in net exports. But the net effect would be a decline in output (income) and the interest rate.

b. Option (i) is the least expansionary because the increase in government expenditure will be financed by taxes, and hence there will be some offsetting reduction in consumption spending. The net effect will be expansionary, however, because some of the tax increase comes from saving. (The net effect is positive

for the same reason that the balanced-budget multiplier is positive in Chapter 10.) Option (ii) is more expansionary than (i) because there is no offsetting tax increase, but the increase in government borrowing will increase interest rates, and this will lead to some crowding out. Option (iii) is the most expansionary in this model, because the government does not borrow (as in footnote 3 in the chapter) and spends newly created money. As a reminder, the model of this chapter assumes a fixed price level so that any expansion in the economy affects output and not prices.

6. The tight monetary policy would drive up interest rates, discouraging investment and causing aggregate output to fall. The simultaneous expansionary fiscal policy would increase the government spending and consumption components of aggregate output, increasing money demand and driving up interest rates further. The policies have opposing effects on aggregate output, so the ultimate effect on Y depends on which effect is stronger. But both policies drive interest rates higher. (In 1981, the prime interest rate rose to 22.75%!)

*8. a. Begin by setting money supply equal to money demand (equilibrium in the money market):

24 000 = 23 000 − 16 000r + 2Y

or 2Y = 1000 + 16 000r

or Y = 500 + 8000r

Continue by setting output (income) equal to planned aggregate expenditure (equilibrium in the goods market):

Y = C + I + G + EX − IM
= 100 + 0.75Y_d + 235 − 1000r + 250 + 50
= 635 + 0.75(Y − 400) − 1000r
= 335 + 0.75Y − 1000r

or 0.25Y = 335 − 1000r

Y = 1340 − 4000r

Solving, 500 + 8000r = 1340 − 4000r
12 000r = 840 or r = 0.07

With r = 0.07, Y = 500 + 8000(0.07) = 1060.

b. If G = 251, we can go through the same steps as before to solve for equilibrium in the goods market to obtain 0.25Y = 336 − 1000r or Y = 1344 − 4000r. Combining this with equilibrium in the money market and solving, 500 + 8000r = 1344 − 4000r or 12 000r = 844. r = 0.07033. With r = 0.07033, Y = 500 + 8000(0.07033) = 1062.7. The government purchases multiplier is 2.7. Expansionary fiscal policy increases output and interest rates. Note that in the simple Keynes cross model the multiplier would have been 1/(1 − MPC) = 1/(1 − 0.75) = 4 but the multiplier has been reduced because the expansion in the economy increases the demand for money, increases interest rates, and reduces investment. The key difference between this question and question 7 is that here the investment function is more sensitive to the interest rate and hence the multiplier is smaller than in question 7.

c. If the money supply falls to 23 000,

23 000 = 23 000 − 16 000r + 2Y

or 2Y = 16 000r, that is, Y = 8000r

As planned aggregate expenditure will still equal output (equilibrium in the goods market) if

Y = 1340 − 4000r, we can solve:

8000r = 1340 − 4000r

12 000r = 1340 or r = 0.1117

With r = 0.1117, Y = 8000(0.1117) = 893.3.

Decreasing the money supply (contractionary monetary policy) pushes up interest rates and reduces output.

2. a.

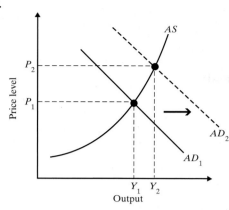

The price level will rise considerably; equilibrium GDP will rise only a little.

b.

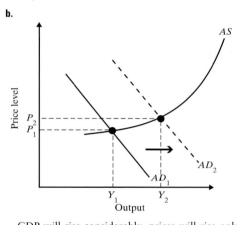

GDP will rise considerably; prices will rise only a little.

c.

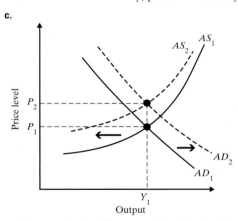

The price level will rise considerably. Equilibrium GDP may fall, but by less than it would if the central bank did not accommodate.

d.

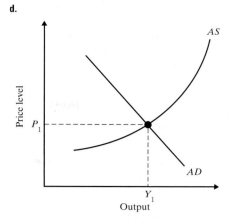

Neither the price level nor output would change. The fiscal and monetary policies have opposing effects on the *AD* curve. If they are of equal strength, there will be no shift in the curve.

4. a.

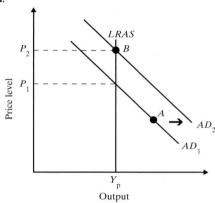

The price level rises, money demand increases, *r* rises, and equilibrium GDP will fall. The expansionary monetary policy reverses the increase in *r* and the decline in *Y*, but increases the rise in the price level that will occur in the long run as the economy adjusts back to full employment (point *B*).

b.

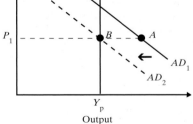

The *AD* curve will shift to the left, and in the long run, GDP will decrease back to its full-employment level. If the shift in *AD* is great enough, the price level will not have to rise during the adjustment process.

c.

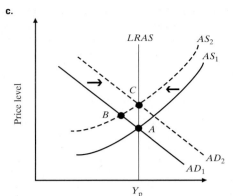

LRAS, AS₂, AS₁, Price level, C, B, A, AD₂, AD₁, Y_p, Output

The oil price shock will cause the *AS* curve to shift leftward. The central bank's accommodation will cause a permanent rightward shift in the *AD* curve. The long-run result will be no change in GDP but a higher price level.

6. Expansionary monetary policy is likely to have a greater effect in country B. Because production costs adjust automatically to price increases in country A, the *AS* curve will be vertical. A rightward shift in the *AD* curve would cause an increase in prices without increasing output because costs increase at the same time as prices. In country B, input prices lag behind output prices, so the short-run *AS* curve is not vertical. In the short run, a rightward shift in the *AD* curve will cause an increase in output.

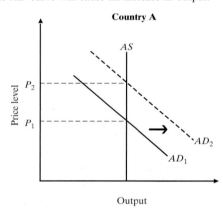

Country A

AS, P_2, P_1, Price level, AD₂, AD₁, Output

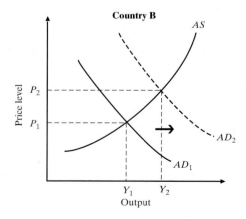

Country B

AS, P_2, P_1, Price level, AD₂, AD₁, Y_1, Y_2, Output

*8. a. This is part of the answer to question 8, Chapter 13.

$$Y = C + I + G + EX - IM$$
$$= 100 + 0.75Y_d + 235 - 1000r + 250 + 50$$
$$= 635 + 0.75(Y - 400) - 1000r$$
$$= 335 + 0.75Y - 1000r$$

or $0.25Y = 335 - 1000r$
$Y = 1340 - 4000r$

Solving, $4000r = 1340 - Y$ or $r = (1340 - Y)/4000$ (for equilibrium in the goods market).

b. Setting $M^s = M^d$,
$24\ 000/P = 23\ 000 - 16\ 000r + 2Y$
or $2Y = 24\ 000/P - 23\ 000 + 16\ 000r$
or $Y = 12\ 000/P - 11\ 500 + 8000r$ (for equilibrium in the money market)

Substituting in for *r* from part **a**,

$Y = 12\ 000/P - 11\ 500 + 8000\ (1340 - Y)/4000$
$= 12\ 000/P - 11\ 500 + 2680 - 2Y$
or $3Y = 12\ 000/P - 8820$ or $Y = 4000/P - 2940$.

This is the *AD* curve as it corresponds to equilibrium in both the goods and money markets.

c. If $Y = 1060$ from the *AS* curve, the *AS* curve meets the *AD* curve at $1060 = 4000/P - 2940$.

Solving $4000 = 4000/P$ or $P = 1$.

d. Doubling M^s,
$48\ 000/P = 23\ 000 - 16\ 000r + 2Y$
or $2Y = 48\ 000/P - 23\ 000 + 16\ 000r$
or $Y = 24\ 000/P - 11\ 500 + 8000r$ (for equilibrium in the money market)

Substituting in for *r* from part a.,

$Y = 24\ 000/P - 11\ 500 + 8000\ (1340 - Y)/4000$
$= 24\ 000/P - 11\ 500 + 2680 - 2Y$
or $3Y = 24\ 000/P - 8820$ or $Y = 8000/P - 2940$. (new *AD* curve)

If $Y = 1060$ from the *AS* curve, the *AS* curve meets the new *AD* curve at $1060 = 8000/P - 2940$.
Solving, $4000 = 8000/P$ or $P = 2$. If the money supply doubles with a vertical *AS* curve, the price level doubles.

e. i. zero, because $\Delta Y = 0$ as output is fixed at 1060.

ii. We need to recalculate the goods market equilibrium equation as
$$Y = C + I + G + EX - IM$$
$$= 100 + 0.75Y_d + 235 - 1000r + 1176.25 + 50$$
$$= 1561.25 + 0.75(Y - 400) - 1000r$$
$$= 1261.25 + 0.75Y - 1000r$$
or $0.25Y = 1261.25 - 1000r$
$Y = 5045 - 4000r$

Solving, $4000r = 5045 - Y$ or $r = (5045 - Y)/4000$ (for equilibrium in the goods market)

Putting that in the money market equilibrium equation:
$Y = 12\ 000/P - 11\ 500 + 8000\ (5045 - Y)/4000$
$= 12\ 000/P - 11\ 500 + 10\ 090 - 2Y$
or $3Y = 12\ 000/P - 1410$ or $Y = 4000/P - 470$ (new *AD* curve)

If $P = 1$ by *AS* curve, $Y = 4000/1 - 470 = 3530$. In this case the multiplier is $(\Delta Y/\Delta G) = (3530 - 1060)/(1176.25 - 250) = 2.7$. This is exactly the same answer as in question 8, Chapter 13 (as it should be, since that question was the same except the price level was always fixed at P = 1.)

iii. Substitute this *AS* curve, $P = 940/(2000 - Y)$, into the new *AD* curve or

$Y = 4000/P - 470 = 4000/[940/(2000 - Y)] - 470$
or $Y = 4000(2000 - Y)/940 - 470$

which implies $940Y = 8\ 000\ 000 - 4000Y - 441\ 800$ by multiplying both sides by 940 or $4940Y = 7\ 558\ 200$ or $Y = 1530$.

The multiplier is $(\Delta Y/\Delta G) = (1530 - 1060)/(1176.25 - 250) = 0.51$ which is between the smallest value zero for the vertical *AS* curve and the largest value for the horizontal *AS* curve.

Chapter 15:

2. These factors indicate that Japan probably has a low rate of frictional unemployment. One part of the natural unemployment rate is made up of movers and workers changing jobs.

4. a. This policy decreases frictional unemployment by helping employers and workers find each other. The time spent in job hunting would be reduced.

b. This policy may decrease structural unemployment by making it profitable to hire workers who would otherwise not be productive enough to employ. (To some extent, however, teenage workers might be substituted for existing workers, thus lessening the impact on unemployment.)

c. This policy reduces structural unemployment by providing workers with skills needed in new or expanding industries.

d. This policy would reduce structural and cyclical unemployment by providing jobs for people who would otherwise be unemployed. The program would cause a direct increase in the demand for labour. A worry might be that to pay them, taxes must be collected, thus reducing demand in the private sector and eliminating some private sector jobs.

e. Reduces frictional unemployment by aiding workers in their job hunt.

f. If the governor is convincing, wage and price hikes would be moderated. This would shift the short-run aggregate supply curve (AS) downward. If the economy is initially above the natural rate of unemployment, the result would be a permanent reduction in cyclical unemployment. Interestingly, the downward shift of the aggregate supply curve would put downward pressure on the price level, reducing inflation and helping to fulfill the governor's assertion. If the economy is at or below the natural rate of unemployment, the AS curve shift will still have the same initial effect. However, once unemployment falls below the natural rate, there will be inflationary pressures and the temporary AS shift will be reversed. If the economy adjusts quickly when output is above potential output, the governor's assertion may not hold.

6. a. While it can be argued that a higher wage tax can increase labour supply (as workers are worse off and adjust by trying to work more), most economists would presume that an additional tax paid on labour income would lead to at least a small reduction in labour-force participation and supply. It is important to the question that only employees' contributions increase. In Canada, both employee and employer contributions are increasing and this complicates matters. In the short run, this will reduce labour demand and with short-run wage rigidity, unemployment will rise. In the long run, the wage will fall and the unemployment will be eliminated.

b. Improved child care reduces the opportunity cost of working. It is likely to attract more parents to the workforce, increasing the labour force and labour supply. It would also reduce the demand for labour by increasing the full costs of hiring a worker. Over the short run, during which some wage rigidity is likely, the effect of an increase in labour supply and a decrease in labour demand would be an increase in the unemployment rate.

c. Increased immigration will increase labour supply at a given wage rate without a corresponding increase in jobs. With short-run wage rigidity, unemployment will rise.

d. Labour supply (and the labour force) should increase as more workers begin to seek even low-paid work to support themselves. With short-run wage rigidity, unemployment will rise.

e. Increased investment might increase or decrease labour demand, depending on whether the new capital is more complementary or substitutable for labour. There would be no immediate impact on labour supply. The effect on employment and unemployment would be ambiguous.

8. We would not expect any increase in unemployment. Wages are changing by the same percentage as prices and this constancy of real wages means that we would move down along a vertical aggregate supply curve. If the prediction of recession causes households to cut back on consumption expenditures and business firms to cut back on investment spending, there will be a leftward shift of the aggregate demand curve. But as long as wages and other input prices fall as fast as prices do, there will be no decline in output or employment.

10. The tradeoffs might be different for the two countries because social contracts and long-term explicit and implicit contracts may keep Japanese firms from laying off workers. Because the labour force in Canada is more transient, layoffs may be more likely. In Japan, a given reduction in inflation would probably require a lower increase in unemployment.

Chapter 16:

2. a.
$$
\begin{aligned}
Y &= C + I + G + EX - IM \\
&= 100 + 0.8Y_d + 60 + 80 + 0 \\
&= 100 + 0.8[Y - (-150 + 0.25Y)] + 60 + 80 \\
&= 100 + 0.8Y + 120 - 0.2Y + 60 + 80 \\
&= 360 + 0.6Y \\
0.4Y &= 360 \\
Y &= 360/0.4 = 900
\end{aligned}
$$

$$
\begin{aligned}
D &= G - T \\
&= 80 - [-150 + 0.25(900)] \\
&= 5
\end{aligned}
$$

b. With $G = 75$:
$$
\begin{aligned}
Y &= C + I + G + EX - IM \\
&= 100 + 0.8Y_d + 60 + 75 + 0 \\
&= 100 + 0.8[Y - (-150 + 0.25Y)] + 60 + 75 \\
&= 100 + 0.8Y + 120 - 0.2Y + 60 + 75 \\
&= 355 + 0.6Y \\
0.4Y &= 355 \\
Y &= 355/0.4 = 887.5
\end{aligned}
$$

$$
\begin{aligned}
D &= G - T \\
&= 75 - [-150 + 0.25(887.5)] \\
&= 3.125
\end{aligned}
$$

The deficit is not zero because the cut in government spending shifts the AD curve to the left, decreasing aggregate output and causing a drop in the net tax revenue. Although the original cut in government spending would seem to eliminate the deficit, the resulting drop in GDP tends to raise the deficit, so the net effect is a deficit that is smaller, but not zero.

c. With $I = 55$:
$$
\begin{aligned}
Y &= C + I + G + EX - IM \\
&= 100 + 0.8Y_d + 55 + 80 + 0 \\
&= 100 + 0.8[Y - (-150 + 0.25Y)] + 55 + 80 \\
&= 100 + 0.8Y + 120 - 0.2Y + 55 + 80 \\
&= 355 + 0.6Y \\
0.4Y &= 355 \\
Y &= 355/0.4 = 887.5 \\
D &= G - T \\
&= 80 - [-150 + 0.25(887.5)] \\
&= 8.125
\end{aligned}
$$

Cutting government spending by the required amount (21.666) means that $G = 80 - 21.666 = 58.33$. Solving again for equilibrium GDP:
$$
\begin{aligned}
Y &= C + I + G + EX - IM \\
&= 100 + 0.8Y_d + 55 + 58.33 + 0 \\
&= 100 + 0.8[Y - (-150 + 0.25Y)] + 55 + 58.33 \\
&= 100 + 0.8Y + 120 - 0.2Y + 55 + 58.33 \\
&= 333.33 + 0.6Y \\
0.4Y &= 333.33 \\
Y &= 333.33/0.4 = 833.33
\end{aligned}
$$

4. U.S. states that must have balanced budgets are unable to use spending and taxing to offset local economic shocks. Moreover, an adverse shock that sends the state budget into deficit requires the state to raise taxes or cut spending, which will cut local spending and exacerbate the impact of the shock. The effect is therefore destabilizing.

   If all states followed this philosophy, the effect would be destabilizing on a national basis for the United States. Adverse shocks would send the economy into recession, causing the federal deficit to swell. If states cannot pursue expansionary policies to help the United States out of the recession, then they must rely more heavily on the federal government to do so. Thus, a larger increase in the federal deficit will be necessary to stimulate the economy than would otherwise be the case.

6. Stabilization policy may be difficult to carry out because there are time lags in the economy's response to such policies. Stabilization policies can thus be destabilizing because they may affect the economy much later, when the adjustments are no longer desirable.

*8. Nominal output growth in percentage terms will equal the percentage increase in real output growth plus inflation. In question 5, you should have shown that real output growth targeting is stabilizing, because any time output growth is above the target, contractionary monetary policy will tend to reduce it and if real output growth is below the target, expansionary monetary policy will tend to increase it. In the text we argued that inflation targeting can be potentially effective if the inflation target is set appropriately and the shocks affecting the economy are aggregate demand shocks. Nominal output growth targeting clearly combines the two approaches, with contractionary monetary policy used if the sum of inflation and real output growth is high and expansionary monetary policy if these are low. It may lead to less contractionary monetary policy than inflation targeting if there is an adverse aggregate supply shock (a leftward movement of the AS curve) because the increase in the inflation rate will be offset by the reduction in real output, so the sum of the two may not increase as much.

   One main problem with nominal output growth targeting is that, like real output targeting, recognition of problems may be slower because the nominal output growth target comes from national accounts data, which are not released as quickly as the consumer price index.

Chapter 17:

2. Probably not, because not that many people have such large mortgages and the fall in longer-term interest rates was not as great as the fall in one-year mortgages. The fall in interest rates (which was partly due to a worldwide fall in interest rates) might be perceived as shorter lasting than a tax cut. Most importantly, the lower interest rates would reduce the consumption of those with interest income, particularly retirees. Of course the effect of the lower interest rates on other components of aggregate expenditure, such as planned investment spending, could make its total effect more stimulative.

4. The value of homes is an important component of household wealth. When home prices rise, household wealth rises and consumption tends to increase. When home prices fall, household wealth falls and consumption decreases. Since changes in consumption are changes in aggregate expenditure, they lead to changes in output and employment in the same direction.

6. A given consumption path requires a given amount of lifetime income to pay for it. But, given initial wealth, lifetime income is determined by working hours. This implies that income is not really an "independent" variable in the consumption function. Rather, the desire to consume and the desire to enjoy leisure together will determine how much income one will earn.

8. Expectations of future sales determine how much capital a firm will want to have in place in the future. To have this capital when it is needed, investment spending must take place in earlier periods. Since expectations of future sales are affected by government policy announcements, release of economic data, and "animal spirits"—all of which can change rapidly—the resulting investment spending is quite volatile.

10. Maintaining inventory stocks helps a firm maintain a smooth production level. When sales unexpectedly increase, goods can be sold out of inventory. When sales unexpectedly decrease, goods can be added to inventories. By smoothing production, a firm can save on the adjustment costs associated with frequent changes in capital stock and employment levels. The cost of this policy is the forgone interest from investing funds in inventory stocks instead of lending out the money in financial markets.

12. If real output growth is 3% and potential GDP grows by 2%, by Okun's Law the extra percentage point of growth will translate into a $1/2.5 = 0.4$ reduction in unemployment, from 9% to 8.6%. Similarly if real output grows by one percentage point more slowly than potential GDP, unemployment will rise by 0.4 to 9.4%.

Chapter 18:

2. a. For a Keynesian, when the economy is below potential output, either tax cuts or increases in government expenditure will increase output and promote growth. However, even below potential output, if there is no accompanying expansionary monetary policy, the effects of the fiscal stimulus will be weak because of offsetting effects involving higher interest rates and a stronger Canadian dollar. In any case, waiting until the budget is balanced is a less expansionary fiscal policy than acting immediately. Remember from the balanced-budget multiplier, back in Chapter 10, that equal increases in government spending and taxes are expansionary and equal reductions in government spending and taxes are contractionary, although the effects are likely to be small.

   For a supply-side economist, the cuts in tax rates are likely to stimulate the economy by increasing incentives. This person would argue that the Progressive Conservative platform would increase growth the most, followed by the Reform platform, while the NDP platform would slow growth to the extent it increased tax rates.

   b. For a Keynesian, expansion when the economy is at potential output can produce at best a short-run increase in output followed by additional inflation. However, for a supply-side economist, the tax-cutting policies are still valuable as they increase potential output by increasing incentives.

4. Nominal income $= M \times V = (\$1000)(5) = \$5000$. If we select the current year as our base year, real income is also $5000. If you are a strict monetarist, you believe V is constant. Therefore, a doubling of the money supply to $2000 will cause a doubling of nominal GDP to $(\$2000)(5) = \$10\,000$. If, however, velocity is a function of the interest rate as well as institutional factors, then it cannot be assumed a constant. In this case, an increase in the money supply (which reduces interest rates) would lower velocity, so $M \times V$ would not increase by as great a percentage as M itself increased, and nominal GDP would rise by a smaller percentage than the money supply increased. If the money supply doubles (rises by 100%), nominal GDP will rise by less than 100%. (We cannot know how the rise in nominal GDP is apportioned between a rise in P and a rise in real GDP without knowing more about the current state of the economy.)

6. Supply-side advocates believe that lower tax rates provide incentives for households to work more hours and to save more and for firms to invest more. These actions would expand the supply of goods and services and, thus, expand aggregate income and the tax base. The tax base would rise by so much that tax revenues would actually rise despite the lower tax rates. Those in the opposing camp believe that incentives are important, but that the effects would not be large enough to raise revenues.

Chapter 19:

2.

TABLE 1

Y/L	Growth Rate
4.28	—
4.23	3.7
4.17	3.6
4.12	3.7

TABLE 2

Y/L	Growth Rate
4.28	—
4.41	3.9
4.53	3.9
4.66	3.9

TABLE 3

Y/L	Growth Rate
4.28	—
4.45	5.0
4.63	5.0
4.81	5.0

In Table 1, L is increasing faster than K and Y, so productivity is falling. In Table 2, K and Y are increasing faster than L, so productivity is growing. The productivity increase is due to more capital per worker. In Table 3, K and L are increasing at the same slow rate, but technology is pushing Y up faster than either is growing.

4. Assuming that the economy stays at full employment, the bill would cause the economy to produce more capital goods and fewer consumption goods. This would lead to a higher growth rate over time. The tradeoff is less consumption today. There are also distributional consequences. Capital income earners (who have higher incomes on average) would benefit. The members of the higher-income households (who spend a smaller fraction of their incomes) would bear relatively less of the consumption-tax burden, while the members of the low-income households (who spend a higher fraction of their incomes) would bear relatively more of the consumption-tax burden.

6. High budget deficits are financed with private saving. That saving otherwise would have found its way through financial markets into private capital production. If the deficit is used to finance current expenditures like paying civil servants, it is not contributing to an expansion of output in the long run. The same is true of a tax cut, which is used to increase current consumption expenditures. But if the government used the money to build capital such as roads and bridges or to increase human capital through better education and job training, it would at least offset part of the reduction in private investment spending. Whether the net result for output growth is positive or negative depends on whether private capital or public capital has a higher rate of return. This is a subject of much debate, and would depend on the specific capital expenditures undertaken by the government.

Chapter 20:

2. a. Manitoba would have an absolute advantage in both wheat and canola.

b. In Manitoba, taking one hectare out of wheat and moving it into canola sacrifices 2.5 tonnes of wheat for 1.7 tonnes of canola. This is 2.5/1.7 = 1.47 tonnes of wheat for each tonne of canola. In Saskatchewan, the sacrifice is 2.4/1.5 = 1.6 tonnes of wheat for each tonne of canola.

c. Based on the calculations in **b** above, Saskatchewan has a comparative advantage in wheat, and Manitoba has a comparative advantage in canola.

d. Yes, the data are consistent with the conclusions in **c** above. While each province grows more wheat than canola, a higher fraction of land in Saskatchewan is in wheat and a higher fraction of land in Manitoba is in canola. Although neither province completely "specializes," each province seems to be devoting more of its resources to producing the good in which it has a comparative advantage.

4. Answers will vary.

6. a. The opportunity cost of a bottle of red wine is 1.5 bottles of white in Australia and 2 bottles of white in New Zealand. Australia, therefore, has a comparative advantage in red wine.

   The opportunity cost of a bottle of white wine is 0.66 bottles of red in Australia and 0.5 bottles of red in New Zealand. New Zealand, therefore, has a comparative advantage in white wine.

b. No. At the current exchange rate, both white and red wine are cheaper in New Zealand. Australians will want to import both types of wine from New Zealand, but New Zealanders will not want to import Australian wine.

c. As Australia has the comparative advantage in red wine and New Zealand in white wine, if there is two-way trade Australia will export red and import white. New Zealand will not import Australian red wine unless it is cheaper, which will require a New Zealand dollar to be worth at least 1.5 Australian dollars. But Australia will only import New Zealand white wine if it is cheaper, which means that the New Zealand dollar can be worth no more than 2 Australian dollars.

8. a. In Ontario, the opportunity cost of one tonne of beef is 30 kilolitres/6 tonnes or 5 kilolitres per tonne. In Quebec, the opportunity cost of one tonne of beef is 24 kilolitres/3 tonnes = 8 kilolitres per tonne.

b. If each province is specializing in a different product, it will be Quebec in milk and Ontario in beef, because the opportunity cost of a tonne of beef is higher in Quebec. (Quebec has the comparative advantage in milk.) Quebec will specialize in milk as long as the price of beef per tonne x 3 is less than 24 kilolitres x $1000, that is, the price of beef is less than $8000 per tonne. Ontario will specialize in beef as long as the price of beef per tonne x 6 is greater than 30 kilolitres x $1000, that is, the price of beef is greater than $5000 per tonne.

10. Such trade can potentially benefit Canada, depending as always on the benefits and the costs. Canada has more fresh water per capita than any country in the world. In general, the way a country sustains imports is by exporting: if Canadians or the government of Canada sells water to the United States, it means Canadians may import more goods from the rest of the world, raising the potential standard of living. Perhaps the principal fear in exporting water comes from a lack of control over this publicly owned resource. For example, such trade would not be beneficial to Canada if foreign tankers were allowed to come to Canadian lakes and take water without charge. Moreover, without some restriction too much water might be taken.

   One proposal to sell water uses Gisborne Lake, Newfoundland. There is considerable dispute over whether free trade agreements that Canada has signed mean that once one private sector firm is allowed to sell bulk water, a precedent is established that prevents the government from stopping other firms from doing the same thing. At time of writing, the government of Canada has imposed a moratorium on water sales.

Chapter 21:

2. a. Answers can include an increase in Canadian incomes, an increase in British interest rates, a decrease in Canadian interest rates, a decrease in the British price level, and an increase in the Canadian price level.

b. All of the above, except for the increase in Canadian incomes, would also cause the supply curve to shift to the left.

c. If the exchange rate floats, none of these policies will affect the balance of payments. However, the two changes in interest rates listed in **a** and **b** above—which would raise the value of the pound without any other simultaneous change in import or export demand—would make British goods relatively more expensive and decrease Britain's trade balance (shrink the surplus, or increase the deficit).

4. a. The consumption function does not change, so instead of spending their money on Japanese goods, U.S. residents will spend it on domestic goods. All else equal, this will stimulate U.S. output and decrease U.S. unemployment, and decrease output and employment in Japan. The Canadian economy is more closely tied to the U.S. economy than with the Japanese, so the increase in exports to the United States due to its increased output will more than offset any loss of Japanese exports. Hence, Canadian output and employment will increase.

b. If income rises, consumers are likely to buy more imports as well as more domestic goods. Imports from Japan will increase somewhat after the initial decrease.

c. If imports decrease, then the demand for yen will also decrease because importers will not need as many yen to purchase Japanese goods.

d. The yen will depreciate and the U.S. dollar will appreciate. With no other changes, one would expect that the Canadian dollar/U.S. dollar exchange rate will not change, meaning the Canadian dollar will also appreciate relative to the yen. Hence, Canada would probably import more from Japan and export less to Japan, reducing Canadian output and employment. The current account deficit will rise, but the total balance of payments will still sum to zero.

e. The quota would have to increase U.S. output and employment, at least in the short run. The increase in the U.S. trade balance increases U.S. output and employment. This causes the U.S. dollar to appreciate, which works to decrease output and employment somewhat. But the only reason that the U.S. dollar appreciates is because of the improvement in the U.S. trade balance. Thus, it is logically impossible for the U.S. dollar to appreciate so much that the trade balance would not improve. And as long as the trade balance improves, U.S. output and employment increase.

*6. a.
$$Y = C + I + G + (EX - IM)$$
$$= 100 + 0.8(Y - 40) + 38 + 75 + 25 - 0.05(Y - 40)$$
$$= 238 + 0.8Y - 0.8(40) - 0.05Y + 0.05(40)$$
$$= 208 + 0.75Y$$
$$0.25Y = 208$$
$$Y = 832$$

Government deficit $= G - T = 75 - 40 = 35$.
Current account balance $= EX - IM$
$$= 25 - 0.05(832 - 40)$$
$$= -14.6$$

b. The multiplier $= 1/[1 - (MPC - MPM)]$
$$= 1/[1 - (0.8 - 0.05)]$$
$$= 4$$

When G increases from 75 to 80, Y will increase by $5(4) = 20$. Imports will rise by $0.05(20) = 1$.

With the quota, the MPM is zero, so the multiplier $= 1/(1 - 0.8) = 5$. Y will rise by $5(5) = 25$. (This assumes that IM is greater than or equal to 40 without the quota, before the increase in G. Actually it is 39.6, but assuming $MPM = 0$ is a very close approximation.) Imports that rise with income act as a leakage and reduce the size of the multiplier.

c. With $EX = 25$, we need $IM = 0.05(Y - 40) = 25$. This implies $Y = 540$. Income is currently 832, so it must be decreased by $832 - 540 = 292$. With a multiplier of 4, this will require a decrease in government spending of $292/4 = 73$.

Chapter 22:

2. a. Capital increases the productivity of labour. A given-sized labour force can produce more output, and output per capita rises.

b. In a market economy, individual household savings decisions determine the pool of aggregate savings. Aggregate savings, in turn, is the amount made available for firms to purchase capital. Savings are matched to investment projects in financial markets, where the interest rate adjusts to equate total desired investment with total desired savings.

c. In developing countries, a greater fraction of output is needed just to ensure the current population's survival. An increase in investment—which requires a decrease in current consumption—cuts dangerously close to this survival level of consumption, and at a minimum causes more discomfort than it would in developed countries.

d. Answers will vary. Market-oriented economists would stress increased incentives for private investment (political stability, lower government budget deficit, and perhaps loans from abroad). Planning-oriented economists might stress government-directed projects, taxes on luxury goods, and capital controls designed to prevent capital flight to developed countries.

4. It is true that poor countries must accumulate capital in order to grow, but many poor countries do indeed have extra output available for savings. The problem is often that the available savings goes abroad (capital flight). Increased political stability and a more stable investment climate would help investment in the domestic economy. In addition, poor countries can get loans and other assistance from developed countries to help them accumulate capital.

6. A country should work to develop both its agricultural and its industrial sectors. Development of the agricultural sector can have high payoffs because it often requires little capital investment and directly benefits the poorest (rural) segment of society. Experience has shown that import substitution is a poor development policy. Its disadvantages include lessened competition in the domestic market, fewer jobs created, and expensive inputs for domestic industries.

Many countries favour industry as a more direct route to growth in the capital stock, and also to emulate the production pattern of already developed countries. Import substitution is attractive because it lessens dependence on unstable foreign demand for exports.

8. Many recent famines have resulted from government policies. In some cases, keeping farm prices artificially low has led to a decrease in production. In other cases, a failure to invest in a distributional infrastructure has led to famine in outlying rural areas.

Appendix 22A:

2. The speaker confuses political systems with economic systems. The Soviet economic system was one of socialism (government ownership of land and capital) and central planning (government direction of resource allocation). Totalitarianism is a political—not an economic—system in which the ruler exercises authoritarian control without the consent of those governed.

4. Disagree. While it is true that central planners can control resource allocation, central planning requires keen and virtuous planners to ensure that scarce resources flow to where they are needed most. In a capitalist market economy, the self-interest of resource owners steers resources to those sectors where they are needed most—that is, those sectors offering the highest rate of return.

Index

A

AAA corporate bond rate, 268
absolute advantage, 403–406
accelerator effect, 355
acquired comparative advantage, 413
actual investment, 182–183
"Adam Smith principle," 473
adjustment costs, 356
administrative costs and inefficiencies, 167
after-tax income, 201
aggregate behaviour, 113, 114
aggregate demand
  and aggregate expenditure, 293–294
  defined, 123–124, 290
  and fiscal policy, 303–305
  and monetary policy, 303–305
  and Phillips Curve, 323–324
  price level increases, 292
  price/net exports link, 293
  real wealth/consumption link, 293
aggregate demand (AD) curve
  complexity of, 291–292
  defined, 291
  deriving the, 290–291
  downward-slope of, 292–293
  and input prices, 325
  price/net exports link, 293
  real wealth/consumption link, 293
  shifts of, 294–295
aggregate expenditure
  and aggregate demand, 293–294
  planned, 183
aggregate income, 176
aggregate output (income) (Y), 117–118,
    176, 277–278
aggregate production function, 383
aggregate supply
  defined, 123–124, 295
  and fiscal policy, 303–305
  and monetary policy, 303–305
  and Phillips Curve, 323–324
  in short run, 296–297
aggregate supply (AS) curve
  and classical labour market, 315–316
  complexity of, 295–296
  cost shocks, 298
  defined, 295
  economic growth, 298
  and input prices, 325
  investment, lack of, 298
  long-run, 300–303, 305–306, 326–329
  and natural disasters, 299
  policy effects on, 305–306
  potential output, 301
  public policy, 299
  shifts in, 297–299
  short-run, 296–300
  stagnation, 298
  supply shocks, 298
  and wars, 299
  weather changes, 299
alienation, 470
all else equal. *See ceteris paribus*
allocative efficiency, 15

alternative rationing mechanisms, 100–101
American Economics Association, 171–172
animal spirits of entrepreneurs, 285,
    354–355
appreciation, 260
Asian economic crisis, 270–271
Asian Tigers, 6
auto pact, 402
automatic destabilizer, 337
automatic stabilizers, 217, 336
autonomous variable, 188
average propensity to consume (APC), 347

B

balance of payments
  balance of trade, 428–429
  balance on capital account, 430
  balance on current account, 429
  capital account, 429–430
  crisis, 437–438
  current account, 428–429
  defined, 427–428
  global, 430–431
  merchandise balance of trade, 429
balance of trade, 428–429, 445–446
balance on capital account, 430
balance on current account, 429
balanced-budget multiplier, 209–210, 222
Bank of Canada, 9, 165, 200, 236
  balance sheet, 240–241
  Bank rate, 242–243, 268
  control of money supply, 241–243
  exchange rate, 248
  fixed exchange rates, 256–258
  flexible exchange rate, 258–261
  functions of, 239–240
  and interest rates, 255–256
    see also interest rate
  and monetary policy, 261–263
  open market operations, 241–242
  response to state of economy, 337–339
  transfers of government deposits, 242
  Web site, 263
Bank of Canada Review, 263
Bank rate, 242–243, 268
banking system
  accounting practices, 235–237
  deposit multiplier, 239–240
  money, creation of, 237
  money multiplier, 239
  reserve ratio, 237
  reserves, 236
banks
  and money creation, 234–239
  run on a, 235
barter, 228
base year, 144
Bennett, R.B., 161
black markets, 101
bonds, 252–253
boom, 125
borders, 420
brain drain, 456
Bretton Woods system, 426–427
British North America (BNA) Act, 58

broad, 231–232
budget, federal. *See* federal budget
budget deficit, 202, 334–335
budget surplus, 202
business cycle, 117–118, 124–125, 126,
    153, 374–375
business inventories, change in, 136–137

C

Canada Health Act, 58
Canada Savings Bonds, 252–253
Canada-United States Automotive Products
    Trade Agreement (APTA), 402
Canada-U.S. Free Trade Agreement, 415,
    416
Canada Yearbook (Statistics Canada), 9
Canadian Alliance, 6
Canadian Anti-Dumping and
    Countervailing Directorate, 414
Canadian dollars
  appreciation, 260
  demand for, 435–436
  depreciation, 260
Canadian economy
  corporations, largest, 53–54
  economic growth in, 388–390
  exports, 61–62
  foreign investment, 138
  gross domestic product (GDP), 56
  imports, 61–62
  major industries, 54–55
  manufacturing sector, 54–55
  national income, 54
  since 1970, 126–128
  policy mix in, 284
  primary sector, 54–55
  private sector in. *See* private sector
  public sector. *See* government; public
      sector
  recession, 6
  service sector, 54–55
  slump in, 304–305
  structural changes, 54–56
  trends and cycles, 124–129
Canadian financial system, 232–233
Canadian foreign aid, 463
Canadian Prairies, 102–105
capital
  account, 428, 429–430
  costs, 285
  as factor of production, 67
  flight, 459
  formation, 455–456
  goods, 31
  human, 386, 456
  market, 67
  physical, 385–386
  private, 298
  public, 298
  resources, 26
  shortages, 455–456
  stock, 180–181
  utilization rates, 285
capital-intensive technology, 354
capitalist economy, 469, 470

Cartesian coordinate system, 20
cashless society, 233
causation, 13
centrally planned economies, collapse of, 471
ceteris paribus, 12, 14
change
  in business inventories, 136–137
  in inventory, 183
China, price rationing and, 102
choice
  capital goods, 31
  consumer, 40
  consumer goods, 31
  in economy of two or more, 28–29
  future costs, 30–31
  in one-person economy, 27
  present costs, 30–31
  production possibility frontier (PPF), 32
  and scarcity, 27, 28–29
circular flow, 66–67, 120–121
classical growth theory, 387
classical models, 114
clipped coins, 231
Club of Rome, 395
command economy, 38–39
commercial paper rate, 268
commodity monies, 229
Common Agricultural Policy (EC), 103–105
communism, 469
Communist Manifesto (Marx), 469
comparative advantage
  absolute advantage, 403–406
  acquired, 413
  defined, 407
  and exchange rate, 411–412
  factor endowments, 412
  Heckscher-Ohlin theorem, 412
  low wage labour, 419–420
  natural, 413
  sources of, 412–413
  specialization, 403, 406–407
  theory of, 29–30, 403
comparative economic systems, 10
Competition Bureau, 107
complementary goods, 72
complements, 72
composition, fallacy of, 13–14
constant dollars, 144
constraints, on market, 100–101
consumer goods, 31
consumer price index (CPI), 145–147, 163–166
consumer sovereignty, 40, 395
consumption
  average propensity to consume (APC), 347
  function, 177–178, 179, 202–203
  household, 20–21, 136
  interest rate effects on, 352
  Keynesian theory of, 347
  life-cycle theory, 347–349
  marginal propensity to consume (MPC), 178
  real wealth, 293
contraction, 125
contractionary fiscal policy, 119, 282–283
contractionary monetary policy, 283
Corn laws, 403
corporate income taxes, 59–60
corporate paper rate, 268
corporate profits, 139
corporations, 52–53

largest in Canada, 53–54
correlation, 13
cost-of-living adjustments (COLAs), 318
cost-push inflation, 307
cost shocks, 298
costs
  adjustment, 356
  external economies of scale, 388
  future, 30–31
  opportunity. See opportunity cost
  present, 30–31
  production, 79
  relative capital, 285
  relative labour, 285
  sunk, 3
counterfeiting, 231
creditors, and inflation, 166–167
crowding-out effect, 280
currency debasement, 230, 231
current account, 428–429
current dollars, 142
curve, slope of, 22
cyclical deficit, 218
cyclical unemployment, 160–161, 314

D

Das Kapital (Marx), 469
debt rescheduling, 466
debtors, and inflation, 166
deficit targeting, 337
deflation, 163, 303, 364
demand
  aggregate, 123–124
  Canadian dollars, 435–436
  changes in, 68
  demand-determined price, 99
  excess, 81–84
  function, 93–95
  gasoline prices, 105–107
  household, 71–73
  law of. *See* law of demand
  market, 75
  mathematics of, 93–95
  in money market, 255
  quantity demanded, 68
  review of, 87–88
  schedule, 69
  shift of, 73–74
demand curve
  aggregate. *See* aggregate demand (AD) curve
  defined, 69
  downward slope, 69–70
  labour, 315
  meaning of, 88
  movement along, 73–74
  other properties, 71
  shift of, 74
demand-pull inflation, 307
demography, 399–400
deposit multiplier, 239–240, 246
depreciation, 137, 140, 260
depression, 118, 154
descriptive economics, 9
desired investment, 183
desired level of inventories, 357
devaluation, 445
developing countries
  see also economic development
  capital shortages, 455–456
  debt, 465–467
  human resources, 456
  infant mortality, 453–454

population, 452–454
  see also population growth
  poverty, 452–454
  pricing policies, 464–465
  productivity, 453
  standards of living, 452
  structural adjustment, 460
diminishing marginal utility, law of, 70
diminishing returns, 384
dirty exchange rate, 258
discouraged worker effect, 158
discretionary fiscal policy, 200
disequilibrium, 187
distributed profits, 53
distribution of output, 40–41
dividends, 53, 123
double-counting, 133
double taxation, 53
dumping, 413–414
Dunning tariff, 414
durable goods, 136

E

Eastern Europe, 42
easy monetary policy, 261
econometrics, 10
economic development
  see also developing countries
  agricultural output, 464–465
  agriculture, 457–458
  brain drain, 456
  capital flight, 455
  capital formation, 455–456
  central planning, 459–460
  debt rescheduling, 466
  vs. economic growth, 460
  entrepreneurial ability, 456
  export substitution, 458, 459
  as field of study, 10
  food shortages, 464
  Green Revolution, 465
  human resources, 456
  import substitution, 458, 459
  industry, 457–458
  issues, 460–467
  market economy, 459–460
  population growth, 460–464
  pricing policies, 464–465
  social overhead capital, 456–463
  sources of, 455–457
  stabilization program, 466
  strategies, 457–460
  Third World debt, 465–467
  vicious-circle-of-poverty hypothesis, 455
economic efficiency, 35
economic growth
  see also productivity
  aggregate supply (AS) curve, 298
  anti-growth argument, 394–396
  artificial needs, creation of, 395
  in Canada, 388–390
  classical growth theory, 387
  since Confederation, 388–389
  consumer sovereignty, 395
  defined, 16, 381
  and demography, 399–400
  in developing countries. See developing
    countries; economic development
  vs. economic development, 460
  education, improvement in, 391
  human capital, increases in, 386
  and income distribution, 396
  in industrial society, 383

and inflation, 167
labour supply, increase in, 383–384
machinery and equipment investment, 391
modern, 381
neoclassical growth theory, 387
new growth theory, 387
openness to trade and investment, 391
physical capital, increases in, 385–386
pro-growth argument, 393–394
production possibility frontier (PPF), 35, 382
and public policy, 390–393
quality of life, 394–395
research and development, 392–393
resources, decline in, 395–396
saving rate, increases in, 391–392
sources of, 383–388
technological change, 386–388
economic history, 10
economic integration, 414–415
economic policy
  efficiency, 15
  equity, 15–16
  full employment, 16
  growth, 16
  price stability, 16
economic problem, 38
economic systems
  capitalist, 469, 470
  command economy, 38–39
  communism, 469
  laissez-faire economy, 39–41
  mixed systems, 41–43
  pure market economies, 39–41
  socialist, 469
economic theory, 9–15
  ceteris paribus, 12
  empirical economics, 14
  evaluation of, 14–15
  fallacy of composition, 13–14
  pitfalls, 13–14
  post hoc, ergo propter hoc, 13
economic thought, history of, 10
economic well-being indexes, 171–172
economics
  analysis, 9
  defined, 2
  descriptive, 9
  empirical, 14
  fields of study, 8, 10
  fundamental concepts of, 2–4
  and global affairs, 5–6
  informed voters, 6
  international, 10
  labour, 10
  and law, 10
  law of demand, 9
  macroeconomics. See macroeconomics
  method of, 8–16
  microeconomics. See microeconomics
  normative, 8
  positive, 8
  public, 10
  regional, 10
  scope of, 7–8
  society, understanding, 4–5
  three basic questions, 27
  urban, 10
  as way of thinking, 2–4
economies of scale, 388
efficiency, 15, 35
efficiency wage theory, 318–319
empirical economics, 14

employed, 154
Engels, Friedrich, 469
entrepreneurs, 65, 285, 354–355
entrepreneurship, 67
environmentalists, 36–37
equations, 12–13
equilibrium
  adjustment, 187–188
  aggregate output (income), 183–192
  changes in, 85–86
  defined, 81, 183–184
  exchange rate, 436–438
  graphing, 82
  interest rate, 254–261, 278
  leakages/injections approach, 185–187, 211–212
  multiplier. See multiplier
  output, 203–204, 431–434
  price level, 299–300
  saving/investment approach, 185–187
  short-run, 301–302
equity, 15–16
Europe, recovery in, 363–364
European Central Bank, 262
European Union (EU), 414–415
excess
  capital effects, 355–357
  demand, 81–84
  labour, 355–357
  supply, 84–85
exchange, 29–30, 410–411
exchange rate
  and balance of trade, 445–446
  and comparative advantage, 411–412
  defined, 248, 409, 426
  devaluation, 445
  dirty, 258
  equilibrium, 436–438
  factors affecting, 438–442
  fixed, 256–258, 444–445
  flexible, 258–261
  floating, 258–261
  foreign exchange market, 435–438
  freely floating, 258
  and interest rate, 441
  and international trade, 408–411
  J curve effect, 445–446
  managed, 258
  McDonalds, 440
  purchasing power parities, 438–441
  pure floating, 258
  revaluation, 445
excise taxes, 60
expansionary fiscal policies, 119, 125, 279–281
expansionary monetary policy, 279, 281–282
expectations, 285
  and financial markets, 372
  and firm decisions, 354–355
  household, 72–73
  and inflation, 308–309
  Phillips Curve, 326
  rational-expectations hypothesis, 371–372, 374
  wage/price adjustment, 372
expectations theory, 267
expenditure approach
  change in business inventories, 136–137
  consumption, household, 136
  defined, 135
  depreciation, 137
  durable goods, 136
  fixed capital formation, 136

government purchases, 139
gross private investment, 136
gross vs. net investment, 137–139
investment, 136–139
net domestic product, 139
net exports (EX-IM), 139
nondurable goods, 136
personal consumption expenditures, 136
semidurable goods, 136
services, 136, 137
experiments, difficulty of, 14
explicit contracts, 318
export subsidies, 413
export substitution, 458, 459
exports
  Canadian, 61–62
  defined, 121
  determinants of, 433–434
  net, 139, 211, 293, 431
  price, 433
external economies of scale, 388

F

factor endowments, 412
factor markets, 66
factors of production
  capital, 67
  labour, 67
  land, 67
fallacy of composition, 13–14
farm income, 140
favored customers, 101
federal budget
  automatic stabilizers, 217
  cyclical deficit, 218
  defined, 212
  economy, influence of, 215–218
  expenditure, 216–217
  and federal debt, 213–215
  fiscal drag, 217–219
  full-employment budget, 218
  international, 218
  overview, 213
  structural deficit, 218
  tax revenues, 215–216
federal debt, 215, 332–333
  burden of, 333–335
  capital expenditures, finance of, 334
  deficit as misleading indicator, 334–335
  deficit reduction, 336–337
  economic stability, 336–337
  and macropolicy, 335–337
  management, 335–337
  and subsequent generations, 333–334
federal deficit, 332, 336–337
federal government, 59, 60
  see also government
fertility rate, 462
fiat money, 229
fields of economics, 8, 10
final goods and services, 133
finance, 10
financial intermediaries, 233
financial market. See money market
fine tuning, 115
firms
  accelerator effect, 355
  animal spirits, 354–355
  behaviour, 359
  corporation, 52–53
  decision-making, 354
  defined, 65
  demand. See demand

employment decisions, 353–354
entrepreneur, 65
excess capital effects, 355–357
excess labour, 355–357
expectations, role of, 354–355
industry, 54
in input markets, 66–67
inventory decisions, 357–359
investment decisions, 353
legal organization of, 52–53
in output markets, 66
partnership, 52
profile of Canadian, 53–54
profit maximization, 354
proprietorship, 52
share of stock, 123
size, 53–54
supply decision, 77
   see also supply
fiscal drag, 217–219
fiscal policy
   balanced-budget multiplier, 209–210
   contractionary, 119, 282–283
   crowding-out effect, 280
   discretionary, 200
   expansionary, 119, 125, 279–281
   federal budget. See federal budget
   under fixed exchange rates, 445
   under flexible exchange rates, 442–443
   government purchases, change in,
      279–281, 282–283
   government spending multiplier, 204–207
   insensitivity of planned investment,
      280–281
   interest sensitivity, 280–281
   lags in economy's response, 339–343
   and macroeconomics, 119
   money supply, increases in, 281
   net taxes, changes in, 279–281, 282–283
   in open economy, 442–443, 445
   policy mix, 283–284
   provincial governments, 216
   response lags, 342
fixed capital formation, 136
fixed exchange rates, 256–258, 444–445
fixed-weight index, 163
fixed-weight price index, 145
flexible exchange rate, 258–261, 434–442
   see also open economy
floating exchange rate, 258–261
flow variable, 253
food shortages, 464
"fool in the shower," 339–340
foreign aid, 463
foreign exchange, 427, 435–438
foreign investment in Canada, 138
franchise, 53
free trade, 415–421
freely floating exchange rate, 258
frictional unemployment, 159, 314
Friedman, Milton, 339, 369
full employment, 16
full-employment budget, 218
future costs, 30–31

G

gasoline prices, 105–107, 110–111
GDP deflator, 144–145
GDP (gross domestic product). *See* gross
      domestic product (GDP)
General Agreement on Tariffs and Trade
      (GATT), 5, 414

*General Theory of Employment, Interest
      and Money* (Keynes), 114, 116, 199,
      347, 365
generalizations, 71
global affairs, 5–6
global balance of payments, 430–431
gold standard, 426
goldsmiths, 234–235
goods
   capital, 31
   complementary, 72
   consumer, 31
   durable, 136
   inferior, 72
   intermediate, 133
   nondurable, 136
   normal, 71
   public, 41–43
   semidurable, 136
   social, 41–43
   substitutes, 72
goods-and-services market. *See* goods
      market
Goods and Services Tax (GST), 60
goods market, 122, 174
   contractionary fiscal policy, 282–283
   contractionary monetary policy, 283
   defined, 273
   expansionary fiscal policy, 279–281
   expansionary monetary policy, 279,
      281–282
   and interest rate, 274–277
   links with money market, 274
government
   see also public sector
   bond rate, 268
   bonds, 123
   borrowing, 123
   budget deficit, 202
   budget surplus, 202
   consumption, effects on, 350–353
   contractionary fiscal policies, 119
   debt, 57, 213–215
      see also federal debt
   deposits, transfers of, 242
   discretionary fiscal policy, 200
   disposable income and, 200–204
   "dissaving," 391
   expansionary fiscal policies, 119
   expenditure, 58–59, 216–217, 279–281
   federal, 59, 60
   federal budget. See federal budget
   fiscal policy. See fiscal policy
   growth policies, 120
   inefficiencies, 41–43
   interest payments, 56
   investment behaviour and, 203
   labour supply, effects on, 350–353
   in macroeconomy, 119–120
   monetary policy. *See* monetary policy
   net taxes, 200–204
   notes, 123
   provincial/local/hospital (PLH), 59, 216
   purchases, 56, 139, 200–204
   redistribution of income, 43
   revenue sources, 58, 59–61
   spending, 56
   stabilization, 43
   structure, 58–59
   subsidies, 141
   supply-side policies, 124
   tax revenues, 215–216, 223–224
   transfer payments, 56, 120, 351
   Treasury bills, 123

government policies
   and economic growth, 390–393
   education, improvement in, 391
   fiscal policy. *See* fiscal policy
   "fool in the shower," 339–340
   growth policies, 390–393
   implementation lags, 341
   and Lucas supply function, 373–374
   machinery and equipment investment,
      391
   monetary policy. See monetary policy
   openness to trade and investment, 391
   recognition lags, 341
   research and development, 392–393
   response lags, 341–343
   saving rate, increases in, 391–392
   stabilization policy, 339
   time lags, 339
government spending multiplier, 204–207,
      222, 224
graphs, 12–13, 19–23
   Cartesian coordinate system, 20
   curve, slope of, 22
   demand function, 94–95
   equilibrium, 82
   household consumption, 20–21
   income, 20–21
   negative relationship, 21
   origin, 20
   positive relationship, 21
   precautions, 22–23
   slope, 21–22
   supply function, 94–95
   time series, 19
   X axis, 20
   Y axis, 20
   Y-intercept, 20
Great Depression, 114–115, 154, 191–192,
      233, 426
Green Revolution, 465
gross domestic product (GDP)
   base year, 144
   calculation of, 135–141
   constant dollars, 144
   consumer price index (CPI), 145–147
   current dollars, 142
   defined, 56, 132
   expenditure approach, 135–139
   final goods and services, 133
   GDP deflator, 144–145
   vs. gross national product (GNP), 134
   income approach, 135
   limitations of concept, 147–149
   nominal, 142–144
   per capita, 148
   potential, 301, 326–329
   price level, measurement of, 144–146
   "produced within given period," 133–134
   purchasing power parities, 148
   real, 143–144
   and social welfare, 147
   underground economy, 147–148
gross investment, 137–139
gross national product (GNP)
   defined, 134
   vs. gross domestic product, 134
   per capita, 148
gross private investment, 136
growth. See economic growth
growth policies, 120

H

Harris, Mike, 57
Heckscher, Eli, 412
Heckscher-Ohlin theorem, 412
Heilbroner, Robert L., 116–117
household(s)
  basic decision-making unit, 65–66
  behaviour, 353
  Canadian, 49–51
  consumption. *See* consumption
  defined, 65–66
  demand, 71–73
  expectations, 72–73
  income, 7, 71–72
  in input markets, 66–67
  labour supply decision, 349–350
  in output markets, 66
  preferences, 72–73
  prices of other goods and services, 72
  quantity demanded, 68
  saving, 177–179
  tastes, 72–73
  wealth, 71–72
human behaviour, 11
human capital, 386, 460
human resources, 26, 460
hyperinflation, 116–117

I

identity, 176
implementation lags, 341
implicit contracts, 317–318
import substitution, 458, 459
imports
  Canadian, 61–62
  defined, 121
  determinants of, 433–434
  and income, 225
  levels, determination of, 431
  marginal propensity to import, 431
  price, 433
incentives, 3–4
income
  after-tax, 201
  aggregate, 176
  approach. *See* income approach
  consumption function, 177–178
  defined, 40, 71
  disposable, 200–204
  distribution of. *See* income distribution
  farm, 140
  gap, 6
  graphs, 20–21
  household, 7
  and household demand, 71–72
  imports and, 225
  interest, 140
  labour, 139
  and money demand, 274
  national, 7
  net national, 142
  nonlabour, 350
  nonwage, 350
  permanent, 348–349
  personal, 141–142
  personal disposable, 142
  personal saving, 142
  personal saving rate, 142
  redistribution of, 43
  tax revenues and, 223–224
  unincorporated business, 140

income approach
  corporate profits, 139
  defined, 135
  depreciation, 140
  farm income, 140
  indirect taxes, 140–141
  interest income, 140
  inventory valuation adjustment, 140
  labour income, 139
  net domestic income, 139–140
  subsidies, 141
  unincorporated business income, 140
income distribution
  and economic growth, 396
  and inflation, 166
income tax
  corporate, 59–60
  legal and economic incidence of a tax, 60
  personal, 59
index, 145
indirect taxes, 140–141
individual production decisions, 40
inductive reasoning, 10–11
industrial organization, 10
Industrial Revolution, 4, 61, 382–383, 386
industry, 54
industry price indexes, 166
inefficiencies, administrative, 167
infant industries, 421
inferior goods, 72
inflation
  administrative costs and inefficiencies, 167
  in Canadian economy, 6
  causes of, 307–309
  consumer price index (CPI), 163–166
  cost-push, 307
  costs of, 166–167
  and creditors, 166–167
  and debtors, 166
  defined, 116, 163
  demand-pull, 307
  economic growth, slower, 167
  effects of high, 116–117
  and expectations, 308–309
  global, 167–168
  income distribution, 166
  industry price indexes, 166
  and money, 309
  Phillips Curve, 322–326
  price, 43
  price indexes, 163–166
  and price level, 322
  problem of, 162–163
  as purely monetary phenomenon, 369
  rate, 127–128, 321
  real interest rate, 166
  risk, increased, 167
  seriousness of costs, 167
  short-run trade-off with unemployment, 326
  stagflation, 115, 308
  supply-side, 307
  sustained, 163, 307, 309
  and unemployment rate, 319–329
information, 3–4
informed voters, 6
infrastructure, 298
Innis, Harold A., 54
innovation, 387
input markets, 66
inputs
  see also factors of production
  defined, 26

prices, 41, 77, 325
insensitivity of planned investment, 280–281
interdependent world economy, 446
interest
  defined, 247
  income, 140
  market rate of, 267
  payments, 56
  rate of. *See* interest rate
  real rate, 267
  sensitivity, 280–281
interest rate
  AAA corporate bond rate, 268
  and Bank of Canada, 256
  Bank rate, 268
  Canadian vs. U.S., 444
  changes and aggregate output, 276–277
  commercial paper rate, 268
  and consumption, 352
  corporate paper rate, 268
  defined, 247
  equilibrium, 254–261, 278
  and exchange rate, 441
  expectations theory, 267
  and goods market, 274–277
  government bond rate, 268
  and investments, 282
  Mundell-Fleming model, 444
  nominal, 267, 284
  overnight rate, 268
  parity, 442
  prime rate, 268
  real, 267, 284–285
  term structure of, 266–268
  three-month Treasury bill rate, 268
intermediate goods, 133
international economic linkages, 5
international economics, 10
international economy
  trade deficit, 402
  trade surplus, 402
International Monetary Fund (IMF), 270–271, 459, 466–467
international sector, 210–212
  defined, 49
  exports, 61–62
  imports, 61–62
  net exports, 431
  and planned aggregate expenditure, 431–433
international trade
  and borders, 420
  comparative advantage. *See* comparative advantage
  and economic integration, 414–415
  and exchange rate, 408–411
  free trade, 415–421
  negotiations, 473–474
  protection. *See* protection
  specialization, 403, 406–407
  terms of trade, 408
  trade barriers, 413–415
  trade flows, explanations for, 412–413
  two-country/two-good example, 410–411
invention, 387
inventories, 180, 183, 357
inventory investment, 353, 357–358
inventory valuation adjustment, 140
investment
  defined, 31, 180
  desired, 183
  expenditure approach, 136–139
  firm decisions, 353

foreign, 138
government effect on, 203
gross, 137
gross private, 136
income, 429
and interest rate, 282
inventory, 353, 357–358
lack of, 298
net, 137–139
openness to, 391
planned, 180–183
plant and equipment, 353
invisible hand, 89

J

J curve effect, 445–446
Japan, deflation in, 364

K

Keynes, John Maynard, 114–115,
    116–117, 119, 285, 347, 355, 365
Keynesian economics, 365–366, 369–370,
    377
Keynesian revolution, 114–115

L

labour
    economics, 10
    as factor of production, 67
    force, 154
    income, 139
    prices of, 41
    productivity, 356, 384
    relative costs, 285
    as resource. See human resources
labour demand curve, 315
labour-force participation rate, 155–156
labour-intensive technology, 354
labour market, 66–67, 122
    and aggregate supply curve, 315–316
    basic concepts, 313–314
    classical view, 314–317
    workforce cuts, 356
labour supply, 383–384
    curve, 314–315
    decision, 349–350
Laffer, Arthur, 376
Laffer Curve, 376
laissez-faire economy
    consumer sovereignty, 40
    defined, 39
    distribution of output, 40–41
    individual production decisions, 40
    price theory, 41
land, 67
land market, 67
law, and economics, 10
law of demand, 9, 69
law of diminishing marginal utility, 70
law of one price, 438
law of supply, 78
leakages/injections approach, 185–187,
    211–212
legal tender, 229–230
Liberals, 6
life-cycle theory of consumption, 347–349
Limits to Growth (Club of Rome), 395
liquidity property of money, 229
long-run aggregate supply (AS) curve,
    300–303, 305–306, 326–329

Lucas, Robert E., 373
Lucas supply function, 373–374

M

M1, 230–231
M2, 231–232
macroeconomics
    "aggregate," use of, 113
    aggregate behaviour, 113, 114
    aggregate output, 117–118
    alternative models, 377–378
    business cycle, 117–118, 124–125, 126
    circular flow, 120–121
    components of macroeconomy, 120–123
    concerns of, 48, 115–119
    contractionary fiscal policies, 119
    defined, 7, 113, 114
    depression, 118
    development of, 114–115
    expansionary fiscal policies, 119
    and federal debt, 335–337
    fine tuning, 115
    fiscal policy, 119
    goods-and-services market, 122
    government in macroeconomy, 119–120
    gross domestic product. See gross
        domestic product (GDP)
    growth policies, 120
    hyperinflation, 116–117
    inflation. See inflation
    inflation rate, 127–128
    labour market, 122
    markets, 174–175
    monetary policy, 119–120
    money market, 122–123
    national income and expenditure
        accounts, 132
    policy mix, 283–284
    price inflation, 43
    recent history, 115
    recession, 118
    stagflation, 115
    sticky prices, 114
    supply-side policies, 124
    unemployment. See unemployment
Malthus, Thomas, 5, 384, 387, 465
managed exchange rate, 258
managerial knowledge, 388
manufacturing sector, 54–55
marginal propensity to consume (MPC),
    178
marginal propensity to import, 431
marginal propensity to save (MPS), 179
marginal utility, 70
marginalism, 3
market coordination, 3–4
market demand, 75
market equilibrium, 81–86
market for goods and services. See goods
    market
market organization, 54
market rate of interest, 267
market supply, 80–81
market system. See price system
markets
    allocation of resources, 88–89
    black, 101
    capital, 67
    constraints on, 100–101
    defined, 39
    factor, 66
    foreign exchange, 435–438

inefficiencies, 41–43
input, 66
labour, 66–67, 122
land, 67
macroeconomics, 174–175
money, 122–123
output, 66
product, 66
redistribution of income, 43
stabilization, 43
supply, 80–81
Marshall, Alfred, 9–11, 69, 94
Martin, Paul, 57
Marx, Karl, 469
Marxian economics
    alienation, 470
    assymmetries of power, 469–470
    centrally planned economies, collapse of,
        471
    means of production, 469–470
    overview, 469
    predictions, 470–471
    profit, nature of, 470
    social relations of production, 471
    tragedy of the commons, 471
mathematics
    of demand and supply, 93–95
    in economics, 12–13
    function, 93
McDonalds, 440
means of payment, 228
means of production, 469–470
medium of exchange, 228
merchandise balance of trade, 429
microeconomics
    classical models, 114
    concerns of, 48
    defined, 7, 113
    working assumption in, 113–114
minimum wage laws, 319, 320
mixed systems
    inefficiencies, 41–43
    redistribution of income, 43
    stabilization, 43
model, 11, 12–13
    see also economic theory
modern economic growth, 381
monetarism
    and inflation, 369
    vs. Keynesian economics, 366, 369–370
    quantity theory of money, 367–369
    velocity of money, 366–367
Monetary Conditions Index (MCI),
    263–264
monetary policy, 200
    and Bank of Canada behaviour, 261–263
    contractionary, 283
    defined, 247
    easy, 261
    expansionary, 279, 281–282
    under fixed exchange rates, 445
    under flexible exchange rates, 443
    lags in economy's response, 339–343
    and macroeconomics, 119–120
    in open economy, 443, 445
    policy mix, 283–284
    preview, 218
    response lags, 342–343
    tight, 262
monetary union, 262
money
    alternate measures of, 232
    appreciation, 260

broad, 231–232
clipped coins, 231
commodity, 229
control of supply, 241–243
counterfeiting, 231
creation of, 237
currency debasement, 230, 231
definitions of, 228–229
demand for. See money demand
depreciation, 260
fiat, 229
and inflation, 309
legal tender, 229–230
liquidity property of, 229
M1, 230–231
M2, 231–232
as means of payment, 228
measurement of Canadian supply of, 230–232
as medium of exchange, 228
multiplier, 239, 246
narrow, 230–231
near-monies, 232
paper, acceptance of, 229–230
quantity theory of, 367–369
as store of value, 228–229
supply, changes in, 256, 281
supply curve, 243
token, 229
as unit of account, 229
velocity of, 366–367
money demand, 248–254
and aggregate output (income), 277–278
curve, shifts in, 255–256
determinants of, 252–254
and income, 274
and money market, 277–278
output, 250–252
pitfalls in thinking, 253–254
and price level, 250–252
vs. saving, 254
speculation motive, 248–249
stock variable, 253
transaction motive, 249–250
transaction volume, 250–252
money market, 175
and aggregate output (income), 277–278
bonds, 252–253
Canada Savings Bonds, 252–253
contractionary fiscal policy, 282–283
contractionary monetary policy, 283
defined, 273
demand in, 255
expansionary fiscal policy, 279–281
expansionary monetary policy, 279, 281–282
and expectations, 372
links with goods market, 274
as macroeconomic component, 122–123
and money demand, 277–278
perpetuities, 252
preview, 218
spending and, 274
supply in, 255
mortality rate, 462
movement along a demand curve, 74
multiplier
algebraic example, 197
autonomous variable, 188
balanced-budget, 209–210, 222
defined, 188
deposit, 239–240, 246
equation, 190–191

fiscal policy, algebraic examples, 221–222
government spending, 204–207, 222, 224
Great Depression, recovery from, 191–192
money, 239, 246
open-economy, 432–433
in practice, 194
in real world, 191
size of, 189–190
spending, 188
tax, 207–209, 222, 224
Mundell, Robert, 444
Mundell-Fleming model, 444

N

NAFTA, 415, 416
narrow money, 230–231
national income, 7
national income and expenditure accounts, 132
natural comparative advantage, 413
natural disasters, and AS curve, 299
natural rate of population increase, 466
natural rate of unemployment, 160
natural resource products, 55
natural unemployment rate, 160, 326–329
near-monies, 232
negative demand shock, 336–337
negative relationship, 21
neoclassical growth theory, 387
neoclassical view of profit, nature of, 470
net domestic income, 139–140
net domestic product, 139
net exports of goods and services (EX-IM), 139, 211, 431
net income, 53
net investment, 137–139
net national income, 142
net worth, 71
new classical macroeconomics
development of, 370–371
Lucas supply function, 373–374
rational-expectations hypothesis, 371–372, 374
real business cycle theory, 374–375
New Democratic Party, 6
new goods bias, 164–165
new growth theory, 387
new housing industry, 282
nominal GDP, 142–144
nominal interest rate, 267, 284
nominal output, 143
nominal rate of interest, 267
nominal wage rate, 349
nondurable goods, 136
nonlabour income, 350
nonwage income, 350
normal goods, 71
normative economics, 8
North American Free Trade Agreement (NAFTA), 415, 416
not in the labour force, 154

O

observed regularities, 10
obstacles to trade. See trade barriers
Ockham's razor, 11
Ohlin, Bertil, 412
oil markets, 105–107
Okun, Arthur, 356
Okun's Law, 356

OPEC (Organization of Petroleum Exporting Countries), 4, 6, 106, 110
open economy
equilibrium output (income), 431–434
exports, determinants of, 433–434
fiscal policy in, 442–443, 445
fixed exchange rates, 445
flexible exchange rates, 434–442
import levels, 431
imports, determinants of, 433–434
marginal propensity to import, 431
monetary policy in, 443, 445
multiplier, 432–433
net exports, 431
trade feedback effect, 434
open-economy multiplier, 432–433
open market operations, 241–242
opportunity cost
and comparative advantage, 29
defined, 2–3, 28
increase in, 34–35
and production possibility frontier (PPF), slope of, 34
and scarcity and choice, 27–28
optimal level of inventories, 357
origin, 20
outlet substitution bias, 165
output markets. See product/output markets
output(s)
aggregate, 176
defined, 27
distribution of, 40–41
equilibrium, 203–204
lost, 160–161
and money demand, 250–252
nominal, 143
overnight rate, 268

P

partnership, 52
payroll taxes, 60
per capita GDP, 148
per capita GNP, 148
perfect substitutes, 72
permanent income, 348–349
perpetuities, 252
personal consumption expenditures, 136
personal disposable income, 142
personal income, 141–142
personal income tax, 59
personal saving, 142
personal saving rate, 142
Phillips, A.W., 322
Phillips Curve
AS/AD analysis, 323–324
defined, 322
expectations, 326
historical perspective, 322
vertical, 327–329
physical capital, 385–386
planned aggregate expenditure (AE), 183, 431–433
planned investment, 180–183, 280–281, 284–285
plant and equipment investment, 353
policy mix, 283–284
population growth
causes of rapid growth, 462–463
concern over, 461
consequences of, 461–462
economic theories of, 463

fertility rate, 462
mortality rate, 462
natural rate of population increase, 462
positive economics, 8
positive relationship, 21
post hoc, ergo propter hoc, 13
potential GDP, 301, 326–329
potential output, 301
Prairie wheat production, 102–105
preferences, 72–73
present costs, 30–31
price
  and aggregate demand, 293
  ceiling, 100
  changes in, 68
  defined, 41
  demand-determined, 99
  in developing countries, 464–465
  exports, 433
  fairness rationale, 100
  floor, 102–103
  gasoline, 105–107, 110–111
  imports, 433
  indexes, 163–166
  inflation, 43
  input, 77, 325
  law of one, 438
  other goods and services, 72
  and quantity demanded, 69–71
  rationing, 84, 97–99, 100, 102
  related products, 80
  and resource allocation, 105
  stability, 16
  sticky, 114
  surprise, 373
  theory, 41
price level
  and aggregate demand, 292
  equilibrium, 299–300
  and inflation, 322
  measurement, 144–146
  and money demand, 250–252
price system
  black markets, 101
  favored customers, 101
  price ceiling, 100
  price rationing, 100, 102
  and price rationing, 97
  queuing, 100
  ration coupons, 101
  resource allocation, 105
primary sector, 54–55
prime rate, 268
Principles of Economics (Marshall), 69, 94
private capital, 298
private sector
  Canadian households, 49–51
  defined, 48–49
  firm, 51–54
producers, 27
product/output markets
  defined, 66
  demand in, 67–75
  supply in, 75–81
production, 26
  costs, 79
  factors of, 67
  inefficiency, 33–34
  periods, 175
  process, 67
production possibility frontier (PPF), 382
  consumer vs. capital goods, 36
  defined, 32
  and economic growth, 35

and economic thinking, 35–36
  and efficiency, 35
  environmental quality, 36
  health care, 35–36
  and opportunity cost, 34
  production inefficiency, 33–34
  slope, 34
    and unemployment, 33
productive efficiency, 35
productivity, 356
  see also economic growth
  of an input, 386–388
  in developing countries, 453
  economies of scale, 388
  environmental regulation, 388
  managerial knowledge, 388
  measurement of changes, 392
  other factors affecting, 388
  "problem," 389–390
  technological change and, 386–388
profit, 77, 470
Progressive Conservative party, 6
promissory note, 123
proprietorship, 52
protection
  infant industries, 421
  and jobs, 418
  low wage labour, 419–420
  and national independence, 420
  and national security, 420
  and trade barriers, 413
  unfair trade practices, 419
provincial/local/hospital (PLH) government,
  59, 60–61, 216
  see also government
public capital, 298
public economics, 10
public goods, 41–43
public policy, 299
  see also government policies
public sector
  see also government
  defined, 49
  gross domestic product (GDP), 56
  size of, 56–58
purchases of goods and services, 56
purchasing power parities, 148, 438–441
purchasing power parity theory, 438
pure floating exchange rate, 258
pure market economies, 39–41

Q

quantitative relationships, 12
quantity demanded, 68, 69–71
quantity supplied, 78
quantity theory of money, 367–369
queuing, 100
quota, 414

R

ration coupons, 101
rational-expectations hypothesis, 371–372,
  374
rationing mechanisms, 97–99, 100–101
real balance effect, 293
real business cycle theory, 374–375
real GDP, 143–144
real interest rate, 166, 284–285
real wage rate, 349
real wealth effect, 293
recession, 6, 118, 125, 154, 162
recognition lags, 341

regional economics, 10
related product price, 80
relative capital costs, 285
relative labour costs, 285
research and development, 387, 392–393
reserve ratio, 237
reserves, 236
resources
  allocation of, 88–89, 105
  capital. See capital
  defined, 26
  finite, decline in, 395–396
  human, 26
  scarce, 2–3
response lags, 341–343
retained earnings, 53
revaluation, 445
Revenue Canada, 59
Ricardo, David, 5, 29, 384, 387, 403, 406,
  407, 473
run on a bank, 235
Russia, 42

S

salaries. *See* wages
sales taxes, 60
saving/investment approach to equilibrium,
  185–187
saving (S)
  defined, 176
  and household consumption, 177–179
  marginal propensity to save (MPS), 179
  vs. money demand, 254
  numerical example, 179–180
  in simple economy, 176
scarce resources, 2–3
scarcity
  capital goods, 31
  and choice, 27, 28–29
  consumer goods, 31
  in economy of two or more, 28–29
  future costs, 30–31
  in one-person economy, 27
  present costs, 30–31
  production possibility frontier (PPF), 32
seasonal adjustment, 157
semidurable goods, 136
service sector, 54–55
services, 136, 137, 429
share of stock, 52, 123, 252
shareholders, 52–53
shift of a demand curve, 74
short-run aggregate supply (AS) curve,
  296–300
simple economy, 176
skilled workers, 358
slope, 21–22
slowdowns, 358
slump, 125
Smith, Adam, 3, 5, 88–89, 469, 473
Smoot-Hawley tariff, 414
social contracts, 317–318
social goods, 41–43
social overhead capital, 456–463
social relations of production, 471
social scientists, 11
social welfare, and GDP, 147
socialist economy, 469
society, and study of economic, 4–5
Solow, Robert, 387
specialization, 29–30, 403, 406–407
speculation motive, 248–249
spending behaviour, 177–180

spending multipliers, 188
stabilization, 43
stabilization policy, 339
stabilization program, 466
stagflation, 115, 308
stagnation, 298
staples, 54
Statistics Canada, 9, 147, 165
sticky prices, 114
sticky wages, 317–318
stock, shares of, 52, 123, 252
stock page, 352
stock variable, 253
store of value, 228–229
Stronach, Frank, 50
structural adjustment, 460
structural deficit, 218
structural unemployment, 159–160, 314
subsidies, 141, 413
substitutes, 72
substitution bias, 163–164
sunk costs, 3
supply
    aggregate, 123–124
    Canadian dollars, 435–436
    change in, 80
    decision, 77
    determinants of, 78–80
    excess, 84–85
    function, 93–95
    gasoline prices, 105–107
    labour, 383–384
    law of, 78
    market, 80–81
    mathematics of, 93–95
    money. See money
    in money market, 255
    production costs, 79
    quantity supplied, 78
    related product price, 80
    review of, 87–88
    schedule, 78
    shift of, 80
supply curve
    aggregate. See aggregate supply (AS)
        curve
    defined, 78
    labour, 314–315
    money, 243
    movement along, 80
supply shocks, 298
supply-side economics
    criticism of, 377
    development of, 375–376
    evaluation of, 376–377
    Laffer Curve, 376
supply-side inflation, 307
supply-side policies, 124
surplus, 474
sustained inflation, 163, 307, 309

T

tables, 12–13
tariff, 413
tastes, 72–73
tax evasion, 148
tax multiplier, 207–209, 222, 224
tax revenues, 215–216, 223–224
taxes
    in Canada, 214
    consumption function, 202–203
    excise, 60
    gasoline, 110–111

Goods and Services Tax (GST), 60
income. See income tax
    indirect, 140–141
    net, 200–204, 279–281, 282–283
    payroll, 60
    sales, 60
technological change, 386–388
term structure of interest rate, 266–268
terms of trade, 408
theories. See economic theory
theory of comparative advantage, 29–30,
    403
Third World debt, 465–467
three basic questions, 27
three-month Treasury bill rate, 268
Tickle Me Elmo, 100–101
tight monetary policy, 262
time lags, 339
time series graph, 19
token money, 229
trade
    balance of, 428–429, 445–446
    and borders, 420
    deficit, 402, 429
    feedback effect, 434
    free, 415–421
    international. See international trade
    merchandise balance of, 429
    obstacles to. See trade barriers
    openness to, 391
    surplus, 402, 429
    terms of, 408
trade barriers
    dumping, 413–414
    Dunning tariff, 414
    and economic integration, 414–415
    export subsidies, 413
    forms of, 413
    quota, 414
    tariff, 413
    World Trade Organization (WTO), 414
tragedy of the commons, 471
transaction motive, 249–250
transfer payments, 56, 120, 351
transfers of government deposits, 242
Treaty of Westphalia, 473–474

U

underground economy, 147–148
unemployed, 154
unemployment, 6
    in Canada, 328
    cost-of-living adjustments (COLAs), 318
    costs of, 158–162
    cyclical, 160–161, 314
    defining, 154–156
    and depression, 154
    duration of, 158
    efficiency wage theory, 318–319
    existence of, 317–319
    explicit contracts, 318
    frictional, 159, 314
    high, 161
    implicit contracts, 317–318
    inevitability of, 159
    letters to R.B. Bennett, 161
    lost output, 161
    as macroeconomic concern, 118–119,
        127
    as macroeconomics concern, 43
    measurement of, 154–156
    minimum wage laws, 319, 320
    natural rate of, 160

production inefficiency, 33–34
    and production possibility frontier (PPF),
        33
    and recession, 154
    short-run trade-off with inflation, 326
    social consequences, 161–162
    social contracts, 317–318
    sticky wages, 317–318
    structural, 159–160, 314
    in U.S., 328
unemployment rate
    and classical view of labour market,
        316–317
    components, 156–158
    defined, 118–119, 155, 313
    demographic groups, 156
    in different industries, 158
    discouraged worker effect, 158
    global, 167–168
    and inflation, 319–329
    natural, 160, 326–329
    Phillips Curve, 322–326
    by province, 157–158
    seasonal adjustment, 157
unfair trade practices, 419
unincorporated business income, 140
unit of account, 229
urban economics, 10
utility, 70

V

value added, 133
variable, 11
velocity of money, 366–367
vicious-circle-of-poverty hypothesis, 455

W

wage/price adjustment, 372
wage rates, 41, 349
wages, 50–51, 349
wars, and AS curve, 299
wealth, 40, 71, 350
Wealth of Nations (Smith), 3, 5
weather changes, and AS curve, 299
weight, 145, 164
William of Ockham, 11
willingness to pay, 98–99
workforce cuts, 356
World Bank, 459
World Petroleum Congress, 110
World Trade Organization (WTO), 5, 414,
    473–474

X

X axis, 20

Y

Y axis, 20
Y-intercept, 20

Photo Credits

5 CP Picture Archive/Elaine Thompson **10** Marko Shark **10** U.S. Geological Survey, U.S. Department of the Interior **39** Greg Girard/Contact Press Images **40** Dallas and John Heaton/Westlight **42** Shepard Sherbell/Saba Press Photos, Inc. **53** Courtesy of General Motors of Canada Limited **61** Prentice Hall archives **66** Leucar Photos/Bob Carroll **99** SuperStock, Inc. **109** James Keyser/Time Pix **116** National Archives **117** Saskatchewan Archives Board, Photograph #R-B9049 (4) **119** Jockel Finck/AP/Wide World Photos **135** Courtesy of Honda Canada Inc. **149** Peter Blakely/Saba Press Photos, Inc. **161** Marge George/Ivy Images **166** City of Toronto Archives, Globe and Mail Collection, Item 114711 **171** Kelly-Mooney/CORBIS/Magma **194** Victor Last/Geographical Visual Aids **229** Jack Fields/Photo Researchers, Inc. **230** Dick Hemingway **231** National Archives of Canada/#C-17069 **233** Reuters/Dima Korotayev/Archive Photos **240** Courtesy of the Bank of Canada and McElligott Photography Limited

250 Dick Hemingway **253** National Post **262** CP Picture Archive, Daniel Maurer **270** CP Picture Archive, Yun Jai-Hyoung Yun **282** Alene McNeill **304** Leduc/Monkmeyer Press **316** National Archives **317** National Archives **322** Andrew Moore/Katz/Saba Press Photos Inc. **328** Photo Researchers Inc. **340** Vic Bider/PhotoEdit **351** Frank Gunn/Canapress **351** Andrew Popper **364** VCL/Master File; Ron Stroud/Master File **372** Terry Ashe/Time Pix **373** Comstock **385** HoHo/Canapress **388** Jeff McIntosh/Canapress **416** Fred Chartrand/Canapress **419** Rory Lysaght. Gamma-Liaison, Inc. **426** PA/AP/Wide World Photos **435** Joel Stettenheim/Saba Press Photos, Inc. **440** CP Picture Archive, Firdia Lisnawati **444** European Union/AP/Wide World Photos **453** Jack Picone Networks/Sygma **463** CIDA Photo; Nancy Durrell McKenna **464** Noel Quidu/Gamma-Liaison, Inc. **473** CP Picture Archive, Itsu Inouye